HUDSON'S

HISTORIC HOUSES & GARDENS

MUSEUMS & HERITAGE SITES

Bringing Britain's Heritage to You

Published by Hudson's Media Ltd
35 Thorpe Road, Peterborough PE3 6AG
Telephone: 01733 296910
Email: info@hudsons-media.co.uk
www.hudsonsheritage.com

Information carried in this Directory is based on that supplied by the owners of the various properties. Every effort has been made to ensure that the information given is accurate at the time of going to press but opening times, admission charges and facilities available at heritage properties may be changed at the discretion of the owners. If long journeys are involved, visitors are advised to check details in advance to ensure that opening times are as published. The publishers do not accept any responsibility for any consequences that may arise from errors or omissions. All rights reserved. No part of this publication may be reproduced, stored in a retrieval system or transmitted in any form or by any means, electronic, mechanical, photocopying, recording or otherwise without the prior permission of Hudson's Media Ltd.

The views expressed by contributors do not necessarily reflect the views of Hudson's Media Ltd or its employees. When branded products are mentioned in editorial or advertising promotions, this should not be taken to imply endorsement of these products by Hudson's Media Ltd or Hudson's Historic Houses & Gardens.

© Hudson's Media Ltd 2016.

Front cover: Holker Hall, Cumbria Insets: jousting at Blenheim Palace, Oxfordshire; children play at Kiplin Hall, Yorkshire; fireworks at Leeds Castle, Kent.

Back cover: Inveraray Castle, Argyll; The Willow Tunnels, Anne Hathaway's Cottage, Warwickshire, the Indian Tea Room, Blenheim Palace, Oxfordshire.

2017

Welcome to HUDSONs

It's 30 years since the first edition of Hudson's – if you can send us a photo of 20 or more editions of Hudson's on your shelf, we will send you next year's for free. Chris Ridgeway at Castle Howard has traced the history of Hudson's for us in this edition. We are also looking at India and its influence not just on country houses but on all of our taste and interior design in the Anglo-India Year of Culture. It's 300 years since the death of Palladian architect James Paine and 30 years since the Great Storm of 1987 devastated gardens in the South East of England. We have been talking to heritage places that are sometimes better known for their regular appearances on screen and I talked to Helen Ghosh, Director of the National Trust. Veteran campaigner Dan Cruickshank alerts us to heritage he cares about and Jonathan Ruffer outlines his inspirational plans for Auckland Castle and the town of Bishop Auckland.

We know the real reason for picking up a copy of Hudson's is for the directory of heritage places to visit. We've filled up our maps for you to include even more historic places and given you lots of information for planning trips. More heritage places than ever are open in the winter – often just the gardens and grounds so the interiors get a rest and space for conservation – so apart from Christmas & Boxing Day you can take the chance to get up close to Britain's history. And, of course, from Easter to October there are thrills and discoveries, days out and places for weddings and overnight. We're delighted to be your companion so get inspired and get out there!

Sarah

Sarah Greenwood, Publisher

Inside

Pictures: Clockwise from opposite page: Antrim Castle Gardens, Antrim; Field to Fork Exhibition at Holkham Hall, Norfolk; dollshouses galore at Newby Hall, Yorkshire; Caerhays Castle, Cornwall, the HHA/Christie's Garden of the Year; *Spirit Jar* by Grayson Perry at Croome NT, Worcestershire.

Thanks to all private owners, local authorities, English Heritage, Historic Royal Palaces, Historic England, Historic Environment Scotland, the National Trust, the National Trust for Scotland, the Royal Collection for their information and for keeping Hudson's accurate and up-to-date. All images are copyright to Hudson's Media Ltd or to the property depicted unless otherwise stated.

Hudson's Historic Houses & Gardens team:
Editorial: Sarah Greenwood, Neil Pope
Production team: Deborah Coulter, Kylie Woolgar, Sarah Phillips
Creative team: Jamieson Eley, Neil Pope
Publishing Managers: Sarah Phillips, Kylie Woolgar
Advertising: James O'Rawe, Kirsten McInroy 01733 296913; Hall-McCartney Ltd, Baldock SG7 5SH
Web team: Sarah Greenwood; Sarah Phillips; Jamieson Eley; NVG www.NVG.net
Printer: Stephens & George, Methyr Tydfil CF48 3TD
Distribution: Compass International Publishing Services, Brentford TW8 9DF
Hudson's Media Ltd, 35 Thorpe Road, Peterborough PE3 6AG 01733 296910

WHAT'S NEW

Watch out for some highlights of the heritage year in 2017.

Year of Heritage, History and Archaeology

HISTORY HERITAGE & ARCHAEOLOGY • 2017 •

The famous monument at Glenfinnan, newly restored this year by the National Trust for Scotland, is a perfect symbol to launch 2017 Scotland's Year of Heritage, History & Archaeology. The tower, at the top of Loch Shiel, was the spot chosen by Bonnie Prince Charlie to rally his forces for the 1745 Jacobite Rising, so is a potent symbol in the Scottish story. From the enigmatic Neolithic village of Skara Brae in Orkney to castles, palaces, ancient townhouses, unrivalled gardens and gracious mansions, this is the year to visit all corners of Scotland and savour its heritage delights.

KEEP ON REMEMBERING
CAPABILITY BROWN! →

Plas Newydd, Hill St, Llangollen, LL20 8AW
Open: Apr, May, Sep, Wed-Mon; Jun-Aug, daily, 10.30-5pm; Oct, Wed-Mon, 10.30-4pm. Adult £6; child £5.

Pride of Place

2017 sees the launch of an initiative from Historic England which will both celebrate and protect the legacy of the LBGT community in Britain. The ambition is to extend statutory protection to historic places associated with the history of lesbian, bisexual, gay and transgender people and allow their stories to take their rightful place in our understanding of Britain's heritage.

Look out this year for LBGT heritage around you and if you want a starting off point how about two famous historic houses. Yorkshire's Shibden Hall, in the care of Calderdale Museums, was home to Anne Lister, today celebrated for her remarkable coded diary, only recently deciphered. The diary describes her life, not just her experience as an independent woman, landowner and farmer in Yorkshire, but also her experiences with the women that she loved and the way in which her independent fortune allowed her to adopt a lesbian lifestyle that was very much at odds with contemporary mores in the 1840s.

A similar household at Plas Newydd in North Wales was home, from 1780, to the Ladies of Llangollen, two Irish noblewomen, Eleanor Butler and Sarah Ponsonby, who became somewhat celebrated as hostesses in Romantic literary circles with writers like Lord Byron, Percy Bysshe Shelley and Sir Walter Scott coming to call.

Do get in touch this year with any LBGT heritage stories from your part of the world. Contact us by emailing info@hudsons-media.co.uk

Right: The reclusive Ladies of Llangollen, pictured in 1828

© THE WELLCOME TRUST

Below: Shibden Hall, Lister's Road, Halifax HX3 6XG
Open: Jan-Feb, Sat-Thur, 11-4pm; Mar-Oct, Sat – Thur, 11-5pm; Nov-Dec, Sat-Mon, 11-4pm. Adult £4.50; child £3.50.

WHAT'S NEW

Keep on remembering Capability Brown

It's no longer Capability Brown's birthday year but his legacy lives on. As part of last year's 'Capability Brown 300 Festival' there were 22 audience development projects aimed at keeping the excitement generated around the festival going long into the future. There are new interpretive schemes to help visitors understand the landscape at Petworth Park, where technology is being harnessed to bring information to visitors out and about in the Park, at Milton Abbey where the creation of a detailed topographical model has brought new insights into the creation of the landscape and at Fenstanton Church, Brown's burial place, where new interpretation boards tell his story.

Milton Abbey, Dorset

There are special trails: a sensory trail at Croome to encourage families with disabilities to discover the parkland and at Blenheim a circular walk that will help all visitors understand how Capability Brown's views and vistas enhance the designed landscape. The new pleasure launch on the lake at Harewood in Yorkshire is called *Capability*. At Kirkharle in Northumberland a whole new landscape has been created around a serpentine lake as a haven for wildlife and a tribute to Brown who was born here. Looks like we won't be forgetting him any time soon.

Above: Experiencing touch on the sensory landscape trail at Croome, Worcestershire
Left: Capability Brown and the plans for Blenheim Palace Park

ANGEL AWARDS

Since 2011 a select group of outstandingly committed groups or individuals have been honoured as Heritage Angels, in England by Historic England and in Scotland by the Scottish Civic Trust, Scottish Archaeology and Historic Environment Scotland. Heritage Angels are any people who have taken extraordinary steps to secure the future of a heritage place. In England, the categories are for best community action project (sponsored by NADFAS), best contribution by a young person, best research project, best rescue and outstanding contribution to heritage. In Scotland they are for Caring & Investigating, Caring & Protecting, Sharing & Celebrating, Young Heritage and Lifetime Contribution. Both schemes are supported by the Andrew Lloyd Webber Foundation. Nominations have to be in by the Autumn, October in England and August in Scotland. If you know of someone who has an exceptional commitment to a heritage project or you are one of those people yourself, put a name forward for an Angel Award in 2017.

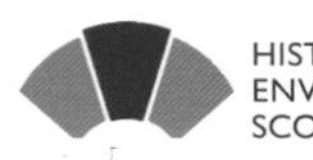

www. historicengland.org.uk/angel-awards.org.uk
www.scottishheritageangelawards.org.uk/

Stokecross Gardens, Berkshire opens for the National Gardens Scheme in 2017

90 years of Charity Gardens

In 2017 the National Gardens Scheme celebrates 90 years of opening private gardens across England & Wales for charity. Over the year there will be plenty of opportunities to celebrate their 90th anniversary, whilst raising money for nursing and caring charities, at the now 3,800 gardens who participate by welcoming visitors and donating the money raised to the Scheme.

NGS have designated the weekend of 27th-29th May as a special celebratory 90th Anniversary weekend. Over 400 gardens will be opening for a weekend of horticultural delight. However the fun doesn't stop there, with special events such as craft fairs, exhibitions and more, 2017 is set to be a truly unforgettable year at the National Gardens Scheme.

You can purchase copies of the 90th anniversary edition of the National Gardens Scheme Yellow Book 2017 at our eShop on www.hudsonsheritage.com

Hatfield House Gardens, Hertfordshire the first garden to open for the National Gardens Scheme in 1927

WHAT'S NEW

HULL CITY
OF CULTURE
2017 →

heritage open days

7 to 10 September 2017

'Let's open the doors!' announced Heritage Open Days patron, Loyd Grossman OBE. This year is set to increase the cavalcade of over 5000 free events and openings taking place between Thursday 7th and Sunday 10th September. From castles to cathedrals, stately homes to swimming baths, palaces to prisons, people of all ages, who might not otherwise engage with heritage become connected with their places through free to access demonstrations, exhibitions, talks and tours. All over the country the pink bunting, balloons and banners of Heritage Open Days are being recognised as a herald of the biggest heritage festival in the country. This year there will be just as much to celebrate, kicking off with a focus on places with a LBGT connections. Thanks to sponsors, the National Trust and the People's Postcode Lottery, 2017's Heritage Open Days weekend will be just as thrilling.

In Scotland, Wales & Northern Ireland things are only slightly different with Doors Open Days, Open Doors and European Heritage Days sparking free access days at weekends throughout September.

Doors Open Days
get into buildings!

© CHRIS LACEY

© ASHMOLEAN MUSEUM, UNIVERSITY OF OXFORD

Celebrating James Paine

In 2017, the Friends of Doncaster Mansion House, the Doncaster Civic Trust, York University and Doncaster Metropolitan Borough Council, celebrate the 300th Anniversary of James Paine's birth by holding a series of architectural and cultural events at the Mansion House and by creating a James Paine website and exhibition. The aim is to work with owners of James Paine's buildings, interested individuals, and organisations in order to develop a new audience for the buildings of James Paine. For further information on the Festival, visit www.mansionhousedoncaster.com.

Hogarth
LIGHTING

Illuminated Turners in the North Gallery of Petworth House with
Andrew Loukes - Curator of Exhibitions.

Our latest commission: to design a new picture light for The National Trust.
Primarily for 'Mr. Turner -An Exhibition' at Petworth House and continuing to
illuminate further works in this great collection.

sales@hogarthlighting.co.uk - www.hogarthlighting.co.uk - 0800 328 8051

WHAT'S NEW

Burton Constable Hall

Hull City of Culture 2017

East Yorkshire is not everyone's top destination but this year Kingston-upon-Hull is the UK's City of Culture so it's a good time to visit. The city itself fell on hard times in the 20th century but has an illustrious past. It was Edward I's King's Town and one of the country's premier ports. Rapid growth as a medieval wool port was followed by prominence in trade with the New World, as a whaling port and as a base for the North Sea fishing fleets. It has taken Hull a long time to recover from 95% destruction by bombing raids in World War II but the restored Old Town brings back its more prosperous past. Hull's most famous son is abolitionist William Wilberforce whose elegant Georgian house is preserved as a museum in the Old Town. As a base, Hull gives you access to the country houses of East Yorkshire, not often visited and well worth the trip. The stars are two Elizabethan prodigy houses. Burton Constable Hall, built by the Constable family in the 1560s, is only 9 miles from Hull. The interiors were remodelled 200 years later with plasterwork of the finest quality, a Cabinet of Curiosities and an exceptional Chinese room. Travel another 20 miles to reach Burton Agnes Hall, well worth the journey for its inspiring mix of antique and contemporary art. Five miles further North takes you to Georgian Sewerby Hall, opened to the public by another famous resident of Hull, Amy Johnson, in 1936. Head back down the coast for 20 miles to picturesque Regency Wassand Hall, overlooking Hornsea Mere, only 15 miles North of Hull.

Burton Agnes (p.258)
Burton Constable Hall (p.258)
Sewerby Hall (p.258)
Wassand Hall (p.258)

Burton Agnes

Sewerby Hall

Discover 1,000 years of history...

- Stunning art & architecture
- Extraordinary stories
- Impressive monuments
- Amazing stained glass
- Drive, walk & cycle trails
- City, town & country locations

visitchurches.org.uk

347 historic churches across England

Registered Charity No: 258612

Hillsborough Castle, the Terrace Garden

Mrs Hudson's Holiday

Mrs Hudson spends her holidays (with dog Walpole) trying out trips to get you thinking about your holidays. This year she's in Northern Ireland.

Why do we never think in our holiday planning – Belfast, that's the place for me! My trip to Northern Ireland was a revelation. First of all, value – I flew, for about the cost of a couple of M&S ready meals. The welcome – everyone is pleased to see you. The beauty – tiny Northern Ireland has sheep-freckled meadows, blue-grey mountains, inland seas, golden sands and craggy coastlines. It also packs in fierce Norman castles, elegant Georgian mansions, Baroque gardens and everywhere paintings of horses and mementoes of the Turf. In six days I didn't even touch all of the six counties.

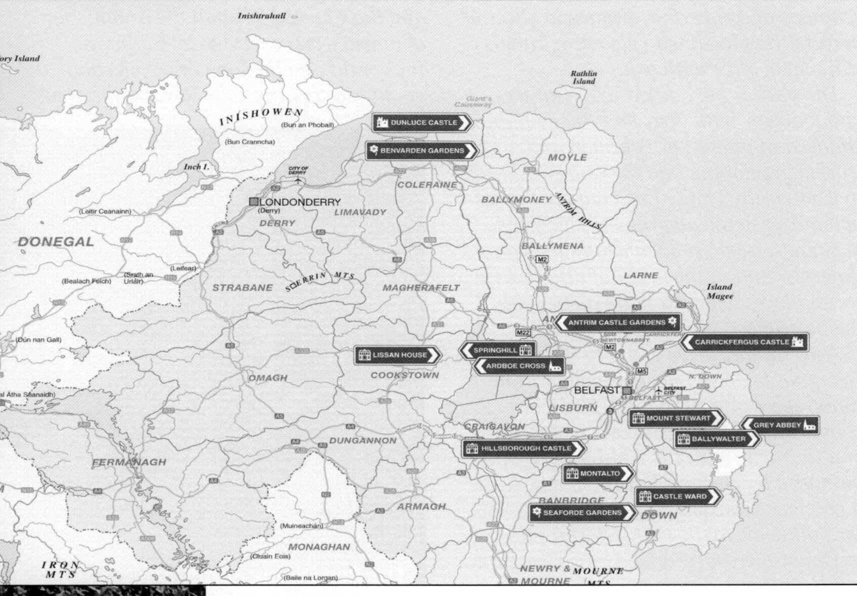

→

You've hardly left the airport before you are in Antrim and right at the heart of Northern Irish history. This was the stronghold of the Clotworthy family, sent to colonise by Elizabeth I; but the castle was burned to the ground during a ball in 1922 (by the IRA?) and only a lonely tower remains. Now a public park preserves the grounds of Antrim Castle and my first encounter with one of several surviving 17th Century gardens in the region. There is nothing quite like this on the mainland. Restored today is a 15 acre garden of the 1680s with pleached hornbeam, flowery parterres of geraniums, echinops and rubeckia, geometric allées of mature trees leading to gleaming canals of still water, alive with fish.

The park is busy, filled with runners and walkers, with dogs and Buggy Babes, children in pursuit of Pokemon and workmen popping into the courtyard café in Clotworthy House for a burger. Stories abound, of heroic wolfhounds, adoring husbands, tragic sudden death and canine funerals. And in the midst of all are wild secret places where you are alone with the birdsong.

A 40 minute drive South to the Georgian town of Hillsborough nestling round the castle on the hill. Hillsborough is now a working royal palace, something of a favourite with the royal family, and managed by Historic Royal Palaces. It is a gracious mansion designed in the 1780s for politician, Wills Hill, 1st Marquess of Downshire, surrounded by a Georgian landscape and Victorian gardens now getting some TLC. It's happening fast – HRP have great plans for Hillsborough and have kicked off with the commission of a new terrace garden by Catherine Fitzgerald and the loan of a collection of old Masters from the Royal Collection which sit happily with Hill family portraits, sparkling Waterford crystal chandeliers and fine Irish silver. The new visitor facilities will be finished by 2019 but that's no reason not to go now.

Antrim Castle Gardens

The Red Dining Room, Hillsborough Castle

Ardboe Cross

Tuesday

The whitewashed exterior of Springhill

A foray into County Tyrone on the West bank of Lough Neagh took me to two early Plantation houses. The crucial date for understanding Irish country houses is 1607, when, with the Flight of the Earls, the old Gaelic aristocracy of Ulster fled into exile and James I pursued a deliberate policy of colonisation, planting a new mainland aristocracy in Ireland.

My first stop, Lissan, is rather a discovery. The exterior is peculiar; a plain Georgian house with a long porte-cochere and a strange domed clock tower at the rear, but this distracts from the fact that this is an old house, dating in parts from the 1620s with a large courtyard of now derelict buildings which housed the domestic offices. Today's interiors are eclectic, with a striking arts and crafts hallway criss-crossed by a staircase like something out of Harry Potter and an 1830s ballroom lit by golden glass above the water garden.

The Staples family were full of characters, Lady Charity, imprisoned after the 1641 Rebellion; peg-legged Henrietta, who lost her leg in a London fire; 'handsome Kitty' whose lovely portrait by Martin Cregan now hangs over the fireplace; and Edwardian society painter and barefoot eccentric, Robert Ponsonby Staples. The Staples family died out in 1999 but by then the wealth accumulated over the centuries through coal and prudent marriages was long gone.

As the fortunes of Lissan declined so they became more entwined with those of the National Trust's nearby Springhill. In 1824 Charlotte Staples married William Lennox-Conyngham of Springhill and so began a process of acquisition accelerated in 1865 when a feud meant that the contents of Lissan were bequeathed to a relative of the Springhill family. Finally, paintings and furniture were acquired for Springhill in a 2-day house sale in the early part of the 20th Century. So at Springhill hangs a marvellous Pompeo Batoni portrait of John Staples on Grand Tour and a magnificent library of nearly 3000 books, one of the most important in Ireland. Springhill was restored by the National Trust so today's house is very much a Plantation house of the 1680s, plain and well balanced. It's intimate, tucked in among trees, and the costume collection is not to be missed.

I finished my day at Ardboe High Cross, a well preserved 9th Century stone cross in evidence of early Irish Christianity on the shores of Lough Neagh, stark in the evening light on the water.

Above, the Library at Springhill, with part of an outstanding collection of books built up by the Conyngham family. Above right, Lissan House

The Rt Hon John Staples (1736-1820) by Pompeo Batoni

Blenheim Palace, Oxfordshire

Woburn Abbey, Bedfordshire

Eastnor Castle, Herefordshire

Blair Castle, Pitlochry, Scotland

Highclere Castle, Berkshire

Arley Hall Gardens, Cheshire

Sausmarez Manor, Guernsey

Benvarden, Northern Ireland

Bolton Castle, Yorkshire

HISTORIC HOUSES ASSOCIATION

Become a Friend of the HHA and discover some of Britain's most special places

Scone Palace, Perth, Scotland

Hundreds of HHA-affiliated, privately-owned historic houses, castles and gardens open regularly to the public. Many of the properties are still lived in, often by families who have owned them for centuries, and many include exquisite gardens. Each is unique, giving you special insights into much-loved homes and their social and historical contexts.

HHA-affiliated properties welcome around 24 million visitors a year, support 41,000 jobs and are often key players in their local communities. The HHA provides practical advice and professional services to these properties, and we represent their views at local, national and European level. As a Friend, you help these properties by understanding their challenges, supporting the HHA's work and spreading the word about the special nature of privately-owned historic houses.

As an HHA Friend your membership gives you outstanding value for money:

- Free entry in normal opening hours to hundreds of historic houses, castles and gardens
- Our quarterly magazine *Historic House*
- Opportunities to join tours to visit properties not usually open to the public

Individual Friend £48
Double Friends (same address) £77
Additional Friends
(same address, including under-16s) £23

Rates shown above are for payment by direct debit.
For payment by credit/debit card or cheque, see www.hha.org.uk.

Check out HHA-affiliated properties with our free app for iPhone, iPad and Android.

To join us, visit www.hha.org.uk or call 01462 896688

Wednesday

Like so many invaders from the past, I arrived at the walls of Carrickfergus Castle. This fearsome Norman fortress glowers over the harbour that protects the entrance to Belfast Lough and to Ireland itself. The castle was first built by Norman invader John de Courcy in 1177 since when it's had an active life, last captured (by the French) in 1760 and an army garrison until 1928. The four square keep and the round headed arches of the banqueting hall are perfect Norman architecture and the whole place feels formidable, though the life size models are a bit disconcerting; the beauty of its reflection in the water is picture perfect.

Whizzing past Belfast on the motorway, I skirt the shores of Northern Ireland's other great body of water, Strangford Lough. Set above it is the National Trust's great 19th Century house, Mount Stewart. The gardens are world famous and the house today is approached through a jungle of exotic growth. I don't know of a more delightful garden for children than the Dodo Terrace with its statues of exotic animals, herms and Noah's Ark. The lake, the romantic Tir N'an Og where the Londonderry family are buried and the walk to the classical Temple of the Winds for views over the Lough filled my day, but this is also a serious treasure house. Home to Foreign Secretary, Lord Castlereagh in the 1810s, the house has always been a political powerhouse. The collection includes romantic portraits by all the great names of the 18th and 19th Centuries, Hoppner, Lawrence, de Lazlo and Sargent. Best of all is a massive canvas by George Stubbs of The Hambletonian, an eloquent study of an exhausted racehorse which dominates the West Stairs. Throughout the house is early English porcelain, Ulster crystal, tapestries and Irish silver all arranged by Edith, Lady Londonderry who revived the house in the 1900s.

Carrickfergus Castle

Mount Stewart; The Dodo Terrace; Dining Room and Central Hall

© NATIONAL TRUST IMAGES/ANDREW BUTLER

© NATIONAL TRUST IMAGES//NAOMI GOGGINS

© NATIONAL TRUST IMAGES/JOHN HAMMOND

© NATIONAL TRUST IMAGES/ELAINE HILL

© CROWN COPYRIGHT. REPRODUCED WITH THE PERMISSION OF THE CONTROLLER OF HER MAJESTY'S STATIONERY OFFICE

Ballywalter Park

Thursday

Moving inland from Strangford Lough, Ballywalter Park is a pink wedding cake of a house, where Lord and Lady Dunleath continue of long tradition of hospitality by leading pre-booked tours. Here the money to build the house was made in the linen mills of 19th Century Belfast, once the largest in the world. It was spent in 1852 commissioning Charles Lanyon to create an Italianate palazzo with a spacious fashionable interior including a domed conservatory, a billiard room and a panelled toplit staircase hall at the heart of the house. The gardens incorporate an earlier walled garden but the Edwardian water gardens set with mature cedars reflect the house's finest period when it was famous for its parties and cricket matches.

To reach Castle Ward from Ballywalter, take the ferry across the Lough to appreciate the size of this inland sea. The National Trust have done much to preserve the East shore from development and once you step through the gates of the Castle Ward estate, it is a hive of activity. There are campers and canoeists, walkers and lodge guests, horse riders, bird watchers and prospective brides. There are also several groups led by guides in wolfskin cloaks on the Game of Thrones trail – there are 10 separate locations for the hit HBO series on the estate. You can trace the layered history. The first castle is now part of the farmyard, the formal canal and temple of a Baroque Plantation house are still part of a later landscape garden, and at the top of the hill stands a pretty Georgian house, Palladian on one side, Gothic on the other. The classical interiors are beautiful but it is the gothic that excites, particularly the fan vaulted ceiling in the Boudoir, but most of all it is the charming eccentricity of this his-and-hers house in two styles that captivates.

Castle Ward's plain Classical front at odds with gothic interiors in the Boudoir and Parnell Bedroom

© NATIONAL TRUST IMAGES/NICK MEERS

© NATIONAL TRUST IMAGES/ ANDREAS VON EINSIEDEL

Seaforde Gardens

Friday

I'm in Co. Down at Georgian Montalto, a restored stuccoed mansion that today is all about luxury. Staying in the exquisitely redecorated rooms which cater to small parties up to 18 is comfort indeed. The best rooms are on the first floor where The Drawing Room has Italian rococo plasterwork and views of the Mourne Mountains having started life as the entrance hall. Montalto is hospitable to all and if you aren't staying in the main house, you might be a wedding guest in The Carriage Rooms. Opening soon for casual visitors, a new gift shop and tea room, and approximately 12 km of trails through the landscaped gardens and woodland. These gardens still have several majestic trees planted by Lord Moira in 1770.

Down the road at Seaforde Gardens, I'm in for a surprise. Lady Anthea Forde has a thing about butterflies and while her late husband Patrick, a celebrated Irish gardener, collected plants for the garden from the Far East, she retaliated by importing butterflies. I spent an hour at least in the Tropical Butterfly House surrounded by the jewel-like wings of swallowtails and monarchs. But the walled garden is the star attraction. Walls protect a micro-climate which has allowed rare sub-tropical plants to flourish. A climb up the Mogul Tower allows you to cheat by tracing a path through the hornbeam maze before trying it for real. Radiating from a group of Victorian conifers, one brought back from the Crimea as a seed, are banks of shrubs and rhododendrons in The Pheasantry Garden. In late summer the garden was full of the subdued tones of blue hydrangeas and the pink and white flowers of some 20 species of Eucryphias, of which the garden has a National Collection.

The gardens at Montalto

Saturday

On the North coast just west from the Giant's Causeway, finding that Dunluce Castle looks Scottish is perhaps no surprise; Scotland is just across the water. Jutting out to sea on a basalt outcrop, Dunluce still looks impregnable even in a ruinous state. Much of the gatehouse towers of the first castle survive but it was seized and largely rebuilt by the deliciously named Sorley Boy McDonnell in the 1550s and was the centre of his resistance to both the local Irish O'Neill chieftains and the English crown. It's a romantic place, full of legend, the cannons came from an Armada wreck, the ruins of a lost town surround it and you must risk a narrow bridge into the inner bailey.

Not far away and back to more civilised times at Benvarden Gardens. The distinctive curved wall of the 2 acre walled garden was already on a map in 1780 and it has been gardened by the Montgomery family since 1798. A rare pleasure is the well maintained kitchen garden, the walls rich with tayberries and espaliered fruit trees and the other half, filled with roses and lavender, is buzzing with bees around clipped topiary bunnies. Surrounding it is a landscaped pleasure ground and a charming stable tearoom with the Montgomery racing colours adorning the walls.

Benvarden Gardens

© CROWN COPYRIGHT. REPRODUCED WITH THE PERMISSION OF THE CONTROLLER OF HER MAJESTY'S STATIONERY OFFICE

Dunluce Castle
Below: the narrow bridge to the inner bailey

Antrim Castle Gardens ***(p.330)***
Hillsborough Castle ***(p.331)***
Lissan House ***(p.331)***
Springhill NT ***(p.332)***
Carrickfergus Castle ***(p.331)***
Mount Stewart NT ***(p.331)***
Ballywalter Park ***(p.330)***
Castle Ward NT ***(p.331)***
Montalto ***(p.331)***
Seaforde Gardens ***(p.332)***
Dunluce Castle ***(p.331)***
Benvarden Gardens ***(p.331)***

Mrs Hudson travelled by Easyjet to Belfast, hired a car at the airport and found no journey longer than an hour. Walpole the dog hates planes. Mrs Hudson is a pseudnym (and so is Walpole).

TARR ON THE ROAD

Peddars & Prince's Feathers

West Norfolk is a region of forests, farmland and open common, peppered with quaint villages and distinctive churches, nestling under a vast sky. Derek Tarr headed southwards visiting great houses and ancient monuments, finishing in gentle Breckland.

DEREK'S WALKS
DAY BY DAY

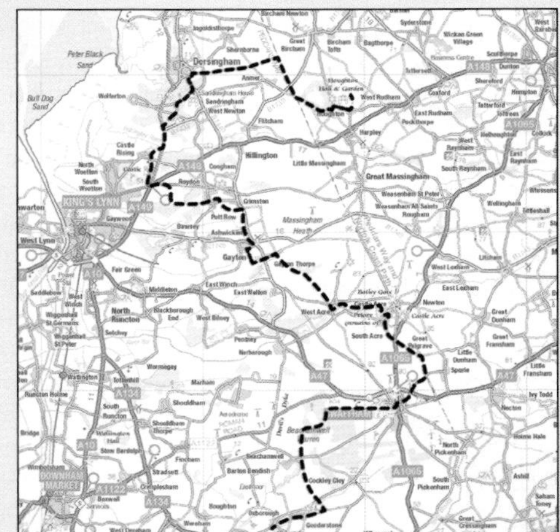

Walk 1: Houghton to Dersingham
Walk 2: Dersingham to Knights Hill
Walk 3: Knights Hill to Castle Acre
Walk 4: Castle Acre to Oxborough

Photos: Nicola Burford

Houghton Hall

WALK 1
Houghton to Dersingham
8 miles approx

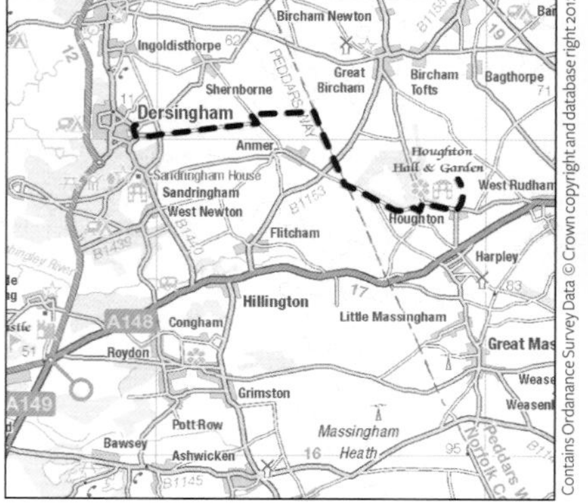

Contains Ordanance Survey Data © Crown copyright and database right 2012

Magnificent Houghton Hall, 18 miles east of Kings Lynn, is the largest country house in Norfolk and the starting point for my ramble. The hall was built in the early 18th Century by Sir Robert Walpole, the first Prime Minister of Great Britain, and is still privately owned by his descendant the 7th Marquess of Cholmondeley. The interior is sumptuous from the intricate plasterwork ceiling of the Stone Hall through to the lavish living quarters. The Great Staircase, where I spent some time discussing the hall with one of the many helpful and informative attendants, is dominated by a bronze copy of the Borghese Gladiator, an ancient marble sculpture housed in the Louvre in Paris.

Following Walpole's death in 1745 the estate fell on hard times due to crippling debts. Many treasures were disposed of including a substantial art collection sold to Katharine the Great of Russia, which now hangs in the Hermitage Museum in St Petersburg. It was not until the 20th Century that Houghton was brought back to its former glory by the 5th Marquess of Cholmondeley and his wife Lady Sybil.

Castle Rising

Outside there is much to see with an array of sculptures both traditional and contemporary. In the stable block is the famed collection of model soldiers, some recreating scenes from historic battles.

I left the estate and followed country lanes before joining the Peddars Way, a footpath following the course of an ancient roadway which I would encounter again later in the walk. So typical of an English summer, the atmosphere became muggy and for a short time the rain lashed down, quickly followed by sunshine over a countryside that was fresh and sparkling.

The Borghese Gladiator

Mortlake tapestries at Houghton

The Feathers Inn

I arrived at Dersingham and visited the church of St Nicholas and its adjoining tithe barn. A short stroll brought me to The Feathers Inn and my stop for the night. Following a delicious meal of local crab with cheese sauce and excellent hospitality, I had a very good night's sleep.

NATIONAL GARDEN SCHEME

Help celebrate our 90th year by visiting a beautiful garden

For more information on our 3,800 gardens open for charity in England and Wales, visit our website **www.ngs.org.uk** or telephone **01483 211535**

The National Gardens Scheme. Registered charity number 1112664

WALK 2

Dersingham to Knights Hill

6.4 miles approx

Suitably refreshed, I left Dersingham the following morning and walked the mile or so to the royal residence of Sandringham House, passing the ornate Norwich Gates on the way. While less imposing than Houghton it has a particular Victorian charm. The house and estate of 7000 acres was purchased in 1862 for the Prince of Wales, later King Edward VII, but was deemed too small for his requirements and so was rebuilt. By 1870 it was completed. The estate has long been held in affection by the Royal Family and every year they spend Christmas here. The Queen's father, King George VI, died here in February 1952. Several rooms are open to the public and there is a fine collection of paintings, porcelain and furniture to be viewed. I was fascinated by a table in the Small Drawing Room from where Her Majesty The Queen has broadcast her Christmas message.

Outside in the gardens, a short distance from the house entrance, stands a wonderful sculpture of a horse, *Estimate*, a favourite of The Queen. It was sculpted by Tessa Campbell Fraser who is the wife of the impressionist and comedian Rory Bremner.

A little way from the house are the coach houses and stable block now converted into a museum, showing an eclectic mix of the Royal Family's state carriages, cars and memorabilia as well as a section dedicated to the Sandringham Company's involvement in the Gallipoli campaign in the First World War. The driveable model of James Bond's Aston Martin DB5 given to Prince Andrew in the mid 1960's brought a nostalgic smile to my face.

I had a bite to eat in the café then strolled through the grounds to visit the parish church of St Mary Magdalene close to the edge of the estate. The church was restored in 1855 and today is a delight. It is used regularly by the Royal Family as a place of worship. Outside is the grave of Prince John, the youngest child of King George VI and Queen Mary. Born at Sandringham in 1905, his story is a tragic one. At an early age it was discovered that he suffered from epilepsy and in 1919, at the age of just 13, he died following a particularly severe attack.

I continued on my travels through the wooded Sandringham Estate and on to the lovely village of Castle Rising. One of the first buildings I came to was Trinity Hospital, an almshouse created in the

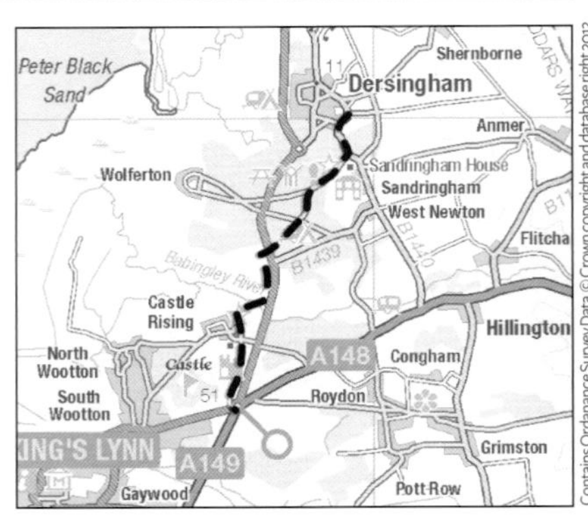

Contains Ordnance Survey Data © Crown copyright and database right 2012

17th Century which houses twelve poor spinsters. Over the years it has been visited by many distinguished people including Alexandra, the last Tsarina of Russia. There is a custom for the residents to attend the Norman church nearby dressed in traditional black hats and red gowns.

The village is dominated by the impressive 12th Century Norman Castle. Much remains of the keep and surrounding earthworks which make it one of the most important medieval structures of this kind in England. It was the dower house for Queen Isabella, the She-wolf of France, following the murder of her husband Edward II at Berkeley Castle. Unlike most other buildings of this era many rooms are still accessible. Since 1544 it has been owned by the Howard family and today is run by English Heritage.

The lane adjacent to the castle led me to the hotel at Knights Hill and the end of the day's journey.

Top, stained glass window in the Norman church of St Lawrence, Castle Rising. Above, Prince Andrew's 007 DB5 in Sandringham Museum.

Left, Daimler Phaeton - the first British Royal car - in Sandringham Museum. Above, Sandringham. Right, Prince John's grave

→

From the top: West Front and fireplace, Castle Acre Priory; Castle gateway, Castle Acre; Roydon Common

WALK 3

Knights Hill to Castle Acre

14.9 miles approx

After two fairly short walks, days three and four were a little more demanding. Following an early start I arrived at Roydon Common, an unusually wild landscape for Norfolk. Maintained by the Norfolk Wildlife Trust this wilderness is home to many species of dragonfly and butterfly, snakes, sheep and even ponies. However, on this day I saw none of these and my abiding memory is sand, and lots of it. Although difficult to walk across, it didn't slow my progress and soon I continued through typical East Anglian countryside of fields and lanes before reaching Gayton by mid-morning. I ventured down the main street passing the village school with its ferocious carved dragon in the playground. The church of St Nicholas was looking resplendent in the sunshine, as was the old windmill a little further along.

I 'ploughed on' past the round towered church at Gayton Thorpe and followed an easy course to Soigne Wood before arriving at West Acre. As I gazed at the 14th Century tower of the church of All Saints, a local gent asked me if I had noticed the clock. *'Very unusual'* he said. As I looked closer I realised that it was adorned with letters instead of numbers spelling out 'WATCH AND PRAY'. Down the lane was the superb Stag Inn where I popped in for a quick pint and a baguette. The walls and ceiling in the bar of this traditional English pub are decorated with an extensive collection of beer mats.

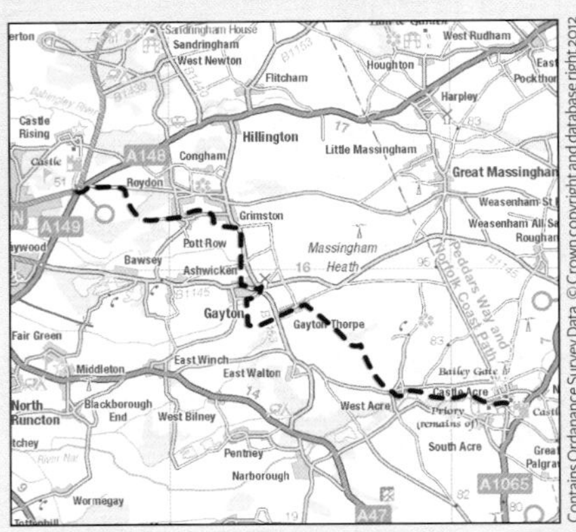

Contains Ordanance Survey Data © Crown copyright and database right 2012

I followed a wooded valley east for a couple of miles, occasionally glimpsing the glistening River Nar, before reaching the picturesque village of Castle Acre. Just on the outskirts is the impressive priory, another site administered by English Heritage. It was dissolved in 1537 but, despite the best efforts of Henry VIII and Thomas Cromwell, much of the priory is still intact. Created by the powerful Warrene family, Earls of Surrey, for over 400 years it was part of the Cluniac order of monks centred on the abbey of Cluny in Burgundy. As with Castle Rising there are many surviving rooms to visit in this most idyllic of settings.

On the village green is the characterful 15th Century Ostrich Inn and that evening's resting place. After dinner I took a stroll to the nearby castle. A lot less of this remains compared with the priory but there is still much to spark the imagination. Pre-dating the priory this Norman stronghold was also a Warrene family creation. It remained important until the late Middle Ages when it was abandoned and subsequently left to deteriorate.

St Nicholas, Gayton

Above (clockwise): the ferocious carved dragon in the village school at Gayton; Watch and Pray clock at All Saints, West Acre; beer mats, Stag Inn, West Acre; the remains of the keep at Castle Acre

Castle Acre Priory

WALK 4

Castle Acre to Oxborough

15 miles approx

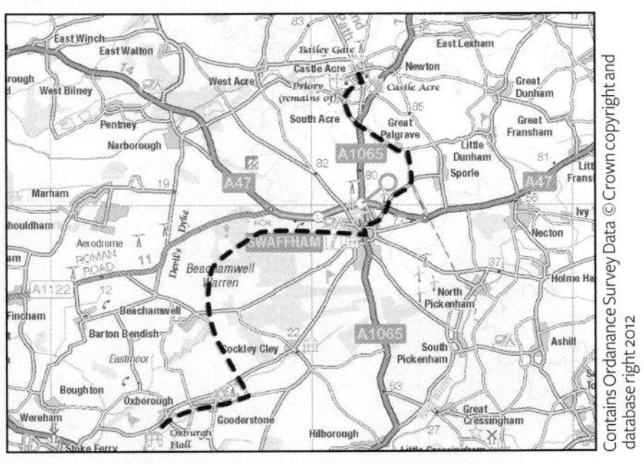

Contains Ordanance Survey Data © Crown copyright and database right 2012

From Castle Acre I rejoined the Peddars Way and headed south pausing to glance back at the priory. In due course I passed Great Palgrave and the site of a long lost medieval village then proceeded into Northern Breckland and the elegant market town of Swaffham. Carvings on the pews of a man, his wife and his dog in the church of St Peter and St Paul hold the key to the tale of the Peddlar of Swaffham, the town's symbol. In 1460 a church warden named John Chapman dreamt of going to London where he would find his fortune. Following his dream he walked to London Bridge where he was told by a stranger to return home and dig under a tree. He followed the advice and found a pot of gold. The story maybe fanciful but Chapman did exist and donated a large sum to rebuild the church. A visit to the small local history museum by the market square is highly recommended. One fascinating section is dedicated to Howard Carter the discoverer of the tomb of the Ancient Egyptian Pharaoh Tutankhamun.

I picked up a sandwich and headed westwards. After a couple of miles of lanes, tracks and forest the route turned south close to the air station at RAF Marham. I lingered for a while to watch pirouetting Tornadoes performing their manoeuvres before continuing on my way to Gooderstone passing hamlets and pig farms and, surprisingly, two American police cars on the driveway of an isolated cottage. Norfolk never fails to surprise!

Reaching the outskirts of the village there was more evidence of the vagaries of the English weather. All day I had walked in glorious sunshine but here the roads were partially flooded due to a recent downpour. Heading towards the centre of the village I discovered a hidden jewel, the Gooderstone Water Gardens. Designed by retired farmer Billy Knights in the early 1970's, these stunning gardens were

Oxburgh Hall

developed in a damp meadow by the River Gadder. Wandering through this little piece of paradise reminded me of Claude Monet's gardens at Giverny in France, without the crowds!

Sadly my time was short and I wanted to reach my final destination, Oxburgh Hall. Intriguingly the hall is located in the village of Oxborough, but has a different spelling. This wonderful Tudor fortified and moated manor house was built in 1482 by Sir Edmund Bedingfeld and, although now owned by the National Trust, his descendants still live here. With an array of towers, chimneys and turrets, little has changed since it was constructed and it is truly a 'fairytale' location. Throughout there is a richness of colour and atmosphere with many delightful rooms. The family were Catholics and fell out of favour at the time of the Reformation. As with other houses of the period, Oxburgh has a priest hole to visit. This small room was cleverly designed to hide a Catholic priest if the Crown's officers came searching. If caught the penalties were severe. A fine way to round off the trip is to climb the stairs to the roof from where there are extensive views of both the countryside in the distance and the house directly below.

Due to high maintenance costs and taxes the family were forced to sell the estate just after the Second World War. Amazingly, this wonderful building was threatened with demolition but, thankfully, the family were able to find the money to buy back the property and donate it to the National Trust in 1952.

Above (clockwise): Triptych, Oxburgh Hall chapel; the library, Oxburgh Hall; Swaffham Museum; Gooderstone Water Gardens

Immediately upon leaving the estate I came across the unusual church of St John. Initially it appeared to be a ruin but in fact half the church is still in use. In 1948 the spire collapsed and it was decided that rather than rebuilding that area of the church it should be left as a shell.

After a hot but enjoyable day, I retired to the stylish and comfortable Bedingfeld Arms, only a short distance from the hall, to enjoy a well-earned dinner.

This area is one of the most tranquil that England has to offer, untouched by the bustling commercial world. The only concessions to advertising I saw were the colourful village name signs, so typical of Norfolk, which adorned the local greens. The friendly demeanour of the people I met guaranteed a warm welcome for this weary heritage traveller.

Houghton Hall (p.214)
Sandringham (p.216)
Castle Rising (p.215)
Castle Acre Priory (p.216)
Oxburgh Hall (p.215)

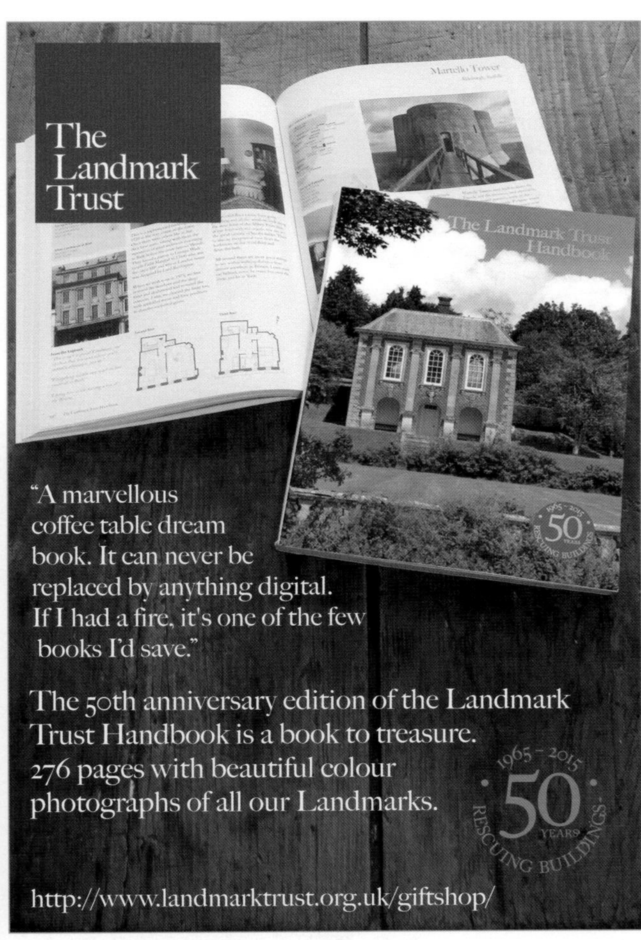

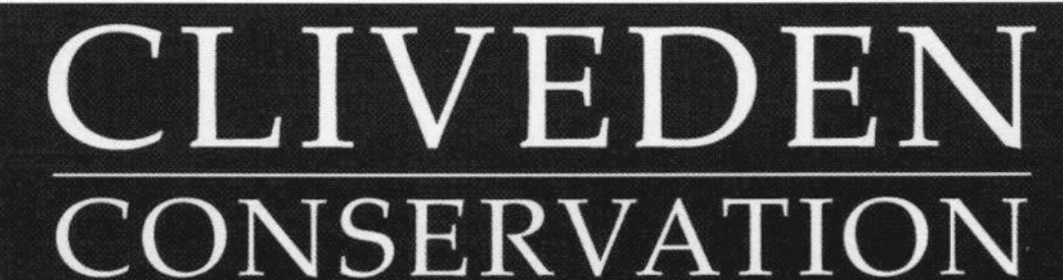

The Landmark Trust
The Landmark Trust Handbook
"A marvellous coffee table dream book. It can never be replaced by anything digital. If I had a fire, it's one of the few books I'd save."
The 50th anniversary edition of the Landmark Trust Handbook is a book to treasure. 276 pages with beautiful colour photographs of all our Landmarks.
1965 – 2015 50 YEARS RESCUING BUILDINGS
http://www.landmarktrust.org.uk/giftshop/

CLIVEDEN CONSERVATION
For the Conservation of Statuary, Masonry, Mosaics, Monuments, Plasterwork & Decorative Arts
Cutlers Hall,City of London. After conservation
City Heritage Award for the Conservation & Refurbishments of the Facade, including Terracotta Frieze & Coat of Arms
With offices at:
Cliveden Estate, near Maidenhead t. 01628 604721
Ammerdown Estate, near Bath t. 01761 420300
Houghton, Norfolk t. 01485 528970
www.clivedenconservation.com
By appointment sculpture conservators to THE NATIONAL TRUST

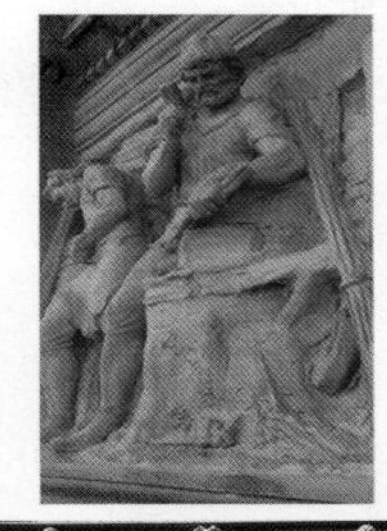

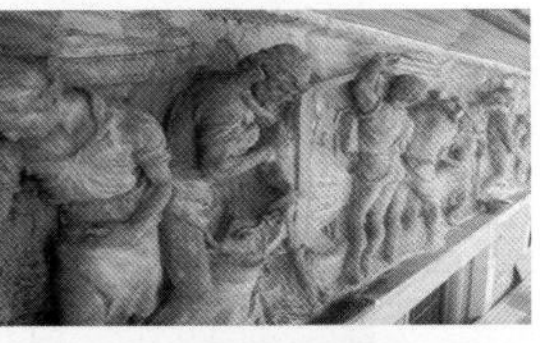

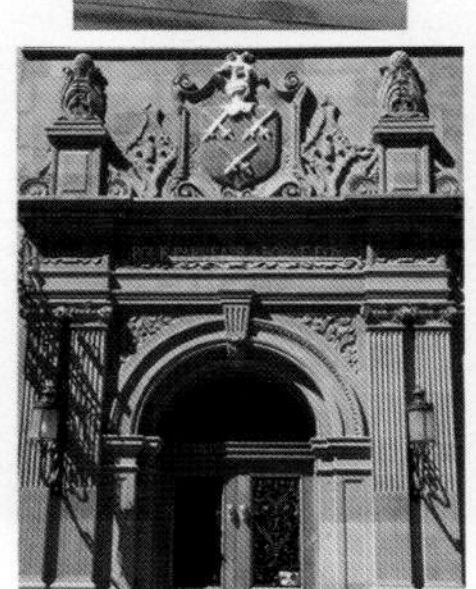

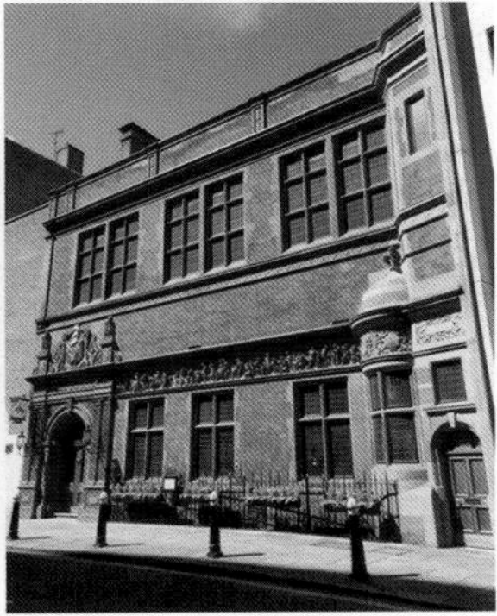

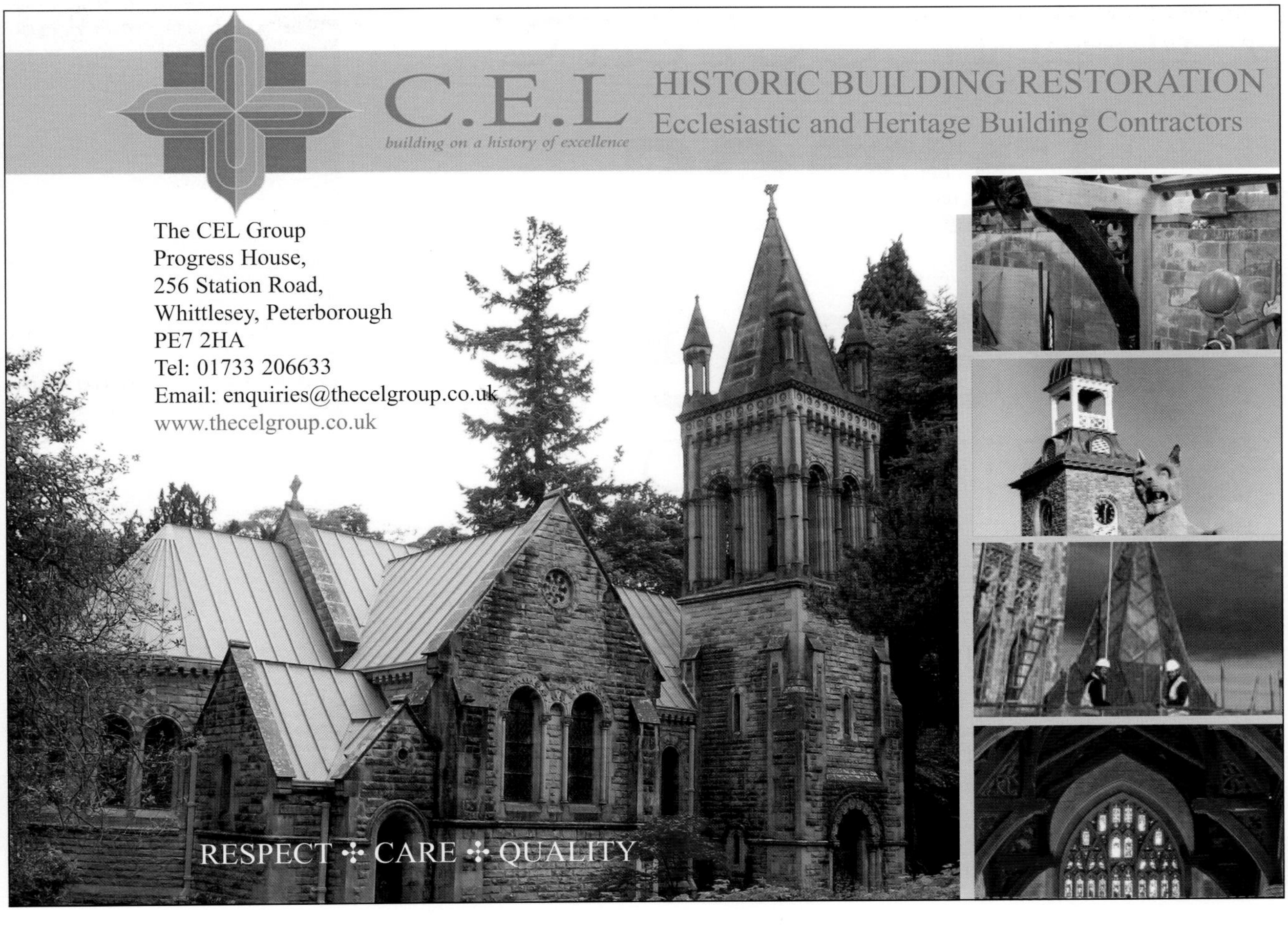

C.E.L
building on a history of excellence
HISTORIC BUILDING RESTORATION
Ecclesiastic and Heritage Building Contractors
The CEL Group
Progress House,
256 Station Road,
Whittlesey, Peterborough
PE7 2HA
Tel: 01733 206633
Email: enquiries@thecelgroup.co.uk
www.thecelgroup.co.uk
RESPECT ✣ CARE ✣ QUALITY

© ASHMOLEAN MUSEUM, UNIVERSITY OF OXFORD

James Paine and his son, James, who was also an architect, painted by Sir Joshua Reynolds and now in the Ashmolean

Defining Architecture
James Paine
1717-1789

James Paine, pioneer Palladian architect, was born 300 years ago this year. Peter Leach, who wrote the definitive biography of Paine, talked to ***Hudson's*** about his legacy.

The Temple of Diana at Weston Park designed James Paine in 1770 to house exotic plants. It is now a holiday let for six, so you can stay in this extraordinarily beautiful and unique building

→

The history of our built and crafted heritage, with its rich cast of creative personalities, has naturally through the passage of time thrown up a wealth of anniversaries to be celebrated. Last year it was the tercentenary of the birth of the landscape gardener 'Capability' Brown and this year it is that of the architect James Paine. The son of a carpenter, Paine was born in the Hampshire town of Andover in the autumn of 1717; and a century later he and his older contemporary Sir Robert Taylor (1714-88) were described as having *'nearly divided the practice of the profession between them ... till Mr. Robert Adam entered the lists'*.

Paine's reaction to 'Capability' Brown was ambivalent. As long as Brown was practising in his chosen metier of landscape gardening, occasionally in conjunction with Paine's own architecture, Paine was prepared to pay tribute to his skill; but his periodic forays as an architect on his own account reduced Paine to grumpy sarcasm:

'*... what surprizing genius's then must those be who are* born architects? *how much above every other order of men? but, as nothing is impossible with the great Author of nature, so we have seen a genius of this kind, who, after having been from his youth confined against his nature, to the serpentine walks of horticulture, emerge, at once, a* compleat architect, *and produce such things, as none but those who were* born *with such amazing* capability *could possibly have done ...*'

Above: The bridge at Chillngton was designed by James Paine to ornament the new landscaped park designed by Lancelot 'Capability' Brown with whom he was a frequent collaborator

Below: Paine's bridge across the Temple Pool at Weston Park, Shropshire; another fine 'Capability' Brown landscape

Francis W Downing

Restoration and Conservation of Paintings

The Studio was established in 1976 to clean and conserve paintings on canvas, panel and fixed structures to the highest standards of conservation for private clients, historic houses, churches, museums and galleries.

- Full professional indemnity insurance
- Full UK and European coverage
- Francis Downing is an Accredited Member of the Institute of Conservation

Over 40 years experience of art conservation, research and care

Francis W Downing ACR
203 Wetherby Road, Harrogate, North Yorkshire HG2 7AE
Tel: 01423 886962 Email: francisdowning@msn.com
www.francisdowning.com

78th EDITION

Cottage in the Wood, Worcestershire

SIGNPOST

SELECTED PREMIER HOTELS 2017

Every Signpost hotel has that something special – the warmest of welcomes, style, comfort, fabulous food and plenty to see and do in the area. All our hotels are inspected by our team, to make sure the highest standards are maintained. The 78th edition continues our tradition of presenting a select collection of premier hotels including luxury country house hotels in beautiful grounds, small hotels with log fires and cosy bedrooms and smart modern townhouse hotels.

www.signpost.co.uk

'Gem of a guide... covers hotels of character'
EXECUTARY NEWS

'For anyone doing any extensive motoring in Britain, this guide would seem invaluable'
NEW YORKER MAGAZINE

'The British Hotel guide for the discerning traveller'
PERIOD LIVING

The Mansion House, Doncaster, a bravado early work for James Paine. Open: All year, on advertised dates, 10-2pm. Tel: 01302 734309

Right: The interior of Doncaster Mansion House

But there was a serious issue at stake here, for Paine, expounding his approach to architecture in the Preface to a volume of his collected designs, was insisting that anybody aspiring to the profession should be *'bred an architect'* and, if he was to *'do justice to his employer'*, should be equipped with the necessary skills and qualifications – knowledge of geometry, proficiency in drawing of all kinds, an understanding of materials and of *'the value of the labour of the several artificers'*, and *'a habit of considering and supplying the conveniences of families of every rank'* derived from *'a constant observation of the wants of mankind'*. In all this he emerges as a spokesman for a new sense of professionalism among architects; and in that capacity he was one of those who helped to lay the foundations of the architectural profession of later centuries.

So how was this professionalism manifested in Paine's work? His career began when, at the age of 19, he was engaged to supervise the erection of Nostell Priory in Yorkshire, a large Palladian country house designed by the amateur architect Colonel James Moyser of Beverley; and then in 1745 he was commissioned to design a prominent public building in the area, the Mansion House at Doncaster. The town, with its famous races, in pre-industrial times functioned as a social centre for the polite society of the locality; and the Mansion House was conceived as a sort of assembly rooms, a venue for the Corporation to *'receive'* the *'neighbouring Nobility and Gentry'* at the *'Entertainments',* as Paine put it.

The striking, original and dramatic design of Stockeld Park in Yorkshire

©NATIONAL TRUST IMAGES/MARK BOLTON

Not surprisingly, it is something of an apprentice work and it has been altered over the years, but its distinctive character is still apparent. It is a rectangular block containing *'Rooms for the Entertainment of Gentlemen'* on the ground floor, and on the piano nobile a double-cube-shaped banqueting room together with tea and card rooms, approached by an imperial staircase. The front, with coupled half-columns and a central Venetian window, and originally crowned by a big pediment across its whole width (replaced by an attic storey in 1803), was copied from one of the centrepieces in the designs for Whitehall Palace published in William Kent's *Designs of Inigo Jones* (1727), Paine simply setting it on a rusticated base; while for the interiors he designed an elaborate scheme of decoration in the characteristic Palladian-cum-rococo manner of his early years. That scheme was only executed in part but in his book of the designs for the building he noted that *'The Ornaments ... are of stucco, executed by Mr. Rose and Mr. Thomas Perritt inferior to none of the Performances of the best Italians that ever work'd in this kingdom'*; and these two Yorkshire plasterers were to work for him on many subsequent occasions. So here we see Paine starting to build up his own team of tried and trusted craftsmen and decorative artists – a strategy which was also adopted a few years later by Robert Adam and was evidently a significant factor in the success of these new professionals.

From these beginnings Paine developed during the 1750s a large country house practice mainly in the North and North Midlands, a particular feature of his work being his pioneering development of the compact, centrally planned Palladian villa form as a model for country houses. One of the finest examples is Stockeld Park near Wetherby in Yorkshire (1758-63), a memorably original and dramatic design in which the Palladian-villa starting point is barely discernible, with a striking triple-pedimented silhouette derived principally from the wings of William Kent's Holkham Hall in Norfolk.

Looking upwards through the staircase to the ceiling detail at Stockeld Park

The chapel commissioned from James Paine in 1760 to ornament the parkland at Gibside, Tyne & Wear now a favourite for weddings →

New Wardour Castle

Inside, the climax is the spectacular toplit central staircase rising right to the attic, with all the main rooms opening conveniently off it. Paine was known during his lifetime as an accomplished designer of staircases, and this fusion of dramatic effect and convenient planning was doubtless one of the qualities which the writer of his obituary in the *Gentleman's Magazine* in 1789 had in mind when he praised Paine's *'uncommon powers in adapting the plans of his buildings with the justest precision, for the purposes to which they were dedicated'*.

During his later years his practice came to be concentrated more in the South, closer to his base in London. Examples from this phase include the new Wardour Castle in Wiltshire (1770-76) and Richmond Bridge, Surrey (1774-7). The latter was one of a group of bridges over the lower Thames which he undertook during these years – evidently competence at bridge-building on a quite ambitious scale was an accomplishment which was expected of architects at this time: this was the finest of the four and apart from being widened in 1937 has been little altered. Wardour Castle however represents the real culmination of Paine's career, for here he used the Palladian villa form for a country house of the largest size – the logical consequence of his progressive development of the villa idea. A big square block flanked by wings of complex form, it is a creative re-working of Palladio's unexecuted project for the Trissino brothers, with the latter's circular central saloon transformed into another magnificent toplit staircase hall now surrounded by the type of circuit of reception rooms which contemporary social mores required. The epitome of the qualities celebrated by Paine's obituarist, the house is one of English Palladianism's defining images.

See James Paine's work at:
Nostell Priory (NT), Yorkshire ***(p.269)***
Stockeld Park, Yorkshire ***(p.266)***
Gibside (NT), Tyne & Wear ***(p.293)***
Wallington (NT), Northumberland ***(p.293)***
Chatsworth, Derbyshire ***(p.225)***
Weston Park, Shropshire ***(p.243)***
Chillington Hall, Staffordshire ***(p.245)***
New Wardour Castle ***is not open to the public.***

For Quality British Coins

RODERICK RICHARDSON

Numismatist

WANTED Choice Collections and Individuals Items

For appointments in London or my latest circular, please contact me at
Old Granary Antiques Centre, Kings Staithe Lane,
King's Lynn, Norfolk, England PE 30 ILZ
Tel: **(+44) 1553 670833**
Email: **roderickrichardson@yahoo.co.uk**
Check out my website: **roderickrichardson.com**

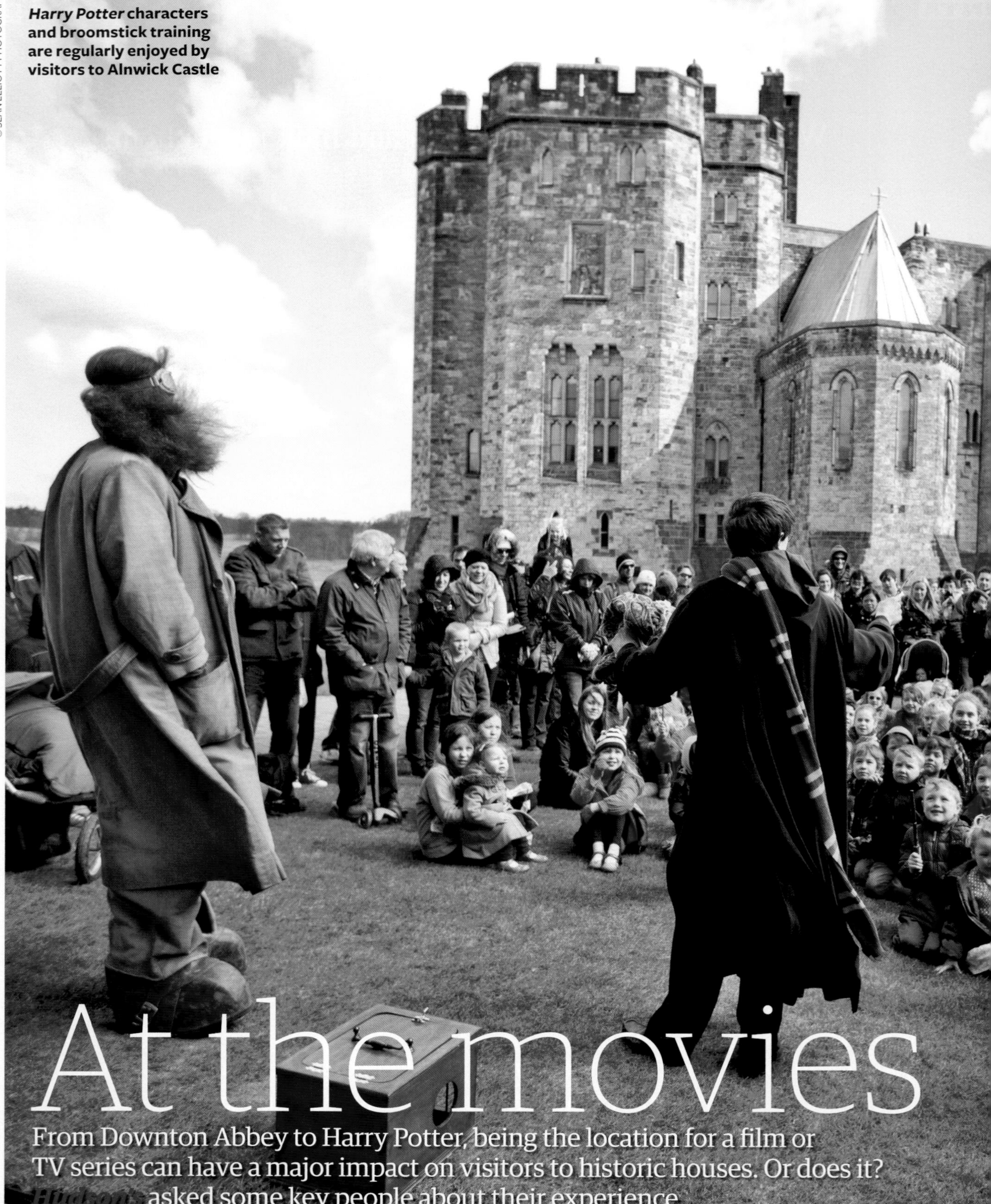

© SEAN ELLIOTT PHOTOGRAPHY

Harry Potter characters and broomstick training are regularly enjoyed by visitors to Alnwick Castle

At the movies

From Downton Abbey to Harry Potter, being the location for a film or TV series can have a major impact on visitors to historic houses. Or does it? *Hudson's* asked some key people about their experience.

Daniel Watkins (pointing) shares secrets with a crowd of Potter fans

Daniel Watkins manages the State Rooms at Alnwick Castle, Northumberland and knows the global response to Harry Potter first hand.

While Alnwick Castle has been home to the Percy family for 700 years, it is perhaps its place as a film location that resonates just as much with many of our visitors.

Most famously, the castle's grounds featured as part of Hogwarts School in the first two *Harry Potter* films. Shooting took place in the early 2000s, but the impact of *Harry Potter* is still apparent today, with visitors particularly eager to fly broomsticks where Harry and friends first flew theirs. It seems that, especially for our international visitors, the impact of Potter is comparable to the likes of Shakespeare, Sherlock Holmes or The Beatles; something intrinsically linked to British culture that they want to experience themselves.

More recently, Alnwick has played host to television crews for *Downton Abbey* and *The Hollow Crown*. *Downton*, in which Alnwick played Brancaster Castle, was given permission to film inside the castle's State Rooms, and so costumes and props have been displayed for visitors there.

We embrace our film connections with daily 'Alnwick On Location' tours, guiding visitors to famous spots from the above productions, as well as the likes of *Robin Hood: Prince of Thieves* and *Blackadder*. With a new cinematic appearance scheduled for 2017, it's a connection we are happy to see continue.

Hatfield Estates, Hertfordshire

Nick Moorhouse is Director of Operations at Hatfield Estates in Hertfordshire and has seen noticeable growth in the number of productions filmed at the house and gardens.

Hatfield House and Gardens has proven to be a very popular setting for a wide variety of TV and feature films over the years. We have found that we are often a popular choice as we are in such close proximity to fantastic production facilities such as Pinewood, Levesden and Elstree Studios. As business at these production studios has blossomed over the last decade, we have been able to benefit from the creative talent of Britain's film industry. Being just 22 minutes from London's Kings Cross there is no doubt the convenience we offer from the capital has also helped us to succeed as a film location.

We understand how important it is to offer privacy and flexibility to those who choose to film here. It's not just that we can offer one of the finest Jacobean Houses in England, the childhood home of Elizabeth I, with a range of different interiors, we also have beautiful 42 acre gardens, planted for year-round colour. Lord and Lady Salisbury, whose home this is, are always keen to support the arts, in particular film, which plays such an important role in the economy of the region.

Oscar winning *The King's Speech* starring Colin Firth and Helena Bonham-Carter was partly filmed at Hatfield.

We have a very long list of productions filmed at Hatfield House, some of the more recent ones include *Wonder Women, Pride and Prejudice and Zombies*, *The Crown* and *Paddington*. Having been used as film location for over 25 years we have a great deal of experience to offer to ensure film makers get the most out of their time with us.

Alan Titchmarsh filming at Hatfield in 2010

Robert Downey Jnr and James Fox in a scene from Hollywood blockbuster, ***Sherlock Holmes*** (2009)

The 2007 production *Orlando* starring Tilda Swinton was filmed both inside and outside at Hatfield. Above right, *Elizabeth: The Golden Age* starring Cate Blanchett made good use of Hatfield's period interiors

HUDSONs

ALL BRITAIN'S BEST HISTORIC PLACES

Explore

Print

Online

Mobile

Visit www.hudsonsheritage.com and sign up to our monthly newsletter for offers, competitions and recommendations throughout the year, and download our app Hudsons UK for up-to-the-minute information when out exploring.

Online

App

BRINGING BRITAIN'S HERITAGE TO YOU

www.hudsonsheritage.com

Scenes from Outlander at Doune Castle

Doune Castle, Scotland

Lisa Robshaw is responsible for marketing Doune Castle for Historic Environment Scotland. Doune has been one of several locations for Outlander, the British-American adaptation of Diana Gabaldon's novels, which is in its third season this year with another to follow.

Scotland's iconic historic attractions not only appeal to visitors, but also inspire film and TV producers as stunning backdrops to tell their stories.

Doune Castle in Stirlingshire has certainly benefited from the TV and film effect. Doune is the stand-in for the fictional Castle Leoch in the hit TV series *Outlander*, popular on both sides of the Atlantic. Doune Castle witnessed a surge in visitor numbers over the last two years, brought by the 'Outlander Effect'. A total of 71,376 people visited the now iconic castle for themselves in 2015, nearly half as many again as the previous year. However, it's worth noting that it's not just *Outlander* that contributes to the popularity and appeal of Doune. If you visit, you may hear the distant sound of horse's hooves, or coconut shells, thanks to the enduring popularity of *Monty Python and the Holy Grail*, also filmed at Doune over 30 years ago.

Other Historic Scotland properties that are also TV and film locations include Blackness Castle, Aberdour Castle and Glasgow Cathedral (*Outlander*), Fort Charlotte (the BBC's *Shetland*) and Caerlaverock Castle (*The Decoy Bride*).

Castle Howard, Yorkshire

Victoria Howard (right, with Phoebe Nicholls and Jeremy Irons) lives at Castle Howard in Yorkshire, firmly associated in many people's minds with Brideshead Revisited, either the 1981 TV series or the 2008 film.

In Autumn 2016, the remaining members of the cast of the TV adaptation of *Brideshead Revisited* returned to Castle Howard for a photo shoot, courtesy of *Vanity Fair*, to mark the 35th anniversary of the iconic Granada production. To fans such as those who constantly leave comments in our Visitors Book or on Trip Advisor, it seems like yesterday .

Brideshead was game changing for Castle Howard but it was the exception that proves the rule. Both before and after *Brideshead*, the house has been used as a film location, from *Lady L* in 1965 to ITV's latest period drama *Victoria*. The list is extensive, including *Garfield*, *Barry Lyndon*, *The Spy with a Cold Nose* and *Death Comes to Pemberley* but most people would be hard pushed to name them all. Given the major disruption caused by filming, the location fees are quite modest. In our experience, the impact on visitors has ranged from zero to a relatively limited increase for a couple of years, with the latter usually only happening if there are recognisable shots of the outside facade.

So why were *Brideshead* and more recently *Downton Abbey* in a different league in their appeal to visitors? I put it down to quality and the part the house plays in the narrative. No-one had ever seen anything quite like *Brideshead* before; the series became a global sensation. *Downton* was a first class example of its genre. In both series, the house was a significant feature or "character" in the storyline and of course provided the title while the building's facade dominated the branding.

So only the stand out period dramas significantly impact visitors. We assess the likely quality of the production before committing, by considering who will be involved, the budget and whether or not the façade will be recognisable. Then it is a question of crossing your fingers.

Channel 4's Phil Spencer at Castle Howard in 2016

***Death Comes to Pemberley* (2013)**

Brideshead Revisited **(1981)**

Unknown Heart (2014)

Lark Rise to Candleford (2008)

Chavenage, Gloucestershire

Caroline Lowsley-Williams lives at Elizabethan Chavenage in Gloucestershire and has successfully promoted the house as a film location.

I came home to Chavenage in the 1990s to oversee the growth and diversification of the 'house business'. Since then we have developed a successful weddings business with a peak of 36 wedding receptions in one calendar year. We host corporate functions: using the estate's 4 x 4 track for car events; running vintage car rallies; hosting seminars etc. I've particularly enjoyed promoting and using Chavenage as a TV/film location. Credits to date include *Cider with Rosie*, *Casualty*, the Hercule Poirot story *The Mysterious Affair at Styles*, *Tess of The D'Urbervilles*, *Lark Rise to Candleford*, *New Worlds*, *Wolf Hall* and *Poldark* in which Chavenage plays the part of Trenwith. We have appeared on several TV productions ourselves including Grayson Perry's *Taste*, *The Salvage Hunters*, *John Bishop's Britain*. Most recently, I was seen on Channel 4's *You Can't Get the Staff*, which was screened in November 2014.

There are thousands of aspects to offering your house and grounds as a film location, apart from the obvious financial benefit. For us, the publicity of having a film or TV programme shot with us is very welcome, visitor numbers went up almost 50% after the BBC's adaptation of *Poldark* was screened. My family all enjoy meeting the cast and crew and appreciate the hearty breakfasts and lunches; the meals are a great bonus and save much cooking. At Chavenage we are delighted with our replacement gravel, eight pairs of new curtains and the fresh lick of paint in many of the rooms. What a way to cheer up a dank English winter's day to look out and see Aidan Turner (*Ross Poldark*) walk by.

Poldark (2016)

Men Are Wonderful (2008)

New Worlds (2014)

Ben Miles and Olivia Grant in *Lark Rise to Candelford* (2008)

→

St Michael's Mount (2012)

National Trust

Harvey Edgington is Head of Filming & Locations at the National Trust. Harvey handles requests for filming at any of the Trust's nearly 500 historic houses, castles, ancient monuments, gardens and parks.

The NT operates an internal film unit which handles all commercial film and still photography enquiries. News enquires are dealt with elsewhere. We have 3-4 crews a day on NT property and although a lot of those are factual crews we have a TV drama or film shoot about twice a month.

Obviously conservation and protection is a priority so we have strict regulations about lighting levels, special effects, candles etc. These have been drawn up in partnership with the conservators and are based on experience as well as best practice. The film unit also issues the contracts, negotiates fees, handle risk assessments, insurance and invoicing. However all of the money goes back to the property who hosted the filming.

Wolf Hall at Montacute (2015)

Burke & Hare filming at Knole, Kent (2016)

→

The BBC's *Wolf Hall* filming at Montacute in Somerset (2015)

We do all this for three reasons. The money, obviously, but also the extra visitors an appearance in a TV show or film can bring. At one property the rise was 146%. The figures may drop later but we find rarely go back to what they were. It has lasting effects. It has been calculated that the famous Colin Firth scene in the BBC's *Pride and Prejudice* is still worth 900,000 to Lyme Park in Cheshire annually. The third reason is that opening up to film crews helps the local economy. A feature film's hotel bill can reach £40k a night. Factual filming has other benefits, it allows the Trust not only to tell its own stories as an organisation but also the history of the places we look after. Be it *Countryfile*, *The One Show* or *Horizon*.

Over the last few years interest in National Trust locations for filming has become more even across the country rather than focusing around London. *Game of Thrones* keeps us busy in Northern Ireland, *Dr Who* led the charge to Wales and *Poldark* of course is Cornwall. Which is why I spend a lot of time on trains.

Alnwick Castle, Northumberland (p.290)
Hatfield House, Hertfordshire (p.211)
Doune Castle, Scotland (p.311)
Castle Howard, Yorkshire (p.259)
Chavenage, Gloucestershire (p.190)
Knole, Kent (p.145)
Montacute, Somerset (p.195)
Tredegar House, Dyffryn (p.322)
St Michael's Mount, Cornwall (p.180)

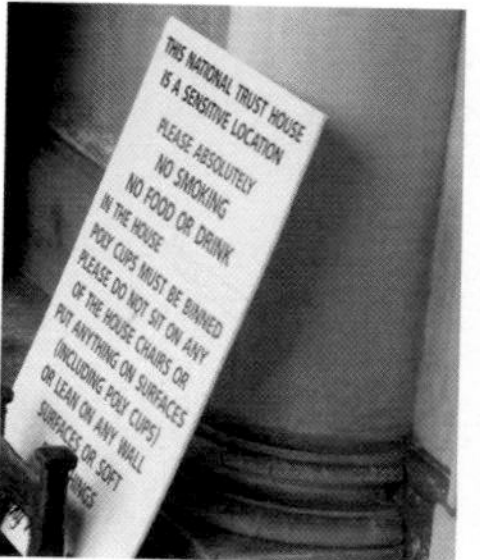

Dr Who at Tredegar House (2005)

Wolf Hall at Montacute (2015)

TM LIGHTING
BRINGING ART TO LIGHT

Waddesdon Manor - Red Drawing Room

TM Goodwood Picture Light

Gold finish, less than 22 watts of power, true colour LED module (+95 CRI), uniform light projection, sized to fit artwork, extra long lamp life - 50,000hrs (approx 15 years). Artworks shown 2.5m (h) x 1.9m (w)

** Please quote 'Waddesdon' when calling for a free consultation.*

SHORTLISTED
WORLD INTERIORS NEWS

WADDESDON
Rothschild Collections

www.tmlighting.com | sales@tmlighting.com | +44 207 278 1600

Conservation Champion

Architectural historian Dan Cruickshank has become a familiar face on TV. We all know his passion for historic places so it should be no surprise to find he is also a spirited campaigner for heritage places. He talked to ***Hudson's*** about his current obsessions.

When I was a child I lived in Warsaw. Ninety percent of the city had been destroyed by the Nazis during the Second World War, mostly in late 1944 after the Warsaw Uprising had been defeated. The Nazis destroyed the city for symbolic reasons, to punish the Poles, to destroy their pride and obliterate them as a nation. For symbolic reasons the Poles resolved to rebuild their ravaged city, particularly the most ancient and beautiful parts, the Old Town, with the Market Square at its heart, and the Royal Castle. Their action was heroic and amazing.

By the mid-1950s much of the Old Town of Warsaw had been rebuilt in a faithful reconstruction that was also inventive, creative and full of vitality. The Poles were determined that a great wrong had to be put right, that the last word on the history of their city should not be left to the perpetrators of evil, to the Nazis with their lust for destructive vengeance.

I lived in the newly rebuilt Old Town in the mid-1950s; I found it an inspiration as a child and I find it an inspiration still. It is a powerful reminder of why history, and historic buildings, matter.

An understanding of the past makes it possible to appreciate the present and to shape the future. It is all-important to learn, understand and apply the lessons of history and nowhere are lessons more powerful, visible and potentially influential than those held by historic buildings.

Buildings are important because our lives are defined by architecture – we live-in, work-in, shop-in, take our pleasures-in or just walk-by buildings, every day of our lives. Architecture is the big, ever-present, artistic and emotional experience.

Warsaw's revival has created a vibrant centre within the restored old city

Destroyed Warsaw, capital of Poland, January 1945

Little remained of the Market Square in Old Warsaw in 1945 →

© JOE ROBSON, AVR LONDON

Reconstructed in 1971-1984, the Royal Castle in Warsaw is today part of a UNESCO World Heritage Site

The Ballroom of the Royal Castle in Warsaw with interiors dating from 1780 created for King Stanislas II Augustus

The Marble Hall of the Royal Castle

I suppose it's the example of Warsaw that, to a degree, has inspired my own reconstruction campaign. This campaign relates to one of Britain's finest early 19th Century architects, Philip Hardwick. In 1837, Hardwick designed the Euston Arch, the first great monument to the Railway Age and one of the finest Greek Revival buildings ever erected.

The Arch was demolished in 1961, in a villainous manner by British Railways in the teeth of great public opposition, with preservation campaigners including John Betjeman and The Victorian Society. Twenty years ago I found over 60 per cent of the carved stones that had comprised the Arch dumped in an East London river. Since then I have campaigned for the rebuilding of the Arch at Euston. It now looks like it will happen with the opportunity created by the reconstruction of Euston Station, as part of HS2.

One of the arguments has been that the Arch rebuilt at Euston would not only 'right a great wrong' but also give the new station distinction, historic pedigree, interest and character. It would draw curious tourists from around the world, entranced by the notion of architectural resurrection and give the new station an individual sense of place, granting a rebuilt Euston some of the interest and attraction of remodelled St Pancras and King's Cross, where repaired old and bold new railway architecture merge in such a creative and memorable manner.

Tourism is all-important to our economy and tourists love history and historic towns and buildings. The immense popularity of Tower of London, Windsor Castle, Bath, Edinburgh and Hampton Court Palace are proof. Castle Howard; Blenheim Palace; Houghton Hall; Holkham Hall are among the most visited attractions in England and I'm happy to report that one of the greatest of England's country houses - certainly the largest and among the architecturally finest as well as one of the most threatened – is now finally on the brink of being saved.

Architectural visualisation by Joseph Robson

Wentworth Woodhouse, the longest facade in Europe

Wentworth Woodhouse in South Yorkshire is stupendous. Built from the late 1720s for the Watson-Wentworth family (they eventually acquired the title of Marquis of Rockingham and united with the Fitzwilliam family), the house acquired a vast and magnificent Palladian front during the 1730s and 40s and was one of the great political 'power houses' of Georgian Britain. But it has been largely empty, partly decaying and seeking a sustainable future for over 30 years.

It miraculously survived the bleak 1950s when hundreds of country houses were destroyed – deemed as surplus to requirements and regarded as hopelessly out of kilter with the modern world. Now SAVE Britain's Heritage, a veteran campaigning conservation group, is brokering an extraordinary deal to save Wentworth Woodhouse. The existing owners, the Newbold family, owned the house for 17 years and completed a series of vital repairs. They have agreed in principle to sell the house for £7 million to the charitable Wentworth Woodhouse Preservation Trust.

Saving this great house for the nation has become a truly national project. The National Heritage Memorial Fund is contributing £3.57 million and support comes from The Monuments Trust; The Art Fund; The John Paul Getty Charitable Trust, and the Sir Siegmund Warburg Voluntary Settlement. Public opening of the house would be supported by the National Trust.

All is not yet settled, many tricky matters have yet to be fully resolved, such as the long term implications of mining subsidence, but the signs are hopeful that one of England's greatest country houses will be saved for the nation – for the enlightenment, inspiration and education of generations to come. A revived Wentworth Woodhouse will be a living monument to why history matters.

Wentworth Woodhouse, Yorkshire ***(p.267)***

A dry-suited Dan Cruickshank oversees the retrieval of one of the lost stones of the Euston Arch

The Great Storm

The storm of October 1987 was the worst for 300 years. Fifteen million trees were felled, of which 70 percent were in private gardens and estates. In Sevenoaks, six of the seven oak trees after which the town is named were blown down. Nearby Riverhill Gardens is home to the Rogers family; Jane Rogers was there that night.

"It is certainly the end of Riverhill as we have known it"

The Waterloo Cedar at Riverhill Himalayan Gardens was planted in 1815 in memory of 19 year old Henry Buckley, the heir to Riverhill House, who was killed by a musket ball at Waterloo. Two hundred years later, it's a massive tree that impresses our visitors but it is also a real survivor. On the night of 15th October 1987, three-quarters of the trees that surrounded it in the woodland gardens at Riverhill were destroyed by winds up to 90mph that devastated the south of England.

I remember the night well, we first noticed that it was unseasonably warm, temperatures apparently rose about 6°C that night, and it had been raining for about 10 days. My husband was worried about the cattle and as the wind rose, got up to check that the gates were secure. As he did so, the lights failed and we quickly decided to move to the basement, afraid that high winds would make the tall chimneys of the house very vulnerable. Luckily, my mother-in-law, who lived in the main part of the house, was away. The winds gusted around 70mph for three or four hours through the course of the night so we were prepared for some damage when it got light. Even so the devastation in the garden was shocking.

We lost 400 trees with a girth of more than 12 inches, a mature monkey puzzle tree came down on top of the house,

©LEIGH CLAPP

©LEIGH CLAPP

©MARK WATTS

©LEIGH CLAPP

©LEIGH CLAPP

a falling Monterey Cedar destroyed the old squash court and fallen trees littered the drive like skittles.

At the time, it seemed like a disaster. The gardens had been started by John Rogers, a friend of Charles Darwin and an enthusiastic amateur botanist, who bought the house in 1840. He was attracted to the house because of its sheltered position and lime-free soil and as a patron of several Victorian plant hunters, he pioneered the planting of many rare trees, including a Turkey Oak planted from a seed brought back from the Crimea. It too survived the storm but many other now mature trees did not.

Immediately after the storm we had to close the woodland rhododendron gardens to visitors and they remained closed for more than a year. Visitor numbers plummeted and funds needed for repairs and conservation were diverted into a four year clean-up. Thirty years on, the garden seems to have returned to normal, but it is a different sort of normal.

The devastation wrought by the storm brought in more light and opened up some areas of woodland which has allowed us to extend the experiences enjoyed by our visitors. The woodland gardens, where the azalea and rhododendrons thrive, gave us the idea for the contemporary gardens here. They are natives of the Himalayas and the hilly site at Riverhill has lent itself perfectly to a garden on a Himalayan theme.

We have been able to continue the family tradition and add to the collection of rare species of azaleas and rhododendrons and also roses. We now have a popular walk to the top of the hill – our Mount Everest – from which visitors can see right over the Weald; it can rightly claim to be the best view in Kent. We took the opportunity to commission world renowned maze designer Adrian Fisher to create a Himalayan maze for us based on the shapes of Tibetan carving; it is a great favourite with children. Space has opened up for our woodland adventure playground and our popular den building areas.

If you want to measure the impact of the Great Storm, perhaps it is significant that in 1987 we opened about eight acres of the gardens to the public but now the gardens cover more than 14 acres and there is so much more to enjoy. If our Waterloo Cedar has been a witness to change in the gardens, it has definitely seen more of a transformation here since the 1987 storm than in the century before.

Riverhill Himalayan Gardens, Kent ***(p.150)***

Faith in the future

Inspired by a series of 17th Century paintings, city financier, Jonathan Ruffer, is now investing £70m to transform Auckland Castle into a faith, art and heritage destination of international significance and help kick start the regeneration of the town of Bishop Auckland, County Durham. He shares his unique vision with ***Hudson's***.

© NEIL WATSON

© GRAEME PEACOCK

© COLIN DAVISON

Jacob from the series *Jacob and his Twelve Sons* by Francisco de Zurbarán

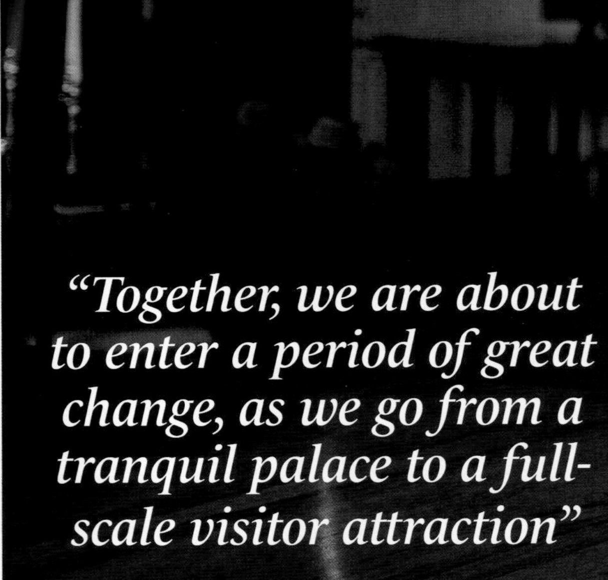

"Together, we are about to enter a period of great change, as we go from a tranquil palace to a full-scale visitor attraction"

In the years when I was growing up – I am now in my mid-60s – I saw the anguish brought about when family homes, which had often been in a family for generations, become an impossible burden to the unfortunate generation who had to face the implacable arithmetic of living beyond its means. As a result I became frightened of these architectural *belles dames sans merci* or, what my old nanny called, those beautiful ladies who wouldn't say 'thank you'.

It is therefore with some surprise that I now find myself in a regeneration project, at the heart of which is Auckland Castle. Home of the Prince Bishops of Durham since the 11th Century, the castle had, until recently, enjoyed no

Jonathan Ruffer, Chairman of the Auckland Castle Trust, pictured in the Long Dining Room at Auckland Castle

© BARRY PELLIS

new building work since the 18th Century, except for the installation of a dumb-waiter between the ground floor and the first in 1938.

It is a place of cross-currents, half the private residence of grandees and half the expression of affairs of state – first as a bastion against the Scots and latterly against Methodism and other heresies.

I had originally intervened to ensure that 13 counter-reformation masterpieces by Francisco de Zurbarán, portraying Jacob and the twelve tribes of Israel, remained in the Long Dining Room of the Castle, where they had been since 1756. I was intrigued by the idea that a very English, Anglican palace should house such deeply Catholic pictures, whose subject matter was Jewish. It spoke of unity in diversity and the message, Methodists welcome too!

It was Neil MacGregor, then Director of the British Museum, who persuaded me to take an altogether bigger step and to acquire not just the pictures, but their container. He explained that the future of Auckland Castle could never be resolved without a solution to the long-term future of the pictures. It would have been eccentric, then, to unlock the possibilities this offered but fail to turn the handle and walk in – so we walked in.

The enormity of what we had taken on was immediately apparent. Bishop Auckland is off the beaten track – even those 20 miles away in Billingham (not to be confused

→

with Blenheim) fail to see the lure. To prove them wrong, we needed to provide enough reason for people to come and we coined the phrase, *'two and a half wows'*, which we thought would be enough to do the trick.

We now have a team of trustees who are greatly engaged and around 70 staff at Auckland Castle, working to create a smorgasbord of offerings to make Bishop Auckland wide enough to wow everyone.

There is also another trust, Eleven Arches, which is responsible for the open air spectacle, Kynren, a community-based exploration of the history of England through the eyes of the North East, which is staged close to Auckland Castle throughout the summer.

Together, we are about to enter a period of great change, as we go from a tranquil palace to a full-scale visitor attraction, where each of its constituent parts echoes the jockey's physique – small, but perfectly formed.

The Castle offering will, when complete, aim to provide a

© COLIN DAVISON

The Zurbarán paintings and other works hanging in Auckland Castle's Long Dining Room

treat for gardeners, with a 17th Century Walled Garden, and five others set in the curtilage around the Castle itself. There will be a complete renovation of the State Rooms and the addition of a new gallery exploring the history of Faith in England since the beginning of time.

This is a hot potato, but it has been the centre of Auckland's purpose for nearly 1,000 years. The history of England is dominated by Christianity but the Jewish faith has a history in England almost as old as the Castle itself. The ups and downs of this country's attitude to the Jews is extreme in both directions, good, I think then, that its story is to be told at the site of one of the luminous highs in this encounter – Bishop Richard Trevor's purchase and proud display of the Zurbarán paintings.

In the town we shall be opening a Spanish Gallery, which has been marvellously supported by many great institutions around the world, including the Museo del Prado, Madrid, which has already held out the hand of friendship. This will

© GRAEME PEACOCK

The Robinson Arch, which was built for Bishop Richard Trevor in the 18th Century and still links Auckland Castle with the town

be complemented by The Zurbarán Centre for Spanish and Latin American Art, which will link world class academic research by Durham University to the Gallery's curatorial programme and support public engagement. The £1.6m centre is being run by the University and has already received a substantial grant from Santander. We will also have the definitive collection of miners' art on permanent show, and a welcome centre which will have a viewing tower allowing a 360° view of the surrounding area that is so rich in history. We intend for Auckland Castle to be a foodie heaven too, with the creation of a contemporary restaurant in the Walled Garden and hope that those who like music might have reason to enjoy concerts in its chapel – the largest private chapel in Europe.

When we are finished I expect to be told that it's all very fine, of course, but in truth the natural advantages afforded by Bishop Auckland are such that even the residents of Billingham might reasonably have been expected to make a visit. In the meantime the work in progress has a dynamism that will make a visit to Bishop Auckland a distinctly energising experience.

Auckland Castle closed to the public for restoration in October 2016, relaunching in 2018, when the Walled Garden will also be open.
Get an early taste of what is in store with the opening of Auckland Castle Trust's Welcome Building and Mining Art Gallery in 2017 or at events in the castle grounds. Auckland Park will remain open to visitors and dog walkers throughout the restoration. Full updates at ***www.aucklandcastle.org***
Open air spectacular Kynren, by Eleven Arches, will return from July to September 2017. ***www.elevenarches.org***

Auckland Castle, County Durham (p.288)

St Peter's Chapel, Auckland Castle, the largest private chapel in Europe

In November 2015 David Cameron designated 2017 the UK-India Year of Culture to celebrate 70 years since Indian independence in 1947. ***Hudson's*** has commissioned a series of three articles to explore the influence of India on country house culture in Britain. In the first, Professor Margot Finn considers the impact of Indian imperial culture on British heritage.

The East India Company at Home

The East India Company was a joint stock company set up in London under Elizabeth I to promote trade with the new lands to the East. By the mid-18th Century the Company had grown in wealth and influence until it effectively administered Britain's empire on the subcontinent, expanding its fiscal, territorial and military grip in the century before its abolition in 1858. By the later 1750s, its civil and military officers enjoyed unprecedented access to Asian goods, through bribes, ceremonial gifts, private commerce and the spoils of war. Together with the Company's official cargoes of Indian and Chinese commodities, these goods helped to transform British families' material sensibilities and homes.

Our study into the East India Company at Home conducted over three years looked at 23 houses, 25 families and a multitude of objects. The research produced a series of case studies which help us evaluate the importance of the influence of the East India trade on British culture.

"Stately and strange it stood, the Nabob's house,
Indian without and coolest Greek within"
John Betjeman, 1960

→

Sir Charles Cockerell's hexagonal pavilion bedroom at Sezincote

Sezincote House and its gardens are a mirage of India in the heart of the Cotswolds. They owe their creation to the collaboration of owner, Sir Charles Cockerell, (1755-1837), his brother, the architect Samuel Pepys Cockerell (1754-1827), the artist Thomas Daniell (1749 -1840) and to a lesser extent the landscape gardener, Humphry Repton (1752-1818). Among them, these men possessed the knowledge, expertise and money to create a distinctive vision of India in the English countryside.

Sir Charles Cockerell was an employee of the East India Company and, inheriting the estate from his brother in 1798, chose the Mughal style of Rajasthan for his new house, complete with onion domes, minarets, peacock-tail windows, jali-work railings and pavilions which explicitly referenced his imperial connections. Thomas Daniell had spent ten years in India recording Indian buildings and had an unparalleled knowledge of Indian architecture, creating at Sezincote perhaps the only 'Indian' country house ever built in England.

Three generations of the Child family at Osterley Park were intimately involved in the East India Company. As far as we know none ever travelled to Asia, or served as employees of the EIC. However, the family was concerned with the governance of the Company, while the family-run bank, Child & Co., was the principal resource funding the grand restoration of Osterley Park in the 1760s. Many of its remarkable examples of decorative art were brought together as a result of the Child family's multi-generational link with the East India Company trade and shipping networks in the Indian Ocean.

India gained a key position in the thriving Indian Ocean trading network through its ability to market a wide range of goods at competitive prices. The port city of Surat was called the "Blessed Port" by India's ruling Mughal dynasty. The Child family played a key role in shaping how Asian textiles entered the British market. At Osterley, the opulent silk embroidered bed pelmet cover and canopy in Mrs Child's bedchamber was likely bought at Surat around 1700-1730. The textiles and many other decorative objects at Osterley highlight the central role of the East India Company sea trade in creating a global economy of artistic exchange that shaped the domestic interior in England.

Pavilion from the gardens, Sezincote

Sezincote, East Front

© JAN SIBTHORPE

Osterley Park, London, home of the Child family, bankers to the East India Company

© NATIONAL TRUST/JOHN MILLER

© NATIONAL TRUST/DENNIS GILBERT

© NATIONAL TRUST

© NATIONAL TRUST/ROBERT MORRIS

Embroidered Indian cotton hangings in Mrs Child's bedchamber Centre: Lacquered furniture imported to Osterley on East India Company ships; Chinese export ware porcelain with the Child family crest is typical of East India Company goods →

Quex Park, Kent

Quex Park in Kent uncovers some of the meanings attributed to 18th and 19th Century East India Company possessions, and how such meanings were adapted to the Victorian and early Edwardian setting. In the 18th Century, the Cotton family had a series of connections to the East India Company.

A number of decorative objects from India and China are believed to have been passed down from these generations to their descendent, Major Percy Powell-Cotton (1866-1940) who actively used this collection in the decoration of Quex Park and added to it as his decorative tastes developed.

Growing up in London, surrounded by Asian pottery, porcelain, furniture, and other objects of interest, the young Percy Powell-Cotton quickly developed a strong sense of the visual arts. Highlighted by the 1851 Great Exhibition in Hyde Park and by the Aesthetic Movement, Indian design became epitomised in the South Kensington Museum's Colonial and Indian Exhibition of 1886. These influences, along with a substantial world trip (1889-91), shaped his later collecting and interior design.

Soon after Percy returned from his world trip and inherited Quex Park, he began to make extensive changes. His travels renewed his love for a family collection deeply shaped by earlier connections to the East India Company and he soon discovered old objects from storage and placed them strategically around the house.

Photographs taken by Percy in 1913 picture the rather

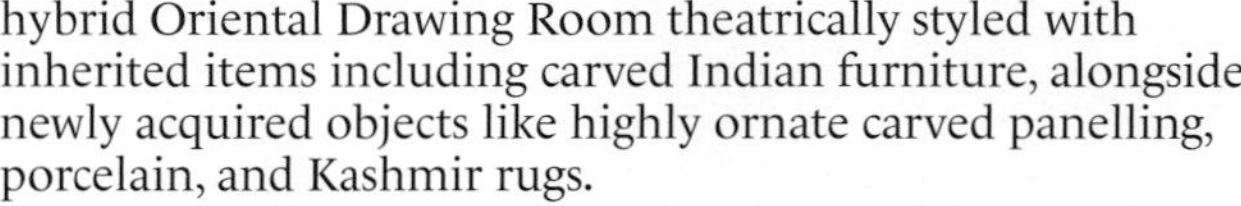

hybrid Oriental Drawing Room theatrically styled with inherited items including carved Indian furniture, alongside newly acquired objects like highly ornate carved panelling, porcelain, and Kashmir rugs.

There is still a dispute about the impact of the British Empire on British culture. At Sezincote and Osterley, direct engagement with India and East India trade created a distinct oriental look to their exterior and interiors. The history of Quex suggests that across generations, objects are still able to conjure specific ideas about a person, a family, or a society. Our study showed that personal relationships and taste were fundamentally changed by living in India, trading with India and circulating goods from the Indian Ocean world.

The Oriental Room at Quex Park in the early 20th Century

Margot Finn is Professor of Modern British History at University College London. She led a three-year project on the impact of the East India Company on British country houses funded by the Leverhulme Trust from 2011-14; she is a trustee of the V&A Museum and President of the Royal Historical Society. Case study contributors included Jan Sibthorpe, Yuthika Shama, Pauline Davies & Alison Bennett. The full findings of the study, The East India Company at Home, c. 1757-1857 edited by Margot Finn and Kate Smith will be published at the end of 2017 by UCL Press as an ebook and on demand.

Sezincote, Gloucestershire(p.194)
Osterley Park NT, Surrey (p.128)
Quex Park, Kent (p.150)

→

The Clive Collection

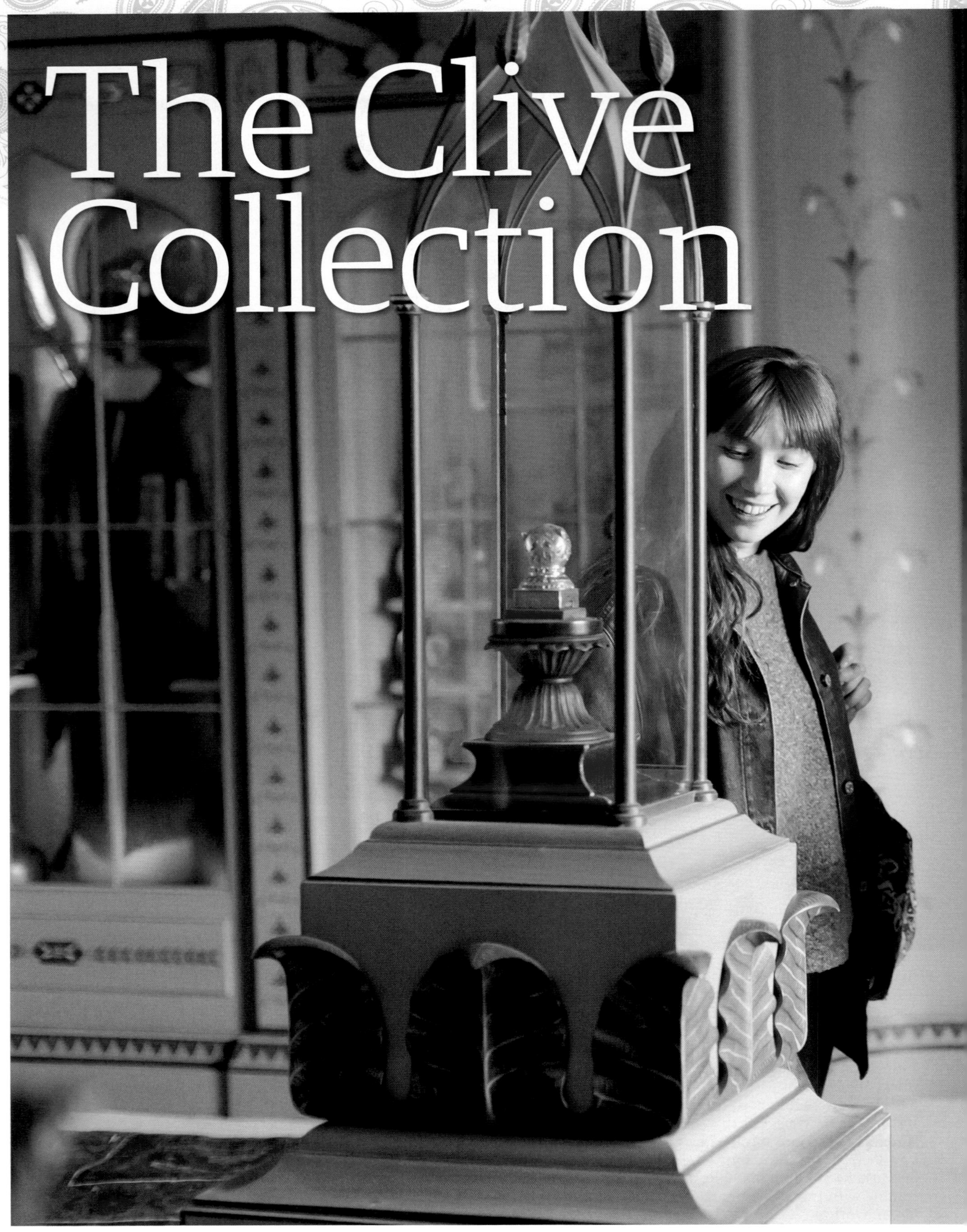

©NATIONAL TRUST/MEGAN TAYL

©NATIONAL TRUST/JOHN HAMMOND

In the second of our UK-India articles, Gareth Sandham, Curator at the National Trust's Powis Castle, assesses the treasures of Clive of India.

Outside London, the finest collection of Indian artefacts in Britain is surely to be found at Powis Castle in mid-Wales. With its foundation as a 13th Century castle of the princes of Powys, and perched high on an escarpment overlooking the wide Severn Valley, this is an unlikely location to find such a wealth of eastern treasures.

The collection began with Robert Clive – 'Clive of India' – and its final home in Wales was due to the marriage of his son, Edward, to Henrietta Herbert, sister of the 2nd Earl of Powis. It was their son, Edward Herbert, who inherited Powis Castle and who gave the eastern artworks a permanent home. Edward's grandson, George Herbert, 4th Earl of Powis died in 1952 and bequeathed the castle to the National Trust who have since acquired the bulk of The Clive Collection.

Left: The Clive Museum at Powis Castle in 2016

Above: Robert Clive, 'Clive of India', painted about 1770 by Nathaniel Dance

→

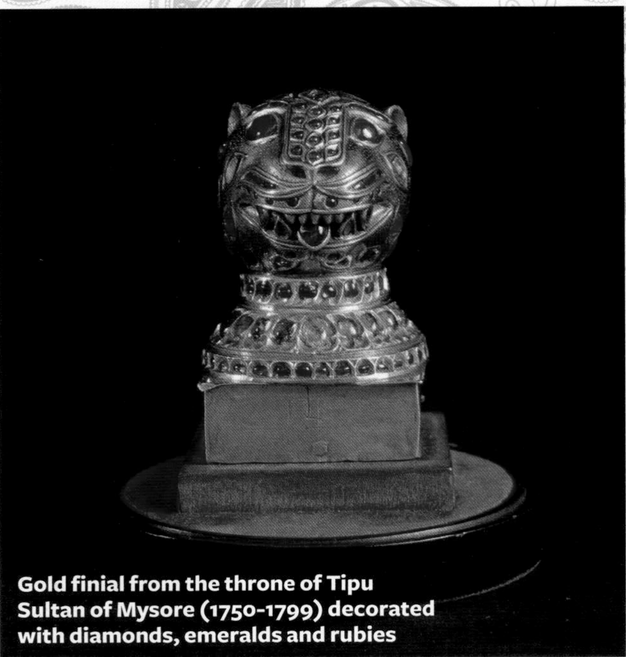
Gold finial from the throne of Tipu Sultan of Mysore (1750-1799) decorated with diamonds, emeralds and rubies

©NATIONAL TRUST/ERIK PELHAM

The son of a Shropshire squire, Robert Clive rose through the ranks of the East India Company, to become one of its most effective military commanders and administrators. Victory at Arcot in 1752 and Plassey in 1757, led him to achieve great power in Bengal, gaining the office of imperial diwan in 1765. His accumulation of riches in the form of loot, gifts and pensions brought him vilification on return to England, and the cause of his death in 1774 at the age of 49 remains obscure.

Despite having little experience in administration, Robert's son Edward was appointed Governor of Madras in 1798, and arrived in India with Henrietta and their daughters just before the outbreak of hostilities between the British and Tipu Sultan. Following the Tiger of Mysore's defeat at Seringapatam, the Clives were presented with several exquisite treasures from his palace. In 1799 Henrietta added to the collection with natural history specimens gathered on an amazing 1000 mile odyssey around southern India.

The Clive Museum itself is striking in its intricacy. Once part of the 18th Century Ballroom, its design by Alec Cobbe is intended to evoke the architecture and style of India, but within an English setting. This style (known in Britain as Hindu-Gothic) is best known from the Brighton Pavilion designed by John Nash, but was also seen closer to Powis at the now demolished Garth Hall in nearby Guilsfield.

The Clives had been perfectly placed to acquire objects of the highest quality, but it is the loss of virtually all the other private collections of this type that now gives The Clive Collection unique value. Even within the subcontinent itself, it is now impossible to find such a cross section of objects from a time when India became embroiled in a wider British imperial conflict.

It was a moment when a rich and ancient culture was only beginning to feel the effects of the dramatic changes which Clive's activities would precipitate. Thus the collection stands as a vivid and unique record of this encounter between very different cultural traditions.

*Powis Castle, Powys (**p.323**)*

©NATIONAL TRUST/ERIK PELHAM

Ivory Ganjifa playing card from the Clive Collection

© NATIONAL TRUST/ERIK PELHAM

© NATIONAL TRUST/ERIK PELHAM

Left: Part of Tipu Sultan's magnificently decorated state tent; the whole tent would fill the castle courtyard

Above: Indian inlaid ivory furniture in the Clive Museum at Powis Castle

© NATIONAL TRUST/ERIK PELHAM

© NATIONAL TRUST/ERIK PELHAM

The sword and (left) the slippers of Tipu Sultan of Mysore

Pleasure Palace

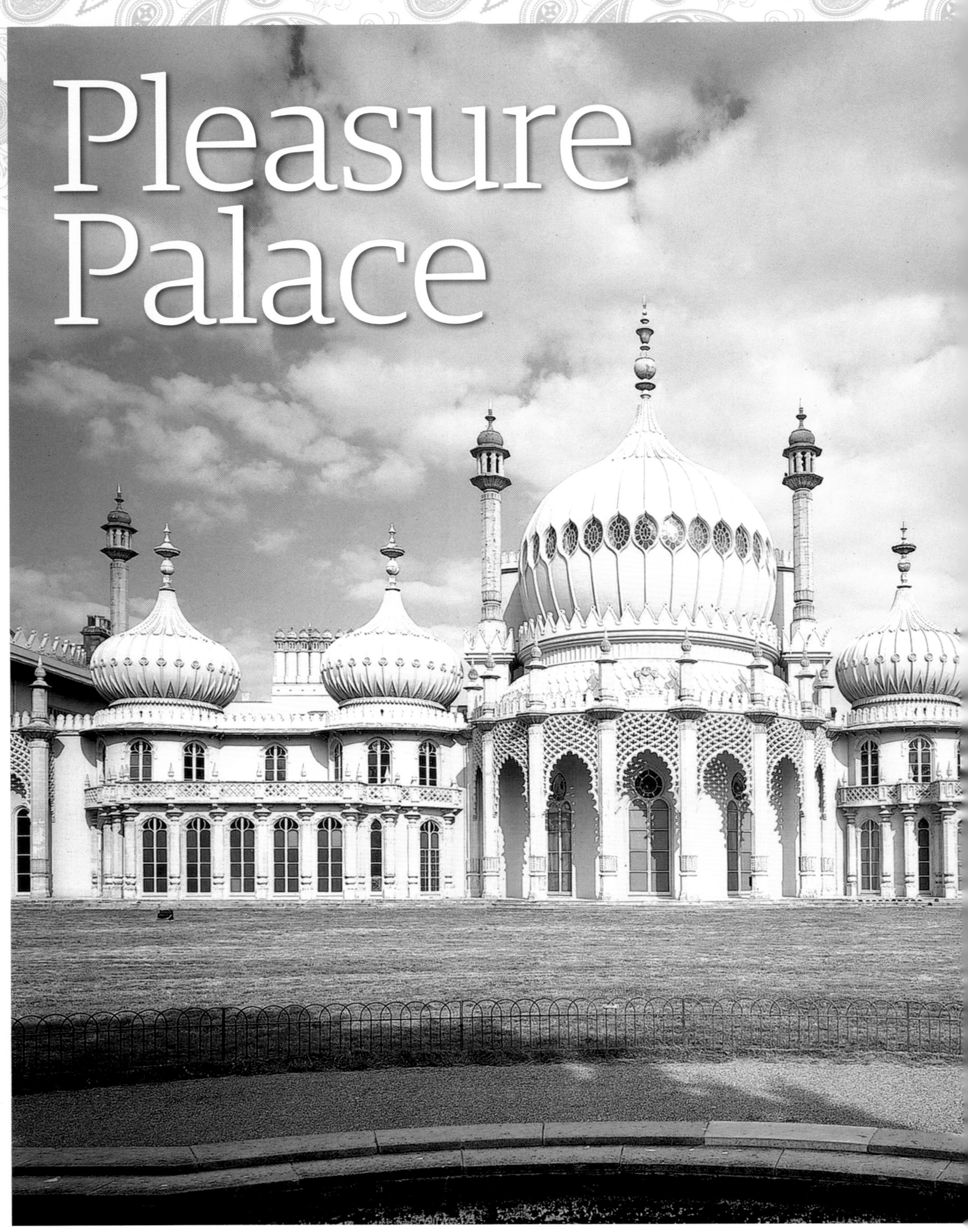

The last in a series of articles to mark the UK-India Year of Culture, ***Hudson's*** asked asked David Beevers, Keeper of the Royal Pavilion in Brighton, to explain the Indian influences at work on this iconic building, the summer palace of the Prince Regent.

The use of the Indian style on the exterior of the Royal Pavilion has mystified visitors since the completion of the building in the 1820s. Contemporaries often likened it to the Kremlin and its Indian origins were forgotten. Today the Indian style is apparent to all. The architect John Nash at the command of the Prince Regent, later George IV, used an unfamiliar style with wit and aplomb so that the Pavilion has in effect become symbolic of the hedonistic town in which it was built.

Exposure to the culture of India was encouraged by trade through the East India Company founded in 1600 but it was only at the end of the 18th Century that a group of artists, scholars, and colonial officials revealed that Indian, especially Mughal art, was aesthetically pleasing. Foremost among these was William Hodges, whose *Select Views in India* was published in 1785-88. He was followed by Thomas and William Daniells' Oriental Scenery (1795-1808). The Daniells' print of the Jami Masjid or Friday Mosque in Delhi inspired the scalloped heads to the stable windows in William Porden's vast and stupendous 1804 design for the Prince's stables and riding house adjoining the Royal Pavilion, the first structure of any size in Europe to use the Indian style.

Left: the exterior of the Royal Pavilion

Above: John Nash, Brighton Pavilion, (c.1826)

"Repton was asked by the Prince to advise on the gardens of the Royal Pavilion and then to produce an Indian design for the building itself"

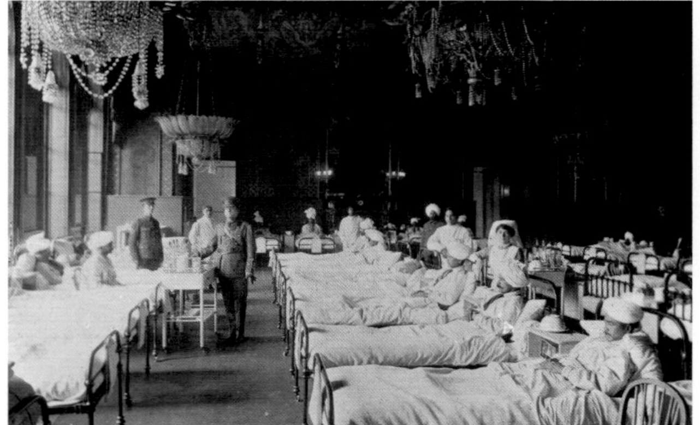

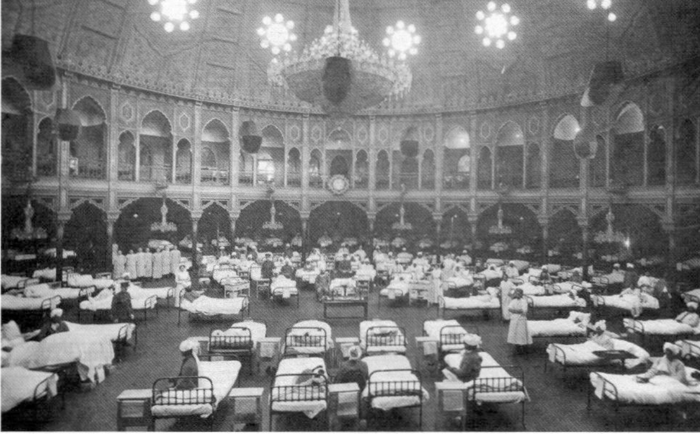

The Royal Pavilion as a First World War military hospital for soldiers from Indian battalions wounded on the Western Front, where they made up almost a third of the British Expeditionary Force in 1914

The use of Indian motifs was the personal decision of Prince George, but it was probably connected with the capture of Delhi by the British in 1803. Porden was a pupil of Samuel Cockerell who with help from the Daniells designed Sezincote in Gloucestershire in 1805 in an Indian style. The landscape gardener and architect Humphry Repton was also part of the Sezincote project; he advised on how Indian motifs might be used on the building. It is surely not coincidental that the two major buildings in Britain in the Indian style were being built at the same time. Shortly after his work at Sezincote, Repton was asked by the Prince to advise on the gardens of the Royal Pavilion and then to produce an Indian design for the building itself. Repton's designs for the gardens and the palace remained unexecuted, but elements from both were used by John Nash who was asked by Prince George in 1814 to remodel the existing neo-classical Pavilion into a Western fantasy of India. The aim was to draw attention away from the superior magnificence of the stables; the Daniells' Indian views again provided the motifs.

The Royal Pavilion as remodelled by Nash became for Prince George a symbol of monarchical continuity after the defeat of Napoleon in 1815; it was also symbolic of Britain's burgeoning Imperial project in India. The shapes of the bulbous domes and minaret-like pinnacles derive from prints of 17th Century mosques such as the Jami Masjid and the Pearl Mosque in Delhi; the delicate jali screens, used in India to lessen the heat, derive from Indian domestic architecture. Indian columns are probably based on the Daniells' illustration of a hall at Allahabad. The covered porch is based on an illustration of a temple on the Ganges.

There is an extraordinary postscript to this episode: the use of the Royal Pavilion as an Indian Military Hospital in 1914-16. More than 2,300 Indian soldiers who had fought on the Western Front were treated in three buildings on the Pavilion Estate. Clifford Musgrave, a former Director of the Royal Pavilion, remarked in 1951 that *'the building achieved a romantic fulfilment beyond the wildest imaginings of its original creators, when it gave shelter to the inhabitants of the land that inspired its fantastic architecture.'*

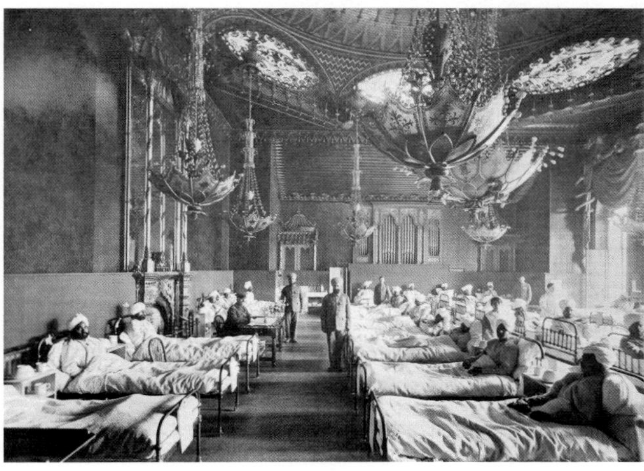

Brighton Pavilion, Sussex (p.171)

Newman Brothers Coffin Fitting Works

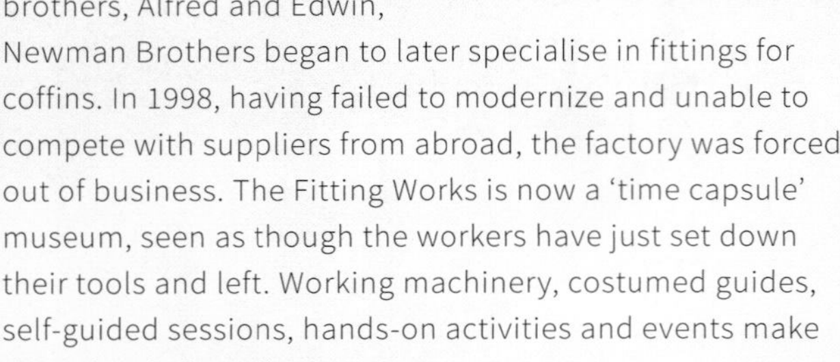

13–15 Fleet Street, Birmingham B3 1JP

Established in 1882 by two brothers, Alfred and Edwin, Newman Brothers began to later specialise in fittings for coffins. In 1998, having failed to modernize and unable to compete with suppliers from abroad, the factory was forced out of business. The Fitting Works is now a 'time capsule' museum, seen as though the workers have just set down their tools and left. Working machinery, costumed guides, self-guided sessions, hands-on activities and events make this a family friendly attraction.

Open: Guided tours on the hour from 12 noon Daily, Tuesday – Sunday and Bank Holiday Mondays

Heritage Open Days: Yes

Parking: On street parking nearby and NCP on Charlotte St

Disabled access: Yes

Admission charge: Yes

T: 0121 233 4790

E: newmanbrothers@coffinworks.org

W: www.coffinworks.org

Nothe Fort

Barrack Road, Weymouth DT4 8UF

Dominating the entrance to Weymouth Harbour, Nothe Fort is a labyrinth of passageways and outdoor areas with stunning views of the Jurassic Coast. It was constructed between 1860 and 1872 on three, easily accessed levels. The Fort is now filled with displays, mammoth guns and cinema areas that chart the history of this magnificent Victorian structure. Nothe Fort is now one of Weymouth's major attractions and a popular venue for events.

Open: Open daily between 25th March – 30th September, for winter opening hours please refer to website for more details.

Heritage Open Days: No

Parking: Public pay & display nearby

Disabled access: Yes

Admission charge: Yes

T: 01305 766 626

E: nothefort@uwclub.net

W: www.nothefort.org.uk

Kensal Green Cemetery

Harrow Road, London W10 4RA

The Grade I listed Kensal Green Cemetery covers 72 acres of beautiful grounds adjoining the Grand Union Canal. One of the world's first garden cemeteries it was inspired by the Père Lachaise Cemetery in Paris. Attractions include the Grade II* listed Dissenters' Chapel, Grade II North Terrace Colonnade, and the Grade II* monument to Emma and Alexis Soyer. Look out for events, exhibitions and guided tours run by the Friends of Kensal Green Cemetery.

Open: Cemetery open 1 April – 30 September: Monday – Saturday 9am – 6pm, Sunday 10am – 6pm. 1 October – 31 March: Monday – Saturday 9am – 5pm, Sunday 10am – 5pm. Bank Holidays 10am – 1pm.

London Open House: No

Parking: Roadside parking on internal cemetery roads

Disabled access: No

Admission charge: No

T: 07530 676 151

E: fokgc@hotmail.com

W: www.kensalgreen.co.uk

Bounds Walls

Ushaw College, Durham DH7 9RH

Ushaw College combines a fascinating history with some of the finest Victorian architecture in the North East. Built in 1852, the Bounds Walls were built to enclose the north and north east sides of a playing field. The games played there were peculiar to Ushaw College; they included handball and a battledore game which were regularly played by students until the 1980s. The wider site offers chapels, a children's bunny trail, beautiful gardens and a varied programme of events.

Open: Free access to the walls, approaching from the drives and car parks to the south and west. For all other parts please check website.

Heritage Open Days: Yes

Parking: Adjacent parking available

Disabled access: Partial access available

Admission charge: No

T: 0191 334 6423

E: tickets@ushaw.org

W: www.ushaw.org

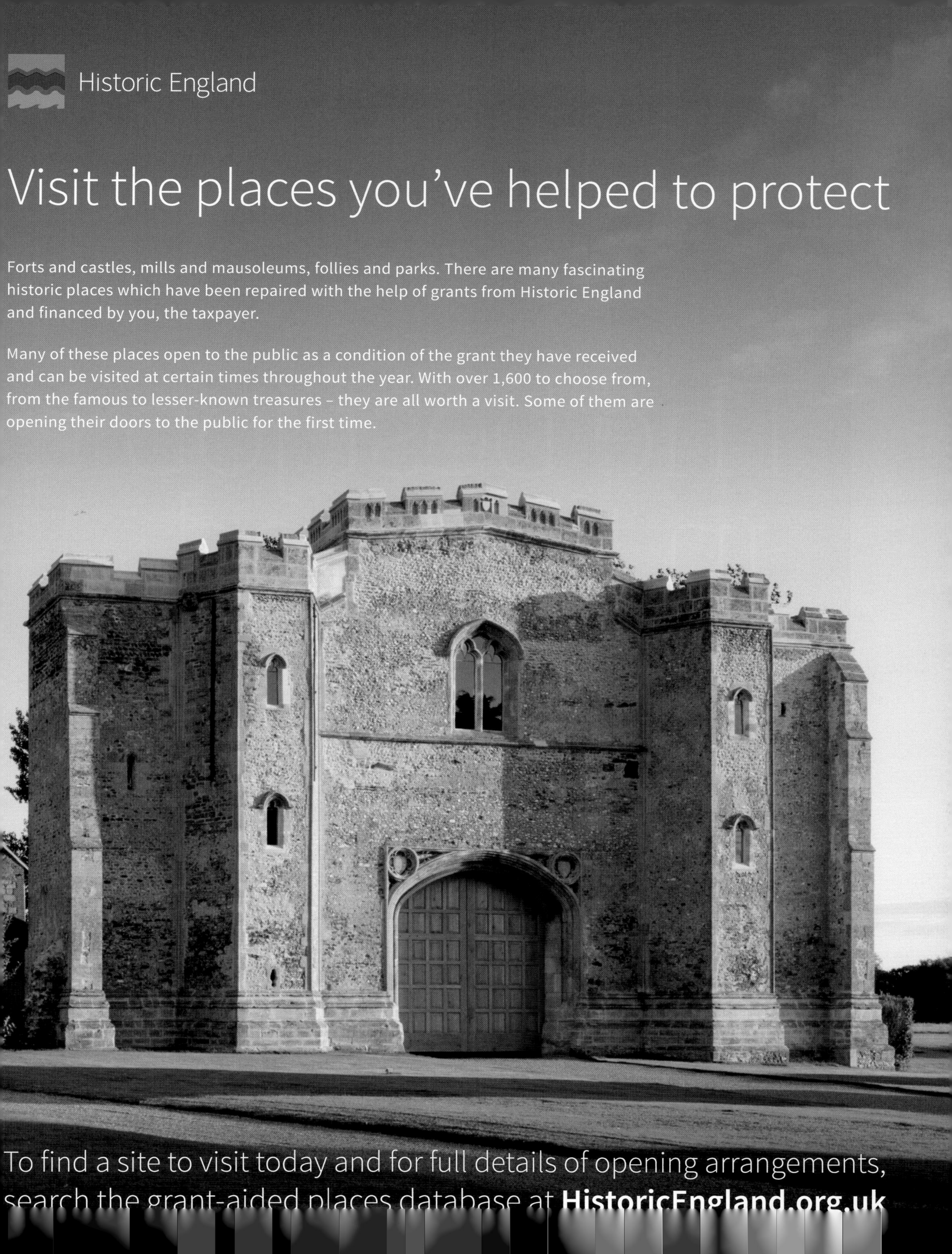

Visit the places you've helped to protect

Forts and castles, mills and mausoleums, follies and parks. There are many fascinating historic places which have been repaired with the help of grants from Historic England and financed by you, the taxpayer.

Many of these places open to the public as a condition of the grant they have received and can be visited at certain times throughout the year. With over 1,600 to choose from, from the famous to lesser-known treasures – they are all worth a visit. Some of them are opening their doors to the public for the first time.

To find a site to visit today and for full details of opening arrangements, search the grant-aided places database at **HistoricEngland.org.uk**

Dame Helen Ghosh, Director General of the National Trust since 2012

The best job in the land

Helen Ghosh became Director General of the National Trust in 2012. Sarah Greenwood met her at Leith Hill Place in Surrey to ask her about her role and about today's National Trust.

©NATIONAL TRUST IMAGES/CHRIS LACEY

©NATIONAL TRUST IMAGES/JOHN MILLER

I've heard you say that you have the best job in the country. Why do you think that?

Yes, the sheer variety of what we look after – everything from the urban properties, like the Birmingham Back to Backs, to walking around places like the Lake District or here in the Surrey hills. Our early founders were as passionate about green open spaces near London as they were with the great landscapes of the North and South West. I try to get out of the office for a couple of days every week.

How important are those founding principles?

I'm a historian by background so I always ask *"What did our founders want us to do?"* I'm very clear that they concentrated on the big conservation challenges of the day. Octavia Hill and Robert Hunter thought about urban spaces; fighting for Parliament Hill Fields and for commons to be protected. When Lord Lothian and later James Lees Milne were collecting houses from the 1930s then what they were effectively saying was *"Right now the conservation challenge is the loss of the country house"*. Last year, we celebrated 50 years of Coast, the Enterprise Neptune campaign against the overdevelopment of the coast. My predecessor, Fiona Reynolds responded to the sense of lack of access, where the challenge was to welcome people to all the places that we had. People felt, particularly with some of our grander houses and estates, *"This isn't for us"*. So we took down the ropes, lit the fires and reminded people that our countryside is as important as our houses. Last year, we had a record 21 million visitors to our pay-on-entry houses, gardens and parkland and about 200 million visits to our free access countryside. So for public benefit, access to landscape is vital.

Extending the season: the gardens at Mottisfont, Hampshire, in the winter

Dame Helen Ghosh

©NATIONAL TRUST IMAGES/CHRIS LACEY

©NATIONAL TRUST IMAGES/DAVID LEVENSON

Visitors at the Birmingham Back to Backs, following a trend towards interest in all types of social housing

©NATIONAL TRUST IMAGES/CAROLE DRAKE

Volunteers helping to construct the Christmas garland in the Great Hall at Cotehele, Cornwall

Are you trying to shake off your traditional middle class image?
It is what people choose for themselves. The number of visitors we get to the whole place – coming in through the gate, going to the café, wandering around the gardens – is rising, the number of people going into historic houses is flat. Therefore, despite all we have done over the last decade to make people feel welcome, there are still a lot of people who think *"It's not for me"*. I personally believe that we will prosper if the nation sees that what we offer them is relevant to their lives, otherwise why would they support us? We need to make sure that we are drawing in people who know less and who might really enjoy and feel enriched by what we have to offer.

What are today's challenges and what is today's big campaign for the National Trust?
We published a new 10 year strategy called *Playing our Part* in 2015. We identified four things that we thought we really needed to focus on. Conservation will always be our No. 1, including looking after our historic houses and collections. The second, something our founder, Octavia Hill, would recognise, is that the biggest conservation challenge that faces the nation is the loss of bio-diversity, whether the result of land management or climate change. So our biggest campaign is to ensure a healthy and beautiful environment, campaigning around better farming methods and cutting energy usage. Thirdly, we want to work with partners and with local communities. Naturalists believe we should create larger scale landscape habitats. We can say to the RSPB, the private landowner and the wildlife trust next door, *"Let's manage this as though it were a single place"*. We do this quite successfully in the Eastern Moors just outside Sheffield, at Wicken Fen and on Hadrian's Wall. Finally, we want to give people experiences that 'move, teach and inspire' to respond to the enormous thirst out there for information.

In the future, what if there are calls to acquire new places that might be under threat?
We have a very clear set of acquisition principles. Is this place under threat? Is it of national significance?Are we the best people to look after it? We would never close our minds to another great country house. Look at relatively recent acquisitions at Tynesfield or Seaton Delaval. We are constantly alive to the question of what is a place of historic interest in terms of the social history of Britain. Without going out with a shopping list, we do need to be open to things that are much more important to the social history of this country than the family in the big house. So I am very interested in social housing issues and we have found people are fascinated by, for example, what social housing looked like In 1968.

©NATIONAL TRUST IMAGES/MEGAN TAYLOR

Tractor at work on Wimpole Home Farm in Cambridgeshire

Wicken Fen National Nature Reserve, Cambridgeshire, in the care of the National Trust since 1899 and now expanding in partnership with local landowners and NGOs

Seaton Delaval Hall, Northumberland, acquired by the National Trust in 2009

©NATIONAL TRUST IMAGES/JOHN MILLER

Is there an element of competition with other organisations like English Heritage, Cadw and the Historic Houses Association who need to attract visitors?

It's not a competition so we all need to grow the cake. Get more people interested, give them experiences which move, teach and inspire them and we all benefit. I think we need to be very careful if people look at the National Trust and think that we can be self-sufficient or that we cannot be flexible enough to fit with a smaller partner. When English Heritage was set up with their £80 million dowry, we said, we don't think it's enough. We carry on saying that to Government. I think they have a very tough financial row to hoe, so we will bend over backwards to help where we can.

You are leaders in the use of volunteers. Is that sustainable and is it a good thing?

Volunteers bring enormous benefits to us. Different skills give us a kind of richness and the sense of being part of a bigger community is fantastically important. I think there is a challenge that the generation that wanted traditional volunteering will move on, so we have to make our opportunities attractive to different kinds of people. We need to be clear that we are offering something that people find rewarding and will fit with the time they have to offer.

You have upwards of 4.5 million members, can you keep growing?

There is a challenge in our success. The more members we have, the more people visit, so handling the sheer volume of numbers at some places is a real challenge. We need to do two things. First of all, spread the load, so get people to visit the places where there is room to grow. We now scan members' cards and we have invested in new tills. So we know a bit about our members and can point people to other places that will interest them. Also, many of our most successful properties have a rolling programme in the spirit of the place but which changes throughout the year.

©NATIONAL TRUST IMAGES/JOHN MILLER

What have you achieved so far as Director General?

I'm most proud of the fact that we have a very clear strategy for the next 10 years. Like any CEO, I have to make sure that we have the right kind of systems, so we have a new finance system. It sounds very dull, but countryside places were very often extremely impoverished; now our rangers and countryside managers have money for every hectare they manage. We are also playing Robin Hood, so if a property has more money than needed for conservation; it goes to the property down the road, putting money with need. I think we've become a bit more confident, so local and senior managers know it is perfectly valid to stand up for our charitable purpose. We had very convoluted decision making processes and I've streamlined some of those as well.

©NATIONAL TRUST IMAGES/STEVE SAYERS

Sheep grazing by the River Exe at Lower Halsdon Farm, Devon →

©NATIONAL TRUST IMAGES/JOHN MILLER

Leith Hill Place, childhood home of composer Ralph Vaughan Williams. Open: 3 Mar-30 Oct, Fri-Mon, 11-5pm. Admission; Adult £5; child £2.50

Hardwick Hall, from the gardens

©NATIONAL TRUST IMAGES/JOHN MILLER

©NATIONAL TRUST IMAGES/ ANDREAS VON EINSIEDEL

The Staircase Hall at The Vyne, Hampshire, created between 1769 and 1771 by John Chaloner Chute

What is the first National Trust property you ever visited?
The first I remember clearly was The Vyne in Hampshire, near where I was brought up; I was 6 or 7. I was fantastically impressed by the staircase and by the name of John Chaloner Chute who commissioned it, and that stuck in my head ever after.

Pick an historical character at the Trust whom you admire?
I'll pick Bess of Hardwick: ambitious in every sense; a very astute businesswoman, who wanted to leave her stamp on the world. The ambition and confidence of the house she created at Hardwick Hall is extraordinary and she clearly had an eye for beauty. So she actually summarises quite a lot about what we are up to and has many of the qualities of our founder, Octavia Hill.

Mottisfont, Hampshire (p.141)
Birmingham Back to Backs (p.252)
Cotehele, Cornwall (p.181)
Seaton Delaval Hall, Northumberland (p.293)
Hardwick Hall, Derbyshire (p.237)
The Vyne, Hampshire (p.141)

©NATIONAL TRUST IMAGES/ JOHN HAMMOND

Elizabeth Talbot, Countess of Shrewsbury, (Bess of Hardwick) (1527-1608) by Rowland Lockey, hanging in the Long Gallery at Hardwick Hall, Derbyshire

The Time Traveller's Guide

Hudson's Historic Houses & Gardens is 30 this year! Dr. Christopher Ridgway, Curator at Castle Howard and Chairman of the Yorkshire Country Houses Partnership, has been looking at why travel is important in the history of heritage places, so we asked him to delve into ours.

Sitting down to read through three decades of *Hudson's Historic Houses and Gardens* might not be everybody's idea of a good time; equally, admitting to owning a complete run of the guide can strike many as peculiar. These pastimes don't have to be the preserve of the heritage anorak though: if challenged with *"You should get out more"*, the reply is surely that *Hudson's* is precisely about getting out more…and more.

Each spring the appearance of the latest edition quickens the heartbeat. It doesn't just signal the end of the winter close season: flicking through the sumptuously illustrated pages, out tumble properties to visit, and ambitious itineraries are devised (if rarely completed). Although these *Hudson's* pilgrims may not reach all their intended sites, they usually manage to add to the names of houses and gardens visited or re-visited each year. The experience of *Hudson's* might begin at home but it invariably ends by going places.

Launched by Norman Hudson in 1987, the *Historic House Travel Trade Manual* (soon afterwards re-named *The Historic House and Garden Directory*) aimed to gather within a single set of covers, a complete set of information on properties open to the public. The primary audience was the travel trade, supplied with up-to-date information on locations, opening times, prices, and other essential details for organised tours; the entries also included a summary of the attractions at each house – architecture, collections, gardens; in addition there was a special interest index, to help readers satisfy their particular need.

Today's Hudson's Publisher, Sarah Greenwood, with founder, Norman Hudson, at Hudson's Heritage Awards presentation in 2016

→

But Norman was essentially looking to serve the needs of the houses, especially those in private ownership, who could not match the range of expertise and resources to be found in organisations such as the National Trust. The Directory enabled these owners to market their properties and a host of amenities aimed beyond the day-visitor; they could advertise conference facilities, special event days for the corporate market, as well as concerts, fireworks, and shooting; they could act as film locations and, after the 1995 Marriage Act, operate as wedding venues. For many owners, appealing to specialist groups was more cost-effective than mounting a regular house-opening operation with all its attendant overheads (leafleting, cafés, lavatories, car parks). Houses, especially the smaller ones, could generate significant income from fewer visits in the form of premium price events. The Directory was thus, as its title suggested, full of hard information; and it distilled Norman's years of experience as Technical Advisor to the Historic Houses Association. Travel operators could locate properties by region, see which ones offered accommodation, opened in winter, had gardens or specialist attractions; and private owners could be sure of a presence in the principal trade manual without costly self-marketing.

Crucially, a third audience who benefited hugely from *Hudson's Directory*, the great visiting public who were keen to know what was on offer amongst the bewildering array of heritage properties throughout the land. In his 1998 foreword Martin Drury, then Director General of the National Trust, reminded the public how in previous centuries visiting country houses had been 'pot luck'; now, with *Hudson's* as a guide, nothing need be left to chance. He deemed the publication, which had dropped the word Directory from its title, to be indispensible, not least of all because it also included information on restaurants and gift shops, which were increasingly part of the visitor experience.

Other changes were afoot too. National Trust and English Heritage properties were included, as were those belonging to their counterparts in Scotland and Wales; houses in receipt of repair grants were listed; and the 1999 issue included a new feature and a sign of things to come – a website index for properties abreast of digital developments. The guide also started to feature introductory articles on properties, and the work of various heritage organisations, giving a context to the bedrock of practical information that remained its great strength. There were themed years too, gardens in 1999, and the year of the sea in 2005, with a spectacular view of Lindisfarne Castle on the front cover.

A fantastic café, as here at Kiplin Hall in Yorkshire, may even be the primary reason for visiting and Hudson's provides a way of checking what to expect

When launched the Directory had featured 137 privately owned properties; by 2007 nearly 2000 properties were promoted – an astonishing density of attractions in such a tiny island, and unrivalled anywhere else in the world. The publication was getting larger, more comprehensive and, inevitably, thicker.

Queues at Blenheim Palace in the 1950s when heritage places first became mass market and (above right) a more interactive and relaxed experience at Blenheim today

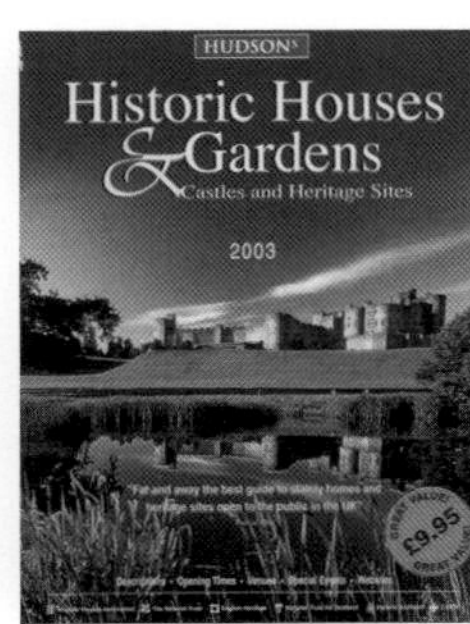

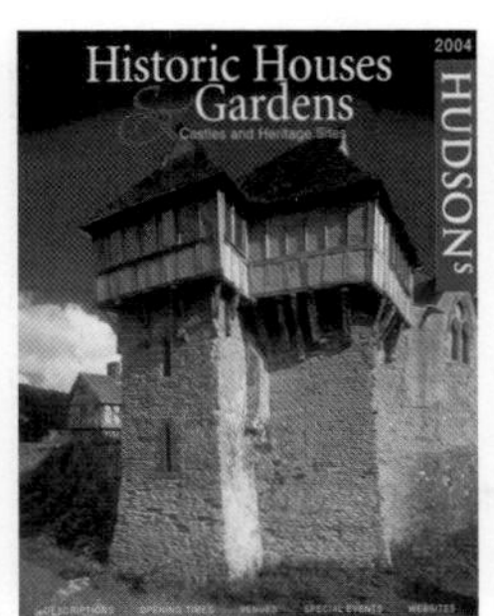

Keeping children busy is a priority at many places; in the new Magic Garden at Hampton Court

©ROBERT MYERS ASSOCIATES

→

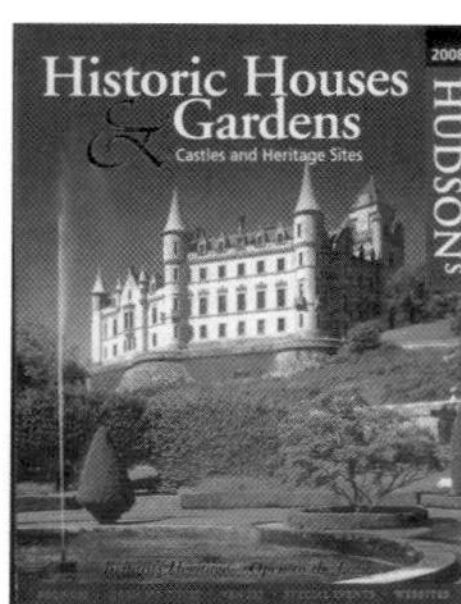

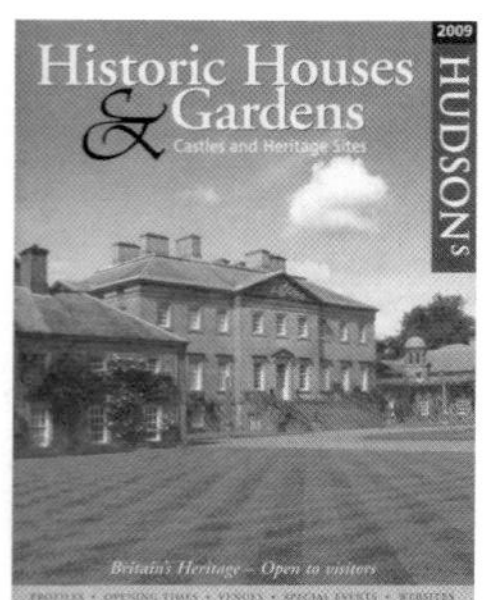

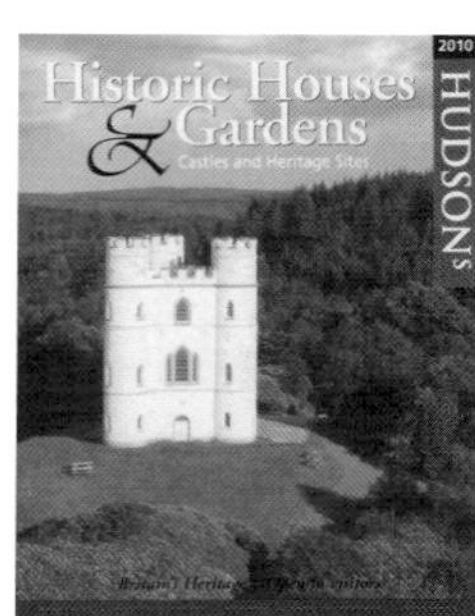

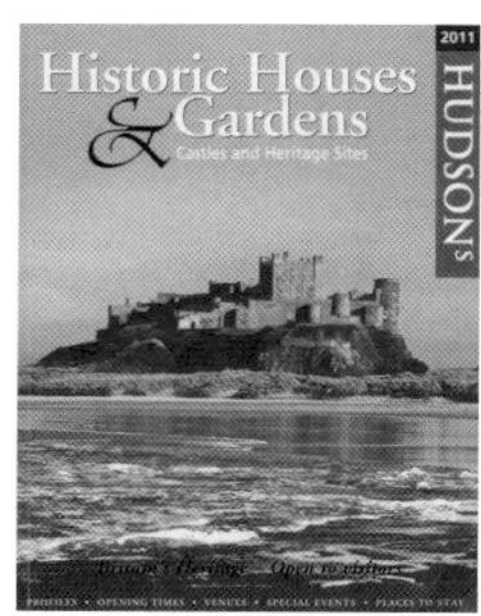

©VISIT ENGLAND/VISIT ESSEX

Today's visitors expect to be able to explore the grounds, kitchens and gardens

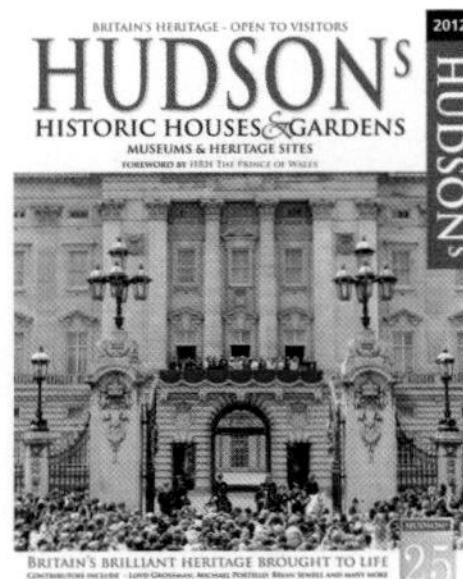

©HISTORIC ENVIRONMENT SCOTLAND/NEIL HANNA

Events are listed online by *Hudson's* and shared with a wide tourism network. These brave knights are at Linlithgow Palace

By comparison, in the 1950s, its predecessor, the ***Historic Houses and Castles of Great Britain and Northern Ireland*** gazetteer, contained less than 50 pages. With a new compact design, it now hovers around a portable 400 pages.

By 2015 the guide included 'Museums and Heritage Sites' in the title strapline, justifying its status as the 'bible' for heritage tourism. Much that had been new or little known in the 1980s was now expected on the part of increasingly demanding visitors. Not all houses could offer everything, but each aspired to present itself as attractive in some way to a range of audiences, which included the traditional day-visitor, families and children (the latter prompting a rise in adventure playgrounds), special interest groups, corporate clients, and the wedding market.

While some might expect the printed version to decline in the digital age, it remains hugely popular. Many people enjoy the portability of the volume, particularly when the wifi signal fails; but ever aware of changing market expectations, ***Hudson's*** has been active online since 2012 and publishes an app aimed at tour operators. The character of ***'Mrs Hudson'*** was created to highlight different itineraries, Tarr on the Road devises walking trips and the launch of ***Hudson's Heritage Awards*** in 2012 has tracked the changing interests of travellers and visitors. In whichever iteration, ***Hudson's*** remains reliable and trusted; one user has described it as *'mind-blowing'*; *'Don't leave home without it'* urged another reviewer.

These testimonials point to the truth that country houses have always been about travel. So many of them are the result of cosmopolitan experiences: owners inspired by architecture and landscapes viewed whilst touring; interiors decorated by itinerant craftsmen; collections that are the fruits of the Grand Tour or further afield in the age of empire. The country house epitomises the movement of people, objects, and ideas, which is why it is so endlessly fascinating to visit and study.

In 2016 the Yorkshire Country House Partnership launched a new collaborative project, on the topic of the country house and travel; this will culminate in a series §of exhibitions like the previously successful *Maids & Mistresses* (2004), *Work & Play* (2007), and *Duty Calls* (2013-14). The focus will include travellers, objects, craftsmen, the technologies and experience of travel (from horse to locomotive to internal combustion engine), travel writing, and much more.

But in-bound tourism is important too, especially in the second half of the 20th Century, which witnessed the rise of the heritage industry we now take for granted. What did houses think they were offering, what did visitors expect to see, and what did they really see? How has the experience of country house visiting changed in terms of the journey to and from properties, the pleasures of the visit itself, or the impressions visitors take away? As good a starting point as any is ***Hudson's*** with its enduring appeal to the armchair voyager and real tourist alike.

To read through this remarkable publication is to gain a unique insight into how the heritage industry sees itself and goes about its business.

Emma's Kitchen

Food has always been important in country houses; couple that with growing interest in the kitchens of the past and the combination is a winner. ***Hudson's*** asked Emma, Viscountess Weymouth to tell us about her new project, *Emma's Kitchen*, launched last year at her home, Longleat in Wiltshire. She shared some recipes with us.

I have a real passion for food – I love to cook for my family and friends and relish any opportunity to entertain. It has been my ambition, for some time, to bring the heart of this house back to life. It all starts with the old kitchens at Longleat. We have more than 300 pieces of antique cooking equipment left behind by people who lived and worked here before my time, including a marvellous collection of copper pans. In the archive, we have menus and guest lists from long ago feasts, including the food and drink served for many royal visitors over the centuries from Henry VIII to HM Queen Elizabeth II. In the Library we have books of recipes, household books and garden manuals. We have a walled kitchen garden and an ancient orchard and we live in a part of Britain with a long tradition of producing delicious and distinctive food from cider to Wiltshire ham.

Putting all of this together has given me the inspiration for a new enterprise at Longleat. Developing *Emma's Kitchen* is allowing me to invite our visitors into the Victorian kitchens for cookery demonstrations and classes, which will launch in 2017, and to start a label to sell produce of all sorts. We have already launched a range of jams and chutneys, including a delicious pineapple chutney. It has a really contemporary taste but I wanted to make it because I know that pineapples were grown here at Longleat in the 18th Century. We are selling delicious home baked cookies, scones and shortbread and have a range of meringues and florentines. We are reviving the kitchen garden, looking for varieties of fruit and vegetables that will work for produce that is appealing and delicious. In time I want to make cider from apples grown in the orchard which dates back to the first John Thynne's purchase of the estate in 1541 – older even than the Elizabethan house.

Before I came to Longleat, I wrote a regular cookery blog and presented programmes on TV's Food Network but it was the BBC's documentary about the house last year, *'All Change at Longleat'*, that gave me a chance to launch the idea of *Emma's Kitchen*. Now the brand is creating a space for me to share my passion for food.

Thynn Truffles

INGREDIENTS

For the Truffles:
220g shredded coconut
400g chopped walnuts
200g cocoa powder
100ml agave nectar
100ml coconut oil
1 tsp sea salt
1 tsp vanilla extract

For the Ganache Coating:
200ml coconut oil
100ml agave nectar
100g cocoa powder
1 tsp sea salt
1 tsp vanilla

METHOD

Mix the coconut and walnuts then add all other truffle ingredients and fold together. Place the mixture in the fridge to chill for 30 mins. Take the mixture from the fridge and roll in your hands to the desired size, then place on baking paper on a baking tray in the freezer for 30 mins.

Combine all the ingredients to make the ganache, and then using a fork, dip the ice-cold truffles to coat.

Sprinkle with a little sea salt or cayenne pepper depending on your mood and preferred flavour, then allow to rest in the freezer for another 10 mins. Remove and enjoy!

White Chocolate Coconut Truffles

INGREDIENTS

350g white chocolate chips
60ml coconut cream
150g shredded coconut

METHOD

Bring the coconut cream to a simmer and then remove from the heat.

Place the white chocolate chips in a bowl and carefully pour over the warmed coconut cream.

Stir until the chocolate has melted and then chill. Scoop out with a teaspoon and roll into balls. Roll in shredded coconut and chill again.

More Truffle Ideas

Milk Chocolate Espresso Truffles

Melt 50% dark chocolate and cream. Add espresso powder, a pinch of salt and a splash of brandy. Cool and scoop out small amounts with a teaspoon to roll into balls. Dust with cocoa powder.

Peanut Crunch Truffles

Blend peanut butter and icing sugar until you have a fluffy mixture, then roll into balls. Using a fork, dip the peanut butter balls into melted chocolate (64% cocoa) and sprinkle with crushed peanuts.

Chilli Truffles

Melt dark chocolate and cream and mix in 2 tsp. hot chilli powder. Chill and roll small amounts into balls. Garnish with a mixture of cayenne pepper and dried chilli flakes.

Salted Caramel Chocolate Brownies

INGREDIENTS

For the Brownies:
200g unsalted butter
200g dark chocolate
4 eggs
130g plain flour
60g cocoa powder

For the Salted Caramel:
200g soft brown sugar
300ml double cream
60g butter
1 tsp sea salt

For the Praline:
150g caster sugar
50g roughly chopped almonds
Squeeze of lemon juice
You will need a sugar thermometer and a silicone baking sheet and a greased and lined brownie tin.
Pre heat oven to 175°C

METHOD

To make the Salted Caramel: Place all ingredients in a pan and whisk until the butter has melted and sugar has dissolved. Bring to the boil and watch carefully whilst it bubbles and thickens. Remove from the heat, carefully transfer to a glass measuring jug and set aside.

To make the Praline: Melt the sugar in a pan. Put the sugar thermometer into the sugar at the start of the process; do not place it in hot melted sugar. Allow to cool before cleaning. Swirl the sugar in the pan to ensure it doesn't burn. Bring it up to 300°C and then carefully pour in chopped almonds and lemon juice. Pour onto baking sheet and allow to cool. Once cool, break into small pieces and set aside.

To make the Brownies: Melt the butter and chocolate in a bain marie. In a food mixer, combine the eggs and sugar. Pour in half of the caramel and combine. When the chocolate mixture has cooled, pour it into the sugar, egg and caramel mixture. Combine the flour and cocoa, then sift into the mixture and gently fold together.

Pour half the batter into the lined tin and evenly scatter some of the praline over the mixture. Pour over the other half and finish off with the rest of the praline. Use a fork to make a pretty feathered pattern on the top.

Bake for 25-30 mins. Allow to cool in the tin before cutting into squares.

The Emma's Kitchen range of products is available from the shop at Longleat.

Longleat House & Gardens, Wiltshire (p.196)

Trustees at the unveiling of the restored grisaille murals on the staircase at Boconnoc, Cornwall in 2009

Just in time

Funding from the Country Houses Foundation

For ten years the Country Houses Foundation has helped plug an important funding gap for the survival of Britain's heritage. The Country Houses Foundation (CHF), set up in 2005, is a charitable grant-giving body which provides funds for the repair and conservation of rural historic buildings and structures in England and Wales.

Its independence has allowed it flexibility to act quickly, and very cost effectively, to help rescue exceptional structures for which the future was uncertain. It has given funds to kick start restoration projects and to provide match funding that has ensured that faltering important projects have gone ahead. Architecturally important structures for which there is no economic use, from ice houses to follies, have been rescued from dereliction.

CHF has worked in close partnership with innumerable other organisations. It is one of the few sources of funds available to private owners, while at the same time securing public benefit and a degree of public access.

To date almost £9 million has been awarded to 165 projects spanning 1,000 years of history, encompassing buildings from castles to cottages, and from iron bridges to orangeries. Most of the properties supported are in the pages of Hudson's and a significant proportion have received national awards acknowledging the quality and importance of the conservation work that the Foundation has enabled.

By often acting as a catalyst for further support and providing even comparatively small sums the Foundation has made a real difference to the survival of buildings and structures that might otherwise have been lost.

Applications, however, always outnumber awards and the Trustees have the difficult task of selecting a short-list of projects that can be supported. Legacies and donations are vital, enabling CHF to continue its work and preserve our architectural heritage. Every gift received increases the level of support that can be offered to the growing number of applications for grants received every year and during this difficult financial climate the CHF's input makes a real difference – not just conserving our built heritage but helping to boost tourism, stimulating learning and providing employment for countless skilled craftsmen and women.

To support the work of CHF or propose a project for grant aid, contact David Price:
0845 402 4102
www.countryhousesfoundation.org.uk

Above left: Restoring the painted scenes of classical deities on the Ballroom ceiling at Stanford Hall in Leicestershire which dates from 1590. Above right: Gilding work in progress at Strawberry Hill

The Large Library at Stowe House, Buckinghamshire, restored and regilded to Sir John Soane's original vision

A restored Sir James Tillie sits eternally over his mausoleum at Pentillie Castle, Cornwall

Wentworth Castle, Yorkshire, the restored Great Conservatory

Celebrating the best visitor experiences

Hudson's Heritage Awards highlight the best. Our team of judges are experts in their field and the lunch we hold allows everyone a chance to be proud of what they have achieved. Thanks are due to our sponsors who make it all possible: Ecclesiastical Insurance; Fortnum & Mason; Jarrold Publishing; and Smith & Williamson. www.hudsons-awards.co.uk

The judges with Dan Cruickshank and Sarah Greenwood. From left: Ken Robinson, Lucinda Lambton, Simon Foster, Jeremy Musson, Norman Hudson

Hudson's Heritage Award winners 2016

2016 Winners

Best Family Day Out
Newby Hall, Yorkshire

First opened in 1948, over the years Newby Hall has quietly developed into an exemplary attraction for all ages while retaining its focus on the superb house, collection and world famous garden. Under 14s love the railway, bushcraft courses, themed days, the adventure gardens and enjoy special children's tours of the house. Over 65s enjoy garden workshops, heritage orchard tours and special events. And everyone appreciates the ice creams, the design led gift shop, the sculpture park and on site Zimbabwean sculptors, theatre performances on the lawn and the acclaimed new dolls' house and teddy bear exhibitions. Over a quarter of the visitors are children and a quarter OAPs, so the age spread is admirable and each year something new has been added to keep the experience fresh.

Newby Hall *(p.263)*

Runner-up: The Shakespeare Birthplace Trust, Stratford-upon-Avon

HUDSONs HERITAGE AWARDS

© HUGO GLENDINNING

Best Shopping

Sponsored by Jarrold Publishing

JARROLD publishing

The Harley Gallery, Welbeck Abbey, Nottinghamshire

The retail development on the estate at Welbeck Abbey includes a prize winning food outlet, Welbeck Farm Shop, as well as The Harley Gallery and the Limehouse Café. The Harley Gallery is a craft and gift shop with a bright contemporary style but an old fashioned approach to selecting and supporting its artists and makers. In particular, the *Made at Welbeck* collection features The Harley Studios resident artists, allowing the estate a direct role in marketing their own tenant artists. The Welbeck Card links the outlets, enhances marketing and encourages customer loyalty. Together the Harley Gallery enterprises have created a lively creative hub for the Midlands and an absorbing shopping destination.

Welbeck Abbey (p.226)

Runner up: Blackwell, the Arts & Crafts House, Windermere

Best Eating Out
Waddesdon Manor, Oxfordshire: The National Trust

At Waddesdon Manor, the National Trust have quickly established an impressive reputation for the quality of their catering. It is a complex business supplying food and drink over multiple outlets from self and full service lunches for visitors to upscale catering for weddings in three separate venues. At the house, the Stables Café caters informally for families, the Manor Restaurant for more formal experience and the nearby Five Arrows Hotel Restaurant offers full service at all times of day. Weddings can be staged at the Five Arrows, in the converted Victorian Dairy building or, now for the first time, in the White Drawing Room. A specially developed range of Rothschild wines from the Old and New Worlds compliment the family history of Waddesdon, the French château built by Lionel de Rothschild in 1873.

Waddesdon Manor (p.137)

Runner-up: Glansevern Gardens, Powys

Waddesdon Manor NT, Oxfordshire

HUDSON'S HERITAGE AWARDS

Best Accommodation

Special award for an outstandingly good idea

Champing with the Churches Conservation Trust

Most of us have been camping, a lucky few have experienced glamping but now, thanks to a brilliant and brave idea from the Churches Conservation Trust, more and more are going champing. If you don't already know, champing is an opportunity to spend the night in the extraordinary surroundings of a medieval church no longer used for regular worship. A night by candlelight, often with a storyteller to set the mood, in the deep quiet of an ancient church before waking in the morning to the coloured light refracted through stained glass windows, is an experience that is definitely designed to create memories. It has also been a new source of income for the Churches Conservation Trust and generated a real media buzz around their activities. An outstandingly good idea.

Best Accommodation
Frampton Court, Gloucestershire

There are few houses of the size and charm of Frampton Court in which one can stay comfortably, and even fewer such houses with an unbroken family history. It is a superbly elegant building with an exceptional gothic orangery and lovely gardens, but the refurbishment of the five main bedrooms has achieved a perfectly pitched style of restrained elegance. Every detail has been considered even to a dog gate on the stairs. Breakfast includes bacon and sausages made from pork bred on the estate and in the bedrooms hang the botanical watercolours from the Frampton Flora, a collection of exquisite wild flower studies made by the ladies of the Clifford family in the 1830s.

Frampton Court *(p.193)*

Runner up: Bruisyard Hall, Suffolk

→

HUDSONS HERITAGE AWARDS

Best New Discovery
Bletchley Park, Hertfordshire

The restored wartime facility at Bletchley Park is telling an extraordinary story of global importance. The public are discovering Bletchley at the same time as they are discovering the history of the World War 2 codebreakers, kept secret for decades. In this sense the whole site at Bletchley is a new discovery but there is one particular discovery which intrigued us. In the roof space of Hut 6, the restoration teams discovered a collection of screwed up pieces of paper which had probably been used as draught excluders. These scraps are the only papers to survive from wartime Bletchley Park and included one of Alan Turing's original Banbury sheets, which used punched holes to decode the messages sent from the German Enigma machine. These scraps of wartime rubbish bring vividly to life the contribution of the codebreakers.

Bletchley Park (p.137)

Runner up: The Judges' Lodging, Presteigne ***Restoration of Ethiopian Shield***

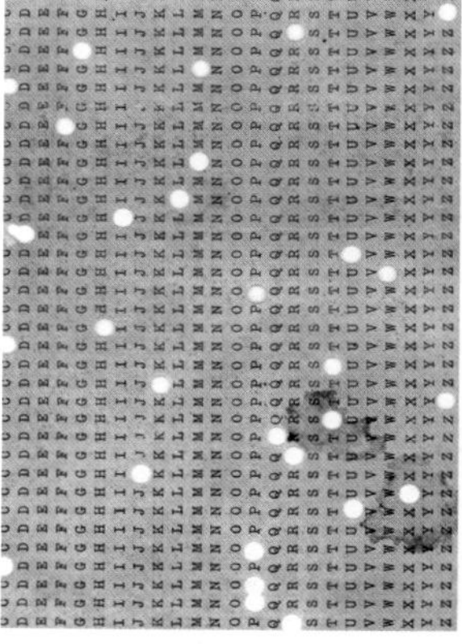

Best Wedding Venue
Combermere Abbey, Shropshire

Combermere Abbey offers an inspired conversion of the walled garden as a multiple wedding venue. Wedding couples have a choice of a conservatory, marquee or innovative fruit tree maze for their ceremony and party. There is extensive accommodation for up to 49 guests and a charming gothic cottage for honeymooners. The idea of planting a commemorative tree for each couple is helping to regenerate the ancient woodland. As a venue, Combermere is well thought out and the main house has been protected as a family home while finding a new use for the walled garden.
Combermere Abbey *(p.277)*
Runner Up: Chiddingstone Castle, Kent

Best Innovation

Special award for an outstandingly good idea

Woburn Abbey Young Curators' Day, Bedfordshire

Woburn Abbey has developed a schools programme with a difference in collaboration with their local primary school. The Young Curators' Day is the culmination of a learning programme for 23 children between seven and nine. Billed as a takeover event, the children lead tours, develop trails, and act as stewards to demonstrate their new found knowledge of the house and its history to cross-generational family groups. The children and visitors are very positive about the experience which delivers real life skills, particularly boosting confidence in public speaking, as well as great exposure to the house and its history for a diverse local community.

Woburn Abbey (*p.204*)

Ai Wei Wei (2015)

Ai Wei Wei (2015)

Ai Wei Wei (2015)

Best Innovation
Blenheim Palace, Oxfordshire

Michelangelo Pistoletto (2016)

The Blenheim Art Foundation was launched with an innovative world class exhibition by a leading contemporary artist with a global reputation. The inaugural exhibition of works by Chinese dissident artist Ai Wei Wei was well orchestrated, merchandised and interpreted particularly given that the artist was under house arrest at the time. The launch of the not-for-profit foundation establishes Blenheim as an arts venue as well as a country house. The impact of this exhibition challenged visitors and attracted new urban audiences and it took the Royal Academy a year to catch up with its own Ai Wei Wei exhibiton. Now the Foundation has plans for exhibitions with a range of contemporary artists over the next few years.
Blenheim Palace (*p.151*)
Runner Up: Croome Court NT, Worcestershire, *The Sky Café*

Laurence Weiner (2015)

Best Loos
Lowther Castle, Cumbria

In setting public toilets into the old stables in the Courtyard at Lowther Castle, the team have set high standards for the conversion and reuse of an historic building. The 5th Earl of Lonsdale - The Yellow Earl - whose stables these were, was a keen hunt follower and racehorse owner. The original loose boxes of the stables have been restored with the retention of many original fittings and appropriate additions to create a series of small groups of public toilets. The essence of the stable has been successfully retained, the basins for example could pass as mangers, but with no compromise on comfort or style.
Lowther Castle (*p.xxx*)
Runner up: The Alnwick Garden, Northumberland

HUDSONS HERITAGE AWARDS

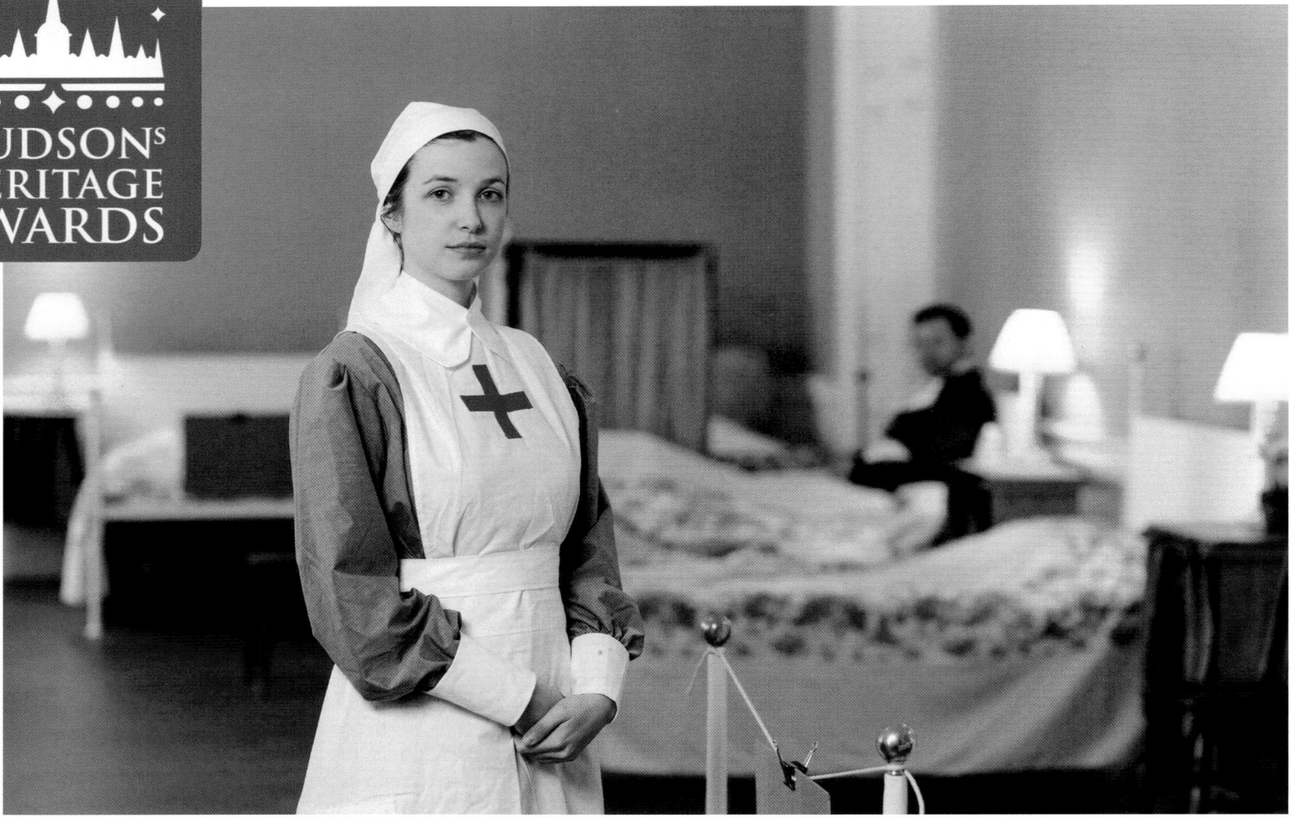

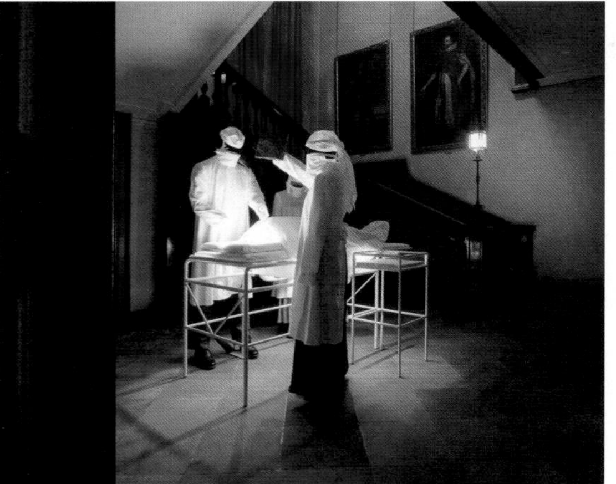

Best Event or Exhibition

Sponsored by Ecclesiastical Insurance

Dunham Massey NT, Cheshire

The recreation of the First World War Stamford Hospital at Dunham Massey was a courageous and imaginative project by the National Trust. Visitors saw the wards, mess room and operating theatre where 282 British and Canadian soldiers injured on the Western Front found a brief sanctuary from the horrors of the trenches of the Great War. The presentation of 30 carefully researched stories of the inmates by professional actors proved thought provoking and engaging and avoided the occasionally awkward interactions between visitors and costumed interpreters. The project has won universal acclaim and been a surprise hit with visitors; it deserved to be the most talked about event of the year.

Dunham Massey (*p.278*)

Runner up: Houghton Hall, Norfolk, *James Turrell exhibition*

Best Hidden Gem

Sponsored by Smith & Williamson

Smith & Williamson
Accountancy · Investment Management · Tax

The Crystal Grotto, Painshill Gardens, Surrey

Charles Hamilton's gardens at Painshill in Surrey, created around 1760, are far less well known than they should be. The landscape with its collection of follies and garden buildings was always entrancing but the restoration of the Crystal Grotto is truly exceptional. The Crystal Grotto, designed by Joseph Lane and made up of 100s of 1000s of crystals of calcite, gypsum, quartz and fluorite, is a real rarity. Now restored to shimmering splendour, enlivened by echoes and splashes of water and light, it gives us once more the exuberant vision of its creator. *Painshill Gardens (p.159)*

Runner up: Keats House, London

Best Picnic Spot

New Lanark, Lanarkshire

FORTNUM & MASON
PICCADILLY SINCE 1707

The World Heritage Site at New Lanark invites a picnic and the team here have done much to encourage families to do just that. The newly laid out picnic site and playground at Clearburn provides plenty of inspiration for a streamside picnic and no shortage of activities, from willow tunnels to storytelling glades and an acting space. It is a well thought out area that makes good use of the natural advantages of the site. New Lanark stage a one day Big Picnic event for picnickers all over the site, at Clearburn and in the founder Robert Owen's gardens. All in all, New Lanark have been thoughtful in providing for picnickers and in doing so have created a special place for families to spread a rug and have a great day out. *New Lanark (p.306)*

Runner up: Lowther Castle Gardens, Cumbria

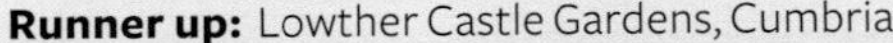

JARROLD
publishing
THE GUIDEBOOK EXPERTS

Jarrold Publishing works with historic houses, gardens, cathedrals, museums and galleries across the UK.

Over the course of a century, we have published 100s of beautiful and informative guidebooks for some of the UK's most interesting places, from Ballindalloch Castle to Howletts Wild Animal Park.

Next time you are out exploring be sure to pick up the latest Jarrold guide for history, intrigue and a beautiful memento of your visit...

...Take a piece of history home with you

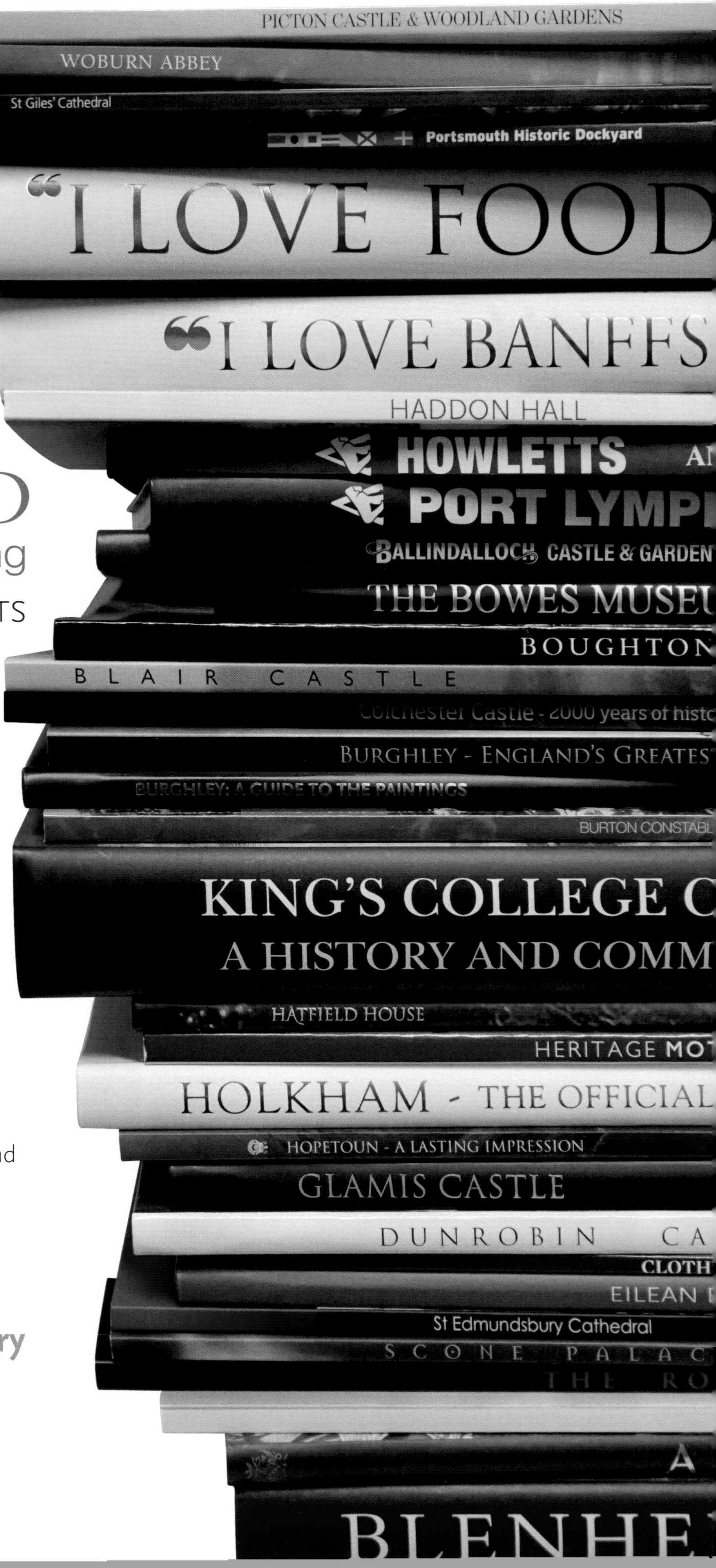

Where is Britain's best heritage picnic spot?

Take a picnic to any heritage place in the UK and you could be picnicking in style with your own classic Fortnum & Mason hamper. All you need to do is nominate your favourite picnic spot. It might be a family picnic on a sunny summer afternoon or a picnic supper during a concert or theatre performance or even a place for a quick sandwich on a cycle ride. We want to know where is the best heritage picnic spot in the UK?

Send us a photograph (or up to four) of your picnic place telling us where it is and describe why it is special to you in 150 words.

If yours is the winning entry you will win the Fortnum & Mason Piccadilly Hamper, fully equipped for four people, and an invitation for two to attend the presentation of Hudson's Heritage Awards, held each year in London. Your winning entry will also feature in next year's Hudson's Historic Houses & Gardens and you will receive a free copy of Hudson's Historic Houses & Gardens 2018.

All entries received will be judged by our independent judging panel chaired by Norman Hudson, OBE. Details can be found at www.hudsons-awards.co.uk where you can also make your nomination online. Make sure you include your name, address, email address and telephone number. You can make a nomination by post to: Hudson's Best Heritage Picnic Award, 35 Thorpe Road, Peterborough PE3 6AG.

The closing date for all entries is 30 September 2017. Winners will be advised by 1 January 2018.

in association with

FORTNUM & MASON

EST 1707

The judges' decision is final and no correspondence will be entered into. Hudson's reserves the right to reproduce all images provided for use in publicity materials.

Blenheim Palace © VISIT BRITAIN IMAGES

Historic House Hotels of the National Trust

Past, Present & Future Perfect

Stay in an Historic House Hotel...

The three Historic House Hotels were each rescued from an uncertain future in the 1980's. They, with their gardens and parks, were restored and converted to hotels, combining historically accurate standards with the provision of traditional yet up-to-date comfort for guests, and offering the very best of British hospitality.

Although very-well suited for their present role, guests should not expect them to be modern hotels like new build in town or country. However, very few allowances need to be made for the fact that the building is more than 300 years old.

Hartwell House & Spa
Vale of Aylesbury,
Buckinghamshire,
HP17 8NR
Tel: 01296 747444
www.hartwell-house.com

Bodysgallen Hall & Spa
Llandudno,
North Wales,
LL30 1RS
Tel: 01492 584466
www.bodysgallen.com

Middlethorpe Hall & Spa
Bishopthorpe Road,
York,
YO23 2GB
Tel: 01904 641241
www.middlethorpe.com

Regional Directory

We want to make Hudson's easy for you to use. Turn to our maps on pages 379 for all sites. Do check opening times before you visit. Many properties are open regularly, but others only occasionally and some may only open for weddings and special events.

Kelmarsh Hall, Northamptonshire

Key to Symbols

- Information
- Shop
- Plant Sales
- Corporate Hospitality / Functions
- Suitable for people with disabilities
- Refreshments / Café / Tearoom
- Restaurant
- Guided Tours
- Audio Tours
- Parking Available
- Education - School Visits
- Suitable for Dogs
- No Dogs
- Accommodation
- Licensed for wedding ceremonies
- Open All Year
- Special Events
- Accept Euros
- Member of the Historic Houses Association but does **not** give free access to Friends
- Member of the HHA giving free access under the HHA Friends Scheme
- Property owned by National Trust
- Property in the care of English Heritage
- Property owned by The National Trust for Scotland
- Property in the care of Historic Scotland
- Properties in the care of Cadw, the Welsh Government's historic environment service
- 2016 Hudson's Heritage Awards Winner
- 2016 Hudson's Heritage Awards Highly Commended

Syon Park, Middlesex

London

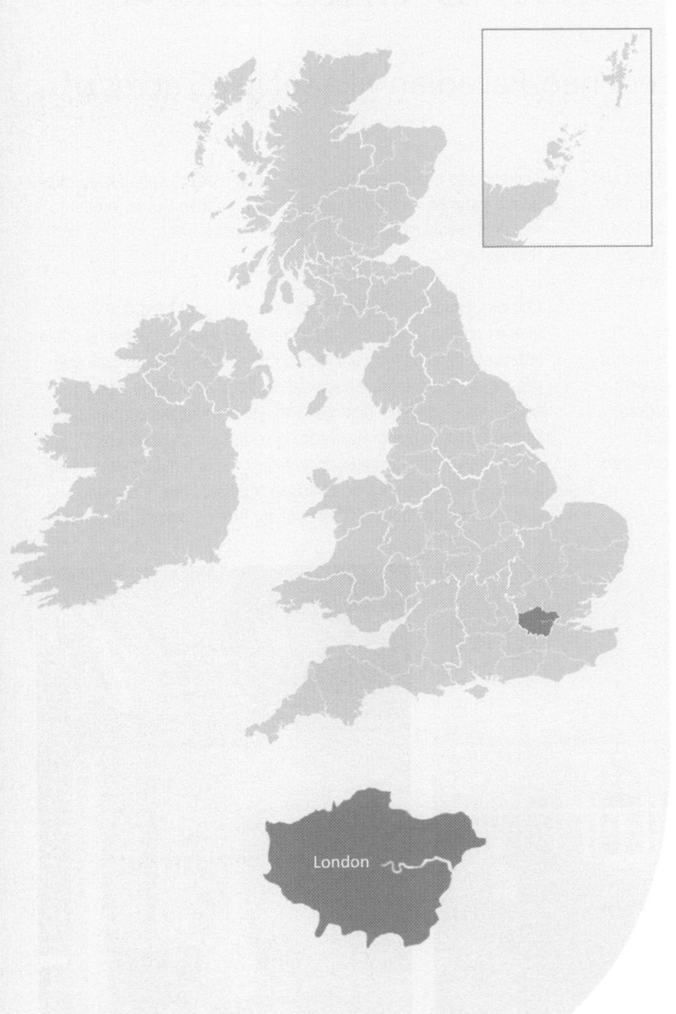

London is the cosmopolitan hub of Great Britain. Look under the surface for stories of kings & queens, ambitious, politicians, artists, musicians, sailors and philosophers. Visit the places where they lived and worked to understand what makes the nation tick.

VISITOR INFORMATION

Owner
Chiswick House and Gardens Trust and English Heritage

Address
Chiswick House
Burlington Lane
London
W4 2RP

Location
Map 19:C8
OS Ref. TQ210 775
Burlington Lane, London W4 2RP.
Rail: Chiswick Station (10 mins walk).
Underground: Turnham Green (25 mins walk)
Bus: 190, E3

Contact
Estate Office
Tel: 020 3141 3350
E-mail: mail@chgt.org.uk

Opening Times
Gardens
7am-dusk all year round.
Chiswick House
Apr-Oct
Sun-Wed and Bank Holidays.
10am-6pm
(5pm Mar & Oct).
Check website for winter 2017 closure.
Café open 7 days a week from 8.30am.

Admission
Gardens:

Entry	Free

House:

Adult	£6.70
Conc.	£6.00
Child	£4.00
Family	£17.40

Discount for groups (11+).

Free for English Heritage and National Art Pass members.

Prices correct at time of press.

Garden & House Tours
House 020 8995 0508
Garden Tours and Camellia Show Group bookings
chgt.org.uk

Special Events
Camellia Show 2017
3 Mar-2 Apr
(Closed Mons).

There is an ongoing programme of community and special events.

Conference/Function

ROOM	Size	Max Cap
Chiswick House		150
Burlington Pavilion		350
The Conservatory		150
The Cafe		80

© Clive Boursnell

CHISWICK HOUSE AND GARDENS

www.chgt.org.uk

Chiswick House is a magnificent neo-Palladian villa set in 65 acres of beautiful historic gardens.

Chiswick House is internationally renowned as one of the first and finest English Palladian villas. Lord Burlington who designed and built the villa from 1725-1729, was inspired by the architecture and gardens of ancient Rome. The opulent interiors created by William Kent, display a rich collection of Old Master paintings.

The Grade I listed gardens surrounding Chiswick House have, at every turn, something to surprise and delight the visitor from the magnificent cedar trees to the beautiful Italianate gardens with their cascade, statues, temples, urns and obelisks. The gardens have been fully restored to their former glory, including the Conservatory, which houses the world famous Camellia collection in bloom during February and March.

There is also a children's play area and a modern café designed by award-winning architects Caruso St John. Open daily it offers seasonal breakfast and lunch menus, snacks, afternoon teas and refreshments.

Chiswick House once acted both as a gallery for Lord Burlington's fine art collection and as a glamorous party venue where he could entertain. Whether you are looking to host a wedding, exclusive private dinner, celebrate a special occasion or arrange a team building day, it is the ideal location. From a stylishly simple civil ceremony to an elaborate wedding reception, champagne celebration in the domed Conservatory, team building days in our Private Walled Gardens or a party in the Café. The House and Gardens are also popular locations for filming and photo shoots.

KEY FACTS

- WCs. Filming, plays, photographic shoots. Weddings, corporate and private events and party hire - please call 020 3141 3351 or events@chgt.org.uk or see chgt.org.uk.
- Chiswick House Shop - see house opening times.
- Private & corporate hospitality.
- See website for access details.
- Open 7 days a week from 8.30am.
- Personal guided tours must be booked in advance.
- House. (Downloadable tours-Garden).
- Pay and display machines (approx. 60 bays).
- Contact Estate Office.
- In gardens except for clearly sign-posted dog-free and short lead only areas. No dogs in house.
- 

© Clive Boursnell

© Richard Bryant

Register for news and special offers at www.hudsonsheritage.com

KENSINGTON PALACE

www.hrp.org.uk/kensingtonpalace

Home to royalty for over 300 years.

Kensington Palace was the childhood home of Queen Victoria. Immerse yourself in the public and private life of this long reigning monarch and explore the different roles she played: queen, wife, mother and widow in the Victoria Revealed exhibition, told through extracts from her own letters and diaries.

Follow in the footsteps of Georgian courtiers in the sumptuous King's State Apartments which show some breathtaking examples of the work of architect and painter William Kent.

Visit the Queen's State Apartments, the intimate, private rooms created for Queen Mary II, who ruled jointly with her husband, King William III, in the 17th Century.

Explore the beautiful gardens, inspired by the famous lawns that existed in the 18th Century and enjoy a leisurely lunch or an indulgent afternoon tea in the splendour of Queen Anne's Orangery, once the setting for the most lavish of court entertainments.

KEY FACTS

- Weddings, dinners, receptions and gala celebrations. Visit hrp.org.uk/hireavenue or call 020 3166 6115.
- Please book, 0844 482 7777.
- Closed 24-26 Dec.

VISITOR INFORMATION

Owner
Historic Royal Palaces

Address
Kensington Gardens
London
W8 4PX

Location
Map 20:I8
OS Ref. TQ258 801
In Kensington Gardens.
Underground:
Queensway on Central Line, High Street Kensington on Circle & District Line.

Contact
Tel: 0844 482 7777
Venue Hire and Corporate Hospitality:
020 3166 6115
E-mail:
kensingtonpalace@hrp.org.uk

Opening Times
Nov-Feb:
Daily, 10am-5pm
(last admission 4pm).

Mar-Oct:
Daily, 10am-6pm
(last admission 5pm).
Closed 24-26 Dec.

Admission
Kids under 16 go free. Visit www.hrp.org.uk/kensingtonpalace or call 0844 482 7777 for more information.

Special Events
Special events throughout the year. See website for details.

Conference/Function
Conferences: Up to 120.
Receptions: Up to 300.
Lunches: Up to 200.
Dinners: 20 to 200.

VISITOR INFORMATION

Owner
The Duke of Northumberland

Address
Syon House
Syon Park
Brentford
Middex
TW8 8JF

Location
Map 19:B8
OS Ref. TQ173 767
Between Brentford & Twickenham, off A4, A310 in SW London.
Sat Nav: TW7 6AZ
Public Transport: Gunnersbury Station then bus 237 or 267. Brentford Rail, Ealing Broadway or Boston Manor Underground, then bus E8. Minicab companies available at the stations.
Air: Heathrow 8m.

Contact
Estate Office
Tel: 020 8560 0882
E-mail: info@syonpark.co.uk

Opening Times
Syon House:
15 Mar-29 Oct 2017
Weds, Thus, Suns and BHs 11am-5pm, last entry 4pm.

Gardens only:
13 Mar-29 Oct 2017
Daily 10.30am-5pm, last entry at 4pm.

House, Gardens and Great Conservatory:
Closed from 30 Oct 2017 - 12 Mar 2018.

Admission
House, Gardens & Conservatory:

Adult	£12.50
Child	£5.50
Conc.	£11.00
Family (2+2)	£28.00
Booked groups (25+)	
Adult	£11.00
Conc.	£10.00
School Group	£4.00

Gardens & Great Conservatory:

Adult	£7.50
Child	£4.00
Conc.	£6.00
Family (2+2)	£16.00
School Group	£3.00

Syon House Ventures reserves the right to alter opening times. Please phone or check website for up to date details and special events.

Conference/Function

ROOM	Size	Max Cap
Great Hall	50'x30'	120
Great Conservatory	60'x40'	150
Summer Marquee		600

SYON PARK

www.syonpark.co.uk

London home of the Duke of Northumberland with magnificent Robert Adam interiors, 40-acres of gardens, including the spectacular Great Conservatory.

Described by John Betjeman as the 'Grand Architectural Walk', Syon House and its 200-acre park is the London home of the Duke of Northumberland, whose family, the Percys, have lived here for 400 years. Originally the site of a late medieval monastery, excavated by Channel 4's Time Team, Syon Park has a fascinating history. Catherine Howard was imprisoned at Syon before her execution, Lady Jane Grey was offered the crown whilst staying at Syon, and the 9th Earl of Northumberland was imprisoned in the Tower of London for 15 years because of his association with the Gunpowder Plot. The present house has Tudor origins but contains some of Robert Adam's finest interiors, which were commissioned by the 1st Duke in the 1760s. The private apartments and State bedrooms are available to view.

The house can be hired for filming and photo shoots subject to availability. Within the 'Capability' Brown landscaped park are 40 acres of gardens which contain the spectacular Great Conservatory designed by Charles Fowler in the 1820s. The House and Great Conservatory are available for corporate and private hire. The Northumberland Room in Syon House is an excellent venue for conferences, meetings, lunches and dinners (max 60). The State Apartments make a sumptuous setting for dinners, concerts, receptions, launches and wedding ceremonies (max 120). Marquees can be erected on the lawn adjacent to the house for balls and corporate events. The Great Conservatory is available for summer parties, launches, filming, photoshoots and wedding receptions (max 150).

KEY FACTS

- No photography in the House.
- Syon Park Visitor Centre, open daily 10.30am-5.00pm during the season. visitorcentre@syonpark.co.uk
- Garden Centre.
- Syon House and the Great Conservatory available for exclusive luncheons, formal dinners, ceremonies, receptions, parties, meetings and corporate events. Contact events@syonpark.co.uk for more info.
- WCs. House - Limited access. Gardens and Great Conservatory - fully accessible.
- The Garden Kitchen Restaurant in the Garden Centre.
- By arrangement.
- Free parking.
- Assistance dogs only.
- London Syon Park Hilton Hotel at www.londonsyonpark.com
- See website for details.

© Historic Royal Palaces

TOWER OF LONDON

www.hrp.org.uk/toweroflondon

The ancient stones reverberate with dark secrets, priceless jewels glint in fortified vaults and pampered ravens strut the grounds.

The Tower of London, founded by William the Conqueror in 1066-7, is one of the world's most famous fortresses, and one of Britain's most visited historic sites. Despite a grim reputation for being a place of torture and death, there are so many more stories to be told about the Tower and its intriguing cast of characters.

This powerful and enduring symbol of the Norman Conquest has been enjoyed as a royal palace, served as an armoury and for over 600 years even housed a menagerie! Don't miss the Crown Jewels in the famous Jewel House, unlocking the story behind the 23,578 gems in the priceless royal jewels. Marvel at the Imperial State Crown and the largest diamond ever found; and see the only treasure to escape destruction in 1649, after the Civil War. For centuries, this dazzling collection has featured in royal ceremonies, and it is still in use today.

Join Yeoman Warder Tours to be entertained by captivating talks of pain, passion, treachery and torture at the Tower. Visit Tower Green and see the memorial to the people who died within the Tower walls. Find out why the last execution at the Tower was in 1941 and see how instruments of torture were used to extract 'confessions' from prisoners. Explore the story of how five coins changed history in the Coins and Kings Exhibition, discover what life was like in the surprisingly luxurious Medieval Palace, and explore the stories of Henry II, Edward I and their courts at work.

See one of the Tower's most famous sights, the ravens. Legend has it Charles II believed that if the ravens were ever to leave the Tower, the fortress and the kingdom would fall. Step into 1,000 years of history every day at the Tower of London.

KEY FACTS

- No photography in Jewel House.
-
- Visit www.hrp.org.uk/hireavenue or call 020 3166 6226.
- WCs.
-
- Licensed.
- Yeoman Warder tours are free and leave front entrance every ½ hr.
-
- None for cars. Coach parking nearby.
- To book 0844 482 7777.
-
-
-

Yeoman Warders

Imperial Crown of India

© The Royal Collection © 2015, Her Majesty Queen Elizabeth II

VISITOR INFORMATION

Owner
Historic Royal Palaces

Address
London
EC3N 4AB

Location
Map 20:P7
OS Ref. TQ336 806
Bus: 15, 42, 78, 100, RV1.
Underground: Tower Hill on Circle/District Line.
Docklands Light Railway: Tower Gateway Station.
Rail: Fenchurch Street Station and London Bridge Station.
Boat: From Embankment Pier, Westminster or Greenwich to Tower Pier. London Eye to Tower of London Express.

Contact
Tel: 0844 482 7777
Venue Hire and Corporate Hospitality: 020 3166 6226
E-mail: visitorservices.tol@hrp.org.uk

Opening Times
Summer:
Mar-Oct, Tue-Sat
9am-5.30pm
(last admission 5pm).
Mon & Sun 10am-5.30pm
(last admission 5pm).

Winter:
Nov-Feb, Tue-Sat
9am-4.30pm
(last admission 4pm).
Mon & Sun 10am-4.30pm
(last admission 4pm).
Closed 24-26 Dec and 1 Jan.

Admission
Visit www.hrp.org.uk/toweroflondon or call 844 482 7777 for more information.

Conference/Function
Conferences: Up to 100.
Meetings: 6 to 100.
Receptions: 20 to 300.
Lunches: Up to 150.
Dinners: 6 to 240.

© National Trust Images / Andrew Butler

OSTERLEY PARK AND HOUSE

JERSEY ROAD, ISLEWORTH, LONDON TW7 4RB

www.nationaltrust.org.uk/osterley

A suburban palace caught between town and country, Osterley Park and House is one of the last surviving country estates in London. Past fields and grazing cattle, just around the lake the magnificent house awaits; presented as it would have been when it was redesigned by Robert Adam in the late 18th Century for the Child family. A place for entertaining friends and clients, fashioned for show and entertaining, the lavish state apartments tell the story of a party palace. Recently returned family portraits and furniture now add a personal touch to grand rooms, and then downstairs, see the contrast of the domestic quarters. Elegant pleasure gardens and hundreds of acres of parkland are perfect for whiling away a peaceful afternoon.

Location: Map 19:C7. OS Ref TQ146 780. A4 between Hammersmith and Hounslow. Main gates at Thornbury & Jersey Road junction. SatNav: TW7 4RD.

Owner: National Trust **Tel:** 020 8232 5050

E-mail: osterley@nationaltrust.org.uk

Open: Gardens & café open all year, 10-5pm (or dusk if earlier). House open fully 25 Feb-5 Nov, 11-5pm; from 6 Nov-31 Dec only basement open for winter exhibition and principle floor open for Christmas weekends, 11-4pm (house entry one hour before closing). Shop open weekends 7 Jan-19 Feb, daily from 25 Feb-5 Nov, weekends 11-26 Nov and daily in Dec, 11-5pm. Park & car park open 7am-7pm all year. Whole property (aside from Park) closed 25 Dec.

Admission: *House & Garden: Adult £12, Child £6, Family £30. Groups (15+) £9.20. *Winter Admission: Adult £9.70, Child £4.85, Family £24.25. Groups (15+) £7.50 *includes voluntary 10% Gift Aid donation. Car Park: £7, free to NT Members. Park and grounds: Free. **Key facts:** No flash photography inside House. NT gift shop with wide range of goods plus second-hand bookshop. Meeting rooms available. WCs, gardens and basement floor of House. Seasonal menus, freshly baked cakes & cream teas. Family friendly. Kids' lunchboxes. Audio-visual guides. Limited for coaches, pre-booking essential. Schools programme. Assistance dogs only in House & Gardens. Park, gardens & café open all year (closed 25 Dec).

© Spencer House Limited / Mark Fiennes. Do not used without the permission of Spencer House Limited.

© Spencer House Limited / Nikolai Cedraeus. Do not used without the permission of Spencer House Limited.

SPENCER HOUSE

27 ST JAMES'S PLACE, LONDON SW1A 1NR

www.spencerhouse.co.uk

Spencer House, built 1756-66 for the first Earl Spencer, an ancestor of Diana, Princess of Wales (1961-97), is London's finest surviving 18th Century town house. The magnificent private palace has regained the full splendour of its late 18th Century appearance after a painstaking ten-year restoration programme. Designed by John Vardy and James 'Athenian' Stuart, the nine State Rooms are amongst the first neo-classical interiors in Europe. Vardy's Palm Room, with its spectacular screen of gilded palm trees and arched fronds, is a unique Palladian set-piece, while the elegant mural decorations of Stuart's Painted Room reflect the 18th Century passion for classical Greece and Rome.

Location: Map 20:L8. OS Ref TQ293 803. Central London: Just off St James's Street, overlooking Green Park.

Contact: Jason Garton, Tours and Facilities Manager

Tel: 020 7514 1958

E-mail: tours@spencerhouse.co.uk

Open: Suns from: 10am-5.30pm (Last tour 16:30). Regular tours throughout the day. Max number on each tour is 20. Mon mornings: for pre-booked groups only. Group size: min 15-60. Closed: Open in Jan for private tours only. Open for private & corporate hospitality except during Aug.

Admission: Adult: £12.00 Conc*: £10.00, *Students, Members of the V&A, Friends of the Royal Academy, Tate Members and senior citizens. For further information please view the website or call us (Mon-Fri only).

Key facts: No photography inside House or Garden. Postcards and Guidebooks House only, ramps and lifts. WC. Obligatory. Comprehensive colour guidebook. Guide Dogs only.

Register for news and special offers at www.hudsonsheritage.com

© Historic Royal Palaces

BANQUETING HOUSE

Whitehall, London SW1A 2ER

www.hrp.org.uk/banquetinghouse

This revolutionary structure was the first in England to be built in a Palladian style. It was designed by Inigo Jones for James I, and work finished in 1622. Intended for the splendour and exuberance of court masques, the Banqueting House is probably most famous for one real life drama: the execution of Charles I which took place here in 1649. One of Charles's last sights as he walked to his death was the magnificent ceiling painted by Peter Paul Rubens in 1630-4.
Location: Map 20:M8. OS Ref TQ30 280. Located on Whitehall in central London, a short walk from Westminster, Charing Cross and Embankment stations.
Owner: Historic Royal Palaces
Contact: Banqueting House Visitor Services **Tel:** 0844 482 7777
E-mail: banquetinghouse@hrp.org.uk
Open: Mon-Sun 10am-5pm. Closed 24, 25, 26 Dec and 1 Jan.
Before visiting, please call or visit our website to confirm we are open.
Admission: Adult £6.00, Cons £5.00, Children free.
Key facts: Weddings, receptions, dinners, award ceremonies.

HOUSES OF PARLIAMENT

Westminster, London SW1A 0AA

www.parliament.uk/visit

Tours of the Houses of Parliament offer visitors a unique combination of 1,000 years of history, modern day politics and stunning art and architecture. See the famous green benches in the Commons Chamber, the gilded throne canopy in the Lords Chamber and the medieval hammer-beam roof in Westminster Hall. Add stylish afternoon tea with a view of the River Thames.
Location: Map 20:M8. OS Ref TQ303 795. Central London, 1km S of Trafalgar Square. Underground: Westminster. **Contact:** Bookings Team
Tel: 020 7219 4114 **E-mail:** visitparliament@parliament.uk
Open: Tours every Sat throughout the year & most weekdays during parliamentary recesses including the summer, Christmas & Easter.
Admission: Check website for tour dates & prices. Discounted group rates for groups of 10 plus if booked in advance.
Key facts: Jubilee Shop off Westminster Hall offers an attractive range of gifts, souvenirs & books. Tour route fully accessible. Alt route via a lift available if required. Jubilee Café - selection of light meals & drinks. Approx. 90 mins. Approx. 60-75 mins. Assistance dogs only. When the Houses are sitting, visitors are welcome to watch debates from the public galleries.

© Dr Johnson's House Trust

DR JOHNSON'S HOUSE

17 Gough Square, London EC4A 3DE

www.drjohnsonshouse.org

A charming 300-year-old townhouse nestled amongst a maze of courts and alleys in the historic City of London. Samuel Johnson, the writer and wit, lived and worked here during the 18th Century, compiling his great 'Dictionary' in the Garret. Today, the House is open to the public with a collection relating to Johnson and his circle of friends, restored interiors, and a wealth of original features. There is a lively programme of events and low-cost education workshops.
Location: Map 20:N7. OS Ref TQ313 812. North of Fleet Street.
Owner: Dr Johnson's House Trust **Contact:** The Curator
Tel: 020 7353 3745 **E-mail:** curator@drjohnsonshouse.org
Open: 11am-5pm Oct-Apr. 11am-5.30pm May-Sep.
Admission: Adults £6.00, Conc. £5.00, Child £2.25, Family £12.50.
Members of the National Trust are entitled to a 50% discount on admission.
Key facts: Small shop selling books, gifts & souvenirs. Available for private hire on evenings and Sundays. Many unavoidable steps. A DVD, audio guide and large-print interpretation can be provided. Pre-booked groups for 10+. £2.00. Available in 10 languages. Disabled bays only in Gough Square & neighbouring streets. English & History workshops, tours/talks for schools, A-level groups & universities. Check website for Christmas closures.

© Keats House, Hampstead

KEATS HOUSE

10 Keats Grove, Hampstead, London NW3 2RR

www.keatshouse.org.uk

Discover the beauty of poetry and place in the former home of the Romantic poet John Keats. Displays of original manuscripts, artefacts and paintings tell the story of how the young poet found inspiration, friendship and love in this stunning Regency villa. Listen to Keats's famous odes, see the engagement ring he gave to his true love Fanny Brawne, or explore our beautiful garden. The House comes alive with regular events, from poetry performances to family fun days.
Location: Map 20:K3. OS Ref TQ272 856. Hampstead Heath (London Overground); Hampstead or Belsize Park (Northern Line).
Owner: City of London Corporation **Tel:** 020 7332 3868
E-mail: keatshouse@cityoflondon.gov.uk
Open: Wed-Sun: 11am-5pm. Also BH Mons.
Admission: Adults £6.50; Seniors (65yrs and over) £5.50; Conc. £4.50; Child 17 & under Free.
Key facts: Books, souvenirs, vintage items & gifts. Available for private hire. Ground floor. Tactile & subtitled AV exhibits. Accessible toilet. 1.30 and 3pm - check before visiting. Disabled parking space. Learning programme. Guide dogs only. Open all year round.

KEW PALACE

Kew Gardens, Kew, Richmond, Surrey TW9 3AB

www.hrp.org.uk/kewpalace

Kew Palace was built as a private house in 1631 but became a royal residence between 1729 and 1818. More like a home than a palace, the privacy and intimacy of this smallest of English royal palaces made it the favourite country retreat for King George III and his family in the late 18th Century. Don't miss the Royal Kitchens; the most perfectly preserved Georgian royal kitchens in existence. At weekends Queen Charlotte's Cottage is also open to visitors.
Location: Map 19:C7. OS Ref TQ188 774.
A307. Junction A307 & A205 (1m Chiswick roundabout M4).
Owner: Historic Royal Palaces
Tel: 0844 482 7777
E-mail: kewpalace@hrp.org.uk
Open: Apr-Sep 10.30am-5.30pm. Last entry 5pm.
Admission: Free of charge, but please note admission tickets to Kew Gardens must be purchased to gain access to Kew Palace. (For gardens admission prices, please visit the Kew Gardens website).
Key facts: Weddings, receptions, dinners, meetings. WCs.

© The Edmond J Safra Fountain Court at Somerset House © Jeff Knowles

SOMERSET HOUSE

Strand, London WC2R 1LA

www.somersethouse.org.uk

Somerset House is an historic building where surprising and original work comes to life. A unique part of the London cultural scene with a distinctive public programme including Skate, concerts, an open-air film season, a diverse range of temporary exhibitions focusing on contemporary culture, an extensive learning programme, free guided tours and 55 fountains that dance in the courtyard in summer. Somerset House currently attracts approximately 2.5 million visitors every year.
Location: Map 20:N7. OS Ref TQ308 809.
Sitting between the Strand and the north bank of the River Thames. Entrances on Strand, Embankment, Lancaster Place and Waterloo Bridge.
Owner: Somerset House Trust
Contact: Visitor Communications
Tel: 020 7845 4600 **Fax:** 020 7836 7613 **E-mail:** info@somersethouse.org.uk
Open: For opening times, please see website.
Admission: For admission prices, please see website.
Key facts: WCs. Licensed. Licensed. By arrangement. On leads.

18 STAFFORD TERRACE

London W8 7BH

From 1875, 18 Stafford Terrace was the home of Punch cartoonist Edward Linley Sambourne, his wife Marion, their two children and live-in servants. Originally decorated by the Sambournes in keeping with fashionable Aesthetic principles, the interiors evolved into wonderfully eclectic artistic statements within the confines of a typical middle-class home.
Location: Map 20:I8. OS Ref TQ252 794.
Parallel to Kensington High St, between Phillimore Gardens & Argyll Rd.
Owner: The Royal Borough of Kensington & Chelsea **Tel:** 020 7602 3316
E-mail: museums@rbkc.gov.uk **Website:** www.rbkc.gov.uk/museums
Open: Mid Sep-Mid Jun. **Admission:** Open access (no need to book) Weds, Sats and Suns 2-5.30pm. Conventional guided tours: Weds and Suns 11am. Costumed guided tours: Sats 11am. Private and Evening tours also available. Visit the website for ticket prices and how to book.
Key facts: Obligatory. None. Guide dogs only.

LEIGHTON HOUSE MUSEUM

12 Holland Park Road, London W14 8LZ

Leighton House Museum is the former studio-house of Victorian artist and President of the Royal Academy, Frederic, Lord Leighton (1830-1896). The only purpose-built studio-house open to the public in the United Kingdom, it is one of the most remarkable buildings of the 19th Century, containing a fascinating collection of paintings and sculpture by Leighton and his contemporaries.
Location: Map 20:M9. OS Ref TQ247 792.
High Street Kensington (10 minute walk); Olympia (5 minute walk)
Owner: The Royal Borough of Kensington and Chelsea
Tel: 020 7602 3316 **E-mail:** museums@rbkc.gov.uk
Website: www.leightonhouse.co.uk
Open: Daily 10am-5:30pm; closed Tues. Private Museum hire during the eve.
Admission: Adult £7.00. Concessions £5.00. National Trust 50%. National Art Pass Free. Admission fees subject to change during exhibitions and public events.
Key facts: Free guided tours on Weds and Suns 3pm.

WESTMINSTER CATHEDRAL

Victoria Street, London SW1P 1QW

The Roman Catholic Cathedral of the Archbishop of Westminster. Spectacular building in the Byzantine style, designed by J F Bentley, opened in 1903, famous for its mosaics, marble and music. Tower viewing gallery has spectacular views across London. Exhibition of vestments, rare ecclesiastical objects and sacred relics. **Location:** Map 20:L9. OS Ref TQ293 791. Off Victoria Street, near Victoria Station. Sat Nav: SW1P 1LT **Owner:** Diocese of Westminster
Contact: Revd Canon Christopher Tuckwell **Tel:** 020 7798 9055
Fax: 020 7798 9090 **Website:** www.westminstercathedral.org.uk
Open: All year: 7am-7pm. Tel. for times at Easter & Christmas. **Admission:** Free. Tower lift/viewing gallery charge: Adult £6, Conc £3, Family (2+4) £12. Exhibition: Adult £5, Conc £2.50, Family £11. Joint Tower & Exhibition tickets: Adult £9, Conc £4.50, Family £18.50. Tel. 020 7798 9028 for Tower/Exhibition opening times. A TripAdvisor 2014 Winner with Certificate of Excellence. **Key facts:** Booking required. Worksheets & tours. Except assistance dogs.

APSLEY HOUSE ⌗

Hyde Park Corner, London W1J 7NT

Apsley House, also known as No. 1 London, is the former residence of the first Duke of Wellington. **Location:** Map 20:L8. OS Ref TQ284 799.
Tel: 020 7499 5676 **Website:** www.english-heritage.org.uk/apsleyhouse
Open: 25 Mar-30 Oct, Wed-Sun & Bank Hols, 11-5 pm, 31 Oct-31 Mar, Sat-Sun, 10-4pm, 24 Dec-1 Jan, closed **Admission:** £9.70 Adult; £5.80 Child.

BUCKINGHAM PALACE

London SW1A 1AA

Buckingham Palace serves as both the office and London residence of Her Majesty The Queen. **Location:** Map 20:L8. OS Ref TQ291 796. Underground: Green Park, Victoria, St James's Park. **Tel:** 020 7766 7300
E-mail: bookinginfo@royalcollection.org.uk **Website:** www.royalcollection.org.uk
Open: 22 Jul-31 Aug, daily, 9.15-7.45pm; 1-30 Sep, daily, 9.15-6.45pm.
Admission: Royal Day Out: Adult £37; Child £20.80.

Register for news and special offers at www.hudsonsheritage.com

HAM HOUSE AND GARDEN

Ham Street, Richmond-upon-Thames, Surrey TW10 7RS

One of London's best kept secrets, this atmospheric Stuart mansion nestles on the banks of Richmond-upon-Thames. **Location:** Map 19:B8. OS Ref TQ172 732. On S bank of the Thames, W of A307 at Petersham between Richmond and Kingston. **Tel:** 020 8940 1950 **E-mail:** hamhouse@nationaltrust.org.uk **Website:** www.nationaltrust.org.uk/ham-house **Open:** All year, daily, 12-4pm; Gardens: 10-5pm. 24 & 25 Dec, closed. **Admission:** Adult £10.40; Child £5.20.

KENWOOD HOUSE

Hampstead Lane, London NW3 7JR

Set in tranquil parkland in fashionable Hampstead, with panoramic views over London. **Location:** Map 20:J1. OS Ref TQ270 874. M1/J2. Signed off A1. **Tel:** 020 8348 1286 **E-mail:** kenwood.house@english-heritage.org.uk **Website:** www.english-heritage.org.uk/kenwoodhouse **Open:** 24 Mar-30 Sep, Sun-Thu & BHs, 10-6pm; 1-24 Oct, Sun-Thu, 10-5pm; 1 Nov-23 Mar, 10-4pm. Daily at half term. 24-6 Dec & 1 Jan, closed. **Admission:** Adult £15; Child £9.

OLD ROYAL NAVAL COLLEGE

King William Walk, Greenwich, London SE10 9NN

One of the most important ensembles in European Baroque architecture and the centrepiece of the Maritime Greenwich World Heritage site. **Location:** Map 19:F7. OS Ref TQ383 778. **Tel:** 020 8269 4747 **E-mail:** boxoffice@ornc.org **Website:** www.ornc.org **Open:** All year, Mon–Sun, 10–5pm. Grounds: daily, 8–11pm. **Admission:** Free.

QUEEN'S HOUSE

Romney Road, Greenwich, London SE10 9NF

16th Century mansion now used to display items from the National Maritime Museum's collection. Come and discover the extraordinary people and events that are key to understanding this iconic building's creation, its history and its significance today. **Location:** Map 19:F7. OS Ref TQ387 776. **Tel:** 020 8858 4422 **Website:** www.rmg.co.uk **Open:** Mon–Sun, 10–5pm, 24–26 Dec, closed. **Admission:** Free.

STRAWBERRY HILL

268 Waldegrave Road, Twickenham TW1 4ST

Strawberry Hill is internationally famous as Britain's finest and first example of Georgian Gothic revival architecture. **Location:** Map 19:C8. OS Ref TQ158 722. Off A310 between Twickenham & Teddington. **Tel:** 020 8744 1241 **E-mail:** enquiry@strawberryhillhouse.org.uk **Website:** www.strawberryhillhouse.org.uk **Open:** Sat-Wed 1 Mar-1 Nov. W/Es 12pm-4pm (last entry). Mon-Wed 1.40pm-4pm (last entry). **Admission:** Adult £12.00, Under 16s free.

18 FOLGATE STREET

Spitalfields, East London E1 6BX

Tel: 020 7247 4013 **E-mail:** info@dennisevershouse.co.uk

2 WILLOW ROAD

2 Willow Road, Hampstead, London NW3 1TH

Tel: 020 7435 6166 **E-mail:** 2willowroad@nationaltrust.org.uk

7 HAMMERSMITH TERRACE

London W6 9TS

Tel: 020 8741 4104 **E-mail:** admin@emerywalker.org.uk

BENJAMIN FRANKLIN HOUSE

36 Craven Street, London WC2N 5NF

Tel: 020 7925 1405

BOSTON MANOR HOUSE

Boston Manor Road, Brentford TW8 9JX

Tel: 0845 456 2800 **E-mail:** victoria.northwood@cip.org.uk

BURGH HOUSE AND HAMPSTEAD MUSEUM

New End Square, Hampstead, London NW3 1LT

Tel: 020 7431 0144 **E-mail:** info@burghhouse.org.uk

CARLYLE'S HOUSE

24 Cheyne Row, Chelsea, London SW3 5HL

Tel: 020 7352 7087 **E-mail:** carlyleshouse@nationaltrust.org.uk

CHELSEA PHYSIC GARDEN

66 Royal Hospital Road, London SW3 4HS

Tel: 020 7352 5646 **E-mail:** enquiries@chelseaphysicgarden.co.uk

ELTHAM PALACE AND GARDENS

Eltham Palace, Court Yard, Eltham, London SE9 5QE

Tel: 020 8294 2548 **E-mail:** customers@english-heritage.org.uk

FENTON HOUSE

Hampstead Grove, London NW3 6SP

Tel: 020 7435 3471 **E-mail:** fentonhouse@nationaltrust.org.uk

FORTY HALL

Forty Hill, Enfield, Middlesex EN2 9HA

Tel: 020 8363 8196 **E-mail:** forty.hall@enfield.gov.uk

FREUD MUSEUM

20 Maresfield Gardens, London NW3 5SX

Tel: 020 7435 2002 **E-mail:** info@freud.org.uk

FULHAM PALACE & MUSEUM

Bishop's Avenue, Fulham, London SW6 6EA

Tel: 020 7736 3233 **E-mail:** admin@fulhampalace.org

HANDEL & HENDRIX

25 Brook Street, London W1K 4HB

Tel: 020 7495 1685 **E-mail:** mail@handelhendrix.org

HOGARTH'S HOUSE

Hogarth Lane, Great West Road, London W4 2QN

Tel: 020 8994 6757 **E-mail:** john.collins@carillionservices.co.uk

MARBLE HILL HOUSE

Richmond Road, Twickenham TW1 2NL

Tel: 020 8892 5115 **E-mail:** customers@english-heritage.org.uk

RANGER'S HOUSE

Chesterfield Walk, Blackheath, London SE10 8QX

Tel: 020 8853 0035 **E-mail:** customers@english-heritage.org.uk

RED HOUSE

Red House Lane, Bexleyheath DA6 8JF

Tel: 0208 303 6359

SOUTHSIDE HOUSE

3 Woodhayes Road, Wimbledon, London SW19 4RJ

Tel: 020 8946 7643 **E-mail:** info@southsidehouse.com

WILLIAM MORRIS GALLERY

Lloyd Park, Forest Road, Walthamstow, London E17 4PP

Tel: 020 8527 9782

Loseley Park, Surrey

The Savill Garden, Windsor

Berkshire
Buckinghamshire
Hampshire
Kent
Oxfordshire
Surrey
Sussex
Isle of Wight

South East

The counties to the South & East of the capital are rich in stories from the past. History makers like Marlborough, Wellington and Churchill made their homes here but so did country squires and Tudor merchants, great nobles and great gardeners.

Find stylish hotels with a personal welcome and good cuisine in the South East. More information on page 348.

- Chase Lodge Hotel
- Deans Place Hotel
- Drakes Hotel
- The Millstream Hotel
- PowderMills Hotel
- The White Horse Hotel

SIGNPOST
RECOMMENDING THE UK'S FINEST HOTELS SINCE 1935
www.signpost.co.uk

THE SAVILL GARDEN

WICK LANE, ENGLEFIELD GREEN, SURREY TW20 0UU

www.windsorgreatpark.co.uk

Discover a world of plants on your doorstep. The Savill Garden showcases plants from around the world, gathered by intrepid plant hunters and refined by nurserymen and breeders, these plants are arranged in stunning displays which recall their areas of origin.

Sir Eric Savill first created his woodland garden in the 1930s. Since then, many others (under the watchful eyes of Kings and Queens) have been on a tireless quest to add their own expertise and creativity. The Rose Garden, opened by HM the Queen in 2010, is a magnificent addition. Visitors can wander the swirls of rose beds and enjoy the perfume at its best from a walkway that rises into the centre of the Rose Garden.

Location: Map 3:G2. OS Ref SU976 707. Located off A30, M25 junction 13 or M4 junction 6. 15 minutes drive from Windsor town centre. Follow the brown tourist road signs. For sat navs, please use postcode TW20 0UJ and note that access to The Savill Garden is only available through public roads. 15 minutes from Heathrow Airport.

Owner: The Crown Estate **Tel:** 01784 485400

E-mail: enquiries@windsorgreatpark.co.uk

Open: Mar-Oct, daily, 10-6pm; Nov-Feb, daily, 10-4.30pm; closed 24 -26 Dec.

Admission: Adult £9.75, Child £4.35.

Key facts: Our gift shop is ideal to pick up a treat for the family, friends, your pet or just yourself! Plants from The Royal Gardens. Enjoy a coffee and cake in our intimate gallery café. A daily selection of hot food, freshly baked cakes, sandwiches, salads and jacket potatoes. Head Gardener's Tour at £150.00 and we offer A Friend of the Savill Garden Guide at £25.00 per 25 people, both last around one hour. Guide dogs only. Closed 24 & 25 Dec.

DORNEY COURT

Nr. Windsor, Berkshire SL4 6QP

www.dorneycourt.co.uk

"One of the finest Tudor Manor Houses in England" - Country Life. Grade I Listed and noted for its outstanding architectural and historical importance. Home of the Palmers for 400 years, passing from father to son over 14 generations. Sitting in a classical setting, highlights include the magnificent Great Hall, oak & lacquer furniture and artwork which combine to tell the story of the House. The stunning Old Coach House Barn with its landscaped courtyard provides a beautiful space for events. **Location:** Map 3:G2. OS Ref SU926 791. 5 mins off M4/J7, 10 mins from Windsor, 2m W of Eton. **Owner/Contact:** Mr James Palmer

Tel: 01628 604638 **Twitter:** @dorneycourt. **E-mail:** info@dorneycourt.co.uk

Open: May Bank Holidays (30 Apr & 1 May; 28 & 29 May) and all Aug - open afternoons 1.30pm-5pm. **Admission:** Adult: £8.50, Child (10yrs+) £5.50. OAPs: £8.00. Groups (10+): £8.00 when open to public. Private group rates at other times. **Key facts:** Film & photo shoots. Weddings. Events. No stiletto heels. Garden centre (www.dckg.co.uk). Events, Activity Days & Wedding Receptions. Video tour of upstairs rooms. Licensed. Licensed. Obligatory. Free. Guide dogs only. By special appointment (Min numbers apply: 20+). €

WINDSOR CASTLE

Windsor, Berkshire SL4 1NJ

Established in the 11th Century by William the Conqueror, Windsor Castle is the oldest and largest occupied castle in the world. **Location:** Map 3:G2. OS Ref SU969 770. M4/J6, M3/J3. 20m from central London.

Tel: 020 7766 7304 **E-mail:** bookinginfo@royalcollection.org.uk

Website: www.royalcollection.org.uk **Open:** Mar-Oct, 9.30am-5pm; Nov-Feb, 9.45am-4.15pm; closed 25 & 26 Dec. **Admission:** Adult £20, Child £11.70.

Dorney Court

Register for news and special offers at www.hudsonsheritage.com

© Chenies Manor House/Marianne Majerus

CHENIES MANOR HOUSE

www.cheniesmanorhouse.co.uk

The Manor House is in the picturesque village of Chenies and lies in the beautiful Chiltern Hills.

The Manor House is approached by a gravel drive leading past the church. Home of the MacLeod Matthews family, this 15th and 16th Century manor house with fortified tower is the original home of the Earls of Bedford, visited by Henry VIII and Elizabeth I. Elizabeth was a frequent visitor, first coming as an infant in 1534 and as Queen she visited on several occasions, once staying for six weeks. The Bedford Mausoleum is in the adjacent church. The house contains tapestries and furniture mainly of the 16th and 17th Centuries, hiding places and a collection of antique dolls. Art exhibitions are held throughout the season in the restored 16th Century pavilion. The Manor is surrounded by five acres of enchanting gardens which have been featured in many publications and on television. It is famed for the Spring display of tulips and late summer Dahlia festival. From early June there is a succession of colour in the Tudor Sunken Garden, the White Garden, herbaceous borders and Fountain Court. The Physic Garden contains a wide selection of medicinal and culinary herbs. In the Parterre is an ancient oak and a complicated yew maze while the Kitchen Garden is in Victorian style with unusual vegetables and fruit. Winner of the Historic Houses Association and Christie's Garden of the Year Award, 2009.

KEY FACTS

Gardens only.

Delicious homemade teas in the Garden Room.

Except Guide Dogs.

© Chenies Manor House/Marianne Majerus

© Chenies Manor House/Marianne Majerus

VISITOR INFORMATION

Owner
Mr and Mrs C Macleod Matthews

Address
Chenies
Buckinghamshire
WD3 6ER

Location
Map 7:D12
OS Ref. TQ016 984
N of A404 between Amersham & Rickmansworth
M25-Ext 18, 3m.

Contact
Chenies Manor House
Tel: 01494 762888
E-mail:
macleodmatthews@btinternet.com

Opening Times
5 Apr-26 Oct
Wed & Thu & Bank Holiday Mons 2-5pm (last entry to the house 4.15pm).

Admission
House & Garden:

Adult	£8.00
Child	£4.50

Garden Only:

Adult	£6.00
Child	£4.00

Groups (20 +) by arrangement throughout the year.

Special Events
17 Apr-Easter BH Mon
House & Garden 2-5pm. The first mention of the distribution of eggs was at Chenies. Children's Egg & Spoon races, Egg Spotting, Homemade teas, Shop & Plants for sale.

1 May-BH Mon
House & Garden 2-5pm "Tulip Festival" Bloms Tulips throughout the house & gardens. Homemade Teas, Shop & Plants for sale.

29 May-BH Mon
House & Garden 2-5pm Homemade Teas, Shop, & Plants for sale.

16 Jul-Sun
Famous Plant & Garden Fair – Gardens 10am-5pm (House opens at 2pm) 70 specialist Nurseries from around the country. Refreshments all day.

28 Aug-BH Mon
House & Garden 2-5pm"Dahlia Festival" a display of a number of different Dahlias throughout the house and gardens.

25 & 26 Oct
House & Garden 2-5pm "Spooks & Surprises", special scary tour of the house for children, visit the difficult maze, Homemade Teas – Shop.

© National Trust Images / Arnhel de Serra

© Claydon Estate

CLAYDON HOUSE AND GARDENS

CLAYDON HOUSE, MIDDLE CLAYDON, BUCKINGHAMSHIRE MK18 2EY

www.nationaltrust.org.uk/claydon

Nestled in peaceful parkland, this Georgian Manor House hides a lavish interior which has been home to the Verney family since 1620. Featuring Rococo carvings, family portraits and an exquisite staircase inlaid with ebony and ivory. The riotous detail continues upstairs in the Chinese Room with a chinoiserie inspired pagoda which is truly one of a kind. To complement the grandeur of the House are Claydon Gardens - a classic example of an English country garden, being both decorative and productive. The gardens include a Kitchen Garden, Pool Garden with 19th Century greenhouse, as well as the formal Box Garden and the Florence Nightingale Centenary Garden. These beautifully tended gardens have something special to offer in any season.

Location: Map 7:C11. OS Ref SP719 253. M40 J9, signposted off A413 (Buckingham) & A41 (Waddesdon crossroads).

Owner: National Trust and Claydon Estate **Contact:** House Manager
Tel: 01296 730349 **Claydon Estate:** 01296 730252.
E-mail: claydon@nationaltrust.org.uk / info@claydonestate.co.uk
Open: House and Gardens: Mar-Oct, Sat-Wed, 11-5pm.
Please visit the website for further details.
Admission: Adult £12.90, Child £3.75.
Please visit the website for further details.
Key facts: Second-hand bookshop with huge variety of genres and authors. The ground floor of the house is accessible with a virtual tour of upstairs. Gardens have some slopes. 01296 730004. Please call for details - tours must be booked in advance. Please call for details or to book your school visit. On leads in park. House & garden.

Stowe House

© National Trust Images / Matthew Antrobus

HUGHENDEN

High Wycombe, Buckinghamshire HP14 4LA

www.nationaltrust.org.uk/hughenden

Amid rolling Chilterns countryside, discover the hideaway and colourful private life of Benjamin Disraeli, the most unlikely Victorian Prime Minister. Follow in his footsteps, stroll through his German forest, relax in his elegant garden and imagine dining with Queen Victoria in the atmospheric manor. Uncover the Second World War story of Operation Hillside, for which unconventional artists painted maps for bombing missions - including the famous Dambusters raid.

Location: Map 3:F1. OS Ref SU866 955.
1½ m N of High Wycombe on the W side of the A4128.
Owner: National Trust **Contact:** The Estate Office **Tel:** 01494 755573
Info Line: 01494 75565 **E-mail:** hughenden@nationaltrust.org.uk
Open: 1 Jan-31 Dec, daily. Closed 24 & 25 Dec. Please see the property website for detailed opening times. **Admission:** House & Garden: Adult £12.00, Child £6.00, Family £30.00. Garden only: Adult £5.00, Child £2.95, Family £12.95. Groups: Adult £10.00. Child £5.00. Free for NT Members. Includes a voluntary 10% donation but visitors can choose to pay the standard prices advised at the property. **Key facts:** Partial. WCs. Hughenden has a Café & Tea Room. Daily. Assistance dogs only in walled gardens and Manor.

Register for news and special offers at www.hudsonsheritage.com

WOTTON HOUSE

Wotton Underwood, Aylesbury Buckinghamshire HP18 0SB

The Capability Brown Pleasure Grounds at Wotton, currently undergoing restoration, are related to the Stowe gardens, both belonging to the Grenville family when Brown laid out the Wotton grounds between 1750 and 1767. A series of man-made features on the 3 mile circuit include bridges, temples and statues.

Location: Map 7:B11. OS Ref SP686 160.
Either A41 turn off Kingswood, or M40/J7 via Thame.
Owner/Contact: David Gladstone
Tel: 01844 238363
Fax: 01844 238380
E-mail: david.gladstone@which.net
Open: 5 Apr-6 Sep: Weds only, 2-5pm. Also: 17 Apr, 29 May, 1 Jul, 5 Aug and 2 Sep: 2-5pm.
Admission: Adult £6.00, Child Free, Conc. £3.00. Groups (max 25).
Key facts: Obligatory.
Limited parking for coaches. On leads.

A room at Wotton House

Chenies Manor House

BLETCHLEY PARK

The Mansion, Bletchley Park, Milton Keynes MK3 6EB

The once top-secret world of iconic WW2 Codebreaking Huts and Blocks set within an atmospheric Victorian estate. **Location:** Map 7:D10. OS Ref SP863 338.
Tel: 01908 640404 **E-mail:** info@bletchleypark.org.uk
Website: www.bletchleypark.org.uk
Open: May-Oct, daily, 9.30-5pm; Nov-Feb, daily, 9.30-4pm; closed 24-26 Dec & 1 Jan. **Admission:** Adult £16, Child £9.

CLIVEDEN

Taplow, Maidenhead SL6 0JA

Relax in grand style as you explore these stunning gardens, woodlands and Thames riverbank. Beautiful floral displays. **Location:** Map 3:F1. OS Ref SU915 851.
Tel: 01628 605069 **E-mail:** cliveden@nationaltrust.org.uk
Website: www.nationaltrust.org.uk/cliveden **Open:** Gardens: 13 Feb-31 Dec, daily,10am-5.30pm; closed 25 & 26 Dec. House: 2 Apr-27 Aug, Thu & Sun, 3-5pm. **Admission:** Adult £10 + £2 for house; Child £5 + £1.

NETHER WINCHENDON HOUSE

Nether Winchendon, Nr Thame, Buckinghamshire HP18 0DY

Medieval Manor Strawberry Hill Gothick. Home last Royal Governor Massachussetts. Continuous family occupation since 1559. **Location:** Map 7:C11. OS Ref SP733 122. **Tel:** 01844 290101 **Website:** www.nwhouse.co.uk
Open: Teas at Church & House: 30 Apr, 1 May, 28 & 29 May, 27 & 28 Aug. Open: 18 Apr-15 May (Closed Sats) 2.30-5.30pm. Guided tours only quarter to each hour. No Conc w/e & BH to HHA/ArtF/OAP. **Admission:** £8.00 Conc.

STOWE HOUSE

Stowe House, Stowe, Buckingham MK18 5EH

The House is known for its spectacular neo-classical interiors and the magnificent views from and towards the House. **Location:** Map 7:C10. OS Ref SP666 366.
Tel: 01280 818002 **Fax:** 01280 818186
E-mail: Houseinfo@stowe.co.uk **Website:** www.stowehouse.org
Open: All year, daily, 11-5pm. House tickets released 1 month in advance & subject to change. **Admission:** Adult £6.20; Child U16 free.

STOWE LANDSCAPE GARDENS

New Inn Farm, Buckingham MK18 5EQ

Picture-perfect views, winding paths, lakeside walks and temples create a timeless landscape, reflecting the changing seasons. **Location:** Map 7:B10. OS Ref SP681 364. Off A422 Buckingham - Banbury Rd. 3m NW of Buckingham.
Tel: 01280 817156 **E-mail:** stowe@nationaltrust.org.uk
Website: www.nationaltrust.org.uk/stowe **Open:** All year, daily, 10-6pm. Closed 24 & 25 Dec. **Admission:** Adult £11.20; Child £5.60.

WADDESDON MANOR

Waddesdon, Nr Aylesbury, Buckinghamshire HP18 0JH

Magnificent house and grounds in the style of a 19th Century French chateau. Built by Baron Ferdinand de Rothschild to display his superb collection of art treasures and entertain the fashionable world. **Location:** Map 7:C11. OS Ref SP740 169. **Tel:** 01296 653226 **Website:** www.nationaltrust.org.uk/waddesdon-manor **Open:** House: Apr-Oct, Wed-Fri, 12-4pm; Sat, Sun & BHs, 11-4; 9 Nov-31 Dec, Wed-Sun, 11.30-6pm. Closed 24-26 Dec. **Admission:** Adult £18; Child £9.

VISITOR INFORMATION

Owner
Lord Montagu

Address
Beaulieu
Hampshire
SO42 7ZN

Location
Map 3:C6
OS Ref. SU387 025
M27 to J2, A326, B3054 follow brown signs.
Bus: Local service within the New Forest.
Rail: Station at Brockenhurst 7m away.

Contact
Visitor Enquiries
Tel: 01590 612345
E-mail:
visit@beaulieu.co.uk

Opening Times
Summer Whitsun-Sep Daily, 10am-6pm. Winter Oct-Whitsun Daily, 10am-5pm Please check website for exact dates. Closed 25 Dec.

Admission
All year Individual and group rates upon application. Groups (15+).

Special Events
Beaulieu hosts a range of family-friendly and motoring themed events throughout the year. Visit www.beaulieuevents.co.uk for details.

All ticket enquiries to our Special Events Booking Office. Tel 01590 612888.

Conference/Function

ROOM	Size	Max Cap
Brabazon (x3)	40' x 40'	85 (x3)
Domus	69' x 27'	150
Palace House		60
Motor Museum		250

Palace House

BEAULIEU

www.beaulieu.co.uk

Beaulieu, at the heart of the New Forest, features a range of heritage attractions.

Palace House
Home of the Montagu family since 1538, Palace House was built around the Great Gatehouse of Beaulieu Abbey. Explore this fantastic gothic styled Victorian country home as costumed guides give you a flavour of life `below stairs' and share with you the fascinating history of the house and the generations who have lived there.

Beaulieu Abbey & Exhibition
Founded on land gifted by King John to Cistercian monks in 1204, Beaulieu Abbey was largely destroyed during the Reformation. The conserved ruins demonstrate the scale of what was once a vast complex. One of the surviving buildings houses an exhibition on the history of the Abbey and the monks that lived and worked here.

The National Motor Museum
Over 250 vehicles tell the story of motoring in Britain from its pioneering origins to the present day. From the earliest motor carriages to classic family saloons, displays include historic sporting motors, modern rally cars, F1 racers, a rustic 1930's country garage and Wheels – a fascinating pod ride through motoring history.

Grounds & Gardens
Explore the informal Wilderness Garden, fragrant Victorian Flower Garden and the Victorian Kitchen Garden. Enjoy the Mill Pond walk through parkland woods and look out for the Rufus Memorial Cairn – to commemorate the death of King William Rufus who, evidence suggests, was killed by an arrow whilst hunting at Beaulieu in 1100.

KEY FACTS

- Allow 4-5 hrs for visits. Helicopter landing point.
- Palace House Kitchen Shop & Main Reception Shop.
- Please see website.
- WC. Wheelchairs in Visitor Reception by prior booking.
- Part of the Brabazon Restaurant- sandwiches to cooked meals and tea & cold drinks.
- Seats 250.
- Attendants on duty.
- Unlimited. Free admission for coach drivers plus voucher.
- Professional staff available to assist.
- In grounds, on leads only.
- Please see www.beaulieu.co.uk/corporate-and-weddings
- Closed 25 Dec.

Register for news and special offers at www.hudsonsheritage.com

© Fergus Baird

AVINGTON PARK

Winchester, Hampshire SO21 1DB

www.avingtonpark.co.uk

From the wrought iron gates and long avenue of limes, approach well-tended lawns, bordering the river Itchen and the elegant Palladian facade. William Cobbett wrote of Avington Park that it was 'one of the prettiest places in the County' and indeed it is true today. Dating back to the 11th Century, and enlarged in 1670, the house enjoys magnificent painted and gilded state rooms overlooking lawns and parkland. Over the years Charles II and George IV stayed at various times. St Mary's, a fine Georgian church, may also be visited. **Location:** Map 3:D4. OS Ref SU534 324. 4m NE of Winchester ½m S of B3047 in Itchen Abbas.

Owner/Contact: Mrs S L Bullen

Tel: 01962 779260 **E-mail:** enquiries@avingtonpark.co.uk

Open: May-Sep: Suns & BH Mons and Mons in Aug, 2.30-5.30pm. Last tour 4.30pm. Group visits welcome by appointment all year.

Admission: Adult £8.00, Child £4.00.

Key facts: Exclusive use for conferences, weddings, films, photoshoots, private parties, seminars and corporate events. Partial (ground floor only) and WC. Obligatory. In grounds, on leads. Guide dogs only in house. By arrangement.

HIGHCLERE CASTLE, GARDENS & EGYPTIAN EXHIBITION

Highclere Castle, Newbury, Berkshire RG20 9RN

www.highclerecastle.co.uk

This spectacular Victorian Castle was the setting for the popular television series, Downton Abbey. Enjoy the splendid State Rooms; the masculine opulence of the Library and the lovely south facing Drawing Room. Explore the Egyptian Exhibition in the Castle Cellars; the Antiquities Room and an amazing recreation of the discovery of Tutankhamun's tomb. Visit Gardens, inspired by Capability Brown, including: Monk's Garden, Secret Garden and new Arboretum.

Location: Map 3:D3. OS Ref SU445 587. M4/J13 - A34 South. M3/J8 - A303 - A34 north. **Owner:** Earl of Carnarvon **Contact:** The Castle Office

Tel: 01635 253210 **Fax:** 01635 255315 **E-mail:** theoffice@highclerecastle.co.uk

Open: Easter Opening: 8-13; 15-23 Apr; (Closed 14 Apr Good Friday). Spring opening: 30 Apr, 1-2 May; 28-30 May; Summer opening: 9 Jul-7 Sep (Sun-Thu each week). (Correct at time of publication). **Admission:** Groups, Concessions, Family Tickets for Castle, Exhibition & Gardens; each element available separately, please check website for prices. **Key facts:** Partial. WCs. Licensed. By arrangement. Free. Guide dogs only.

© John Anderson

EXBURY GARDENS & STEAM RAILWAY

Exbury, Southampton, Hampshire SO45 1AZ

www.exbury.co.uk

A tranquil 200-acre woodland garden world-famous for dazzling displays of rhododendrons, azaleas and camellias in spring. Summer brings hydrangeas and showpiece exotics heat up the Herbaceous Borders. The extensive tree collection ensures year-round interest and stunning autumn colour. A ride on the 1¼ mile steam railway will delight visitors of all ages. **Location:** Map 3:D6. OS Ref SU425 005. 20 mins Junction 2, M27 west. In the New Forest.

Owner: Exbury Gardens Ltd. **Contact:** Estate Office

Tel: 023 8089 1203 **Fax:** 023 8089 9940 **E-mail:** info@exbury.co.uk

Open: 22 Mar-10 Nov 2017, 10am-5.30pm last admission 4.30pm.

Admission: Please see website for up to date admission prices. Prices and opening dates subject to variations. Please visit www.exbury.co.uk. **Key facts:** Gift shop on site offering a wonderful selection of local produce, gift ideas & keepsakes Our plant sales are open from Apr-Jun & stock a stunning collection of plants & shrubs A fully licensed restaurant is on site serving freshly cooked homemade meals, afternoon teas & cakes By arrangement with our knowledgeable staff to show you the best parts of the gardens Free car & coach park Dogs are allowed everywhere on short leads, even the train!

© National Trust

HINTON AMPNER

Bramdean, Alresford, Hampshire SO24 0LA

www.nationaltrust.org.uk/hinton-ampner

This elegant country manor and tranquil garden sit so harmoniously within the landscape that one cannot exist without the other. Enjoy the exquisite collection of ceramics and art and avenues of sculptured topiary leading to breathtaking views across the South Downs. With newly opened parkland, one can experience all Hinton Ampner has to offer.

Location: Map 3:E5. OS Ref SU597 275. M3/J9 or A3 on A272, 1m W of Bramdean.

Owner: National Trust

Contact: Property office

Tel: 01962 771305

E-mail: hintonampner@nationaltrust.org.uk

Open: 18 Feb-18 Dec, daily, 11am-4.30pm. Closed 27 Nov- Dec.

Admission: Please see website for details.

Key facts: WCs. Licensed. By arrangement. Limited for coaches. Dogs are welcome on parkland, estate and tea-room courtyard. Closed Christmas Eve and Christmas day.

KING JOHN'S HOUSE & HERITAGE CENTRE

Church Street, Romsey, Hampshire SO51 8BT

www.kingjohnshouse.org.uk

Three historic buildings on one site: Medieval King John's House, containing 14th Century graffiti and rare bone floor, Tudor Cottage complete with traditional Tea Room and Victorian Heritage Centre with recreated shop and parlour. Beautiful period gardens, special events/exhibitions and children's activities throughout the year. Gift shop and Tourist Information Centre. Available for hire for small private parties, meetings and corporate functions.

Location: Map 3:C5. OS Ref SU353 212. M27/J3. Opposite Romsey Abbey, next to Post Office. **Owner:** King John's House & Tudor Cottage Trust Ltd

Contact: Anne James **Tel:** 01794 512200 **E-mail:** info@kingjohnshouse.org.uk

Open: Mon-Sat, 10am-4pm. Limited opening on Suns. Evenings also for pre-booked groups. Open all year except Christmas week.

Admission: Adult £4.00, Child £1.00, Conc. £3.00. Family & Season tickets.

Key facts: Main Plant sale in May - cuttings etc. on outside table Hall with kitchen available or Tea Room can provide catering Partial. Traditional Tea Room with homemade cakes, cream teas & light lunches. Pre-booking for groups Off Latimer St, through King John's Garden. Re-enactment days - Stone age to WW1. Guide dogs only.

TUDOR HOUSE AND GARDEN

Bugle Street, Southampton SO14 2AD

www.tudorhouseandgarden.com

Southampton's most important historic building, Tudor House and Garden reveals over 800 years of history in one fascinating location; at the heart of the old town. The timber-framed building was built in the late 15th Century, with King John's Palace, an adjacent Norman house accessible from Tudor House Garden, dating back a further 300 years. **Location:** Map 3:D5. OS Ref SU419 113. Off A3057 Town Quay Rd, opposite Red Funnel **Owner:** Southampton City Council

Tel: 023 8083 4536 **E-mail:** museums@southampton.gov.uk

Open: Tue-Fri 10am-3pm, Sat-Sun 10am-5pm. Closed Mons (except BHs, 10am-5pm). **Admission:** Adult: £5.00, Over 5s: £4.00, Under 5s: Free, Family (2 adults, 3 children): £13.75, Concessions: £4.00. **Key facts:** Our shop has a range of quality Tudor & Victorian inspired gifts & books. We offer a wide range of rooms which can be laid out in different styles. All areas are accessible, with the exception of the cellar and attic. Our café serves a delicious range of lunches, cakes & refreshments. Guided tours are available by booking in advance. Education visits are available by booking in advance. The venue is licensed for weddings & civil ceremonies. Closed 24 Dec-1 Jan inclusive.

©SSPT

STRATFIELD SAYE HOUSE

Stratfield Saye, Hampshire RG7 2BZ

www.stratfield-saye.co.uk

After the Duke of Wellington's victory against Napoleon at the Battle of Waterloo in 1815, the Duke chose Stratfield Saye as his country estate. The house contains many of the 1st Duke's possessions and is still occupied by his descendents being a family home rather than a museum.

Location: Map 3:E2. OS Ref SU700 615.
Equidistant from Reading (M4/J11) & Basingstoke (M3/J6) 1½m W of the A33.

Owner: The Duke of Wellington

Contact: Estate Office

Tel: 01256 882694

Open: Thu 13-Mon 17 Apr. Fri 4-Tue 29 Aug.

Admission: Weekdays: Adult £11.00, Child £4.00, Over 60s/Student £10.00.
Weekends: Adult £13.00, Child £5.00, Over 60s/Student £12.00.
Groups by arrangement only.

Key facts: WC. Obligatory. Guide dogs only.

GILBERT WHITE & THE OATES COLLECTIONS

High St, Selborne, Alton GU34 3JH

Explores the lives of three explorers of the natural world. Home of the naturalist Gilbert White, and surrounded by 25 acres of garden and parkland. The Oates Collections celebrates the lives of 19th Century explorer Frank Oates, and Lawrence Oates who travelled on the ill-fated Terra Nova Expedition. **Location:** Map 3:E4. OS Ref SU741 336. Selborne is on B3006 from Alton to A3. **Tel:** 01420 511275 **E-mail:** info@gilbertwhiteshouse.org.uk

Website: www.gilbertwhiteshouse.org.uk

Open: 1 Jan-19 Feb, Fri-Sun, 10.30am-4.30pm. 20 Feb-31 Mar, Tue-Sun, 10.30am-4.30pm. 1 Apr-31 Oct, Tue-Sun, 10.30am-5.00pm. 1 Nov-24 Dec, 10.30am-4.30pm. Jul & Aug 7 days a week 10.30-5pm. **Admission:** Adult £9.50, Conc £8.50, U16 £4.00, U5 Free, Family Ticket (2A+3C) £24.50. Pre-booked group of 10+ £7.50. Garden Only £7.50. **Key facts:** Books, local produce & gifts. Buy plants from garden. Suitable. Assistance provided. Elegantly restored dining room. In village, 2 min walk. In grounds only.

Houghton Lodge Gardens

Register for news and special offers at www.hudsonsheritage.com

HOUGHTON LODGE GARDENS

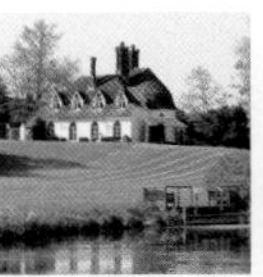

Stockbridge, Hampshire SO20 6LQ

An 18th Century Grade II* listed Gothic cottage idyllically set above the tranquil River Test. Peaceful formal and informal gardens with fine trees. Chalk Cob walls enclose traditional Kitchen Garden with espaliers, themed herb garden, wild flowers and orchid house. 14 acres of picturesque countryside, meadow walks, four charming Alpacas, topiary Peacock Garden and snorting dragon! Tea House offers light refreshments. **Location:** Map 3:C4. OS Ref SU344 332. 1½m S of Stockbridge (A30) on minor road to Houghton village.
Owner: Daniel Busk **Contact:** Sophie Busk **Tel:** 01264 810502
E-mail: sophie@houghtonlodge.co.uk **Website:** www.houghtonlodge.co.uk
Open: Daily from 1 Apr-30 Sep, 10am-5pm. House tours & garden tours are available to pre-booked groups. **Admission:** Adult £6.50, Children £3.00, Under 3 Free. Coach tours & groups are welcome on any day by appointment only.
Key facts: Plant sales Fishing to rent Tea House - Light refreshments. By arrangement. Hard standing for 2 coaches. On short leads. Yes.

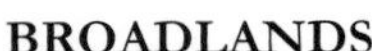

BROADLANDS

Romsey, Hampshire SO51 9ZD

Broadlands is the historic home of the Brabourne family.
Location: Map 3:C5. OS Ref SU353 202.
Tel: 01794 505080
Website: www.broadlandsestates.co.uk
Open: Jun-Sep. Please see our website for details.

HARCOMBE HOUSE

Park Lane, Ropley, Alresford, Hampshire SO24 0BE

House tour and grounds available for picnics.
Location: Map 3:E4. OS Ref SU636 309. **Tel:** 07796 195550
Open: Please call for details.
Admission: Please call for details.

STAY CLOSE TO HISTORY

Go to the quick guide at the back of this book to find great places to stay

HUDSON'S

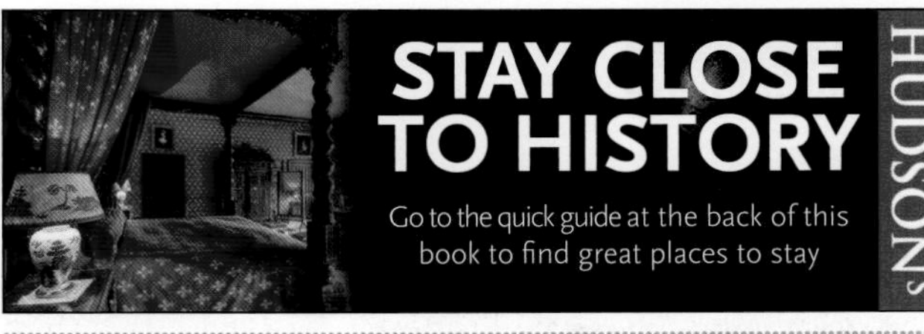

MOTTISFONT

Mottisfont, Nr Romsey, Hampshire SO51 0LP

A romantic house and gallery, crafted from a medieval priory, set in beautiful riverside gardens. **Location:** Map 3:C5. OS Ref SU327 270.
Tel: 01794 340757 **E-mail:** mottisfont@nationaltrust.org.uk
Website: www.nationaltrust.org.uk/mottisfont **Open:** Gardens: All year, daily, 10-5pm. House: 1 Mar-31 Oct, daily, 11-5pm; 1 Nov-31 Dec, daily, 11-4pm. Closed 24 & 25 Dec. **Admission:** Adult £13.60; Child £6.80.

THE VYNE

Sherborne St John, Basingstoke RG24 9HL

Five centuries of history are brought to life in this former Tudor palace turned 17th Century family home, set in 1500 acres of gardens, woodland and wetlands.
Location: Map 3: E3. OS Ref SU637 565.
Tel: 01256 883858 **E-mail:** thevyne@nationaltrust.org.uk
Website: www.nationaltrust.org.uk/the-vyne **Open:** All year, daily, 10am-5pm. Closed 24 & 25 Dec. **Admission:** Adult £11.75; Child £5.90.

WINCHESTER CITY MILL

Bridge Street, Winchester SO23 9BH

Winchester City Mill is a working watermill dating back to at least Saxon times.
Location: Map 3D:4. OS Ref SU486 293. M3/J9 & 10.
Tel: 01962 870057 **E-mail:** winchestercitymill@nationaltrust.org.uk
Website: www.nationaltrust.org.uk/winchestercitymill
Open: Open Daily: 1 Jan-19 Feb 10am-4pm, 20 Feb-29 Oct 10am-5pm, 30 Oct-24 Dec 10am-4pm, Closed 25-31 Dec. **Admission:** Adults £4, Children £2.

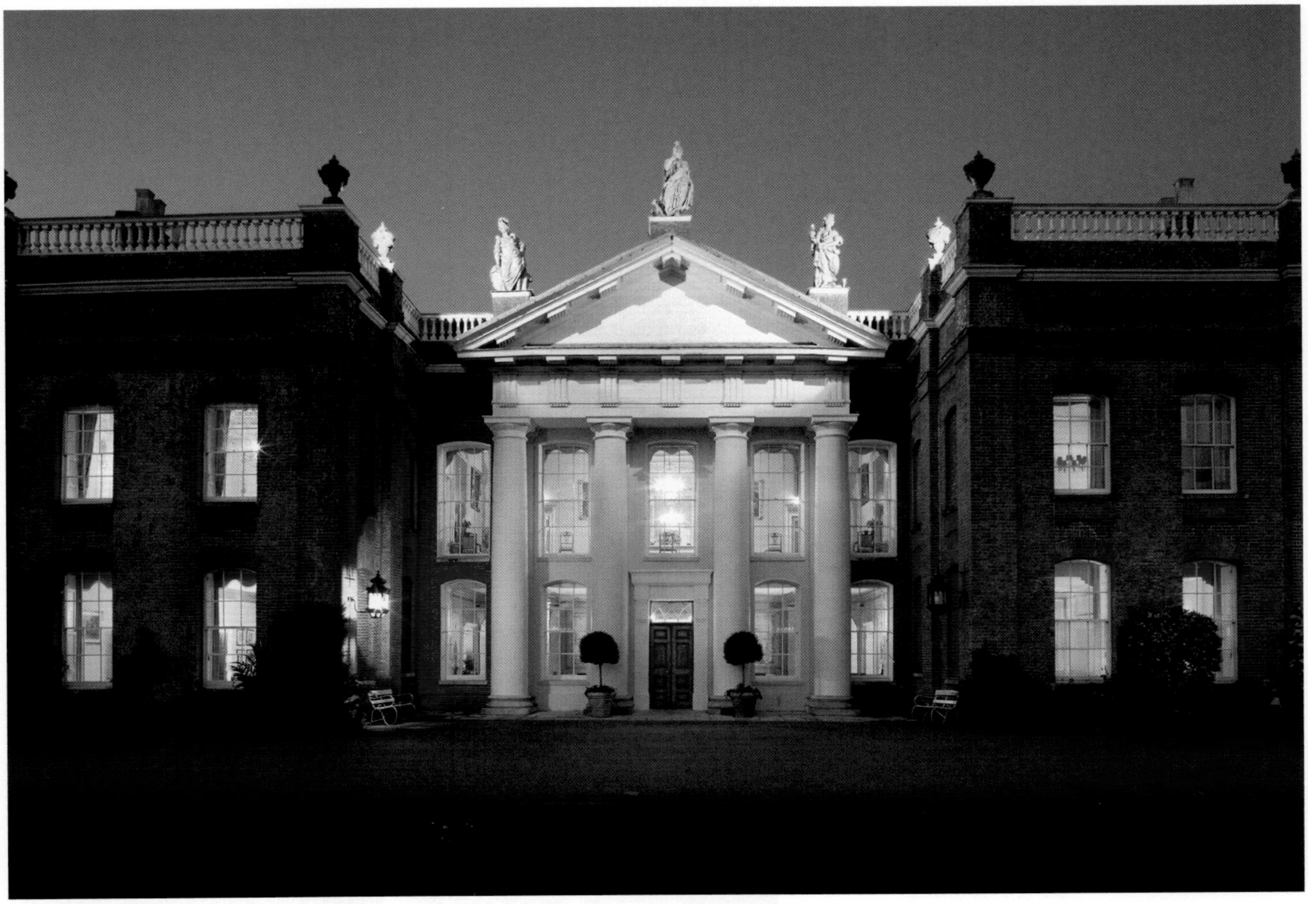

Avington Park at Night

VISITOR INFORMATION

Owner
The Denys Eyre Bower Bequest, Registered Charitable Trust

Address
Chiddingstone Castle
Nr Edenbridge
Kent
TN8 7AD

Location
Map 19:G12
OS Ref. TQ497 452
10m from Tonbridge, Tunbridge Wells and Sevenoaks. 4m Edenbridge. Accessible from A21 and M25/J5. London 35m.
Bus: Enquiries: Tunbridge Wells TIC 01892 515675.
Rail: Tonbridge, Tunbridge Wells, Edenbridge then taxi. Penshurst then 2m walk.
Air: Gatwick 15m.

Contact
Tel: 01892 870347
E-mail: events@chiddingstonecastle.org.uk

Opening Times
Sun, Mon, Tue, Wed & Bank Holidays from Apr until the end of Oct (check the website for any unforeseen alterations to this).

Times: 11am-5pm. Last entry to house 4:15pm.

Admission
Adults	£9.00
Children (5-13)	£4.00
Family (2 adults + 2 children or 1 adult + 3 children)	£23.50
Grounds and Tea Rooms	Free
Parking	£2.00

Special Events
We have a series of special event days, including the Wedding Fair in March, the Literary Festival in May, the Summer Vintage Fair in June, the Country Fair in September and the Christmas Fair in November. Please visit the website What's On page for more information.

CHIDDINGSTONE CASTLE

www.chiddingstonecastle.org.uk

Chiddingstone Castle is a hidden gem in the Garden of England; a unique house with fascinating artefacts and beautiful grounds.

Situated in an historic village in the heart of the idyllic Kentish Weald, Chiddingstone Castle has Tudor origins and delightful Victorian rooms. Lying between Sevenoaks and Tunbridge Wells, it is conveniently located close to the M25 (Junction 5 - Sevenoaks or Junction 6 - Oxted). We welcome individuals, families and groups - guided tours are available. There is ample parking available in the large car park. Delicious light lunches, homemade cakes and traditional cream teas can be enjoyed in the cosy Tea Room set in the Old Buttery or in the delightful sheltered courtyard. The Castle's Gift Shop can be found in the former Well Tower. There is also an antiques and second-hand bookshop located next to the Tea Room courtyard.

Set in 35 acres this attractive country house originates from the 1550s when High Street House, as the Castle was known, was home to the Streatfeild family. Several transformations have since taken place and the present building dates back to 1805 when Henry Streatfeild extended and remodelled his ancestral home in the 'castle style' which was then fashionable. Rescued from creeping dereliction in 1955 by the gifted antiquary Denys Eyre Bower, the Castle became home to his amazing and varied collections - Japanese Samurai armour, swords and lacquer, Egyptian antiquities, Buddhist artefacts, Stuart paintings and Jacobite manuscripts. Visitors can also visit Bower's Study and learn of his eccentric and complicated life, which featured a notorious scandal.

Further exhibition rooms are open showing the Victorian history of the Castle - the Victorian Kitchen and Scullery and the fascinating Housekeeper's Room. From the Servants' Hall, group visitors can climb the secret back stairs and discover the Servant's Bedroom in the attic – a real 'upstairs downstairs' experience!

The large, informal gardens feature a lake, sweeping lawns, herbaceous borders, woodland, a Victorian Orangery with a contemporary glazed roof and an Ancient Egyptian-themed conceptual garden - a unique grass maze and treasure trail that complements the antiquities found indoors.

KEY FACTS

- Museum, scenic gardens and lake, picnics, fishing available.
- Well stocked gift shop.
- Available for private and corporate functions. Licensed for Civil Ceremonies. Wedding receptions.
- WCs.
- Cream teas a speciality.
- By arrangement.
- We welcome visits from schools who wish to use the collections in connection with classroom work.
-  In grounds and Tea Room courtyard on leads.

© English Heritage

VISITOR INFORMATION

Owner
English Heritage

Address
Dover Castle
Castle Hill
Dover
Kent
CT16 1HU

Location
Map 4:O4
OS Ref. TR325 419
Easy access from A2 and M20. Well signposted from Dover centre and east side of Dover. 2 hrs from central London.
Bus: 0870 6082608.
Rail: London St. Pancras Intl (fast train); London Victoria; London Charing Cross.

Contact
Visitor Operations Team
Tel: 01304 211067
E-mail: customers@english-heritage.org.uk

Opening Times
Jan-Mar & Nov-Dec, Sat & Sun, 10am-4pm; daily at half term;
Apr-Oct, daily, 10am-5pm.
Closed 24-26 Dec & 1 Jan.

Admission

Adult:	£20.20
Child:	£12.10

Special Events
Please visit www.english-heritage.org.uk for the most up-to-date information on our exciting days out and events.

DOVER CASTLE

www.english-heritage.org.uk/dovercastle

Explore over 2,000 years of history at Dover Castle.

Immerse yourself in the medieval world and royal court of King Henry II as you climb the stairs into the Great Tower and meet the first of the many life like projected figures which will guide you round the six great recreated rooms and several lesser chambers of the palace. On special days throughout the year interact with costumed characters as they bring to life the colour and opulence of medieval life.

Take an adventurous journey into the White Cliffs as you tour the maze of Secret Wartime Tunnels. Children will love dressing up in wartime uniforms, exploring the tunnels, the interactive displays and virtual tour. Through sight, sound and smells, re-live the wartime drama of a wounded pilot fighting for his life. Discover what life would have been like during the dark and dramatic days of the Dunkirk evacuation with exciting audio-visual experiences. See the pivotal part the Secret Wartime Tunnels played in Operation Dynamo.

Above ground, enjoy magnificent views of the White Cliffs from Admiralty Lookout and explore the Fire Command Post, re-created as it would have appeared 90 years ago in the last days of the Great War. Also see a Roman Lighthouse and Anglo-Saxon church, as well as an intriguing network of medieval underground tunnels, fortifications and battlements.

Dover Castle was used as a film location for 'The Other Boleyn Girl' starring Natalie Portman and Scarlett Johanssen and Zaffirelli's Hamlet amongst others.

KEY FACTS

- WCs. No flash photography within the Great Tower.
- Two.
-
- Licensed.
- Tour of tunnels. Last tour 1 hr before closing.
- Ample.
- Education centre. Pre-booking essential.
- Dogs on leads only.
-
-

© English Heritage

© English Heritage

VISITOR INFORMATION

Owner
Hever Castle Ltd

Address
Hever Castle
Hever
Edenbridge
Kent
TN8 7NG

Location
Map 19:G12
OS Ref. TQ476 450
See website for directions.

Contact
Estate Office
Tel: 01732 865224
Fax: 01732 866796
E-mail:
info@hevercastle.co.uk

Opening Times
See website for opening times or call 01732 865224.

Admission
INDIVIDUAL

Castle & Gardens:

Adult	£16.90
Senior	£14.70
Student	£14.20
Child	£9.50
Family	£44.50

Gardens only:

Adult	£14.20
Senior	£12.70
Student	£12.10
Child	£9.00
Family	£38.90

Group (15+)

Castle & Gardens:

Adult	£12.90
Senior	£12.00
Student	£10.00
Child	£7.00

Gardens only:

Adult	£10.90
Senior	£10.35
Student	£8.60
Child	£6.70

Special Events
An extensive events programme. See website for details.

HEVER CASTLE & GARDENS

www.hevercastle.co.uk

Experience 700 years of colourful history and spectacular award-winning gardens at the childhood home of Anne Boleyn.

Dating back to the 13th Century, Hever Castle was once the childhood home of Anne Boleyn, second wife of Henry VIII and mother of Elizabeth I and formed the unlikely backdrop to a sequence of tumultuous events that changed the course of Britain's history, monarchy and religion.

Its splendid panelled rooms contain fine furniture, tapestries, antiques and an important collection of Tudor portraits. Two beautifully illuminated prayer books on display in the Book of Hours Room belonged to Anne and bear her inscriptions and signature. One is believed to be the prayer book Anne took with her to her execution at the Tower.

The charming castle at Hever has a rich and varied history.

Today much of what you see is the result of the remarkable efforts of a wealthy American, William Waldorf Astor, who used his fortune to restore and extend the Castle in the early 20th Century. A section of the Castle is dedicated to its more recent history, containing pictures and memorabilia relating to the Astor family and the Edwardian period.

The award-winning gardens are set in 125 acres of glorious grounds. Marvel at the Pompeiian wall and classical statuary in the Italian Garden; admire the giant topiary chess set and inhale the fragrance of over 4,000 rose bushes in the quintessential English Rose Garden. The Loggia, overlooking the 38-acre Lake, is the perfect spot to relax before exploring the Tudor Garden, Blue Corner and Rhododendron Walk.

KEY FACTS

- No photography in the Castle. Accommodation, venue hire and golf.
- Gift and garden. Guide books.
- Seasonal variety of plants.
- Meetings, training & conferences. Team building & golf days. Parties and banqueting.
- Partial. WCs. See website.
- Seasonal opening. See website.
- Choice of restaurants. Seasonal opening. See website.
- Castle & Garden Guided Tours by arrangement. Min 15 persons.
- English, French, German, Dutch, Russian & Chinese. Children's version available.
- Free parking.
- Discounted rates, education room and school packs.
- Well behaved dogs on leads in grounds.
- Luxury B&B & holiday cottage in Astor Wing of the Castle.
- Choice of venues on the estate.
- An extensive events programme. See website.

Register for news and special offers at www.hudsonsheritage.com

© National Trust / Jo Hatcher

KNOLE

www.nationaltrust.org.uk/knole

More of a town than a house: six hundred years of history.

Knole is a house full of hidden treasures. Built as an archbishop's palace and nestled in Kent's last medieval deer park, the house passed through royal hands to the Sackville family – its inhabitants from 1603 to today. Knole is in the midst of a huge project to conserve and restore its remarkable showrooms and collection, with the support of the Heritage Lottery Fund. This year, some of the restored showrooms will re-open to visitors, whilst several others will be closed for specialist conservation.

Marvel at the world-class collection of paintings and furniture in the showrooms, before climbing to the top of the newly restored Gatehouse Tower and exploring the private rooms of former resident Eddy Sackville-West. Visit the new conservation studio and watch as conservators care for Knole's treasures.

After exploring Knole's 1,000 acre deer park, relax in the refurbished Brewhouse Café or soak up the atmosphere in the historic courtyards. Lord Sackville's private garden is open on Tuesdays (April to September). Restoration work continues in Knole's showrooms until 2018. There is always something new to discover as we continue to peel back the layers of six hundred years of history.

KEY FACTS

- Conservation work continues in the showrooms, which means that some rooms are closed to visitors in 2017.
- Gift shop in the Brewhouse Café and specialist bookshop in Green Court.
- Plant sales in the Brewhouse Courtyard.
- Please view our website for full access information.
- Brewhouse Café, rooftop terrace, Grab & Go kiosk, outdoor picnic area.
- Highlights tours of the showrooms Tue-Sun, 11am-12pm. Limited availability, included in admission price.
- Free to National Trust members. £4 for non-members. Car park open 10am-6pm.
- Dogs on leads allowed in park and courtyards. Assistance dogs only in garden, tower and showrooms.
- There is a busy programme of events year round. Please check our website for details.

© National Trust Images / Robert Morris

© National Trust / Caron McCrickard

VISITOR INFORMATION

Owner
National Trust

Address
Knole
Sevenoaks
Kent
TN15 0RP

Location
Map 19:H10
OS Ref. TQ532 543
Satnav postcode: TN13 1HU. Follow brown signs to Sevenoaks High Street. Concealed entrance opposite St Nicholas Church. The nearest railway station is Sevenoaks, which is 1.5 miles away.

Contact
Tel: 01732 462100
E-mail: knole@nationaltrust.org.uk

Opening Times
Showrooms: 4 Mar-5 Nov. Guided tours from 11am-12pm, subject to availability. Free flow visits from 12-4pm. Last entry at 3.30pm. Closed on Mons. Open on BHs (except 25 & 26 Dec 2017 & 1 Jan 2018).

Gatehouse Tower, Conservation Studio, Brewhouse Cafe and Shop: Daily from 10am-5pm (closes at 4pm in winter).

Courtyards (Visitor Centre, Bookshop, Orangery, Estate Office): Daily from 10am-5pm (closes at 4pm in winter).

Parkland: All year. Car park open 10am-6pm.

Lord Sackville's private garden: Tues, 4 Apr-26 Sep, 11am-4pm. Last entry at 3.30pm.

Please note that Knole is closed 24 and 25 Dec.

Admission
National Trust members and under 5s: Free

Conservation studio, courtyards, parkland: Free

Showrooms and Gatehouse Tower:

Adult:	£12.50
Child:	£6.75
Family:	£29.75

Group rates available (15+). Advance booking required. Coach parking and tours available.

Email: knolebookings@nationaltrust.org.uk

VISITOR INFORMATION

Owner
Viscount De L'Isle MBE

Address
Penshurst
Nr Tonbridge
Kent
TN11 8DG

Location
Map 19:H12
OS Ref. TQ527 438
From London M25/J5 then A21 to Hildenborough, B2027 via Leigh; from Tunbridge Wells A26, B2176. Follow brown signs.
Metro Bus: 231, 233 from Tunbridge Wells and Edenbridge.
Rail: Charing Cross/ Waterloo East-Hildenborough, Tonbridge or Tunbridge Wells; then bus or taxi.

Contact
Tel: 01892 870307
E-mail: contactus@ penshurstplace.com

Opening Times
11 Feb-31 Mar
Weekends only.
10.30am-6pm.
House:
12-4pm.
Grounds:
10.30-6pm or dusk if earlier.

1 Apr-29 Oct
Daily, 10.30am-6pm.
House:
12-4pm.
Grounds:
10.30am-6pm.
Last entry 5pm.

Shop & Porcupine Pantry: Open all year.
Winter: Open to Groups by appointment only.

Admission
For 2017 individual and group prices, please see www.penshurstplace.com.

Special Events
Weald of Kent Craft & Design Show: First May BH weekend (Sat-Mon) and second weekend in Sept (Fri-Sun).
Maize Maze: Open during school Summer Holidays.

Conference/Function
A small selection of private banqueting and conference rooms are available, details of which can be found at www.penshurstplace.com.

© Darryl Curzon Photography

The Italian Garden in Spring

PENSHURST PLACE & GARDENS

www.penshurstplace.com

One of England's greatest family-owned historic houses with a history spanning nearly seven centuries.

In some ways time has stood still at Penshurst; the great House is still very much a medieval building with improvements and additions made over the centuries but without any substantial rebuilding. Its highlight is undoubtedly the medieval Baron's Hall, built in 1341, with its impressive 60ft-high chestnut-beamed roof. A marvellous mix of paintings, tapestries and furniture from the 15th, 16th and 17th Centuries can be seen throughout the House, including the helm carried in the state funeral procession to St Paul's Cathedral for the Elizabethan courtier and poet, Sir Philip Sidney, in 1587. This is now the family crest.

Gardens

The Gardens, first laid out in the 14th Century, have been developed over generations of the Sidney family, who first came to Penshurst in 1552. A major restoration and replanting programme undertaken by the 1st Viscount De L'Isle has been continued by his son the 2nd Viscount De L'Isle, to ensure they retain their historic splendour. The 1st Viscount De L'Isle is commemorated with an Arboretum, planted in 1991.

The Gardens are divided by a mile of yew hedges into 'rooms', each planted to give a succession of colour as the seasons change, with the completion of a major redevelopment project on the Jubilee Walk and a more recent regeneration to the Blue and Yellow Border. There is also an Adventure Playground, Woodland Trail, Toy Museum and Garden Restaurant, with the Porcupine Pantry café and a Gift Shop open all year. A variety of events in the park and grounds take place throughout the year.

KEY FACTS

- Guidebook available to purchase. No photography in house.
- Gift Shop outside paid perimeter.
- Small plant centre.
- Conference and private banqueting facilities including weddings.
- Partial. Contact for details.
- Porcupine Pantry outside paid perimeter.
- Garden Restaurant in the grounds.
- Guided tours available by arrangement before the House opens to the public. Garden tours available 10.30am-4.30pm.
- Ample for cars and coaches.
- All year by appointment, discount rates, education room and teachers' packs.
- Registered assistance dogs only.
- Wedding ceremonies and receptions.
- See opening times.
- See www.penshurstplace.com/whats-on

© Jigsaw Design and Publishing

The Barons Hall

© Sam Bond

The Heraldic Garden

Register for news and special offers at www.hudsonsheritage.com

© National Trust Images/Chris Lacey

© National Trust Images/Zoë Colbeck

CHARTWELL

MAPLETON ROAD, WESTERHAM, KENT TN16 1PS

www.nationaltrust.org.uk/chartwell

Chartwell was the much-loved Churchill family home and the place from which Sir Winston drew inspiration from 1924 until the end of his life. The house is still much as it was when the family lived here with pictures, books and personal mementos. The studio is home to a collection of Churchill's paintings which have been saved for the nation. The gardens reflect Churchill's love of the landscape and nature. The woodland estate offers family walks, trails, den building, a Canadian Camp, dormouse dens, bomb crater and opportunities to stretch your legs and enjoy the spectacular views of Chartwell house. The Mulberry Room above the Landemare Café can be booked for meetings, conferences, lunches and dinners.

Location: Map 19:F11. OS Ref TQ455 515.
2m S of Westerham, forking left off B2026.

Owner: National Trust **Contact:** Marketing & Development Manager

Tel: 01732 868381 **E-mail:** chartwell@nationaltrust.org.uk

Open: House: 25 Feb-29 Oct, Daily, 11am-5pm last entry 4.15pm. Garden, Shop, Café, Exhibition & Studio, and everyday 1 Jan-31 Dec, times vary please call for further details. The studio is closed in Jan, by tour only in Feb. The exhibition closes for short periods to change the display. All visitors require a timed ticket to visit the house, please obtain upon arrival at the Visitor Welcome Centre - places limited. **Admission:** House, Garden & Studio: Adult £15.00, Child £7.50, Family £37.50. Garden, Exhibition, Studio & Winter season only: Adult £7.50, Child £3.75, Family £18.75. Gift Aid prices. Groups (15+) Adult £12.50, Child £6.25.

Key facts: Conference & function facilities. The Mulberry Room can accommodate up to 80 people. Partial. There are steep slopes and steps through the garden to the house. Wheelchairs are available from the Visitor Welcome Centre. Accessible toilets. Licensed. By arrangement. £3.00 for non-members. In grounds on leads. Estate open all year except 24 & 25 Dec. House open from Mar until Oct.

LEEDS CASTLE

MAIDSTONE, KENT ME17 1PL

www.leeds-castle.com

Set in 500 acres of beautiful Kent parkland, there's something to discover every day at "the loveliest castle in the world". During its 900 year history, Leeds Castle has been a Norman stronghold, the private property of six of England's medieval Queens and a palace used by Henry VIII. In the 1930s the Castle was a playground for the rich and famous, as Lady Baillie, the last private owner, entertained high society down from London for the weekends.

During your visit discover the glorious gardens and grounds, spiraling yew maze, free-flying falconry displays, leisurely punting trips and the unique Dog Collar Museum. Children will enjoy riding on Elsie the Castle Land Train, taking a trip on the ferry boat and the adventure playgrounds.

Location: Map 4:L3. OS Ref TQ835 533. From London to A20/M20/J8, 40m, 1 hr. 7m E of Maidstone, ¼m S of A20.

Owner: Leeds Castle Foundation

Tel: 01622 765400 **Fax:** 01622 735616

E-mail: enquiries@leeds-castle.co.uk

Open: Summer: 1 Apr-30 Sep Daily, 10.30am-4.30pm (last adm).
Winter: 1 Oct-31 Mar Daily, 10.30am-3pm (last adm).

Admission: Annual Tickets (prices valid until 31 Mar 2017). Adult £24.50; Senior Citizen £21.50; Student £21.00; Visitor with disabilities £21.00;
Child (4-15yrs) £16.50; Infants (under 4yrs) Free.

Key facts: Residential and day conferences, weddings, team building days, falconry, golf course, golf coaching, banquets, events. Banquets, meetings, seminars, presentations and conferences. WCs. Licensed. Licensed. Free parking. Guide dogs only. B&B, Holiday Cottages & Glamping. Closed to visitors on the first weekend of November (for Fireworks) and Christmas Day. €

RESTORATION HOUSE

17-19 CROW LANE, ROCHESTER, KENT ME1 1RF

www.restorationhouse.co.uk

Fabled city mansion deriving its name from the stay of Charles II on the eve of The Restoration. This complex ancient house has beautiful interiors with exceptional early paintwork related to decorative scheme 'run up' for Charles' visit. The house also inspired Dickens to create 'Miss Havisham' here. "Interiors of rare historical resonance and poetry", Country Life. Fine English furniture and strong collection of English portraits (Mytens, Kneller, Dahl, Reynolds and several Gainsboroughs). Charming interlinked walled gardens and ongoing restoration of monumental Renaissance water garden A private gem. "There is no finer pre- Civil war town house in England than this" - Simon Jenkins, The Times. "Deserves a medal" -Jools Holland. *New for 2017- unveiling of Renaissance garden, including access to monumental gazebo, dramatic tiered terracing with presiding Matthew Darbyshire Farnese Hercules and other compelling antique statues.

Location: Map 4:K2. OS Ref TQ744 683.

In Historic centre of Rochester, off High Street, opposite the Vines Park. 5 minutes' walk from Rochester Station with Hi Speed to St Pancras and regular services to Victoria and Charing Cross.

Owner: R Tucker & J Wilmot

Contact: Robert Tucker

Tel: 01634 848520

E-mail: robert.tucker@restorationhouse.co.uk

Open: 8 Jun-29 Sep, Thu & Fri, 10am-5pm, plus Sat 10 Jun, 12-5pm. Photographer's hour Fridays 10-11am during opening times.

Admission: Adult £8.50 (includes 36 page illustrated guidebook), Child £4.25 Conc £7.50 Booked group (8+) tours: £10.00pp.

Tea Shop: Open same days as house.

Key facts: No stilettos. No photography in house except Fri morns 10-11am. Garden & Tea shop wheelchair accessible. Open when house is open. By arrangement. £10 per head, min 8 per tour or £80. Guide dogs only.

© David Archer

BELMONT HOUSE & GARDENS

Belmont Park, Throwley, Faversham, Kent ME13 0HH

www.belmont-house.org

Belmont is an elegant 18th Century house, home to six generations of the Harris family. It contains many mementos of the family's history and travels; including, fine paintings, furniture, Indian silverware and perhaps the finest private clock collection in the country. The gardens contain a Pinetum complete with grotto, a walled ornamental garden, specimen trees and a large kitchen garden with Victorian greenhouses, all set in parkland.

Location: Map 4:M3. OS Ref TQ986 564. 4½m SSW of Faversham, off A251.

Owner: Harris (Belmont) Charity

Tel: 01795 890202 **E-mail:** administrator@belmont-house.org

Open: Open Apr-Sep. Please visit our website for opening hours, tour times & special events. Gardens open daily, 10am-6pm or dusk if earlier. Groups Tue & Thu by appointment. Pre-booked specialist clock tours 1.30pm last Sat of the month.

Admission: House & Garden: Adult £8.00, Child (Under 12's free) £5.00, Conc. £7.00. Garden Only: Adult £5.00, Child (12-16yrs) £2.50, Conc. £4.00. Clock Tour £15.00. **Key facts:** No photography in house. In the kitchen garden. Partial. WCs. Tea Room open from 1pm on Sat & Sun for cream teas & cakes. Self-service Mon-Fri. The interior of the House can only be viewed by guided tour. Limited for coaches. In the gardens, on lead only. Gardens. See opening times.

Chartwell

Register for news and special offers at www.hudsonsheritage.com

THE GRANGE

St Augustine's Road, Ramsgate, Kent CT11 9NY

www.landmarktrust.org.uk

Augustus Pugin is regarded as being one of Britain's most influential architects and designers and to stay here in the home he designed for himself and his family offers a unique chance to step into his colourful and idiosyncratic world.
Location: Map 4:O2. OS Ref TR377 643.
Owner: The Landmark Trust
Tel: 01628 825925
E-mail: bookings@landmarktrust.org.uk
Open: Self-catering accommodation. Parts of house open Wed afternoons; there are eight Open Days. Please contact for further details.
Admission: Free, visits by appointment. Contact Catriona Blaker 01843 596401.
Key facts: This house was designed as a family home and it works as well today as it did in 1844.

IGHTHAM MOTE

Mote Road, Ivy Hatch, Sevenoaks, Kent TN15 0NT

www.nationaltrust.org.uk/ighthammote

Moated manor dating from 1320, reflecting seven centuries of history, from the medieval Crypt to a 1960s Library. Owned by knights, courtiers to Henry VIII and society Victorians. Highlights include Great Hall, Drawing Room, Tudor painted ceiling, Grade 1 listed dog kennel and apartments of US donor.
Location: Map 19:H11. OS Ref TQ584 535.
6m E of Sevenoaks off A25. 2½m S of Ightham off A227.
Owner: National Trust **Contact:** Administrator
Tel: 01732 810378 **Fax:** 01732 811029
E-mail: ighthammote@nationaltrust.org.uk
Open: Daily all year, excl 24 & 25 Dec. 10am-5pm or dusk if earlier. House: 11am, last entry half hour before closing. Some areas may be partially open during certain times of the year. See website for full details.
Admission: See website for details.
Key facts: No flash photography. Volunteer 8 seated electric buggy. WCs. 3 wheelchairs ground floor access only. Photograph album of upstairs. Licensed. Outside patio area with views of house. House tour £4.00pp. Garden tours with Head Gardener £5.00pp.

Tulips in Italian Garden at Penhurst Place

GOODNESTONE PARK GARDENS

Goodnestone Park, Nr Wingham, Canterbury, Kent CT3 1PL

'The most perfect English garden' 14 acres of beautiful tranquillity including a woodland area, large walled garden and Tea Room.
Location: Map 4:N3. OS Ref TR254 544. 8m Canterbury, 1½m E of B2046 - A2 to Wingham Road, signposted from this road. Postcode of Car Park: CT3 1PJ.
Contact: Francis Plumptre
Tel/Fax: 01304 840107
E-mail: enquiries@goodnestoneparkgardens.co.uk
Website: www.goodnestoneparkgardens.co.uk
Open: Apr: Sun 12-4, May-Aug: Wed/Thu/Fri 11-5pm and Sun 12-5pm, Sep: Sun 12-4pm.
Admission: Adult: £7.00, Concessions: £6.50, Child (6-16): £2.00, Season Ticket: £20.00, Family Season Ticket (2+2): £38.00, Groups (20+): £6.50 (out of opening hours £8.00).
Key facts: Suitable. WCs. Licensed. Partial. By arrangement.

MOUNT EPHRAIM GARDENS

Hernhill, Faversham, Kent ME13 9TX

In these enchanting 10 acres of Edwardian gardens, terraces of fragrant roses lead to a small lake and woodland area. A grass maze, unusual topiary, Japanese-style rock garden, arboretum, herbaceous border and many beautiful mature trees are other highlights. Peaceful, unspoilt atmosphere set in Kentish orchards with magnificent views over the Thames Estuary. **Location:** Map 4:M3. OS Ref TR065 598.
In Hernhill village, 1m from end of M2. Signed from A2 & A299.
Owner: William Dawes & Family
Tel: 01227 751496 / 07516 664151 **E-mail:** info@mountephraimgardens.co.uk
Website: www.mountephraimgardens.co.uk
Open: Apr-end Sep: Wed, Thu, Fri, Sat & Sun, 11am-5pm and BH Mons. Groups Mar-Oct by arrangement.
Admission: Adult £7.00, Child (4-16) £2.50. Groups (10+): £6.00.
Key facts: Partial. WCs. Licensed. Licensed. By arrangement. On leads. 4 B&B rooms. Licensed for civil weddings.

NURSTEAD COURT

Nurstead Church Lane, Meopham Kent DA13 9AD

Nurstead Court is a Grade I listed manor house built in 1320 of timber-framed, crownposted construction, set in extensive gardens and parkland. The additional front part of the house was built in 1825. Licensed weddings are now held in the house with receptions and other functions in the garden marquee.

Location: Map 4:K2. OS Ref TQ642 685. Nurstead Church Lane is just off the A227 N of Meopham, 3m from Gravesend.

Owner/Contact: Mrs S Edmeades-Stearns **Tel:** 01474 812368 / 01474 812121

E-mail: info@nursteadcourt.co.uk **Website:** www.nursteadcourt.co.uk

Open: Every Tue & Wed in Sep, and first Tue & Wed in Oct 2-5pm or all year round by arrangement.

Admission: Adult £5.00, Child £2.50, OAP/Student £4.00 Group (max 54): £4.00.

Key facts: Weddings/Functions. Licensed. Obligatory, by arrangement. Limited for coaches. Guide Dogs only. 2 bed cottage.

COBHAM HALL

Cobham, Kent DA12 3BL

Magnificent Jacobean, Elizabethan manor house with Repton designed gardens set in 150 acres of parkland. **Location:** Map 4:K2. OS Ref TQ683 689.

Tel: 01474 823371 **Fax:** 01474 825902

E-mail: enquiries@cobhamhall.com **Website:** www.cobhamhall.com

Open: Specific days only. Check website or phone for details.

Admission: Adult £5.50, Conc. £4.50, Self-guided garden tour £2.50.

COBHAM WOOD AND MAUSOLEUM

Cobham DA12 3BS

Restored 18th Century mausoleum & ancient woodland.

Location: Map 4:K2. OS Ref TQ432 608.

Via the M2 and A2. Exit A2 at Shorne/Cobham.

Tel: 01732 810378 **E-mail:** cobham@nationaltrust.org.uk

Website: www.nationaltrust.org.uk/cobham-wood

Open: Woods open all year. Mausoleum see website for details.

DOWN HOUSE

Luxted Road, Downe, Kent BR6 7JT

It was here that Charles Darwin worked on his scientific theories and wrote 'On the Origin of Species by Means of Natural Selection'.

Location: Map 19:F9. OS Ref TQ431 611.

Tel: 01689 859119 **Website:** www.english-heritage.org.uk/darwin

Open: 1 Nov-31 Mar, Sat & Sun, 10-4pm; Apr-Oct, daily 10-5pm; daily at half term & 27-31 Dec. **Admission:** Adult £12.30; Child £7.40.

LULLINGSTONE CASTLE & WORLD GARDEN

Eynsford, Kent DA4 0JA

Fine state rooms. Site for the World Garden of Plants.

Location: Map 19:G9. OS Ref TQ530 644. 1m S Eynsford W side of A225.

Tel: 01322 862114 **Fax:** 01322 862115 **E-mail:** info@lullingstonecastle.co.uk

Website: www.lullingstonecastle.co.uk **Open:** Apr-Sep: Fris, Sats, Suns and BHs. Oct: Suns 12-5pm Closed Good Fri. **Admission:** Adult £8.00, Child £4.00, OAP £6.50, Family £18.00, Groups, Tours and Special Events - please see website.

Knole

OWLETTS

The Street, Cobham, Gravesend DA12 3AP

Former home of the architect Sir Herbert Baker. Highlights include an impressive Carolean staircase, plasterwork ceiling and large kitchen garden.

Location: Map 4:K2. OS Ref TQ665 687. 1m south of A2 at west end of village. Limited parking at property. Parking nearby in Cobham village.

Tel: 01732 810378 **E-mail:** owletts@nationaltrust.org.uk

Website: www.nationaltrust.org.uk/owletts **Open:** See website for details.

QUEX PARK

Birchington, Kent CT7 0BH

Fine Regency country house with beautiful gardens set in the heart of an historic estate. Powell Cotton Museum houses natural history specimens and cultural objects from Africa, Asia and the Far East. **Location:** Map 4:O2. OS Ref TR309 682. **Tel:** 01843 841119 **Website:** www.quexpark.co.uk

Open: Museum & Gardens: 10 Jan-16 Dec, Tue-Sun & BHs, 10am-5pm. House: 1 Apr-29 Oct, Tue-Sun & BHs, 1-4pm. **Admission:** Adult £8.50; Child £6.

RIVERHILL HIMALAYAN GARDENS

Sevenoaks, Kent TN15 0RR

Privately-owned historic gardens. Spectacular views, remarkable plant and tree collection, contemporary sculpture. Shop and Café. **Location:** Map 4:J3. OS Ref TQ541 522. 2m S of Sevenoaks on A225, just off A21. **Tel:** 01732 459777

E-mail: sarah@riverhillgardens.co.uk **Website:** www.riverhillgardens.co.uk

Open: 18 Mar-10 Sep. Weds-Sun & BH Mons, 10.30am-5pm.

Admission: Adult £8.25, Child £5.95

SCOTNEY CASTLE

Lamberhurst, Tunbridge Wells, Kent TN3 8JN

Scotney Castle is quite simply one of the most stunning, picturesque gardens in England, with two celebrated former homes on one site.

Location: Map 4:K4. OS Ref TQ688 353. Signed off A21 1m S of Lamberhurst.

Tel: 01892 893820 **E-mail:** scotneycastle@nationaltrust.org.uk

Website: www.nationaltrust.org.uk/scotneycastle **Open:** All year, daily, 10-5pm, timed tickets. Closed 24 & 25 Dec. **Admission:** Adult £13; Child £6.50.

ST JOHN'S JERUSALEM

Sutton-at-Hone, Dartford, Kent DA4 9HQ

13th Century chapel surrounded by a tranquil moated garden, once part of the former Commandery of the Knight's Hospitallers.

Location: Map 4:J2. OS Ref TQ558 703. 3 miles south of Dartford

Tel: 01732 810378 **E-mail:** stjohnsjerusalem@nationaltrust.org.uk

Website: www.nationaltrust.org.uk/st-johns-jerusalem/

Open: See website for details. **Admission:** See website for details.

SISSINGHURST CASTLE

Sissinghurst, Cranbrook, Kent TN17 2AB

One of the world's most celebrated gardens and a sensory paradise of colour and beauty throughout the year.

Location: Map 4:L4. OS Ref TQ807 383. 1m E of Sissinghurst village.

Tel: 01580 710700 **E-mail:** sissinghurst@nationaltrust.org.uk

Website: www.nationaltrust.org.uk/sissinghurst

Open: 12 Mar-31 Oct, daily, 11-5.30pm. **Admission:** Adult £12.05; Child £5.85.

TONBRIDGE CASTLE

Castle Street, Tonbridge, Kent TN9 1BG

One of the finest Gatehouse Castles in England. **Location:** Map 19:H11. OS Ref TQ590 466. 5 mins walk from Tonbridge Train Station, 30 minutes by train from London. Short drive off A21. **Tel:** 01732 770929

E-mail: tonbridge.castle@tmbc.gov.uk **Website:** www.tonbridgecastle.org

Open: Open all year: Mon-Sat, 9am-5pm last tour 4pm. Suns & BHs, 10.30am-4.30pm last tour 3.30pm. **Admission:** Adult £8.50; Concession £5.

WALMER CASTLE AND GARDENS

Deal, Kent CT14 7LJ

A tudor fort transformed into an elegant stately home. Beautiful gardens including the Queen Mother's garden. **Location:** Map 4:O3. OS Ref TR378 501.

Tel: 01304 364288 **E-mail:** customers@english-heritage.org.uk

Website: www.english-heritage.org.uk/walmer **Open:** 2 Jan-31 Mar & Nov-Dec, Sat & Sun, 10-4pm; 1 Apr-30 Sep, daily, 10-5pm; daily at half term and 27-31 Dec. Closed 24-26 Dec & 1 Jan. **Admission:** Adult £11.20; Child £6.70.

Register for news and special offers at www.hudsonsheritage.com

BLENHEIM PALACE

www.blenheimpalace.com

Spend an inspiring day exploring a National Treasure.

Receive a warm welcome into the home of the 12th Duke and Duchess of Marlborough and the birthplace of Sir Winston Churchill. Wonder at this masterpiece of 18th Century Baroque architecture, which houses some of the finest antique collections in Europe. Take a tour of the State Rooms and admire the portraits, tapestries and exquisite furniture while learning about the 300-year history of this National Treasure.

Explore this World Heritage Site amongst over 2000 acres of 'Capability' Brown landscaped parkland. Take a stroll and admire some of the finest views in England. Discover the array of Formal Gardens, including the Rose Garden, Water Terraces and Secret Garden. A short miniature train ride away from the Palace is the Pleasure Gardens, which boast a Giant Hedge Maze, Butterfly House, Lavender Garden and 'Blenheim Bygones' exhibition.

Blenheim Palace hosts a wealth of events, exhibitions and tours throughout the year. From firm favourites to new experiences, there is something for everyone to enjoy.

Relax in one of the on-site cafés and restaurants, serving everything from informal coffee and cake to luxury afternoon teas, fine dining and more. Spend some time in the award-winning East Courtyard shop and find locally produced crafts and gifts with many ranges that are exclusive to Blenheim Palace.

Blenheim Palace is Britain's Greatest Palace, and offers visitors a precious time, every time.

KEY FACTS

- Popular filming location and available for private hire.
- Two shops selling a range of gifts and souvenirs.
- Corporate Hospitality available.
- Toilet facilities & lift access to the Palace. Blue Badge Holder parking & carers go free.
- The Oxfordshire Pantry & Water Terrace Café serve seasonal hot & cold food.
- The Orangery Restaurant serves lunch and Afternoon Teas.
- Guided tours available from Mon-Sat year-round.
- Free parking for cars and coaches.
- Trails and tours are available for school groups.
- Dogs allowed in the Park only and must be kept on leads. Assistance dogs welcome.
- We have a number of rooms licensed for evening wedding ceremonies.

VISITOR INFORMATION

Owner
The 12th Duke and Duchess of Marlborough

Address
Blenheim Palace
Woodstock
Oxfordshire
OX20 1PP

Location
Map 7:A11
OS Ref. SO441 161
From London, M40, A44 (1.5 hrs), 8 miles North West of Oxford. London 63 miles Birmingham 54 miles.
Bus: No.S3 from Oxford
Coach: From London (Victoria) to Oxford.
Rail: Oxford Parkway Station.

Contact
Visitor Information
Tel: 0800 8496 500
E-mail: operations@blenheimpalace.com

Opening Times
Open daily all year with the exception of Christmas Day.

Palace and Pleasure Gardens
Open daily from 10.30am-5.30pm (last admission 4.45pm). The Formal Gardens open at 10am
Park
Open daily from 9am-6pm (last admission 4.45pm).

Admission
Palace, Park & Gardens

Adult	£24.90
Concessions*	£19.90
Child**	£13.90
Family	£59.90

Park & Gardens

Adult	£15.30
Concessions	£11.20
Child*	£7.10
Family	£41.00

*65+ or students with valid ID. Discounted concessionary rates are available Mon-Fri only.
**5-16 yrs.

Prices are subject to change.

Annual Pass Offer
Buy one day get 12 months free!

Discounts on group bookings (15+): contact group sales on 01993 815600 email groups@blenheimpalace.com.

Conference/Function
Contact the Events Team: 01993 813874, sales@blenheimpalace.com

VISITOR INFORMATION

Owner
Lord Saye & Sele

Address
Broughton Castle
Broughton
Nr Banbury
Oxfordshire
OX15 5EB

Location
Map 7:A10
OS Ref. SP418 382
Broughton Castle is 2½m SW of Banbury Cross on the B4035, Shipston-on-Stour - Banbury Road. Easily accessible from Stratford-on-Avon, Warwick, Oxford, Burford and the Cotswolds. M40/J11.
Rail: From London/ Birmingham to Banbury.

Contact
Manager, Mrs James
Tel: 01295 276070
E-mail:
info@broughtoncastle.com

Opening Times
Summer
Weds, Suns and Bank Holiday Mons
2-5pm, 1 Apr-30 Sep.

Open all year on any day, at any time, for group bookings - by appointment only.

Admission

Adult	£9.00
Child (5-15yrs)	£5.00
OAP/Student	£8.00
Garden only	£5.00

Groups

Adult	£9.00
OAP	£9.00
Child (5-10yrs)	£5.00
Child (11-15yrs)	£6.00
Garden only	£6.00

(There is a minimum charge for groups - please contact the manager for details).

BROUGHTON CASTLE

www.broughtoncastle.com

"About the most beautiful castle in all England...for sheer loveliness of the combination of water, woods and picturesque buildings." Sir Charles Oman (1898).

Broughton Castle is essentially a family home lived in by Lord and Lady Saye & Sele and their family. The original medieval Manor House, of which much remains today, was built in about 1300 by Sir John de Broughton. It stands on an island site surrounded by a 3 acre moat. The Castle was greatly enlarged between 1550 and 1600, at which time it was embellished with magnificent plaster ceilings, splendid panelling and fine fireplaces. In the 17th Century William, 8th Lord Saye & Sele, played a leading role in national affairs. He opposed Charles I's efforts to rule without Parliament and Broughton became a secret meeting place for the King's opponents. During the Civil War William raised a regiment and he and his four sons all fought at the nearby Battle of Edgehill. After the battle the Castle was besieged and captured. Arms and armour from the Civil War and other periods are displayed in the Great Hall. Visitors may also see the gatehouse, gardens and park together with the nearby 14th Century Church of St Mary, in which there are many family tombs, memorials and hatchments.

Gardens

The garden area consists of mixed herbaceous and shrub borders containing many old roses. In addition, there is a formal walled garden with beds of roses surrounded by box hedging and lined by more mixed borders.

KEY FACTS

- Photography allowed in house.
-
- Partial.
- Teas on Open Days. Groups may book morning coffee, light lunches and afternoon teas.
- Available for booked groups.
- Limited.
-
- Guide dogs only in house. On leads in grounds.
- Open all year for groups.

Register for news and special offers at www.hudsonsheritage.com

© National Trust/Paul Watson

BUSCOT PARK

www.buscotpark.com

One of Oxfordshire's best kept secrets.

Buscot Park is the home of the Henderson Family and the present Lord and Lady Faringdon, with their eldest son James and his wife Lucinda. They look after the property on behalf of the National Trust as well as the family collection of pictures, furniture, ceramics and objects d'art, known as the Faringdon Collection, which is displayed in the House.

Built between 1780 and 1783 for a local landowner, Edward Lovedon Townsend, the estate was purchased in 1889 by Lord Faringdon's great-grandfather, Alexander Henderson, a financier of exceptional skill and ability, who in 1916 was created the 1st Lord Faringdon. He greatly enlarged the House, commissioned Harold Peto to design the famous Italianate water garden, and laid the foundations of the Faringdon Collection. Among his many purchases were Rembrandt's portrait of Pieter Six, Rossetti's portrait of Pandora, and Burne-Jones's famous series, The Legend of the Briar Rose.

His grandson and heir, Gavin Henderson, added considerably to the Collection, acquiring important furniture designed by Robert Adam and Thomas Hope, and was instrumental in returning the House to its late 18th Century appearance.

The family, together with their fellow Trustees, continue to add to the Collection, to freshen its display, and to enliven the gardens and grounds for the continuing enjoyment of visitors.

KEY FACTS

- No photography in house.
- Small shop selling peppermint products, local cider and honey, along with guide books and a selection of postcards and other items showing images of the House, Grounds and the Art Collection.
- A selection of plants and surplus kitchen garden produce available when in season.
- Partial. WC's, some ramps, motorised PMVs available – please contact Estate Office prior to visit for more information. Steps to House.
- Open the same days as the House, offering cream teas, a range of cakes and slices, cheese scones, and a selection of hot and cold drinks.
- Ample car parking, 2 coach spaces.
- Guide dogs only.

The Peto Water Garden

'Pandora' by Dante Gabriel Rossetti

VISITOR INFORMATION

Owner

The National Trust (Administered on their behalf by Lord Faringdon)

Address

Buscot Park
Faringdon
Oxfordshire
SN7 8BU

Location

Map 6:P12
OS Ref. SU239 973
Between Faringdon and Lechlade on A417.
Bus: Stagecoach 65/66 Oxford to Swindon, alight Faringdon; Stagecoach 64 Swindon to Carterton, alight Lechlade.
Taxi: Faringdon or Lechlade.
Rail: Oxford or Swindon.

Contact

The Estate Office
Tel: 01367 240786
Fax: 01367 241794
Info Line: 01367 240932
E-mail: estbuscot@aol.com

Opening Times

House, Grounds and Tea Room:
25 Mar-30 Sep, Wed-Fri and BH's and weekends as listed below, 2pm-6pm (last entry to House 5pm, Tea Room last orders 5.30pm).
Apr 1/2, 15/16/17, 29/30.
May 1, 13/14, 27/28/29.
Jun 10/11, 24/25.
Jul 8/9, 22/23.
Aug 12/13, 26/27/28.
Sep 9/10, 23/24.

Grounds Only:
3 Apr-26 Sep, Mon-Tue, 2pm-6pm.

Admission

House & Grounds:

Adult	£10.00
Over 65s	£8.00
Child (5-15)	£5.00
Under 5 Free.	

Grounds only:

Adult	£7.00
Over 65s	£5.00
Child (5-15)	£3.50
National Trust members	Free

Groups:
Advance booking must be made with the Estate Office.

VISITOR INFORMATION

Owner
The Lord & Lady Camoys

Address
Stonor Park
Henley-On-Thames
Oxfordshire
RG9 6HF

Location
Map 3:E1
OS Ref. SU743 893
1 hr from London, M4/J8/9. A4130 to Henley-On-Thames. A4130/B480 to Stonor. On B480 NW of Henley. M40/J6. B4009 to Watlington. B480 to Stonor.
Bus: None
Taxi: Henley-On-Thames 5m
Rail: Henley-On-Thames 5m, or Reading 9m
Air: Heathrow

Contact
Jonathan White
Tel: 01491 638587
E-mail:
administrator@stonor.com

Opening Times
House, Gardens and Chapel:
Apr-Sep 2017

Stonor Adventure Valley:
Apr-Oct 2017

For up to date open days and times please visit our website www.stonor.com or phone 01491 638587

Private Groups:
Open all year on any day, at any time, for group bookings - by appointment only.

Admission
For up to date admission prices please visit our website www.stonor.com or phone 01491 638587.

Special Events
4 Jun 2017
VW Owners' Rally.

25-28 Aug 2017
Chilterns Craft & Design Show.

Conference/Function
Please contact the Administrator for further details.

STONOR

www.stonor.com

Stonor - a story of continuity. The same family have lived here for over 850 years and have always been Roman Catholics.

Stonor has been home to the Stonor family for over 850 years and is now home to The Lord and Lady Camoys. The history of the house inevitably contributes to the atmosphere; unpretentious yet grand. A facade of warm brick with Georgian windows conceals older buildings dating back to the 12th Century and a 14th Century Catholic Chapel sits on the south east corner. Stonor nestles in a fold of the beautiful wooded Chiltern Hills with breathtaking views of the park where Fallow deer have grazed since medieval times.

It contains many family portraits, old Master drawings and paintings, Renaissance bronzes and tapestries, along with rare furniture and a collection of modern ceramics. St Edmund Campion sought refuge at Stonor during the Reformation and printed his famous pamphlet 'Ten Reasons', in secret, on a press installed in the roof space. A small exhibition celebrates his life and work.

Mass has been celebrated since medieval times in the Chapel. The stained glass windows were executed by Francis Eginton: installed in 1797. The Chapel decoration is that of the earliest Gothic Revival, begun in 1759, with additions in 1797. The Stations of the Cross were carved by Jozef Janas, a Polish prisoner of war in World War II and given to Stonor by Graham Greene in 1956.

The gardens offer outstanding views of the Park and valley and are especially beautiful in May and June, containing fine displays of daffodils, irises, peonies, lavenders and roses along with other herbaceous plants and shrubs.

New for 2017: Stonor Adventure Valley play area, offering fun and excitement for ages 2-15.

KEY FACTS

- No photography in house.
- Small gift shop with local crafts and honey from the estate.
- Please contact the Administrator for further details.
- Partial.
- Stonor Pantry serves a selection of hot and cold lunches and homemade cakes and scones. Group visits - all refreshments must be prebooked.
- Open all year on any day, at any time, for private guided tours - by appointment only.
- 100yds away.
- Please contact the Administrator for further details.
- On leads in park at all times. Assistance dogs only in House & Gardens.

Register for news and special offers at www.hudsonsheritage.com

KINGSTON BAGPUIZE HOUSE

KINGSTON BAGPUIZE, ABINGDON, OXFORDSHIRE OX13 5AX

www.kbhevents.uk

This lovely family home circa 1660 was remodelled in the early 1700's for the Blandy family. With English and French furniture in the elegant panelled rooms the entrance hall is dominated by a handsome cantilevered staircase. The house is surrounded by mature parkland and gardens notable for an interesting collection of cultivated plants which give year round interest including snowdrops & Magnolia in spring, flowering trees & shrubs in summer and autumn colour from September. Raised terrace leads to the 18th Century panelled pavilion looking over the gardens towards the house. Available for filming & featured as Lord Mertons home in Downton Abbey series 5 & 6 and the finale of Downton Abbey. Venue for weddings and small conferences.

Location: Map 7:A12. OS Ref SU408 981. In Kingston Bagpuize village, off the A415 Abingdon to Witney road South of the A415/A420 intersection. Abingdon 5m, Oxford 9m. **Owner:** Mrs Francis Grant **Contact:** Virginia Grant

Tel: 01865 820259 **E-mail:** info@kbhevents.uk

Open: Gardens Only (Snowdrops): 5,12,19 & 26 Feb. House & Gardens: 12, 13, 26 & 27 Mar. 9,10, 23 & 24 Apr. 7, 8, 21, 22, 28 & 29 May. 11, 12, 25 & 26 Jun. 9-11 & 23-25 Jul. 6-8 & 20-22 Aug. 10,11,17 & 18 Sep. All days 2-5pm (last entry to house 4pm). Free flow visits to ground floor of house.

Admission: House & Garden: Adult £9.00, Child/Student (11-21) £5.50. Garden only: Adult £6.00, Child/Student (11-21) £4.00. Family & Season tickets available. Group rates 20+ by appointment weekdays throughout the year. NB: Please visit website to confirm before travelling as dates & times may be subject to change.

Key facts: No photography in house on open days. Cards & pottery in Tea Room. Rare Plant Fair 28 May 2017 www.rareplantfair.co.uk. See website. WCs. Homemade teas. Free flow visits to ground floor only on advertised open days. Guided tours for pre-booked groups only. Guide dogs only. See website. Group visits by Appointment.

© Harpur Garden Images

© Harpur Garden Images

ROUSHAM HOUSE

NR STEEPLE ASTON, BICESTER, OXFORDSHIRE OX25 4QX

www.rousham.org

Rousham represents the first stage of English landscape design and remains almost as William Kent (1685-1748) left it. One of the few gardens of this date to have escaped alteration. Includes Venus' Vale, Townesend's Building, seven-arched Praeneste, the Temple of the Mill and a sham ruin known as the 'Eyecatcher'. The house was built in 1635 by Sir Robert Dormer. Dont miss the walled garden with their herbaceous borders, small parterre, pigeon house and espalier apple trees. A fine herd of Longhorn cattle are to be seen in the park.

Excellent location for fashion, advertising, photography etc.

Location: Map 7:A10. OS Ref SP477 242. E of A4260, 12m N of Oxford, S of B4030, 7m W of Bicester.

Owner/Contact: Charles Cottrell-Dormer Esq

Tel: 01869 347110 / 07860 360407 **E-mail:** ccd@rousham.org

Open: Garden: All year: daily, 10am-4.30pm (last adm). House: Pre-booked groups, May-Sep (Mon-Thu).

Admission: Garden: £6.00. No children under 15yrs.

Key facts: Rousham is an ideal Oxfordshire venue for wedding receptions, offering a site to pitch a marquee together with acres of landscape and formal gardens that can be used for photographs and pre-reception drinks. We have also held some car rallies, The Bentley, MG and Aston Martin owners clubs have all held rallies at Rousham. These events are held in the park, immediately next to the house. Open access to the house and garden can be arranged. Partial.

MAPLEDURHAM HOUSE AND WATERMILL

Mapledurham, Reading RG4 7TR

www.mapledurham.co.uk

Beautiful late 16th Century Elizabethan home of the Blount family and 15th Century watermill fully restored producing flour, semolina & bran. Hydro powered turbine producing green electricity. Delightful setting on the river Thames. Delicious teas served in the Old Manor Tea Rooms. A passenger boat service runs from nearby Caversham on open days. **Location:** Map 3:E2. OS Ref SU670 767. N of River Thames. 4m NW of Reading, 1½ m W off A4074.

Owner: The Mapledurham Trust **Contact:** Mrs Lola Andrews

Tel: 0118 9723350 **E-mail:** enquiries@mapledurham.co.uk

Open: Easter-Sep: Suns & BHs (not Aug Bank Holiday) 1-5.30pm (last admission 5pm). Suns in Oct 1-4.30pm (last admission 4pm).

Sat and midweek guided private parties by arrangement only.

Admission: Please call 0118 9723 350 for details. Mapledurham Trust reserves the right to alter or amend opening times or prices without prior notification.

Key facts: Gift shop located in the watermill. Ideal venue for fairs, shows & wedding receptions. Partial. Tea Room serving sandwiches, cream teas & cakes. Guided tours for midweek party visits & some Suns. School visits welcome at the watermill throughout the year. Dogs welcome on leads in the grounds only. Guide dogs only in the house, watermill or Tea Rooms.

MILTON MANOR HOUSE

Milton, Abingdon, Oxfordshire OX14 4EN

Dreamily beautiful mellow brick house, traditionally designed by Inigo Jones. Celebrated Gothick library and Catholic chapel. Lived in by family; pleasant relaxed and informal atmosphere. Park with fine old trees, stables, walled garden and woodland walk. Picknickers welcome. Free parking, refreshments and pony rides usually available.

Location: Map 3:D1. OS Ref SU485 924. Just off A34, village and house signposted, 9m S of Oxford, 15m N of Newbury. 3m from Abingdon & Didcot.

Owner: Anthony Mockler-Barrett Esq

Contact: By email for weddings, special events etc. florentinagifts@hotmail.co.uk or 020 899 32580. Please write to The Administrator for group visits giving contact details & proposed dates & numbers.

Tel: 01235 831287 **Fax:** 01235 862321

Open: Easter Sun & BH Mon, 16-17 Apr; 30 Apr-1 May; 21 May-4 Jun; 18 Aug-31 Aug.

Admission: Adult £8; Child (under 14) £2.

Gardens & grounds only: Adult £4, Child (under 14) £1.

Key facts: Grounds. Obligatory. Free. Guide dogs only.

SULGRAVE MANOR

Manor Road, Sulgrave, Nr Banbury, Oxfordshire OX17 2SD

www.sulgravemanor.org.uk

Ancestral Home of George Washington, the manor house was built by Lawrence Washington in the middle of the 16th Century and has a later 18th Century wing. With three acres of beautiful gardens, designed by the renowned architect Sir Reginald Blomfield, the Manor is open to the public between April and October but will take bookings for small private parties and larger groups all year round.

Location: Map 7:B10. OS Ref SP560 455.

Contact: Cymon Snow

Tel: 01295 760205

E-mail: enquiries@sulgravemanor.org.uk

Open: Please see website for details.

Admission: Adult £7.90, Concs £7.40, Child (4-15yrs) £3.60, Family (2 Adults and up to 3 children) £21.00. Garden only £3.60, Infant (under 4yrs) Free.

Key facts: Picnic site, Coach parties/groups welcomed, Credit cards accepted. Partial. Light Refreshments. Entertaining and informative tours. Free. In grounds only. Small private parties and larger groups by appointment.

Blenheim Palace lake in Autumn

Register for news and special offers at www.hudsonsheritage.com

HAMPTON COURT PALACE

www.hrp.org.uk/hamptoncourtpalace

Discover the magnificence of this former royal residence, once home to the flamboyant King Henry VIII.

Marvel at the two distinct and contrasting Tudor and Baroque architectural styles and soak up the atmosphere in 60 acres of stunning gardens. Extended and developed in grand style in the 1520s by Henry VIII, the present day elegance and romance of the palace owes much to the Christopher Wren designed baroque buildings commissioned by William and Mary at the end of the 17th Century.

At the palace you are able to step back in time and relive some of the extraordinary moments in the life of Henry VIII and the Glorious Georgians. Try on a courtier gown and explore the majestic environment where kings have entertained, celebrated and mourned. Marvel at the grandeur of the magnificent Great Hall and Great Watching Chamber, see the stunning vaulted ceiling of the Chapel Royal and explore the enormous kitchens, the most extensive surviving 16th Century kitchens in Europe today.

Explore the Magic Garden, our exciting new interactive play garden for families. Populated by mysterious mythical beasts, with battlements to storm, towers to besiege, and even a secret grotto to discover, the Magic Garden is a new and unique way for your family to explore the palace's past.

The palace is surrounded by formal gardens and sits in 60 acres of parkland gardens, including the 18th Century Privy Garden and world famous maze.

KEY FACTS

- Information Centre.
-
- Weddings, dinners, receptions.
- WCs.
-
- Licensed.
-
- Ample for cars, coach parking nearby.
- Rates on request 0844 482 7777.
- Guide dogs only.
-
- Closed 24-26 Dec.
-

VISITOR INFORMATION

Owner
Historic Royal Palaces

Address
Hampton Court Palace
Surrey
KT8 9AU

Location
Map 19:B9
OS Ref. TQ155 686
From M25/J15 or M25/J12 or M25/J10.
Rail: 30 minutes from Waterloo, zone 6 travelcard
Boat: From Richmond, Kingston or Runnymede

Contact
Historic Royal Palaces
Tel: 0844 482 7777
Venue Hire and Corporate Hospitailty:
hrp.org.uk/hireavenue,
020 3166 6507.
E-mail:
hamptoncourt@hrp.org.uk

Opening Times
Mar-Oct:
Daily, 10am-6pm.
(last admission 5pm).

Nov-Feb:
Daily, 10am-4.30pm.
(last admission 3.30pm).

Closed 24-26 Dec.

The Magic Garden is closed during the winter.

Please check our website before visiting for full details.

Admission
Visit www.hrp.org.uk for admission prices, or call 0844 482 7777.

Special Events
Special events year round, visit website for details.

Conference/Function
Conferences: Up to 250.
Receptions: Up to 400.
Lunches: Up to 220.
Dinners: Up to 270.
Marquees: Up to 3000.

VISITOR INFORMATION

Owner
National Trust

Address
Great Bookham
Nr Dorking
Surrey
RH5 6BD

Location
Map 19:B10
OS Ref. TQ136 522
5m NW of Dorking, 2m S of Great Bookham, off A246.

Contact
Tel: 01372 452048
E-mail: polesdenlacey@nationaltrust.org.uk

Opening Times
Gardens, table service café, coffee shop and gift shop:
Daily from 10am-5pm (4pm in winter).
Closed 24 & 25 Dec.

House:
1 Jan-29 Oct
10am-5pm.
30 Oct-31 Dec
10am-4pm.

Admission
Seasonal admission charges. Please check our website for details.

Special Events
Throughout Easter, the house is decorated with stunning displays of seasonal flowers.

To celebrate the 75th anniversary of the National Trust owning Polesden Lacey in 2017, we will be launching the Greville rose, specially cultivated by our garden team.

At Christmas, the house and grounds are dressed to impress in keeping with Edwardian traditions and evoking the warming spirit of Christmas. An 18ft Christmas tree welcomes guests into the hall of the house, Christmas music floats through the air and our room guides can answer any questions dressed in full period costume.

Discover this Edwardian party house

POLESDEN LACEY

www.nationaltrust.org.uk/polesdenlacey

Polesden Lacey is an Edwardian party house set in an area of Outstanding Natural Beauty overlooking the Surrey Hills. Explore the house or stroll through the grounds enjoying the view and leave feeling revitalised.

'This is a delicious house...' remarked Queen Elizabeth, the Queen Mother on her honeymoon at Polesden Lacey. This country retreat, with glorious views across the rolling Surrey Hills, was home to famous Edwardian hostess Mrs Greville, who entertained royalty and the celebrities of her time. The house has stunning interiors and contains a fabulous collection of art and ceramics. The gardens offer something for every season, including climbing roses, herbaceous borders and a winter garden. There are four waymarked countryside walks around the estate.

Margaret Greville bought Polesden Lacey in 1906, and left it to the National Trust in 1942. She inherited a fortune from her father, William McEwan, and she mixed with royalty and politicians. She was loved by many, but not all, mainly because she liked to gossip and wasn't afraid to speak her mind. Mrs Greville was renowned for being a wonderful hostess as well as generous to those less fortunate than her.

'Tea is at 5 o'clock, and at Polesden 5 o'clock means 5 o'clock and not 5 minutes past. Which in its turn means the Spanish ambassador, who has gone for a walk down the yew avenue, hastily retraces his steps, and the Chancellor of the Exchequer, whoever he may be, hurries down the great staircase, followed by several members of the House of Lords, and that the various ladies belonging to these gentlemen rise from their chaise-longues on which they have been resting in their bedrooms.' Down the Kitchen Sink by Beverley Nichols.

KEY FACTS

- The gift shop stocks homeware, luxury gifts, books, delicious nibbles and drinks.
- Accessible WC, catering & retail. Courtesy shuttle. Grounds mostly accessible. Free wheelchairs & powered mobility vehicles. Hearing loops available.
- Hot and cold food, homemade cakes and drinks.
- The house is open every day except Christmas eve and Christmas day, tours daily until half 12 followed by free flow, access by timed tickets at certain times. Free garden tours.
- Gardens only.
- P
- In the grounds (excluding formal gardens). Assistance dogs welcome.
- Grounds only.

© Polesden Lacey
Discover Mrs Greville's rags to riches story

© Polesden Lacey
Enjoy the splendour of the Edwardian formal garden

Register for news and special offers at www.hudsonsheritage.com

HATCHLANDS PARK

East Clandon, Guildford, Surrey GU4 7RT

www.nationaltrust.org.uk/hatchlands-park

Hatchlands Park was built in 1756 for Admiral Boscawen. The house is set in a beautiful 430-acre Repton park, with a variety of way-marked walks and there is a stunning bluebell wood in the spring. The house contains the Cobbe Collection of Old Master paintings and also the Cobbe Collection of keyboard instruments, the world's largest group of early keyboard instruments owned or played by famous composers such as Purcell, J C Bach, Mozart and Elgar.

Location: Map 19:A10. OS Ref TQ065 518.
Off the A246. Follow brown signs.
Owner: National Trust
Tel: 01483 222482
E-mail: hatchlands@nationaltrust.org.uk
Open: 7 Apr-30 Oct, Tues-Thus & Suns, BHs and Fris in Aug, 2-5.30pm.
Admission: House £10.00, Park walks £6.00, Groups £7.00. (includes voluntary donation - visitors can pay standard prices shown at property and on website).
Key facts: No photography inside the house. Please call for details. Open as shop. Thus. Free parking. Under close control in designated areas of parkland.

LOSELEY PARK

Guildford, Surrey GU3 1HS

www.loseleypark.co.uk

Loseley Park, built in 1562 by Sir William More, is a fine example of Elizabethan architecture. The rooms contain fascinating works of art, furniture from the 17th Century and many unique features. The Walled Garden is compared favourably to gardens of national renown.

Location: Map 3:G3. OS Ref SU975 473. 30m SW of London, leave A3 S of Guildford on to B3000. Signposted. **Owner:** Mr Michael More-Molyneux
Contact: Joanna Phillips **Tel:** 01483 304440 / 01483 405112
Wisteria Tea Room bookings: 01483 457103
E-mail: enquiries@loseleypark.co.uk
Open: House: May-Aug Mon-Thu 12pm-4pm. Sun: 1pm-5pm & BHs.
Gardens & Grounds: May-Sep: Sun-Thu: 11am-5pm & BHs
Admission: House & Gardens Adult £10.00. Child (5-16yrs) £5.00. Conc. £8.50. Child (under 5yrs) Free. Family (2 + 3) £26.00. Gardens & Grounds only: Adult £5.50. Child (5-16yrs) £2.75. Conc. £5.00. Please contact for Group bookings.
Key facts: Ground floor of house accessible to non-motorized wheelchairs only. Full Access Statement available. Lunches and teas. Fully licensed. Obligatory: 45 mins. Pre-booked Garden tours available. 150 cars, 6 coaches. Guide dogs only. Dogs on leads in car park only. For weddings, private and corporate functions.

© Painshill

PAINSHILL LANDSCAPE GARDEN

Portsmouth Road, Cobham, Surrey KT11 1JE

www.painshill.co.uk

Painshill is a beautiful 18th Century landscape garden. The 158 acre wonderland has something for everyone. Discover magical follies, including the restored crystal Grotto (limited opening times), historic plantings, the John Bartram Heritage Collection of North American trees and shrubs (Plant Heritage) and spectacular vistas. Visitor entrance is off Between Streets, Cobham.

Location: Map 19:B9. OS Ref TQ100 601. M25/J10/A3 to London. W of Cobham on A245. Signposted. Closest Sat Nav Ref KT11 1AA.
Owner: Painshill Park Trust **Contact:** Visitor Operations Team
Tel: 01932 868113 **Fax:** 01932 868001 **E-mail:** info@painshill.co.uk
Open: All Year (Closed 25-26 Dec). Mar-Oct 10am-6pm or dusk (last entry 4.30pm). Nov-Feb 10am to 4pm or dusk (last entry 3pm).
Admission: Adult £8.00 Concessions £7.00, Child (5-16 yrs) £4.50, Family (2 Adults & 4 Children) £27.00, U5's & Disabled Carer: Free. Group rates available.
Key facts: Books, gifts, Painshill Sparkling Wine & Painshill Honey. Abercorn Room with small courtyard (seats 50). WCs. Accessible route. Free pre-booked wheelchair loan. Pre-booked guided buggy tours. Licensed. Picnic area. Pre-book 10+ groups. Free. Coaches must book. Pre-book via Education Dept. On short fixed leads. Closed 25-26 Dec.

GREAT FOSTERS

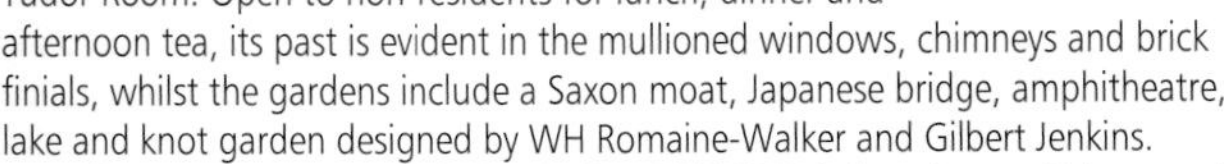

Stroude Road, Egham, Surrey TW20 9UR

Set in 50 acres of stunning gardens and parkland Great Fosters is a fine example of Elizabethan architecture and is now a luxury hotel with two restaurants, The Estate Grill and The Tudor Room. Open to non-residents for lunch, dinner and afternoon tea, its past is evident in the mullioned windows, chimneys and brick finials, whilst the gardens include a Saxon moat, Japanese bridge, amphitheatre, lake and knot garden designed by WH Romaine-Walker and Gilbert Jenkins.

Location: Map 3:G2. OS Ref TQ015 694. M25 J/13, follow signs to Egham and then brown historic signs for Great Fosters.
Owner: The Sutcliffe family
Contact: Amanda Dougans
Tel: 01784 433822 **E-mail:** reception@greatfosters.co.uk
Website: www.greatfosters.co.uk
Open: All year. **Admission:** No charge.
Key facts: WC. Licensed. Guide dogs only.

CLAREMONT LANDSCAPE GARDEN

Portsmouth Road, Esher, Surrey KT10 9JG

One of the earliest surviving English landscape gardens, restored to its former glory. Features include a lake, island with pavilion, grotto, turf amphitheatre, viewpoints and avenues. **Location:** Map 19:B9. OS Ref TQ128 632.
Tel: 01372 467806 **E-mail:** claremont@nationaltrust.org.uk
Website: www.nationaltrust.org.uk/claremont **Open:** Jan-Mar & Nov-Dec, daily, 10am-5pm; Apr-Oct, daily, 10am-6pm. **Admission:** Adult £7.65; Child £3.85.

VISITOR INFORMATION

Owner
Arundel Castle Trustees Ltd

Address
Arundel Castle
Arundel
West Sussex
BN18 9AB

Location
Map 3:G6
OS Ref. TQ018 072
Central Arundel, N of A27.
Brighton 40 mins,
Worthing 15 mins,
Chichester 15 mins. From London A3 or A24, 1½ hrs.
M25 motorway, 30m.
Bus: Bus stop 100 yds.
Rail: Station 1½m.
Air: Gatwick 25m.

Contact
Bryan McDonald,
Castle Manager
Tel: 01903 882173
E-mail:
visits@arundelcastle.org

Opening Times
1 Apr-29 Oct 2017:
Tues to Suns, Good Fri & Easter Mon. May BH Mons, and Mons in Aug.

Fitzalan Chapel, Gardens & Grounds, Gift Shop:
10am-5pm.

Castle Keep, Restaurant & Coffee Shop:
10am-4.30pm.

Main Castle Rooms:
12 noon-5pm.
Last entry 4pm.

Admission
Please contact us or see website for up-to-date admissions rates.
Group rates available.

ARUNDEL CASTLE & GARDENS

www.arundelcastle.org

Ancient Castle, Stately Home, Gardens & The Collector Earl's Garden.

A thousand years of history is waiting to be discovered at Arundel Castle in West Sussex. Dating from the 11th Century, the Castle is both ancient fortification and stately home of the Dukes of Norfolk and Earls of Arundel.

Set high on a hill, this magnificent Castle commands stunning views across the River Arun and out to sea. Climb the Keep, explore the battlements, wander in the grounds and recently restored Victorian gardens and relax in the garden of the 14th Century Fitzalan Chapel.

In the 17th Century during the English Civil War the Castle suffered extensive damage. The process of structural restoration began in earnest in the 18th Century and continued up until 1900. The Castle was one of the first private residences to have electricity and central heating and had its own fire engine.

Inside the Castle over 20 sumptuously furnished rooms may be visited including the breathtaking Barons' Hall with 16th Century furniture; the Armoury with its fine collection of armour and weaponry, and the magnificent Gothic library entirely fitted out in carved Honduras mahogany. There are works of art by Van Dyck, Gainsborough, Canaletto and Mytens; tapestries; clocks; and personal possessions of Mary Queen of Scots including the gold rosary that she carried to her execution.

There are special event days throughout the season, including, Shakespeare in The Collector Earl's Garden, Arundel International Jousting & Medieval Tournament, and medieval re-enactments.

Do not miss the magnificent Collector Earl's Garden based on early 17th Century classical designs.

KEY FACTS

- No photography or video recording inside the Castle.
- Distinctive and exclusive gifts.
- WCs, ramps, lifts. Please see website.
- Licensed.
- Licensed.
- By prior arrangement. Tour time 1½-2 hrs. Tours available in various languages - please enquire.
- Ample car and coach parking in town car park. Free admission and refreshment voucher for coach driver.
- Norman Motte & Keep, Armoury & Victorian bedrooms. Special rates for schoolchildren (aged 5-16) and teachers.
- Registered Assistance dogs only.
- On special event days admission prices may vary.

GOODWOOD HOUSE

www.goodwood.com

Goodwood House, ancestral home of the Dukes of Richmond and Gordon with magnificent art collection.

Goodwood is one of England's finest sporting estates. At its heart lies Goodwood House, the ancestral home of the Dukes of Richmond and Gordon, direct descendants of King Charles II. Today, it is lived in by the present Duke's son and heir, the Earl of March and Kinrara, with his wife and family. Their home is open to the public on at least 60 days a year.

The art collection includes a magnificent group of British paintings from the 17th and 18th Centuries, such as the celebrated views of London by Canaletto and superb sporting scenes by George Stubbs. The rooms are filled with fine English and French furniture, Gobelins tapestries and Sèvres Porcelain. Special works of art are regularly rotated and displayed and the books can be viewed by written application to the Curator (there is a special charge for these viewings). Each Summer there is an exhibition focusing on items in the collection and the family history.

Goodwood is also renowned for its entertaining, enjoying a reputation for excellence. Goodwood's own organic farm provides food for the table in the various restaurants on the estate. With internationally renowned horseracing and motor sport events, the finest downland golf course in the UK, its own aerodrome and hotel, Goodwood offers an extraordinarily rich sporting experience.

KEY FACTS

- Conference and wedding facilities. No photography. Very well informed guides. Shell House optional extra on Connoisseurs' Days.
- WCs.
- Obligatory.
- Ample.
- Guide dogs only.
- Goodwood Hotel.
- Civil Wedding Licence. Call Wedding Line or email estatesalesofficenquiries@goodwood.com.

VISITOR INFORMATION

Owner

The Goodwood Estate Co.Ltd. (Earl of March and Kinrara).

Address

Goodwood House
Goodwood
Chichester
West Sussex
PO18 0PX

Location

Map 3:F6
OS Ref. SU888 088
3½m NE of Chichester. A3 from London then A286 or A285. M27/A27 from Portsmouth or Brighton.
Rail: Chichester 3½m Arundel 9m.
Air: Heathrow 1½ hrs Gatwick ¾hr.

Contact

Assistant to the Curator
Tel: 01243 755012
Fax: 01243 755005
Recorded Info: 01243 755040.
Weddings: 01243 775537.
E-mail: curator@goodwood.com or curators.assistant@goodwood.com

Opening Times

House
12 Mar-22 Oct:
Suns & Mons, 1-5pm (last admission 4pm).
6 Aug-7 Sep:
Sun-Thu, 1-5pm (last admission 4pm).
Please note these dates are provisional. Please always check the website or call the Ticket office 01243 755055 before visiting.
Special tours for booked groups of 20+ only.
Closures
Closed for some special events and around Members Meeting, the Festival of Speed and Revival Meeting.

Admission

House

Adult	£9.50
Young Person (12-18yrs)	£5.00
Child (under 12yrs)	Free
Booked Groups (20-60)	
Open Day (am - by request only)	£14.00
Open Day (pm)	£12.00

Please note these rates are provisional.

Special Events

75th Members' Meeting, Festival of Speed, Qatar Goodwood Festival & Goodwood Revival Meeting:
Please visit our website.

Conference/Function

ROOM	Size	Max Cap
Ballroom	79' x 23'	180

VISITOR INFORMATION

Owner
The Great Dixter Charitable Trust

Address
Northiam
Rye
East Sussex
TN31 6PH

Location
Map 4:L5
OS Ref. TQ817 251
Signposted off the A28 in Northiam.

Contact
Perry Rodriguez
Tel: 01797 252878
E-mail: office@greatdixter.co.uk

Opening Times
1 Apr-29 Oct:
Tue-Sun, House 2-5pm.
Garden 11am-5pm.

Specialist Nursery Opening times:
Apr-Oct
Mon-Fri, 9am-5pm.
Sat 9am-5pm.
Sun 10am-5pm.

Nov-End of Mar
Mon-Fri, 9am-12.30pm, 1.30-4.30pm.
Sat 9am-12.30pm.
Sun Closed.

Admission
House & Garden:

Adult	£10.50
Child	£1.50

Garden only:

Adult	£8.50
Child	£1.00

A Gift Aid on admission scheme is in place.

Special Events
Study days on a wide range of subjects available. Please check the website for details.

GREAT DIXTER HOUSE & GARDENS

www.greatdixter.co.uk

A very special garden with a great deal of character, planted with flair, always something to see, whatever the season.

Great Dixter, built c1450, is the birthplace of the late Christopher Lloyd, gardening author. Its Great Hall is the largest medieval timberframed hall in the country, restored and enlarged for Christopher's father (1910-12). The house was largely designed by the architect, Sir Edwin Lutyens, who added a 16th Century house (moved from elsewhere) knitting the buildings together as a family home. The house retains much of the collections of furniture and other items put together by the Lloyds early in the 20th Century, with some notable modern additions by Christopher. The gardens feature a variety of topiary, ponds, wild meadow areas and the famous Long Border and Exotic Garden. Featured regularly in 'Country Life' from 1963, Christopher was asked to contribute a series of weekly articles as a practical gardener - he never missed an issue in 42 years. There is a specialist nursery which offers an array of unusual plants of the highest quality, many of which can be seen in the fabric of the gardens. Light refreshments are available in the gift shop as well as tools, books and gifts. The whole estate is 57 acres which includes ancient woodlands, meadows and ponds which have been consistently managed on a traditional basis. Coppicing the woodlands, for example, has provided pea sticks for plant supports and timber for fencing and repairs to the buildings. There is a Friends programme available throughout the year. Friends enjoy invitations to events and educational courses as well as regular newsletters.

KEY FACTS

- No photography in House.
- Obligatory.
- Limited for coaches.
- Guide dogs only.

© Lancing College

The glorious gothic architecture of Lancing College Chapel

LANCING COLLEGE CHAPEL

www.lancingcollege.co.uk

'I know of no more spectacular post-Reformation ecclesiastical building in the kingdom.' Evelyn Waugh, former pupil.

Lancing College Chapel is the place of worship for the community of Lancing College, the Central Minster of the Woodard Schools and a well-loved Sussex landmark. The Chapel stands prominently on the South Downs. The exterior, with its pinnacles and flying buttresses, is a testament to Victorian structural bravado. Designed by Herbert Carpenter in the 13th Century French gothic style, it is the fourth tallest ecclesiastical building in England.

The foundations were laid in 1868 and the atmospheric crypt came into use in 1875. The upper chapel was dedicated in 1911 but the west wall and rose window were added in the 1970s. There is now a plan to complete the building with a west porch. A beautiful war memorial cloister was built in the 1920s.

The interior is breathtaking. Soaring columns branch out into fan vaulting, perfectly proportioned arches and vast clerestory windows. There are stained glass windows by Comper and Dykes Bower and one commemorating former pupil Fr Trevor Huddleston made by Mel Howse in 2007. Behind the high altar are superb tapestries woven on the William Morris looms in the 1920s. The oak stall canopies are by Gilbert Scott. There are two organs (Walker 1914 and Frobenius 1986) with intricately carved oak cases.

The Chapel has a fascinating history which is still unfolding and it is a treasure house of ecclesiastical art. Lancing Chapel welcomes visitors both as an important heritage landmark and as a place of quiet reflection and prayer.

KEY FACTS

- Guide books, information leaflets and a DVD.
- Stall with guide books and postcards at entrance to the Chapel.
- The upper chapel (but not the crypt) is easily accessible for the disabled.
- Guided tours and brief talks about the Chapel can be booked with the Verger. Groups should be booked in advance.
- It is usually possible to park very near the entrance to the Chapel.
- School and other educational groups are welcome and may request guided tours and other information.
- Guide dogs only in Chapel. Dogs on leads welcome in College grounds.
- Open all year except Christmas Day, Boxing Day and New Year's Day.

© Lancing College

Interior of Lancing College Chapel looking East

© Lancing College

The splendid rose window and Walker organ

VISITOR INFORMATION

Owner
Lancing College Chapel Trust

Address
Lancing
West Sussex
BN15 0RW

Location
Map 3:H6
OS Ref. TQ196 067
North of the A27 between Shoreham-by-Sea and Lancing at the Coombes Road/Shoreham Airport traffic lights. Filter right if coming from the east. Turn off Coombes Road at sign for Lancing College and proceed to the top of Lancing College drive. It is usually possible to park outside the Chapel.
Rail: Train to Shoreham-by-Sea or Lancing on the London-Littlehampton and Portsmouth line and take a taxi.
Bus: The nearest bus routes are Brighton and Hove Buses 2A, Compass Buses, 106 and Coastliner 700.

Contact
The Verger
Tel: 01273 465949
Fax: 01273 464720
Enquiries may also be made at Reception, Lancing College on 01273 452213.
E-mail:
verger@lancing.org.uk

Opening Times
10am-4pm Mon-Sat.
12 noon-4pm on Sun.
Every day of the year except for Christmas Day, Boxing Day and New Year's Day.

Admission
Admission Free.
Donations are requested for the Friends of Lancing Chapel.
Visitors are asked to sign in for security purposes as they enter the Chapel.
The other College buildings are not open to the public.

Special Events
Visitors can reserve seats for Public Carol Services by applying in writing to Lancing College Chapel, Lancing, West Sussex, BN15 0RW with a stamped, self-addressed envelope.
Visitors wishing to attend other services should contact the Verger.

© National Trust Images / John Miller

© National Trust Images/Geoffrey Frosh

BATEMAN'S

BURWASH, ETCHINGHAM, EAST SUSSEX TN19 7DS

www.nationaltrust.org.uk/batemans

"A good and peaceable place" was how Rudyard Kipling described Bateman's, a beautiful Sussex sandstone manor house and garden where the Kiplings lived from 1902-1936. Originally built in 1634 this mellow house, with its little watermill, was a sanctuary to the most famous writer in the English speaking world. Set in the glorious landscape of the Sussex Weald, the house and gardens are kept much as they were in Kipling's time and visitors can discover a fascinating collection of mementos of Kipling's time in India.

Location: Map 4:K5. OS Ref TQ671 238.
0.5 m S of Burwash off A265.

Owner: National Trust

Contact: The Administrator **Tel:** 01435 882302

E-mail: batemans@nationaltrust.org.uk

Open: House/Shop/Tea Room/Garden: Open all year (closed Christmas Eve and Christmas Day) Please call 01435 882302 or visit our website for details of seasonal opening times.

Admission: For 2017 prices please call 01435 882302 or visit our website. Group discount available (15+ pre-booked).

Key facts: Garden available for wedding receptions and functions. The shop has a large selection of new and second-hand Kipling books. Partial. WC. Ground floor access only. Virtual tour of upstairs. Licensed. Our Tea Room offers a selection of snacks, hot and cold meals as well as delicious cakes. Limited for coaches. Closed Christmas Eve and Christmas Day.

FIRLE PLACE

FIRLE, NR LEWES, EAST SUSSEX BN8 6LP

www.firle.com

The family's 500 year old history at Firle Place commenced when Sir John Gage (1479-1556) completed his manor house c.1543, in the lee of the chalk folds of the Sussex South Downs. The house was remodelled in the 18th Century, providing its present Georgian façade, including the rare Serlian window on the entrance front. The celebrated works of art now housed at Firle, comprising Old Master paintings, furniture and Sèvres porcelain, reflect the taste of successive generations of collectors and familial relationships, significant additions arriving in the mid-1950s from the Cowper collection at Panshanger House, Hertfordshire and the Grenfell collection from Taplow Court, Berkshire.

Location: Map 4:J6. OS Ref TQ473 071.
4m SE of Lewes on A27 Brighton/Eastbourne Road.

Owner: The Rt Hon Viscount Gage

Tel: 01273 858567

E-mail: enquiries@firle.com

Open: Jun-Sep, Sun-Thu, 2.00-4.30pm. Last admission 4.15pm.
(Dates and times subject to change. Please check before your visit).
Tea Room open (without charge) on House opening days only, from 12.30-4.30pm.

Admission: Adult £9.00, Child £4.50, Conc. £8.00

Private Tours: Private group tours can be arranged by prior appointment. Please telephone 01273 858307 for details or please visit the website.

Key facts: No photography in house. Available for private hire. Ground floor & Tea Room. Licensed. In grounds on leads.

Register for news and special offers at www.hudsonsheritage.com

© National Trust Images/Lisa Davies

© National Trust Images/Lisa Davies

NYMANS

HANDCROSS, HAYWARDS HEATH, WEST SUSSEX RH17 6EB

www.nationaltrust.org.uk/nymans

One of the National Trust's premier gardens, Nymans was a country retreat for the creative Messel family, and has views stretching out across the Sussex Weald. From vibrantly colourful summer borders to the tranquillity of ancient woodland, Nymans is a place of experimentation with constantly evolving planting designs and a rare and unusual plant collection. The comfortable yet elegant house, a partial ruin, reflects the personalities and stories of the talented Messel family, from the Countess of Rosse to Oliver Messel and photographer Lord Snowdon.
Location: Map 4:I4. OS Ref SU187:TQ265 294. At Handcross on B2114, 12 miles south of Gatwick, just off London-Brighton M23.
Owner: National Trust **Contact:** Nymans
Tel: 01444 405250
E-mail: nymans@nationaltrust.org.uk
Open: Garden, woods, café, shop and garden centre, gallery in the House, and second hand bookshop: 1 Jan-28 Feb, daily, 10am-4pm. 1 Mar-31 Oct, daily, 10am-5pm. 1 Nov-31 Dec, daily, 10am-4pm. House open for special events only from 1 Nov-28 Feb. Closed 24 & 25 Dec. Last admission to Gallery 30 mins before closing and for short periods during the year to change exhibitions. For more information and any other changes please check the website.
Admission: Please see website.
Key facts: WC, some level paths. Licensed. Daily, free. Special interest tours for groups £2.50pp booked in advance. Guide dogs only. No dogs in garden. Closed 24 & 25 Dec.

© Parham Park Limited, photography E Zeschin

© Parham Park Limited, photography E Zeschin

PARHAM HOUSE & GARDENS

PARHAM PARK, PULBOROUGH, WEST SUSSEX RH20 4HS

www.parhaminsussex.co.uk

One of the top twenty in Simon Jenkins's book 'England's Thousand Best Houses'. Idyllically set in the heart of an ancient deer park, below the South Downs, the Elizabethan House contains an important collection of needlework, paintings and furniture. The spectacular Long Gallery is the third longest in England. The Gardens include a four-acre Walled Garden with stunning herbaceous borders, plus Pleasure Grounds. Parham has always been a well-loved family home, and only three families have lived here since its foundation stone was laid in 1577. Its tranquillity and timeless beauty have changed little over the years. Now owned by a charitable trust, and lived in by Lady Emma Barnard, her husband James and their family.
Location: Map 3:G5. OS Ref TQ060 143. Midway between Pulborough & Storrington on A283. SatNav: RH20 4HR.
Owner: Parham Park Ltd **Contact:** Estate Office
Tel: 01903 742021 **Facebook:** ParhamHouseAndGardens
Twitter: @parhaminsussex **E-mail:** enquiries@parhaminsussex.co.uk
Open: Easter Sun-end of Sep, Sun to Wed. Suns only in Oct.
Gardens open 12 noon, House at 2pm.
Please see website for up-to-date information and additional events.
Admission: House & Gardens: Adult £11.00, Concession £10.00, Child £6.00, Family £32. Gardens only: Adult £9.00, Senior £8.00, Child £5.00, Family £26.00. Season Ticket: Single £24.00, Double £42.00, Family £66.00.
Key facts: Gifts including Parham's own jams & preserves. Plants grown by our own Garden Team. Exclusive packages by arrangement, on Thus & Fris during the open season. Disabled access in the gardens & ground floor of the house. Full accessibility statement on website. Open on House & Garden open days only. Licensed. House & Garden tours are available by arrangement, led by Parham Guides & members of the Gardening Team. Ample free parking. Designated parking for coaches & disabled visitors is within 50 metres. Please enquire. In Gardens only, on leads.

© ©Jenny Porrett

© ©National Trust Images/Andreas von Einsiedel

PETWORTH HOUSE & PARK

CHURCH STREET, PETWORTH, WEST SUSSEX GU28 0AE

www.nationaltrust.org.uk/petworth

Shaped by a family of collectors over the past 800 years, this 17th Century 'house of art' inspired countless artists, including England's greatest landscape painter JMW Turner. The finest collection of art and sculpture in the care of the National Trust, including world famous paintings by Van Dyck, Reynolds, Blake and Turner, is displayed in the opulent state rooms and North Gallery. In contrast the atmospheric Servants' Quarters evoke the hustle and bustle of 'below stairs' life. Outdoors is a woodland Pleasure Ground and 700 acres of 'Capability' Brown landscaped deer park with glorious views of the South Downs National Park.

Location: Map 3:G5. OS Ref SU976 218. Both house and park car parks located on A283; Follow signs from centre of Petworth (A272/A283). Sat-Nav: GU28 9LR

Owner: National Trust

Contact: The Administration Office

Tel: 01798 342207

E-mail: petworth@nationaltrust.org.uk

Open: House: 18 Mar-5 Nov, 7 days a week, 11am-5pm last admission 4:30pm. Pleasure Grounds, Café & Gift Shop: 10am-5pm daily all year. Closes dusk if earlier. *Closed 24 & 25 Dec*

Admission: Adult £15.00, Child (5-17yrs) £7.50, Family £37.50, Groups (pre-booked) £12.00.

Key facts: WCs. Licensed. By arrangement. 700 meters from house. Parking charge for non-members (£4.00), NT Members parking Free. Assistance dogs only.

© Anthony Capo-Bianco

ST MARY'S HOUSE & GARDENS

BRAMBER, WEST SUSSEX BN44 3WE

www.stmarysbramber.co.uk

Enchanting medieval house, winner of Hudsons Heritage 'Best Restoration' award in 2011. Features in Simon Jenkins' book 'England's Thousand Best Houses'. Fine panelled interiors, including unique Elizabethan 'Painted Room'. Interesting family memorabilia and other collections including English costume dolls.

Five acres of grounds. Formal gardens with amusing topiary, and exceptional example of prehistoric tree Ginkgo biloba. 'Secret' Garden, with Victorian fruit-wall and rare pineapple pits, Rural Museum, Jubilee Rose Garden, Terracotta Garden, King's Garden, unusual circular Poetry Garden, woodland walk and Landscape Water Garden with island and waterfall. Traditional cottage-style Tea Room.

A place of fascination, charm and friendliness.

Location: Map 3:H6. OS Ref TQ189 105. Bramber village off A283. From London 56m via M23/A23 or A24. Buses from Brighton, Shoreham and Worthing.

Owner: Mr Peter Thorogood MBE and Mr Roger Linton MBE

Tel: 01903 816205 **E-mail:** info@stmarysbramber.co.uk

Open: May-end Sep: Suns, Thus & BH Mons, 2-6pm. Extra Weds in Aug, 2-6pm. Last entry 5pm. Groups at other days and times by arrangement.

Admission: House & Gardens: Adult £9.00, Conc. £8.50, Child £4.00. Groups (25+) £9.00. Gardens only: Adult £6.00, Child £2.00, Groups £6.00.

Key facts: No photography in house. Partial. Obligatory for groups (max 55).Visit time 2½-3 hrs. 20 cars or 2 coaches. The elegant Victorian Music Room is licensed for up to 90 people. Exclusive use of the historic reception rooms and delightful formal gardens for up to two hours.

Register for news and special offers at www.hudsonsheritage.com

© National Trust Images/Chris Roe

© National Trust Images/Lisa Barnard

SHEFFIELD PARK AND GARDEN

SHEFFIELD PARK, UCKFIELD, EAST SUSSEX TN22 3QX

www.nationaltrust.org.uk/sheffield-park-and-garden

The garden is a horticultural work of art formed through centuries of landscape design, with influences of 'Capability' Brown and Humphry Repton. Four lakes form the heart of the garden, with paths circulating through the glades and wooded areas surrounding them. Each owner has left their impression, which can still be seen today in the layout of the lakes, the construction of Pulham Falls, the planting of Palm Walk and the many different tree and shrub species from around the world. Our historic parkland forms a larger footprint for the Sheffield Park estate. Dating back several centuries, it has had many uses including a deer park and WWII camp, and is now grazed with livestock. (Please note house is privately owned). **Location:** Map 4:I5. OS Ref TQ415 240. Midway between East Grinstead and Lewes, 5m NW of Uckfield on E side of A275.
Owner: National Trust **Contact:** Property Office
Tel: 01825 790231 **Fax:** 01825 791264
E-mail: sheffieldpark@nationaltrust.org.uk
Open: Garden/Shop/Tea Room: Open all year (closed Christmas Eve & Christmas Day). Please call 01825 790231 or visit our website for details of seasonal opening times. Parkland: Open all year, dawn to dusk.
Admission: For 2017 prices, please call 01825 790231 or visit our website. Groups discount available (15+ pre-booked) NT, RHS Individual Members and Great British Heritage Pass holders Free. Discounts available in conjunction with the Bluebell Railway for groups. **Key facts:** Gifts, condiments, books, gardening accessories & outdoor wear. Extensive, well-stocked plant sales area. Accessible route in garden. WCs in Tea Room & reception. Mobility scooters & wheelchairs. Coach House Tea Room. Tues & Thus 11am-12pm. Coach parking area & accessible spaces. Garden: Dogs on leads are now allowed after 1.30pm. Parkland: Dogs allowed on leads all day.

© National Trust Images / Nadia Mackenzie

© National Trust Images / Chris Hill

STANDEN

WEST HOATHLY ROAD, EAST GRINSTEAD, WEST SUSSEX RH19 4NE

www.nationaltrust.org.uk/standen

Designed by Philip Webb in the 1890s for wealthy solicitor, James Beale, and his family, Standen is a family home with nationally important Arts & Crafts interiors, most famous for its Morris & Co. designs. The 12 acre hillside garden has been recently restored to uncover lost features and conserve the historic plant collection. A licensed café serves seasonal dishes and Arts & Crafts inspired gifts are available in the shop.
Location: Map 4:I4. OS Ref TQ389 356.
2m S of East Grinstead, signposted from B2110.
Owner: National Trust **Contact:** Property Office
Tel: 01342 323029
Twitter, Facebook & Instagram: Search for StandenNT.
E-mail: standen@nationaltrust.org.uk
Open: Open daily: 1 Jan-31 Jan & 1 Nov-31 Dec: Garden, Café, Shop 10am-4pm. House: 11am-3.30pm (last entry 3pm. Tours only Mon-Fri).
1 Feb-31 Oct: Garden, Café, Shop 10am-5pm, House 11am-4.30pm (last entry 4pm). Closed 24 & 25 December. Please check website for full details and events.
Admission: Admission is free for National Trust members. For admission prices for non-members, please check the website or call us on 01342 323029.
Key facts: Year round events programme. Gifts, exhibition souvenirs, condiments, books, gardening accessories & more.
WCs. Wheelchairs available to borrow. Barn Café (Licensed).
Guided tours available at certain times, check website for details.
Dogs welcome in the gardens on short leads. Morris Apartment (Self-catering, sleeps 2+2) available to hire. Closed 24 & 25 Dec.

BORDE HILL GARDEN

Borde Hill Lane, Haywards Heath, West Sussex RH16 1XP

www.bordehill.co.uk

Botanical heritage and stunning landscapes make Borde Hill the perfect day out for horticulture enthusiasts, country lovers, and families. The Elizabethan House nestles in the centre of the formal garden which is set as outdoor 'rooms', including the Azalea, Rhododendron, Rose and Italian gardens. Themed events, gift shop, café, tea garden, restaurant, and gallery. Dog friendly.

Location: Map 4:15. OS Ref TQ323 265.
1½ miles north of Haywards Heath, 20 mins N. of Brighton, or S. of Gatwick on A23 taking exit 10a via Balcombe & Cuckfield.
Contact: Joanna Stewart
Tel: 01444 450326 **E-mail:** info@bordehill.co.uk
Open: 8 Apr-1 Oct, daily, 10am-5pm; Jul-Aug, daily, 10am-6pm; Oct half term, daily, 10am-5pm.
Admission: Adult £8.20; Child £5.50.
Key facts: WCs. Maps. Homemade food. Award-winning. Garden & House. Free parking. On leads.

CHICHESTER CATHEDRAL

Chichester, West Sussex PO19 1PX

www.chichestercathedral.org.uk

Ancient and modern, this magnificent 900 year old Cathedral has treasures from every age, from medieval stone carvings to world famous contemporary artworks. Open every day and all year with free entry. Free guided tours and special trails for children. Regular exhibitions, free weekly lunchtime concerts and a superb Cloisters Café and Shop. A fascinating place to visit.

Location: Map 3:F6. OS Ref SU860 047. West Street, Chichester.
Contact: Visitor Services Officer
Tel: 01243 782595 **Fax:** 01243 812499
E-mail: visitors@chichestercathedral.org.uk
Open: Summer: 7.15am-7pm, Winter: 7.15am-6pm. Choral Evensong daily (except Wed).
Admission: Free entry. Donations greatly appreciated.
Key facts:

CHARLESTON

Firle, Nr Lewes, East Sussex BN8 6LL

www.charleston.org.uk

Charleston, with its unique interiors and beautiful walled garden, was the home of artists Vanessa Bell and Duncan Grant from 1916 and the country meeting place of the Bloomsbury group. They decorated the house, painting walls, doors and furniture and filling the rooms with their own paintings and works by artists they admired, such as Picasso, Derain and Sickert.

Location: Map 4:J6. OS Ref TQ490 069.
7 miles east of Lewes on A27 between Firle and Selmeston
Owner: The Charleston Trust **Tel:** 01323 811626 **E-mail:** info@charleston.org.uk
Open: Apr-Oct: Wed-Sat, guided tours from 1pm (12pm Jul-Sep) Last entry 5pm. Sun & BH Mon open 1-5.30pm.
Admission: Please check website for full details of admission costs.
Key facts:
Obligatory, except Sunday.

CLINTON LODGE GARDEN

Fletching, E Sussex TN22 3ST

www.clintonlodgegardens.co.uk

A formal but romantic garden around a Caroline and Georgian house, reflecting the gardening fashions throughout its history, particularly since the time of Sir Henry Clinton, one of Wellington's generals at Waterloo. Lawn and parkland, double blue and white herbaceous borders between yew and box hedges, a cloister walk swathed in white roses, clematis and geraniums, a Herb Garden where hedges of box envelop herbs, seats are of turf, paths of camomile. A Pear Walk bursts with alliums or lilies, a Potager of flowers for cutting, old roses surround a magnificent water feature by William Pye, and much more. Private groups by appointment - Lunches can be arranged for groups of 10-30.

Location: Map 4:I5. OS Ref TQ428 238. In centre of village behind tall yew and holly hedge. **Owner/Contact:** Lady Collum
Tel: 01825 722952 **Fax:** 01825 723967 **E-mail:** garden@clintonlodge.com
Open: NGS Open Days: Sun 7 May, Mon 12 Jun, Mon 26 Jun & Mon 31 Jul. Other days by appointment. **Admission:** NGS Entrance £5.00, Children Free.
Key facts: WC. NGS days only By arrangement. Limited. Guide dogs only.

HAMMERWOOD PARK

East Grinstead, Sussex RH19 3QE

www.hammerwoodpark.co.uk

The best kept secret in Sussex, with house and park preserved "untouched by a corporate plan". Built by White House architect Latrobe in Greek Revival style in 1792 as a temple to Bacchus, left derelict by Led Zeppelin, painstakingly restored by the Pinnegar family over the last 30 years and brought to life with guided tours, concerts some including Finchcocks' instruments and filming.

Location: Map 4:J4. OS Ref TQ442 390.
3.5 m E of East Grinstead on A264 to Tunbridge Wells, 1m W of Holtye.
Owner: David and Anne-Noelle Pinnegar
Tel: 01342 850594 **E-mail:** antespam@gmail.com
Open: 1 Jun-end Sep: Wed, Sat & BH Mon, 2-5pm. Guided tour starts 2.05pm. Private groups: Easter-Jun. Coaches strictly by appointment. Small groups any time throughout the year by appointment. **Admission:** House & Park: Adult £8.50, Child £2.00. Private viewing by arrangement.
Key facts: Conferences. Helipad (see Pooley's - prior permission required). Obligatory. In grounds. B&B. €

© National Trust

UPPARK HOUSE & GARDEN

South Harting, Petersfield, West Sussex GU31 5QR

www.nationaltrust.org.uk/uppark

Admire the Georgian grandeur of Uppark from its stunning hilltop location on the South Downs. Discover the fascinating world of Sir Harry Fetherstonhaugh, Lady Emma Hamilton and the dairymaid who married her master. See the famous doll's house, Victorian servants' quarters, lovely garden and breathtaking views.
Location: Map 3:F5. OS Ref 197 SU775 177.
In Between Petersfield & Chichester on B2146.
Owner: National Trust
Contact: The Property Office
Tel: 01730 825415 **Fax:** 01730 825873
E-mail: uppark@nationaltrust.org.uk
Open: All year, daily, House: 1-4pm. Gardens:10-5pm. Closed 24 & 25 Dec.
Admission: Adult £11; Child £5.50.
Key facts: No photography in the house. WCs at carpark, in shop and in house. Lift to basement of house. Available for hire. Guide dogs only.

STANSTED PARK

Rowlands Castle, Hampshire PO9 6DX

www.stanstedpark.co.uk

Stansted House and its Chapel stand in 1750 acres of parkland and ancient forest within the South Downs National Park. The state rooms are furnished as though the 10th Earl was still at home giving the visitor a real sense of a bygone era, the extensive servants' quarters below stairs are filled with historic artefacts that are brought to life by the very knowledgeable and friendly stewards who will guide you through the vibrant history of Stansted Park.
Location: Map 3:F5. OS Ref SU761 103. Follow brown heritage signs from A3(M) J2 Emsworth or A27 Havant **Owner:** Stansted Park Foundation
Contact: Reception **Tel:** 023 9241 2265 **Fax:** 023 9241 3773
E-mail: enquiry@stanstedpark.co.uk
Open: House & Chapel: Easter Sun-end Sep; Sun, Mon, Tue & Wed 1-5pm (last adm. 4pm). Tea Room, Farm Shop & Garden Centre: open every day. Maze: weekends and school holidays 11am-4pm (Feb-Oct). Light Railway: weekends and Weds. **Admission:** House & Chapel: Adult £10.00, Child (5-15yrs) £5.00, Conc. £8.00, Family (2+3) £25.00. Groups/educational visits by arrangement.
Key facts: Private & corporate hire. Suitable. WCs. Licensed. By arrangement. By arrangement. Guide dogs only. Grounds.

© Weald & Downland Open Air Museum

WEALD & DOWNLAND OPEN AIR MUSEUM

Town Lane, Singleton, Chichester, West Sussex PO18 0EU

www.wealddown.co.uk

The Museum is home to over 50 rescued historic rural buildings, reconstructed in 40 acres of beautiful parkland in the South Downs. Six of its historic houses include carefully researched period gardens, showcasing plants, herbs and flowers grown by our ancestors. See the working smithy, watermill and Tudor kitchen. Watch seasonal domestic, craft and farming demonstrations. Enjoy the tranquillity of the site, with working Shire horses and oxen, plus traditional breed farm animals and poultry. **Location:** Map 3:F5. OS Ref SU875 127.
Off A286 Chichester to Midhurst road at Singleton.
Contact: Katie Jardine **Tel:** 01243 811363 / 24-hours 01243 811348
E-mail: office@wealddown.co.uk **Open:** 10.30am-6pm during British Summer Time. 10.30am-4pm at other times. Winter opening dates vary - see website for details. **Admission:** Adult £13, Child £7, Over 65 £12, Family £36 (2 adults plus 3 children), Disabled plus carer £5. Prices include optional Gift Aid donation.
Key facts: Partial. WCs. Parking. New café opening spring 2017 Pre-bookable. Free. On leads. Limited winter opening.

WILMINGTON PRIORY

Wilmington, Nr Eastbourne, East Sussex BN26 5SW

www.landmarktrust.org.uk

The Priory is part of an outstanding now mostly ruinous monastic site in the South Downs, combined with the comfort of rooms improved by the Georgians. This area was beloved by the Bloomsbury set whose influential houses are nearby; it's close to Glyndebourne and a few miles from the sea.
Location: Map 3:F5. OS Ref TQ544 042.
Owner: Leased to The Landmark Trust by Sussex Archaeological Society
Tel: 01628 825925
E-mail: bookings@landmarktrust.org.uk
Open: Self-catering accommodation. 30 days Apr-Oct, contact for details.
Admission: Free on Open Days, visits by appointment.
Key facts: A vaulted medieval entrance porch leading off the large farmhouse kitchen makes an atmospheric summer dining room and the monastic ruins are yours to wander.

ARUNDEL CATHEDRAL

London Road, Arundel, West Sussex BN18 9AY

French Gothic Cathedral, church of the RC Diocese of Arundel and Brighton built by Henry, 15th Duke of Norfolk and opened 1873. **Location:** Map 3:G6. OS Ref TQ015 072.
Above junction of A27 and A284.
Owner: Diocese of Arundel and Brighton
Contact: Rev. Canon T. Madeley
Tel: 01903 882297 **Fax:** 01903 885335
E-mail: aruncath1@aol.com
Website: www.arundelcathedral.org
Open: Summer: 9am-6pm. Winter: 9am-dusk. Tue, Wed, Fri, Sat: Mass 10am; Mon and Thu: Mass 8.30am (at Convent of Poor Clares, Crossbush); Sat: Vigil Mass 6.15pm (at Convent of Poor Clares, Crossbush); Sun: Masses 9.30am and 11.15am. Shop open in the summer, Mon-Fri, 10am-4pm and after services and on special occasions and otherwise on request. **Admission:** Free.
Key facts: By arrangement.

COWDRAY HERITAGE TRUST

River Ground Stables, Midhurst, West Sussex GU29 9AL

Cowdray is one of the most important survivals of a Tudor nobleman's house. Set within the stunning landscape of Cowdray Park, the house was partially destroyed by fire in 1793. Explore the Tudor Kitchen, Buck Hall, Chapel, Gatehouse, Vaulted Storeroom and Cellars, Visitor Centre and Shop.
Location: Map 3:F5. OS Ref TQ891 216. On the outskirts of Midhurst on A272.
Owner: Cowdray Heritage Trust **Contact:** The Manager **Tel:** 01730 812423
Visitor Centre Tel: 01730 810781 (during opening hours only).
E-mail: heritage@cowdray.co.uk **Website:** www.cowdray.co.uk
Open: Please check our website for opening times. Groups all year round by arrangement. **Admission:** Check website for details.
Key facts: Full level access, WCs, limited disabled parking.
Free audio guides. Children's tour available.
In Midhurst by bus stand, a short walk along causeway.

1066 BATTLE OF HASTINGS

Battle, Sussex TN33 0AD

Founded in penance by William the Conqueror following the Norman defeat of the English in 1066. **Location:** Map 4:K5. OS Ref TQ749 157. Top of Battle High St.
Tel: 01424 775705 **E-mail:** customers@english-heritage.org.uk
Website: www.english-heritage.org.uk/1066
Open: 1 Nov-31 Mar, Sat & Sun, 10am-4pm; Apr-Oct, daily 10am-5pm; daily at half term & 27-31 Dec. **Admission:** Adult £11.20; Child £6.70.

ANNE OF CLEVES HOUSE

52 Southover High Street, Lewes, East Sussex BN7 1JA

Location: Map 4:I5. OS Ref TQ412 096.
Tel: 01273 474610
E-mail: Anne@sussexpast.co.uk
Open: Feb, 1 Nov-16 Dec, Tue-Sun, 10am-4pm; Mar-Oct, Tue-Sat, 10am-5pm, Sun, Mon & BH, 11am-5pm; Nov-16 Dec, Tue-Sun, 11am-5pm.
Admission: Adult £5.60; Child £3.10.

BODIAM CASTLE

Bodiam, Nr Robertsbridge, East Sussex TN32 5UA

Built in 1385 to defend the surrounding countryside and as a comfortable dwelling for a rich nobleman. One of the finest examples of medieval architecture.
Location: Map 4:K5. OS Ref TQ785 256. 3m S of Hawkhurst, 2m E of A21 Hurst Green. **Tel:** 01580 830196 **E-mail:** bodiamcastle@nationaltrust.org.uk
Website: www.nationaltrust.org.uk/bodiam-castle
Open: All year, daily, 10-5pm. Closed 24 & 25 Dec.

DENMANS GARDEN

Denmans Lane, Fontwell, Denmans Lane BN18 0SU

Unique 4 acre garden. **Location:** Map 3:G6. OS Ref SU944 070.
Tel: 01243 542808
E-mail: denmans@denmans-garden.co.uk
Website: www.denmans-garden.co.uk
Open: 10am-4pm daily all year - check website for winter opening times.
Admission: Adults £5.95; OAP £5.50.

FISHBOURNE ROMAN PALACE

Salthill Road, Fishbourne, Chichester, Sussex PO19 3QR

The remains of a palatial Roman building constructed in the 1st Century AD. View the stunning Roman mosaics and the replanted Roman garden.
Location: Map 3:F6. OS Ref SU838 047. 1.5m W of Chichester in Fishbourne village off A27/A259. **Tel:** 01243 785859 **E-mail:** adminfish@sussexpast.co.uk
Website: www.sussexpast.co.uk/fishbourne **Open:** Feb & Nov-15 Dec, daily, 10-4pm; Mar-Oct, daily, 10-5pm. **Admission:** Adult £8.90; Child £4.20.

GLYNDE PLACE

Glynde, East Sussex BN8 6SX

Glynde Place is a magnificent example of Elizabethan architecture commanding exceptionally fine views of the South Downs. **Location:** Map 4:J5. OS Ref TQ456 092. Signposted off the A27, 4m SE of Lewes at top of village.
Tel: 01273 858224 **E-mail:** info@glynde.co.uk **Website:** www.glyndeplace.co.uk
Open: Wed, Thu, Sun, May & Jun, plus Aug BHs, 2-5pm.
Admission: Adult £5; Child £3.

HASTINGS CASTLE

Castle Hill Road, West Hill, Hastings, East Sussex TN34 3AR

Location: Map 5:L5. OS Ref TQ825 094.
Tel: 01424 444412
E-mail: bookings@discoverhastings.co.uk
Open: All year, daily, 10-5pm.
Admission: Adult £4.25; Child £3.95.

HIGH BEECHES WOODLAND & WATER GARDEN

High Beeches Lane, Handcross, West Sussex RH17 6HQ

A hidden gem in the High Weald of Sussex sensitively planted with many rare trees and plants. **Location:** Map 4:I4. OS Ref TQ274 309. **Tel:** 01444 400589
Website: www.highbeeches.com **Open:** Apr-1 Nov: except Weds, 1-5pm (last adm. 4.30pm). Tours anytime, by appointment only. **Admission:** Adult £7.50

LEWES CASTLE & MUSEUM

Barbican House, 169 High Street, Lewes, East Sussex BN7 1YE

Climb to the top of this 1000 year old Norman Castle for stunning panoramic views across Sussex and explore the Museum of Sussex Archaeology.
Location: Map 4:I6. OS Ref TQ414 100. **Tel:** 01273 486290
Website: www.sussexpast.co.uk/properties-to-discover/lewes-castle
Open: Nov-Feb, daily, 10am-3.45pm; Mar-Oct, Tue-Sat, 10am-5.30pm, Sun, Mon & BH, 11am-5pm. **Admission:** Adult £7.40; Child £4.

MICHELHAM PRIORY

Upper Dicker, Hailsham, East Sussex BN27 3QS

England's longest medieval water filled moat surrounds the site which dates back to 1229. **Location:** Map 4:J6. OS Ref TQ557 094.
Tel: 01323 844224 **E-mail:** adminmich@sussexpast.co.uk
Open: 13-28 Feb, daily, 11am-4pm; Mar-Oct, daily, 10.30am-5pm; Nov-20 Dec, daily, 11am-4pm.
Admission: Adult £8.90; Child £4.50.

PASHLEY MANOR GARDENS

Pashley Manor, Ticehurst, Wadhurst, East Sussex TN5 7HE

Pashley offers a sumptuous blend of romantic landscaping, imaginative plantings, fine old trees, fountains and ponds. **Location:** Map 4:K4. OS Ref TQ702 296. On B2099 between A21 and Ticehurst Village.
Tel: 01580 200888 **E-mail:** info@pashleymanorgardens.com
Website: www.pashleymanorgardens.com **Open:** All year, Tue-Sat, 10am-5pm; Sun, 2-5pm. **Admission:** Adult £6.60; Child £3.50.

PRESTON MANOR

Preston Drove, Brighton, East Sussex BN1 6SD

A delightful Manor House which powerfully evokes the atmosphere of an Edwardian gentry home both 'upstairs' and 'downstairs'. **Location:** Map 4:I6. OS Ref TQ303 064. 2m N of Brighton seafront on A23 London Road.
Tel: 03000 290900 **E-mail:** visitor.services@brighton-hove.gov.uk
Website: www.prestonmanor.virtualmuseum.info **Open:** All year, Tue-Sat, 10am-5pm; Sun, 2-5pm. **Admission:** Adult £6.60; Child £3.50.

THE ROYAL PAVILION

Brighton, East Sussex BN1 1EE

Universally acclaimed as one of the most exotically beautiful buildings in the British Isles, the Royal Pavilion is the former seaside residence of King George IV.
Location: Map 4:I6. OS Ref TQ312 041. **Tel:** 03000 290900
E-mail: visitor.services@brighton-hove.gov.uk
Website: www.royalpavilion.org.uk **Open:** Jan-Mar, daily, 10am-5.15pm; Apr-Sep, daily, 9.30am-5.45pm; Oct-Dec, daily, 10am-5.15pm. Closed 24-26 Dec.

SACKVILLE COLLEGE

High Street, East Grinstead, West Sussex RH19 3BX

Built in 1609 for Robert Sackville, Earl of Dorset, as an almshouse and overnight accommodation for the Sackville family. **Location:** Map 4:I4. OS Ref TQ397 380. A22 to East Grinstead, College in High Street (town centre).
Tel: 01342 323414 **E-mail:** admin@sackvillecollege.org.uk
Website: www.sackvillecollege.org.uk **Open:** Mid-Jun-mid-Sep, Wed-Sun, 2-5pm. Groups all year by arrangement. **Admission:** Adult £4.50; Child £1.

WEST DEAN COLLEGE & GARDENS

West Dean, Chichester, West Sussex PO18 0RX

An impressive collection of working Victorian Glasshouses, a 300 foot pergola, a spring garden and the occasional surreal fibreglass tree offer year-round interest.
Location: Map 3:F5. OS Ref SU865 129.
Tel: Gardens: 01243 818210 **E-mail:** enquiries@westdean.org.uk
Website: www.westdean.org.uk **Open:** Feb-24 Dec, Mon-Fri, 10.30am-5pm, Sat & Sun, 9am-5pm. **Admission:** Adult £8.50; Feb, Nov, Dec: Adult £5.50.

WOOLBEDING GARDENS

Midhurst, West Sussex GU29 9RR

Woolbeding is a modern garden masterpiece, with constantly evolving colour-themed garden rooms surrounding the house and magical landscape garden.
Location: Map 3:F5. OS Ref SU872 227. No parking in the local area, apart from disabled. **Tel:** 0844 249 1895 **E-mail:** woolbedinggardens@nationaltrust.org.uk
Website: www.nationaltrust.org.uk/woolbeding **Open:** 7 Apr-30 Sep, Tue & Fri, 10.30am-4.30pm. **Admission:** Adult £8.40; Child £4.20. Booking essential.

Chichester Cathedral

VISITOR INFORMATION

Owner
English Heritage

Address
Osborne House
East Cowes
Isle of Wight
PO32 6JX

Location
Map 3:D6
OS Ref. SZ516 948
1 mile SE of East Cowes.
Ferry: Isle of Wight ferry terminals. Red Funnel, East Cowes 1½ miles Tel: 02380 334010. Wightlink, Fishbourne 4 miles Tel: 0870 582 7744

Contact
The House Administrator
Tel: 01983 200022
Venue Hire and Hospitality Tel: 01983 203055
E-mail: customers@english-heritage.org.uk

Opening Times
2 Jan-31 Mar, 1-13 Nov,
Sat & Sun, 10am-4pm;
Apr-Oct, 3-4 Dec,
daily, 10am-5pm; 27-31 Dec,
daily, 10am-4pm.

Admission
Adult: £16.50
Child: £9.50

Special Events
There is an exciting events programme available throughout the year, for further details please contact the property or visit the website.

Conference/Function

ROOM	Max Cap
Duchess of Kent Suite	Standing 70 Seated 30
Durbar Hall	Standing/Seated 40
Marquee	Large scale events possible
Upper Terrace	Standing 250
Victoria Hall	Standing 120 Seated 80

© English Heritage

OSBORNE HOUSE

www.english-heritage.org.uk/osborne

Take an intimate glimpse into the family life of Britain's longest reigning monarch and the house Queen Victoria loved to call home.

Osborne House was a peaceful, seaside retreat of Queen Victoria, Prince Albert and their family. Step inside and marvel at the richness of the State Apartments including the lavish Indian Durbar Room.

The Queen died at the house in 1901 and many of the rooms have been preserved almost unaltered ever since. The nursery bedroom remains just as it was in the 1870s when Queen Victoria's first grandchildren came to stay.

Don't miss the Swiss Cottage, a charming chalet in the grounds built for teaching the royal children domestic skills. Enjoy the beautiful gardens with their stunning views over the Solent, the fruit and flower Victorian Walled Garden and Queen Victoria's private beach – now open to visitors for the first time.

Osborne hosts events throughout the year, and Queen Victoria's palace-by-the-sea offers both the superb coastal location and facilities for those who want to entertain on a grand scale in style.

KEY FACTS

- Available for corporate and private hire. Suitable for filming, concerts, drama. No photography in the house.
- Private and corporate hire.
- WCs.
- Nov-Mar for pre-booked guided tours only. Tours allow visitors to see the Royal Apartments and private rooms.
- Ample.
- Please book. Education room.

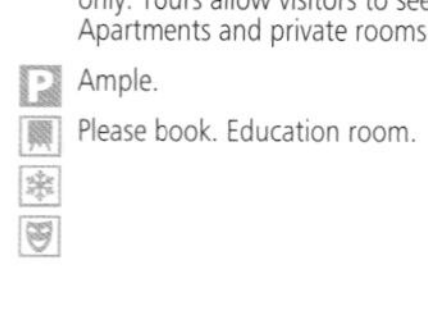

© English Heritage

© English Heritage

Register for news and special offers at www.hudsonsheritage.com

ASHDOWN HOUSE
Lambourn, Newbury, Berkshire RG17 8RE
Tel: 01494 755569 **E-mail:** ashdown@nationaltrust.org.uk

BASILDON PARK
Lower Basildon, Reading, Berkshire RG8 9NR
Tel: 0118 984 3040 **E-mail:** basildonpark@nationaltrust.org.uk

SHAW HOUSE
Church Road, Shaw, Newbury, Berkshire RG14 2DR
Tel: 01635 279279 **E-mail:** shawhouse@westberks.gov.uk

ASCOTT
Wing, Leighton Buzzard, Buckinghamshire LU7 0PR
Tel: 01296 688242 **E-mail:** info@ascottestate.co.uk

WEST WYCOMBE PARK
West Wycombe, High Wycombe, Buckinghamshire HP14 3AJ
Tel: 01494 513569

BREAMORE HOUSE & MUSEUM
Breamore, Fordingbridge, Hampshire SP6 2DF
Tel: 01725 512858 **E-mail:** breamore@btinternet.com

JANE AUSTEN'S HOUSE MUSEUM
Chawton, Alton, Hampshire GU34 1SD
Tel: 01420 83262 **E-mail:** enquiries@jahmusm.org.uk

PORTCHESTER CASTLE
Portsmouth, Hampshire PO16 9QW
Tel: 02392 378291 **E-mail:** customers@english-heritage.org.uk

SIR HAROLD HILLIER GARDENS
Jermyns Lane, Ampfield, Romsey, Hampshire SO51 0QA
Tel: 01794 369318 **E-mail:** info@hilliergardens.org.uk

WINCHESTER CATHEDRAL
9 The Close, Winchester SO23 9LS
Tel: 01962 857200 **E-mail:** visits@winchester-cathedral.org.uk

CARISBROOKE CASTLE
Newport, Isle Of Wight PO30 1XY
Tel: 01983 522107 **E-mail:** customers@english-heritage.org.uk

NUNWELL HOUSE & GARDENS
Coach Lane, Brading, Isle Of Wight PO36 0JQ
Tel: 01983 407240 **E-mail:** info@nunwellhouse.co.uk

BOUGHTON MONCHELSEA PLACE
Boughton Monchelsea, Nr Maidstone, Kent ME17 4BU
Tel: 01622 743120 **E-mail:** mk@boughtonplace.co.uk

CHILHAM CASTLE
Canterbury, Kent CT4 8DB
Tel: 01227 733100 **E-mail:** chilhamcastleinfo@gmail.com

DEAL CASTLE
Victoria Road, Deal, Kent CT14 7BA
Tel: 01304 372762 **E-mail:** customers@english-heritage.org.uk

EMMETTS GARDEN
Ide Hill, Sevenoaks, Kent TN14 6BA
Tel: 01732 750367 **E-mail:** emmetts@nationaltrust.org.uk

Hever Castle

GODINTON HOUSE AND GARDENS
Godinton Lane, Ashford, Kent TN23 3BP
Tel: 01233 620773 **E-mail:** info@godinton-house-gardens.co.uk

GREAT COMP GARDEN
Comp Lane, Platt, Borough Green, Kent TN15 8QS
Tel: 01732 886154 **E-mail:** info@greatcompgarden.co.uk

GROOMBRIDGE PLACE GARDENS
Groombridge, Tunbridge Wells, Kent TN3 9QG
Tel: 01892 861 444 **E-mail:** carrie@groombridge.co.uk

HALL PLACE & GARDENS
Bourne Road, Bexley, Kent DA5 1PQ
Tel: 01322 526574 **E-mail:** info@hallplace.org.uk

LULLINGSTONE ROMAN VILLA
Lullingstone Lane, Eynsford, Kent DA4 0JA
Tel: 01322 863467 **E-mail:** customers@english-heritage.org.uk

QUEBEC HOUSE
Westerham, Kent TN16 1TD
Tel: 01732 868381

ROCHESTER CASTLE
The Lodge, Rochester-Upon-Medway, Medway ME1 1SW
Tel: 01634 402276 **E-mail:** customers@english-heritage.org.uk

ST AUGUSTINE'S ABBEY
Longport, Canterbury, Kent CT1 1TF
Tel: 01227 767345 **E-mail:** customers@english-heritage.org.uk

SMALLHYTHE PLACE
Smallhythe, Tenterden, Kent TN30 7NG
Tel: 01580 762334

TUDOR HOUSE
King Street, Margate, Kent CT9 1QE
Tel: 01843 577577 **E-mail:** visitorinformation@thanet.gov.uk

ARDINGTON HOUSE
Wantage, Oxfordshire OX12 8QA
Tel: 01235 821566 **E-mail:** info@ardingtonhouse.com

CHASTLETON HOUSE
Chastleton, Nr Moreton-In-Marsh, Oxfordshire
Tel: 01608 674981 **E-mail:** chastleton@nationaltrust.org.uk

GREYS COURT
Rotherfield Greys, Henley-On-Thames, Oxfordshire RG9 4PG
Tel: 01491 628529 **E-mail:** greyscourt@nationaltrust.org.uk

MINSTER LOVELL HALL & DOVECOTE
Minster Lovell, Oxfordshire OX29 0RR
Tel: 0870 333 1181

NUFFIELD PLACE
Huntercombe, Henley on Thames RG9 5RY
Tel: 01491 641224 **E-mail:** nuffieldplace@nationaltrust.org.uk

WATERPERRY GARDENS
Waterperry, Nr Wheatley, Oxfordshire OX33 1JZ
Tel: 01844 339226 **E-mail:** office@waterperrygardens.co.uk

GODDARDS
Abinger Common, Dorking, Surrey RH5 6TH
Tel: 01628 825925 **E-mail:** bookings@landmarktrust.org.uk

RHS GARDEN WISLEY
Nr Woking, Surrey GU23 6QB
Tel: 0845 260 9000

VANN
Hambledon, Godalming GU8 4EF
E-mail: vann@caroe.com

ALFRISTON CLERGY HOUSE
The Tye, Alfriston, Nr Polegate, East Sussex BN26 5TL
Tel: 01323 871961 **E-mail:** alfriston@nationaltrust.org.uk

LEWES PRIORY
Town Hall, High Street, Lewes, East Sussex BN7 2QS
Tel: 01273 486185 **E-mail:** enquiries@lewespriory.org.uk

PALLANT HOUSE GALLERY
9 North Pallant, Chichester, West Sussex PO19 1TJ
Tel: 01243 774557 **E-mail:** info@pallant.org.uk

PEVENSEY CASTLE
Pevensey, Sussex BN24 5LE
Tel: 01323 762604 **E-mail:** customers@english-heritage.org.uk

WAKEHURST PLACE
Ardingly Road, North of Ardingly, West Sussex RH17 6TN
Tel: 01444 894004 **E-mail:** wakehurst@kew.org

Great Fosters Entrance

Register for news and special offers at www.hudsonsheritage.com

THE COLLEGES OF OXFORD UNIVERSITY

For further details contact
Oxford Information Centre,
15-16 Broad Street, Oxford OX1 3AS
Tel: +44 (0)1865 726871
Email: tic@oxford.gov.uk
Fax: +44 (0)1865 240261
www.visitoxford.org

BIDWELLS

All Souls' College
High Street
Tel: 01865 279379
Founder: Archbishop Henry Chichele 1438
Open: Mon-Fri, 2-4pm (4.30pm in summer)

Balliol College
Broad Street
Tel: 01865 277777
Founder: John de Balliol 1263
Open: Daily, 1-5pm (or dusk)

Brasenose College
Radcliffe Square
Tel: 01865 277830
Founder: William Smythe, Bishop of Lincoln 1509
Open: Daily, 10-11.30am (tour groups only) & 2-4.30pm (5pm in summer)

Christ Church
St. Aldates
Tel: 01865 286573
Founder: Cardinal Wolsey/Henry VIII 1546
Open: Mon-Sat 9am-5.30pm; Sun, 1-5.30pm (last adm 4.30pm)

Corpus Christi College
Merton Street
Tel: 01865 276700
Founder: Bishop Richard Fox 1517
Open: Daily, 1.30-4.30pm

Exeter College
Turl Street
Tel: 01865 279600
Founder: Bishop Stapleden of Exeter 1314
Open: Daily, 2-5pm

Green College
Woodstock Road
Tel: 01865 274770
Founder: Dr Cecil Green 1979
Open: By appointment only

Harris Manchester College
Mansfield Road
Tel: 01865 271011
Founder: Lord Harris of Peckham 1996
Open: Chapel only: Mon-Fri, 8.30am-5.30pm. Sat, 9am-12 noon

Hertford College
Catte Street
Tel: 01865 279400
Founder: TC Baring MP 1740
Open: Daily, 10am-noon & 2pm-dusk

Jesus College
Turl Street
Tel: 01865 279700
Founder: Dr Hugh Price (Queen Elizabeth I) 1571
Open: Daily, 2-4.30pm

Keble College
Parks Road
Tel: 01865 272727
Founder: Public money 1870
Open: Daily, 2-5pm

Kellogg College
Banbury Road
Tel: 01865 61200
Founder: Kellogg Foundation 1990
Open: Mon-Fri, 9am-5pm

Lady Margaret Hall
Norham Gardens
Tel: 01865 274300
Founder: Dame Elizabeth Wordsworth 1878
Open: Gardens: 10am-5pm

Linacre College
St Cross Road
Tel: 01865 271650
Founder: Oxford University 1962
Open: By appointment only

Lincoln College
Turl Street
Tel: 01865 279800
Founder: Bishop Richard Fleming of Lincoln 1427
Open: Mon-Sat, 2-5pm; Sun, 11 am-5pm

Magdalen College
High Street
Tel: 01865 276000
Founder: William of Waynefleete 1458
Open: Oct-Jun: 1-6pm/dusk (whichever is the earlier) and Jul-Sept 12 noon-6pm

Mansfield College
Mansfield Road
Tel: 01865 270999
Founder: Free Churches 1995
Open: Mon-Fri, 9am-5pm

Merton College
Merton Street
Tel: 01865 276310
Founder: Walter de Merton 1264
Open: Mon-Fri, 2-4pm; Sat & Sun, 10am-4pm

New College
New College Lane
Tel: 01865 279555
Founder: William of Wykeham, Bishop of Winchester 1379
Open: Daily, 11 am-5pm (summer); 2-4pm (winter)

Nuffield College
New Road
Tel: 01865 278500
Founder: William Morris (Lord Nuffield) 1937
Open: Daily, 9am-5pm

Oriel College
Oriel Square
Tel: 01865 276555
Founder: Edward II/Adam de Brome 1326
Open: By arrangement with TIC

Pembroke College
St Aldates
Tel: 01865 276444
Founder: James I 1624
Open: By appointment only

The Queen's College
High Street
Tel: 01865 279120
Founder: Robert de Eglesfield 1341
Open: By arrangement with TIC

Somerville College
Graduate House, Woodstock Road
Tel: 01865 270600
Founder: Association for the Education of Women 1879
Open: 2-5.30pm

St. Anne's College
56 Woodstock Road
Tel: 01865 274800
Founder: Association for the Education of Women 1878
Open: 9am-5pm

St. Antony's College
62 Woodstock Road
Tel: 01865 284700
Founder: M. Antonin Bess 1948
Open: By appointment only

St. Catherine's College
Manor Road
Tel: 01865 271700
Founder: Oxford University 1964
Open: 9am-5pm

St. Edmund Hall
Queens Lane
Tel: 01865 279000
Founder: St. Edmund Riche of Abingdon c.1278
Open: Mon-Sun, Term time, 12 noon-4pm

St. Hilda's College
Cowley Place
Tel: 01865 276884
Founder: Miss Dorothea Beale 1893
Open: By appointment only

St. Hugh's College
St. Margarets Road
Tel: 01865 274900
Founder: Dame Elizabeth Wordsworth 1886
Open: 10am-4pm

St. John's College
St. Giles
Tel: 01865 277300
Founder: Sir Thomas White 1555
Open: 1-5pm (or dusk)

St. Peter's College
New Inn Hall Street
Tel: 01865 278900
Founder: Rev. Christopher Charvasse 1928
Open: 10am-5pm

Trinity College
Broad Street
Tel: 01865 279900
Founder: Sir Thomas Pope 1554-5
Open: Mon-Fri 10am-noon and 2-4pm. Sat & Sun in term, 2-4pm; Sat & Sun in vacation 10am-12 noon and 2-4pm

University College
High Street
Tel: 01865 276602
Founder: Archdeacon William of Durham 1249
Open: Contact College for details

Wadham College
Parks Road
Tel: 01865 277900
Founder: Nicholas & Dorothy Wadham 1610
Open: Term time: daily, 1-4.15pm.
Vacation: daily, 10.30-11.45am & 1-4.15pm

Wolfson College
Linton Road
Tel: 01865 274100
Founder: Oxford University 1966
Open: Daylight hours

Worcester College
Worcester Street
Tel: 01865 278300
Founder: Sir Thomas Cookes 1714
Open: Daily, 2-5pm

Christchurch College, Oxford

Colleges are working buildings; times are subject to change and charges may apply. Groups must book in advance. Many halls are only open before 12pm. Libraries & Fellows' Gardens are generally private. Please call at the Porters' Lodge first.

Caerhays Castle, Cornwall

Mapperton, Dorset

Cornwall
Devon
Dorset
Gloucestershire
Somerset
Wiltshire

South West

From Poldark in Cornwall to Hardy in Wessex, there is plenty of romance in the South West. The airy gothic villas of Devon and Cornwall, Tudor mansions of Gloucestershire and stunning gardens of Dorset and Somerset make this a region to find your own secret places.

Find stylish hotels with a personal welcome and good cuisine in the South West. More information on page 348.

- Alexandra Hotel
- Berry Head Hotel
- The Cottage Hotel
- Hannafore Point Hotel
- Ilsington Country House Hotel
- The Inn at Fossebridge
- The Lordleaze Hotel
- The Manor Hotel
- Mortons House Hotel
- Northcote Manor
- The Pear Tree at Purton
- Plumber Manor
- Purbeck House Hotel

www.signpost.co.uk

VISITOR INFORMATION

■ Owner
English Heritage

■ Address
Tintagel
Cornwall
PL34 0HE

■ Location
Map 1:F7
OS Ref. SX054 885
On Tintagel Head, ½m along uneven track from Tintagel.

■ Contact
Visitor Operations Team
Tel: 01840 770328
E-mail: tintagel.castle@english-heritage.org.uk

■ Opening Times
2 Jan-31 Mar & Nov-Dec, Sat & Sun, 10am-4pm; daily at half term;
Apr-Oct, daily, 10am-5pm.
Closed 24-26 Dec & 1 Jan.

■ Admission

Adult:	£6.20
Child:	£3.70

■ Special Events
There is an exciting events programme available throughout the year, for further details please contact the property or visit the website.

© EHPL / Skyscan

TINTAGEL CASTLE ⌗

www.english-heritage.org.uk/tintagel

Tintagel Castle is a magical day with its wonderful location, set high on the rugged North Cornwall coast.

Steeped in legend and mystery; said to be the birthplace of King Arthur, you can still visit the nearby Merlin's Cave. The castle also features in the tale of Tristan and Isolde.

Joined to the mainland by a narrow neck of land, Tintagel Island faces the full force of the Atlantic. On the mainland, the remains of the medieval castle represent only one phase in a long history of occupation.

The remains of the 13th Century castle are breathtaking. Steep stone steps, stout walls and rugged windswept cliff edges encircle the Great Hall, where Richard Earl of Cornwall once feasted.

KEY FACTS

- WC. Video film shown about the Legend of Arthur.
- (shop)
- (refreshments)
- P No vehicles. Parking (not EH) in village only.
- (guide book)
- Dogs on leads only.
- (open all year)
- (English Heritage)

© English Heritage

© English Heritage

Register for news and special offers at **www.hudsonsheritage.com**

BOCONNOC

THE ESTATE OFFICE, BOCONNOC, LOSTWITHIEL, CORNWALL PL22 0RG

www.boconnoc.com

Boconnoc House, the winner of the 2012 HHA/Sotheby's Award for Restoration and the Georgian Group Award, was bought with the proceeds of the Pitt Diamond in 1717. Three Prime Ministers, a history of duels and the architect Sir John Soane play a part in the story of this unique estate. The beautiful woodland garden, the Georgian Bath House, Soane Stable Yard, 15th Century Church and naturesque landscape tempt the explorer. The Boconnoc Music Award for ensembles from the Royal College of Music, the Cornwall Spring Flower Show and fairytale weddings are part of Boconnoc today, in between filming, fashion shoots, corporate days and private parties. Groups by appointment (15-150).

Location: Map 1:G8. OS Ref SX146 606. A38 from Plymouth, Liskeard or from Bodmin to Dobwalls, then A390 to East Taphouse and follow signs.

Owner: Boconnoc Trustees **Contact:** Sima Gordiz

Tel: 01208 872507 **Fax:** 01208 873836 **E-mail:** office@boconnoc.com

Open: Garden: 7, 14, 21, 28 May. 2-5pm. Private Tours 2017: 8 May, 23 May, 13 Jun, 25 Jul, 14 Aug, 12 Sep. Special Events: Cornwall Garden Society Spring Flower Show: 1, 2 Apr, Boconnoc Music Award concerts with the Royal College of Music 18 & 20 Jul, Steam Fair at Boconnoc 28-30 Jul, Motorsport Carnival 12 Aug, Landscape Art Course 22-24 Sep, Glow in the Park Night Run 14 Oct. Group bookings daily by appointment.

Admission: House £14.00; Garden £4.00; Child (under 12yrs) Free.

Key facts: Conferences and accommodation. Partial. Licensed. By appointment. Yes. By appointment. In grounds, on leads. 18 doubles (9 en suite). Holiday and residential houses to let. Church or Civil ceremony. By Appointment.

CAERHAYS CASTLE & GARDEN

CAERHAYS, GORRAN, ST AUSTELL, CORNWALL PL26 6LY

www.caerhays.co.uk

One of the very few Nash built castles still left standing - situated within approximately 140 acres of informal woodland gardens created by J C Williams, who sponsored plant hunting expeditions to China at the turn of the century. As well as guided tours of the house from March to June visitors will see some of the magnificent selection of plants brought back by the intrepid plant hunters of the early 1900s these include not only a national collection of magnolias but a wide range of rhododendrons and the camellias which Caerhays and the Williams family are associated with worldwide.

Location: Map 1:F9. OS Ref SW972 415. S coast of Cornwall - between Mevagissey and Portloe. 9m SW of St Austell.

Owner: F J Williams Esq **Contact:** Lucinda Rimmington

Bookings and Enquiries: Sophie Hodge

Tel: 01872 501310 **Fax:** 01872 501870 **E-mail:** enquiries@caerhays.co.uk

Open: House: 20 Mar-16 Jun: Mon-Fri only (including BHs), tours 11.30am, 1pm and 2.30pm, booking recommended. Gardens: 20 Feb-18 Jun: daily (including BHs), 10am-5pm (last admission 4pm).

Admission: House £8.50; Gardens £8.50; House & Gardens £13.50. Group tours: by arrangement. Groups please contact Estate Office.

Key facts: No photography in house. Selling a range of Caerhays products & many other garden orientated gifts. Located beside entrance point. The Georgian Hall is available for hire for meetings. The Magnolia Tea Rooms serve a wide range of foods using locally sourced produce. Obligatory. By arrangement. Limited for large coaches. On leads. Caerhays has a selection of 5* properties available for hire for self-catering holidays. Weddings can be held at The Vean or the Coastguard's Lookout with marquee receptions in the castle grounds.

PRIDEAUX PLACE

PADSTOW, CORNWALL PL28 8RP

www.prideauxplace.co.uk

Tucked away above the busy port of Padstow, the home of the Prideaux family for over 400 years, is surrounded by gardens and wooded grounds overlooking a deer park and the Camel estuary to the moors beyond. The house still retains its 'E' shape Elizabethan front and contains fine paintings and furniture. Now a major international film location, this family home is one of the brightest jewels in Cornwall's crown. The historic garden is undergoing major restoration work and offers some of the best views in the county. A cornucopia of Cornish history under one roof.

Location: Map 1:E8. OS Ref SW913 756. 5m from A39 Newquay/Wadebridge link road. Signposted by Historic House signs.

Owner/Contact: Peter Prideaux-Brune Esq

Tel: 01841 532411 **Fax:** 01841 532945 **E-mail:** office@prideauxplace.co.uk

Open: Easter Sun 16 Apr-Thu 5 Oct (closed Sun 30 Apr-Wed 3 May). Grounds and Tea Room: 12.30-5pm. House Tours: 1.30-4pm (last tour).

Admission: House & Grounds: Adult £9.00, Child 12-16 years £5.00, Child U12 free. Grounds only: Adult £4.00, Child 12-16 years £2.00, Child U12 free. Groups (15+) discounts apply. **Key facts:** Open air theatre, open air concerts, car rallies, art exhibitions, charity events. By arrangement. Partial. Ground floor & grounds. Fully licensed. Obligatory. By arrangement. On leads. By arrangement.

© National Trust / St Michael's Mount

© National Trust / St Michael's Mount

ST MICHAEL'S MOUNT

MARAZION, NR PENZANCE, CORNWALL TR17 0EL

www.stmichaelsmount.co.uk / www.nationaltrust.org.uk

This beautiful island has become an icon for Cornwall and has magnificent views of Mount's Bay from its summit. There the church and castle, whose origins date from the 12th Century, have at various times acted as a Benedictine priory, a place of pilgrimage, a fortress, a mansion house and now a magnet for visitors from all over the world. **Location:** Map 1:C10. OS Ref SW515 300. 3 miles East of Penzance. **Owner:** National Trust **Contact:** St Aubyn Estates

Tel: 01736 710507 **Tide Information:** 01736 710265

E-mail: enquiries@stmichaelsmount.co.uk

Open: Castle:19 Mar-2 Jul 10.30am-5pm, 3 Jul-1 Sep 10.30am-5.30pm, 3 Sep-27 Oct 10.30am-5pm.

Gardens:17 Apr-2 Jul 10.30am-5pm (Mon-Fri), 3 Jul-1 Sep 10.30am-5.30pm (Thu & Fri), 3 Sep-29 Sep 10.30am-5pm (Thu & Fri).

Admission: Castle: Adult £9.50, Child (Under 5) Free, Child (5-16) £4.50, Family (2 adults & up to 3 children) £23.50, Single Adult Family (up to 3 children) £14.00. Gardens: Adult £7.00, Child (Under 5) Free, Child (5-16) £3.50.

Key facts: For a full events calendar throughout the season, please check the website. Visit the Island Gift Shop or the Courtyard Shop for unique crafted objects, accessories & Cornish produce. Partial. WCs. Our Island Café offers expansive sea views from its garden. Opt for a light bite from the good value menu which includes pasties, coffees, freshly prepared sandwiches & cake. Our licensed restaurant serves a wide selection of light lunches, homemade breads & cakes plus fresh fish specials, using the best local, seasonal & sustainable ingredients. By arrangement. On mainland, including coach parking (not NT.) Guide dogs only. Limited opening hours in the winter.

© Pencarrow

PENCARROW HOUSE & GARDENS

Washaway, Bodmin, Cornwall PL30 3AG

www.pencarrow.co.uk

Owned, loved and lived in by the family. Georgian house and Grade II* listed gardens. Superb collection of portraits, furniture and porcelain. Marked walks through 50 acres of beautiful formal and woodland gardens, Victorian rockery, Italian garden, over 700 different varieties of rhododendrons, lake, Iron Age hill fort and icehouse. Childrens playground, Café and gift shop. Guided tours of the house Sundays to Thursdays **Location:** Map 1:F8. OS Ref SX040 711. Between Bodmin and Wadebridge. 4m NW of Bodmin off A389 & B3266 at Washaway.
Owner: Molesworth-St Aubyn family **Contact:** Administrator
Tel: 01208 841369 **E-mail:** info@pencarrow.co.uk
Open: House: 2 Apr-28 Sep, 11am-4pm (guided tour only - the last tour of the House is at 3pm). Café & Shop are open same dates & days as the house. Shop 10am-5pm. Café 11am-5pm (House, Café & shop closed Fri & Sat.) Gardens: 1 Mar-31 Oct, Daily, 10am-5.30pm. **Admission:** House & Gardens: Adult £10.75, Concession £9.75, Gardens: Adult £5.75, Concession £5.25, under 16's now free, group rates available and coaches welcome.
Key facts: Café, Gift, Plant shop & small children's play area. Partial disability access. Obligatory. Free. In grounds.

TREWITHEN GARDENS

Grampound Rd, Nr Truro, Cornwall TR2 4DD

A historic estate near Truro, Cornwall that has been lived in by the same family for 300 years. The Woodland Gardens are outstanding with 22 Champion Trees, rare and highly prized plants and Trewithen is 1 of 39 gardens internationally (1 of only 5 in the UK) recognised as a Camellia Society Garden of Excellence.
Location: Map 1:E9. OS Ref SW914 524. Grampound Road, near Truro, Cornwall on the A390. **Owner:** A M J Galsworthy
Contact: The Estate Office (Liz White) **Tel:** 01726 883647 **Fax:** 01726 882301
Liz White: secretary@trewithenestate.co.uk.
E-mail: info@trewithengardens.co.uk **Website:** www.trewithengardens.co.uk
Open: Gardens: Mar 1-Jun 31 daily 10am-4pm. House: Mar-Jun Mon & Tue afternoons 2-4pm (guided tours only - booking advisable).
Admission: Adult £8.50, Child U12 Free. Combined entry & group rates available. Concessions also available - contact us or visit website.
Key facts: No inside pics. WCs. On leads.

COTEHELE

Saint Dominick, Saltash, Cornwall PL12 6TA

Tudor house with superb collections, garden, quay and estate.
Location: Map 1:H8. OS Ref SX422 684.
Tel: 01579 351346 **E-mail:** cothele@nationaltrust.org.uk
Website: www.nationaltrust.org.uk/cotehele
Open: Gardens: All year, daily, dawn-dusk. House: Mar-Dec, daily, 11am-4pm.
Admission: Adult £10; Child £5.

LANHYDROCK

Lanhydrock, Bodmin, Cornwall PL30 5AD

The grandest house in Cornwall, set in a glorious landscape of gardens, parkland & woods overlooking the valley of the River Fowey. **Location:** Map 1:F8. OS Ref SX085 636. **Tel:** 01208 265950 **E-mail:** lanhydrock@nationaltrust.org.uk
Website: www.nationaltrust.org.uk/lanhydrock **Open:** Gardens: 14 Feb-31 Dec, 10am-5.30pm. House: 1 Mar-31 Oct, 11am-5.30pm, Dec, 11am-4pm; 5 Nov-27 Nov, Sat & Sun, 11am-4pm. **Admission:** Adult £12.65; Child £6.30.

THE LOST GARDENS OF HELIGAN

Pentewan, St Austall, Cornwall PL26 6EN

200 acres of garden history, mystery and romance.
Location: Map 1:E9. OS Ref SW999 464.
Tel: 01726 845100 **E-mail:** info@heligan.com
Website: www.heligan.com
Open: Jan-Mar, daily, 10am-5pm; Apr-Aug, daily, 10am-6pm; 1-30 Sep, daily, 10am-6pm; 1 Oct-31 Dec, daily, 10am-5pm. **Admission:** Adult £13.50; Child £6.

PENTILLIE CASTLE & ESTATE

Paynters Cross, St Mellion, Saltash, Cornwall PL12 6QD

Built in 1698 by the eccentric Sir James Tillie, Pentillie Castle sits in a beautiful position above the River Tamar, surrounded by 500 acres of parkland and gardens.
Location: Map 1:H8. OS Ref SX040 645. 7m West of Plymouth.
Tel: 01579 350044 **Fax:** 01579 212002 **E-mail:** contact@pentillie.co.uk
Website: www.pentillie.co.uk **Open:** Gardens: BH Mons in May & 21 May, tours at 2pm. Book a wedding or a group tour. **Admission:** Adult £16.50.

PENDENNIS CASTLE

Falmouth, Cornwall TR11 4LP

Explore one of Henry VIII's finest coastal fortresses, Pendennis Castle, which has defended Cornwall against foreign invasion since Tudor times.
Location: Map 1:E10. OS Ref SW824 318. On Pendennis Head.
Tel: 01326 316594 **E-mail:** pendennis.castle@english-heritage.org.uk
Website: www.english-heritage.org.uk/pendennis **Open:** Mar-Sep, daily, 10-5pm; Oct, daily, 10-4pm. **Admission:** Adult £8.70; Child £5.20.

PORT ELIOT HOUSE & GARDENS

St. Germans, Saltash, Cornwall PL12 5ND

Port Eliot is an ancient, hidden gem, set in stunning fairytale grounds which nestle beside a secret estuary in South East Cornwall. **Location:** Map 1:H8. OS Ref SX359 578. Situated in the village of St Germans on B3249 in SE Cornwall.
Tel: 01503 230211 **E-mail:** info@porteliot.co.uk
Website: www.porteliot.co.uk
Open: 27 Feb-25 Jun, Sun-Fri, 2-5.30pm. **Admission:** Adult: £8; Child £4.

RESTORMEL CASTLE

Lostwithiel, Cornwall PL22 0EE

Hilltop Norman castle, with remains of circular keep, deep moat, keep gate and Great Hall visible. **Location:** Map 1:F8. OS Ref OS200, SX104 614. 1½m N of Lostwithiel off A390. **Tel:** 01208 872687 **E-mail:** customers@english-heritage.org.uk **Website:** www.english-heritage.org.uk/restormel
Open: 2 Jan-31 Mar & Nov-Dec, Sat & Sun, 10-4pm; daily at half term;1 Apr-31 Oct, 10-5pm. Closed 24-26 Dec & 1 Jan. **Admission:** Adult £4.50; Child £2.70.

ST CATHERINE'S CASTLE

St Catherine's Cove, Fowey, Cornwall PL23 1JH

One of a pair of small artillery forts built by Henry VIII in the 1530s to defend Fowey Harbour, consisting of two storeys with gun ports at ground level.
Location: Map 1:F9. OS Ref SX118 509.
Tel: 0370 333 1181
Website: www.english-heritage.org.uk
Open: Open any reasonable time during daylight hours. **Admission:** Free.

Boconnoc

© Nick Carter

GREAT FULFORD

DUNSFORD, NR. EXETER, DEVON EX6 7AJ

www.greatfulford.co.uk

On a hill overlooking a lake and set in a landscaped park Great Fulford has been the home of the Fulford family since at least the 12th Century. The current house reflects the financial ups and downs of the family over the centuries, with a major rebuilding and enlargement taking place in 1530 and again in 1580 while in 1690 the house, which had been badly damaged in the Civil War, was fully restored. Internally then there is a stunning suite of Great Rooms which include a superb Great Hall replete with some of the finest surviving examples of early Tudor carved panelling as well as a William & Mary period Great Staircase which leads to the recently restored Great Drawing Room or Ballroom. Other rooms in the house are in the 'gothic' taste having been remodelled, as was the exterior, by James Wyatt in 1805.

Location: Map 2:J7. OS Ref SX790 917. In centre of Devon. 10m W of Exeter. South of A30 between villages of Cheriton Bishop and Dunsford.
Owner/Contact: Francis Fulford
Tel: 01647 24205 **Fax:** 01647 24401
E-mail: francis@greatfulford.co.uk
Open: All year by appointment for parties of any size but with a minimum fee of £150. Alternatively individuals can book tours on prearranged dates via www.invitationtoview.co.uk.
Admission: £9.00 per person.
Key facts: Obligatory.

HARTLAND ABBEY

NR BIDEFORD, NORTH DEVON EX39 6DT

www.hartlandabbey.com

Built in 1160, Hartland Abbey is a hidden gem on the stunning North Devon coast. Passing down generations from the Dissolution, it remains a fascinating, lived-in family home: architecture from 1160 to 1850 by Meadows and Sir George Gilbert Scott, murals, important paintings and furniture, porcelain, early photographs, documents and family memorabilia. Exhibitions: 'Filming at Hartland Abbey since 1934' and 'William Stukeley-Saviour of Stonehenge'. Woodland gardens and walks lead to the Jekyll designed Bog Garden and Fernery, restored 18th Century Walled Gardens of flowers, fruit and vegetables, the Summerhouse, Gazebo and the beach at Blackpool Mill, location for BBC's 'Sense and Sensibility' and 'The Night Manager'. Beautiful daffodils, bluebells & tulips in spring. Delicious home cooking in The Old Kitchens. 1 mile from Hartland Quay. 2016 Winner 'Best Garden and/or Country House in N Devon'. Special Events - see website. **Location:** Map 1:G5. OS Ref SS240 249. 15m W of Bideford, 15m N of Bude off A39 between Hartland and Hartland Quay on B3248.

Owner: Sir Hugh Stucley Bt **Contact:** Theresa Seligmann
Tel: 01237 441496/234 / 01884 860225 **E-mail:** ha_admin@btconnect.com
Open: House, Gardens, Grounds & Beachwalk: Sun 26 Mar-1 Oct, Sun-Thu 11am-5pm. (House 2-5pm - last admission 4.15pm). Tea Room, Light lunches & cream teas. 11am-5pm. **Admission:** House, Gardens, Grounds & Beachwalk: Adult £12.50, Child (5-15ys) £5.00, Under 5 Free, Registered disabled £8.50, Family (2+2) £29.00. Gardens, Grounds, Beachwalk & Exhibition: Adult £8.50, Child (5-15ys) £4.00, Under 5 Free, Registered disabled £5.00, Family (2+2) £22.00. Groups & coaches: Concs 20+. Open at other dates and times. Booking essential. Large car park adjacent to the house.
Key facts: Small shop in the museum selling a wide range of gifts. Plants produced in our gardens. Wedding receptions. Corporate events. Partial. WC. Homemade lunches and cream teas. By arrangement. Flat parking adjacent to house. In grounds, on leads. Five separate venues.

Register for news and special offers at **www.hudsonsheritage.com**

POWDERHAM CASTLE

KENTON, NR EXETER, DEVON EX6 8JQ

www.powderham.co.uk

Powderham Castle is the magnificent 600 year old family home of the Earl & Countess of Devon. The Castle is grade 1 listed. It sits within an ancient Deer Park and enjoys breathtaking views across the Exe Estuary. Powderham Castle and its extensive woods and gardens are open to visitors from April to October and are available all year for private functions. Visitors enjoy the unique architecture, fascinating history and exquisite interiors, furniture and artwork of the Castle on entertaining guided tours which run frequently each day. The courtyard café offers a selection of home cooked food. The gift shop, walled garden, animal and play area and an extensive calendar of events create a wonderful day out.

Location: Map 2:K7. OS Ref SX965 832. 6m SW of Exeter, 4m S M5/J30. Access from A379 in Kenton village.

Owner: The Earl & Countess of Devon **Contact:** Iain Beaumont, Castle Director

Tel: 01626 890243

E-mail: castle@powderham.co.uk

Open: Apr-Oct 2017. Please visit our website for specific dates and times. Belvedere closes on 1 Aug and American Garden on 1 Sep 2017.

Admission: Please visit www.powderham.co.uk for admission prices.

Key facts: Available for private hire, including corporate events, all year. Powderham Castle is licenced for Marriages and Civil Partnerships and offers a bridal suite and extensive accommodation. Partial. WCs. Licensed. Licensed. Obligatory. Included. 1hr. Free. Victorian Learning Programme - suitable for Key Stage 1 and 2 - An excellent learning resource to supplement children's learning outside of the classroom. Guide Dogs Welcome.

CADHAY

Ottery St Mary, Devon EX11 1QT

www.cadhay.org.uk

Cadhay is approached by an avenue of lime-trees, and stands in an extensive garden, with herbaceous borders and yew hedges, with excellent views over the original medieval fish ponds. The main part of the house was built in about 1550 by John Haydon who had married the de Cadhay heiress. He retained the Great Hall of an earlier house, of which the fine timber roof (about 1420-1460) can be seen. An Elizabethan Long Gallery was added by John's successor at the end of the 16th Century, forming a unique courtyard with statues of Sovereigns on each side, described by Sir Simon Jenkins as one of the 'Treasures of Devon'.

Location: Map 2:L6. OS Ref SY090 962. 1m NW of Ottery St Mary. From W take A30 and exit at Pattesons Cross, follow signs for Fairmile and then Cadhay. From E, exit at the Iron Bridge and follow signs as above.

Owner: Mr R Thistlethwayte **Contact:** Jayne Covell **Tel:** 01404 813511

Open: May-Sep, Fri 2pm-5pm. Also: Late May & Summer BH Sat-Sun-Mon. Last tour 4pm. **Admission:** House (Guided tour) and Gardens: Adult £8.00, Child £3.00. Gardens Only: Adults £4.00, Child £1.00. Parties of 15+ by prior arrangement. **Key facts:** Ground floor & grounds. The Apple Store is now a Tea Room Obligatory. Guide dogs only.

CASTLE HILL GARDENS

Castle Hill, Filleigh, Barnstaple, Devon EX32 0RQ

www.castlehilldevon.co.uk

Set in the rolling hills of Devon, Castle Hill Gardens offers a tranquil visit. Stroll through the spectacular gardens, dotted with mystical temples, follies, statues, vistas and a sham castle. The path through the Woodland Gardens, filled with flowering shrubs, leads you down to the river, the magical Satyr's temple and Ugley Bridge. The newly restored 18th Century Kennel dedicated to Lady Margaret Fortescue sits on the edge of Oxford Down and the Holwell Temple perches high in the woods. **Location:** Map 2:I14. OS Ref SS661 362. A361, take B3226 to South Molton. Follow brown signs to Castle Hill.

Owner: The Earl and Countess of Arran **Contact:** Marie Tippet

Tel: 01598 760421 / 01598 760336 Ext 1 **E-mail:** gardens@castlehill-devon.com

Open: Daily except Sats Apr-Sep 11am-5pm. Oct-Mar 11am-dusk. Refreshments are available from Apr-Sep. Groups and coach parties are welcome at all times by prior arrangement. **Admission:** Adults £6.00, Senior citizens £5.50, Family £15.00, Children 5-15 £2.50, Under 5's Free, Groups (20+) £5.00.

Key facts: Partial. WCs. By arrangement. Free parking. On leads. Daily except Sats.

FURSDON HOUSE AND GARDENS

Cadbury, Nr Thorverton, Exeter, Devon EX5 5JS

www.fursdon.co.uk

Fursdon House is at the heart of a small estate where the family has lived for over 750 years. Set within a hilly and wooded landscape the gardens and grounds are attractive with walled and open areas with far reaching views. Family memorabilia with fine costume and textiles are displayed on informal guided tours. Two spacious apartments and a restored Victorian cottage offer stylish holiday accommodation. **Location:** Map 2:K6. OS Ref SS922 046.
By car- Off A3072 between Bickleigh & Crediton. 9m N of Exeter signposted through Thorverton from A396 Exeter to Tiverton road **Owner:** Mr E D Fursdon
Contact: Mrs C Fursdon **Tel:** 01392 860860 **E-mail:** admin@fursdon.co.uk
Open: Gardens & Tea Room, Weds, Thus and BH Mons from Easter-end Sep 2-5pm; House open for guided tours BH Mons & Wed & Thus from Jun-Sep inclusive at 2.30pm & 3.30pm. Group Tours at other times by arrangement. Some special openings on Suns. See website for details.
Admission: House and Garden Adult £8.50, Child Free. Garden only £4.50.
Key facts: Conferences. No photography or video. Coach Hall suitable for small meetings & conferences. Max 45 seated. Coach Hall Tea Room serving cream teas & selection of cakes. Obligatory. Limited for coaches. Dogs on leads are allowed in the gardens Self-catering.

SAND

Sidbury, Sidmouth
EX10 0QN

www.SandSidbury.co.uk

Sand is one of East Devon's hidden gems. The beautiful valley garden extends to six acres and is the setting for the lived-in Tudor house, the 15th Century Hall House, and the 16th Century Summer House. The family, under whose unbroken ownership the property has remained since 1560, provide guided house tours.
Location: Map 2:L7. OS Ref SY146 925. Well signed, 400 yards off A375 between Honiton and Sidmouth. Do not rely on SatNav by postcode.
Contact: Mr & Mrs Huyshe-Shires
Tel: 01395 597230
E-mail: info@SandSidbury.co.uk
Open: Suns & Mons in Jun and BH Suns & Mons. For other dates see website. Open 2-6pm. Last tour 5pm. Groups by appointment.
Admission: House & Garden: Adult £7.50, Child/Student £1.00.
Garden only: Adult £3.00, accompanied Child (under 16) Free.
Key facts: No photography in house Partial.
Obligatory. On leads.

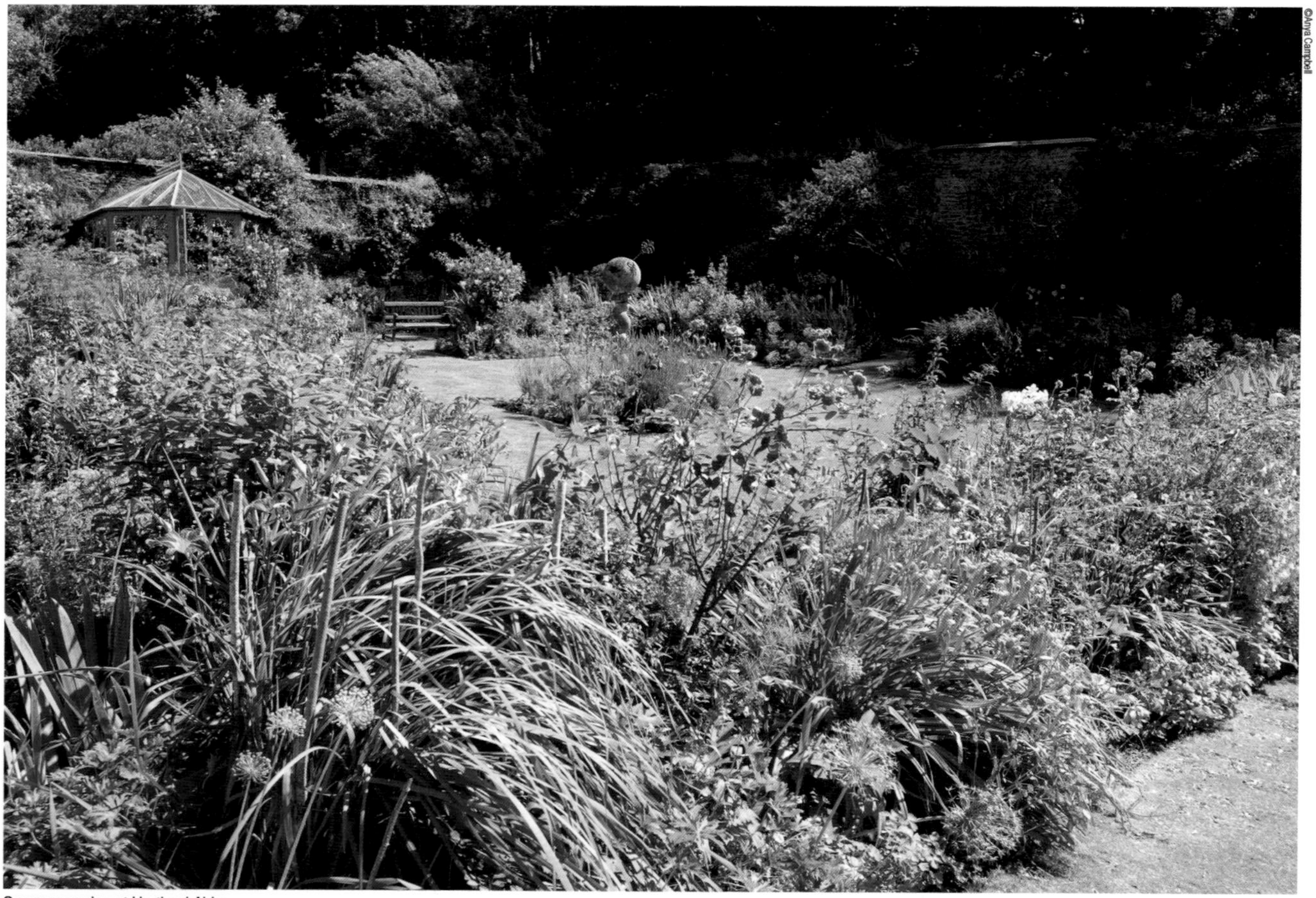

©Anya Campbell

Summer garden at Hartland Abbey

TIVERTON CASTLE

Park Hill, Tiverton, Devon EX16 6RP

www.tivertoncastle.com

Part Grade I Listed, part Scheduled Ancient Monument, few buildings evoke such immediate feeling of history. Originally built 1106, but later altered. Home of medieval Earls of Devon & Princess Katherine Plantagenet. Captured by Fairfax during English Civil War. Fun for children: try on armour; ghost stories, secret passages, medieval loos, beautiful walled gardens, interesting furniture, pictures. Super holiday accommodation - modern comforts in medieval surroundings. Make a Castle your home.
Location: Map 2:K5. OS Ref SS954 130. Just N of Tiverton town centre.
Owner: Mr and Mrs A K Gordon **Contact:** Mrs A Gordon
Tel: 01884 253200 **Fax:** 01884 254200 **Alt Tel:** 01884 255200.
E-mail: info@tivertoncastle.com
Open: Easter-end Oct: Sun, Thu, BH Mon, 2.30-5.30pm. Last admission 5pm. Open to groups (12+) by prior arrangement at any time.
Admission: Adult £7.00; Child 7-16yrs £3.00, under 7 Free; Garden only £2.00.
Key facts: Partial. By arrangement. Limited for coaches. Guide dogs only. 5 properties

HEMERDON HOUSE

Plympton, Devon PL7 5BZ

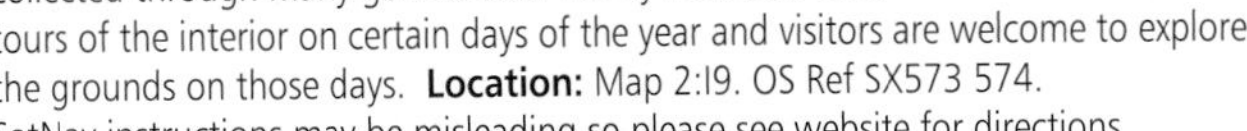

Built in the late 18th Century by the current owners' ancestors, Hemerdon House is a trove of local history, containing naval and military mementos, paintings, furniture, china and silver collected through many generations. Family members offer tours of the interior on certain days of the year and visitors are welcome to explore the grounds on those days. **Location:** Map 2:I9. OS Ref SX573 574. SatNav instructions may be misleading so please see website for directions.
Tel: 07704 708416 **E-mail:** hemerdon.house@gmail.com
Website: www.hemerdonhouse.co.uk
Open: See website for 2017 dates.
Admission: £7.50, HHA members and children under 12 no charge.
Key facts: Parties of 6 or more please contact us in advance; parties of 10 or more by prior arrangement only. Partial access. Two tours of approximately 1 hour 15 minutes each, starting at 2.15pm and 4pm - last entry at 4pm. Free parking. Dogs on leads are permitted in the grounds while the house is open.

A LA RONDE

Summer Lane, Exmouth, Devon EX8 5BD

A unique 16 sided house, completed c1796. Built for two spinster cousins, Jane and Mary Parminter, on the return from a European grand tour. **Location:** Map 2:L7. OS Ref SY004 834. 2m N of Exmouth on A376. **Tel:** 01395 265514 **E-mail:** alaronde@nationaltrust.org.uk **Website:** www.nationaltrust.org.uk/a-la-ronde **Open:** 28 Jan-10 Mar, daily, guided tour; Feb half term & 12 Mar-30 Oct, daily, 11-5pm. **Admission:** Adult £8.40; Child £4.20.

CASTLE DROGO

Drewsteignton, Nr Exeter EX6 6PB

Extraordinary granite and oak castle which combines the comforts of the 20th Century with the grandeur of a Baronial castle. **Location:** Map 2:J7. OS Ref SX724 902. **Tel:** 01647 433306 **E-mail:** castledrogo@nationaltrust.org.uk **Website:** www.nationaltrust.org.uk/castle-drogo **Open:** Gardens: All year, daily, 11am-4pm, 5.30pm in summer. House: 6 Mar-29 Oct, daily, 11am-5pm; 4 Nov-17 Dec, Sat & Sun, guided tour, 11am-4pm. **Admission:** Adult £9; Child £4.45

CHAMBERCOMBE MANOR

Ilfracombe, Devon EX34 9RJ

Eleventh Century Manor house set in three acres of beautiful gardens and surrounding woodland.
Location: Map 2:I3. OS Ref SS532 468.
Tel: 01271 862624
Website: www.chambercombemanor.org.uk
Open: 20 Mar-27 Oct, Mon-Fri & Sun, 12-3pm **Admission:** Adult £8.50.

DOWNES

Crediton, Devon EX17 3PL

Built in 1692 and faced with Beer stone in 1794 before undergoing extensive changes during the 19th Century. The historic home of General Sir Redvers Buller VC, celebrated in a small museum. **Location:** Map 2:K6. OS Ref SX852 997. Approx 1m from Crediton town centre. **Tel:** 01363 775142 **E-mail:** info@downes.co.uk **Website:** www.downesestate.co.uk **Open:** Easter Mon-11 Jul & Aug BH weekend, tours at 2.15pm. **Admission:** Contact for details.

GREENWAY

Greenway Road, Galmpton, nr Brixham, Devon TQ5 0ES

'The loveliest place in the world'. Take this extraordinary glimpse into the beloved holiday home of the famous author Agatha Christie. **Location:** Map 2:K8. OS Ref SX876 548. **Tel:** 01803 842382 **E-mail:** greenway@nationaltrust.org.uk **Website:** www.nationaltrust.org.uk/greenway **Open:** 13 Feb-30 Oct, daily, 10.30-5pm; 4 Nov-17 Dec, Sat & Sun, 11-4pm; 27 Dec-31 Dec, Wed-Sun, 11-4pm. **Admission:** Adult £10.30; Child £5.10.

KILLERTON

Broadclyst, Exeter EX5 3LE

Spectacular hillside garden surrounded by parkland and woods. The house includes a costume collection. **Location:** Map 2:K6. OS Ref SS976 001. Off Exeter - Cullompton Rd (B3181). M5 N'bound J30, M5 S'bound J28. **Tel:** 01392 881345 **E-mail:** killerton@nationaltrust.org.uk **Website:** www.nationaltrust.org.uk **Open:** Mar-Oct, 11am-5pm; 18 Nov-31 Dec, 11am-4pm. Closed 25 & 26 Dec. **Admission:** Adult £10.50; Child £5.25.

KILWORTHY FARM

Tavistock, Devon PL19 0JN

Described as one of Devon's Hidden Gems, and is well known for its range of Victorian farm buildings built in 1851-1853 by Francis, the 7th Duke of Bedford. **Location:** Map 2:I7. OS Ref SX481 769. **Tel:** 01822 618042 **E-mail:** info@kilworthyfarm.co.uk **Website:** www.kilworthyfarm.co.uk **Open:** 14, 15, 17 Apr, 29 & 30 Apr, 1 May, 27, 28, & 29 May, 1–31 Aug Excluding all Thus. **Admission:** Free

KNIGHTSHAYES

Bolham, Tiverton, Devon EX16 7RQ

One of the finest surviving Gothic Revival houses. A rare example of the work of architect William Burges. Garden renowned for rare trees, shrubs and seasonal colours. **Location:** Map 2:K5. OS Ref SS960 151. 7 miles from M5 exit 27 A361. Switch off Sat Nav and follow signs. **Tel:** 01884 254665 **E-mail:** knightshayes@nationaltrust.org.uk **Website:** www.nationaltrust.org.uk **Open:** Jan-Dec, daily, 10am-4pm. **Admission:** Adult £9.30; Child £4.65.

SALTRAM

Plympton, Plymouth, Devon PL7 1UH

Saltram was largely created between 1740-1820s by the Parker family, featuring some of Robert Adam's finest rooms. The gardens are beautiful throughout the year. **Location:** Map 2: I9. OS Ref SX521 555. **Tel:** 01752 333500 **E-mail:** saltram@nationaltrust.org.uk **Website:** www.nationaltrust.org.uk **Open:** 1 Jan-28 Feb, 11am-3.30pm; 1 Mar-31 Oct, 11am-4.30pm; 1 Nov-31 Dec, 11am-3.30pm. Gardens: 10am-4pm. **Admission:** Adult £10.70; Child £5.30.

VISITOR INFORMATION

Owner
Mr & Mrs Patrick Cooke

Address
Athelhampton
Dorchester
Dorset
DT2 7LG

Location
Map 2:P6
OS Ref. SY771 942
Athelhampton House is located just 5 miles East of Dorchester, between the villages of Puddletown and Tolpuddle.
Follow the brown tourist signs for Athelhampton from the A35.

Contact
Owen Davies or Laura Pitman
Tel: 01305 848363
E-mail: enquiry@athelhampton.co.uk

Opening Times
1 Mar-1 Nov, Sun-Thus, 10am-5pm. Closed every Fri & Sat (also open every Sun throughout the Winter months). Please see the website for further details on opening times.

Admission
House & Gardens:

Adult	£13.75
Senior	£12.50
Child (under 16)	£3.00
Disabled	£8.50
Student	£9.00
Gardens Only Ticket	£9.50

Please contact us for group booking rates and hospitality.
Some Fridays may be available by appointment.

Special Events
Flower Festival
Spring Plant Sale
MG Car Rally
Quarterly Car Auctions
Christmas Food Fair
Outdoor Theatre
Traditional Village Fete
Autumn Plant Sale

Athelhampton has a thriving Conference and Wedding business and offers exclusive use for Wedding parties and private functions on Fridays and Saturdays throughout the year.

Please contact us by phone or visit our website for more information.

Conference/Function

ROOM	Size	Max Cap
Long Hall	13mx6m	80
Conservatory	16mx11m	120
Media Suite/ Cinema	fixed seating	75
Great Hall	12mx8m	82

ATHELHAMPTON HOUSE & GARDENS

www.athelhampton.co.uk

One of the finest 15th Century Houses in England nestled in the heart of the picturesque Piddle Valley in the famous Hardy county of rural Dorset.

Athelhampton House has been privately owned for over 500 years. The Cooke family moved to Athelhampton from Bristol in 1957 and have continued to restore, improve and protect this historic place for future generations.

The House dates from 1485 and is a magnificent example of early Tudor architecture. Sir William Martyn was granted a licence by Henry VII to enclose 160 acres of deer park and to build the fortified manor. His Great Hall, with a roof of curved brace timbers and an oriel window with fine heraldic glass is now one of the finest examples from this period. The House has an array of fine furniture from Jacobean to Victorian periods. The west wing hosts an exhibition of paintings and sketches by the Russian artist, Marevna (1892-1984). The collection of her works, painted mainly in the cubist style, includes pieces painted throughout her lifetime including her travels, life in Paris, her time whilst she lived at Athelhampton during the 1940's and 50's and her years in Ealing.

In 1891 Alfred Carte de Lafontaine (the then owner of Athelhampton) commissioned the building of the formal gardens. The Grade 1 listed gardens which have won the HHA 'Garden of the Year' award surround the main house, with Elizabethan style ham stone courts. The famous 30 foot high yew pyramids dominate the Great Court and the 15th Century Dovecote is still home to a colony of beautiful white fantail doves. Water forms a recurring theme throughout the garden with pools, fountains and the River Piddle.

In 2015, the kitchen garden was opened for the first time in a generation. The garden had been lost to the wild and over the next few years it will be lovingly restored to its former glory, providing our thriving restaurant and pub with fresh and seasonal produce, as well as enhancing our visitor experience.

KEY FACTS

- www.athelhampton.co.uk
- Books, local produce, plants & gifts.
- Plants for sale from the gift shop.
- By arrangement, for a range of activities & catering please contact us.
- Limited access to upper floors in the House.
- Coffee, lunches & afternoon tea.
- Home-cooked lunches & a Sunday Carvery.
- Guided tours by arrangement.
- Free car & coach parking.
- Educational staff are available.
- Dogs on leads welcome, grounds only.
- Delightful holiday cottage on the estate.
- Civil wedding ceremonies indoor & outdoor locations.
- Open all year round on a Sunday.
- Special events throughout the year.

Register for news and special offers at **www.hudsonsheritage.com**

CLAVELL TOWER

Kimmeridge, near Wareham, Dorset BH20 5PE

www.landmarktrust.org.uk

This four storey, circular tower stands high on the cliff overlooking one of the most striking bays on the Dorset coast. Built in 1830 its location has captivated many including writers like Hardy and PD James.
Location: Map 2:A7. OS Ref SY915 796.
Owner: The Landmark Trust
Tel: 01628 825925
E-mail: bookings@landmarktrust.org.uk
Open: Self-catering accommodation.
2 Open Days per year.
Other visits by appointment.
Admission: Free on Open Days and visits by appointment.
Key facts: A four storey tower with each room on a different floor. The bedroom, on the first floor, has a door onto a balcony that encircles the whole building.

MAPPERTON

Beaminster, Dorset DT8 3NR

www.mapperton.com

Voted 'The Nation's Finest Manor House' by Country Life and principal location of 2015 film 'Far from the Madding Crowd'. Glorious Jacobean manor with Sandwich family collection overlooking 15 acre Italianate garden, with orangery, topiary and borders, descending to ponds and arboretum. Outstanding views of Dorset hills and woodlands.
Location: Map 2:N6. OS Ref SY503 997. 2m southeast of Beaminster, follow brown signs on B3163. **Owner/Contact:** The Earl & Countess of Sandwich
Tel: 01308 862645 **E-mail:** office@mapperton.com
Open: House: 2 Apr-31 Oct daily (exc. Fri & Sat) 12-4pm. Gardens: 1 Mar-31 Oct: daily (exc. Sat) 11am-5pm. Café: 2 Apr-31 Oct: daily (exc. Sat) 11am-5pm.
Admission: House & Gardens: Adult £12.00, Child (under 15yrs) free.
Gardens only: Adult £9.00, Child (under 15yrs) free. Gardens in March only £4.50.
House & Gardens: £10.00 per person for groups over 20, by appointment only.
Key facts: Partial. WCs. Licensed. By arrangement.
Limited for coaches. Guide dogs only.

LULWORTH CASTLE & PARK

East Lulworth, Wareham, Dorset BH20 5QS

www.lulworth.com

Impressive 17th Century Castle & historically important 18th Century Chapel set in extensive parkland, with views towards the Jurassic Coast. Built as a hunting lodge to entertain Royalty, the Castle was destroyed by fire in 1929. Since then it has been externally restored and internally consolidated by English Heritage. The Castle houses informative displays & exhibitions on its history, and the delightful Castle Tea Room offering a place to relax and enjoy your surroundings.
Location: Map 3:A7. OS Ref ST853 822.
In E Lulworth off B3070, 3m NE of Lulworth Cove. **Owner:** The Weld Estate
Tel: 01929 400352 **Fax:** 01929 40563 **E-mail:** info@lulworth.com
Open: Castle & Park: Typically open Sun-Fri from Mar-Dec. Opening dates & times may vary throughout the year, check website or call before visiting. Last admission to Castle is 1hr before closing. **Admission:** Pay & Display parking £3.00, allowing access to Park walks, Play & Picnic areas, Castle Tea Room. Admission applies for Castle & Chapel - please see website. EH & HHA members Free entry.
Key facts: Concerts, corporate & private hire/events, weddings by arrangement. WCs. Lift access to Upper Ground floor. Licensed.
By arrangement. Guide dogs only. Open Mar-Dec.

MINTERNE GARDENS

Minterne Magna, Nr Dorchester, Dorset DT2 7AU

www.minterne.co.uk

Landscaped in the manner of 'Capability' Brown, Minterne's unique garden has been described by Simon Jenkins as 'a corner of paradise'. 20 wild, woodland acres of magnolias, rhododendrons and azaleas providing new vistas at each turn, with small lakes, streams and cascades. Private House tours, dinners, corporate seminars, wedding and events. As seen on BBC Gardeners' World. Voted one of the ten Prettiest Gardens in England by The Times.
Location: Map 2:O6. OS Ref ST660 042.
On A352 Dorchester/Sherborne Rd, 2m N of Cerne Abbas.
Owner/Contact: The Hon Mr & Mrs Henry Digby
Tel: 01300 341370 **Fax:** 01300 341747
E-mail: enquiries@minterne.co.uk
Open: Mid Feb-9 Nov: daily, 10am-6pm.
Admission: Adult £5.00, accompanied children free. Free to RHS members.
Key facts: Seminars/Team Building/Away Days. Unsuitable.
By arrangement. Tours personally guided by Lord Digby. Free. Picnic tables in car park. In grounds on leads. 4 rooms licenced for Civil Ceremonies. Capacity between 60-160.

SHERBORNE CASTLE & GARDENS

New Road, Sherborne, Dorset DT9 5NR

www.sherbornecastle.com

Discover the historic Digby stately home built by Sir Walter Raleigh in 1594. View magnificent staterooms besides Raleigh's kitchen and a museum in the castle's cellars. Explore acres of impressive lakeside gardens in a stunning setting forming one of 'Capability' Brown's finest landscapes in the south west.

Location: Map 2:O5. OS Ref ST649 164. 1/4m from town and main line railway station. Follow brown signs from A30 or A352. ½m S of the Old Castle.
Owner: Mr E. Wingfield Digby
Contact: Robert B. Smith
Tel: 01935 812072 **Fax:** 01935 816727
E-mail: enquiries@sherbornecastle.com
Open: 1 Apr 2017 to 29 Oct 2017. Gardens & Tea Room from 10am. Castle & Gift Shop from 11am with last admission 4.30pm. Closes at 5pm.
Admission: Castle & Gardens: Adult £12.00, Senior £11.00, Child Free (max 4 per full paying adult). Gardens only: Adult £6.50, Senior £6.00, Child Free (max of 4 per adult). Groups +15 discount options available on application.
Key facts: WCs. By arrangement. On leads.

WOLFETON HOUSE

Nr Dorchester, Dorset DT2 9QN

A fine medieval and Elizabethan manor house lying in the water-meadows near the confluence of the rivers Cerne and Frome. It was embellished around 1580 and has splendid plaster ceilings, fireplaces and panelling. To be seen are the Great Hall, Stairs and Chamber, Parlour, Dining Room, Chapel and Cyder House.

Location: Map 2:O6. OS Ref SY678 921. 1½m from Dorchester on the A37 towards Yeovil. Indicated by Historic House signs.
Owner: Capt N T L L T Thimbleby
Contact: The Steward
Tel: 01305 263500
E-mail: kthimbleby.wolfeton@gmail.com
Open: Jun-end Sep: Mon, Wed & Thu, 2-5pm. Groups by appointment throughout the year.
Admission: £8.00
Key facts: Catering for groups by prior arrangement. By arrangement. By arrangement. Limited for coaches.

© Justin Barton

ST GILES HOUSE

Wimborne St Giles, Dorset BH21 5NA

www.stgileshouse.com

This beautiful family house has a long and rich history. In the past 400 years it has been at the heart of politics, philosophy and social thought. In recent times an award winning restoration has seen it brought back to life and become a family home once again. We are now excited to share it with you. Call us for corporate hire, weddings and bespoke events.

Location: Map 3:A5. OS Ref SU031 119. Wimborne St Giles, 4mls SE of A354, past almshouses and church.
Owner: The Earl of Shaftesbury
Contact: Nick Ashley-Cooper
Tel: 01725 517214
E-mail: catherine@stgileshouse.com
Open: By appointment for groups and for bespoke events.
Key facts: By appointment only.

© Jayson Hutchins

Sherborne Castle

Register for news and special offers at **www.hudsonsheritage.com**

CHURCH OF OUR LADY & ST IGNATIUS

North Chideock, Bridport, Dorset DT6 6LF

Built by Charles Weld of Chideock Manor in 1872 in Italian Romanesque style, it is a gem of English Catholicism and the Shrine of the Dorset Martyrs. Early 19th Century wall paintings in original barn-chapel (priest's sacristy) can be seen by arrangement. A museum of local history & village life displayed in adjoining cloister.

Location: Map 2:A7. OS Ref SY090 786.
A35 to Chideock, turn into N Rd & ¼mile on right.
Owner: The Weld Family Trust
Contact: Mrs G Martelli **Tel:** 01308 488348
E-mail: amyasmartelli40@hotmail.com
Website: www.chideockmartyrschurch.org.uk
Open: All year: 10am-4pm.
Admission: Donations welcome.
Key facts: Partial. Limited for coaches. Guide dogs only.

DEANS COURT

Deans Court Lane, Wimborne, Dorset BH21 1EE

An historic private house and garden that has been lived in for 1,300 years. **Location:** Map 3:B6. OS Ref SZ010 998. Follow signs to Wimborne Town Centre; pass through the Square and at the end of the High Street cross the junction (opposite Holmans TV shop) into Deans Court Lane. **Owner:** Sir William & Lady Hanham **Contact:** Jonathan Cornish **Tel:** 01202 849314 **E-mail:** info@deanscourt.org **Website:** www.deanscourt.org **Open:** May 1,3,10,17,24; Jun 7,14,21,28; Jul 5,12,16,19,23,25,26,30; Aug 2,6,9,13,15,20,23,27,28,29,30. Tours start on Weds at 1pm, 2.20pm, 3.40pm; Suns & BH Mons at 10am, 11.20am, 12.40pm. Meet at gate on Deans Court Ln. NGS openings: May 16; Jun 27. See NGS website **Admission:** Guided tours only, approx. 70 mins for house & garden. Adults £8; Senior & Disabled £6; Child (under-16) & HHA Friends-Free. **Key facts:** Homestore. Contact us. Healthfood Café. Tours only. Only NGS. 20 pers. max. Only NGS. No for tours. Holiday lets. May-Aug. €

EDMONDSHAM HOUSE & GARDENS

Cranborne, Wimborne, Dorset BH21 5RE

Charming blend of Tudor and Georgian architecture with interesting contents. Organic walled garden, six acre garden with unusual trees and spring bulbs. 12th Century church nearby.

Location: Map 3:A5. OS Ref SU062 116. Off B3081 between Cranborne and Verwood, NW from Ringwood 9m, Wimborne 9m.
Owner/Contact: Mrs Julia E Smith
Tel: 01725 517207
Open: House & Gardens all BH Mons, Weds in Apr & Oct only, 2-5pm. Gardens Apr-Oct Suns & Weds 2-5pm. Groups by arrangement (max 50).
Admission: House & Garden: Adult £5.00, Child £1.00 (under 5yrs free). Garden only: Adult £2.50, Child 50p (under 5yrs free).
Key facts: Partial. WCs. Only Weds Apr & Oct. Obligatory. Limited. Guide dogs only.

SANDFORD ORCAS MANOR HOUSE

Sandford Orcas, Sherborne, Dorset DT9 4SB

Tudor manor house with gatehouse, fine panelling, furniture, pictures. Terraced gardens with topiary and herb garden. Personal conducted tour by owner.

Location: Map 2:O5. OS Ref ST623 210. 2½m N of Sherborne, Dorset 4m S of A303 at Sparkford. Entrance next to church.
Owner/Contact: Sir Mervyn Medlycott Bt
Tel: 01963 220206
Open: Easter Mon, 10am-5pm. May & Jul-Sep: Suns & Mons, 2-5pm.
Admission: Adult £5.00, Child £2.50. Groups (10+): Adult £4.00, Child £2.00.
Key facts: Unsuitable. Obligatory. Parking available. In grounds, on leads.

Forde Abbey

ABBOTSBURY SUBTROPICAL GARDENS

Abbotsbury, Weymouth, Dorset DT3 4LA

The Garden is a mixture of formal and informal flowers, world famous for it's Camellia groves and magnolias. **Location:** Map 2:N7. OS Ref SY564 851. Off A35 nr Dorchester, on B3157 between Weymouth & Bridport. **Tel:** 01305 871387 **E-mail:** info@abbotsbury-tourism.co.uk **Website:** www.abbotsbury-tourism.co.uk / www.abbotsburyplantsales.co.uk **Open:** 2 Jan-17 Dec, daily, 10-5pm; 4pm winter closing. **Admission:** Adult £12; Child £6.

CORFE CASTLE

Wareham, Dorset BH20 5EZ

Thousand-year-old royal castle shaped by warfare.

Location: Map 3:A7. OS Ref SY960 820.
Tel: 01929 477 062 **E-mail:** corfecastle@nationaltrust.org.uk
Website: www.nationaltrust.org.uk/corfe-castle
Open: All year, daily. Jan, Feb, Nov, Dec, 10am-4pm; Mar & Oct, 10am-5pm; Apr-Sep, 10am-6pm. **Admission:** Adult £8.50; Child £4.25

FORDE ABBEY & GARDENS

Forde Abbey, Chard, Somerset TA20 4LU

More than 900 years of history are encapsulated in this elegant former Cistercian monastery and its 30 acres of award-winning gardens. **Location:** Map 2:N6. OS Ref ST358 041. Just off the B3167 4m SE of Chard. **Tel:** 01460 221290 **E-mail:** info@fordeabbey.co.uk **Website:** www.fordeabbey-gardens-dorset.co.uk **Open:** Gardens: All year, daily, 10am-5.30pm. House: 6 May-29 Oct, Tue-Fri, Sun & BH Mons, 12-4pm. **Admission:** Adult £12.50; U15 free.

HIGHCLIFFE CASTLE

Highcliffe-On-Sea, Christchurch BH23 4LE

Built in the 1830s in the Romantic/Picturesque style.

Location: Map 3:B6. OS Ref SZ200 930. Off the A337 Lymington Road, between Christchurch and Highcliffe-on-Sea.
Tel: 01425 278807 **Fax:** 01425 280423 **E-mail:** enquiries@highcliffecastle.co.uk
Website: www.highcliffecastle.co.uk **Open:** 1 Feb-23 Dec, daily, 11-5pm.
Admission: Adult £3.50; U16 free. Guided tour: Adult £6.

KINGSTON LACY

Wimborne Minster, Dorset BH21 4EA

Explore this elegant country mansion, built to resemble an Italian Palace, and discover an outstanding collection of fine works of art. **Location:** Map 3:A6. OS Ref ST980 019. **Tel:** 01202 883402 **E-mail:** kingstonlacy@nationaltrust.org.uk **Website:** www.nationaltrust.org.uk/kingston-lacy **Open:** Gardens: Jan, Feb, Nov, Dec, daily, 10-4pm; Mar-Oct, daily 10-6pm. House: Mar-Oct, daily, 11-5pm; Oct-Dec, daily, 11-4pm. **Admission:** Adult £13.50; Child £6.70.

STOCK GAYLARD HOUSE

Nr Sturminster Newton, Dorset DT10 2BG

A Georgian house overlooking ancient deer park.

Location: Map 2:P5. OS Ref ST722 130. Turning off A3030 almost opposite B3143 junction. **Tel:** 01963 23511 **E-mail:** Office@stockgaylard.com
Website: www.stockgaylard.com
Open: 22 Apr-1 May; 22-30 May; 22-30 Sep. 2-5pm. Groups by appointment.
Admission: Adult £5.00.

VISITOR INFORMATION

Owner
Mr David Lowsley-Williams

Address
Chavenage House
Chavenage
Tetbury
Gloucestershire
GL8 8XP

Location
Map 3:A1
OS Ref. ST872 952
Less than 20m from M4/J16/17 or 18. 1¾m NW of Tetbury between the B4014 & A4135. Signed from Tetbury. Less than 15m from M5/J13 or 14. Signed from A46 (Stroud-Bath road). Coaches - access the site through the Coach Entrance.
Taxi: The Pink Cab 07960 036003
Rail: Kemble Station 7m.
Air: Bristol 35m. Birmingham 70m. Grass airstrip on farm.

Contact
Caroline Lowsley-Williams
Tel: 01666 502329
Fax: 01666 504696
E-mail: info@chavenage.com

Opening Times
Summer
May-Sep
Thu, Sun, 2-5pm.
Last admission 4pm.
Also Easter Sun, Mon & BH Mons.

NB. Will open on any day and at other times by prior arrangement for groups.

Winter
Oct-Mar
By appointment only for groups.

Admission
Guided Tours are inclusive in the following prices.

Summer

Adult	£8.00
Child (5-16 yrs)	£4.00

Winter
Groups only
(any date or time)
Rates by arrangement.

Conference/Function

ROOM	Size	Max Cap
Ballroom	70' x 30'	120
Oak Room	25' x 20'	30

© James Kerr - Photography

CHAVENAGE HOUSE

www.chavenage.com

The Elizabethan Manor Chavenage House, a TV/Film location, is still a family home, offers unique experiences, with history, ghosts and more.

Chavenage is a wonderful Elizabethan house of mellow grey Cotswold stone and tiles which contains much of interest for the discerning visitor. The approach aspect of Chavenage is virtually as it was left by Edward Stephens in 1576. Only two families have owned Chavenage; the present owners since 1891 and the Stephens family before them. A Colonel Nathaniel Stephens, MP for Gloucestershire during the Civil War was cursed for supporting Cromwell, giving rise to legends of weird happenings at Chavenage since that time.

There are many interesting rooms housing tapestries, fine furniture, pictures and relics of the Cromwellian period. Of particular note are the Main Hall, where a contemporary screen forms a minstrels' gallery and two tapestry rooms where it is said Cromwell was lodged.

Recently Chavenage has been used as a location for TV and film productions: credits include, 'Barry Lyndon', the Hercule Poirot story 'The Mysterious Affair at Styles','The House of Elliot', 'Casualty', 'Cider with Rosie', Jeremy Musson's 'The Curious House Guest'; 'Dracula', 'Lark Rise to Candleford'; 'Bonekickers'; 'Tess of the D'Urbervilles', New Worlds and scenes from critically acclaimed 'Wolf Hall' . Chavenage now features as Trenwith House in hugely popular 'Poldark'. Chavenage is the ideal attraction for those wishing a personal tour, usually conducted by the owner or his family, or for groups wanting a change from large establishments. Meals for pre-arranged groups have proved hugely popular. It also provides a charming venue for wedding receptions, conferences, seminars and other functions.

KEY FACTS

- Suitable for filming, photography, corporate entertainment, activity days, seminars, receptions & product launches. No photography inside house.
- Occasional.
- Corporate entertaining. Private drinks parties, lunches, dinners, anniversary parties & wedding receptions.
- Partial. WCs.
- Refreshments, meals & teas can be booked for groups in advance
- By owner & family. Large groups given a talk prior to viewing. Couriers/group leaders should arrange tour format prior to visit.
- Up to 100 cars. 2-3 coaches (by appointment). Coaches access from A46 (signposted) or from Tetbury via B4014, enter back gates for parking area.
- Chairs can be arranged for lecturing.
- Assistance Dogs Only.
- Out of season - only by appointment.

© Mammoth Productions

Aidan Turner as Ross Poldark

© James Kerr - Photography

The tapestried 'Oliver Cromwell Room'.

SUDELEY CASTLE & GARDENS

www.sudeleycastle.co.uk

A must-see on any visit to The Cotswolds, Sudeley Castle & Gardens is the only private castle in England to have a queen – Katherine Parr – buried within the grounds.

Located only eight miles from the picturesque Broadway, Sudeley Castle & Gardens has played an important role in England's history, boasting royal connections that stretch back over 1,000 years - and is now a much-loved family home with award-winning gardens.

Inside, the castle contains many fascinating treasures from ancient Roman times to the present day. Outside, the castle is surrounded by award-winning gardens and a breathtaking 1,200 acre estate.

It is also the only private castle in England to have a queen buried within the grounds. The last of Henry VIII's six wives, Katherine Parr lived and died in the castle. She is now entombed in a beautiful 15th Century church found within the award-winning gardens.

Sudeley Castle's magnificent gardens are world-renowned, providing variety and colour from spring through to autumn. The centerpiece is the Queens Garden, so named because four of England's queens – Anne Boleyn, Katherine Parr, Lady Jane Grey and Elizabeth I – once admired the hundreds of varieties of roses found in the garden.

A pheasantry, adventure playground with picnic area, gift shop and Terrace Café in the banqueting hall complete the perfect day out.

KEY FACTS

- www.sudeleycastle.co.uk / 01242 604244.
- Open daily from 6 Mar-29 Oct 2017.
- Weddings & Events.
- Partial. WCs.
- Light lunches, afternoon tea, cakes, snacks, tea, coffee & soft drinks.
- Licensed.
- By arrangement. Call the Estate Office.
- Ample parking.
- Contact Estate Office for schools materials.
- Guide dogs only.
- Country Cottages.
- The family's Private Library situated within the family's apartments is available for civil ceremonies & civil partnerships.
- See website.

VISITOR INFORMATION

Owner
Elizabeth, Lady Ashcombe and family

Address
Sudeley Castle & Gardens
The Cotswolds
Gloucestershire
GL54 5JD

Location
Map 6:O10
OS Ref. SP032 277
8m NE of Cheltenham, at Winchcombe off B4632. From Bristol or Birmingham M5/J9. Take A46 then B4077 towards Stow-on-the-Wold.
Coaches: Marchants Coaches
Rail: Cheltenham Station 8m.
Air: Birmingham or Bristol 45m.

Contact
Visitor Centre
Tel: 01242 604 244
Fax: 01242 602 959
Estate Office: 01242 602 308.
E-mail: enquiries@sudeley.org.uk

Opening Times
6 Mar-29 Oct, daily, 10am-5pm.

Admission
Adult:	£14.50
Child:	£5.50

Special Events
Special events throughout the season. See www.sudeleycastle.co.uk, Facebook.com/SudeleyCastle and Twitter @SudeleyCastle.

Conference/Function

ROOM	Size	Max Cap
Chandos Hall		60
Banqueting Hall + Pavilion		100
Marquee		Unlimited
Long Room		80
Library		50

Frampton Court, Gloucestershire

© Stephen Randall Photography

KELMSCOTT MANOR

KELMSCOTT, NR LECHLADE, GLOUCESTERSHIRE GL7 3HJ

www.kelmscottmanor.org.uk

'The loveliest haunt of ancient peace'. Kelmscott Manor, a Grade I listed Tudor farmhouse adjacent to the River Thames, was William Morris's summer residence from 1871 until his death in 1896. Morris loved Kelmscott Manor, which seemed to him to have 'grown up out of the soil'. Its beautiful gardens with barns, dovecote, meadow and stream provided a constant source of inspiration.
The house contains an outstanding collection of the possessions and work of Morris, his family and associates, including furniture, textiles, pictures, carpets and ceramics.

Location: Map 6:P12. OS Ref SU252 988. At SE end of the village, 2m due E of Lechlade, off the Lechlade - Faringdon Road.

Owner: Society of Antiquaries of London

Tel: 01367 252486

E-mail: admin@kelmscottmanor.org.uk

Open: House and Garden Apr-Oct: Weds and Sats, 11am-5pm (Ticket office opens 10.30am). Last admission to the house, 4.30pm. Limited advance bookings on public open days. House has limited capacity; timed ticket system operates. Group visits Apr-Oct: Thus. Must be booked in advance.

Admission: Adult £9.50, Child/Student £5.00. Family £26.00. Garden only: £3.50. Carer accompanying disabled person Free.

Key facts: No flash photography in house. Partial. WCs. Licensed. Licensed. By arrangement. 8 minutes walk. Limited for coaches. Guide dogs only.

RODMARTON MANOR

CIRENCESTER, GLOUCESTERSHIRE GL7 6PF

www.rodmarton-manor.co.uk

A Cotswold Arts and Crafts house, one of the last great country houses to be built in the traditional way, containing beautiful furniture, ironwork, china and needlework specially made for the house. The large garden complements the architecture and contains many areas of great beauty and character including the magnificent herbaceous borders, topiary, roses, rockery and kitchen garden. Available as a film location and for small functions.

Location: Map 6:N12. OS Ref ST934 977. Off A433 between Cirencester and Tetbury.

Owner: Mr Simon Biddulph

Contact: John & Sarah Biddulph

Tel: 01285 841442

E-mail: enquiries@rodmarton-manor.co.uk

Open: For 2017 opening details please see website. (www.rodmarton-manor.co.uk) or telephone 01285 841442.

Admission: House & Garden: £8.00, Child (5-15yrs) £4.00. Garden only: £5.00, Child (5-15yrs) £1.00. Guided tour of Garden: Entry fee plus £40.00 per group.

Key facts: Colour guidebook & postcards on sale. Available for filming. No photography in house. WCs in garden. Garden & ground floor. Open days & groups by appointment. By arrangement. Guide dogs only.

STANWAY HOUSE & WATER GARDEN

STANWAY, CHELTENHAM, GLOUCESTERSHIRE GL54 5PQ

www.stanwayfountain.co.uk

'As perfect and pretty a Cotswold manor house as anyone is likely to see' (Fodor's Great Britain 1998 guidebook). Stanway's beautiful architecture, furniture, parkland and village are complemented by the restored 18th Century water garden and the magnificent fountain, 300 feet, making it the tallest garden and gravity fountain in the world. Teas available. Beer for sale. Wedding reception venue.

The Watermill in Church Stanway, now fully restored as a working flour mill, was recently re-opened by HRH The Prince of Wales. Its massive 24-foot overshot waterwheel, 8th largest waterwheel in England, drives traditional machinery, to produce stoneground Cotswold flour.

Location: Map 6:O10. OS Ref SP061 323.
N of Winchcombe, just off B4077.
Owner: The Earl of Wemyss and March
Contact: Debbie Lewis **Tel:** 01386 584528
Fax: 01386 584688 **E-mail:** stanwayhse@btconnect.com
Open: House & Garden: Jun-Aug: Tue & Thu, 2-5pm.
Private tours by arrangement at other times.
Admission: Please see website for up-to-date admission prices.
Key facts: Film & photographic location. Wedding receptions. By arrangement. Call 07850 585539 for details. School Tours of the Water Mill by arrangement. In grounds on leads.

FRAMPTON COURT, THE ORANGERY AND FRAMPTON MANOR

Frampton on Severn, Gloucestershire GL2 7EP

www.framptoncourtestate.co.uk

Built in 1731 & now run as a luxury B&B, Frampton Court has a superb panelled interior, antique furniture & 'Frampton Flora' watercolours. The 18th Century 'Strawberry Hill' gothic Orangery sits, breath-takingly, at the end of a Dutch ornamental canal in The Court grounds & is a self-catering holiday house. Frampton Manor is said to be the birthplace of 'Fair Rosamund' Clifford mistress of Henry II & has an impressive 16th Century Wool Barn; its walled garden is a plantsman's delight.
Location: Map 6:M12. OS Ref SO748 080. 2 miles from M5 J13 via A38 & B4071.
Owner: Mr & Mrs Rollo Clifford **Contact:** Janie Clifford **Tel:** 01452 740268
E-mail: events@framptoncourtestate.co.uk **Open:** Frampton Court & Manor by appointment for groups (10+). Manor Garden: Mon & Fri 2.30-5pm, 24 Apr-1 Jul.
Admission: Frampton Court: House & Garden £10.00. Frampton Manor: House, Garden & Wool Barn £10.00. Garden only £5.00. Wool Barn only £3.00. **Key facts:** Filming, Parkland for hire. Pan-Global Plants. Wedding receptions. Partial. For pre-booked groups. B&B at The Court: 01452 740267 Self-catering at The Orangery: 01452 740698 By arrangement.

NEWARK PARK

Ozleworth, Wotton-Under-Edge Gloucestershire GL12 7PZ

www.nationaltrust.org.uk/newark-park

Newark Park is Cotswold escarpment estate with at its heart Newark House. Originally a Tudor hunting lodge, the house has been extended over 450 years into a fascinating and eclectic home. The estate offers woodland walks and the gardens provide space to play, explore and contemplate with spectacular views.
Location: Map 2:P1. OS Ref 172. ST786 934. Approx. 10 minutes' drive from M5 junctions 13 & 14. Off A4135 Tetbury/Dursley, follow signs for Newark Park.
Owner: National Trust **Tel:** 01453 842644
E-mail: newarkpark@nationaltrust.org.uk
Open: Main season: 1 Mar-30 Oct: 11am-5pm. Closed Tues. Winter opening: 4-5 Feb, 11-27 Feb, 4 & 5, 11 & 12, 18 & 19, 25 & 26 Nov, 2 & 3 and 9 & 10 Dec: 11am-4pm. **Admission:** Adult £9.00, Child £4.50, Family £22.50.
Key facts: Gift shop on first floor of Newark House. Ground floor ramp access. Tea pavilion offering light lunches, drinks, cakes & ice creams. Contact us for availability. On leads in gardens and estate. Holiday cottage.

Register for news and special offers at www.hudsonsheritage.com

OWLPEN MANOR

Uley, Nr Dursley, Gloucestershire GL11 5BZ

www.owlpen.com

The romantic Tudor manor house stands in a picturesque valley setting with church, Court House and watermill. Stuart terraced gardens with magnificent yew topiary. Unique painted cloths, and family and Arts and Crafts collections. "By far the finest small manor house in all of England" - Prof Francis Comstock. "Owlpen, in Gloucestershire: ah, what a dream is there!"- Vita Sackville-West. "The loveliest place in England" - Fodor's Guide. **Location:** Map 6:M12. OS Ref ST800 983. One mile east of Uley, off the B4066. **Owner:** Sir Nicholas and Lady Mander
Contact: Bella Wadsworth **Tel:** 01453 860261 **E-mail:** sales@owlpen.com
Open: The house will be open by appointment only for groups of 15 people or more. Apr-Oct, Mon-Fri. **Admission:** Group tours £15.00. Cream Tea £26.00 per person including a tour of the House & Gardens. Or, a two course lunch for £36.00 per person including a tour of the House & Gardens.
Key facts: Accessible by coach only via Uley Village. Restaurant open for cream teas and lunches by appointment. Usually by owner. At top of drive. Disabled parking next to manor house. 9 Self-catering holiday cottages. Licensed for up to 100 people, weddings for up to 150 in garden marquee. Open all year for weddings and restaurant bookings.

SEZINCOTE

Moreton-In-Marsh, Gloucestershire GL56 9AW

www.sezincote.co.uk

Exotic oriental water garden by Repton and Daniell. Large semi-circular orangery. House by S P Cockerell in Indian style was the inspiration for Brighton Pavilion.
Location: Map 6:P10. OS Ref SP183 324. 2 miles west of Moreton-in-Marsh on the A44 opposite entrance to Batsford Arboretum.
Contact: Dr E Peake
Tel: 01386 700444
E-mail: enquiries@sezincote.co.uk
Open: Garden: Thus, Fris & BH Mons, 2-6pm except Dec.
House: As above May-Sep. Teas in Orangery when house open.
Admission: House: Adult £10.00 (guided tour).
Garden: Adult £5.00, Child £1.50 (under 5yrs Free).
Groups welcomed weekdays, please contact for details.
Key facts: Please see our website for up-to-date events and special openings. For full information for disabled visitors please email enquiries@sezincote.co.uk. Obligatory. Except assistance dogs. Weddings.

KIFTSGATE COURT GARDENS

Chipping Campden, Gloucestershire GL55 6LN

Magnificently situated garden on the edge of the Cotswold escarpment with views towards the Malvern Hills. Many unusual shrubs and plants including tree peonies, abutilons, specie and old-fashioned roses.
Winner HHA/Christie's Garden of the Year Award 2003.
Location: Map 6:O9. OS Ref SP173 430.
4m NE of Chipping Campden. ¼ m W of Hidcote Garden.
Owner: Mr and Mrs J G Chambers
Contact: Mr J G Chambers
Tel: 01386 438777 **E-mail:** info@kiftsgate.co.uk
Website: www.kiftsgate.co.uk
Open: May, Jun, Jul, Sat-Wed, 12 noon-6pm. Aug, Sat-Wed, 2-6pm.
Apr & Sep, Sun, Mon & Wed, 2-6pm.
Admission: Adult: £8.50, Child £2.50. Groups (20+) £7.50.
Key facts: Partial. Limited for coaches. Guide dogs only.

ABLINGTON MANOR

Bibury, Cirencester, Gloucestershire GL7 5NY

Ablington Manor is a grade I, 16th Century manor house with a 4 acre garden through which the River Coln runs. **Location:** Map 6: O12. OS Ref SP102 075. Ablington is situated off the B4425 Cirencester to Burford road.
Tel: 01285 740363 **E-mail:** prue@ablingtonmanor.com
Open: By appointment and on advertised days for charity.
Admission: By arrangement.

BERKELEY CASTLE

Berkeley, Gloucestershire GL13 9BQ

The Castle, once a fortress, is now a comfortable family home. Visit the Norman Keep, dungeon, medieval kitchens, Great Hall and State Apartments. Enjoy eight acres of gardens. **Location:** Map 6:M12. OS Ref ST685 990.
Tel: 01453 810303 **Fax:** 01453 512995 **E-mail:** info@berkeley-castle.com
Website: www.berkeley-castle.com **Open:** Good Fri-29 Mar, daily, 11-5pm; 1 Apr-31 Oct, Sun-Wed, 11-5pm. **Admission:** Adult £11; Child £6.

DYRHAM PARK

Dyrham, Nr Bath, Gloucestershire SN14 8ER

Spectacular late 17th Century mansion, garden and deer park. Discover fascinating interiors little changed in 300 years. **Location:** Map 2:P2. OS Ref ST741 757.
Tel: 0117 937 2501 **E-mail:** dyrhampark@nationaltrust.org.uk
Website: www.nationaltrust.org.uk/dyrham-park
Open: Gardens: 1 Jan-5 Feb, Sat & Sun, 10am-4pm; 13 Feb-31 Dec, 10am-5pm. House: 4 Mar-29 Oct, 10am-5pm. **Admission:** Adult £11.20; Child £5.80.

HIDCOTE MANOR GARDEN

Hidcote Bartrim, Nr Chipping Campden, Gloucs GL55 6LR

One of the most delightful gardens in England, created in the early 20th Century by the great horticulturist Major Lawrence Johnston.
Location: Map 6:O10. OS Ref SP176 429. **Tel:** 01386 438333
E-mail: hidcote@nationaltrust.org.uk **Website:** www.nationaltrust.org.uk/hidcote
Open: 11 Feb-26 Feb & 4 Nov-17 Dec, Sat & Sun, 11-4pm; 27 Feb-29 Oct, daily, 10-5pm. **Admission:** Adult £10.90; Child £5.45.

HIGHGROVE GARDENS

The Garden Tours Office, The Barn, Close Farm, Gloucestershire GL8 8PH

Gardens created by His Royal Highness the Prince of Wales over the last 35 years; a series of interlinked organic gardens that reflect his artistry and commitment to sustainability. **Location:** Map 3:A1. OS Ref ST884 918. **Tel:** 0303 123 7310
Website: www.highgrovegardens.com **Open:** Apr-Oct, booked tours on selected dates. **Admission:** Adult, from £17.50.

WHITTINGTON COURT

Cheltenham, Gloucestershire GL54 4HF

Elizabethan & Jacobean manor house with church.
Location: Map 6:N11. OS Ref SP014 206. 4m E of Cheltenham on N side of A40.
Tel: 01242 820556
E-mail: lucy@whittingtoncourt.co.uk
Open: 15-30 Apr & 12-28 Aug: 2-5pm.
Admission: Adult £5.00; Child £1.00; OAP £4.00.

FAIRFIELD

Stogursey, Bridgwater, Somerset TA5 1PU

Elizabethan and medieval house. Occupied by the same family (Acland-Hoods and their ancestors) for over 800 years. Woodland garden. Views of Quantocks and the sea. House described in Simon Jenkins' book 'England's Thousand Best Houses'.

Location: Map 2:L4. OS Ref ST187 430. 11m W Bridgwater, 8m E Williton. From A39 Bridgwater/Minehead turn North. House 1m W Stogursey.

Tel: 01278 732251

Open: 17 Apr-29 May, 7-23 Jun. Wed, Thu, Fri & BH Mon. Guided house tours at 2.30 & 3.30pm. Garden also open.

Admission: £6.00 in aid of Stogursey Church. Advisable to contact to confirm dates.

Key facts: No inside photography. Obligatory. No coach parking. Guide dogs only.

GLASTONBURY ABBEY

Magdalene Street, Glastonbury BA6 9EL

A hidden jewel in the heart of Somerset, Glastonbury Abbey is traditionally associated with the earliest days of Christianity in Britain. It is also the resting place for the legendary King Arthur.

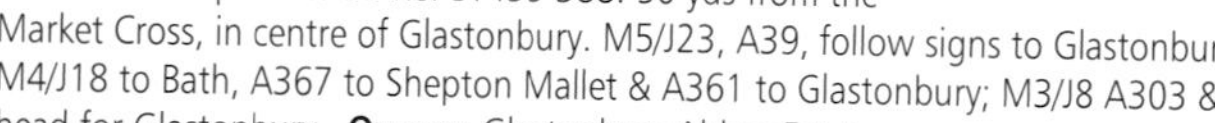

Location: Map 2:N4. OS Ref ST499 388. 50 yds from the Market Cross, in centre of Glastonbury. M5/J23, A39, follow signs to Glastonbury; M4/J18 to Bath, A367 to Shepton Mallet & A361 to Glastonbury; M3/J8 A303 & head for Glastonbury. **Owner:** Glastonbury Abbey Estate

Tel: 01458 832267 **Fax:** 01458 836117 **Twitter:** @glastonburyabbe

E-mail: info@glastonburyabbey.com **Website:** www.glastonburyabbey.com

Open: Open 364 days a year, except 25 Dec. Nov-Feb 9am-4pm. Mar-May 9am-6pm. Jun-Aug 9am-8pm. Sep-Oct 9am-6pm. Events held throughout year.

Admission: For the latest information visit the website - reduced tickets available online up until 6pm the day before you visit **Key facts:** Summer. Mar-Oct (groups pre-book Nov-Feb). Pay & display nearby. Primary to University, RE, History, workshops & activities 01458 8361103. On leads.

BARRINGTON COURT

Barrington, Nr Ilminster, Somerset TA19 0NQ

Discover the echoes of history in the heart of Somerset, in breathtaking gardens and working orchards. **Location:** Map 2:N5. OS Ref ST395 183.

Tel: 01460 241938 **E-mail:** barringtoncourt@nationaltrust.org.uk

Website: www.nationaltrust.org.uk/barrington-court

Open: 2 Jan-Mar & Nov-Dec, Sat & Sun,10.30am-3pm; Apr-Oct, 10.30am-5pm.

Admission: Adult £8.30; Child £4.10.

Glastonbury Abbey

COTHAY MANOR & GARDENS

Greenham, Wellington, Somerset TA21 0JR

Twelve acres of magical, romantic gardens surround what is reputedly the most perfect example of a small classic medieval manor. A plantsman's paradise.

Location: Map 2:L5. OS Ref ST085 213. **Tel:** 01823 672283

E-mail: cothaymanor@btinternet.com **Website:** www.cothaymanor.co.uk

Open: Apr-Sep, Tue-Thu, Sun & BH Mons, 11am-5pm.

Admission: Adult £14.75; Child (gardens only) £3.90.

DODINGTON HALL

Nr Nether Stowey, Bridgwater, Somerset TA5 1LF

Small Tudor manor house on the lower slopes of the Quantocks. Great Hall with oak roof. Semi-formal garden with roses and shrubs.

Location: Map 2:L4. OS Ref ST172 405. ½m from A39, 11m W of Bridgwater, 7m E of Williton. **Tel:** 01278 741400 **Open:** 3-12 Jun, 2-5pm.

Admission: Donations to Dodington Church. No coach parking.

HESTERCOMBE GARDENS

Cheddon Fitzpaine, Taunton, Somerset TA2 8LG

Exquisite Georgian landscape garden designed by Coplestone Warre Bampfylde, Victorian terrace/shrubbery, and Edwardian Lutyens/Jekyll formal gardens.

Location: Map 2:M5. OS Ref ST241 287. **Tel:** 01823 413923

E-mail: info@hestercombe.com **Website:** www.hestercombe.com

Open: All year, daily, 10-6pm; 5pm winter closing. Closed 25 Dec.

Admission: Adult £11; Child £5.50.

KENTSFORD

Washford, Watchet, Somerset TA23 0JD

Location: Map 2:L4. OS Ref ST058 426.

Tel: 01984 632309

E-mail: wyndhamest@btconnect.com

Open: Please contact for details.

Admission: Please contact for details.

MONTACUTE HOUSE

Montacute, Somerset TA15 6XP

A glittering Elizabethan house, adorned with elegant chimneys, carved parapets and other Renaissance features. **Location:** Map 2:N5. OS Ref ST499 172.

Tel: 01935 823289 **E-mail:** montacute@nationaltrust.org.uk

Website: www.nationaltrust.org.uk/montacute-house **Open:** 1 Jan-26 Feb, Sat & Sun, 12-3pm; 4 Mar- 29 Oct, daily, 11-4.30pm; 4 Nov-31 Dec, Sat & Sun, 12-3pm. Closed 24 & 25 Dec. **Admission:** Adult £11.40; Child £5.70.

ORCHARD WYNDHAM

Williton, Taunton, Somerset TA4 4HH

English manor house. Family home for 700 years encapsulating continuous building and alteration from the 14th to the 20th Century.

Location: Map 2:L4. OS Ref ST072 400. 1m from A39 at Williton.

Tel: 01984 632309 **E-mail:** wyndhamest@btconnect.com

Website: www.orchardwyndham.com

Open: Please telephone for details. **Admission:** Please telephone for details.

PRIOR PARK LANDSCAPE GARDEN

Ralph Allen Drive, Bath BA2 5AH

Beautiful and intimate 18th Century landscape garden created by Bath entrepreneur Ralph Allen with advice from Alexander Pope and 'Capability' Brown.

Location: Map 2:P3. OS Ref ST762 628. **Tel:** 01225 833422

E-mail: priorpark@nationaltrust.org.uk **Website:** www.nationaltrust.org.uk/prior-park **Open:** 1-29 Jan, Sat & Sun, 10-4pm; 30 Jan-29 Oct, daily, 10-5.30pm; 4 Nov-31 Dec, Sat & Sun, 10-4pm. **Admission:** Adult £6.50: Child £3.40.

TYNTESFIELD

Wraxall, North Somerset BS48 1NX

Extraordinary Victorian Estate. The House is a Gothic revival extravaganza with surrounding formal & kitchen gardens and extensive woodland.

Location: Map 2:N2. OS Ref ST506715. **Tel:** 0844 800 4966 **E-mail:** tyntesfield@nationaltrust.org.uk **Website:** www.nationaltrust.org.uk/tyntesfield

Open: Gdns: Jan, Feb, Nov, Dec 10am-5pm (Hse: 11-3pm); Mar-Oct, 10-6pm (Hse: 11-5pm). Closed 25 Dec **Admission:** Adult £14.05; Child £7.15.

Register for news and special offers at **www.hudsonsheritage.com**

LONGLEAT

LONGLEAT, WARMINSTER, WILTSHIRE BA12 7NW

www.longleat.co.uk

Set within 900 acres of 'Capability' Brown landscaped grounds, Longleat House is widely regarded as one of the best examples of high Elizabethan architecture in Britain and one of the most beautiful stately homes open to the public.
Visited by Elizabeth I in 1547, Longleat House was built by Sir John Thynne from 1568 and is currently home of the 7th Marquess of Bath. Many treasures are included within; the fine collection of paintings ranges from English portraits dating from the 16th Century to Dutch landscapes and Italian Old Masters. The ceilings are renowned for their ornate paintings and abundance of gilt made by the firm of John Dibblee Crace in the 1870s and 1880s. The furniture collection includes English pieces from as early as the 16th Century, fine French furniture of the 17th and 18th Centuries and a collection of major Italian pieces.
Don't miss the Safari Drive-Through, Animal Discovery and Adventure Zone for a fun filled day out for all the family.

Location: Map 2:P4. OS Ref ST809 430. Just off the A36 between Bath-Salisbury (A362 Warminster-Frome) 2 hrs from London following M3, A303, A36, A362 or M4/J18. A46, A36.
Owner: Marquess of Bath
Tel: 01985 844400
E-mail: enquiries@longleat.co.uk
Open: 11-19 Feb, daily; 24 Feb-26 Mar, Fri-Sun only; 31 Mar-29 Oct, daily excl. 12, 19, 26 Sept & 3, 10, 17 Oct. Limited House route available during Christmas period, selected dates from 10 Nov-2 Jan. Please see website for details.
Admission: Please see website for details: www.longleat.co.uk.
Key facts: Lady Bath's Shop; Emma's Kitchen Book indoor & outdoor events from 45 -500+ Orangery The Cellar Café House tours from 12 noon daily; private chattels tours on advertised dates

WILTON HOUSE

WILTON, SALISBURY SP2 0BJ

www.wiltonhouse.com

Wilton House has been the Earl of Pembroke's ancestral home for 470 years. Inigo Jones and John Webb rebuilt the house in the Palladian style after the 1647 fire whilst further alterations were made by James Wyatt from 1801. Recipient of the 2010 HHA/Sotheby's Restoration Award, the chief architectural features are the 17th Century state apartments (Single and Double Cube rooms), and the 19th Century cloisters. The House contains one of the finest art collections in Europe and is set in magnificent landscaped parkland featuring the Palladian Bridge. A large adventure playground provides hours of fun for younger visitors.
Location: Map 3:B4. OS Ref SU099 311. 3m W of Salisbury along the A36.
Owner: The Earl of Pembroke **Contact:** The Estate Office
Tel: 01722 746728 **Fax:** 01722 744447 **E-mail:** tourism@wiltonhouse.com
Open: House: 14 Apr-17 Apr inclusive; 29 Apr-31 Aug, Sun-Thu plus BH Sats, 11.30am-5pm, last admission 4.30pm.
*Please check website for up-to-date information.
Grounds: 9 Apr-23 Apr; 29 Apr-17 Sep, Sun-Thu plus BH Sats, 11am-5.30pm. Private groups at other times by arrangement.
Admission: House & Grounds*: Adult £15.00, Child (5-15) £7.75, Concession £13.00, Family £37.75 *includes admission to Dining & South Ante Rooms when open. Grounds: Adult £6.25, Child (5-15) £4.75, Concession £5.75, Family £17.50. Group Admission: Adult £12.75, Child £6.25, Concession £10.75. Guided Tour: £8.00. Exhibitions: "Cecil Beaton at Wilton". An exhibition of photographs from The Cecil Beaton Studio Archive at Sotheby's: Lord Pembroke's Classic Car Collection, in the Old Riding School.
Key facts: Film location, equestrian events, antiques fairs, vehicle rallies. No photography in house. Open 5 days a week during the season. WCs. Licensed. Licensed. By arrangement. £8.00. 200 cars & 12 coaches. Free coach parking. Group rates (min 15), drivers' meal voucher. National Curriculum KS1/2. Sandford Award Winner 2002 & 2008. Guide dogs only.

© Lydiard Park

BOWOOD HOUSE & GARDENS

Calne, Wiltshire SN11 0LZ

www.bowood.org

Set within one of 'Capability' Brown's finest landscapes, Bowood is home to the Lansdowne family. Visit the Georgian House and discover over 250 years of art and historical memorabilia and the laboratory where Joseph Priestley discovered oxygen gas. Award-winning gardens and outstanding children's adventure playground.
Location: Map 3:A2. OS Ref ST974 700. Follow the Brown Tourist signs 'Bowood House & Gardens'. The entrance in through white gates just off Derry Hill.
If using a Satnav please use the postcode SN11 9NF.
Owner: The Marquis of Lansdowne **Contact:** Bowood House and Gardens
Tel: 01249 812102 **E-mail:** houseandgardens@bowood.org
Open: Apr-Oct 2017. See website for up-to-date opening & admission details.
Key facts: Limited disabled parking spaces near House & WC available. Treehouse Café. Stables Restaurant. Pre-booked guided tours available. Free ample parking.

© Philip Pearce

IFORD MANOR: THE PETO GARDEN

Lower Westwood, Bradford-on-Avon, Wiltshire BA15 2BA

www.ifordmanor.co.uk

Unique Grade 1 Italian-style garden set on a romantic hillside above the River Frome. Designed by Edwardian architect Harold Peto, who lived at Iford from 1899-1933, the garden features terraces, colonnades, cloisters, casita, statuary, evergreen planting and magnificent rural views. Winner of the 1998 HHA/Christie's Garden of the Year Award. 2016 is year four of a five year historic replant in the rose garden and Great Terrace. **Location:** Map 2:P3. OS Ref ST800 589. 7m SE of Bath. Coaches must call in advance for directions.
Owner: The Cartwright-Hignett Family **Contact:** Mr William Cartwright-Hignett
Tel: 01225 863146 **E-mail:** info@ifordmanor.co.uk
Open: Apr 1-Sep 30: Tue, Wed, Thu, Sat, Sun & BH Mons, 2-5pm. Oct: Suns only, 2-5pm. Tea Room at weekends May-Sep, 2:30-5pm; cake of the day at other times. **Admission:** Adult £5.50, Conc. £5.00. Groups (10+) also welcome (exclusive use) outside normal opening hours, strictly by appointment.
Key facts: No professional photography without permission. Children under 10yrs preferred weekdays for safety. Please enquire about private events. Partial. WCs. Tea Room open at weekends 2:30-5pm. Subject to availability for groups booked in advance. Limited for coaches. On leads.

LYDIARD PARK

Lydiard Tregoze, Swindon, Wiltshire SN5 3PA

www.lydiardpark.org.uk

Lydiard Park is the ancestral home of the Viscounts Bolingbroke. The Palladian house contains original family furnishings and portraits, exceptional plasterwork and rare 17th Century window. The Georgian ornamental Walled Garden has beautiful seasonal displays of flowers and unique garden features. Exceptional monuments, including the Golden Cavalier, in the church.
Location: Map 3:B1. OS Ref SU104 848. 4m W of Swindon, 1½m N M4/J16.
Owner: Swindon Borough Council
Contact: Lydiard Park
Tel: 01793 466664 **E-mail:** lydiardpark@swindon.gov.uk
Open: Please check the Lydiard Park website for 2017 opening times.
Admission: Adult £6.50, Child (3-16 yrs) £3.50, Senior £6.00
Key facts: No photography in house. Small gift shop. Seasonal plants available. Designated parking, WCs. Forest Café open all year. By arrangement. Car parking charges apply.

CORSHAM COURT

Corsham, Wiltshire SN13 0BZ

Historic collection of paintings and furniture.
Extensive gardens. Tours by arrangement.
Location: Map 3:A2. OS Ref ST874 706.
Sign-posted from the A4, approx. 4m W of Chippenham.
Owner: Lord Methuen **Contact:** The Curator
Tel: 01249 712214 \ 01249 701610 **E-mail:** staterooms@corsham-court.co.uk
Website: www.corsham-court.co.uk
Open: Tue, Wed, Thu, Sat, Sun 20 Mar-30 Sep 2-5.30pm.
Weekends only: 1 Oct-19 Mar 2-4.30pm (Closed Dec).
Admission: House & gardens: Adult £10.00; Child £5.00.
Gardens only: Adult £5.00; Child £2.50. **Key facts:** No photography in house. Guide books, postcards, etc at cash desk. Platform lift & WC. Max 45. If requested the owner may meet the group. Morning tours preferred. 120yds from house. Coaches may park in Church Square. Coach parties must book in advance. Available: rate negotiable. A guide will be provided.

LACOCK ABBEY

Lacock, Nr Chippenham, Wiltshire SN15 2LG

Founded in 1232 and coverted to a country house in c1540, once home to William Henry Fox Talbot. **Location:** Map 3:A2. OS Ref ST919 684.
Tel: 01249 730459 **E-mail:** lacockabbey@nationaltrust.org.uk
Website: www.nationaltrust.org.uk/lacock **Open:** House: 1 Jan-12 Feb & 4-26 Nov, Sat & Sun, 11.30-3.30pm; 13 Feb-29 Oct, daily, 11-5pm; 1-31 Dec, Thus-Sun, 11.30-3.30pm. **Admission:** Adult £12.10; Child £6.

MOMPESSON HOUSE

Cathedral Close, Salisbury, Wiltshire SP1 2EL

Elegant, spacious house in the Cathedral Close, built 1701. **Location:** Map 3:B4. OS Ref SU142 297. On N side of Choristers' Green in Cathedral Close, nr High Street Gate. **Tel:** 01722 335659 **E-mail:** mompessonhouse@nationaltrust.org.uk
Website: www.nationaltrust.org.uk **Open:** 11 Mar-26 Jul, Sat-Wed, 11-5pm; 27 Jul-6 Sep, 11-5pm; 9 Sep-29 Oct, Sat-Wed, 11-5pm; 25 Nov-17 Dec, Sat & Sun, 11-3.30pm. **Admission:** Adult £6.30; Child £3.

Register for news and special offers at **www.hudsonsheritage.com**

NEWHOUSE

Redlynch, Salisbury, Wiltshire SP5 2NX

A brick, Jacobean 'Trinity' House, c1609, with two Georgian wings and a basically Georgian interior. **Location:** Map 3:B5. OS Ref SU218 214. 9m S of Salisbury between A36 & A338. **Tel:** 01725 510055
E-mail: events@newhouseestate.co.uk **Website:** www.newhouseestate.co.uk
Open: 1 Mar-10 Apr, Mon-Fri & 28 Aug: 2-5pm. **Admission:** Adult £5.00, Child £3.00, Conc. £5.00. Groups (15+): Adult £4.00, Child £3.00, Conc. £4.00.

NORRINGTON MANOR

Alvediston, Salisbury, Wiltshire SP5 5LL

Built in 1377 it has been altered and added to in every century since, with the exception of the 18th Century.
Location: Map 3:AS. OS Ref ST966 237. Signposted to N of Berwick St John and Alvediston road (half way between the two villages).
Tel: 01722 780 259 **Open:** By appointment in writing.
Admission: A donation to the local churches is asked for.

OLD WARDOUR CASTLE

Nr Tisbury, Wiltshire SP3 6RR

Ruins of a 14th Century castle by a lake, in landscaped grounds, with grotto. Wedding venue. **Location:** Map 3:A5. OS Ref OS184, ST939 263. Off A30 2m SW of Tisbury. **Tel:** 01747 870487 **E-mail:** customers@english-heritage.org.uk
Website: www.english-heritage.org.uk/oldwardour
Open: 1 Jan-31 Mar, daily, 10-4pm; 1 Apr-30 Sep, daily, 10-6pm; 1 Nov-31 Dec, daily, 10-4pm. Closed 24-26 Dec & 1 Jan. **Admission:** Adult £5.20; Child £3.10.

STONEHENGE

Wiltshire SP4 7DE

One of the wonders of the world and the best-known prehistoric monument in Europe. **Location:** Map 3: B4. OS Ref SU121423.
Tel: 0870 333 1181 **E-mail:** customers@english-heritage.org.uk
Website: www.english-heritage.org.uk/visit/places/stonehenge **Open:** All year, 9.30am-dusk; 1 Jun-31 Aug, 9am-8pm. Closed 24 & 25 Dec. Subject to change around summer solstice. **Admission:** Adult £18.20; Child £10.90.

STOURHEAD

Stourton, Nr Warminster BA12 6QD

Explore the world-famous landscape garden, experience the Grand Tour in the Palladian mansion. **Location:** Map 2:P4. OS Ref ST776 340. At Stourton off the B3092, 3m NW of A303 (Mere), 8m S of A361 (Frome). **Tel:** 01747 841152
E-mail: stourhead@nationaltrust.org.uk **Website:** www.nationaltrust.org.uk
Open: Gdns: All year, 9-5pm. Hse: 25 Feb-22 Oct, 11-4.30pm, 23 Oct-12 Nov, 11-3.30pm, 25 Nov-20 Dec, 11-3pm. **Admission:** Adult £14.20; Child £7.10.

ANTONY HOUSE & GARDEN

Torpoint, Cornwall PL11 2QA
Tel: 01752 812191 **E-mail:** antony@nationaltrust.org.uk

CHYSAUSTER ANCIENT VILLAGE

Nr Newmill, Penzance, Cornwall TR20 8XA
Tel: 07831 757934 **E-mail:** customers@english-heritage.org.uk

LAUNCESTON CASTLE

Castle Lodge, Launceston, Cornwall PL15 7DR
Tel: 01566 772365 **E-mail:** customers@english-heritage.org.uk

LAWRENCE HOUSE MUSEUM

9 Castle Street, Launceston, Cornwall PL15 8BA
Tel: 01566 773277 **E-mail:** lawrencehousemuseum@yahoo.co.uk

MOUNT EDGCUMBE HOUSE & COUNTRY PARK

Cremyll, Torpoint, Cornwall PL10 1HZ
Tel: 01752 822236

ST MAWES CASTLE

St Mawes, Cornwall TR2 5DE
Tel: 01326 270526 **E-mail:** stmawes.castle@english-heritage.org.uk

TREBAH GARDEN

Mawnan Smith, Nr Falmouth, Cornwall TR11 5JZ
Tel: 01326 252200 **E-mail:** mail@trebah-garden.co.uk

TRELISSICK GARDEN

Feock, Truro, Cornwall TR3 6QL
Tel: 01872 862090 **E-mail:** trelissick@nationaltrust.org.uk

TRERICE

Kestle Mill, Nr Newquay, Cornwall TR8 4PG
Tel: 01637 875404 **E-mail:** trerice@nationaltrust.org.uk

ARLINGTON COURT

Nr Barnstaple, North Devon EX31 4LP
Tel: 01271 850296 **E-mail:** arlingtoncourt@nationaltrust.org.uk

BERRY POMEROY CASTLE

Totnes, Devon TQ9 6LJ
Tel: 01803 866618 **E-mail:** customers@english-heritage.org.uk

BUCKLAND ABBEY

The National Trust, Yelverton, Devon PL20 6EY
Tel: 01822 853607 **E-mail:** bucklandabbey@nationaltrust.org.uk

CLOVELLY

Clovelly, Nr Bideford, N Devon EX39 5TA
Tel: 01237 431781 **E-mail:** visitorcentre@

COLETON FISHACRE

Brownstone Road, Kingswear, Dartmouth TQ6 0EQ
Tel: 01803 842382 **E-mail:** coletonfishacre@nationaltrust.org.uk

COMPTON CASTLE

Marldon, Paighton TQ3 1TA
Tel: 01803 843235 **E-mail:** compton@nationaltrust.org.uk

DARTMOUTH CASTLE

Castle Road, Dartmouth, Devon TQ6 0JN
Tel: 01803 833588 **E-mail:** dartmouth.castle@english-heritage.org.uk

THE GARDEN HOUSE

Buckland Monachorum, Yelverton PL20 7LQ
Tel: 01822 854769 **E-mail:** office@the gardenhouse.org.uk

RHS GARDEN ROSEMOOR

Great Torrington, Devon EX38 8PH
Tel: 01805 624067 **E-mail:** rosemooradmin@rhs.org.uk

SHILSTONE

Modbury, Devon PL21 0TW
Tel: 01548 830888 **E-mail:** abi@shilstonedevon.co.uk

TOTNES CASTLE

Castle Street, Totnes, Devon TQ9 5NU
Tel: 01803 864406 **E-mail:** customers@english-heritage.org.uk

HIGHER MELCOMBE
Melcombe Bingham, Dorchester, Dorset DT2 7PB
Tel: 01258 880251 **E-mail:** mc.woodhouse@hotmail.co.uk

PORTLAND CASTLE
Castletown, Portland, Weymouth, Dorset DT5 1AZ
Tel: 01305 820539 **E-mail:** customers@english-heritage.org.uk

BATSFORD ARBORETUM
Batsford, Moreton-in-Marsh, Gloucestershire GL56 9QB
Tel: 01386 701441 **E-mail:** arboretum@batsfordfoundation.co.uk

BOURTON HOUSE GARDEN
Bourton-on-the-Hill, Gloucestershire GL56 9AE
Tel: 01386 700754 **E-mail:** info@bourtonhouse.com

CHEDWORTH ROMAN VILLA
Yanworth, Cheltenham, Gloucestershire GL54 3LJ
Tel: 01242 890256 **E-mail:** chedworth@nationaltrust.org.uk

CIRENCESTER PARK GARDENS
Cirencester, Gloucestershire GL7 2BU
Tel: 01285 653135

PAINSWICK ROCOCO GARDEN
Painswick, Gloucestershire GL6 6TH
Tel: 01452 813204 **E-mail:** info@rococogarden.org.uk

WOODCHESTER MANSION
Stonehouse, Gloucestershire GL10 3TS
Tel: 01453 861541 **E-mail:** info@woodchestermansion.org.uk

ACTON COURT
Latteridge Road, Iton Acton, Bristol, Gloucestershire BS37 9TL
Tel: 01454 228224 **E-mail:** info@actoncourt.com

THE AMERICAN MUSEUM & GARDENS
Claverton Manor, Bath BA2 7BD
Tel: 01225 460503 **E-mail:** info@americanmuseum.org

ASSEMBLY ROOMS
Bennett Street, Bath BA1 2QH
Tel: 01225 477785 **E-mail:** costume_enquiries@bathnes.gov.uk

DUNSTER CASTLE
Dunster, Nr Minehead, Somerset TA24 6SL
Tel: 01643 821314 **E-mail:** dunstercastle@nationaltrust.org.uk

FARLEIGH HUNGERFORD CASTLE
Farleigh Hungerford, Bath, Somerset BA2 7RS
Tel: 01225 754026 **E-mail:** customers@english-heritage.org.uk

THE MERCHANT'S HOUSE
132 High Street, Marlborough, Wiltshire SN8 1HN
Tel: 01672 511491 **E-mail:** admin@merchantshousetrust.co.uk

ROMAN BATHS
Abbey Church Yard, Bath BA1 1LZ
Tel: 01225 477785 **E-mail:** romanbaths_bookings@bathnes.gov.uk

OLD SARUM
Castle Road, Salisbury, Wiltshire SP1 3SD
Tel: 01722 335398 **E-mail:** customers@english-heritage.org.uk

Sezincote

Register for news and special offers at **www.hudsonsheritage.com**

HUDSONs

ALL BRITAIN'S BEST HISTORIC PLACES

Explore

Print

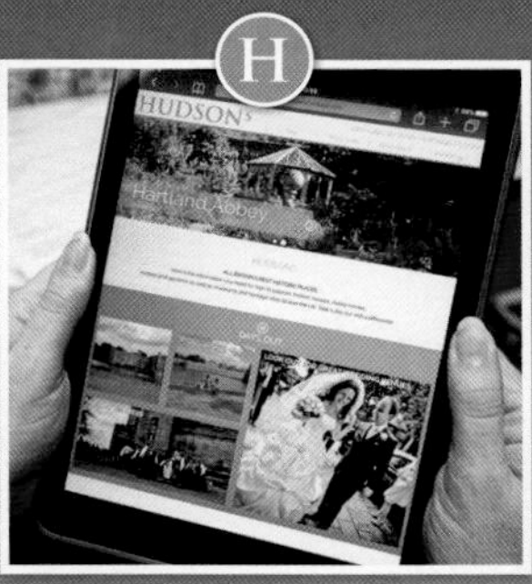

Online

Mobile

Visit www.hudsonsheritage.com and sign up to our monthly newsletter for offers, competitions and recommendations throughout the year, and download our app Hudsons UK for up-to-the-minute information when out exploring.

Online

App

BRINGING BRITAIN'S HERITAGE TO YOU

www.hudsonsheritage.com

Holkham Hall, Norfolk

Bedfordshire
Cambridgeshire
Essex
Hertfordshire
Norfolk
Suffolk

East of England

Few regions shelter such an architectural variety as East Anglia from timbered moated manor houses to magnificent Palladian mansions with gardens and great art collections to stop you in your tracks.

VISITOR INFORMATION

Owner
The Duke and Duchess of Bedford & The Trustees of the Bedford Estates

Address
Woburn
Bedfordshire
MK17 9WA

Location
Map 7:D10
OS Ref. SP965 325
Signposted from M1 J12/J13 and A4012. Easy access from A5 via Hockliffe, follow signs to Woburn village.

Contact
Woburn Abbey
Tel: 01525 290333
E-mail: admissions@woburn.co.uk

Opening Times
Woburn Abbey, Gardens and Deer Park.

Please telephone or visit our website for details.

Admission
Please telephone or visit our website for details.

Group rates available.

Special Events
Please visit our website for a full list of our events, guided tours and study days.

Don't miss the Woburn Abbey Garden Show on 24th & 25th Jun 2017. Set against the stunning backdrop of Woburn Abbey, 'The Gardener's Garden Show' offers visitors an informative day out.

© The Duke and Duchess of Bedford & The Trustees of the Bedford Estates

WOBURN ABBEY AND GARDENS

www.woburnabbey.co.uk

Step inside Woburn Abbey and immerse yourself in 400 years of family stories and British history, explore 28 acres of award-winning gardens and enjoy a drive through the extensive deer park.

Woburn Abbey has belonged to the Russell family since the mid-16th Century and is today the family home of the Duke and Duchess of Bedford. Visit the Abbey to view the unique indoor Grotto and explore the state rooms to learn more about the lives of the Earls and Dukes of Bedford, discover great tales of imprisonment, beheadings, love affairs, Royal Pardons political reforms and Royal state visits.

Discover an art collection including an unrivalled group of 16th and 17th Century portraits, works by Reynolds and Van Dyck and the largest private collection of Canaletto's Venetian views on public display, together with a treasury of silver, porcelain and fine English and French furniture.

The English tradition of Afternoon Tea was popularised by Anna-Maria, Duchess of Bedford, in the 19th Century and can still be enjoyed at Woburn today.

The 28 acres of Woburn Abbey Gardens are exceptional. Enjoy elegant horticultural designs, woodland glades, ponds and architectural features; much of which were the inspiration of Humphry Repton who contributed to their design. The restoration of Repton's original Pleasure Grounds from 200 years ago continues today.

KEY FACTS

- Gift and souvenir shop.
- Woburn grown plants available to buy throughout the main season.
- Conferences, exhibitions, banqueting, luncheons and dinners.
- Very limited access in the house. Good access in the gardens.
- Licensed Tea Room. Freshly prepared, homemade meals, snacks and sweet treats as well as afternoon tea.
- By arrangement.
- Free parking.
- Please telephone for details.
- Except assistance dogs in Gardens only.
- The Woburn Hotel in the village of Woburn
- Weddings are held in the Sculpture Gallery, visit website or call for more information.
- www.woburnabbey.co.uk/events

© The Duke and Duchess of Bedford & The Trustees of the Bedford Estates

© The Duke and Duchess of Bedford & The Trustees of the Bedford Estates

QUEEN ANNE'S SUMMERHOUSE

Shuttleworth, Old Warden, Bedfordshire SG18 9DU

www.landmarktrust.org.uk

Hidden in a pine wood on the edge of the Shuttleworth estate is this intriguing folly with high quality 18th Century brickwork. Inside is the most elegant bedsit and a staircase in which one of the turrets winds up to the roof terrace or down to the vaulted basement, now a bathroom, where the servants once prepared refreshments. Surrounded by the flora and fauna of beautiful woodland, this is a magical spot.

Location: Map 7:E10. OS Ref TL154 444.
Owner: The Landmark Trust
Tel: 01628 825925
E-mail: bookings@landmarktrust.org.uk
Open: Self-catering accommodation. Visits by appointment.
Admission: Free for visits by appointment.
Key facts: A bedsit with kitchen, dining, sitting and sleeping on the ground floor. A spiral staircase leads down to the bathroom.

TURVEY HOUSE

Turvey, Bedfordshire MK43 8EL

A neo-classical house set in picturesque parkland bordering the River Great Ouse. The principal rooms contain a fine collection of 18th and 19th Century English and Continental furniture, pictures, porcelain, objets d'art and books. Walled Garden.

Location: Map 7:D9. OS Ref SP939 528.
Between Bedford and Northampton on A428.
Owner: The Hanbury Family **Contact:** Daniel Hanbury
Tel: 01234 881621 **E-mail:** danielhanbury@hotmail.com
Website: www.turveyhouse.co.uk
Open: May 1, 10, 14, 24, 28 & 29.
Jun 7,11, 21 & 25.
Jul 5, 9, 19, 23, 24, 25, 26, 27, 28, 30 & 31.
Aug 1, 2, 3, 4, 6, 20, 27 & 28.
Admission: Adult £6.00, Child £3.00.
Key facts: No photography in house. Obligatory.
Ample for cars, none for coaches.

SWISS GARDEN

Old Warden Park, Bedfordshire SG18 9EP

The Swiss Garden is a late Regency garden created between 1820 and 1835 by the third Lord Ongley and is an outstanding example of the Swiss picturesque.

Location: Map 7:E10. OS Ref TL150 447.
Tel: 01767 627927 **Website:** www.theswissgarden.org
Open: 1 Jan-12 Feb, daily, 10-4pm; Feb half term-31 Oct, daily, 9.30-5pm; 1 Nov-31 Dec, daily, 10-4pm. **Admission:** Adult £8; Child Free.

WREST PARK

Silsoe, Luton, Bedfordshire MK45 4HS

Take a stroll through three centuries of landscape design at Wrest Park.

Location: Map 7:E10. OS Ref 153. TL093 356.
Tel: 01525 860000 **E-mail:** customers@english-heritage.org.uk
Website: www.english-heritage.org.uk/wrest
Open: 2 Jan-31 Mar, Sat & Sun, 10-4pm; daily at half term; Apr-Oct, daily, 10-5pm; Nov-Dec, daily, 10-4pm. **Admission:** Adult £10.80; Child £6.50.

HUDSON'S

NEED THE PERFECT SETTING FOR YOUR DREAM DAY?

Go to the quick guide at the back of this book for the best wedding venues

www.hudsonsweddings.com

©English Rose Weddings

ELTON HALL

ELTON HALL AND GARDENS, ELTON, CAMBRIDGESHIRE PE8 6SH

www.eltonhall.com

Elton Hall is a fascinating mixture of styles and has evolved as a family house since the late 15th Century. The house contains wonderful furniture, porcelain and magnificent paintings. Artists represented in the collection include Gainsborough, Constable, Reynolds and Old Masters from the early Italian Renaissance. The library is one of the largest in private ownership and contains such treasures as Henry VIII's prayer book.

The formal gardens have been restored during the last 30 years and include a Gothic Orangery, a Flower Garden with spectacular fountain, Shrub Garden and Box Walk. Billowing borders surround the lily pond, while topiary, parterres and immaculately kept lawns and paths give structure to the many unusual plants.

Location: Map 7:E7. OS Ref TL091 930. Close to A1 in the village of Elton, off A605 Peterborough - Oundle Road.

Owner: Sir William Proby Bt, CBE **Contact:** Catherine Lockwood

Tel: 01832 280468 **E-mail:** events@eltonhall.com

Open: 2pm-5pm: May: Last May BH, Sun & Mon. Jun & Jul: Wed, Thu. Aug: Wed, Thu, Sun & BH Mon. Private groups by arrangement daily May-Sep.

Admission: Please see website www.eltonhall.com for current house and garden prices. Children under 16 free. Or call 01832 280468.

Key facts: No photography in house. Walled Garden Plant Centre and Tea Room. For meetings and dinners, Parkland for outdoor activities. Garden suitable. Obligatory. Except Bank Holidays when Room Guides. At Walled Garden Plant Centre, adjacent to Elton Hall. Contact events@eltonhall.com No dogs in Hall and Formal Gardens. Guide dogs in gardens only. Two licensed wedding venues.

ISLAND HALL

Godmanchester, Cambridgeshire PE29 2BA

www.islandhall.com

An important mid-18th Century mansion of great charm, owned and restored by an award-winning interior designer. This family home has lovely Georgian rooms, with fine period detail, and interesting possessions relating to the owners' ancestors since their first occupation of the house in 1800. A tranquil riverside setting with formal gardens and ornamental island forming part of the grounds in an area of Best Landscape. Octavia Hill wrote 'This is the loveliest, dearest old house; I never was in such a one before'.

Location: Map 7:F8. OS Ref TL244 706. Centre of Godmanchester, Post Street next to free car park. 1m S of Huntingdon, 15m NW of Cambridge A14.

Owner: Mr Christopher & Lady Linda Vane Percy **Contact:** Mr C Vane Percy

Tel: Groups 01480 459676. **Individuals via Invitation to View:** 01206 573948.

E-mail: enquire@islandhall.com

Open: Groups by arrangement: All year round. Individuals via Invitation to View.

Admission: Groups (40+) £8.00 per person, (30+) £8.50 and Parties under 20 a minimum charge of £180.00.

Key facts: See website for more details. Homemade teas.

© National Trust

Peckover House

KIMBOLTON CASTLE

Kimbolton, Huntingdon, Cambridgeshire PE28 0EA

www.kimbolton.cambs.sch.uk/castle

Vanbrugh and Hawksmoor's 18th Century adaptation of 13th Century fortified house. Katherine of Aragon's last residence. Tudor remains still visible. Courtyard by Henry Bell of Kings Lynn. Outstanding Pellegrini murals. Gatehouse by Robert Adam. Home of Earls and Dukes of Manchester, 1615-1950. Family portraits in State Rooms. Now Kimbolton School.
Location: Map 7:E8. OS Ref TL101 676. 7m NW of St Neots on B645.
Owner: Governors of Kimbolton School
Contact: Mrs N Butler
Tel: 01480 860505 **Fax:** 01480 861763
Open: 5 Mar & 5 Nov 2017, 1-4 pm.
Admission: Adult £5.00, Child £2.50, OAP £4.00. Groups by arrangement throughout the year, including evenings, special rates apply.
Key facts: Unsuitable. By arrangement. On leads. In grounds only.

THE MANOR, HEMINGFORD GREY

Norman Court, High Street, Hemingford Grey, Cambridgeshire PE28 9BN

www.greenknowe.co.uk

One of the oldest continuously inhabited houses in Britain built about 1130. The three walls of The Music Room have seen and heard nearly nine hundred years of family life. The house was made famous as 'Green Knowe' by the author Lucy M. Boston. The internationally known patchwork collection sewn by Lucy Boston is also shown. Surrounded by a moat and on the fourth side by a river the four acre garden, laid out by Lucy Boston, has topiary, old roses, award-winning irises and herbaceous borders. **Location:** Map 7:F8. OS Ref TL290 706. A14, 3m SE of Huntingdon. 12m NW of Cambridge. Access via small gate on riverside.
Owner/Contact: Diana Boston **Tel:** 01480 463134
E-mail: diana_boston@hotmail.com **Open:** House: All year to individuals or groups by prior arrangement. Also in May guided tours daily at 2pm (booking advisable). Garden: All year, daily, 11am-5pm (4pm in winter).
Admission: House & Garden: Adult £8.00, Concessions £7, Child £3.00, Family £22.00. Garden only £4 adults £3.50 concessions children free. **Key facts:** No photography in house. Cash, cheque or bank transfer payments only. Partial. Access to hall and dining room only. Garden has some gravel areas. Obligatory. Cars: Disabled plus a few spaces if none in High Street. Coaches: Nearby. Particularly suitable for children. Guide dogs only.

PECKOVER HOUSE & GARDEN

North Brink, Wisbech, Cambs PE13 1JR

An oasis hidden away in an urban environment. A classic Georgian merchant's townhouse, lived in by the Peckover family for 150 years, reflecting their Quaker lifestyle. The house is open over three floors, including the basement service area and our Banking Wing. Outstanding gardens - two acres of sensory delight, with summerhouses, Orangery, over 60 varieties of rose and specimen trees.
Location: Map 7:G6. OS Ref TF458 097. N bank of River Nene, Wisbech B1441.
Owner: National Trust **Contact:** The Property Secretary **Tel:** 01945 583463
Fax: 01945 587904 **E-mail:** peckover@nationaltrust.org.uk
Website: www.nationaltrust.org.uk/peckover **Open:** We are open on varying days throughout the year. See website or call for full opening information.
Admission: NT members free. Groups discount: (min 15 people) book in advance with Property Secretary. See website for full admission prices.
Key facts: PMV Partial. WCs. Licensed. By arrangement. Signposted. Guide dogs only. www.nationaltrustcottages.co.uk

ANGLESEY ABBEY, GARDENS & LODE MILL

Quy Road, Lode, Cambridgeshire CB25 9EJ

A passion for tradition and style inspired one man to transform a run-down country house and desolate landscape. **Location:** Map 7:G9. OS Ref TL533 622. 6m NE of Cambridge on B1102, signs from A14 jct35. **Tel:** 01223 810080
E-mail: angleseyabbey@nationaltrust.org.uk **Website:** www.nationaltrust.org.uk/angleseyabbey **Open:** Gdns: 10-4.30pm; Apr-Oct, 10-5.30pm. Hse: Tue-Sun, 7-26 Mar, 11-3pm; 29 Mar-29 Oct, 11-4pm. **Admission:** Adult £12.45; Child £6.45.

CAMBRIDGE UNIVERSITY BOTANIC GARDEN

1 Brookside, Cambridge CB2 1JE

Opened in 1846, designed for year round interest & seasonal inspiration.
Location: Map 7:G9. OS Ref TL453 573.
1 mile S of city centre between A1309 & A1307
Tel: 01223 336265 **E-mail:** enquiries@botanic.cam.ac.uk
Website: www.botanic.cam.ac.uk **Open:** All year, daily, 10-4pm; Apr-Sep, 10-6pm. **Admission:** Adult £5, Child U16 Free.

DENNY ABBEY

Ely Road, Chittering, Waterbeach, Cambridgeshire CB25 9PQ

Benedictine monastery founded 1159 with Farmland Museum & 1940s farm labourer's cottage.
Location: Map 7:G8. OS Ref TL488 685. 6m N of Cambridge on the A10.
Tel: 01223 860988 **E-mail:** info@farmlandmuseum.org.uk
Website: www.dennyfarmlandmuseum.org.uk
Open: Apr-Oct, daily, 12-5pm. **Admission:** Adult £5; Child £3.

LONGTHORPE TOWER

Thorpe Rd, Longthorpe, Cambridgeshire PE1 1HA

One of most important set of 14th Century wall painting in Northern Europe.
Location: Map 7:E7. OS Ref TL192 984. 2m W of Peterborough just off A47.
Tel: 01733 864663 **E-mail:** customers@english-heritage.org.uk
Website: www.english-heritage.org.uk/longthorpetower
Open: Apr-Oct, Sat, Sun & BH Mons, 10am-5pm.
Admission: Adult £3; Child £2.

WIMPOLE ESTATE

Arrington, Royston, Cambridgeshire SG8 0BW

A unique working estate still guided by the seasons, an impressive mansion at its heart with beautiful interiors by Gibbs, Flitcroft and Soane.
Location: Map 7:F9. OS Ref 154, TL336 510. **Tel:** 01223 206000
E-mail: wimpolehall@nationaltrust.org.uk **Website:** www.nationaltrust.org.uk/wimpole-estate **Open:** House & Farm: 11 Feb-29 Oct, daily, 11am-5pm. Gardens: Daily, all year, 11am-4pm. **Admission:** Adult £16.25; Child £8.

East of England

VISITOR INFORMATION

Owner
English Heritage

Address
Audley End House
Audley End
Saffron Walden
Essex
CB11 4JF

Location
Map 7:G10
OS Ref. TL525 382
1m W of Saffron Walden on B1383, M11/J8 & J10.
Rail: Audley End 1¼ m.

Contact
Visitor Operations Team
Tel: 01799 522842
E-mail: customers@english-heritage.org.uk

Opening Times
Gardens & Stables:
2 Jan-Mar & Nov-Dec, Sat & Sun, 10-4pm; daily at half term; Apr-Oct, daily, 10-5pm.
House:
Apr-Oct, daily, 12-4pm.

Please visit www.english-heritage.org.uk for opening times, admission prices and the most up-to-date information.

Admission
Adult:	£18.30
Child:	£11.00

Special Events
There is an exciting events programme available throughout the year, for further details please contact the property or visit the website.

© English Heritage

AUDLEY END ⌗

www.english-heritage.org.uk/audleyend

One of England's finest country houses, Audley End is also a mansion with a difference. Enjoy a great day out.

Experience the daily routine of a Victorian stable yard as it is brought to life. Complete with resident horses and a costumed groom, the stables experience includes an exhibition where you can find out about the workers who lived on the estate in the 1880s, the tack house and the Audley End fire engine. There is also a children's play area and Café which are ideal for family visitors.

Every great house needed an army of servants and the restored Victorian Service Wing shows a world 'below stairs' that was never intended to be seen. Immerse yourself in the past as you visit the kitchen, scullery, pantry and laundries with film projections, introductory wall displays and even original food from the era.

The cook, Mrs Crocombe, and her staff can regularly be seen trying out new recipes and going about their chores.

Audley End House is itself a magnificent house, built to entertain royalty. Among the highlights is a stunning art collection including works by Masters Holbein, Lely and Canaletto. Its pastoral parkland is designed by 'Capability' Brown and there is an impressive formal garden to discover. Don't miss the working Organic Kitchen Garden with its glasshouses and vinery growing original Victorian varieties of fruit and vegetables. Audley End also boasts Cambridge Lodge a two storey detached holiday cottage. The sitting room enjoys magnificent views of the grounds of Audley End House.

KEY FACTS

- Open air concerts and other events. WCs.
- Service Yard and Coach House Shops.
- By arrangement for groups.
- Coaches to book in advance. Free entry for coach drivers and tour guides.
- Dogs on leads only.

© English Heritage

© English Heritage

Register for news and special offers at **www.hudsonsheritage.com**

© National Trust Images / David Levenson

PAYCOCKE'S HOUSE & GARDEN

www.nationaltrust.org.uk/paycockes

"One of the most attractive half-timbered houses of England" - Nikolaus Pevsner

A magnificent half-timbered Tudor wool merchant's house with a beautiful and tranquil arts-and-crafts style cottage garden. Visitors can follow the changing fortunes of the house over its five hundred year history as it went from riches to rags and discover how it was saved from demolition and restored to its former glory as one of the earliest buildings saved by the National Trust.

Thomas Paycocke was an affluent merchant whose home reflected the wealth of the wool industry in Coggeshall. The House passed to the Buxton family, descendants of Paycocke but after the decline of the wool trade it saw harder times passing through different hands and uses and by the 19th Century was used as tenements and a haulier's store and office and threatened with dereliction. In 1904 it was bought by Noel Buxton, a descendent of the family who owned the House from the late 16th Century. He began a 20 year renovation of the building to restore it to how he thought it might have looked in 1509 when it was built. During this time it was lived in by friends and relatives of Buxton including Conrad Noel the 'red' vicar of Thaxted and composer Gustav Holst. Buxton bequeathed Paycocke's to the National Trust on his death in 1924.

The House has a charming Coffee Shop and relaxing garden. The House has recently benefited from a substantial investment in interpretation and hosts changing exhibitions of art.

KEY FACTS

- Cream tea, coffee and cake offer.
- At Grange Barn, Coggeshall.
- 
- On leads in gardens only.
- Open 7 days a week excluding closing 22-27 Dec for Christmas.
- Events through the year.

Coffee Shop

© National Trust Images/David Levenson

Study

© National Trust Images/David Levenson

VISITOR INFORMATION

Owner
National Trust

Address
25 West Street
Coggeshall
Essex
C06 1NS

Location
Map 8:I11
OS Ref. TL848 225
Parking available nearby at Grange Barn (also NT), a five minute walk away, 1/3 of a mile. Limited on street parking on West Street.

Contact
The Manager
Tel: 01376 561305
E-mail: paycockes@nationaltrust.org.uk

Opening Times
Open 7 days a week excluding 22-26 Dec for Christmas.

18 Mar-1 Oct
11am-5pm

2 Oct-29 Oct
11am-4pm

30 Oct-21 Dec
11am-3pm

27 Dec-1 Mar 2018
11am-3pm

Garden opens at 10.30am, last admission and last service in the coffee shop at 4.30pm.

Reduced room opening in winter season (Oct-Mar) and garden closed due to conservation work.

Admission

Adult:	£7.00
Child:	£3.50
National Trust Members:	Free

Ticket also gives admission to our sister property in Coggeshall, Grange Barn.

BOURNE MILL

BOURNE ROAD, COLCHESTER, ESSEX CO2 8RT

www.nationaltrust.org.uk/bourne-mill/

In 1591 Sir Thomas Lucas built Bourne Mill, an ornate building that served as both a genteel fishing lodge for him to entertain guests and for milling grain. In around 1640 it was converted for 'fulling' wool-cloth but after the collapse of the wool trade in Colchester in the 1840s it was converted back into a grain mill; it continued producing flour until 1935. Bourne Mill is set in tranquil grounds, next to a millpond and babbling stream. The waterwheel and cog wheels still turn and the grounds hold woodlands and wetlands and a Tudor Physic Garden, a good place for a tea or coffee by the pond. One can follow the Bourne stream to see the sites of two lower mills further down its course.

Location: Map 8:J11. OS Ref TM005 238. 1 mile south of centre of Colchester, on Bourne Road, off Mersea Road (B1025).

Owner: National Trust

Contact: The House Manager

Tel: 01206 549799 **E-mail:** bournemill@nationaltrust.org.uk

Open: Weds to Suns and BH Mons from 15 Mar-29 Oct, 11am-5pm, closes at 4pm in Oct.

Admission: Adult £3.75, Child £1.90, free for National Trust Members.

Key facts: Info point. Gift shop Plant sales. Hire the Mill. Limited access to some areas - please call. Teas, coffees, cakes & cold drinks. Welcome talk for groups. Limited parking; undesignated parking on surrounding streets. Schools by appointment. Well behaved dogs allowed on a lead in the grounds.

© Peter Gamble

COPPED HALL

Crown Hill, Epping, Essex CM16 5HS

www.coppedhalltrust.org.uk

Mid-18th Century Palladian mansion under restoration. Situated on ridge overlooking landscaped park. Ancillary buildings including stables and racquets court. Former elaborate gardens being rescued from abandonment. Large 18th Century walled kitchen garden - adjacent to site of 16th Century mansion where 'A Midsummer Night's Dream' was first performed. Ideal film location.

Location: Map 7:G12. OS Ref TL433 016. 4m SW of Epping, N of M25.

Owner: The Copped Hall Trust

Contact: Alan Cox

Tel: 020 7267 1679

E-mail: coxalan1@aol.com

Open: Ticketed events and special open days. See website for dates. Private tours by appointment.

Admission: Open Days £8.00. Guided Tour Days £8.00. Gardens Only £5.00.

Key facts: Partial. In grounds on leads.

INGATESTONE HALL

Hall Lane, Ingatestone, Essex CM4 9NR

www.ingatestonehall.com

16th Century mansion, with 11 acres of grounds (formal garden and wild walk), built by Sir William Petre, Secretary of State to four Tudor monarchs, which has remained in his family ever since. Furniture, portraits and memorabilia accumulated over the centuries - and two Priests' hiding places.

Location: Map 7:H12. OS Ref TQ654 986. Off A12 between Brentwood & Chelmsford. From London end of Ingatestone High St., take Station Lane, cross level crossing and continue for ½ mile.

Owner/Contact: The Lord Petre

Tel/Fax: 01277 353010 **Additional Contact:** Mrs Lynne Pykerman

E-mail: house@ingatestonehall.co.uk

Open: 2017: 16 Apr-27 Sep Wed, Suns & Bank Holidays, 12 noon-5pm.

Admission: Adult £7.00, Child £3.00 (under 5yrs Free), Conc. £6.00. (Groups of 20+ booked in advance: Adult £6.00, Child £2.00, Conc. £5.00).

Key facts: No photography in house. Capacity for receptions - 100. Capacity for dinners - 65. Partial. WCs. Available out of normal hours by arrangement. Free parking. Guide dogs only.

Register for news and special offers at **www.hudsonsheritage.com**

HATFIELD HOUSE

www.hatfield-house.co.uk

Over 400 years of culture, history and entertainment.

Hatfield House is the home of the 7th Marquess and Marchioness of Salisbury and their family. The Estate has been in the Cecil family for over 400 years. Superb examples of Jacobean craftsmanship can be seen throughout the House.

In 1611, Robert Cecil, 1st Earl of Salisbury built his fine Jacobean House adjoining the site of the Old Palace of Hatfield. The House was splendidly decorated for entertaining the Royal Court, with State Rooms rich in paintings, fine furniture and tapestries.

Superb examples of Jacobean craftsmanship can be seen throughout Hatfield House such as the Grand Staircase with its fine carving and the rare stained glass window in the private chapel. Displayed throughout the House are many historic mementos collected over the centuries by the Cecils, one of England's foremost political families.

The garden at Hatfield House dates from the early 17th Century when Robert Cecil employed John Tradescant the Elder to collect plants for his new home. Tradescant was sent to Europe where he found and brought back trees, bulbs, plants and fruit trees, which had never previously been grown in England.

In the Park, an oak tree marks the place where the young Princess Elizabeth first heard of her accession to the throne. Visitors can enjoy extensive walks in the park, following trails through the woods and along the Broadwater. The Veteran Tree Trail also provides the opportunity to learn more about our ancient oaks.

KEY FACTS

- No flash photography in house. Tours of Old Palace when building is not in use.
- Newly refurbished Stable Yard home to variety of independent retailers & Hatfield House Gift Shop.
- Weddings, Banquets & Conferences venue & catering. Tel 01707 262055.
- All floors of House accessible via lift.
- The Coach House Restaurant. Morning coffee, afternoon tea, cakes, hot & cold lunches. Tel: 01707 262030.
- Group tours by arrangement, please call 07107 287052.
- Audio tours of House.
- Free.
- Living History Schools programme.
- On leads. Park only.

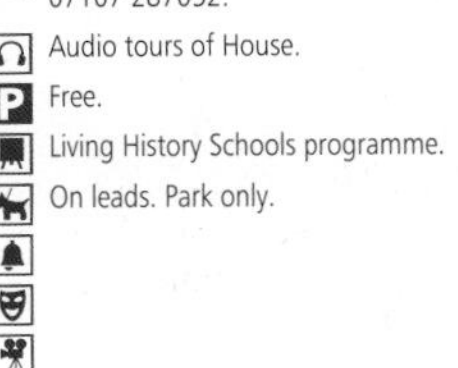

VISITOR INFORMATION

Owner
The 7th Marquess of Salisbury

Address
Hatfield House
Hatfield
Hertfordshire
AL9 5NQ

Location
Map 7:F11
OS Ref. TL237 084
21 miles north of London, M25 Jct 23, A1(M) Jct 4. Pedestrian Entrance directly opposite Hatfield Railway Station.
Bus: Nearest stop at Hatfield Station, also regular buses from surrounding towns.
Rail: Kings Cross to Hatfield 22mins. Station is opposite entrance to Park. Underground links to main line at Finsbury Park.

Contact
Visitors Department
Tel: 01707 287010
E-mail: visitors@hatfield-house.co.uk

Opening Times
House:
15 Apr-30 Sep 2017 Wed-Sun & BH 11-5pm (last admission 4pm).

Garden, Park, Farm, Shops and Restaurant:
Tues-Sun & BH
10am - 5.30pm.

Admission
House, Park and West Garden:

Adult	£19.00
Seniors	£18.00
Child	£9.00

Group rates available.

East Garden:
(Wed only) £4.00
per person.

West Garden and Park only:

Adult	£11.00
Seniors	£10.00
Child	£7.00

Group rates available.

Special Events
There are a number of events held throughout the year, please see the website for more details.

Conference/Function

ROOM	Size	Max Cap
The Old Palace	112' x 33'	280
Riding School Conference Centre	100' x 40'	170

KNEBWORTH HOUSE

Knebworth Park, Knebworth, Hertfordshire SG1 2AX

www.knebworthhouse.com

A fantastic day out for all the family. Home of the Lytton family since 1490, Knebworth's romantic gothic exterior hides a much earlier Tudor house. Explore the delightful formal gardens with dinosaur trail, wilderness garden, walled garden and a huge adventure playground in the historic deer park. Events programme throughout the year. Knebworth is well known for its rock concerts and as a popular TV/feature film location. Knebworth Barns are open all year for weddings & corporate hospitality. **Location:** Map 7:E11. OS Ref TL234 223. Direct access off the A1(M) J7 Stevenage, SG1 2AX, 28m N of London, 15m N of M25/J23
Contact: The Estate Office **Tel:** 01438 812661
E-mail: info@knebworthhouse.com **Open:** Mar-Sep, Please check website for open dates and times for Knebworth House, Gardens & Park. Knebworth Barns are open all year for events, corporate and social functions. **Admission:** See website for current prices. Children under 3 admitted free of charge. HHA members free on non-event days. RHS Partner Garden. Discount admission for Art Fund members.
Key facts: See Access statement online. Admission generally by guided tour. See website for details of free flow days. Free of charge. See Education section of Website. Sandford award winning programmes. In Park on leads only.

GORHAMBURY

St Albans, Hertfordshire AL3 6AH

Late 18th Century house by Sir Robert Taylor. Family portraits from 15th-21st Centuries.
Location: Map 7:E11. 2m W of St Albans. Access via private drive off A4147 at St Albans. For SatNav please enter AL3 6AE for unlocked entrance to estate at Roman Theatre.
Owner: Gorhambury Estates Co Ltd
Contact: The Administrator
Tel: 01727 854051
E-mail: office@grimstontrust.co.uk
Website: www.gorhamburyestate.co.uk
Open: Due to impending refurbishment, the regular House opening hours have changed for 2017. We can accommodate visitors by appointment from Apr-Jun. Please check the Gorhambury website or call for further details.
Admission: House: Adult £8.00; Senior: £7.00; Child: £5.00.
Key facts: No photography. Partial. Obligatory.

BENINGTON LORDSHIP GARDENS

Benington Lordship, Benington, Stevenage, Hertfordshire SG2 7BS

7 acre garden in timeless parkland setting. **Location:** Map 7:F11. OS Ref TL296 236. In village of Benington next to the church. 4m E of Stevenage.
Tel: 01438 869668 **E-mail:** garden@beningtonlordship.co.uk
Website: www.beningtonlordship.co.uk **Open:** See website for details. Snowdrops in Feb, Chilli Festival Aug BH w/e. **Admission:** See website

SHAW'S CORNER

Ayot St Lawrence, Welwyn, Hertfordshire AL6 9BX

Home of Edwardian playwright, George Bernard Shaw.
Location: Map 7:E11. OS Ref TL194 166. At SW end of village, 2m NE of Wheathampstead, approximately 2m N from B653. A1(M)/J4, M1/J10.
Tel: 01438 829221 **E-mail:** shawscorner@nationaltrust.org.uk
Website: www.nationaltrust.org.uk/shawscorner
Open: Apr-Oct, Wed-Sun, 12-5pm. **Admission:** Adult £7.50; Child £3.75.

Hatfield House

Register for news and special offers at **www.hudsonsheritage.com**

© www.garethhacon.com

HOLKHAM HALL

www.holkham.co.uk

A breath-taking Palladian house with an outstanding art collection, panoramic landscapes and the best beach in England.

Holkham is a special place where a stunning coastal landscape meets one of England's great agricultural estates.

At the heart of this thriving, privately-owned, 25,000 acre estate stands Holkham Hall, an elegant 18th Century Palladian-style mansion, based on designs by William Kent and built by Thomas Coke, 1st Earl of Leicester. The Marble Hall, with its 50ft domed ceiling, is a spectacular entrance with stairs leading to the magnificent state rooms displaying superb collections of ancient statuary, original furniture, tapestries and paintings.

Visitors can also enjoy the 'Field to Fork' exhibition which tells the fascinating story of Holkham's unique farming heritage through fun and engaging interactive displays. Or there is the tranquillity and colourful plantings of the 18th Century walled garden, currently undergoing an extensive project to restore the six-acre garden to its former glory. For shopping and refreshments, the cobbled courtyard houses a spacious gift shop and café both showcasing the work and produce of local artisans and suppliers.

Families will love the children's woodland adventure play area with its tree houses in the sky, rope walkways and a zip wire. There's a chance to discover the wildlife and landscape of Holkham Park too, with walks and cycle or boat hire.

At the north entrance to the park is Holkham village with the estate-owned inn, The Victoria, several shops and the entrance to Holkham Beach and National Nature Reserve, with its golden sands and panoramic vista.

KEY FACTS

- Photography allowed. Stair climbing machine in hall offers access for most manually operated wheelchairs.
- Courtyard Gift Shop. Norfolk produce.
- Hall, Lady Elizabeth Wing and grounds.
- WC in courtyard. Full access statement on Holkham website.
- Courtyard Café. Licensed. Local produce.
- The Victoria, Holkham village. Licensed.
- Private guided tours by arrangement.
- Ample. Parking charge.
- Comprehensive education programme for early years, primary, secondary and further education.
- On leads in park. Assistance dogs only in the hall.
- The Victoria, Holkham village.
- Civil ceremonies and partnerships.
- Open for events and functions outside of main visitor season.
- Outdoor and indoor events.

VISITOR INFORMATION

Owner

Trustees of the Holkham Estate. Home of the Earls of Leicester.

Address

Holkham Estate
Wells-next-the-Sea
Norfolk, NR23 1AB

Location

Map 8:14
OS Ref. TF885 428
London 120m, Norwich 35m, King's Lynn 30m.
Sat Nav: NR23 1RH.
Bus: King's Lynn to Cromer.
Rail: Norwich 35m. King's Lynn 30m.
Air: Norwich Airport 32m.

Contact

Marketing Manager
Laurane Herrieven
Tel: 01328 710227
E-mail: enquiries@holkham.co.uk

Opening Times

Hall:
1 Apr-31 Oct 12-4pm, Sun, Mon, Thus & 14-15 Apr, 27-28 Oct.
NB Closed 28-29 May, 22-23 Jul.
NB Chapel, Libraries & Strangers' Wing, open at family's discretion.
'Field to Fork', Walled Garden, Courtyard Café, Gift Shop & Play Area:
1 Apr-31 Oct 10am-5pm, every day.1 Nov-17 Dec.
For winter opening & admission see website.
Cycle Hire & Lake Activities: See website.

Admission

Holkham Hall, 'Field to Fork' & Walled Garden

Adult:	£15
Child (5-16yrs):	£7.50
Family:	£41

'Field to Fork' & Walled Garden

Adult:	£7
Child (5-16yrs):	£3.50
Family:	£19

'Field to Fork' Only:

Adult:	£5
Child (5-16yrs):	£2.50
Family:	£13.50

NB Family ticket = 2 adults & up to 3 children.
Car parking charge £3
Redeemable in Gift Shop.
Pre-booked groups:
15+, 20% discount, free coach parking, organiser free entry, coach driver's refreshments.
Private Guided Tours:
12 people minimum.
Price per person £21.00

Special Events

Full events programme.

Conference/Function

Corporate events, dinners, conferences, parties, rallies, product launches, filming, weddings & receptions.

© Houghton Hall and Richard Long Full Moon Circle

© Houghton Hall Walled Garden

HOUGHTON HALL & GARDENS

HOUGHTON, KING'S LYNN, NORFOLK PE31 6UE

www.houghtonhall.com

Houghton Hall is one of the finest examples of Palladian architecture in England. Built in the 1720s for Sir Robert Walpole, Britain's first Prime Minister. Original designs by James Gibbs & Colen Campbell, interior decoration by William Kent. The Hall is currently home to the 7th Marquess of Cholmondeley, Walpole's descendant, and his family.

The Award-winning 5-acre Walled Garden is divided into themed areas and includes a double-sided herbaceous border, formal rose parterre, mixed kitchen garden, fountains and statues. Contemporary Sculptures by world-renowned artists are displayed in the grounds. In 2017 a special exhibition by British Sculptor and Turner Prize Winner, Richard Long will be held May to October. See website for details.

Location: Map 8:15. OS Ref TF792 287. 13m E of King's Lynn, 10m W of Fakenham, 1½m N of A148.
Owner: The Marquess of Cholmondeley
Contact: The Estate Office
Tel: 01485 528569
Fax: 01485 528167
E-mail: info@houghtonhall.com
Open: See website www.houghtonhall.com
Admission: See website for prices / booking details. www.houghtonhall.com
Key facts: WCs. Allocated parking near the House. Licensed. By arrangement. Please contact Estate Office. See www.houghtoneducation.co.uk Assistance Dogs Only.

Holkham Hall

CASTLE RISING CASTLE

Castle Rising, King's Lynn, Norfolk PE31 6AH

www.castlerising.co.uk

Possibly the finest mid-12th Century Keep in England: it was built as a grand and elaborate palace. It was home to Queen Isabella, grandmother of the Black Prince. Still in good condition, the Keep is surrounded by massive ramparts up to 120 feet high. Picnic area, adjacent Tea Room. Audio tour.

Location: Map 7:H5. OS Ref TF666 246.
Located 4m NE of King's Lynn off A149.
Owner: Lord Howard
Contact: The Custodian
Tel: 01553 631330 **Fax:** 01533 631724
Open: 1 Apr-1 Nov: daily, 10am-6pm (closes at dusk if earlier in Oct). 2 Nov-31 Mar: Wed-Sun, 10am-4pm. Closed 24-26 Dec.
Admission: Adult £4.50, Child £3.00, Conc. £3.80, Family £14.00. 15% discount for groups (11+). Opening times and prices are subject to change.
Key facts: Picnic area. Suitable.

HINDRINGHAM HALL AND GARDENS

Blacksmiths Lane, Hindringham, Norfolk NR21 0QA

www.hindringhamhall.org

House: Beautiful Tudor Manor House surrounded by 12th Century moat. A scheduled Ancient Monument, along with the adjacent 3 acres of fishponds. Gardens: Four acres of peaceful gardens within and without the moat surrounding the house. Working walled vegetable garden, herb parterre, daffodil walk, bluebell and cyclamen copse, stream garden, bog garden, herbaceous borders, Autumn border, Victorian nut tunnel, rose and clematis pergolas. A garden with something for all seasons. **Location:** Map 8:J4. OS Ref TF978 366. Turn off the A148 halfway between Fakenham and Holt at the Crawfish P.H. Drive to Hindringham and pass the Village Hall, on the right take the next left into Blacksmiths Lane.
Owner/Contact: Mr & Mrs Charles Tucker
Tel: 01328 878226 **E-mail:** info@hindringhamhall.org
Open: House: 5 times a year for a 2hr guided history tour. Groups on other days by arrangement. Gardens & Tea Room: Sun afternoons 2-5pm & Wed mornings 10am-1pm Apr-Sep inclusive. See website for dates & times. **Admission:** House: Tour £18 inc refreshments. Garden: Adults £7, Child (under 15yrs) Free.
Key facts: Many plants for sale from seeds & cuttings from the gardens. No hills or steps but some gravel paths. Teas, coffee, other beverages & cakes. Large car park on the right as you enter the drive. 3 detached holiday cottages within the grounds, each with own garden - sleep 2 and 4.

© National Trust Images/John Hammond

OXBURGH HALL

Oxborough, King's Lynn, Norfolk PE33 9PS

www.nationaltrust.org.uk/oxburgh-hall

Peel back the layers of 500 years of rich and turbulent history at this romantic, moated manor house 7 miles SW of the market town of Swaffham. You'll find hidden doors, panoramic rooftop views, a secret priest's hole which you can crawl inside and embroideries worked by Mary, Queen of Scots. Outside, the 70 acres of gardens and woodland are dog friendly and you'll be charmed by My Lady's Wood.
Location: Map 8:16. OS Ref TF742 012. 7m SW of Swaffham on S side of Stoke Ferry road. **Owner:** National Trust
Tel: 01366 328258 **E-mail:** oxburghhall@nationaltrust.org.uk
Open: Whole property open daily from 11 Mar-29 Oct at 11am and 12pm-3pm daily from 11 Feb-10 Mar. Garden, shop & Tea Room also open most weekends in Jan, Feb, Nov, Dec. Detailed opening information available on our website.
Admission: House & Garden: (Gift Aid On Entry) Adult £11.60, Garden only: £6.50. Special child and family tickets available. For full list of prices/group bookings please refer to website. **Key facts:** Free garden tours daily. Gift shop & second-hand bookshop Light lunches, hot and cold drinks. By arrangement. Limited for coaches. Welcome in gardens & woodland. Assistance dogs only in house. Holiday cottage on the estate.

Castle Acre Priory

© Raveningham Estate

RAVENINGHAM GARDENS

Raveningham, Norwich, Norfolk NR14 6NS

www.raveningham.com

Superb herbaceous borders, 19th Century walled kitchen garden, Victorian glasshouse, herb garden, rose garden, time garden, contemporary sculptures, Millennium lake, arboretum with newly created stumpery, 14th Century church, all in a glorious parkland setting surrounding Raveningham Hall. Tea Room serving homemade cake and refreshments. **Location:** Map 8:L7. OS Ref TM399 965. Between Norwich & Lowestoft off A146 then B1136.
Owner: Sir Nicholas Bacon Bt OBE DL **Contact:** Dr Barbara Linsley
Tel: 01508 548480 **E-mail:** barbara@raveningham.com
Open: Snowdrop season: Feb, Sun-Fri (closed Sats) 11am-4pm. National Gardens Scheme opening: Sun 5 Mar. Main season: Apr 3-Aug 31, Mon-Fri, 11am-4pm. Summer Suns: 16, 23 & 30 Jul; 6,13, 20 & 27 Aug. Bank Holidays: 14 Apr, 17 Apr, 1 May, 29 May & 28 Aug.
Admission: Adult £5.00, Child (under 16yrs) Free, Concessions £4.50. Groups welcome by prior arrangement.
Key facts: Disabled toilet, gardens accessible via gravel paths. Tea Room, homemade cakes, quiches & other refreshments. Well behaved dogs on leads welcome.

MANNINGTON GARDENS & COUNTRYSIDE

Mannington Hall, Norwich NR11 7BB

Gardens known for large collection of classic roses also feature trees and shrubs and other plants surrounding medieval moated manor with lake, board walk across meadow with bird hide and interesting events programme.
Location: Map 8:K5. OS Ref TG144 320.
Owner: The Lord & Lady Walpole **Contact:** Lady Walpole
Tel: 01263 584175 **E-mail:** admin@walpoleestate.co.uk
Website: www.manningtongardens.co.uk
Open: Walks open every day of the year. Events from Apr and Gardens from late May-Aug; Suns 12-5, Wed, Thu & Fri 11-5. Party visits and appointments may be possible on other days.
Admission: Please see website.
Key facts: Grounds. WCs. Licensed. By arrangement. £2.00 car park fee (walkers only). In park only. Park. €

SANDRINGHAM

The Estate Office, Sandringham, Norfolk PE35 6EN

Sandringham House, the Norfolk retreat of Her Majesty The Queen, is set in 60 acres of beautiful gardens. The main ground floor rooms used by The Royal Family, still maintained in the Edwardian style, are open to the public, as well as the fascinating Museum and the charming parish church.
Location: Map 7:H5. OS Ref TF695 287.
8m NE of King's Lynn on B1440 off A148.
Owner: HM The Queen **Contact:** The Public Enterprises Manager
Tel: 01485 545408 **Fax:** 01485 541571 **E-mail:** visits@sandringhamestate.co.uk
Website: www.sandringhamestate.co.uk
Open: 15 Apr-late Jul & early Aug-late Oct.
Admission: House, Museum & Gardens, Adult £15.50, Child £7.00, Conc. £13.50. Museum & Gardens, Adult £10.00, Child £5.00, Conc. £9.00.
Key facts: No photography in house. Plant Centre. Visitor Centre only. WCs. Licensed. Licensed. By arrangement. Private evening tours. Ample. Guide dogs only.

WALSINGHAM ABBEY GROUNDS & THE SHIREHALL MUSEUM

Common Place, Walsingham, Norfolk NR22 6BP

Ruins of the medieval Augustinian Priory and place of pilgrimage. Peaceful gardens, woodland and river walks open all year, with spectacular naturalised snowdrops throughout in February. Visitor entry is at The Shirehall Museum, a preserved Georgian Courthouse, where you can discover Walsingham's unique history since 1061. **Location:** Map 8:J4. OS Ref TF934 367. 4 miles N of Fakenham, on B1105. **Owner:** Walsingham Estate
Tel: 01328 820510 **E-mail:** museum@walsinghamabbey.com
Website: www.walsinghamabbey.com
Open: Snowdrop walks: 30 Jan-5 Mar, Mon-Sun, 10am-4pm. From 6 Mar: Sat & Sun, 11am-4pm. Mar weekdays, Mon-Fri 11am-1pm & 2-4pm. 25 Mar-5 Nov, Mon-Sun 11am-4pm. 6 Nov to end Jan 2018, Mon-Fri, 11am-1pm & 2pm-4pm.
Admission: Adult £5.00, Child 6-16 £2.50. Under 6 free.
Key facts: Coaches please follow route marked. Gift shop. Feb snowdrops. Partial access. By arrangement. Dogs on leads.

BLICKLING ESTATE

Blickling, Norwich, Norfolk NR11 6NF

Built in the early 17th Century, Blickling boasts one of England's finest Jacobean house. **Location:** Map 8:K5. OS Ref TG176 285. See website for directions.
Tel: 01263 738030 **E-mail:** blickling@nationaltrust.org.uk
Website: www.nationaltrust.org.uk/blickling
Open: House: Mar-Oct, Wed-Mon, 12-5pm; 4 Nov-19 Nov, Sat & Sun, 12-4pm; 24 Nov-3 Dec, Fri-Sun, 12-4pm. **Admission:** Adult £12.65; Child £6.80.

CASTLE ACRE PRIORY

Stocks Green, Castle Acre, King's Lynn, Norfolk PE32 2XD

Explore the romantic ruins of this 12th Century Cluniac priory, set in the picturesque village of Castle Acre. **Location:** Map 8:I5. OS Ref TF814 148.
Tel: 01760 755394 **E-mail:** customers@english-heritage.org.uk
Website: www.english-heritage.org.uk/castleacrepriory **Open:** 2 Jan-31 Mar, Sat & Sun, 10-4pm; 1 Apr-30 Sep, 10-6pm; 1-31 Oct, 10-5pm; 1 Nov-31 Dec, Sat & Sun, 10-4pm. Closed 24-26 Dec & 1 Jan. **Admission:** Adult £7.30; Child £4.40.

EUSTON HALL

Thetford, Suffolk IP24 2QP

Home to the Dukes of Grafton for over 350 years.
Location: Map 8:L8. OS Ref TL895 781.
Tel: 01842 766366 **E-mail:** info@euston-estate.co.uk
Website: www.eustonhall.co.uk **Open:** 2 Jan-31 Mar, Sat & Sun, 10-4pm; daily at half term; Apr-Oct, daily, 10-5pm; 1 Nov-23 Dec, Sat & Sun, 27-31 Dec, daily, 10-4pm. **Admission:** Adult £8.40; Child £5.50.

FELBRIGG HALL

Felbrigg, Norwich, Norfolk NR11 8PR

One of the finest 17th Century country houses in East Anglia.
Location: Map 8:K4. OS Ref TG193 394. Nr Felbrigg village, 2m SW of Cromer, entrance off B1436, signposted from A148 & A140. **Tel:** 01263 837444
E-mail: felbrigg@nationaltrust.org.uk **Website:** www.nationaltrust.org.uk
Open: Gdns: Mar-Oct, 11-5.30pm; Nov-18 Dec, Tue-Sat, 11-3pm. Hse: Mar-Oct, Sat-Wed, 11-4pm; 17 Jul-15 Sep, 11-5pm. **Admission:** Adult £9.90; Child £4.70.

SHERINGHAM PARK

Upper Sheringham, Norfolk NR26 8TL

One of Humphry Repton's most outstanding achievements, the landscape park contains fine mature woodlands. **Location:** Map 8:K4. OS Ref TG139 410. 2m SW of Sheringham, access for cars off A148 Cromer-Holt road; 5m W of Cromer, 6m E of Holt. **Tel:** 01263 820550 **E-mail:** sheringhampark@nationaltrust.org.uk
Website: www.nationaltrust.org.uk **Open:** All year, daily. Café & Visitor Centre: Winter, Sat & Sun, 11-4pm; Apr-Oct, daily, 10-5pm. **Admission:** Free.

© National Trust Images/Jane Gosling

© Technique Productions

LAVENHAM: THE GUILDHALL OF CORPUS CHRISTI

THE MARKET PLACE, LAVENHAM, SUDBURY CO10 9QZ

www.nationaltrust.org.uk/lavenham

Once one of the wealthiest towns in Tudor England, Lavenham oozes charm and character. The rich clothiers who thrived here left a legacy of buildings that now make up the streets of crooked timber-framed houses that are so beloved of visitors today. With its timber-framed houses and magnificent church, a visit to picturesque Lavenham is a step back in time. The early 16th Century Guildhall is the ideal place to begin with its exhibitions on local history bringing to life the fascinating stories behind this remarkable village.

Once you have explored the Guildhall and sampled some homemade fare in our Tea Room, why not visit some of the unique shops and galleries in the village. Lavenham truly has something for everyone.

Location: Map 8:J9. OS Ref OS155, TL915 942.
6m NNE of Sudbury. Market Place in village centre. A1141 & B1071.

Owner: National Trust **Contact:** Jane Gosling
Tel: 01787 247646 **E-mail:** lavenhamguildhall@nationaltrust.org.uk
Open: Guildhall, shop & Tea Room: 7 Jan-26 Feb, Sat & Sun, 11am-4pm. 1 Mar-29 Oct, Mon-Sun, 11am-5pm. 2 Nov-24 Dec, Thu-Sun, 11am-4pm.
Admission: Adult £7.15, Child £3.55, Family £17.85, Groups £5.75. School parties by arrangement. **Key facts:** The perfect present or holiday memory to take home. Books, cards & National Trust gifts. A selection of seasonal plants to remind you of your time at Lavenham. Access to ground floor, shop & Tea Room. Photo album, virtual tour & large print guides available. Tea Room serving delicious homemade fare, light lunches & cream teas. By arrangement. No on-site parking but free parking in Lavenham village. Open all year with reduced hours Nov-Feb.

Framlingham Castle

FRESTON TOWER

Nr Ipswich, Suffolk IP9 1AD

www.landmarktrust.org.uk

Freston Tower is a six-storey Tudor folly that looks out over the River Orwell. There is a single room on each floor with the sitting room at the top to take advantage of the unrivalled views.
Location: Map 8:K9. OS Ref TM177 397.
Owner: The Landmark Trust
Tel: 01628 825925
E-mail: bookings@landmarktrust.org.uk
Open: Self-catering accommodation. Open Days on 8 days per year, other visits by appointment.
Admission: Free on Open Days and visits by appointment.
Key facts: Six storeys joined by a steep spiral staircase. There is a room on each floor and a roof terrace.

GAINSBOROUGH'S HOUSE

46 Gainsborough Street, Sudbury, Suffolk CO10 2EU

www.gainsborough.org

Gainsborough's House is the childhood home of the artist Thomas Gainsborough, R.A. (1727–1788) and shows the most comprehensive collection of his paintings, drawings and prints on display within a single setting. A varied programme of temporary exhibitions is also shown throughout the year. The historic house dates back to the 16th Century and has an attractive walled garden filled with 18th Century plant species. **Location:** Map 8:I10. OS Ref TL872 413. From Sudbury town centre head down Gainsborough Street towards Weaver's Lane.
Owner: Gainsborough's House Society **Contact:** Liz Cooper **Tel:** 01787 372958
Fax: 01787 376991 **E-mail:** mail@gainsborough.org **Open:** All year: Mon-Sat, 10am-5pm; Sun, 11am-5pm. Closed: Good Friday & Christmas to New Year.
Admission: Please phone for details of admission charges or see our website.
Key facts: No photography in the Exhibition Gallery. The new shop offers a range of themes based on the heritage of Gainsborough and the Georgian period. A small selection of plants from Gainsborough's Garden are available for sale. Suitable WCs. By arrangement. Guide dogs only.

HELMINGHAM HALL GARDENS

Helmingham, Stowmarket, Suffolk IP14 6EF

www.helmingham.com

Grade 1 listed gardens, redesigned by Lady Tollemache (a Chelsea Gold Medallist) set in a 400 acre deer park surrounding a moated Tudor Hall.
Visitors are enchanted by the stunning herbaceous borders, the walled kitchen garden, herb, knot, rose and wild gardens. A delicious range of local food is served in the Coach House Tea Rooms and the Stable Shops offer a wide range of local produce, plants, garden accessories and local crafts.
Coach bookings warmly welcomed. There are a variety of events throughout the season including The Festival of Classic & Sports Cars and Suffolk Dog Day.
Location: Map 8:K9. OS Ref TM190 578.
B1077, 9m north of Ipswich, 5m south of Debenham.
Owner: The Lord & Lady Tollemache **Contact:** Events Office
Tel: 01473 890799 **E-mail:** events@helmingham.com
Open: Gardens only: 1 May-17 Sep 2017. 12-5pm Tue, Wed, Thu, Sun & all BH's.
Admission: Adults £7.00, Child (5-15yrs) £3.50. Groups (30+) £6.00.
Key facts: WCs. Licenced. By arrangement. Pre-booking required. Dogs on leads only.

ICKWORTH HOUSE, PARKLAND, WOODLAND & GARDENS

Horringer, Bury St Edmunds, Suffolk IP29 5QE

www.nationaltrust.org.uk/ickworth

A touch of classical Italy brought to Suffolk. Enjoy an entertaining day at this idiosyncratic and beautiful country estate. The grand Rotunda is filled with treasures collected by the Hervey family and sits in tranquil, landscaped parkland with waymarked walks and cycle routes. Discover one of the earliest Italianate gardens in England. Experience 1930's life in the newly restored Servants' basement. **Location:** Map 8:19. OS Ref TL816 611. In Horringer, 3m SW of Bury St Edmunds on W side of A143. **Owner:** The National Trust **Contact:** Property Administrator **Tel:** 01284 735270 **E-mail:** ickworth@nationaltrust.org.uk
Open: House: 4 Mar-29 Oct, Thu-Tue, 11am-4pm (Tours only 11am-12pm & 4-5pm, last entry 4pm). 30 Oct-31 Dec 11am-3pm tours only. Parkland & Gardens: Daily 9am-5.30pm all year. Shop & Café: Daily 10.30am-5pm. Closed Christmas Eve & Day. **Admission:** Gift Aid Admission: House, Park & Gardens £14.00, Child £7.00, Family £35.00. Groups (15+) £11.00pp. **Key facts:** Prices correct as of Aug 2016. Mar-Oct. Weekends only Nov & Dec. Lift in main house. Mobility scooters available. West Wing drop off point. Tours available everyday. Basement audio tour on selected days. Assistance dogs only in Italianate gardens. All dogs on leads on the Estate. 5 Holiday cottages.

Register for news and special offers at **www.hudsonsheritage.com**

OTLEY HALL

Hall Lane, Otley, Suffolk IP6 9PA

www.otleyhall.co.uk

The outstanding late medieval house in East Suffolk. Stunning medieval Moated Hall (Grade I) frequently described as 'one of England's loveliest houses'. Noted for its richly carved beams, superb linenfold panelling and 16th Century wall paintings. The unique 10 acre gardens include historically accurate Tudor re-creations and voted among the top 10 gardens to visit in Great Britain.
Location: Map 8:K9. OS Ref TM207 563. 7m N of Ipswich, off the B1079.
Owner: Dr Ian & Reverend Catherine Beaumont
Contact: Bronyia Tebenham **Tel:** 01473 890264
Facebook: facebook.com/otleyhallsuffolk. **Twitter:** @OtleyHall
E-mail: events@otleyhall.co.uk
Open: Gardens and café every Wed May-Sep. 11am-5pm. £3.00 entrance, café serving light lunches and afternoon tea. The House and grounds are available for wedding ceremonies and receptions where we offer exclusive access to the venue on the wedding day. Tours by appointment all year round. For more info please visit our website. **Admission:** By appointment only. No commercial photography.
Key facts: Partial. Licensed. By arrangement. In grounds only and on a short lead.

SOMERLEYTON HALL & GARDENS

Somerleyton, Lowestoft, Suffolk NR32 5QQ

www.somerleyton.co.uk

Originally Jacobean, re-modelled in 1844 to a magnificent Anglo-Italian styled stately home. 12 acres of beautiful gardens include the famous yew hedge maze, 300ft pergola, Vulliamy tower clock, Paxton glasshouses, restored Nesfield's parterre and new white sunken garden. Please see website for special events.
Location: Map 8:M7. OS Ref TM493 977. 5m NW of Lowestoft on B1074, 7m SW of Great Yarmouth off A143. **Owner:** Lord and Lady Somerleyton.
Contact: Emily **Tel:** 08712 224244 (office) **Twitter:** @SomerleytonHall
Facebook: SomerleytonHall. **E-mail:** info@somerleyton.co.uk
Open: Times vary throughout the season - please check website for details.
Admission: Please visit website for prices & special events.
Key facts: No photography in house. Selling books, postcards and gifts. Kitchen garden produce available and Peter Beales roses. Available for receptions, conferences, weddings and exclusive Private Hire of the entire Hall. Suitable. WCs. Partial disabled access. Kitchen Garden Café. Obligatory. Available by pre-arrangement. Guide dogs only. The Fritton Arms.

HAUGHLEY PARK

Stowmarket, Suffolk IP14 3JY

Grade 1 listed red-brick manor house of 1620 set in gardens, park and woodland. Original five-gabled east front, north wing rebuilt in Georgian style, 1820. Varied six acre gardens including walled kitchen garden. Way-marked woodland walks. 17th Century barn bookable for weddings, meetings etc.
Location: Map 8:J8. OS Ref TM005 618. Signed from J47a and J49 on A14 on black-on-white road signs. Approx. 10m west of Bury St Eds.
Owner: Mr & Mrs Robert Williams **Contact:** Barn Office
Tel: 01359 240701 **E-mail:** info@haughleypark.co.uk
Website: www.haughleypark.co.uk
Open: Garden only: May-Sep: Tues, 2-5.30pm. Bluebell Sundays: last in Apr, first in May. Weird & Wonderful Wood: see website.
Admission: Garden: £4.00, Child under 16 Free.
Key facts: Picnics allowed. WCs. By arrangement. On leads.

FLATFORD

Bridge Cottage, East Bergholt, Suffolk CO7 6UL

In the heart of the beautiful Dedham Vale. **Location:** Map 8:J10. OS Ref TM076 332. On N bank of Stour, 1m S of East Bergholt B1070.
Tel: 01206 298260 **E-mail:** flatfordbridgecottage@nationaltrust.org.uk
Website: www.nationaltrust.org.uk/flatford
Open: Jan-Feb, Sat & Sun, 10.30-3.30pm; Mar, Wed-Sun, 10.30-5pm; Apr-Oct, 10.30-5.30pm; Nov-23 Dec, Sat & Sun, 10.30-3.30pm. **Admission:** Free.

FRAMLINGHAM CASTLE

Framlingham, Suffolk IP13 9BP

Framlingham is a magnificent 12th Century castle. **Location:** Map 8:L8. OS Ref TM287 637. In Framlingham on B1116. NE of town centre.
Tel: 01728 724189 **E-mail:** customers@english-heritage.org.uk
Website: www.english-heritage.org.uk/framlingham **Open:** 2 Jan-31 Mar, Sat & Sun, 10-4pm; daily at half term; Apr-Oct, daily, 10-5pm; 1 Nov-23 Dec, Sat & Sun, 27-31 Dec, daily, 10-4pm. **Admission:** Adult £8.40; Child £5.50.

KENTWELL HALL & GARDENS

Long Melford, Suffolk CO10 9BA

A beautiful mellow redbrick Tudor Mansion, surrounded by a broad moat, with rare service building of c1500. Interior 'improved' by Thomas Hopper in 1820s.
Location: Map 8:I9. OS Ref TL863 479. Off the A134. 4m N of Sudbury.
Tel: 01787 310207 **E-mail:** info@kentwell.co.uk **Website:** www.kentwell.co.uk
Open: Feb-Oct, weekends; 11-5pm; Apr-Sep, special events and Tudor re-enactments. **Admission:** Adult from £14.99; Child from £8.95.

MELFORD HALL

Long Melford, Sudbury, Suffolk CO10 9AA

For over two centuries Melford Hall has been the much loved family home of the Hyde Parkers. **Location:** Map 8:I9. OS Ref TL866 461. In Long Melford off A134, 14m S of Bury St Edmunds, 3m N of Sudbury.
Tel: 01787 379228 **E-mail:** melford@nationaltrust.org.uk
Website: nationaltrust.org.uk/melfordhall
Open: Apr-Oct, Wed-Sun, 12-5pm. **Admission:** Adult £7.50; Child £3.75.

ORFORD CASTLE

Orford, Woodbridge, Suffolk IP12 2ND

It has a warren of passageways and chambers to be explored with a winding staircase right to the top. **Location:** Map 8:M9. OS Ref TM420 498.
Tel: 01394 450472 **E-mail:** customers@english-heritage.org.uk
Website: www.english-heritage.org.uk/orford
Open: 2 Jan-31 Mar & 1 Nov-23 Dec, Sat & Sun, 10-4pm; Apr-Oct, daily, 10-5pm; 27-31 Dec, daily, 10-4pm. **Admission:** Adult £7.60; Child £4.60.

CECIL HIGGINS ART GALLERY
Castle Lane, Bedford MK40 3RP
Tel: 01234 718618 **E-mail:** thehiggins@bedford.gov.uk

HOUGHTON HOUSE
Ampthill, Bedford, Bedfordshire
Tel: 01223 582700 (Regional Office) **E-mail:** customers@english-heritage.org.uk

THE LUTON HOO WALLED GARDEN
Luton Hoo Estate, Luton, Bedfordshire LU1 3TQ
Tel: 01582 879089 **E-mail:** office@lhwg.org.uk

MOGGERHANGER PARK
Park Road, Moggerhanger, Bedfordshire MK44 3RW
Tel: 01767 641007 **E-mail:** enquiries@moggerhangerpark.com

ELY CATHEDRAL
The Chapter House, The College, Ely, Cambridgeshire CB7 4DL
Tel: 01353 667735 ext.261

HILL HALL
Theydon Mount, Essex CM16 7QQ
Tel: 01799 522842

HYLANDS ESTATE
Hylands Park, London Road, Chelmsford CM2 8WQ
Tel: 01245 605500 **E-mail:** hylands@chelmsford.gov.uk

LAYER MARNEY TOWER
Nr Colchester, Essex CO5 9US
Tel: 01206 330784 **E-mail:** info@

THE MUNNINGS ART MUSEUM
Castle House, Castle Hill, Dedham, Essex CO7 6AZ
Tel: 01206 322127 **E-mail:** enquiries@munningsmuseum.org.uk

RHS HYDE HALL
Creephedge Lane, Rettendon, Chelmsford, Essex CM3 8ET
Tel: 0845 265 8071 **E-mail:** hydehall@rhs.org.uk

ASHRIDGE GARDENS
Berkhamsted, Hertfordshire HP4 1NS
Tel: 01442 843491 **E-mail:** reception@ashridge.org.uk

BACONSTHORPE CASTLE
Baconsthorpe, Norfolk
Tel: 01223 582700 **E-mail:** customers@english-heritage.org.uk

CLIFTON HOUSE
Queen Street, King's Lynn PE30 1HT
E-mail: anna@kingstaithe.com

DRAGON HALL
115-123 King Street, Norwich, Norfolk NR1 1QE
Tel: 01603 663922 **E-mail:** info@dragonhall.org

FAIRHAVEN WOODLAND AND WATER GARDEN
School Road, South Walsham, Norfolk NR13 6DZ
Tel: 01603 270449 **E-mail:** fairhavengarden@btconnect.com

KIMBERLEY HALL
Wymondham, Norfolk NR18 0RT
Tel: 01603 759447 **E-mail:** events@kimberleyhall.co.uk

NORWICH CASTLE MUSEUM & ART GALLERY
Norwich, Norfolk NR1 3JU
Tel: 01603 493625 **E-mail:** museums@norfolk.gov.uk

BELCHAMP HALL
Belchamp Walter, Sudbury, Suffolk CO10 7AT
Tel: 01787 881961

BRUISYARD HALL
Bruisyard Hall, Bruisyard, Saxmundham, Woodbridge IP17 2EJ
Tel: 01728 639000 **E-mail:** info@bruisyardhall.com

GLEMHAM HALL
Little Glemham, Woodbridge, Suffolk IP13 0BT
Tel: 01728 746704 **E-mail:** events@glemhamhall.co.uk

LANDGUARD FORT
Felixstowe, Suffolk IP11 3TX
Tel: 01394 675900 **E-mail:** customers@english-heritage.org.uk

THE RED HOUSE - ALDEBURGH
Golf Lane, Aldeburgh, Suffolk IP15 5PZ
Tel: 01728 452615 **E-mail:** enquiries@brittenpears.org

SUTTON HOO
Woodbridge, Suffolk IP12 3DJ
Tel: 01394 389700 **E-mail:** suttonhoo@nationaltrust.org.uk

WYKEN HALL GARDENS
Stanton, Bury St Edmunds, Suffolk IP31 2DW
Tel: 01359 250287

Holkham Hall

Register for news and special offers at **www.hudsonsheritage.com**

UNIVERSITY OF CAMBRIDGE

For further details contact
(general enquiries):
+44 (0) 1223 337733

BIDWELLS

Christ's College
St Andrew's Street, Cambridge CB2 3BU
Tel: 01223 334900
Website: www.christs.cam.ac.uk
Founder: Lady Margaret Beaufort
Founded: 1505

Churchill College
Madingley Road, Cambridge CB3 0DS
Tel: 01223 336000
Website: www.chu.cam.ac.uk
Founded: 1960

Clare College
Trinity Lane, Cambridge CB2 1TL
Tel: 01223 333200
Website: www.clare.cam.ac.uk
Founded: 1326

Clare Hall
Herschel Road, Cambridge CB3 9AL
Tel: 01223 332360
Website: www.clarehall.cam.ac.uk
Founded: 1965

Corpus Christi College
King's Parade, Cambridge CB2 3BU
Tel: 01223 338000
Website: www.corpus.cam.ac.uk
Founded: 1352

Darwin College
Silver Street, Cambridge CB3 9EU
Tel: 01223 335660
Website: www.dar.cam.ac.uk
Founded: 1964

Downing College
Regent Street, Cambridge CB2 1DQ
Tel: 01223 334800
Website: www.dow.cam.ac.uk
Founded: 1800

Emmanuel College
St Andrew's Street, Cambridge CB2 3AP
Tel: 01223 334200
Website: www.emma.cam.ac.uk
Founded: 1584

Fitzwilliam College
Huntingdon Road, Cambridge CB2 0DG
Tel: 01223 332000
Website: www.fitz.cam.ac.uk
Founded: 1966

Girton College
Huntingdon Road, Cambridge CB3 0JG
Tel: 01223 338999
Website: www.girton.cam.ac.uk
Founded: 1869

Gonville & Caius College
Trinity Street, Cambridge CB2 1TA
Tel: 01223 332400
Website: www.cai.cam.ac.uk
Founded: 1348

Homerton College
Hills Road, Cambridge CB2 2PH
Tel: 01223 507111
Website: www.homerton.cam.ac.uk
Founded: 1976

Hughes Hall
Wollaston Road, Cambridge CB1 2EW
Tel: 01223 334897
Website: www.hughes.cam.ac.uk
Founded: 1885

Jesus College
Jesus Lane, Cambridge CB5 8BL
Tel: 01223 339339
Website: www.jesus.cam.ac.uk
Founded: 1496

King's College
King's Parade, Cambridge CB2 1ST
Tel: 01223 331100
Website: www.kings.cam.ac.uk
Founded: 1441

Lucy Cavendish College
Lady Margaret Road, Cambridge CB3 0BU
Tel: 01223 332190
Website: www.lucy-cav.cam.ac.uk
Founded: 1965

Magdalene College
Magdalene Street, Cambridge CB3 0AG
Tel: 01223 332100
Website: www.magd.cam.ac.uk
Founded: 1428

New Hall
Huntingdon Road, Cambridge CB3 0DF
Tel: 01223 762100
Website: www.newhall.cam.ac.uk
Founded: 1954

Newnham College
Grange Road, Cambridge CB3 9DF
Tel: 01223 335700
Website: www.newn.cam.ac.uk
Founded: 1871

Pembroke College
Trumpington Street, Cambridge CB2 1RF
Tel: 01223 338100
Website: www.pem.cam.ac.uk
Founded: 1347

Peterhouse
Trumpington Street, Cambridge CB2 1RD
Tel: 01223 338200
Website: www.pet.cam.ac.uk
Founder: The Bishop of Ely
Founded: 1284

Queens' College
Silver Street, Cambridge CB3 9ET
Tel: 01223 335511
Website: www.girton.cam.ac.uk
Founder: Margaret of Anjou, Elizabeth Woodville
Founded: 1448

Ridley Hall
Ridley Halll Road, Cambridge CB3 9HG
Tel: 01223 741080
Website: www.ridley.cam.ac.uk
Founded: 1879

Robinson College
Grange Road, Cambridge CB3 9AN
Tel: 01223 339100
Website: www.robinson.cam.ac.uk
Founded: 1979

St Catharine's College
Kings Parade, Cambridge CB2 1RL
Tel: 01223 338300
Website: www.caths.cam.ac.uk
Founded: 1473

St Edmund's College
Mount Pleasant, Cambridge CB3 0BN
Tel: 01223 336086
Website: www.st-edmunds.cam.ac.uk
Founded: 1896

St John's College
St John's Street, Cambridge CB2 1TP
Tel: 01223 338600
Website: www.joh.cam.ac.uk
Founded: 1511

Srlwyn College
Grange Road, Cambridge CB3 9DQ
Tel: 01223 335846
Website: www.sel.cam.ac.uk
Founded: 1882

Sidney Sussex College
Sidney Street, Cambridge CB2 3HU
Tel: 01223 338800
Website: www.sid.cam.ac.uk
Founded: 1596

Trinity College
Trinity Street, Cambridge CB2 1TQ
Tel: 01223 338400
Website: www.trin.cam.ac.uk
Founded: 1546

Trinity Hall
Trinity Lane, Cambridge CB2 1TJ
Tel: 01223 332500
Website: www.trinhall.cam.ac.uk
Founded: 1350

Wesley House
Jesus Lane, Cambridge CB5 8BJ
Tel: 01223 350127 / 367980
Website: www.wesley.cam.ac.uk

Westcott House
Jesus Lane, Cambridge CB5 8BP
Tel: 01223 741000
Website: www.ely.anglican.org/westcott

Westminster & Cheshunt
Madingley Road, Cambridge CB3 0AA
Tel: 01223 741084
Website: www.westminstercollege.co.uk

Wolfson College
Grange Road, Cambridge CB3 9BB
Tel: 01223 335900
Website: www.wolfson.cam.ac.uk
Founded: 1965

Colleges are working buildings; times are subject to change and charges may apply. Groups must book in advance.
Many halls are only open before 12pm. Libraries & Fellows' Gardens are generally private. Please call at the Porters' Lodge first.

Burghley House, Lincolnshire

Doddington Hall, Lincolnshire

Derbyshire
Leicestershire & Rutland
Lincolnshire
Northamptonshire
Nottinghamshire

East Midlands

The East Midlands boasts some of Britain's finest stately homes and great estates. Heritage is one of the prime reasons for coming to this lovely part of Britain, so make the most of it.

HADDON HALL

ESTATE OFFICE, HADDON HALL, BAKEWELL, DERBYSHIRE DE45 1LA

www.haddonhall.co.uk

There has been a dwelling here since the 11th Century but the house we see today dates mainly from the late 14th Century with alterations in the 16th & 17th Centuries. Haddon was the home of the Vernon family until the late 16th Century when the estate passed by marriage to the Manners family, who still live in the hall today. When the Dukedom of Rutland was conferred on the Manners family in 1703 they moved to Belvoir Castle, and Haddon was left deserted for 200 years. The 9th Duke returned in the 1920's and began restoring the hall. Haddon is a popular location for film and television productions, featuring as Thornfield Hall in several renditions of 'Jane Eyre', as well as appearing in 'The Princess Bride' and 'The Hollow Crown'.

Location: Map 6:P2. OS Ref SK234 663. From London 3 hrs, Sheffield ½hr, Manchester 1 hr. Haddon is on E side of A6 1½m S of Bakewell. M1/J29.

Owner: Lord Edward Manners **Contact:** Selina King

Tel: 01629 812855 **E-mail:** info@haddonhall.co.uk

Open: Apr: Sat, Sun & Mon and Easter 8-24 Apr. May-Sep: Open daily (except 20 & 21 May). Oct: Sat, Sun & Mon and half-term 23-27 Oct.
Opening times: 10.30am-5pm (last admission 4pm).
Christmas: 1-17 Dec 10.30am-4pm (last admission 3.30pm).
Haddon Hall is closed during Jan, Feb, Mar & Nov.

Admission: Please see website for admission prices & further information.

Key facts: Ideal film location due to authentic & genuine architecture requiring little alteration. Suitable locations also on Estate.
Gatehouse Gift Shop, local & specially selected souvenirs, gifts, cards & plants.
WCs. Further accessibility information can also be found on our website.
Pre-bookable. Ample. 450yds from house. Parking charge applies.
Assistance dogs only. Licensed for civil ceremonies.

© Renishaw Hall & Gardens

RENISHAW HALL AND GARDENS

RENISHAW, NR SHEFFIELD, DERBYSHIRE S21 3WB

www.renishaw-hall.co.uk

Renishaw Hall and Gardens have been home to the Sitwell family for over 400 years. Its present owner, Alexandra, welcomes you. Renishaw Hall is set in eight acres of Italianate gardens, designed by Sir George Sitwell featuring statues, yew hedges, beautiful herbaceous borders and ornamental ponds. Mature woodlands and lakes offer wonderful walks. The hall offers an intriguing insight into the Sitwell family's history, with a fascinating collection of paintings including work by John Piper. The hall & gardens are open for group and public tours, see website for details. The Café, shop and museum are in the stables. Tours of the vineyard are available throughout the season. The hall & gardens can be hired for film and photo shoots. **Location:** Map 7:A2. OS Ref SK435 786.
On A6135, 3m from M1/J30, located between Sheffield and Chesterfield.

Owner: Mrs Hayward **Contact:** The Hall & Visitor Manager **Tel:** 01246 432310
Fax: 01246 430760 **E-mail:** enquiries@renishaw-hall.co.uk

Open: 22 Mar-1 Oct. Gardens open Wed-Sun & BH Mons, 10.30am-4.30pm. Hall open to public on Fris throughout season 1pm or 2.30pm & weekends in Aug, pre-booking advisable for guided tours. Hall, garden & vineyard tours available throughout year for private groups & coach tours, by appointment only.

Admission: HHA /RHS members free entry to Gardens. Guided Hall Tours £6.50. Discounts for coach/group bookings over 20 people. Parking £1.00. Non-member entry Gardens Adults £6.50, Concessions £5.50, Children £3.25, under 5's free. Non-member Guided Hall Tour Adults £13.00, Concessions £12.00.

Key facts: Café, Gift Shop, WC available during garden opening.
Plant sales by Handley Rose Nursery available at the visitor centre.
Partial. WCs. Licensed. By arrangement throughout season for groups & on Fridays to public. £1.00 per car for the day.
On leads.

Register for news and special offers at www.hudsonsheritage.com

CHATSWORTH

Bakewell, Derbyshire DE45 1PP

www.chatsworth.org

Chatsworth, home of the Duke and Duchess of Devonshire, is set in the heart of the Peak District in Derbyshire. You can explore the historic house for fascinating stories and one of Europe's most significant art collections, in the garden you'll discover water features, giant sculptures and beautiful flowers. Or come face to face with our farm animals in our working farmyard and adventure playground.

Location: Map 6:P2. OS Ref SK260 703. From London 3 hrs M1/J29, signposted via Chesterfield. 3m E of Bakewell, off B6012,10m W of Chesterfield.
Rail: Chesterfield Station, 11m. Bus: Chesterfield - Baslow 1½m.

Owner: Chatsworth House Trust **Contact:** The Booking Office

Tel: 01246 565430 **Fax:** 01246 583536 **E-mail:** visit@chatsworth.org

Open: Visit www.chatsworth.org for details.

Admission: Visit www.chatsworth.org for details.

Key facts:

MELBOURNE HALL & GARDENS

Melbourne, Derbyshire DE73 8EN

www.melbournehall.com

This beautiful house of history, in its picturesque poolside setting, was once the home of Victorian Prime Minister William Lamb. The fine gardens, in the French formal style, contain Robert Bakewell's intricate wrought iron arbour and a fascinating yew tunnel. Upstairs rooms available to view by appointment.

Location: Map 7:A5. OS Ref SK389 249.
8m S of Derby. From London, exit M1/J24.

Owner: Lord & Lady Ralph Kerr **Contact:** Mrs Gill Weston

Tel: 01332 862502 **Fax:** 01332 862263 **E-mail:** melbhall@globalnet.co.uk

Open: Hall: Every day Aug only (not first 3 Mons) 2-5pm. Last admission 4.15pm. Gardens: 1 Apr-30 Sep: Weds, Sats, Suns, BH Mons, 1.30-5.30pm. Additional days in Aug whenever the Hall is open.

Admission: Please see website or telephone for up-to-date admission charges.

Key facts: No photography in house. Visitor centre shops, hospice shop, gift shop, antiques, jewellery, cakes & furniture restorer. Selection for sale at garden entrance. Partial. WCs. Melbourne Hall Tea Room. Obligatory in house Tue-Thus. Limited. No coach parking. Guide dogs only.

Haddon Hall

© The Portland Collection

WELBECK ABBEY

Welbeck, Worksop, Nottinghamshire S80 3LL

www.welbeck.co.uk

The Welbeck Estate covers some 15,000 acres, nestled between Sherwood Forest & Clumber Park. At its heart lies Welbeck Abbey, a stately home which dates back to 1153 when it was founded as a Premonstratensian monastery.
Location: Map 7:B2. OS Ref SK557 752. From the M1 – leave the motorway at Junction 30 and follow brown signs for Welbeck. From the A1 – leave the A1 at Worksop and follow brown signs to Welbeck.The car park entrance is marked on the A60 with a brown sign for The Harley Gallery.
Owner: Welbeck Estates Company Limited
Contact: The Harley Gallery
Tel: 01909 501700 **E-mail:** info@harleygallery.co.uk
Open: Tours run during the summer. Please always check the website before visiting for full details. **Admission:** £16.50 per person.
Key facts: No photography. The Harley Shop. By prior arrangement. Ground floor only. The Harley Café. Obligatory. Free parking. Please park at The Harley Gallery.

CATTON HALL

Catton, Walton-On-Trent, South Derbyshire DE12 8LN

Catton, built in 1745, has been in the hands of the same family since 1405 and is still lived in by the Neilsons as their private home. This gives the house a unique, relaxed and friendly atmosphere, with its spacious reception rooms, comfortable bedrooms and delicious food and wine. The acres of parkland alongside the River Trent are ideal for all types of corporate and public events.
Location: Map 6:P5. OS Ref SK20 6153. Birmingham NEC 20m.
Owner/Contact: Robin & Katie Neilson
Tel: 01283 716311 **E-mail:** estateoffice@catton-hall.com
Website: www.catton-hall.com
Open: By prior arrangement all year, for corporate hospitality, shooting parties, or private groups. Guided tours at 2pm prompt. BH Mons, and all Mons in Aug.
Key facts: By arrangement. By arrangement. 4 x four posters, 5 twin, all en suite.

BOLSOVER CASTLE

Castle Street, Bolsover, Derbyshire S44 6PR

An enchanting and romantic spectacle, situated high on a wooded hilltop dominating the surrounding landscape. **Location:** Map 7:A2. OS Ref SK471 705.
Tel: 01246 822844 **E-mail:** customers@english-heritage.org.uk
Website: www.english-heritage.org.uk/bolsover **Open:** 2 Jan-31 Mar, Sat & Sun, 10-4pm; 1 Apr-30 Sep, daily, 10-6pm; 1-31 Oct, 10-5pm; 1 Nov-31 Dec, Sat & Sun, 10-4pm. Closed 24-26 Dec & 1 Jan. **Admission:** Adult £11.30; Child £6.80.

CALKE ABBEY

Ticknall, Derbyshire DE73 7LE

The house that time forgot, this baroque mansion, built 1701-3 for Sir John Harpur, is set in a landscaped park. **Location:** Map 7:A5. OS Ref SK366 226. 10m S of Derby, on A514 at Ticknall between Swadlincote and Melbourne.
Tel: 01332 863822 **E-mail:** calkeabbey@nationaltrust.org.uk
Website: www.nationaltrust.org.uk/calke **Open:** Gardens: 11 Feb-29 Oct, 10am-5pm. House: 25 Feb-29 Oct, 11am-5pm. **Admission:** Please see website.

ELVASTON CASTLE AND COUNTRY PARK

Borrowash Road, Elvaston, Derby DE72 3EP

Elvaston Castle Country Park encompasses approximately 321 acres of open parkland, woodland and more formal historical gardens.
Location: Map 7:A5. OS Ref SK406 330.
Tel: 01629 533870 **E-mail:** countrysideservice@derbyshire.gov.uk
Website: www.derbyshire.gov.uk **Open:** Jan-Mar, daily, 9-5pm; Apr-Sep, daily, 9-8pm; Oct-Dec, daily, 9-5pm. **Admission:** Free; car parking charges.

HARDWICK ESTATE

Doe Lea, Chesterfield, Derbyshire S44 5QJ

One of the most splendid houses in England. Built by the extraordinary Bess of Hardwick in the 1590's, and unaltered. **Location:** Map 7:A3. OS Ref SK456 651. See website for directions. **Tel:** 01246 850430 **Fax:** 01246 858424 **E-mail:** hardwickhall@nationaltrust.org.uk **Website:** www.nationaltrust.org.uk/hardwick
Open: Gardens: All year, daily, 10-6pm. Hall: 11 Feb-29 Oct, Wed-Sun, 11-5pm; 25 Nov-17 Dec, Wed-Sun, 11-3pm. **Admission:** Adult £6.55; Child £3.30.

HOPTON HALL

Hopton, Wirksworth, Matlock, Derbyshire DE4 4DF

Formal gardens with 1 acre walled garden. Recently restored.
Location: Map 6:P3. OS Ref SK261 533.
Tel: 01629 540923 **E-mail:** bookings@hoptonhall.co.uk
Website: www.hoptonhall.co.uk
Open: 1 Feb-5 Mar, 13 Jun-24 Aug, Tue-Thu, 10.30-4pm.
Admission: Adult £4.

KEDLESTON HALL

Derbyshire DE22 5JH

Kedleston Hall boasts the most complete and least altered sequence of Robert Adam interiors in England. Take in the 18th Century pleasure grounds and 800 acre park. **Location:** Map 6:P4. OS Ref SK312 403.
Tel: 01332 842191 **E-mail:** kedlestonhall@nationaltrust.org.uk
Website: www.nationaltrust.org.uk/kedleston **Open:** Park: All year, daily,10am-dusk. Hall: 25 Feb-29 Oct, Sat-Thu, 12-5pm. **Admission:** Adult £12; Child £6.

OGSTON HALL AND GARDENS

Ogston New Road, Brackenfield, Derbyshire DE55 6AP

Part Jacobean, Georgian house extensively remodelled by T.C Hine 1850-64. Beautiful terraced gardens with views over mature parkland.
Location: Map 7:A3. OS Ref SK372 592. 6 miles E of Matlock, 1 mile N.E of Brackenfield, by Ogston Reservoir. Entrance opposite Ogston Lodge, Brackenfield.
Tel: 01773 520970 / 07796 130677 **Open:** 1-28 Aug, 2-5pm.
By appointment only. **Admission:** £10 per head.

SUDBURY HALL & MUSEUM OF CHILDHOOD

Ashbourne, Derbyshire DE6 5HT

17th Century family home & museum; a place to share stories of vision & imagination. **Location:** Map 6:O7. OS Ref SK157 323. **Tel:** 01283 585337
E-mail: sudburyhall@nationaltrust.org.uk **Website:** www.nationaltrust.org.uk
Open: Hall: 11 Feb-29 Oct, Wed-Sun & BH Mons, tours on Tue, 1-5pm. Museum: 11 Feb- 26 Mar, Wed-Sun, 10.30am-5pm; 27 Mar-29 Oct, 10.30am-5pm; 2 Nov-17 Dec, Thu-Sun, 10.30am-4pm. **Admission:** Adult £15; Child £7.50.

TISSINGTON HALL

Ashbourne, Derbyshire DE6 1RA

Tissington Hall stands at the centre of its estate, built in 1609 by Francis FitzHerbert it still remains in the family. **Location:** Map 6:P3. OS Ref SK175 524. 4m N of Ashbourne off A515 towards Buxton.
Tel: 01335 352200 **E-mail:** events@tissingtonhall.co.uk
Website: www.tissingtonhall.co.uk **Open:** 17-20 Apr, 1 May, 29-31 May, 12-3pm; 31 Jul-24 Aug, Mon-Thu, 12-3pm. **Admission:** Adult £10; Child £5.

WINGFIELD MANOR

South Wingfield, Derbyshire DE55 7NH

Ruins of palatial medieval manor house buit in the 1440s for Ralph, Lord Cromwell, Treasurer of England.
Location: Map 7:A3. OS Ref SK375 552.
Tel: 0870 333 1181 **Website:** www.english-heritage.org.uk
Open: Apr-Sep, first Sat each month, pre-booked tours only.
Admission: Adult £6.90; Child £4.10.

Register for news and special offers at **www.hudsonsheritage.com**

STANFORD HALL

LUTTERWORTH, LEICESTERSHIRE LE17 6DH

www.stanfordhall.co.uk

Stanford has been the home of the Cave family, ancestors of the present owner since 1430. In the 1690's, Sir Roger Cave commissioned the Smiths of Warwick to pull down the old Manor House and build the present Hall. Throughout the house are portraits of the family and examples of furniture and objects which they collected over the centuries. There is also a collection of Royal Stuart portraits. The Hall and Stables are set in an attractive Park on the banks of Shakespeare's Avon. There is a walled Rose Garden and an early ha-ha.

Location: Map 7:B7. OS Ref SP587 793.
M1/J18 6m. M1/J20, 6m. M6 exit/access at J1, 4m. Historic House signs.
Owner: Mr & Mrs N Fothergill
Contact: Nick Fothergill
Tel: 01788 860250
E-mail: enquiries@stanfordhall.co.uk

Open: Special 3 week Easter opening – Mon 3 Apr-Fri 7 Apr and Sun 9 Apr-Mon 24 Apr 2017. Open other days in conjunction with park events and bank holidays. See our website or telephone for details. House open any weekday or weekday evening for pre-booked groups. **Admission:** House & Grounds: Adult £8.00, Child (5-15 yrs) £2.50. Private group tours (20+): Adult £8.00, Child £2.50. Special admission prices will apply on event days.

Key facts: Craft centre (event days and Bank Hols). Corporate days, clay pigeon shoots, filming, photography, small conferences, accommodation. Parkland, helicopter landing area, lecture room, Stables Tea Room. Caravan site. Lunches, dinners & wedding receptions. Partial. WCs. Stables Tea Room. Tour time: 3/4 hr in groups of approx 25. 1,000 cars and 6-8 coaches. Coach parking on gravel in front of house. Dogs on leads only. Accommodation available. Group bookings only.

BELVOIR CASTLE

Belvoir, Grantham, Leicestershire NG32 1PE

Belvoir Castle stands high on a hill overlooking 16,000 acres of woodland and farmland. Events in the park, weddings, world famous pheasant and partridge shoot, tours of the Castle, art collection and renovated gardens.

Location: Map 7:C4. OS Ref SK820 337. A1 from London 110m. Leicester 30m. Grantham 7m. **Tel:** 01476 871001 **Website:** www.belvoircastle.co.uk
Open: Mar-Sep, selected days, 11-5pm. **Admission:** Adult £15; Child £8.

VISITOR INFORMATION

Owner
Burghley House Preservation Trust Ltd

Address
House Manager
Stamford
Lincolnshire
PE9 3JY

Location
Map 7:E7
OS Ref. TF048 062
Burghley House is 1m SE of Stamford. From London, A1 2hrs. Visitors entrance is on B1443.
Rail: London - Peterborough 1hr (East Coast mainline). Stamford Station 12mins, regular service from Peterborough.
Taxi: Direct line 01780 481481.

Contact
The House Manager
Tel: 01780 752451
Fax: 01780 480125
E-mail: burghley@burghley.co.uk

Opening Times
House & Gardens:
18 Mar-29 Oct 2017 (closed 31 Aug-3 Sep).
Open daily (House closed on Fris), 11am-5pm, (last admission 4.30pm).

Admission
House & Gardens

Adult	£18.00
Child (3-15 yrs)	£9.00
Family	£52.00

Groups (20+)

Adult	£12.50

Gardens Only

Adult	£12.00
Child (3-15 yrs)	£8.00
Family	£38.00

Special Events
South Gardens Opening
18 Mar-30 Apr.
Burghley Horse Trials
Aug 31-3 Sep.
Battle Proms
8 Jul.
Flower Festival
30 Sep-8 Oct.

Conference/Function

ROOM	Size	Max Cap
Great Hall	70' x 30'	160
Orangery	100' x 20'	120
Summer House	17.5' x 17.5'	25

BURGHLEY HOUSE

www.burghley.co.uk

Burghley House, home of the Cecil family for over 400 years is one of England's Greatest Elizabethan Houses.

Burghley was built between 1555 and 1587 by William Cecil, later Lord Burghley, principal adviser and Lord High Treasurer to Queen Elizabeth. During the 17th and 18th Centuries, the House was transformed by John 5th Earl of Exeter and Brownlow, the 9th Earl; travelling to the cultural centres of Europe and employing many of the foremost craftsmen of their day. Burghley contains one of the largest private collections of Italian art, unique examples of Chinese and Japanese porcelain and superb items of 18th Century furniture. Principal artists and craftsmen of the period are to be found at Burghley: Antonio Verrio, Grinling Gibbons and Louis Laguerre all made major contributions to the beautiful interiors.

Park and Gardens

The house is set in a 300-acre deer park landscaped by 'Capability' Brown and is one of the finest examples of his work. A lake was created by him and delightful avenues of mature trees feature largely in his design. Brown also carried out alterations to the architecture of the House and added a summerhouse in the South Gardens. The park is home to a large herd of Fallow deer, established in the 16th Century. The Garden of Surprises is a modern oasis of flowing water and fountains, statues, and obelisks. The contemporary Sculpture Garden was reclaimed from 'Capability' Brown's lost lower gardens in 1994 and is dedicated to exhibiting innovative sculptures. The private gardens around the house are open from mid-March to mid-April for the display of spring bulbs.

KEY FACTS

- Suitable for a variety of events, large park, golf course, helicopter landing area, cricket pitch. No photography in house.
- 
- WCs.
- Licensed.
- Licensed.
- By Arrangement.
- Ample. Free refreshments for coach drivers.
- Welcome. Guide provided.
- Guide dogs only.
- Civil Wedding Licence.

GRIMSTHORPE CASTLE, PARK AND GARDENS

GRIMSTHORPE, BOURNE, LINCOLNSHIRE PE10 0LZ

www.grimsthorpe.co.uk

Building styles from 13th Century. North Front is Vanbrugh's last major work. State Rooms and picture galleries including tapestries, furniture and paintings. Interesting collection of thrones, fabrics and objects from the old House of Lords, associated with the family's hereditary Office of Lord Great Chamberlain. 3,000 acre park with lakes, ancient woods, walking and cycle trail, cycle hire shop. Extensive gardens including unusual ornamental kitchen garden. Groups can explore the park in their own coach by booking a one-hour, escorted park tour. Tailor-made group visits available on request including Head Gardener tour. Full and half day bespoke visits for groups of 15+. **Location:** Map 7:D5. OS Ref TF040 230. 4m NW of Bourne on A151, 8m E of Colsterworth Junction of A1. **Owner:** Grimsthorpe & Drummond Castle Trust Ltd. A Charity registered in England, Wales & Scotland SCO39364.

Contact: Ray Biggs **Tel:** 01778 591205 **E-mail:** ray@grimsthorpe.co.uk **Open:** Castle: Apr & May: Sun, Thu & BH Mons. Jun-Sep: Sun-Thu inclusive. 12-4pm (last admission 3pm). Park & Gardens: same days as Castle, 11am-6pm (last admission 5pm). Groups: Apr-Sep: by arrangement. Closed Fris and Sats **Admission:** Castle, Park & Garden: Adult £11.00, Child £5.00, Conc. £10.00, Family (2+3) £27.00. Park & Gardens: Adult £6.00, Child £2.50, Conc. £5.00, Family (2+3) £14.50. Group rates: from £9.50. **Key facts:** No photography in house. Locally produced food and drink plus other gifts and souvenirs. WCs. Morning coffee from 11am, Light lunches 12-2.30. Afternoon tea service. Closes 5pm. Obligatory except Suns & BH Mons. Ample. Dogs on leads only. Please avoid formal gardens & adventure playground.

AYSCOUGHFEE HALL MUSEUM & GARDENS

Churchgate, Spalding, Lincolnshire PE11 2RA

www.ayscoughfee.org

Ayscoughfee Hall, a magnificent Grade I listed building, was built in the 1450s. The Hall is set in five acres of extensive landscaped grounds which include amongst other features a memorial designed by Edwin Lutyens. The Museum features the history of the Hall, the people who lived there and the surrounding Fens. **Location:** Map 7:F5. OS Ref TF249 223. E bank of the River Welland, 5 mins walk from Spalding town centre. Follow brown signs if driving. **Owner:** South Holland District Council **Contact:** Museum Officer **Tel:** 01775 764555 **E-mail:** museum@sholland.gov.uk **Open:** Hall: 10.30am-4pm Wed-Sun (open on BH Mon), closed over Christmas period. Gardens: 8am until dusk every day (except Christmas Day). **Admission:** Free. **Key facts:** Photography allowed, apart from in temporary exhibition Gallery. Small shop in Hall. Email for info. WCs, lift. Open 7 days a week. By arrangement. Large public pay and display car park next door. Email for info. Guide dogs only in Hall, all dogs allowed in Gardens (on lead). Email for info. Closed at Christmas.

DODDINGTON HALL & GARDENS

Lincoln LN6 4RU

www.doddingtonhall.com

Romantic Smythson house standing today as it was built in 1595. Still a family home. Georgian interior with fascinating collection of porcelain, paintings & textiles. Five acres of wild & walled formal gardens plus kitchen garden provide colour & interest year-round. Award-winning Farm Shop, Café & Restaurant. Country Clothing, Large Bicycle Shop, Farrow & Ball & Home Stores. **Location:** Map 7:D2. OS Ref SK900 710. 5m W of Lincoln on the B1190, signposted off the A46 and B1190. **Owner:** Mr & Mrs J J C Birch **Contact:** The Estate Office **Tel:** 01522 812510 **E-mail:** info@doddingtonhall.com **Open:** Gardens only: Sun 12 Feb-16 Apr & Oct, Suns only, 11am-4.30pm. Last admission 4pm. Hall & Gardens: Sun 16 Apr–Weds 27 Sep, Suns, Weds & B.H Mons 12-4.30pm (Gardens 11am). Last admission 4pm. **Admission:** Gardens only: Adult £7.00, Child £3.50, Family £18.00 (2 adults + up to 4 children). House & Gardens: Adult £10.50, Child £4.75, Family £28.00. Group visits (guided tours for 20+) £11.00pp. **Key facts:** Photography permitted, no flash. No stilettos. Seasonal. Virtual tour. Garden accessible - mixed surface. Open 7 days. Breakfast, lunches & teas. No booking. Open 7 days and Fri/Sat eve. By arrangement. Workshops for KS1/2. Guide dogs only. Holidays Cottages within the Estate boundaries.

LINCOLN CASTLE

Castle Hill, Lincoln LN1 3AA

www.lincolncastle.com

Discover Lincoln Castle, home to one of the four surviving Magna Cartas, the attraction has undergone a £22m refurbishment. Bringing 1,000 years of history to life – right where it happened.
Location: Map 7:D2. OS Ref SK976 718. Set next to Lincoln Cathedral in the Historic Quarter of the city. Follow signs from A1 Newark or A15 North and South.
Owner: Lincolnshire County Council **Contact:** Lincoln Castle
Tel: 01522 554559 **E-mail:** lincoln_castle@lincolnshire.gov.uk
Open: Apr-Sep 10am-5pm, Oct-Mar 10am-4pm.
Admission: Adults £12.00, Conc £9.60, Child 5 & over £7.20, Under 5's free. Walk, Prison and Vault included. Entry to Castle grounds, shop and café are free.
Key facts: Events through the year. Some events will have separate admission prices. Set within the Prison with a range to suit all pockets. Tailor made packages. Accessible including part of the Medieval Wall. Set within the Prison and licenced. A variety of tours available. Audio tour included in admission price. Please contact us for education visits. Assistance dogs only. Closed 24-26 Dec & 31 Dec-1 Jan.

AUBOURN HALL

Lincoln LN5 9DZ

Nine acres of lawns and floral borders surround this homely Jacobean manor house. Garden tours are available. The Gardens are also available for Wedding Receptions. We can provide a stunning setting for your bespoke marquee wedding and other celebrations.
Location: Map 7:D3. OS Ref SK928 628. 6m SW of Lincoln. 2m SE of A46.
Owner: Mr & Mrs Christopher Nevile
Contact: Paula Dawson, Estate Office
Tel: 01522 788224 **Fax:** 01522 788199
E-mail: estate.office@aubournhall.co.uk **Website:** www.aubournhall.co.uk
Open: Garden open for Events, Groups and Garden visits from May-Sep. Please contact the Estate Office or go to our website www.aubournhall.co.uk for details.
Admission: Adult £4.50; Child Free.
Key facts: Partial. WCs. By arrangement. Limited for coaches. Guide dogs only.

FULBECK MANOR

Fulbeck, Grantham, Lincolnshire NG32 3JN

Built c1580. 400 years of Fane family portraits. Open by written appointment. Guided tours by owner approximately 1¼ hours. Tea Rooms at Craft Centre, 100 yards, for light lunches and teas.
Location: Map 7:D3. OS Ref SK947 505. 11m N of Grantham. 15m S of Lincoln on A607. Brown signs to Craft Centre & Tearooms and Stables.
Owner/Contact: Mr Julian Francis Fane
Tel: 01400 272231
E-mail: fane@fulbeck.co.uk
Open: By written appointment.
Admission: Adult £7.00. Groups (10+) £6.00.
Key facts: No photography. Partial. WCs. Obligatory. Ample for cars. Limited for coaches. Except assistance dogs.

ARABELLA AUFRERE TEMPLE

Brocklesby Park, Grimsby, Lincolnshire DN41 8PN

Garden Temple of ashlar and red brick with coupled doric columns.
Location: Map 11:E12. OS Ref TA139 112. Off A18 in Great Limber Village.
Tel: 01469 560214
E-mail: office@brocklesby.co.uk
Open: 1 Apr–31 Aug: viewable from permissive paths through Mausoleum Woods at all reasonable times. **Admission:** None.

BELTON HOUSE

Grantham, Lincolnshire NG32 2LS

Begun for Sir John Brownlow in 1685, Belton was designed to impress & across its 300 year history, each generation left their creative mark. **Location:** Map 7:D4. OS Ref SK929 395. **Tel:** 01476 566116 **E-mail:** belton@nationaltrust.org.uk
Website: www.nationaltrust.org.uk **Open:** Grounds: 1 Jan-28 Feb, 9.30am-4pm; 1 Mar-29 Oct, 9.30am-5.30pm; 30 Oct-31 Dec, 9.30am-4pm. House: 11 Mar-29 Oct, Wed-Sun, 12.30-5pm. **Admission:** Adult £13.10; Child £8.40.

BROCKLESBY MAUSOLEUM

Brocklesby Park, Grimsby, Lincolnshire DN41 8PN

Family Mausoleum designed by James Wyatt and built between 1787 and 1794.
Location: Map 11:E12. OS Ref TA139 112. Off A18 in Great Limber Village.
Tel: 01469 560214
E-mail: office@brocklesby.co.uk
Open: By prior arrangement with Estate Office.
Admission: Modest admission charge for interior.

EASTON WALLED GARDENS

Easton, Grantham, Lincolnshire NG33 5AP

400 year old gardens with snowdrops, roses, daffodils, iris, a cut flower garden, cottage garden and 80m of poppies. **Location:** Map 7:D5. OS Ref SK929 268. 1m from A1 (between Stamford and Grantham) North of Colsterworth, onto B6403 and follow signs. **Tel:** 01476 530063 **E-mail:** info@eastonwalledgardens.co.uk
Website: www.visiteaston.co.uk **Open:** Mar-Oct, Wed-Fri, Sun & BH Mons, 11am-4pm. **Admission:** Adult £7; Child £3.

GUNBY HALL

Spilsby, Lincolnshire PE23 5SL

A homely country house dated 1700 set in Victorian walled gardens at the foot of the Lincolnshire Wolds. **Location:** Map 7:G3. OS Ref TF470 672.
Tel: 01754 890102 **E-mail:** gunbyhall@nationaltrust.org.uk
Website: www.nationaltrust.org.uk/gunby-estate-hall-and-gardens
Open: Gardens: Apr-Oct, daily, 11am-5pm. House: Apr-Oct, Sat-Wed, 11am-5pm; 25 Nov-10 Dec, Sat & Sun, 11am-3pm. **Admission:** Adult £7.50; Child £3.75.

LEADENHAM HOUSE

Lincolnshire LN5 0PU

Late 18th Century house in park setting. **Location:** Map 7:D3. OS Ref SK949 518. Entrance on A17 Leadenham bypass (between Newark and Sleaford).
Tel: 01400 272680 **E-mail:** leadenhamhouse@googlemail.com
Open: 3-7; 10-12; 19-21 Apr; 8-12; 15-19; 22-24; 30,31 May; Spring & Aug BHs.
Admission: £5.00. Please ring door bell.
Groups by prior arrangement only.

MARSTON HALL

Marston, Grantham NG32 2HQ

The ancient home of the Thorold family containing Norman Plantagenet Tudor & Georgian elements. Telephone to avoid disruptive restoration work.
Location: Map 7:D4. OS Ref SK893 437. 5m N of Grantham and 1m E of A1.
Tel: 07812 356237 **Fax:** 0208 7892 857 **E-mail:** johnthorold@aol.com
Open: Feb 17-22, Apr 12-19 (Easter), Apr 29-30, May 1, 27-31 & Aug 24-29.
Admission: Adult £4.00, Child £1.50. Groups must book.

WOOLSTHORPE MANOR

Water Lane, Woolsthorpe by Colsterworth NG33 5PD

Isaac Newton, was born in this 17th Century manor house in 1642 & developed his ideas about light & gravity here. **Location:** Map 7:D5. OS Ref SK924 244.
Tel: 01476 862823 **E-mail:** woolsthorpemanor@nationaltrust.org.uk
Website: www.nationaltrust.org.uk **Open:** Science Centre: Jan-Dec, 11am-3pm; 5pm in Summer. House: Winter, Fri-Mon, 11am-3pm; Apr-Oct, Wed-Sun, 11am-5pm. **Admission:** Adult £6.45; Child £3.47.

DEENE PARK

www.deenepark.com

Home of the Brudenell family since 1514, this 16th Century house incorporates a medieval manor with important Georgian additions.

Seat of the 7th Earl of Cardigan who led the charge of the Light Brigade at Balaklava in 1854, today the house is the home of Robert Brudenell, his wife Charlotte and their son William. The rooms on show are regularly used by the family, their friends and family guests. The house has grown in size since its medieval origins as successive generations extended the house during the Tudor and Georgian periods, providing the visitor with an interesting yet complementary mixture of styles. There is a considerable collection of family portraits and possessions, including memorabilia from the Crimean War.

The gardens are mainly to the south and west of the house and include long borders, old-fashioned roses and specimen trees. The most impressive feature of the garden is a parterre designed by David Hicks in the 1990's. The topiary teapots, inspired by the finial on the Millenium obelisk, form a fine feature as they mature. The most recent addition is the Golden Garden inspired by Charlotte Brudenell and her love of bold, warm colours. Open parkland lies across the water from the terraced gardens providing enchanting vistas in many directions. The more energetic visitor can discover these during a rewarding walk in the tranquil surroundings. As well as the flora, there is also a diversity of bird life ranging from red kites to kingfishers and black swans to little grebes.

On public open days homemade lunches and delicious cakes are available in the Old Kitchen Tea Room, while souvenirs and mementos of your visit can be found in the Gift Shop. Guided Group Tours are available between Apr and the end of Sep by prior arrangement on Tues, Weds and Thus, we advise groups to pre-book their catering in advance. Formal dining opportunities in the Regency Dining Room are also available in the form of hosted lunches and evening dinners, subject to the availability of Robert and Charlotte Brudenell.

KEY FACTS

- No photography in house or large bags.
- Shop.
- Various plants for sale in May, Jun & Jul.
- Buffets, lunches & dinners by arrangement. Selected rooms available for private functions.
- Access to ground floor & garden.
- Light lunches, afternoon tea & refreshments. Groups bookings taken.
- In house private dining by arrangement.
- Group visits (approx 90 mins).
- Unlimited for cars in visitor parking area. Space for 2 coaches 10 yds from house.
- Dogs allowed in car park & parkland only
- Regency Dining Room licensed for Civil Ceremonies. Walled Garden available for marquee receptions. Ceremony room max capacity is 60 people.
- Parkland suitable for events & filming.

VISITOR INFORMATION

Owner
Mr and Mrs Robert Brudenell

Address
Deene Park
Corby
Northamptonshire
NN17 3EW

Location
Map 7:D7
OS Ref. SP950 929
6m NE of Corby off A43. From London via M1/J15 then A43, or via A1, A14, A43 - 2 hrs. From Birmingham via M6, A14, A43, 90 mins.
Rail: Corby Station 10 mins & Kettering Station 20mins.
Satellite navigation:
Travelling by car: use postcode NN17 3EG
Coaches only: use postcode NN17 3EW

Contact
The Administrator
Tel: 01780 450278
Fax: 01780 450282
E-mail: admin@deenepark.com

Opening Times
Apr: Sun 16, 23, 30, BH Mon 17
May: Sun 7, 14, 21, 28 BH Mon 1 & 29
Jun: Sun 4, 11, 18, 25
Jul: Sun 2, 9, 16, 23, 30
Aug: Sun 6, 13, 20, 27 BH Mon 28
Sep: Wed 6, 13, 20, 27

Gardens & Tea Room:
Gardens are also open on selected weekdays throughout the summer, please see website for 2017 opening dates & times.

Admission
Public Open Days
House & Gardens:

Adult	£10.00
Conc.	£9.00
Child (5-16yrs)	£5.00

Under 5 free with an adult.

Gardens only:

Adult & Conc.	£6.00
Child (5-16yrs)	£3.00

Under 5 free with an adult.

Groups (20+) by arrangement:

Tue-Thu, Suns	£10.00
(Min 20	£200.00)

Under 5 free with an adult.

Special Events
Snowdrop Sundays:
Feb, Sun 19, 26. Gardens & tea room from 11am - 4pm. Last adm. 3pm. Adults £4, children F.O.C.

© Althorp Estate

ALTHORP

NORTHAMPTON NN7 4HQ

www.spencerofalthorp.com

Althorp House was built in 1508, by the Spencers, for the Spencers, and that is how it has remained for over 500 years. Today, Althorp contains one of the finest private collections of art, furniture and ceramics in the world, including numerous paintings by Rubens, Reynolds, Lely, Gainsborough and Van Dyck. Visitors can enjoy a guided tour of the House in the company of one of Althorp's expert tour guides, discovering the fascinating history of one of England's most beautiful, private and historic houses. Wander around the Gardens, the current Exhibitions and visit the Café and Gift Shop in the Stables.

Location: Map 7:C9. OS Ref SP682 652. From the M1, 7m from J16 and 10m from J18. Situated on A428 Northampton - Rugby. Rail: 5m from Northampton station and 14m from Rugby station. Sat Nav Postcode: NN7 4HQ.

Owner: The Rt Hon The 9th Earl Spencer

Contact: Althorp

Tel: 01604 770107

E-mail: mail@althorp.com

Open: Please visit website for current opening dates and times.

Admission: Garden, Exhibition and guided tour of the House: Adults £18.50, Conc £16.00, 5-16 years £11.00, Family £45.00, 0-4 years and HHA Members free entry. Please call 01604 770107 or email groups@althorp.com to pre-book coach parties and group visits.

Key facts: No indoor photography with still or video cameras. House and Estate accessible to wheelchairs, except the first floor of the House. The Stables Café serves a wide selection of drinks, cakes, sandwiches & snacks. Althorp is available to view by guided tour only, departing frequently from the Wootton Hall. Free parking with a 5/10 minute walk to the House. Disabled parking available. Guide dogs only.

COTTESBROOKE HALL & GARDENS

COTTESBROOKE, NORTHAMPTONSHIRE NN6 8PF

www.cottesbrooke.co.uk

Dating from 1702 the Hall's beauty is matched by the magnificence of the gardens and the excellence of the picture, furniture and porcelain collections. The Woolavington collection of sporting pictures is possibly the finest of its type in Europe and includes paintings by Stubbs, Ben Marshall and artists renowned for works of this genre. Portraits, bronzes, 18th Century English and French furniture and fine porcelain are among the treasures.

The formal gardens are continually being updated and developed by influential designers. The Wild Gardens, a short walk across the Park, are planted along the course of a stream.

Location: Map 7:B8. OS Ref SP711 739. 10m N of Northampton near Creaton on A5199 (formerly A50). Signed from Junction 1 on the A14.

Owner: Mr & Mrs A R Macdonald-Buchanan

Contact: The Administrator

Tel: 01604 505808

E-mail: welcome@cottesbrooke.co.uk

Open: May-end of Sep. May & Jun: Wed & Thu, 2-5.30pm. Jul-Sep: Thu, 2-5.30pm. Open BH Mons (May-Sep), 2-5.30pm.
The first open day is Mon 1 May 2017.

Admission: House & Gardens: Adult £8.50, Child £5.00, Conc £7.50.
Gardens only: Adult £6.00, Child £4.00, Conc £5.50.
Group & private bookings by arrangement.

Key facts: No large bags or photography in house. Filming & outside events. Partial. WCs. Hall guided tours obligatory. Guide dogs only.

Register for news and special offers at www.hudsonsheritage.com

HOLDENBY HOUSE

NORTHAMPTON NN6 8DJ

www.holdenby.com

Once the largest private houses in England and subsequently the palace of James I and prison of Charles I, Holdenby has appeared in the BBC's acclaimed adaptation of 'Great Expectations'. Sitting on a hill overlooking thousands of acres of rolling countryside, its suite of elegant state rooms open onto beautiful Grade I listed gardens making it an enchanting and ever popular venue for weddings. Its combination of grandeur and intimacy make it a magnificent location for corporate dinners and meetings, while the spacious grounds have accommodated many large events from Civil War battles to Formula One parties. Day visitors enjoy Sunday garden openings and other special events days with Icarus Falconry located in the walled garden.

Location: Map 7:B8. OS Ref SP693 681. M1/J15a.
7m NW of Northampton off A428 & A5199.

Owner: James Lowther
Contact: Commercial Manager
Tel: 01604 770074
Fax: 01604 770962
E-mail: office@holdenby.com
Open: Gardens: Apr-Sep; Suns & BH Mons; 1-5pm
Admission: Adult £5, Child £3.50, Concession £4.50, Family (2+2) £15
Prices will vary on special event days. Please see our website for details.
Key facts: Children's play area. Victorian Kitchen Teas available on special event days; Refreshments available on Sunday garden openings May-Aug. Obligatory, by arrangement. Limited for coaches. 7 times Sandford Award Winner. On leads.

KELMARSH HALL AND GARDENS

KELMARSH, NORTHAMPTON NN6 9LY

www.kelmarsh.com

Built in the Palladian style to a James Gibbs design, 18th Century Kelmarsh Hall is set in beautiful gardens with views over the surrounding parkland. The former home of society decorator, Nancy Lancaster, Kelmarsh still reflects the essence of her panache and flair. The award-winning gardens include a formal terrace, rose gardens and the historic walled kitchen garden. Summer 2017 will see the opening of the Heritage Lottery Funded project, Tunnelling Through the Past, which will open up the 'below stairs' areas. Kelmarsh Hall, gardens and parkland can be hired exclusively for weddings, corporate events and private parties.

Location: Map 7:C8. OS Ref SP736 795. Sat Nav: NN6 9LX.
See website for directions.

Owner: The Kelmarsh Trust
Tel: 01604 686543
E-mail: enquiries@kelmarsh.com
Open: Please visit our website or call 01604 686 543 for the latest opening times. Season Apr-Oct.
Admission: Please visit our website or call 01604 686 543 for the latest admission prices.
Key facts: Suitable for corporate events & functions.
Disabled parking and WCs. Licensed.
On leads.

© Clive Nichols

LAMPORT HALL & GARDENS

NORTHAMPTONSHIRE NN6 9HD

www.lamporthall.co.uk

Lamport Hall was the home of the Isham family from 1560 until 1976, and is an architectural gem. It still houses the fine collection of furniture and paintings accumulated by the family, including many beautiful items acquired on the Grand Tour in the 1670s. Surrounded by parkland, the delightful 10-acre gardens are famous as the home of the world's oldest garden gnome, and there are fascinating examples of changes in garden design across the centuries. Added attractions include a large exhibition in the Edwardian stable block and the quirky Museum of Rural Life. Group visits to the Hall and gardens are very welcome, and a range of themed tours are available for groups

Location: Map 7:C8. OS Ref SP759 745. Entrance on A508. Midway between Northampton and Market Harborough, 3m S of A14 J2.

Owner: Lamport Hall Preservation Trust

Contact: Executive Director

Tel: 01604 686272 **Fax:** 01604 686224

E-mail: admin@lamporthall.co.uk

Open: Every Wed & Thu from 5 Apr-26 Oct (guided house tours at 2.15 and 3pm; free-flow around gardens). Also open most BH Sun/Mon (free-flow). Private tours at other times by arrangement. Please check website for opening times and prices.

Admission: House & Garden: Adult £9, Senior £8.50, Child (11-18) £4.
Gardens Only: Adult £6, Senior £5.50, Child (11-18) £3.
Private groups: House & gardens £9, Gardens only £6. Minimum charges apply.

Key facts: No photography in house. Available for filming. Partial. WCs. Licensed. Group visits welcome by prior arrangement. Limited for coaches. Guide dogs only in the Hall, but all dogs welcome on leads in the gardens. Groups only.

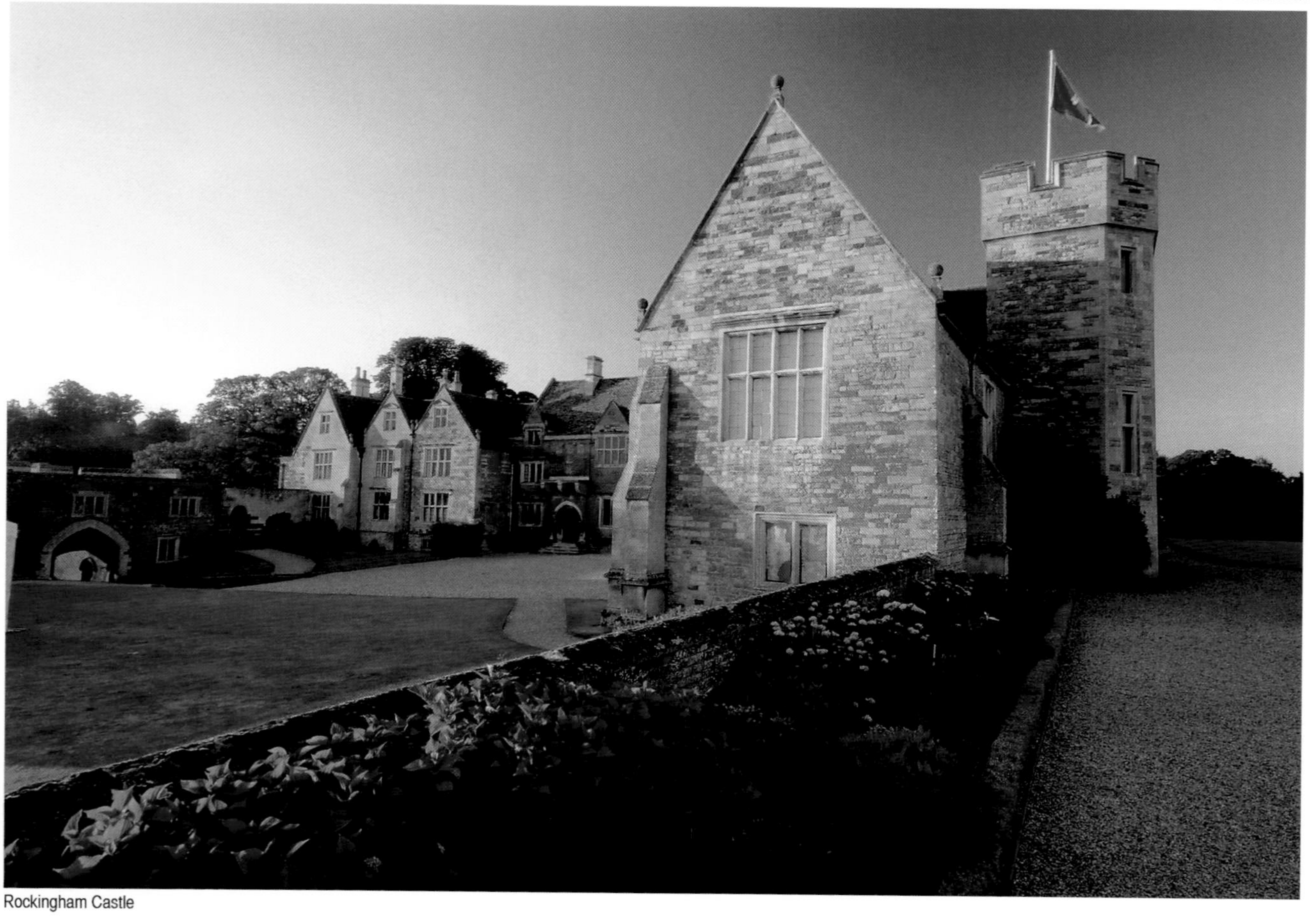

Rockingham Castle

ROCKINGHAM CASTLE

ROCKINGHAM, MARKET HARBOROUGH, LEICESTERSHIRE LE16 8TH

www.rockinghamcastle.com

Rockingham Castle stands on the edge of an escarpment giving dramatic views over five counties and the Welland Valley below. Built by William the Conqueror, the Castle was a royal residence for 450 years. In the 16th Century Henry VIII granted it to Edward Watson and for 450 years it has remained a family home. The predominantly Tudor building, within Norman walls, has architecture, furniture and works of art from practically every century. Surrounding the Castle are 18 acres of gardens following the foot print of the medieval castle. The 400 year old 'Elephant Hedge' bisects the formal terraced gardens.

Location: Map 7:D7. OS Ref SP867 913. 1m N of Corby on A6003. 9m E of Market Harborough. 14m SW of Stamford on A427.

Owner: James Saunders Watson **Contact:** Laurie Prashad, Operations Manager

Tel: 01536 770240 **E-mail:** estateoffice@rockinghamcastle.com

Open: Easter Sun to the end of May, Suns & BH Mons. Jun-Sep, Tues, Suns & BH Mons. Open 12-5pm. Grounds open at noon. Castle opens at 1pm. Last entry 4.30pm. **Admission:** House & Gardens: Adult £11.00, Child (5-16 years) £6.50, Family (2+2) £28.50. Grounds only: (Incl. Gardens, Salvin's Tower, Gift Shop & Licensed Tea Room) Adult or Child £6.50 (Not when special events held in grounds). Groups: (min 20) Adult £11.00 (on open days), Adult £12.50 (private guided tour), Child (5-16 years) £6.50. School groups: (min 20) Adult £11.00, Child £5.50 (1 Adult free with 15 Children). Groups/school parties on most days by arrangement.

Key facts: No photography in Castle. The Castle, situated in a spectacular setting in beautiful and peaceful grounds, provides an ideal backdrop for a conference, a seminar, product launch, photo shoot or simply an out of office meeting. Partial. WCs. Licensed. Licensed. By arrangement. Limited for coaches. On leads. For centuries royalty & private guests have been entertained in the medieval Great Hall. Built in 1200, it is a superb room for both civil wedding ceremonies & wedding receptions.

© Haddonstone Ltd

HADDONSTONE SHOW GARDENS

The Forge House, Church Lane, East Haddon Northampton NN6 8DB

www.haddonstone.com

See Haddonstone's classic garden ornaments and architectural stonework in the beautiful walled manor gardens including: planters, fountains, statues, bird baths, sundials and balustrades - even an orangery, gothic grotto and other follies. As featured on BBC TV. New features include replicas of Soane Museum designs and the acclaimed new bust of Lancelot 'Capability' Brown. Gastro pub nearby.

Location: Map 7:B8. OS Ref SP667 682. 7m NW of Northampton off A428. Located in village centre opposite school. Signposted.

Owner: Haddonstone Ltd **Contact:** Simon Scott, Marketing Director

Tel: 01604 770711 **E-mail:** info@haddonstone.co.uk

Open: Mon-Fri, 9am-5.30pm. Closed weekends, BHs and Christmas period. Check Haddonstone website for details of NGS weekend opening and Sat openings in Summer. **Admission:** Free (except NGS). Groups by appt only. No coach parties.

Key facts: No photography without permission. Haddonstone designs can be ordered for delivery to addresses worldwide. Almost all areas of garden accessible. By arrangement. Limited. Except assistance dogs. €

SOUTHWICK HALL

Southwick, Nr Oundle, Peterborough, Northamptonshire PE8 5BL

Well off the beaten track, Southwick Hall - a family home for 700 years - offers a friendly and informal welcome. Featuring an unusual variety of family and local artefacts and archives, with building additions throughout its history, the house vividly illustrates the development of the English Manor House - medieval towers and finials, Elizabethan hall and Georgian and Victorian alterations.

Location: Map 7:E7. OS Ref TL022 921. 3m N of Oundle, 4m E of Bulwick.

Owner: Christopher Capron **Contact:** G Bucknill

Tel: 01832 274064 **E-mail:** southwickhall@hotmail.co.uk

Website: www.southwickhall.co.uk

Open: Please see Southwick Hall website for open days and times.

Admission: Please see Southwick Hall website for admission prices.

Key facts: Partial. Groups welcome. Dogs on leads in the grounds only. No dogs permitted inside.

© Hardy Plant

Kelmarsh Gardens

BOUGHTON HOUSE

Kettering, Northamptonshire NN14 1BJ

Boughton is a Tudor manor house transformed into a vision of Louis XIV's Versailles. The house displays a staggering collection of fine art.

Location: Map 7:D8. OS Ref SP900 815.

Tel: 01536 515731 **E-mail:** blht@boughtonhouse.co.uk

Website: www.boughtonhouse.co.uk

Open: 15-17 Apr, 1-30 Aug, daily, 12-5pm. **Admission:** Adult £10; Child £8.

CANONS ASHBY

Daventry, Northamptonshire NN11 3SD

Home of the Dryden family since the 16th Century, this Elizabethan manor house was built c1550. **Location:** Map 7:B9. OS Ref SP577 506. Access from M40/J11, or M1/J16. Signposted from A5, 3m S of Weedon crossroads. **Tel:** 01327 861900 **E-mail:** canonsashby@nationaltrust.org.uk **Website:** www.nationaltrust.org.uk/canonsashby **Open:** Apr-Oct, Fri-Wed, 11am-5pm; Nov, Sat & Sun, 11am-3pm; 9-15 Dec, daily, 11am-3pm. **Admission:** Adult £9.54; Child £4.77.

STOKE PARK PAVILIONS

Stoke Bruerne, Towcester, Northamptonshire NN12 7RZ

The two pavilions, dated c1630 and attributed to Inigo Jones, formed part of one of the first Palladian country houses built in England. They have extensive gardens and overlook parkland. **Location:** Map 7:C10. OS Ref SP740 488. 7m S of Northampton. **Tel:** 07768 230325 **Open:** Aug: daily, 3-6pm. Other times by appointment only. **Admission:** Adult £3.00; Child Free.

WAKEFIELD LODGE

Potterspury, Northamptonshire NN12 7QX

Georgian hunting lodge with deer park.

Location: Map 7:C10. OS Ref SP739 425.

4m S of Towcester on A5. Take signs to farm shop for directions.

Tel: 01327 811395

Open: House: 16 Apr-29 May: Mon-Fri (closed BHs), 12 noon-4pm. Appointments by telephone. Access walk open Apr & May. **Admission:** £5.00.

WESTON HALL

Towcester, Northamptonshire NN12 8PU

A Queen Anne Northamptonshire manor house with an interesting collection associated with the literary Sitwell family.

Location: Map 7:B10. OS Ref SP592 469. 5 miles W of Towcester.

Tel: 07710 523879 **E-mail:** george@crossovercapital.co.uk

Open: Most weekends by appointment.

Admission: £8.00. Free on Open Days.

Althorpe

CARLTON HALL

Carlton-On-Trent, Nottingham NG23 6LP

Carlton Hall is a grade II* listed building built in 1765. Typical of period with pedimented central block flanked by lower wings. Contains its original collection of fine family portraits, as well as 17th/18th Century paintings and antique continental furniture. The ornamental stable block completed in 1769 is possibly by John Carr of York.

Location: Map 7:C3. OS Ref SK799 639.

Owner/Contact: George Vere-Laurie

Tel: 07775 785344

E-mail: carltonhallnotts@gmail.com

Open: 1 Apr-30 Sep, Wed only. 2pm-5pm. 24 hour notice required for tours only. Other dates and times by appointment.

Admission: £10.00pp, inc. tour and tea.

Key facts: Saddlery shop in stable block. 24 hour notice required. €

PAPPLEWICK HALL

Papplewick, Nottinghamshire NG15 8FE

A beautiful classic Georgian house, built of Mansfield stone, set in parkland, with woodland garden laid out in the 18th Century. The house is notable for its very fine plasterwork, and elegant staircase. Grade I listed.

Location: Map 7:B4. OS Ref SK548 518.

Halfway between Nottingham & Mansfield, 3m E of M1/J27. The Hall is 1/2 mile north of Papplewick village, off Blidworth Waye (B683)

Owner/Contact: Mr J R Godwin-Austen

Tel: 0115 9632623

E-mail: mail@papplewickhall.co.uk

Website: www.papplewickhall.co.uk

Open: 1st, 3rd & 5th Wed in each month 2-5pm, and by appointment.

Admission: Adults £5.00 each; Groups (10+) £4.00 per head.

Key facts: No photography. Obligatory. Limited for coaches.

CLUMBER PARK

Worksop, Nottinghamshire S80 3AZ

Clumber Park was once the country estate of the Dukes of Newcastle.

Location: Map 7:B2. OS Ref SK625 745. 4½m SE of Worksop, 6½m SW of Retford, just off A1/A57 via A614. 11m from M1/J30. **Tel:** 01909 544917 **Fax:** 01909 500721 **E-mail:** clumberpark@nationaltrust.org.uk **Website:** www.nationaltrust.org.uk/clumberpark **Open:** Winter, daily, 10-4pm; Summer, daily, 10-5pm. **Admission:** £7 per vehicle.

HOLME PIERREPONT HALL

Holme Pierrepont, Nr Nottingham NG12 2LD

This charming 16th Century manor house set in thirty acres of Park and gardens with a carved Charles II Staircase. **Location:** Map 7:B4. OS Ref SK628 391. 5m ESE of central Nottingham. Follow signs to the National Water Sports Centre and continue for 1.5m. **Tel:** 0115 933 2371 **E-mail:** rplb@holmepierrepont hall.com **Website:** www.holmepierreponthall.com **Open:** Feb & Mar, Sun-Tue, 2-5pm; Apr, Sun, 2-5pm; not Easter Sun. **Admission:** Adult £5; Child Free.

NEWSTEAD ABBEY

Ravenshead, Nottingham, Nottinghamshire NG15 8GE

The house is best known as the ancestral home of Lord Byron, and displays many personal items that belonged to the great Romantic poet. **Location:** Map 7:3B. OS Ref SK539 538. **Tel:** 01623 455900 **E-mail:** sallyl@newsteadabbey.org.uk **Website:** www.newsteadabbey.org.uk **Open:** Grounds: All year, daily, 10am-5pm. House: All year, Sat, Sun & BH Mons, 12-5pm; half terms, Mon-Sun, 10am-4pm. **Admission:** Adult £7; Child £5.

EYAM HALL
Eyam, Hope Valley, Derbyshire S32 5QW
Tel: 01433 631976 **E-mail:** nicolawright@eyamhall.co.uk

HARDWICK OLD HALL
Doe Lea, Nr Chesterfield, Derbyshire S44 5QJ
Tel: 01246 850431 **E-mail:** customers@english-heritage.org.uk

THE PAVILION GARDENS
St John's Road, Buxton, Derbyshire SK17 6XN
Tel: 01298 23114 **E-mail:** terry.crawford@highpeak.gov.uk

PEVERIL CASTLE
Market Place, Castleton, Hope Valley S33 8WQ
Tel: 01433 620613 **E-mail:** customers@english-heritage.org.uk

SUTTON SCARSDALE HALL
Hall Drive, Sutton Scarsdale, Chesterfield, Derbyshire S44 5UR
Tel: 01246 822844 **E-mail:** bolsover.castle@english-heritage.org.uk

ASHBY DE LA ZOUCH CASTLE
South Street, Ashby De La Zouch LE65 1BR
Tel: 01530 413343 **E-mail:** customers@english-heritage.org.uk

DONINGTON LE HEATH MANOR HOUSE
Manor Road, Heath, Coalville, Leicestershire LE67 2FW
Tel: 01530 831 259 **E-mail:** richard.knox@leics.gov.uk

KIRBY MUXLOE CASTLE
Kirby Muxloe, Leicestershire LE9 2DH
Tel: 01162 386886 **E-mail:** customers@english-heritage.org.uk

OAKHAM CASTLE
Castle Lane (Off Market Place), Oakham, Rutland LE15 6DF
Tel: 01572 758440

STAUNTON HAROLD HALL
Staunton Harold, Ashby de la Zouch, Leicestershire LE65 1RT
Tel: 01332 862599 **E-mail:** rowan@stauntonharoldhall.co.uk

STONEYWELL
Ulverscroft, Markfield, Leicestershire LE67 9QE
Tel: 01530 248040 **E-mail:** emily.wolfe@nationaltrust.org.uk

ELSHAM HALL GARDENS & COUNTRY PARK
Elsham Hall, Brigg, Lincolnshire DN20 0QZ
Tel: 01652 688698 **E-mail:** enquiries@elshamhall.co.uk

GAINSBOROUGH OLD HALL
Parnell Street, Gainsborough, Lincolnshire DN21 2NB
Tel: 01427 677348 / **E-mail:** gainsborougholdhall@lincolnshire.gov.uk

NORMANBY HALL COUNTRY PARK
Normanby, Scunthorpe DN15 9HU
Tel: 01724 720588 **E-mail:** normanby.hall@northlincs.gov.uk

TATTERSHALL CASTLE
Sleaford Road, Tattershall, Lincolnshire LN4 4LR
Tel: 01526 342543 **E-mail:** tattershallcastle@nationaltrust.org.uk

78 DERNGATE: THE CHARLES RENNIE MACKINTOSH HOUSE & GALLERIES
Tel: 01604 603407 **E-mail:** info@78derngate.org.uk

Haddonstone Show Gardens - Soane Shakespear

COTON MANOR GARDEN
Nr Guilsborough, Northamptonshire NN6 8RQ
Tel: 01604 740219 **E-mail:** pasleytyler@cotonmanor.co.uk

KIRBY HALL
Deene, Corby, Northamptonshire NN17 5EN
Tel: 01536 203230 **E-mail:** customers@english-heritage.org.uk

RUSHTON TRIANGULAR LODGE
Rushton, Kettering, Northamptonshire NN14 1RP
Tel: 01536 710761

HODSOCK PRIORY GARDENS
Blyth, Nr Worksop, Blyth S81 0TY
Tel: 01909 591204

KELHAM HALL
Newark, Nottinghamshire NG23 5QX
Tel: 01636 650000 **E-mail:** info@kelham-hall.com

MR STRAW'S HOUSE
5-7 Blyth Grove, Worksop S81 0JG
Tel: 01909 482380 **E-mail:** mrstrawshouse@nationaltrust.org.uk

NOTTINGHAM CASTLE AND ART GALLERY
Lenton Road, Nottingham NG1 6EZ
Tel: 0115 876 1400 **E-mail:** nottingham.castle@nottinghamcity.gov.uk

WOLLATON HALL AND PARK
Wollaton Park, Nottingham NG8 2AE
Tel: 0115 915 3900 **E-mail:** maria.narducci@nottinghamcity.gov.uk

Stokesay Court, Shropshire

Charlecote Park, Warwickshire

Herefordshire
Shropshire
Staffordshire
Warwickshire
West Midlands
Worcestershire

Heart of England

Tourists flock to Warwick and Stratford, but many overlook the number of less celebrated heritage treasures in this fascinating region.

EASTNOR CASTLE

NR LEDBURY, HEREFORDSHIRE HR8 1RL

www.eastnorcastle.com

Eastnor Castle was built 200 years ago by John, 1st Earl Somers, and is an example of Norman Revival. Standing at the southern end of the Malvern Hills, the castle is still a family home. The inside is dramatic: a 60' high Hall leads to the State Rooms, including the Pugin Gothic Drawing Room and an Italian-style Library, each with a view of the lake. The castle is surrounded by an arboretum housing a collection of mature specimen trees, a lake and a deer park. Within the grounds are a maze, children's adventure playground, Burma Bridge tree top walkway, junior assault course, woodland play area, Land Rover little off-roaders and full-size play Land Rover. Exclusive use is offered for weddings, private and corporate events and filming.

Location: Map 6:M10. OS Ref SO735 368. 2m SE of Ledbury on A438 Tewkesbury road. M50/J2 & from Ledbury take the A449/A438. Tewkesbury 20 mins, Malvern 20 mins, Hereford 25 mins, Cheltenham 30 mins, B'ham 1 hr.

Owner: Mr J Hervey-Bathurst **Contact:** Castle Office

Tel: 01531 633160 **Fax:** 01531 631776 **E-mail:** enquiries@eastnorcastle.com

Open: Easter Opening: Fri 14-Thu 20 Apr. May Day BH: Sun 30 Apr-Mon 1 May. Spring BH: Sun 28-Mon 29 May. May Half Term: Tue 30 May-Thu 1 Jun. 4 Jun-16 Jul: Every Sun. 23 Jul-31 Aug: Sun to Thu. Sep: Every Sun.

Admission: Castle & Grounds: Adult £11.00, Child (3-15yrs) £7.00, Family (2+3) £30.00. Grounds Only: Adult £7.00, Child (3-15yrs) £5.00, Family (2+3) £20.00, Groups (20+) Guided £12.00, Self-guided £10.00, Schools £7.50 Groups (40+) Guided £11.50, Self-guided £9.50.

Key facts: Gift shop. Exclusive hire for corporate events, parties & filming. Wheelchair stairclimber to state rooms. Licensed. Pre-booked on Mons & Tues all year. Ample. Guides available. Dogs welcome. Exclusive use accommodation. Wedding ceremonies & receptions.

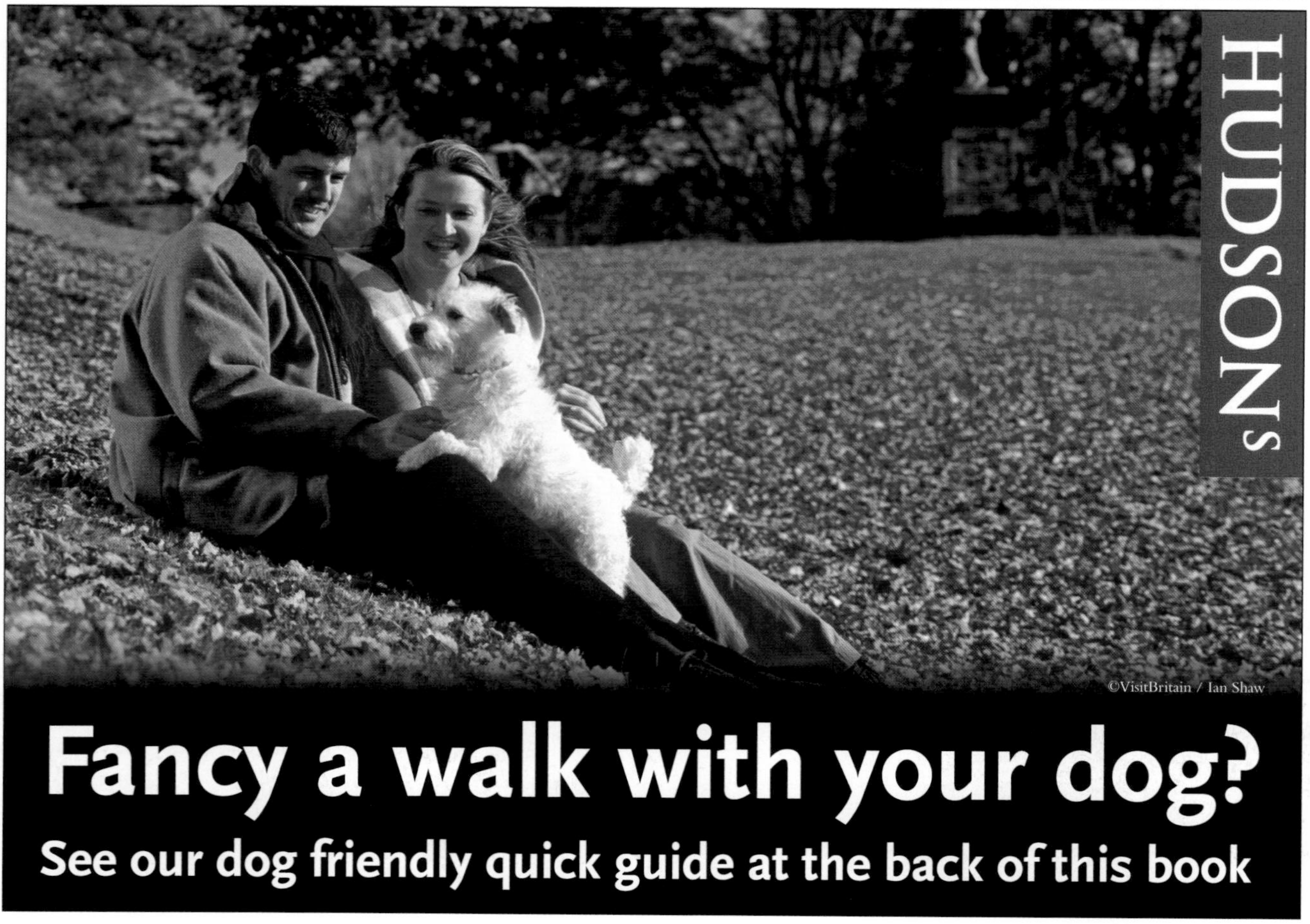

HUDSON'S

©VisitBritain / Ian Shaw

Fancy a walk with your dog?

See our dog friendly quick guide at the back of this book

HERGEST CROFT GARDENS

Kington, Herefordshire HR5 3EG

Garden for all Seasons; set in 70 acres containing spring bulbs and summer borders, old fashioned kitchen garden with unusual vegetables, brightly coloured azaleas & rhododendrons over 30ft high followed by spectacular autumn colour.
Location: Map 6:J9. OS Ref SO281 565. Follow brown tourist signs along A44.
Owner: Mr Edward Banks **Contact:** Mrs Melanie Lloyd **Tel:** 01544 230160
E-mail: gardens@hergest.co.uk **Website:** www.hergest.co.uk
Open: Daily from 1 Apr-29 Oct 12 noon-5.30pm. Season tickets covers 365 days; groups by arrangement. Flower Fair: Mon, 1 May, 10am-5.30pm.
Plant Fair: Sun, 15 Oct, 10am-4.30pm. **Admission:** Adult £6.50, Child (under 16) free. Pre-booked groups (20+) £5.50 each. Pre-booked group with guided tour (20+) £7.50 each. Season Tickets £25.00 each.
Key facts: Interesting gardening gifts. Rare & unusual plants. Limited disabled access. Ridgeway Catering provide homemade lunches & teas. Dog on leads welcome. Haywood Cabin - holiday let.

OLD SUFTON

Mordiford, Hereford HR1 4EJ

A 16th Century manor house which was altered and remodelled in the 18th and 19th Centuries and again in this Century. The original home of the Hereford family (see Sufton Court) who have held the manor since the 12th Century.
Location: Map 6:L10. OS Ref SO575 384.
Mordiford, off B4224 Mordiford - Dormington road.
Owner: Trustees of Sufton Heritage Trust
Contact: Mr & Mrs J N Hereford
Tel: 01432 870268/01432 850328.
E-mail: james@sufton.co.uk
Open: By Appointment to: james@sufton.co.uk
Key facts: Partial. Obligatory.
Small school groups. No special facilities.

SUFTON COURT

Mordiford, Hereford HR1 4LU

Sufton Court is a small Palladian mansion house. Built in 1788 by James Wyatt for James Hereford. The park was laid out by Humphry Repton whose 'red book' still survives. The house stands above the rivers Wye and Lugg giving impressive views towards the mountains of Wales.
Location: Map 6:L10. OS Ref SO574 379.
Mordiford, off B4224 on Mordiford- Dormington road.
Owner: J N Hereford
Contact: Mr & Mrs J N Hereford
Tel: 01432 870268/01432 850328
E-mail: james@sufton.co.uk
Open: 16-29 May & 15-28 Aug: 2-5pm. Guided tours: 2, 3 and 4pm.
Admission: Adult £5.00; Child 50p.
Key facts: Obligatory. Only small coaches.
Small school groups. No special facilities.
In grounds, on leads.

BERRINGTON HALL

Nr Leominster, Herefordshire HR6 0DW

The creation of Thomas Harley, the 3rd Earl of Oxford's remarkable son, who made a fortune from supplying pay and clothing to the British Army in America and became Lord Mayor of London in 1767 at the age of 37. **Location:** Map 6:L8. OS Ref SO509 636. 3m N of Leominster, 7m S of Ludlow. **Tel:** 01568 615721 **E-mail:** berrington@nationaltrust.org.uk **Website:** www.nationaltrust.org.uk/berrington
Open: Please see website for up-to-date opening times and admission prices.

BROCKHAMPTON ESTATE

Bringsty, Nr Bromyard WR6 5TB

Timber framed medieval moated manor house and romantic chapel set in 19th Century parkland. **Location:** Map 6:M9. OS Ref SO684 549. 2m E of Bromyard on A44. **Tel:** 01885 488099 **E-mail:** brockhampton@nationaltrust.org.uk
Website: www.nationaltrust.org.uk
Open: 2 Jan-Mar & 4 Nov-17 Dec, Sat & Sun, 11-4pm; Apr-Oct, daily, 11-5pm.
Admission: Adult £7.80; Child £3.90.

CROFT CASTLE

Aymestrey, Nr Leominster, Herefordshire HR9 9PW

Home to the Croft family for nearly 1000 years and set in 1500 acres of woodland.
Location: Map 6:K8. OS Ref SO580 210. **Tel:** 01568 780246
E-mail: croftcastle@nationaltrust.org.uk **Website:** www.nationaltrust.org.uk
Open: Mar-Oct & Feb half term, daily, 10-5pm; 4 Nov-17 Dec, Sat & Sun, 10-4pm.
Admission: Adult £9.45; Child £4.72.

GOODRICH CASTLE

Ross-On-Wye, Herefordshire HR9 6HY

Completely walled Norman castle commanding the passage of the river Wye.
Location: Map 6:L11. OS Ref SO577 200. 5m S of Ross-on-Wye, off A40.
Tel: 01600 890538 **E-mail:** customers@english-heritage.org.uk
Website: www.english-heritage.org.uk/goodrich
Open: 2 Jan-Mar & Nov-22 Dec & Feb half term, Sat & Sun, 10-4pm; Apr-Oct, daily, 10-5pm. **Admission:** Adult £7.70; Child £4.60.

KINNERSLEY CASTLE

Kinnersley, Herefordshire HR3 6QF

Marches castle renovated around 1580. Fine plasterwork solar ceiling.
Location: Map 6:K9. OS Ref SO3460 4950.
Tel: 01544 327407 **E-mail:** katherina@kinnersley.com
Website: www.kinnersleycastle.co.uk **Open:** See website for more information.
Admission: Adult £7.50. Child £2.00. Concs. & Groups over 8: £6.50.

LANGSTONE COURT

Llangarron, Ross on Wye, Herefordshire HR9 6NR

Mostly late 17th Century house with older parts. Interesting staircases, panelling and ceilings. **Location:** Map 6:L11. OS Ref SO534 221. Ross on Wye 5m, Llangarron 1m. **Tel:** 01989 770254 **E-mail:** richard.jones@langstone-court.org.uk
Website: www.langstone-court.org.uk
Open: Under discussion with HMRC. Please see www.langstone-court.org.uk for up-to-date information. **Admission:** Free.

Eastnor Castle

LUDLOW CASTLE

CASTLE SQUARE, LUDLOW, SHROPSHIRE SY8 1AY

www.ludlowcastle.com

Ludlow Castle is one of the country's finest medieval ruins set in the glorious Shropshire countryside at the heart of the bustling black and white town of Ludlow. The castle was a Norman fortress extended over the centuries to become a fortified Royal Palace. Castle House has been restored and now has Gift Shops, Tea Room and Terrace; three beautifully appointed self-catering apartments and is also a unique wedding venue. **Location:** Map 6:L8. OS Ref SO509 745. Ludlow is situated on the A49. From Birmingham, head west on the A456 through Kidderminster. Continue on the A456 through Tenbury Wells. Turn right onto the A49 and follow signs for Ludlow. From the M5 leave at Junction 3 and continue on the A456 through Kidderminster. Continue on the A456 through Tenbury Wells. Turn right onto the A49 and follow signs for Ludlow.
Owner: The Earl of Powis & The Trustees of the Powis Estates
Contact: Sonja Belchere (The Custodian) **Tel:** 01584 874465

Facebook: Ludlow Castle **Twitter:** @LudlowCastle1
E-mail: info@ludlowcastle.com
Open: Weekends Only: Jan-3rd Mon in Feb. 7 Days a week: Oct-Mar 10am-4pm. Apr-Sep 10am-5pm. Visit the website for Closure details.
Admission: Visit the website for up-to-date admission charges.
Key facts: There are 3 gift shops around the Castle - Castle Gift Shop, Castle Gallery & Picture Framing, The Art Room. The grounds are accessible but uneven in places. We provide WCs. Traditional Tea Rooms with waiting staff. Licensed. By arrangement. £3.00 each. Welcome throughout Castle, Tea Room & the Sir Henry Sidney Apartment. Three 4-5* self-catering apartments. Civil ceremonies & receptions in The Round Chapel & Castle House function rooms. There is also an option for a marquee.
The Castle is closed for events set ups. Always check website before visiting.

UPTON CRESSETT HALL AND GATEHOUSE

BRIDGNORTH, SHROPSHIRE WV16 6UH

www.uptoncressetthall.co.uk

Moated Grade 1 Elizabethan manor and romantic turreted Gatehouse set in unspoilt Shropshire countryside near Bridgnorth and Ludlow. Group Tours all year and weekend opening in the summer. The Gatehouse offers luxury award-winning accommodation on separate floors (B&B or self-catering) with sumptuous poster beds in either the Prince Rupert Bedroom or Thatcher Suite. Runner-up last year for Best Accommodation at Hudson's awards and a previous winner of Best Hidden Gem. The Gatehouse is perfect for romantic honeymoons and mini-breaks, standing in the middle of expansive moated topiary gardens. In 'The Thousand Best Houses of Britain', Simon Jenkins describes Upton Cressett as as an 'Elizabethan gem'. Country Life says the Hall is 'a splendid example of the English manor house at its most evocative' whilst John Betjeman describes our hamlet as a 'remote and beautiful place', The Hall was the historic home of the royalist Cressett family before Sir Bill Cash MP renovated the Hall in the early 1970s. The young king Edward V - the Prince in the Tower - stayed in 1483 and Prince Rupert stayed in the Gatehouse in the Civil War.
Location: Map 6:M7. OS Ref OS506 592. Bridgnorth 4 miles. Ludlow 17 miles. Brown tourist signs to Hall are located two miles from A 458 Bridgnorth-Shrewsbury road. **Owner:** William and Lady Laura Cash **Contact:** Laura Cash **Tel:** 01746 714616 **E-mail:** laura@uptoncressett.co.uk **Open:** Group tours all year. For summer public opening days see website. **Admission:** Adults £12.50 (including entry to gardens, Hall tour and homemade scones and tea). Gardens and Tea Room entry, including scones/tea £7.50. No concessions. Group tours min 10, max 45. Group lunches and private dining in Great Hall, prices on request. **Key facts:** No photography in the house. Millinery Tea Room on all open days, 'Bosworth Tea Pavilion' tea tent open in good weather.
Free with admission. On leads only.

WESTON PARK

WESTON-UNDER-LIZARD, NR SHIFNAL, SHROPSHIRE TF11 8LE

www.weston-park.com

The former home of the Earls of Bradford, the House, Park and Gardens is now owned and maintained by the Weston Park Foundation, an independent charitable trust. Built in 1671, by Lady Elizabeth Wilbraham, this warm and welcoming house is home to internationally important paintings including works by Van Dyck, Gainsborough and Stubbs; furniture and objets d'art, providing enjoyment for all visitors. Step outside to enjoy the 1,000 acres of glorious Parkland, take one of a variety of woodland and wildlife walks, all landscaped by the legendary 'Capability' Brown in the 18th Century.

Location: Map 6:N6. OS Ref SJ808 107. Birmingham 40 mins. Manchester 1 hr 30 mins. Motorway access M6/J12 or M54/J3 and via the M6 Toll road J12.

Owner: The Weston Park Foundation **Contact:** Andrea Webster

Tel: 01952 852100

E-mail: enquiries@weston-park.com

Open: Open daily from Sat 27 May-Sun 3 Sep (Except 16-23 Aug inc.) House is closed on Sats. Granary Deli & Café & Art Gallery. Free entry and open all year round (Deli is closed on Mons). Granary Grill open daily all year round for lunch. Dates are correct at the time of going to print.

Admission: Park & Gardens: Adult £6.50, Child (3-14yrs) £3.50, Family (2+3/1+4) £25.00, OAP £6.00 House admission + £3.00, Granary Grill & Deli and Art Gallery, Free entry & open all year. Prices are correct at the time of going to print.

Key facts: Granary Deli & Café is open all year round. (Closed on Mons). The Granary Deli & Café serves coffee, homemade cakes & light bites. Granary Grill. Licensed. By arrangement. Ample free parking. Award-winning educational programme available during all academic terms. Private themed visits aligned with both National Curriculum and QCA targets. In grounds. On leads. Civil Wedding Licence.

Drawing Room at Stokesay Court

SOULTON HALL

Soulton, Nr. Wem, Shrewsbury, Shropshire SY4 5RS

www.soultonhall.co.uk

An ancient manor surrounded by its own woodland and farm with a history reaching back before the Domesday Book. Candle lit restaurant, serving own and local produce. Accommodation available in the Manor House and Carriage House, with self-catering cottages around the farm, including the Keeper's Cottage in the bluebell wood. Soulton Court, an 18th Century barn and gardens welcomes exclusive use conferences and celebrations of 100 or so; larger events can be accommodated by arrangement.
Location: Map 6:L5. OS Ref SJ541 302. Located off the B5065 (Soulton Road), access off the A49 north of Shrewsbury at Prees Green.
Owner: Mrs Ashton **Tel:** 01939 232786 **E-mail:** enquiries@soultonhall.co.uk
Open: Please visit the website for up-to-date opening times.
Admission: Please visit the website for up-to-date admission prices.
Key facts: Meeting facilities in Soulton Court are disabled accessible.

© Stokesay Court

STOKESAY COURT

Onibury, Craven Arms, Shropshire SY7 9BD

www.stokesaycourt.com

Unspoilt and secluded, Stokesay Court is an imposing late Victorian mansion with Jacobean style façade, magnificent interiors and extensive grounds containing a grotto, woodland and interconnected pools. Set in the rolling green landscape of South Shropshire near Ludlow, the house and grounds featured as the Tallis Estate in award-winning film 'Atonement'. During WW1 Stokesay Court played an important role as a military hospital and displays bring this history to life.
Location: Map 6:K7. OS Ref SO444 786. A49 Between Ludlow and Craven Arms.
Owner/Contact: Ms Caroline Magnus
Tel: 01584 856238 **E-mail:** info@stokesaycourt.com
Open: Guided tours Apr-Sept for booked groups (20+). Groups (up to 60) can be accommodated by arrangement. Tours for individuals take place on dates advertised on website. Booking essential.
Admission: Please check website for up-to-date admission prices.
Key facts: No stilettos. No photography in house. Partial. WCs. Tea & home baked refreshments included in ticket price. Obligatory. Dogs on leads - gardens only. Apr-Sep on selected dates

HODNET HALL GARDENS

Hodnet, Market Drayton, Shropshire TF9 3NN

Over 60 acres of brilliant coloured flowers, magnificent forest trees, sweeping lawns and a chain of ornamental pools which run tranquilly along the cultivated garden valley to provide a natural habitat for waterfowl and other wildlife. No matter what the season, visitors will always find something fresh and interesting to ensure an enjoyable outing. **Location:** Map 6:L5. OS Ref SJ613 286. 12m NE of Shrewsbury on A53; M6/J15, M54/J3.
Owner: Sir Algernon and the Hon Lady-Percy
Contact: Secretary **Tel:** 01630 685786 **Fax:** 01630 685853
E-mail: secretary@heber-percy.freeserve.co.uk
Website: www.hodnethallgardens.org
Open: Every Sun and BH Mon from Sun 2 Apr–Sun 24 Sep. Also the following Wed 10 May, 14 Jun & 19 Jul. Please see our website and Facebook page for upcoming special days and events.
Admission: Adult £7; Child (aged 5-15) £1; Under 5's free.
Key facts: Partial. WCs. On leads.

LONGNER HALL

Uffington, Shrewsbury, Shropshire SY4 4TG

Designed by John Nash in 1803, Longner Hall is a Tudor Gothic style house set in a park landscaped by Humphry Repton. The home of one family for over 700 years. Longner's principal rooms are adorned with plaster fan vaulting and stained glass.
Location: Map 6:L6. OS Ref SJ529 110. 4m SE of Shrewsbury on Uffington road, ¼m off B4380, Atcham.
Owner: Mr R L Burton
Contact: Sara Watts
Tel: 07903 842235
Open: Tours at 2pm & 3.30pm on weekdays from Mon 29 May-Fri 30 Jun & BH Mons: 17 Apr, 1 May & 28 Aug. Groups at any time by arrangement.
Admission: Adult £5.00; Child/OAP £3.00.
Key facts: No photography in house. Partial. Obligatory. Limited for coaches. By arrangement. Guide dogs only.

COUND HALL

Cound, Shropshire SY5 6AH

Queen Anne red brick Hall.
Location: Map 6:L6. OS Ref ST560 053.
Tel: 01743 761721 **Fax:** 01743 761722
Open: Mon 13 Feb–Fri 17 Feb 2017, 10am-4pm.
Admission: Adult £4.50, Child £2.30, Conc. £3.40, Family £11.30.

DUDMASTON ESTATE

Quatt, Bridgnorth, Shropshire WV15 6QN

Enchanted wooded parkland, sweeping gardens and a house with a surprise.
Location: Map 6:M7. OS Ref SO748 888. **Tel:** 01746 780866
E-mail: dudmaston@nationaltrust.org.uk **Website:** www.nationaltrust.org.uk/dudmaston-estate **Open:** Gardens:19-23 Mar, 26 Mar-28 Sep, 1-31 Oct, Mon-Thu & Sun, 12-5pm. House: 26 Mar-31 Sep, Mon-Thu & Sun, 1-5pm.
Admission: Adult £8.95; Child £4.50.

STOKESAY CASTLE

Nr Craven Arms, Shropshire SY7 9AH

Stokesay is England's most delightful fortified medieval manor. **Location:** Map 6:L8. OS Ref OS137, SO688 753. 7m NW of Ludlow off A49. **Tel:** 01588 672544 **E-mail:** customers@english-heritage.org.uk **Website:** www.english-heritage.org.uk **Open:** 2 Jan-31 Mar, Sat & Sun, 10-4pm; 1 Apr-30 Sep, daily, 10-6pm; 1-31 Oct, daily, 10-5pm; 1 Nov-23 Dec, Sat & Sun, 10-4pm; 27-31 Dec, daily, 10-4pm. **Admission:** Adult £7.70; Child £4.60.

CHILLINGTON HALL

Codsall Wood, Wolverhampton, Staffordshire WV8 1RE

www.chillingtonhall.co.uk

Home of the Giffards since 1178, the present house dates from the 18th Century, firstly by the architect Francis Smith of Warwick in 1724 and completed by John Soane in 1786. Parkland laid out by 'Capability' Brown in the 1760s with additional work by James Paine. Chillington was the winner of the HHA/Sotheby's Restoration Award 2009 for work done on Soane's magnificent Saloon. The Georgian Model Farm has undergone major renovation over the past 8 years and has an educational/meeting area. **Location:** Map 6:N6. OS Ref SJ864 067.
2m S of Brewood off A449. 4m NW of M54/J2.
Owner: Mr & Mrs J W Giffard **Contact:** Estate Office
Tel: 01902 850236 **E-mail:** office@chillingtonhall.co.uk
Open: House & Grounds: 2-4pm (last entry 3.30pm)16-19 & 30 Apr; 1-4 & 28-31 May; 5-7 Jun; 31 Jul; 1-3, 7-10 & 14-17 Aug. Private groups at other times by prior arrangement.
Admission: Adult £8.00; Child £4.00. Grounds only: Half price.
Key facts: Available for Weddings, Corporate Events, Filming, Hire of the Park & Private Parties. WCs & Car parking. In grounds.
Licensed for up to 130 guests.

WHITMORE HALL

Whitmore, Newcastle-Under-Lyme, Staffordshire ST5 5HW

Whitmore Hall is a Grade I listed building, designated as a house of outstanding architectural and historical interest. Parts of the hall date back to a much earlier period and for 900 years has been the seat of the Cavenagh-Mainwarings, who are direct descendants of the original Norman owners. The hall has beautifully proportioned light rooms and has recently been refurbished; it is in fine order. There are good family portraits to be seen with a continuous line dating from 1624 to the present day. The park encompasses an early Victorian summer house and the outstanding and rare Elizabethan stables.
Location: Map 6:M4. OS Ref SJ811 413.
On A53 Newcastle-Market Drayton Road, 3m from M6/J15.
Owner/Contact: Mr Guy Cavenagh-Mainwaring
Tel: 01782 680 478 **E-mail:** whitmore.hall@yahoo.com
Open: 1 May-31 Aug: Tues and Weds, open 2-4.30pm with guided tours at 2.15pm, 3pm and 3.45pm. **Admission:** Adult £5.00; Child 50p.
Key facts: Ground floor and grounds. Afternoon teas for booked groups (15+), May-Aug. Ample. Except assistance dogs. Please contact us for information on Weddings at Whitmore.

BIDDULPH GRANGE GARDEN

Grange Road, Biddulph, Staffordshire ST8 7SD

This amazing Victorian garden was created by James Bateman for his global collection of plants. **Location:** Map 6:N3. OS Ref SJ891 592.
Tel: 01782 517999 **E-mail:** biddulphgrange@nationaltrust.org.uk
Website: www.nationaltrust.org.uk **Open:** 1 Jan-28 Feb, 11-3.30pm; 1 Mar-22 Oct, 11-5.30pm; 23 Oct-22 Dec, 11-3.30pm; 26 Dec-31 Dec, Mon-Sat, 11-3.30pm. **Admission:** Adult £8.10; Child £4.05.

BOSCOBEL HOUSE & THE ROYAL OAK

Bishop's Wood, Brewood, Staffordshire ST19 9AR

This 17th Century hunting lodge played a vital part in Charles II's escape from the Roundheads. **Location:** Map 6:N6. OS Ref OS127, SJ838 082.
Tel: 01902 850244 **E-mail:** customers@english-heritage.org.uk
Website: www.english-heritage.org.uk/boscobel **Open:** 2 Jan-31 Mar, Sat & Sun, 10-4pm; 1 Apr-31 Oct, Wed-Sun & BH Mons, 10-5pm; 1 Nov-31 Dec, Sat & Sun, 10-4pm. Closed 24-26 Dec & 1 Jan. **Admission:** Adult £7.70; Child £4.60.

THE HEATH HOUSE

Tean, Stoke-On-Trent, Staffordshire ST10 4HA

Set in rolling parkland with fine formal gardens, Heath House is an early Victorian mansion built 1836-1840 in the Tudor style.
Location: Map 6:O4. OS Ref SK030 392. **Tel:** 01538 722212
E-mail: info@theheathhouse.co.uk **Website:** www.theheathhouse.co.uk
Open: 2-6pm. Last entries 4.30pm. See our website for dates - please telephone in advance to confirm. **Admission:** £6.50pp. No concessions.

SHUGBOROUGH ESTATE

Milford, Stafford, Staffordshire ST17 0XB

Rare survival of a complete estate, with all major buildings including mansion house, servants' quarters, model farm and walled garden.
Location: Map 6:N5. OS Ref SJ990 215. **Tel:** 08454 598900
E-mail: shugborough@nationaltrust.org.uk **Website:** www.nationaltrust.org.uk
Open: Apr-Oct, daily, 11am-5pm. House: Closed Tues.
Admission: Adult £15; Child £9.

SINAI PARK HOUSE

Shobnall Road, Burton upon Trent, Staffordshire DE13 0QJ

Built in the 15th, 16th, 17th and 18th Centuries, Grade II* listed Sinai Park House is a timber-framed building. **Location:** Map 6:O6. OS Ref SK221 230.
Tel: 01889 598600 **E-mail:** kate@brookesandco.net
Website: www.sinaiparkhouse.co.uk **Open:** Guided tours only, advanced booking needed. **Admission:** Please see website.

© English Heritage

Boscobel House

VISITOR INFORMATION

■ Owner
The Viscount Daventry

■ Address
Arbury Hall
Nuneaton
Warwickshire
CV10 7PT

■ Location
Map 6:P7
OS Ref. SP335 893
London, M1, M6/J3 (A444 to Nuneaton), 2m SW of Nuneaton. 1m W of A444. Nuneaton 5 mins. Birmingham City Centre 20 mins. London 2 hrs, Coventry 20 mins.
Bus/Coach: Nuneaton Station 3m.
Air: Birmingham International 17m.

■ Contact
Events Secretary
Tel: 024 7638 2804
Fax: 024 7664 1147
E-mail: info@arburyestate.co.uk

■ Opening Times
Hall & Gardens:
BH weekends only (Sun & Mon). Easter-Aug from 1-6pm.
Last guided tour of the Hall 4.30pm.
Groups/Parties (25+) by arrangement.

■ Admission
Hall & Gardens

Adult	£8.50
Child (up to 14 yrs)	£4.50
Family (2+2)	£20.00

Gardens Only

Adult	£5.50
Child (up to 14 yrs)	£4.00

Conference/Function

ROOM	Size	Max Cap
Dining Room	35' x 28'	120
Saloon	35' x 30'	70
Room 3	48' x 11'	40
Stables Tearooms	31' x 18'	80

ARBURY HALL

www.arburyestate.co.uk

Arbury Hall, original Elizabethan mansion house, Gothicised in the 18th Century surrounded by stunning gardens and parkland.

Arbury Hall has been the seat of the Newdegate family for over 450 years and is the ancestral home of Viscount Daventry. This Tudor/Elizabethan House was Gothicised by Sir Roger Newdegate in the 18th Century and is regarded as the 'Gothic Gem' of the Midlands. The principal rooms, with their soaring fan vaulted ceilings and plunging pendants and filigree tracery, stand as a most breathtaking and complete example of early Gothic Revival architecture and provide a unique and fascinating venue for corporate entertaining, product launches, fashion shoots and activity days. Exclusive use of this historic Hall, its gardens and parkland is offered to clients. The Hall stands in the middle of beautiful parkland with landscaped gardens of rolling lawns, lakes and winding wooded walks. Spring flowers are profuse and in June rhododendrons, azaleas and giant wisteria provide a beautiful environment for the visitor. George Eliot, the novelist, was born on the estate and Arbury Hall and Sir Roger Newdegate were immortalised in her book 'Scenes of Clerical Life'.

KEY FACTS

- Corporate hospitality, film location, small conferences, product launches and promotions, marquee functions, let day shooting. No cameras or video recorders indoors.
- Small selection of souvenir gifts.
- Exclusive lunches and dinners for corporate parties in dining room, max. 50, buffets 80.
- Partial, WCs.
- Stables Tea Rooms (on first floor) open from 1pm.
- Obligatory. Tour time: 50min.
- 200 cars and 3 coaches 250 yards from house. Follow tourist signs. Approach map available for coach drivers.
- Dogs on leads in garden. Guide dogs only in house.

Register for news and special offers at **www.hudsonsheritage.com**

© Jana Eastwood

CHARLECOTE PARK

www.nationaltrust.org.uk/charlecote-park

A Victorian home set in landscaped deer park.

A home for the Lucy's for c.800 years, the family still live in one private wing today. The house holds surprising treasures from early editions of Shakespeare to an impressive Beckford table and stories to discover. The Tudor Gatehouse draws visitors from park to court walking in the same processional footsteps as Queen Elizabeth I. The outbuildings were a bustle of activity as laundry was washed, beer brewed and food cooked.

Protected by the Rivers Dene & Avon and by its distinctive cleft-oak paling fencing Charlecote Park presents a picture of peace and repose. The wider parkland is open to explore with stunning views along the river Avon. There are opportunities to get closer to nature with the Spinney wildlife area open every day. The fallow deer roam the estate freely, along with a flock of Jacob sheep, they are a great photo opportunity for anyone who has their camera ready.

If plants and flowers are of interest then the gardens offer colourful displays in the parterre, shady walks in the woodland garden whilst the long border is great for getting ideas to take home with you.

When it's time for a cup of tea or an ice cream we have a variety of food and drink available in our Orangery, kiosks and two shops. Whether you are here for a full day or just half an hour, there's plenty of space to explore and new experiences to discover.

KEY FACTS

- Visitor Reception in the main car park.
- Servants Hall Shop and Pantry Shop.
- Variety of Plants in the Tea Garden.
- Wheelchairs can be borrowed for the day.
- Orangery Tea Room.
- Guided tours of the House & Outbuildings on Weds and in shoulder months.
- Main car park adjacent to the park.
- Contact the office for more booking school visits.
- Assistance dogs only.
- Holiday Flat (Sleeps 6).
- Excluding 25 & 26 Jan and Christmas Day when the whole property is closed.
- See events listing on the National Trust website.

© Jana Eastwood

© Jana Eastwood

VISITOR INFORMATION

Owner

National Trust

Address

Wellesbourne
Warwick
Warwickshire
CV35 9ER

Location

Map 6:P9
OS Ref. SP263 562
1m W of Wellesbourne 5m E of Stratford-upon-Avon. Exit 15 from M40 (Take A429 marked Stow & follow brown NT signs).
Rail: Stratford-upon-Avon, 51/2ml. Leamington Spa 8ml.

Contact

Property Office
Tel: 01789 470277
Fax: 01789 470544
E-mail: charlecotepark@nationaltrust.org.uk

Opening Times

Grounds & Outbuildings: Daily through the year 10am-6pm (Closing at 4pm in winter or at dusk if earlier)
Shop & Tea Room: Daily throughout the year 10.30am-5pm (Closing at 4pm in winter)
House: 18 Feb-24 Mar, 11.30am-3.30pm (Guided tours Wed), 25 Mar-5 Nov, 11am-4pm (Guided tours Wed), 11 Nov-17 Dec, 11.30am-3pm Sat & Sun only.
Christmas: 18 Dec-24 Dec, 11.30am-3pm.
Guided Tours: Available daily 1 Jan-17 Feb & 6 Nov-31 Dec.
Whole property: Closed 25 & 26 Jan & 25 Dec.

Admission

House, Garden & Park:
Gift Aid (Standard)
Adult £12.00 (£10.90)
Child £6.00 (£5.45)
Family £30.00 (£27.27)
Grounds & Outbuildings Only:
Gift Aid (Standard)
Adult £8.00 (£7.27)
Child £4.00 (£3.63)
Family £20.00 (£18.18).

Special Events

Join Charlecote throughout the year for our programme of seasonal events. April for the Easter egg hunt, outdoor children's activities in the Summer Holidays, October for the Halloween trail and December to get fully festive with the traditional Christmas. Special events are listed on the National Trust website.

VISITOR INFORMATION

Owner
The Shakespeare Birthplace Trust

Address
Henley Street
Stratford-upon-Avon
CV37 6QW

Location
Map 6:P9
OS Ref.
Birthplace: SP201 552
Hall's Croft: SP200 546
Hathaway's: SP185 547
Arden's: SP166 582
New Place: SP200 548

Car: 2 hrs from London. 45 mins from Birmingham. 4m from M40/J15 and well signed from all approaches.

Rail: Service from London (Marylebone).

Contact
The Shakespeare Birthplace Trust
Tel: 01789 204016 (General Enquiries)
Tel: 01789 201806 (Group Visits).
E-mail:
info@shakespeare.org.uk / groups@shakespeare.org.uk

Opening Times
The Shakespeare Family Homes are open daily throughout the year except Christmas Day and Boxing Day (Shakespeare's Birthplace is open on Boxing Day).

Mary Arden's Farm closes for Winter from Nov-Mar.

Opening times vary throughout the year. Please see www.shakespeare.org.uk for up-to-date information.

Admission
Visit the website for full details on ticket prices.

You can enjoy 12 months' free admission with every pass as tickets to the Shakespeare Houses are valid for a year with unlimited entry.

Pay for a day and take the whole year to explore!

Visit the website for further details www.shakespeare.org.uk.

SHAKESPEARE'S FAMILY HOMES ✦

www.shakespeare.org.uk

Discover Shakespeare's homes, farm and gardens in Stratford-upon-Avon, including Shakespeare's New Place.

Shakespeare's Birthplace - Where the story began
Explore the extraordinary story of William and the house he was born and grew up in. Our fascinating guides will captivate you with tales of his father's business ventures. Take centre stage with our costumed troupe, Shakespeare Aloud!

Mary Arden's Farm - A working Tudor farm
Visit the family farm where Shakespeare's mother grew up. Experience the sights, sounds and smells of a working Tudor farm and follow our resident Tudors as they work. Meet rare breed animals, enjoy archery and falconry, or explore the nature trails and playground. Don't miss our free events throughout the school holidays.

Anne Hathaway's Cottage - Love and marriage
Follow young Shakespeare's footsteps to the Cottage where he courted an older woman. Our guides will bring this Tudor love story to life in its original setting with nine acres of beautiful cottage gardens, woodland walks and sculpture trail to explore. Enjoy refreshments in the delightful Cottage Garden Café.

Shakespeare's New Place - His family home
The only home Shakespeare ever bought and where he lived for 19 years. Reopened in 2016 for the 400th anniversary of Shakespeare's death, come and walk in his footsteps and trace the footprint of his family home in a contemporary landscape setting. Enjoy specially commissioned sculptures and see a new side of Shakespeare with an exhibition of his world.

Hall's Croft - Daughter and Granddaughter
The luxurious Jacobean home of Shakespeare's daughter Susanna and her husband Dr John Hall. Stroll round the walled garden planted with fragrant herbs used in his remedies. Browse in the gift shop or unwind in the Café .

KEY FACTS

- City Sightseeing bus tour connecting town houses with Anne Hathaway's Cottage and Mary Arden's Farm.
- Gifts available.
- Available, tel for details.
- Partial. WCs.
- Mary Arden's Farm, Anne Hathaway's Cottage, Hall's Croft.
- By special arrangement.
- Free coach terminal for groups drop off and pick up at Birthplace. Max stay 15 mins. Parking at Mary Arden's Farm. Pay & display parking at Anne Hathaway's Cottage.
- Available for all houses. For information 01789 201806.
- Guide dogs only.
- Please check for full details.
- Please check website for details.

LORD LEYCESTER HOSPITAL

HIGH STREET, WARWICK CV34 4BH

www.lordleycester.com

This magnificent range of 14th and 15th Century half-timbered buildings was adapted into almshouses by Robert Dudley, Earl of Leycester, in 1571. The Hospital still provides homes for ex-Servicemen and their wives. The Guildhall, Great Hall, chantry Chapel, Brethren's Kitchen and galleried Courtyard are still in everyday use. The regimental museum of the Queen's Own Hussars is housed here. The historic Master's Garden was featured in BBC TV's 'Gardener's World', and the Hospital buildings in many productions including, most recently, 'Dr Who' and David Dimbleby's 'How We Built Britain'.

Location: Map 6:P8. OS Ref SP280 647. 1m N of M40/J15 on the A429 in town centre. Rail: 10 minutes walk from Warwick Station.

Owner: The Governors
Contact: The Master
Tel: 01926 491422
Open: All year: Tue-Sun & BHs (except Good Fri & 25 Dec), 10am-5pm (4pm in winter). Garden: Apr-Sep: 10am-4.30pm.
Admission: Adult £5.90, Child £4.90, Conc. £5.40. Garden only £2.00.
Key facts: Partial. WCs.
By arrangement.
Limited for cars. No coaches.
Except assistance dogs.

ASTLEY CASTLE

Nuneaton, Warwickshire CV10 7QS

www.landmarktrust.org.uk

Groundbreaking modern accommodation has been inserted within the ruined walls of this ancient moated site to combine the thrill of modern architecture with the atmosphere of an ancient place. Large glass walls now frame views of medieval stonework and the adjacent church and surrounding countryside.

Location: Map 7:A7. OS Ref SP310 894.
Owner: The Landmark Trust
Tel: 01628 825925
E-mail: bookings@landmarktrust.org.uk
Open: Self-catering accommodation. Part of grounds open Mon and Fri, 8 Open Days per year, contact office.
Admission: Free on Open Days and visits by appointment.
Key facts: The living accommodation is on the first floor and the bedrooms and bathrooms on the ground floor. A lift enables easy access for all.

COMPTON VERNEY ART GALLERY & PARK

Warwickshire CV35 9HZ

www.comptonverney.org.uk

Set within a Grade I listed mansion remodelled by Robert Adam in the 1760s, Compton Verney offers a unique art gallery experience. Relax and explore the 120 acres of 'Capability' Brown landscaped parkland, discover a collection of internationally significant art, enjoy free tours and a programme of popular events.

Location: Map 7:A9. OS Ref SP312 529. 9m E of Stratford-upon-Avon, 10 mins from M40/J12, on B4086 between Wellesbourne and Kineton. Rail: Nearest station is Banbury or Leamington Spa. Air: Nearest airport Birmingham International.
Owner: Compton Verney House Trust **Contact:** Ticketing Desk
Tel: 01926 645500 **Fax:** 01926 645501 **Ticket Desk Hours:** 10.30am-4.30pm Tue-Sun. **E-mail:** info@comptonverney.org.uk
Open: 18 Mar-11 Dec 2017; Tue-Sun and BH Mons, 10.30am-5pm. Last entry to Gallery 4.30pm. Groups welcome, please book in advance.
Admission: Please call for details. Group discounts are available.
Key facts: Photography is not permitted in some areas of the Gallery.
WCs. and access throughout the building on all floors. Licensed.
Licensed and waitress service. By arrangement. Ample.
Guide dogs only.

HILL CLOSE GARDENS TRUST

Bread and Meat Close, Warwick, Warwickshire CV34 6HF

www.hillclosegardens.com

16 hedged Victorian gardens overlooking Warwick racecourse with delightful listed brick summerhouses. Created by tradespeople to escape the congestion and pollution of the town. Spring bulbs, old varieties of soft fruit and vegetables, unusual fruit trees and extensive herbaceous borders. Glasshouse for tender plants. Plant, produce and gift sales. Café serving lunches and teas at weekends and Bank Holidays in summer. Teas and snacks all year. Events throughout the year listed on website. **Location:** Map 6:P8. OS Ref SP277 647. M40 Junction 15 Follow A429 & signs for racecourse, enter main racecourse gate off Friars Street. Bear right to entrance to Gardens. **Owner:** Hill Close Gardens Trust **Contact:** Centre Manager
Tel: 01926 493339 **E-mail:** centremanager@hcgt.org.uk
Open: Apr-Oct Gardens every day 11am-5pm. Café Sat & Sun & BH Mons. Nov-Mar Gardens Mon-Fri 11am-4pm. Teas & snacks available during all opening times. Closed Christmas-New Year. Check website for full details.
Admission: Adults £4.00, Child £1.00 (to include garden trail). Under 5s free. HCGT & RHS Members free. **Key facts:** Gifts & cards. Plants sales & produce sales. Corporate, party & community. Access, toilet & parking. Hot & cold drinks, cakes, quiche, soup, teacakes, scones & snacks. On request. Min 10 max 48. 2 hours free. On request. Assistance only.

WARWICK CASTLE

Warwick CV34 4QU

www.warwick-castle.com

Over 1000 years of jaw-dropping history, where ancient myths and spell-binding tales will set your imagination alight. Meet history face to face and be prepared to participate fully in Castle life. **Location:** Map 6:P8. OS Ref SP283 647.
Tel: 01926 495421 **E-mail:** customer.information@warwick-castle.com
Open: All year, daily, 10am-dusk. Events throughout the day.
Admission: Adult £25.20; Child £22.20.
Key facts: Corporate events, receptions, Feasts, Dungeon's After Dark and Highwayman's Suppers. Guide books in English, French, German, Japanese and Spanish. Ghosts & Ghouls evenings. Three shops. For groups (pre-booked). Guides in most rooms. Ideal location, being a superb example of military architecture dating back to the Norman Conquest and with elegant interiors up to Victorian times. Group rates apply. To qualify for group rates please call 0870 442 2371. Education packs available. Group rates apply. To qualify for group rates please call 0870 442 2371. Education packs available.

HONINGTON HALL

Shipston-On-Stour, Warwickshire CV36 5AA

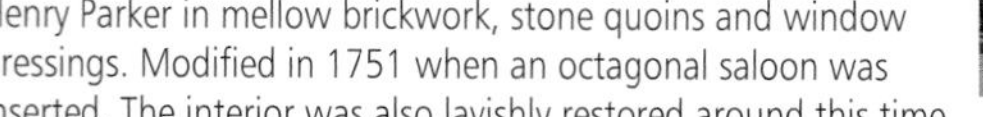

This fine Caroline manor house was built in the early 1680s for Henry Parker in mellow brickwork, stone quoins and window dressings. Modified in 1751 when an octagonal saloon was inserted. The interior was also lavishly restored around this time and contains exceptional mid-Georgian plasterwork. Set in 15 acres of grounds.
Location: Map 6:P9. OS Ref SP261 427.
10m S of Stratford-upon-Avon. 1½m N of Shipston-on-Stour.
Take A3400 towards Stratford, then signed right to Honington.
Owner/Contact: Benjamin Wiggin Esq
Tel: 01608 661434
Fax: 01608 663717
E-mail: bhew@honingtonhall.plus.com
Open: By appointment for groups (10+).
Admission: Email for details.
Key facts: Obligatory.

KENILWORTH CASTLE & GARDEN

Kenilworth, Warwickshire CV8 1NE

Kenilworth's varied buildings and architectural styles reflect its long connection with successive English monarchs. **Location:** Map 6:P8. OS Ref OS140, SP278 723. **Tel:** 01926 852078 **E-mail:** customers@english-heritage.org.uk
Website: www.english-heritage.org.uk/kenilworth **Open:** 2 Jan-31 Mar, Sat & Sun, 10-4pm; 1 Apr-30 Sep, 10-6pm; 1-31 Oct, 10-5pm; 1 Nov-23 Dec, Sat & Sun, 10-4pm; 27-31 Dec, 10-4pm. **Admission:** Adult £11.20; Child £6.70.

STONELEIGH ABBEY

Kenilworth, Warwickshire CV8 2LF

A Cistercian monastery converted into a stately home. Stoneleigh hosted Jane Austen and Queen Victoria. **Location:** Map 6:P8. OS Ref SP320 712. Off B4115 Ashow Road. **Tel:** 01926 858535 **E-mail:** enquire@stoneleighabbey.org
Website: www.stoneleighabbey.org
Open: Good Fri-31 Oct. Guided tour only - times on website. Grounds 11am-5pm.
Admission: Adults £9.50, Child £4.50.

© VisitBritain / Martin Brent

Warwick Castle

© Birmingham Museums Trust

BIRMINGHAM MUSEUMS

www.birminghammuseums.org.uk

Take a journey back into Birmingham's rich and vibrant past.

Birmingham Museum & Art Gallery - Free Entry
From Renaissance masterpieces to Egyptian mummies and the Staffordshire Hoard, Birmingham Museum & Art Gallery showcases a world class collection that offers fascinating glimpses into Birmingham's vibrant past.

Aston Hall
Experience the splendour of this 17th Century Jacobean mansion. Take a tour through majestic state rooms, including the imposing Long Gallery, and the beautiful Lady Holte's Garden. Display rooms illustrate the part Aston Hall played in the English Civil War, and how it prepared to receive royalty on more than one occasion.

Blakesley Hall
Visit one of Birmingham's finest timber-framed houses, built in 1590. With a herb garden and orchard within its grounds, Blakesley Hall is a peaceful haven set in an urban location.

Museum of the Jewellery Quarter
Enjoy a lively guided tour of the perfectly preserved Smith & Pepper jewellery factory, which reveals Birmingham's jewellery heritage and offers a unique glimpse of working life in the city's famous Jewellery Quarter.

Sarehole Mill
Discover the idyllic childhood haunt of J.R.R.Tolkien. One of only two surviving working watermills in Birmingham, gain a unique insight into the lives of the millers who once worked there. Today, the mill retains its tranquil atmosphere and the millpond provides a peaceful haven for kingfishers, moorhens and herons.

Soho House
Discover the elegant Georgian home of the pre-eminent industrialist and entrepreneur Matthew Boulton. Soho House was also the meeting place of the leading 18th Century intellectuals of the Lunar Society.

KEY FACTS

- Gift shops located at all sites.
- Available for corporate hire and special events. See Birmingham Museums website for full details.
- Wheelchair access across sites.
- Tea Rooms located at all sites.
- Expert-led Heritage Tours are available across all heritage sites. See Birmingham Museums website for full details.
- Parking available across sites. See Birmingham Museums website for full details.
- School visits are welcome. See Birmingham Museums for full details of our educational programme.
- Guide dogs only.
- Weddings and receptions available at some sites. See Birmingham Museums website for full details.

© Birmingham Museums Trust

© Birmingham Museums Trust

VISITOR INFORMATION

Owner
Birmingham Museums Trust

Address
Registered address:
Birmingham Museums Trust
Birmingham Museum & Art Gallery
Birmingham
B3 3DH

Location
Map 6:O7
OS Ref. SP066 869

Contact
Birmingham Museums Trust
Tel: 0121 348 8000 (General Enquiries)
Tel: 0121 348 8001 (Group Bookings)
E-mail: enquiries@birminghammuseums.org.uk

Opening Times
Opening times vary throughout the year. See Birmingham Museums website for up-to-date information.

Admission
See Birmingham Museums website for up-to-date admission prices.

Entry into grounds, gardens, visitor centres and Tea Rooms at our heritage sites is free.

You can enjoy 12 months unlimited entry across all Birmingham Museums heritage sites, and exhibitions at Birmingham Museum & Art Gallery with an annual membership. Adult membership starts at £25.00, with concession, joint, family and life options available.

With Membership Plus, you can enjoy all of these benefits plus unlimited admission into Thinktank, Birmingham Science Museum.

Thinktank, Birmingham Science Museum
Journey to the stars in the Planetarium, discover Birmingham's Spitfire Story in the Spitfire Gallery, uncover the Thinktank ichthyosaur and get hands-on with giant-sized exhibits in the outdoor Science Garden. Plus, with four floors of interactive exhibits dedicated to science, technology and industry, Thinktank offers mind-boggling days out for all the family.

Winterbourne House and Gardens

BIRMINGHAM BOTANICAL GARDENS

Westbourne Road, Edgbaston, Birmingham B15 3TR

15 acres of beautiful historic landscaped gardens with 7000 shrubs, plants and trees. Four glasshouses, Roses and Alpines, Woodland and Rhododendron Walks, Rock Pool, Herbaceous Borders, Japanese Garden. Children's playground, aviaries, gallery, bandstand, Tea Room giftshop, parking.
Location: Map 6:O7. OS Ref SP048 855. 2m W of city centre. Follow signs to Edgbaston then brown tourist signs.
Owner: Birmingham Botanical & Horticultural Society
Contact: Kim Hill **Tel:** 0121 454 1860 **Fax:** 0121 454 7835
E-mail: Kim@birminghambotanicalgardens.org.uk
Website: www.birminghambotanicalgardens.org.uk
Open: Daily: 10am-dusk. Closed Christmas Day and Boxing Day. Refer to website for details.
Admission: Adult £7.00, Family £22.00. Groups, Conc. £4.75, Children U5 free.
Key facts: On application. Guide dogs only. Closed 25/26 Dec.

CASTLE BROMWICH HALL GARDENS TRUST

Chester Road, Castle Bromwich, Birmingham B36 9BT

10 acres of historic walled gardens, rescued by volunteers, and restored to 17/18th Century formal English style, pre-'Capability' Brown. Formal walks, espaliered fruit and holly maze contrasts with informal wildlife areas beyond the walls. **Location:** Map 6:O6. OS Ref SP141 899. Off B4114, 5m E of Birmingham City Centre, 1 mile from M6/J5 exit N only.
Owner: Castle Bromwich Hall & Gardens Trust **Contact:** Sue Brain
Tel: 0121 749 4100 **Twitter:** @cbhallgardens. **E-mail:** admin@cbhgt.org.uk
Website: www.cbhgt.org.uk **Open:** 1 Apr-31 Oct: Tue-Thu, 11am-4pm. Sat, Sun BH Mon 12.30-4.30pm. 1 Nov-31 Mar: Tue-Thu 11am-3pm.
Admission: Summer: Adults £4.50/£4.00, Child £1.00. Winter: All Adults £4.00, Child £1.00.
Key facts: Guide and books. WCs, wheelchairs. By arrangement. Limited for coaches. On leads.

BACK TO BACKS

55-63 Hurst Street, Birmingham, West Midlands B5 4TE

Take an exciting step back into Birmingham's industrial past by visiting the last remaining courtyard of Back to Back houses in Birmingham. Guided Tours.
Location: Map 6:O7. OS Ref SP071 861.
E-mail: backtobacks@nationaltrust.org.uk **Website:** www.nationaltrust.org.uk
Open: Term time, Tue-Thu, 1-5pm; Fri-Sun, BH Mons, School Hols, 10am-5pm. Closed Tue after BH weekends. **Admission:** Adult £7.85; Child £4.55.

BADDESLEY CLINTON

Rising Lane, Baddesley Clinton, Warwickshire B93 0DQ

A 500 year old moated medieval manor house with hidden secrets!
Location: Map 6:P8. OS Ref SP199 715. **Tel:** 01564 783294
E-mail: baddesleyclinton@nationaltrust.org.uk
Website: www.nationaltrust.org.uk/baddesley-clinton
Open: l Jan-11 Feb, daily, 9-4pm; 12 Feb-29 Oct, daily, 9-5pm; 30 Oct-31 Dec, daily, 9-4pm. Closed 24 & 25 Dec. **Admission:** Adult £10.45; Child £5.15.

HAGLEY HALL

Hall Lane, Hagley, Nr. Stourbridge, Worcestershire DY9 9LG

This elegant Palladian house, completed in 1760, contains some of the finest examples of Italian plasterwork. **Location:** Map 6:N7. OS Ref SO919 806.
Tel: 01562 882408 **E-mail:** info@hagleyhall.com
Website: www.hagleyhall.com
Open: 9 Jan-12 Mar, daily, 1.30-4.30pm, guided tours.
Admission: Adult £10; Child £5.

KINVER EDGE AND THE ROCK HOUSES

Compton Road, Kinver, Nr Stourbridge, Staffordshire DY7 6DL

These wonderful cave houses were inhabited until the 1950's and are now open to the public. **Location:** Map 6:N7. 4m W of Stourbridge, 4m N of Kidderminster.
Tel: 01384 872553 **E-mail:** kinveredge@nationaltrust.org.uk
Website: www.nationaltrust.org.uk/kinver-edge-and-the-rock-houses
Open: Apr-Oct & Feb half term, Sat-Wed, 11-5pm; 4 Nov-17 Dec, Sat & Sun, 11-4pm; 18 Dec-20 Dec, Mon-Wed, 11-3pm. **Admission:** Adult £5; child £2.50.

WIGHTWICK MANOR & GARDENS

Wightwick Bank, Wolverhampton, West Midlands WV6 8EE

Wightwick is in every way an idyllic time capsule of Victorian nostalgia for medieval England. **Location:** Map 6:N6. OS Ref SO869 985.
Tel: 01902 761400 **E-mail:** wightwickmanor@nationaltrust.org.uk
Website: www.nationaltrust.org.uk **Open:** Gardens: All year, daily, 11-4pm (5pm in sum). House: 1 Jan-30 Jun, daily except Tue, 12-4pm; 1 Jul-31 Aug, 12-5pm; 1 Sep-31 Dec, daily except Tue, 12-4pm. **Admission:** Adult £10.30; Child £5.15.

WINTERBOURNE HOUSE AND GARDEN

58 Edgbaston Park Road, Birmingham B15 2RT

Winterbourne is set in 7 acres of botanic garden. Exhibition spaces tell the history of the previous owners and the garden. **Location:** Map 6:O7. OS Ref SP052 839.
Tel: 0121 414 3003 **E-mail:** enquiries@winterbourne.org.uk **Website:** www.winterbourne.org.uk **Open:** Jan-Mar/Nov-Dec 10am-4pm Mon-Fri, 11am-4pm Sat-Sun; Apr-Oct 10am-5.30pm Mon-Fri, 11am-5.30pm Sat-Sun. Closed Christmas period. **Admission:** Adult £5.45, Conc £4.45, Family £16.00.

Where is Britain's Best Heritage Picnic Spot?

HUDSON'S HERITAGE AWARDS 2017

Nominate your favourite UK heritage picnic spot and tell us why you like it and you could win a fabulous Fortnum & Mason picnic hamper and tickets to the awards

Enter now at www.hudsons-awards.co.uk

Entries will be judged by our independent panel of heritage experts. The judges' decision will be final.

© National Trust Images/Andrew Butler

© National Trust Images/James Dobson

CROOME

NEAR HIGH GREEN, WORCESTERSHIRE WR8 9DW

www.nationaltrust.org.uk/croome

There's more than meets the eye at Croome. A secret wartime airbase, now a visitor centre, was once a hub of activity for thousands of people. Outside is the grandest of English landscapes, 'Capability' Brown's masterful first commission, with commanding views over the Malverns. The parkland was nearly lost, but is now great for walks and adventures with a surprise around every corner. At the heart of the park lies Croome Court, once home to the Earls of Coventry. The 6th Earl was an 18th Century trend-setter, and today Croome follows his lead using artists and craftspeople to tell the story of its eclectic past in inventive ways.
Location: Map 6:N9. OS Ref SO878 448. Approximately 10 miles south of Worcester. Leave M5 motorway at Junction 7 and follow B4084 towards Pershore. Alternatively, access from the A38. Follow Brown Signs.
Owner: National Trust
Tel: 01905 371006 **Fax:** 01905 371090
E-mail: croome@nationaltrust.org.uk
Open: See National Trust website nationaltrust.org.uk/croome for full opening times. Park, House, Restaurant & Shop open every day except 24 & 25 Dec.
Admission: See National Trust website for full prices.
Key facts: A visit to the shop at the Visitor Centre is a relaxing way to spend some time looking for that perfect souvenir or gift. A great selection of plants at our Gardener's Bothy. Pleasure grounds accessible (gravel path). Manual wheelchair and powered mobility vehicle available to book. Designated mobility parking. Access to house via wheelchair stairclimber. A 1940s style restaurant in the Visitor Centre & Tea Room in the House. By arrangement. By arrangement. Dogs welcome.

BEWDLEY MUSEUM

12 Load Street, Bewdley, Worcestershire DY12 2AE

www.bewdleymuseum.co.uk

Situated in the delightful Georgian town of Bewdley this unique museum can be enjoyed by the whole family. Beautiful gardens, imaginative displays, a café with fresh local produce. Exhibitions, events and plenty of activities for children. The Tourist Information Centre is based on site at the entrance to the museum.
Location: Map 6:M8. OS Ref SO786 753. 4 miles to the west of Kidderminster on the B1490 in the centre of Bewdley. Two public car parks are within walking distance. **Owner:** Wyre Forest District Council **Contact:** Alison Bakr
Tel: 0845 603 5699 **E-mail:** Alison.bakr@wyreforestdc.gov.uk
Open: Mar-Oct 10am-4.30pm. Nov and Dec 11am-3pm. Fri, Sat and Sun. Café and access to the gardens Mar-Dec. **Admission:** Free.
Key facts: Situation at the entrance to the museum. Situated in the herb garden. Private events and functions are held on site. Full access on site. Shambles café set in the museum. Serving hot and cold drinks, snacks, lightbites, hot meals and alcohol. Guided tours and walks. Blitz and evacuation, river and rail plus bespoke programmes. Welcome on site. Wedding receptions and parties held in the museum and gardens.

Harvington Hall

HARVINGTON HALL

Harvington, Kidderminster, Worcestershire DY10 4LR

www.harvingtonhall.com

Tucked away in a peaceful corner of Worcestershire, Harvington Hall is a remarkable moated manor house with the largest surviving series of priest hides in the country and a rare collection of original Elizabethan wall paintings. The Hall is surrounded by beautiful walled gardens in a peaceful moatside setting. The Moatside Tea Room offers superb homemade cakes, scones and light lunches, and the Hall's gift shop offers a selection of Fairtrade and unusual gifts.

Location: Map 6:N8. OS Ref SO877 745. On minor road, ½m NE of A450/A448 crossroads at Mustow Green. 3m SE of Kidderminster.

Owner: Roman Catholic Archdiocese of Birmingham **Contact:** Hall Manager

Tel: 01562 777846 **E-mail:** harvingtonhall@btconnect.com

Open: Wed-Sun, Mar-Oct, from 11.30am (closing times vary). Open B/H Mons. Closed Good Fri. Pre-booked groups & schools also available.

Admission: Adult £9.00, Child (5-16) £5.00, OAP £8.00, Family (2 adults & 3 children) £25.00, Garden & Malt House Visitor Centre: £3.50.

Key facts: Partial. WCs. Limited for coaches. Guide dogs only.

LITTLE MALVERN COURT

Nr Malvern, Worcestershire WR14 4JN

Prior's Hall, associated rooms and cells, c1489. Former Benedictine Monastery. Oak-framed roof, five bays. Library, collection of religious vestments and relics. Embroideries and paintings. Gardens: 10 acres of former monastic grounds with spring bulbs, blossom, old fashioned roses and shrubs.

Access to Hall only by flight of steps. **Location:** Map 6:M9. OS Ref SO769 403. 3m S of Great Malvern on Upton-on-Severn Road (A4104).

Owner: Trustees of the late T M Berington

Contact: Mrs T M Berington **Tel:** 01684 892988 **Fax:** 01684 893057

E-mail: littlemalverncourt@hotmail.com **Website:** www.littlemalverncourt.co.uk

Open: 19 Apr-20 Jul, Weds & Thus, 2.15-5pm, last admission 4pm. Open for NGS Mon 1 May, with Flower Festival in the Priory.

Admission: House & Garden: Adult £8.00, Child £3.00. Garden only: Adult £7.00, Child £2.00. Groups by prior arrangement.

Key facts: Garden (partial). Tea & cake. House only.

MADRESFIELD COURT

Madresfield, Malvern WR13 5AJ

Moated family home with mainly Victorian architecture and fine collection of furniture and art. Extensive gardens and arboretum.

Location: Map 6:M9. OS Ref SO808 472. 6m SW of Worcester. 1½ m SE of A449. 2m NE of Malvern.

Owner: The Trustees of Madresfield Estate

Contact: Mrs Cheryl Stone

Tel: 01684 573614

E-mail: tours@madresfieldestate.co.uk

Website: www.madresfieldestate.co.uk

Open: Guided tours of about 1.5 hours on specified dates and times between Mar and Sep. Numbers are restricted and prior booking is essential to avoid disappointment. We have no refreshment facilities.

Admission: £13.00. No concessions and no Under 16s.

Key facts: Guide books. WCs. Obligatory.

THE TUDOR HOUSE MUSEUM

16 Church Street, Upton-upon-Severn, Worcestershire WR8 0HT

Exhibits of Upton past and present, local pottery and "Staffordshire Blue".

Location: Map 6:N10. OS Ref SO852 406. Centre of Upton-upon-Severn, 7miles SE of Malvern by B4211.

Owner: Tudor House Museum Trust

Tel: 01684 438820

E-mail: lavendertudor@talktalk.net

Website: www.tudorhousemuseum.org

Open: Apr-Oct. Tue-Sun and BH afternoons. 1.30-4.30pm. Nov-Mar Suns 2-4pm

Key facts: Garden and ground floor only. Pre-booked.

HANBURY HALL

Droitwich, Worcestershire WR9 7EA

Completed in 1701, this homely William & Mary-style house is famed for its fine painted ceilings and staircase. Stunning 20 acre garden.

Location: Map 6:N8. OS Ref SO944 637.

Tel: 01527 821214 **E-mail:** hanburyhall@nationaltrust.org.uk

Website: www.nationaltrust.org.uk **Open:** Jan-Mar & Oct-Dec, daily, 11-1pm; Apr-Oct, daily, 11-5pm. **Admission:** Adult £10.45; Child £5.15.

SPETCHLEY PARK GARDENS

Spetchley Park, Worcester WR5 1RS

Surrounded by glorious countryside and a deer park this 30 acre Victorian paradise was created to boast an enviable collection of plant treasures from every corner of the globe. **Location:** Map 6:N9. OS Ref SO895 539.

Tel: 01453 810303 **E-mail:** hb@spetchleygardens.co.uk

Website: www.spetchleygardens.co.uk **Open:** Apr-Sep, Wed-Sun, 11-6pm; Oct, Sat & Sun, 11-4pm. **Admission:** Adult £7; Child £2.50.

WITLEY COURT & GARDENS

Great Witley, Worcestershire WR6 6JT

Witley Court was one of England's great country houses. Today it is a spectacular ruin. **Location:** Map 6:M8. OS Ref OS150, SO769 649.

Tel: 01299 896636 **E-mail:** customers@english-heritage.org.uk

Website: www.english-heritage.org.uk **Open:** 2 Jan-31 Mar, Sat & Sun, 10-4pm; 1 Apr-30 Sep, 10-6pm; 1-31 Oct, 10-5pm; 1 Nov-23 Dec, Sat & Sun, 10-4pm; 27-31 Dec, 10-4pm. **Admission:** Adult £8.60; Child £5.20.

Croome

ACTON BURNELL CASTLE
Acton Burnell, Shrewsbury, Shropshire SY5 7PF
Tel: 0121 625 6832 **E-mail:** andrea.fox@english-heritage.org.uk

ATTINGHAM PARK
Atcham, Shrewsbury, Shropshire SY4 4TP
Tel: 01743 708170/162 **E-mail:** attingham@nationaltrust.org.uk

BENTHALL HALL
Broseley, Shropshire TF12 5RX
Tel: 01746 780838 **E-mail:** wendy.barton@nationaltrust.org.uk

HAWKSTONE HALL & GARDENS
Marchamley, Shrewsbury, Shropshire SY4 5LG
Tel: 01630 685242 **E-mail:** hawkhall@aol.com

MAWLEY HALL
Cleobury Mortimer DY14 8PN
Tel: 0208 298 0429 **E-mail:** rsharp@mawley.com

MUCH WENLOCK PRIORY
Much Wenlock, Shropshire TF13 6HS
Tel: 01952 727466 **E-mail:** customers@english-heritage.org.uk

CASTERNE HALL
Ilam, Nr Ashbourne, Derbyshire DE6 2BA
Tel: 01335 310489 **E-mail:** mail@casterne.co.uk

ERASMUS DARWIN HOUSE
Beacon Street, Lichfield, Staffordshire WS13 7AD
Tel: 01543 306260 **E-mail:** enquiries@erasmusdarwin.org

MOSELEY OLD HALL
Moseley Old Hall Lane, Wolverhampton WV10 7HY
Tel: 01902 782808 **E-mail:** moseleyoldhall@nationaltrust.org.uk

SANDON HALL
Sandon, Staffordshire ST18 OBZ
Tel: 01889 508004 **E-mail:** info@sandonhall.co.uk

THE TRENTHAM ESTATE
Stone Road, Trentham, Staffordshire ST4 8AX
Tel: 01782 646646 **E-mail:** enquiry@trentham.co.uk

BAGOTS CASTLE
Church Road, Baginton CV8 3AR
Tel: 07786 438711 **E-mail:** delia@bagotscastle.org.uk

COUGHTON COURT
Alcester, Warwickshire B49 5JA
Tel: 01789 400777 **E-mail:** office@throckmortons.co.uk

FARNBOROUGH HALL
Banbury OX17 1DU
Tel: 01295 690002 **E-mail:** farnboroughhall@nationaltrust.org.uk

PACKWOOD HOUSE
Packwood Lane, Lapworth, Warwickshire B94 6AT
Tel: 01564 783294 **E-mail:** packwood@nationaltrust.org.uk

UPTON HOUSE & GARDENS
Upton, Near Banbury, Warwickshire OX15 6HT
Tel: 01295 670266 **E-mail:** uptonhouse@nationaltrust.org.uk

Charlecote Park

Burton Constable Hall, East Yorkshire

Kiplin Hall, North Yorkshire

East Yorkshire
North Yorkshire
South Yorkshire
West Yorkshire

Yorkshire & The Humber

Yorkshire has more than its fair share of historic places to visit and since Hull is the UK's City of Culture this year, you may find yourself crossing the Humber Bridge into little visited East Yorkshire. Don't miss Yorkshire's treasure houses, particularly Castle Howard and Harewood House, but make time for some of the region's wide variety of heritage places and gardens.

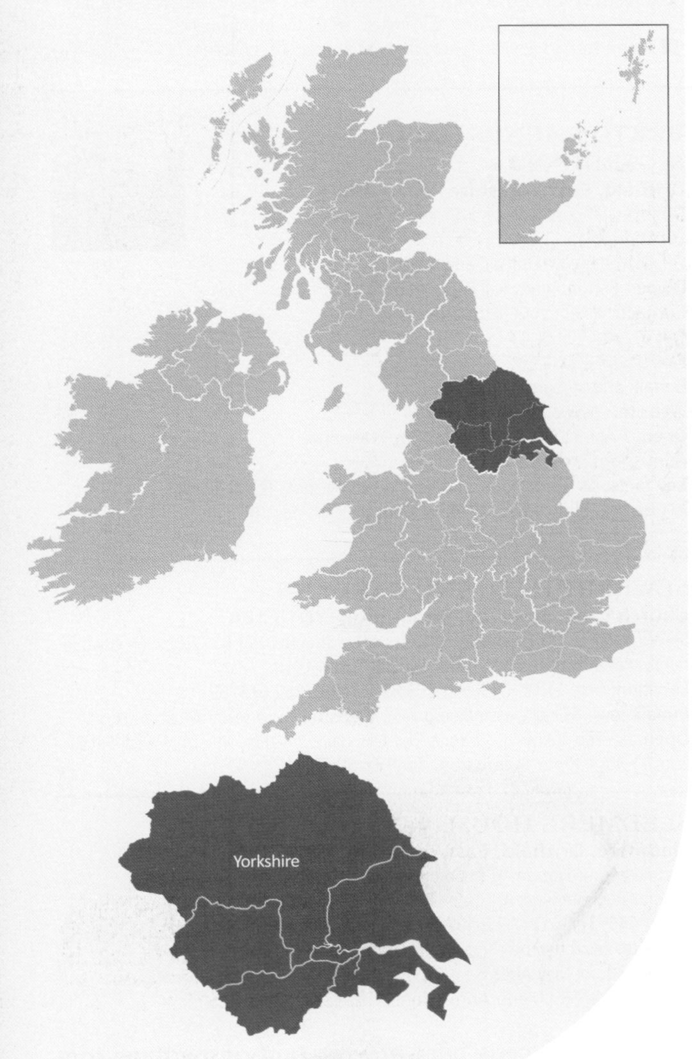

WASSAND HALL

SEATON, HULL, EAST YORKSHIRE HU11 5RJ

www.wassand.co.uk

Fine Regency house 1815 by Thomas Cundy the Elder. Beautifully restored walled gardens, woodland walks, Parks and vistas over Hornsea Mere, part of the Estate since 1580. The Estate was purchased circa 1520 by Dame Jane Constable and has remained in the family to the present day, Mr Rupert Russell being the great nephew of the late Lady Strickland-Constable.

The house contains a fine collection of 18/19th Century paintings, English and Continental silver, furniture and porcelain. Wassand is very much a family home and retains a very friendly atmosphere. Homemade afternoon teas are served in the conservatory on Open Days.

Location: Map 11:F9. OS Ref TA174 460. On the B1244 Seaton-Hornsea Road. Approximately 2m from Hornsea.

Owner/Contact: R E O Russell - Resident Trustee

Tel/Fax: 01964 534488 **E-mail:** rupert@reorussell.co.uk

Open: 26-29 May (May 29 Vintage Car Rally), 14-18 (Jun 18 Plant Fair) & 29-30 Jun, 1-3 & 12-16 Jul (Jul 16 Concert Hall Closed), 2-8 (Aug 5 Closed) & 25-28 Aug.

Admission: Hall & Gardens: Adult £6.50, OAP £6.00, Child (11-15) £3.50, Child (under 10) Free. Hall: Adult £4.50, OAP £4.00, Child (11-15) £2.00, Child (under 10) Free. Grounds & Garden: Adult £4.50, OAP £4.00, Child (11-15) £2.00, Child (under 10) Free

Key facts: Group Bookings - Guided Tours, Bird Hide inclusive ticket contact Shirley Power 01964-537474. Limited. By arrangement Ample for cars, limited for coaches. In grounds, on leads.

BURTON CONSTABLE HALL & GROUNDS

Skirlaugh, Hull, East Yorks HU11 4LN

www.burtonconstable.com

East Yorkshire's best kept secret. Meander upstairs and downstairs through 30 evocative grand rooms filled with fine art and furniture. Visit the stable lad's bedchamber, blacksmith's shop, tack rooms and the restored workings of the 18th Century stable clock and of course see the skeleton of a 60' sea monster. Explore the historic grounds, with their woodland and parkland walks, follow the wildlife trail or just find a favourite spot to relax in this glorious setting. **Location:** Map 11:E10. OS Ref TA193 369. Beverley 14m, Hull 10m. Signed from Skirlaugh. **Owner:** Burton Constable Foundation **Contact:** Mrs Helen Dewson **Tel:** 01964 562400 **E-mail:** enquiries@burtonconstable.com **Open:** Easter Sat-29 Oct: Stables, Grounds, Tea Room & Gift Shop open daily 11am-5pm. Hall: Sat-Thu inclusive (every day in Jul & Aug). Hall: 12noon-5pm (last admission 1 hour before closing). Christmas Opening 18 Nov-10 Dec (tbc) Hall, 11am-4pm (last admission 1 hour before closing). Tea Room, Gift Shop, Stables & Grounds 11am to approx. 4.30pm. Please telephone to confirm opening times prior to your visit as they may be subject to change. **Admission:** Adult £10.00, Child £5.00, OAP £9.50. Family £26.00 (2 adults & 2 children). Prices include 10% Gift Aid. **Key facts:** Photography. Small gift shop. Seminars/meetings. Mostly accessible. Stables Tea Room. Tours can be arranged in advance. Ample free parking. Indoor & outdoor. On leads in grounds. Guide dogs only in hall.

BURTON AGNES HALL & GARDENS

Driffield, East Yorkshire YO25 4NB

Elizabethan house with award winning gardens.

Location: Map 11:E9. OS Ref TA103 633. Off A614 between Driffield and Bridlington.

Owner: Burton Agnes Hall Preservation Trust Ltd

Contact: Mr Simon Cunliffe-Lister

Tel: 01262 490324

Fax: 01262 490513

E-mail: office@burtonagnes.com

Website: www.burtonagnes.com

Open: 1 Apr-31 Oct & 14 Nov-23 Dec 11am-5pm.

Admission: See website.

Key facts: Gift Shop and home and garden shop. WCs. Licensed. Licensed. Dogs on leads only.

SEWERBY HALL AND GARDENS

Church Lane, Sewerby, Bridlington YO15 1EA

Sewerby Hall is a grade one listed building constructed 1714-1720 by the Greame family. Recently restored to how it would look in 1910.

Location: Map 11:F8. OS Ref TA203 690. **Tel:** 01262 673769

E-mail: sewerby.hall@eastriding.gov.uk **Website:** www.sewerbyhall.co.uk

Open: Jan-Feb, daily, 11.30-3pm; Mar-Oct, daily, 11-4pm; Nov-Dec, Wed, Sat & Sun, 11.30-3.30pm. **Admission:** Adult £6.50; Child £4.40.

SLEDMERE HOUSE

Sledmere, Driffield, East Yorkshire YO25 3XG

Sledmere House exudes 18th Century elegance with each room containing decorative plasterwork by Joseph Rose Junior. **Location:** Map 11:D9. OS Ref SE931 648. **Tel:** 01377 236637 **E-mail:** info@sledmerehouse.com **Website:** www.sledmerehouse.com **Open:** Apr & Oct, Tue, Thu, Sun, 11am-3.30pm; May-Jun & Sep, Tue-Thu, Sun, 11am-3.30pm; Jul & Aug, Tue-Sun, 11am-3.30pm; BH Mons. **Admission:** Adult £7.50; Child £3.50.

CASTLE HOWARD

www.castlehoward.co.uk

Designed by Sir John Vanbrugh in 1699 Castle Howard is undoubtedly one of Britain's finest private residences.

Built for Charles Howard the 3rd Earl of Carlisle and taking over 100 years to complete, today Castle Howard remains home to the Howard family. Discover the rich and varied history, dramatic interiors and sweeping parklands of this magnificent house.

Free flowing tours of the house allow you to explore at your leisure, with friendly and knowledgeable guides throughout happy to share stories. From decadent bedrooms and lavish drawing rooms to the stunning Great Hall and vast Long Gallery, there are architectural wonders and world renowned collections in every room.

The house façade bristles with carvings and the gold topped dome reaches skyward giving Castle Howard its iconic silhouette.

Spend a day exploring the beautiful gardens; with meandering woodland paths, lakeside terraces and sweeping vistas dotted with temples, statues and follies. The walled garden is the perfect place to relax with a stunning collection of roses, herbaceous borders and a formal potager. Seasonal highlights include daffodils, rhododendrons, bluebells, roses and striking autumnal hues.

Enjoy a changing programme of exhibitions and events, including Christmas opening when the house is decorated for the festive season. Plus free outdoor tours, illustrated children's trail, adventure playground and summer boat trips on the Great Lake (weather permitting). Treat yourself at a range of cafés and shops, including garden centre, farm shop and gift shops.

KEY FACTS

- Photography allowed.
- Gift shops, farm shop and garden centre.
- Available for private events.
- Access to all areas except High South, Exhibition Wing and Chapel.
- Choice of four Cafés.
- Guides in each room.
- Free parking.
- School parties welcome.
- Dogs on leads welcome in gardens only. Assistance dogs welcome in house.
- Camping and caravanning.
- Great Hall licensed for weddings.
- Gardens, shops and cafés open all year.
- Full programme for all the family.

VISITOR INFORMATION

Owner
Castle Howard Estate Ltd

Address
Castle Howard
York
North Yorkshire
YO60 7DA

Location
Map 11:C8
OS Ref. SE716 701
From the North: From the A1 take the A61 to Thirsk then the A170 to Helmsley. Before Helmsley turn right onto the B1257 and follow the brown signs.
From the South: Take the A1M to Junction 44 and follow the A64 east to York. Continue past York and follow the brown signs.
Bus: Service from York.
Rail: London Kings Cross to York 1hr. 50 mins. York to Malton Station 30 mins.

Contact
Visitor Services
Tel: 01653 648333
E-mail: house@castlehoward.co.uk

Opening Times
House & Grounds:
Visit www.castlehoward.co.uk for details of opening times.

Grounds:
Open all year except Christmas Day.

Stable Courtyard Shops, Café & Garden Centre:
Visit website for details of opening times.

For more information please contact Castle Howard Estate Office on 01653 648444.

Admission
Visit www.castlehoward.co.uk for details of admission prices.

Conference/Function

ROOM	Size	Max Cap
Long Gallery	197' x 24'	200
Grecian Hall	40' x 40'	70

VISITOR INFORMATION

Address
Skipton Castle
Skipton
North Yorkshire
BD23 1AW

Location
Map 10:O9
OS Ref. SD992 520
In the centre of Skipton, at the N end of High Street. Skipton is 20m W of Harrogate on the A59 and 26m NW of Leeds on A65.
Rail: Regular services from Leeds & Bradford.

Contact
Penny Cannon
Tel: 01756 792442
E-mail:
info@skiptoncastle.co.uk

Opening Times
All year
Mon-Sat 10am-5pm
Sun 11am-5pm
(Oct-Mar 4pm)
(Closed 23-25 Dec).

Admission

Adult	£8.10
Child (0-4yrs)	Free
Child (5-17yrs)	£5.10
OAP	£7.00
Student (with ID)	£7.00
Family (2+3)	£25.90
Groups (15+)	
Adult	£6.90
Child (0-17yrs)	£5.10

Includes illustrated tour sheet in a choice of ten languages, plus free badge for children.

Groups welcome - Coach parking and guides available for pre-booked groups at no extra charge.

Special Events
Historical Re-enactments. Plays. Art Exhibitions. For up-to-date information and events, visit our website www.skiptoncastle.co.uk.

Conference/Function

Room	Size	Max Cap
Oak Room		30
Granary		100

SKIPTON CASTLE

www.skiptoncastle.co.uk

Skipton Castle, over 900 years old, one of the best preserved, most complete medieval castles in England.

Guardian of the gateway to the Yorkshire Dales for over 900 years, this unique fortress is one of the most complete, well-preserved medieval castles in England. Standing on a 40-metre high crag, fully-roofed Skipton Castle was founded around 1090 by Robert de Romille, one of William the Conqueror's Barons, as a fortress in the dangerous northern reaches of the kingdom.

Owned by King Edward I and Edward II, from 1310 it became the stronghold of the Clifford Lords withstanding successive raids by marauding Scots. During the Civil War it was the last Royalist bastion in the North, yielding only after a three-year siege in 1645. 'Slighted' under the orders of Cromwell, the Castle was skilfully restored by the redoubtable Lady Anne Clifford and today visitors can climb from the depths of the Dungeon to the top of the Watch Tower, explore the Banqueting Hall, Kitchens, the Bedchamber and even the Privy!

Every period has left its mark, from the Norman entrance and the medieval towers, to the beautiful Tudor courtyard with the great yew tree planted by Lady Anne in 1659.

In the grounds visitors can see the Tudor wing built as a royal wedding present for Lady Eleanor Brandon, niece of Henry VIII, the beautiful Shell Room decorated in the 1620s with shells and Jamaican coral and the ancient medieval chapel of St. John the Evangelist. The Chapel Terrace, with its delightful picnic area, has fine views over the woods and Skipton's lively market town.

KEY FACTS

- Fully roofed. Photography allowed for personal use only.
- Specialist books, cards, gifts. Online shop.
- Unusual plants grown in grounds.
- Corporate hospitality. Wedding ceremonies. Champagne receptions.
- Unsuitable.
- Licensed. Open all year.
- Licensed. Open all year.
- By arrangement.
- Large public coach and car park nearby.
- Tour guides, educational rooms and teachers packs available.
- Dogs on leads only.
- Civil Wedding Licence. Max 80 guests.
- Open all year except 23-25 Dec.

Register for news and special offers at www.hudsonsheritage.com

© Ed. Remsberg, University of Maryland.

© Ed. Remsberg, University of Maryland.

KIPLIN HALL AND GARDENS

NR SCORTON, RICHMOND, NORTH YORKSHIRE DL10 6AT

www.kiplinhall.co.uk

This award-winning house & garden was the Jacobean country seat of founder of Maryland, George Calvert. 'Gothic' wing added in 1820s & redesigned in 1887 by W.E. Nesfield. This intriguing property is now furnished as a comfortable Victorian home with an eclectic mix of previous owners' furniture & personalia plus enough original 16th-19th Century paintings to fill a small gallery! Special Exhibition - 'Home Sweet Home'! Attractive Gardens, productive Walled Garden, woodland/ lakeside walks & small garden museum. Tea Room serving homemade scones, cakes & lunches. Family fun - Activities Room, Play Ship, garden games, dipping-pond, croquet, natural play-area, table tennis & more!

Location: Map 11:A7. OS Ref SE274 976. Midway between Richmond & Northallerton, 5 miles east of A1M, on B6271 Scorton - Northallerton road.

Owner: Kiplin Hall CIO **Contact:** D. Webster, Curator

Tel: 01748 818178 **E-mail:** info@kiplinhall.co.uk

Open: Gardens and Tea Room: Sat, Sun, Mon, Tue & Wed from 4 Feb-1 Nov, 10am-5pm (4pm Feb & Mar). Also Good Fri.
Hall: Sat, Sun, Mon, Tue & Wed from 1 Apr-1 Nov, also Good Fri, 11am-5pm.
Christmas: Fri, Sat & Sun 1-3 and 8-10 Dec, 10am-4pm.

Admission: Hall/Gardens/Grounds: With Gift Aid/Without G/A - Adult £10/9.10, Conc. £9/8.10, Child £5.30/4.80, Family (2+2) £26/23.60. Gardens/Grounds only: Adult £6.50/5.90, Conc. £5.50/5, Child £3.50/3.20, Family (2+2) £19.50/17.70.

Key facts: Special Events, incl. Christmas. Small, but well-stocked. Fruit/Veg & Plants from Walled Garden in season. Please telephone to discuss. Wheelchair access to ground floor & gardens. Accessible W.C. Homemade cakes, scones & lunches. Local produce & fruit and veg from Walled Garden used in season. Pre-booked for groups of 18 or more. In gardens only. Assistance dogs are welcome in Hall.

MARKENFIELD HALL

NR RIPON, NORTH YORKSHIRE HG4 3AD

www.markenfield.com

"This wonderfully little-altered building is the most complete surviving example of the medium-sized 14th Century country house in England" John Martin Robinson 'The Architecture of Northern England'. Tucked privately away down a mile-long winding drive, Markenfield is one of the most astonishing and romantic of Yorkshire's medieval houses: fortified, completely moated, and still privately owned. Winner of the HHA and Sotheby's Finest Restoration Award 2008.

Location: Map 10:P8. OS Ref SE294 672. Access from W side of A61. 2½ miles S of the Ripon bypass.

Owner: Mr Ian & Lady Deirdre Curteis **Contact:** The Administrator

Tel: 01765 692303 **Fax:** 01765 607195 **E-mail:** info@markenfield.com

Open: 30 Apr-14 May and 11-25 Jun daily 2-5pm. Last entry 4:30pm.
Group bookings can be accepted all year round by appointment.

Admission: Adult £6.00, Conc. £5.00. Booked groups from £8.00 per person for a guided tour (min charge £120.00).

Key facts: Partial. Wheelchair access to the ground floor only. Dogs in grounds only.

© Merchant Adventurers' Hall

© Merchant Adventurers' Hall

MERCHANT ADVENTURERS' HALL

FOSSGATE, YORK YO1 9XD

www.theyorkcompany.co.uk

The Merchant Adventurers' Hall is one of York's medieval marvels. Set in beautiful gardens in the heart of historic York, it is open for public use as a museum, wedding and hospitality venue and meeting place some 650 years after construction began in 1357.

Location: Map 11:B9. OS Ref SE605 517. On Foot: In the City Centre between Fossgate & Piccadilly. Disabled parking available on Fossgate. Park & Ride: www.yorkparkandride.co.uk. Public Transport: 2 miles from York station.

Owner: The Company of Merchant Adventurers of the City of York

Contact: Lauren Marshall **Tel:** 01904 654818

E-mail: enquiries@theyorkcompany.co.uk

Open: Mar-Oct: Mon-Thu: 9am-5pm. Fri-Sat: 9am-3.30pm. Sun: 11am-4pm Nov-Feb: Mon-Thu: 10am-4pm. Fri-Sat: 10am-3.30pm. Sun: Closed. Closed: 24 Dec-3 Jan. Last admission to Hall is 30 minutes prior to closing time. Occasionally the Hall is closed for private functions or maintenance work, so you may wish to telephone in advance.

Admission: Adult £6.00; Concessions(60+/Students) £5.00; Children (16 and under) FREE.

Key facts: Accept Groups by prior booking. Public toilets are for visitors use only. The Merchant Adventurers' Hall is a unique and prestigious venue offering an unrivalled setting for your corporate events. Audio tour in English free with admission. Except Assistance Dogs The Merchant Adventurers' Hall provides a beautiful setting for your wedding. This ancient medieval guildhall is over 650 years old and can be yours exclusively for your special day.

© Ed. Remsberg, University of Maryland

Kiplin Hall with the Yorkshire Dales in the distance

© Peter Packer

© Jerry Hardman Jones

NEWBY HALL & GARDENS

NEWBY HALL, RIPON, NORTH YORKSHIRE HG4 5AE

www.newbyhall.com

Designed under the guidance of Sir Christopher Wren, this graceful country house, home to the Compton family, epitomises the Georgian 'Age of Elegance'. Its beautifully restored interior presents Robert Adam at his best with rare Gobelins tapestries and one of the UK's largest private collections of classical statuary. The award-winning gardens created in the early 1920s, boast one of Europe's longest double herbaceous borders and are of interest to specialist and amateur gardeners alike. Newby also offers a large Adventure Garden for children, miniature railway, excellent restaurant, shop, plant centre, Dollshouse Exhibition and Gyles Brandreth's Teddy Bear Collection.

Events: 10-11 Jun Tractor Fest and 16 Jul Historic Vehicle Rally

Location: Map 11:A8. OS Ref SE348 675. Midway between London and Edinburgh, 4m W of A1(M), towards Ripon. From north use J49, from south use J48 and follow brown tourist signs. 40 mins from York, 30 mins from Harrogate.

Owner: Mr Richard Compton **Contact:** The Administrator

Tel: 01423 322583 opt 3 **Fax:** 01423 324452 **E-mail:** info@newbyhall.com

Open: Summer- House*, 1 Apr-24 Sep. Apr, May, Jun & Sep: Tue-Sun & BH Mons; Jul-Aug: Daily. See website for tour times. *Areas of the House can be closed to the public from time to time, please check website for details. Garden, dates as House, 11am-5.30pm. Last admission 5pm. Winter, Oct-end Mar closed.

Admission: See website for 2017 prices.

Key facts: Allow a full day for viewing house and gardens. Suitable for filming and for special events. No indoor photography. 'The Shop @ Newby Hall' - Modern British Art and Craftsmanship. Quality toys. Quality plants available, reflecting the contents of the garden. Wedding receptions & special functions. Licensed for civil ceremonies. Suitable. WCs. Parking. Electric and manual wheelchairs available - booking essential. Licensed. Licensed. Obligatory. Ample. Hard standing for coaches. Welcome. Rates on request. Woodland discovery walk, adventure gardens and train rides. Guide/hearing dogs only in Gardens/Woodland. Dog exercise area for other dogs not permitted into gardens or woodland walk. House licensed.

PLUMPTON ROCKS

PLUMPTON, KNARESBOROUGH, NORTH YORKSHIRE HG5 8NA

www.plumptonrocks.com

A Grade 2* listed man-made lake and surrounding pleasure gardens against a backdrop of towering rocks eroded by the wind. It has been described by English Heritage to be of outstanding interest. The large picturesque garden was formed in the 1760s by creating a lake at the foot of an extensive range of weathered and contorted gritstone outcrops. The 30 acre park provides seemingly endless opportunities to explore, with tranquil lakeside walks, dramatic Millstone Grit rock formations, romantic woodland walks winding through bluebells and rhododendrons. Painted by Turner and described by Queen Mary as 'Heaven on earth'. The lake, woodlands and dam have recently been restored to their 18th Century magnificence.

Location: Map 11:A9. OS Ref SE353 535. Between Harrogate and Wetherby on A661, 1m SE of A661 junction with Harrogate southern bypass.

Owner/Contact: Robert de Plumpton Hunter

Tel: 01289 382322

E-mail: info@plumptonrocks.com

Open: May-Oct on Sats, Suns & BH's at 11am-6pm

Admission: Adult £3.50, Concessions: £2.50 (Prices subject to change)

Key facts: The rocks are steep, footpaths uneven & lake is deep. Stout walking shoes are essential. Unsuitable. Limited for coaches. In grounds, on leads.

RIPLEY CASTLE

RIPLEY, HARROGATE, NORTH YORKSHIRE HG3 3AY

www.ripleycastle.co.uk

Home to the Ingilby Family, Ripley Castle dates from the 1555 Tudor Tower and Priests Hole to elegant Georgian rooms. A unique collection of objects and paintings reflecting the family's 700 year history. Guided tours are informative and amusing with themed and family tours available. Extensive Gardens, Parkland and Lakes, Garden tours and family activities.

Location: Map 10:P9. OS Ref SE283 605. W edge of village. Just off A61 between Harrogate and Ripon.
Owner: Sir Thomas Ingilby Bt
Contact: Estate & Events Admin Team
Tel: 01423 770152
Fax: 01423 771745
E-mail: enquiries@ripleycastle.co.uk
Open: Gardens open daily. Castle by guided tour.
Please see website for times.

Admission: Gardens & Parkland FREE, Castle from £4.50 on weekdays.
Castle & Gardens Weekends: Adults £10, Concessions £9, Child £7, Family £25.
Gardens Only Weekends: Adult £5, Concession/child £4.50. Family £15

Key facts: No photography in Castle unless by prior written consent. Parkland for outdoor activities & concerts. Check website for event details. The Castle Gift Shop is where you go to purchase your tickets for the Castle and Gardens. Here you will find greetings cards and gifts for every occasion, including soft toys, cushions, soaps and perfumes. A stall outside the Gift Shop offers a wide range of; flowers, plants and herbs especially selected by our Ripley Castle Gardeners, including a selection from the Castle's own gardens. Dinners, Weddings and all types of corporate events. 12-120 guests. Hearing Loop system. Licensed. Licensed. Tour time 60 mins. 290 cars & 300 yards from Castle entrance. Coach park 50 yards. Free. By prior arrangement. Guide dogs only. 100 yards from the Castle with 25 bedrooms.

BROUGHTON HALL ESTATE

Skipton, Yorkshire BD23 3AE

www.broughtonhall.co.uk

Broughton Hall on the edge of the stunning Yorkshire Dales National Park has now become available for private hire. With sixteen en suite bedrooms, Broughton provides the ultimate destination for family reunion's, house parties, corporate retreats or a base to explore the surrounding countryside. Guests can also exclusively hire any one of the four other exquisite venues on the 3000 acre estate from contemporary Utopia or luxury holiday retreats Eden, Higher Scarcliffe or Yellison. **Location:** Map 10:N9. OS Ref SD943 507. On A59, 2m W of Skipton.
Owner: The Tempest Family **Contact:** The Estate Office
Tel: 01756 799608 **Fax:** 01756 700357
E-mail: tempest@broughtonhall.co.uk / info@broughtonhall.co.uk
Open: Utopia, set in the Dan Pearson designed walled garden at Broughton is open for Breakfast and Lunch, Mon-Fri. Viewings of other properties are by prior arrangement only. **Admission:** Please contact for prices.
Key facts: Company retreats & board meetings at the Hall. Meetings & Events space available at Utopia. Breakfast & Lunch - Licensed. By arrangement. Ample car parking. Must be pre-booked. 16 luxury bedrooms with stunning en suite bathrooms. Further accommodation available on the estate. Chapel on site for Catholic services.

CONSTABLE BURTON HALL GARDENS

Leyburn, North Yorkshire DL8 5LJ

www.constableburton.com

A delightful terraced woodland garden of lilies, ferns, hardy shrubs, roses and wild flowers surrounds this beautiful Palladian house designed by John Carr. Garden trails and herbaceous borders and stream garden with large architectural plants and reflection ponds. Stunning seasonal displays of snowdrops and daffodils. An annual Tulip Festival takes place over the early May Bank Holiday weekend. Group tours of the House and Gardens are invited by prior arrangement.
Location: Map 10:P7. OS Ref SE164 913. 3m E of Leyburn off the A684.
Owner/Contact: D'Arcy & Imogen Wyvill
Tel: 01677 450428 **Fax:** 01677 450622 **E-mail:** gardens@constableburton.com
Open: Garden opening 2017: 25 Mar- 17 Sep, 10am-4pm daily.
Tulip Festival: Sat 29, Sun 30 Apr & Mon 1 May. Please consult website for exceptional closures for private events. House closed to the public. Private tours and venue for classic car rallies available by arrangement through the estate office.
Admission: Adult £4.00, Child (5-16yrs) 50p, OAP £3.00.
Key facts: Woodland walks. Partial. Limited for coaches. On leads only.

DUNCOMBE PARK

Helmsley, North Yorkshire YO62 5EB

www.duncombepark.com

The sweeping grass terraces, towering veteran trees, and now newly-restored classical temples are described by historian Christopher Hussey as 'the most spectacularly beautiful among English landscape conceptions of the 18th Century'. Beside superb views over the Rye valley, visitors will discover woodland walks, ornamental parterres, and a 'secret garden' at the Conservatory.

Location: Map 11:B7. OS Ref SE604 830. Entrance just off Helmsley Market Square, signed off A170 Thirsk-Scarborough road.

Owner/Contact: Hon Jake Duncombe

Tel: 01439 770213 **Fax:** 01439 771114 **E-mail:** info@duncombepark.com

Open: Garden Only: 17 Apr-31 Aug, Sun-Fri, 10:30am-5pm. The garden may close for private events and functions - please check website for information.

Admission: Gardens & Parkland: Adult £5.00, Conc £4.50, Child (5-16yrs) £3.00, Child (0-5yrs) Free, Groups (15+) £4.00

Parkland: Adult £1.00, Child (0-16yrs) Free.

Key facts: Wedding receptions, conferences, corporate hospitality, country walks, nature reserve, orienteering, film location, product launches, vehicle rallies. Banqueting facilities. For 15+ groups only.

THE FORBIDDEN CORNER LTD

Tupgill Park Estate, Coverham, Nr Middleham North Yorkshire DL8 4TJ

www.theforbiddencorner.co.uk

A unique labyrinth of tunnels, chambers, follies and surprises created in a four acre garden in the heart of the Yorkshire dales. The Temple of the Underworld, The Eye of the Needle, a large pyramid made of translucent glass paths and passageways that lead nowhere. Extraordinary statues at every turn. A day out with a difference that will challenge and delight children and adults of all ages.

Location: Map 10:07. OS Ref SE094 866. A6108 to Middleham, situated 2½ miles west of Middleham on the Coverham Lane.

Owner: Colin R Armstrong CMG, OBE **Contact:** John or Wendy Reeves

Tel: 01969 640638 **E-mail:** forbiddencorner@gmail.com

Open: 1 Apr-31 Oct daily, then every Sun until Christmas. Mon-Sat 12-6pm. Sun & B/H's 10am-6pm (or dusk if earlier). **Admission:** Admissions are by pre-booked tickets only, please phone or book online before your visit. Please see website for up-to-date info & prices. **Key facts:** Gifts & branded mementoes. WCs. Ramps into shop & café. Limited access in gardens. Own blend of barista served coffee, locally sourced food & award-winning pies & teas. Free parking. Special rates available. Guide dogs only. Self-catering cottages all year. Free day pass with all stays over 2 days.

© Fairfax House

FAIRFAX HOUSE

Castlegate, York, North Yorkshire YO1 9RN

www.fairfaxhouse.co.uk

Come and unlock the splendour within one of the finest Georgian townhouses in England. A classical architectural masterpiece with superb period interiors, incomparable stucco ceilings and the outstanding Noel Terry collection of furniture, Fairfax House transports you to the grandeur of 18th Century city living. Don't miss a programme of special events and exhibitions.

Location: Map 11:B9. Centrally located, close to Clifford's Tower & Jorvik Centre. Park & Ride 2 mins away. **Tel:** 01904 655543 **E-mail:** info@fairfaxhouse.co.uk

Open: 5 Feb-31 Dec (closed 24-26 Dec). Tue-Sat & BHs: 10am-5pm. Sun: 11am-4pm. Mon: Guided tours at 11am and 2pm.

Admission: Adult £6.00, Conc. £5.00, Children Free. Daytime and exclusive access evening group tours available, plus catering package options.

Key facts: Suitable for filming. Stunning venue for private dining & drinks receptions. Audio guides in French, German, Italian, Spanish, Polish, Japanese & Chinese Parking in adjacent Clifford's Tower car park. Guide dogs only.

HOVINGHAM HALL

Hovingham, York, North Yorkshire YO62 4LU

www.hovingham.co.uk

Attractive Palladian family home, designed and built by Thomas Worsley. The childhood home of Katharine Worsley, Duchess of Kent. It is entered through a huge riding school and has beautiful rooms with collections of pictures and furniture. The house has attractive gardens with magnificent Yew hedges and cricket ground.

Location: Map 11:C8. OS Ref SE666 756.
18m N of York on Malton/Helmsley Road (B1257).

Owner: Sir William Worsley **Contact:** The Estate Office

Tel: 01653 628771 **Fax:** 01653 628668 **E-mail:** office@hovingham.co.uk

Open: 1-28 Jun inclusive 12.30-4.30pm; Guided tours only (last tour at 3.30pm); Tea Room open daily 1-4.30pm.

Admission: Adult £9.50, Concessions £9.00, Child £5.00, Gardens only £5.00. Family ticket £25.00 (2 adults, 3 children).

Key facts: No photography permitted in the Hall. Partial ground floor only. Obligatory. Limited. None for coaches. Except assistance dogs.

NEWBURGH PRIORY

Coxwold, York, North Yorkshire YO61 4AS

www.newburghpriory.co.uk

Home to the Earls of Fauconberg and the Wombwell family the house was built in 1145 with alterations in 1538 & 1720 and contains the tomb of Oliver Cromwell together with the family collection of art and furniture. The beautiful grounds contain a lake, water garden, walled garden, amazing topiary yews and woodland walks set against the backdrop of the White Horse. The Tea Rooms set in the old kitchens sell a range of delicious teas and homemade cakes. **Location:** Map 11:B8. OS Ref SE541 764. 4m E of A19, 18m N of York, ½ m E of Coxwold.
Owner/Contact: Stephen Wombwell
Tel: 01347 868372 **E-mail:** estateoffice@newburghpriory.co.uk
Open: 2 Apr-28 Jun, Wed & Sun. BH Mon 17 Apr & 28 Aug. Gardens 2-6pm, House 2.30-4.45pm. Tours every ½ hour. Bus parties by prior arrangement. Special tours of private apartments Wed 5, 12, 19, 26 Apr & 3 May, £5.00pp.
Admission: House & Gardens: Adult £8.00, Child £2.00. Gardens only: Adult £4.00, Child Free. **Key facts:** No photography in house. Available for corporate hospitality. Partial. Tea Rooms sells a range of homemade cakes & teas. Obligatory apart from 9 Apr & 28 Aug. New car park for 45 cars & two coaches, additional car parking available. In grounds, on leads. Civil weddings & Wedding receptions throughout the year.

STOCKELD PARK

Off the A661, Wetherby, North Yorkshire LS22 4AN

www.stockeldpark.co.uk

A gracious Palladian mansion by James Paine (1763), featuring a magnificent cantilevered staircase in the central oval hall. Surrounded by beautiful gardens and set in 18th Century landscaped parkland at the heart of a 2000 acre estate. Popular for filming and photography. In 2012 Stockeld Park was winner of Hudsons Best Family Day Out for its Adventure attraction, with interactive, imaginative play indoor and out and famous Enchanted forest.
Location: Map 11:A9. OS Ref SE376 497. York 12m, Harrogate 5m, Leeds 12m.
Owner: Mr and Mrs P G F Grant **Contact:** Mr P Grant
Tel: 01937 586101 **Fax:** 01937 580084 **E-mail:** office@stockeldpark.co.uk
Open: House: Privately booked events and tours only. Contact Estate Office 01937 586101. Please see website for further opening of the adventure site and special events www.stockeldpark.co.uk. Please note we are open throughout all the local school holidays. **Admission:** Prices on application.
Key facts: Fantastic seasonal gift emporium filled with gift ideas. Private event & Wedding enquiries welcome. Homemade & Local, Fully Licensed. Groups, Tours and Groups welcome by appointment. Free Parking. Schools welcome by appointment.

SION HILL HALL

Kirby Wiske, Thirsk, North Yorkshire YO7 4EU

www.sionhillhall.co.uk

A tree lined sweeping driveway leads to the elegant hall, set in 5 acres of inspiring gardens. 'A Masterpiece in the neo-Georgian Style' designed in 1912 by the renowned York architect Walter H Brierley 'the Lutyens of the North'. The hall is exquisitely furnished and hosts a fine collection of art and antiques. Graceful gardens include a formal parterre with clipped box and hornbeam, Long Walk with bountiful herbaceous borders, charming woodland Lower Walk, and a traditional Kitchen Garden. **Location:** Map 11:A7. OS Ref SE373 844.
7m E of A1. 6m S of Northallerton off A167. 4m W of Thirsk.
Owner: Herbert William Mawer Charitable Trust **Contact:** Michael Mallaby
Tel: 01845 587206 **E-mail:** sionhill@btconnect.com
Open: Open throughout the year, by prior arrangement. Please contact to book.
Admission: £14.00 per person (minimum group of 12). Includes a personal welcome and introduction, guided tour of the hall and gardens, and tea/coffee with biscuits served in the original Edwardian kitchens.
Key facts: No photography in the hall. Partial. WC. By arrangement. Min of 12 people. Ample for cars and coaches. Guide dogs only.

© Ed. Remsberg, University of Maryland

The green bedroom at Kiplin Hall

BROCKFIELD HALL

Warthill, York YO19 5XJ

Georgian house (1804) by Peter Atkinson for Benjamin Agar Esq. Mrs. Wood's father was Lord Martin Fitzalan Howard, son of Lady Beaumont of Carlton Towers, Selby. Brockfield has portraits of her Stapleton family. There is a permanent exhibition of paintings by Staithes Group artists, by appointment outside August.
Location: Map 11:C9. OS Ref SE664 550. 5m E of York off A166 or A64.
Owner: Mr & Mrs Simon Wood **Contact:** Simon Wood
Tel: 01904 489362 **E-mail:** simon@brockfieldhall.co.uk
Website: www.brockfieldhall.co.uk
Open: Spring BH Mon (29 May). Daily in Aug from 1-5pm except Mons but including BH Mon. On all the above days there will be three conducted tours by the owner at 1pm, 2.30pm and 4pm.
Admission: Adult £7.00.
Key facts: No photography inside house. By arrangement. In grounds, on leads.

NORTON CONYERS

Wath, Nr Ripon, North Yorkshire HG4 5EQ

Won the 2014 HHA/Sotheby's Restoration Award. Visited by Charlotte Bronte & an original of "Thornfield Hall". Has belonged to the Grahams for 393 years; possesses a special atmosphere in consequence. Family pictures and furniture. Romantic mid-18th Century walled garden with outstanding herbaceous borders. NEW ATTRACTION: Display of historic garden tools.
Location: Map 11:A8. OS Ref SF319 763. 4m NW of Ripon. 3 ½ m from the A1.
Owner: Sir James and Lady Graham **Contact:** Visits Secretary
Tel: 01765 640333 **E-mail:** info@nortonconyers.org.uk
Website: www.nortonconyers.org.uk/www.weddingsatnortonconyers.co.uk
Open: House: 27 Apr-1 May,13-16 & 25-29 May,9-13 & 20-23 Jul, 24-28 Aug, 2-5pm. Last adms. 4.30pm. Garden: Please see our website. Wedding receptions by arrangement. **Admission:** House: £15.00 (Flat shoes MUST be worn). Garden: Free, except for charity days & group bookings. **Key facts:** Orangery and garden for hire. Partial. WC. By arrangement. On leads in garden only.

SUTTON PARK

Sutton-On-The-Forest, N. Yorkshire YO61 1DP

The Yorkshire home of Sir Reginald and Lady Sheffield. Early Georgian architecture. Magnificent plasterwork by Cortese. Rich collection of 18th Century furniture. Award-winning gardens attract enthusiasts from home and abroad. Tranquil Caravan and Camping Club CL Site also available for Rallies. Woodland Walk. Tea Rooms. **Location:** Map 11:B9. OS Ref SE583 646. 8 miles N of York on B1363 York-Helmsley Road follow brown signs
Contact: Administrator **Tel:** 01347 810249 **Fax:** 01347 811251
E-mail: suttonpark@statelyhome.co.uk **Website:** www.statelyhome.co.uk
Open: Private parties all year by appointment (min. charge for 15).
For House and gardens opening dates in 2017, tour times & admission prices see website for details.
Key facts: No photography. Flower Power Fairs www.flowerpowerfairs.co.uk Partial. WCs. Tea Rooms. Obligatory. Limited for coaches. Woodland Walk only.

ASKE HALL

Richmond, North Yorkshire DL10 5HJ

A predominantly Georgian collection of paintings, furniture and porcelain in house which has been the seat of the Dundas family since 1763.
Location: Map 10:P6. OS Ref NZ179 035. 4m SW of A1 at Scotch Corner, 2m from the A66, B6274. **Tel:** 01748 822000 **E-mail:** mandy.blenkiron@aske.co.uk
Website: www.aske.co.uk **Open:** 7 & 8 Sep (Heritage Open Days)
Tours at 10, 11 & 12. **Admission:** Free.

HELMSLEY CASTLE

Castlegate, Helmsley, York YO62 5AB

Discover how the castle evolved over the centuries, from a mighty medieval fortress to a luxurious Tudor mansion, to a Civil War stronghold and a romantic Victorian ruin. **Location:** Map 11:B7. OS Ref SE612 837. **Tel:** 01904 601946
Website: www.english-heritage.org.uk **Open:** Jan-Mar, Sat & Sun, 10-4pm; daily at half term; Apr-Oct, daily, 10-5pm; Nov-Dec, daily, 10-4pm.
Admission: Adult £6.40; Child £3.80.

NUNNINGTON HALL

Nunnington, North Yorkshire YO62 5UY

Picturesque Yorkshire manor house with organic garden and exciting exhibitions.
Location: Map 11:C8. OS Ref SE669 793. **Tel:** 01439 748283
E-mail: nunningtonhall@nationaltrust.org.uk
Website: www.nationaltrust.org.uk/nunnington-hall
Open: Mar-Oct, Wed-Sun, 11-5pm; 4 Nov-10 Dec, Sat & Sun, 11-4pm.
Admission: Adult £8.25; Child £4.15.

SCAMPSTON WALLED GARDEN

Scampston Hall, Malton, North Yorkshire YO17 8NG

A contemporary garden with striking perennial meadow planting that explodes with colour in the summer. Created by acclaimed designer and plantsman, Piet Oudolf. **Location:** Map 11:D8. OS Ref SE865 755.
Tel: 01944 759111 **E-mail:** info@scampston.co.uk
Website: www.scampston.co.uk/gardens **Open:** 14 Apr- 30 Oct, Tue-Sun, BH Mons, 10-5pm. **Admission:** Adult £7.50; Child £4.

TREASURER'S HOUSE

Minster Yard, York, North Yorkshire YO1 7JL

Named after the Treasurer of York Minster, the house is not all that it first seems! The size and splendour and contents of the house are a constant surprise.
Location: Map 11:B9. OS Ref SE604 523. **Tel:** 01904 624247
Website: www.nationaltrust.org.uk/treasurers-house-york
Open: 1 Mar-31 Oct, daily, 11am-4.30pm; 9 Nov-17 Dec, Thu-Sun, 11am-4.30pm. **Admission:** Adult £7.20; Child £3.50.

BRODSWORTH HALL & GARDENS

Brodsworth, Nr Doncaster, Yorkshire DN5 7XJ

Inside this beautiful Victorian country house almost everything has been left exactly as it was when it was still a family home. **Location:** Map 11:B12. OS Ref SE506 070. **Tel:** 01302 722598 **E-mail:** customers@english-heritage.org.uk
Website: www.english-heritage.org.uk/brodsworthhall
Open: Gardens: Weekends all year, 10-4pm; half terms, Apr-Sep, 10-6pm; 1-31 Oct, 10-5pm. House: Apr-Oct, 11-5pm. **Admission:** Adult £11.50; Child £6.90.

CONISBROUGH CASTLE

Castle Hill, Conisbrough, Doncaster DN12 3BU

Medieval fortress with unique cylindrical keep; setting of Sir Walter Scott's Ivanhoe.
Location: Map 7:A1. OS Ref SK515 989.
Tel: 01709 863329 **E-mail:** enquiries@english-heritage.org.uk
Website: www.conisbroughcastle.org.uk
Open: Winter, Sat & Sun, 10-4pm; Mar-Sep, daily, 10-6pm; Oct, daily 10-5pm.
Admission: Adult £5.70; Child £3.40.

WENTWORTH WOODHOUSE

The Mansion, Wentworth, Rotherham S62 7TQ

A grand Georgian house with two distinct façades. **Location:** Map 7:A1. OS Ref SK393 978. Enter by driveway on Cortworth Lane, (opp Clayfields Lane) & ignore Private Signs. Park near house. **Tel:** 01226 351161 **E-mail:** tours@wentworthwoodhouse.co.uk **Website:** www.wentworthwoodhouse.co.uk
Open: Consult our website **Admission:** Consult our website.

Markenfield Hall

VISITOR INFORMATION

Owner
The Earl and Countess of Harewood

Address
Harewood House
Harewood
Leeds
West Yorkshire
LS17 9LG

Location
Map 10:P10
OS Ref. SE311 446
A1 N or S to Wetherby. A659 via Collingham, Harewood is on A61 between Leeds and Harrogate. Easily reached from A1, M1, M62 and M18. 40 mins from York, 20 mins from centre of Leeds or Harrogate.

Bus: No. 36 from Leeds or Harrogate.

Rail: London Kings Cross to Leeds/Harrogate 2hrs 20 mins. Leeds/Harrogate Station 7m.

Air: Leeds Bradford Airport 9m.

Contact
Harewood House
Tel: 0113 218 1010
E-mail:
info@harewood.org

Opening Times
House, Gardens, Grounds, Bird Garden, Farm Experience, Courtyard, and Bookshop open from 24 Mar-29 Oct 2017.

Please see website or call our team for details.

Admission
Please see website.

Conference/Function
Private venue hire available.

The North Front, Harewood House

© Simon Warner & Harewood House Trust

HAREWOOD HOUSE & GARDENS

www.harewood.org

Explore one of Yorkshire's most loved country houses with award winning gardens and grounds.

Built 1759, Harewood House is the seat of the Earl and Countess of Harewood. The magnificent Georgian building has remained within the Lascelles family since its construction and has retained much of its original splendour. Designed by renowned Georgian architect John Carr, furnished by Thomas Chippendale and with interiors by Robert Adam, Harewood House offers visitors the chance to unearth striking, original features and experience the grandeur of one of Yorkshire's finest country houses.

In each room, friendly guides are on hand to offer insights into the history and detail of the house, including the extensive art collections. From El Greco, JMW Turner and Joshua Reynolds to Epstein, Sidney Nolan and Gaudier-Brzeska, there is a diverse range on offer, spanning centuries of patronage.

Representing one of Capability Brown's most important designs, the Grade 1 listed parkland has remained unchanged since it was created in the late 18th Century. With a 32 acre lake, soft rolling hills and mature, established tree lines, you can experience the idyllic, picturesque views Brown imagined for Harewood.

With over 100 acres of grounds and gardens to explore, from the informal Himalayan Garden which bursts into life in May, to the productive Walled Garden surrounded by warm red brick walls, visitors won't be disappointed.

Visitors can also enjoy contemporary art exhibitions, the rare Bird Garden, the Farm Experience, and a selection of popular cafés. Whether you want to visit the house and its awe-inspiring collections or enjoy the beautiful gardens, Harewood provides a wonderful day of discovery.

The house was recently used as a set for ITV's 'Victoria' series. Throughout 2017, the opulent rooms on the State Floor will come to life with costumes from the programme including dresses worn by Jenna Coleman who plays Queen Victoria. These will be on display alongside personal objects from Harewood's collection. Highlights includes a beautiful miniature by the English School of Queen Victoria, a writing set she owned, and letters written by the 2nd Countess of Harewood about Victoria's visit to the house in 1835.

KEY FACTS

- Please see website for further information.
- Gifts, souvenirs, postcards and publications.
- Fine Dining in house and private venue hire available.
- WCs. No access to State Rooms for electric wheelchairs. Courtesy wheelchair.
- Terrace Café. Licensed.
- Courtyard Café - Licensed.
- Guided tours by prior arrangement.
- Free. Designated for blue badge holders.
- Sandford Award for Education. School parties welcome.
- On leads. Service dogs welcome except in Bird Garden and Farm Experience.

The Music Room, Harewood House

© Paul Barker & Harewood House Trust

The Terrace, Harewood House

© Lee Beel & Harewood House Trust

LOTHERTON HALL

Aberford, Leeds, West Yorkshire LS25 3EB

www.leeds.gov.uk/lothertonhall

Explore this Edwardian country estate with extensive grounds, historic house, deer park, gardens and children's playgrounds. Discover the stories of this fantastic country home, once the home of the Gascoigne family; housing a wonderful collection of fine and decorative arts, as well as a dedicated Fashion Gallery. From the bird garden, to the woodland play area, to stunning nature trails, this historic estate really has got something for everyone.

Location: Map 11:B10. OS Ref SE450 360.
Owner: Leeds City Council
Contact: Visitor Services
Tel: 0113 378 2959
E-mail: lotherton.hall@leeds.gov.uk
Open: Please check the website or call for seasonal opening dates.
Admission: Please check the website for current admission prices.
Key facts: We welcome group visits, please call to arrange your day out. Passenger lift in the House.

TEMPLE NEWSAM

Temple Newsam Road, Leeds LS15 OAE

www.leeds.gov.uk/templenewsam

Discover 500 years of history in this beautiful country mansion set within 1500 acres of parkland. Explore rooms filled with fine and decorative art treasures and uncover the secrets of past residents. One of the great country houses of England, this Tudor-Jacobean mansion was the birthplace of Lord Darnley, husband of Mary Queen of Scots. Rich in beautifully restored interiors, the house includes a wealth of paintings, Chippendale furniture, textiles, silver and ceramics.

Location: Map 10:P10. OS Ref SE358 321. 4m E of city centre B6159 or 2m from M1 junction 46. 4 miles from city centre.
Owner: Leeds City Council
Contact: Visitor Services
Tel: 0113 3367460 **E-mail:** temple.newsam.house@leeds.gov.uk
Open: Please check the website or call 0113 336 7460 for seasonal opening times.
Admission: Please check the website or call 0113 336 7460 for admission prices.
Key facts: We welcome group visits, please call to arrange your day out.

© John Whitaker

YORK GATE GARDEN

Back Church Lane, Adel, Leeds LS16 8DW

www.yorkgate.org.uk

Inspirational one acre garden widely recognised as one of Britain's finest small gardens. A series of smaller gardens with different themes and in contrasting styles are linked by a succession of delightful vistas. Striking architectural features play a key role throughout the garden which is noted for its exquisite planting details and Arts and Crafts features.

Location: Map 10:P10. OS Ref 275 403. 2¼m SE of Bramhope, just off A660.
Owner: Perennial - Gardeners' Royal Benevolent Society
Contact: Garden Administrator
Tel: 0113 267 8240 **E-mail:** yorkgate@perennial.org.uk
Open: 2 Apr-27 Sep, Sun to Thu and BH Mons, 12:30pm-4:30pm.
Admission: Standard £5.00. Gift Aid £5.50. Child (16 & under) and Carers Free. Annual Friends Membership £25.00 per annum. POA for groups.
Key facts: Groups welcome by appointment. Please call for additional details. Wide selection of locally sourced items, garden gear, cards and gifts. Seasonal plants available from greenhouse and garden selected by Head Gardener. Private catering available. Cheery Tea Room open for drinks, freshly made cakes & light bites. By arrangement and on most Sundays. Local parking by the church on Church Lane. Assistance dogs only.

EAST RIDDLESDEN HALL

Bradford Road, Riddlesden, Keighley, W. Yorkshire BD20 5EL

Once the home of 17th Century merchant James Murgatroyd. No visit is complete without a relaxing stroll around the intimate gardens.
Location: Map 10:O10. OS Ref SE07914 208. **Tel:** 01535 607075
E-mail: eastriddlesden@nationaltrust.org.uk **Website:** www.nationaltrust.org.uk
Open: Apr-Oct & Feb half term, Sat-Wed, 10.30-4.30pm; 4 Nov-17 Dec, Sat & Sun, 11-4pm. **Admission:** Adult £6.20; Child £3.

LEDSTON HALL

Hall Lane, Ledston, Castleford, West Yorkshire WF10 2BB

17th Century mansion with some earlier work, lawned grounds.
Location: Map 11:A11. OS Ref SE437 289. 2m N of Castleford, off A656.
Tel: 01423 707838 **E-mail:** victoria.walton@carterjonas.co.uk
Website: www.whelerfoundation.co.uk
Open: Exterior only: May-Aug: Mon-Fri, 9am-4pm. Other days by appointment.
Admission: Free.

NOSTELL PRIORY & PARKLAND

Doncaster Road, Wakefield, West Yorkshire WF4 1QE

One of Yorkshire's jewels, an architectural treasure by James Paine with later additions by Robert Adam. **Location:** Map 11:A11. OS Ref SE403 175.
Tel: 01924 863892 **E-mail:** nostellpriory@nationaltrust.org.uk **Website:** www.nationaltrust.org.uk **Open:** Gardens: 1 Jan-28 Feb, 10-4pm; 1 Mar-29 Oct, 10-5pm; 30 Oct-31 Dec, 10-4pm. House: 1 Mar-29 Oct, Wed-Sun, 1-5pm; 2 Dec-17 Dec, Sat & Sun, 10-4pm. **Admission:** Adult £10.50; Child £5.25.

ALLERTON PARK
Knaresborough, North Yorkshire HG5 0SE
Tel: 01423 330927

BARLEY HALL
2 Coffee Yard, Off Stonegate, York YO1 8AR
Tel: 01904 610275 **E-mail:** dscott@yorkat.co.uk

BENINGBROUGH HALL & GARDENS
Beningbrough, North Yorkshire YO30 1DD
Tel: 01904 472027 **E-mail:** beningbrough@nationaltrust.org.uk

BOLTON ABBEY
Skipton, North Yorkshire BD23 6EX
Tel: 01756 718009 **E-mail:** tourism@boltonabbey.com

BOLTON CASTLE
Nr Leyburn, North Yorkshire DL8 4ET
Tel: 01969 623981 **E-mail:** info@boltoncastle.co.uk

CLIFFORD'S TOWER
Tower Street, York YO1 9SA
Tel: 01904 646940 **E-mail:** customers@english-heritage.org.uk

FOUNTAINS ABBEY & STUDLEY ROYAL
Ripon, North Yorkshire HG4 3DY
Tel: 01765 608888 **E-mail:** fountainsabbey@nationaltrust.org.uk

THE GEORGIAN THEATRE ROYAL
Victoria Road, Richmond, North Yorkshire DL10 4DW
Tel: 01748 823710 **E-mail:** admin@georgiantheatreroyal.co.uk

HELMSLEY WALLED GARDEN
Cleveland Way, Helmsley, North Yorkshire YO62 5AH
Tel: 01439 771427 **E-mail:** info@helmsleywalledgarden.org.uk

JERVAULX ABBEY
Ripon, North Yorkshire HG4 4PH
Tel: 01677 460226

MIDDLEHAM CASTLE
Castle Hill, Middleham, Leyburn, North Yorkshire DL8 4QR
Tel: 01969 623899

ORMESBY HALL
Ladgate Lane, Ormesby, Middlesbrough TS7 9AS
Tel: 01642 324188 **E-mail:** ormesbyhall@nationaltrust.org.uk

PARCEVALL HALL GARDENS
Skyreholme, Nr Appletreewick, North Yorkshire BD23 6DE
Tel: 01756 720311 **E-mail:** parcevallhall@btconnect.com

RHS GARDEN HARLOW CARR
Crag Lane, Harrogate, North Yorkshire HG3 1QB
Tel: 01423 565418 **E-mail:** harlowcarr@rhs.org.uk

RICHMOND CASTLE
Richmond, North Yorkshire DL10 4QW
Tel: 01748 822493 **E-mail:** caroline.topps@english-heritage.org.uk

RIEVAULX TERRACE & TEMPLES
The National Trust, Rievaulx, North Yorkshire YO62 5LJ
Tel: 01723 870423 **E-mail:** nunningtonhall@nationaltrust.org.uk

RIPON CATHEDRAL
Ripon, North Yorkshire HG4 1QR
Tel: 01765 602072

SCARBOROUGH CASTLE
Castle Road, Scarborough, North Yorkshire YO11 1HY
Tel: 01723 383636 **E-mail:** scarborough.castle@english-heritage.org.uk

SHANDY HALL
Coxwold, Thirsk, North Yorkshire YO61 4AD
Tel: 01347 868465 **E-mail:** shandyhall@dial.pipex.com

THORP PERROW ARBORETUM
Bedale, North Yorkshire DL8 2PR
Tel: 01677 425323 **E-mail:** enquiries@thorpperrow.com

WHITBY ABBEY
Whitby, North Yorkshire YO22 4JT
Tel: 01947 603568 **E-mail:** customers@english-heritage.org.uk

CANNON HALL MUSEUM, PARK & GARDENS
Cawthorne, Barnsley, South Yorkshire S75 4AT
Tel: 01226 790270 **E-mail:** cannonhall@barnsley.gov.uk

CUSWORTH HALL, MUSEUM & PARK
Cusworth Lane, Doncaster DN5 7TU
Tel: 01302 782342 **E-mail:** museum@doncaster.gov.uk

WENTWORTH CASTLE GARDENS
Lowe Lane, Stainborough, Barnsley, South Yorkshire S75 3ET
Tel: 01226 776040 **E-mail:** heritagetrust@wentworthcastle.org

BRAMHAM PARK
The Estate Office, Bramham Park, Bramham LS23 6ND
Tel: 01937 846000 **E-mail:** enquiries@bramhampark.co.uk

BRONTE PARSONAGE MUSEUM
Church Street, Haworth BD22 8DR
Tel: 01535 642323 **E-mail:** lauren.livesey@bronte.org.uk

CLIFFE CASTLE MUSEUM
Spring Gardens Lane, Keighley BD20 6LH
Tel: 01274 431212 **E-mail:** cartwright.hall@bradford.gov.uk

OAKWELL HALL & RED HOUSE
Nutter Lane, Birstall WF17 9LG / Oxford Rd, Gomersal BD19 4JP
E-mail: oakwell.hall@kirklees.gov.uk / red.house@kirklees.gov.uk

PONTEFRACT CASTLE
Castle Chain, Pontefract, West Yorkshire WF8 1QH
Tel: 01977 723 440 **E-mail:** castles@wakefield.gov.uk

SHIBDEN HALL
Lister's Road, Halifax, West Yorkshire HX3 6XG
Tel: 01422 352246 **E-mail:** shibden.hall@calderdale.gov.uk

Harewood House & Gardens, State Bedroom, Leeds

© Paul Barker and Harewood House Trust

Holker Hall, Cumbria

Bramall Hall, Merseyside

Cheshire
Cumbria
Lancashire
Manchester
Merseyside

North West

The English Lakes are famous as a holiday destination but your efforts to go a little further into less frequented parts of Cumbria and Lancashire will be well rewarded.

ADLINGTON HALL & GARDENS

MILL LANE, ADLINGTON, MACCLESFIELD, CHESHIRE SK10 4LF

www.adlingtonhall.com

Adlington Hall, home of the Leghs from 1315 was built on the site of a Hunting Lodge in the Forest of Macclesfield in 1040. Two oaks, part of the original building, remain rooted in the ground supporting the east end of the Great Hall. Between the trees in the Great Hall stands an organ built by 'Father' Bernard Smith. Played on by Handel.

The Gardens, laid out over many centuries, include a Lime walk planted in 1688 and a Regency rockery surrounding the Shell Cottage. The Wilderness area includes a Rococo styled landscape garden containing the chinoserie T'Ing House, a Pagoda bridge and the classical Temple to Diana. The 60 acres of gardens also include the stunning Rose Garden and Yew Tree Maze.

Location: Map 6:N2. OS Ref SJ905 804. 5m N of Macclesfield, A523,13m S of Manchester. London 178m.

Contact: Emma Joyce or Philippa Reed **Tel:** 01625 827595

E-mail: enquiries@adlingtonhall.com

Open: Apr 16, 17, 23, 30. May 1, 7, 14, 21, 28, 29. Jun 4, 11, 18, 25. Jul 2, 9, 16, 23, 30. Aug 6, 13, 20, 27, 28. Sep 3, 10, 17, 24.

Admission: House & Gardens: Adult £9.00, Child £5.00, Student £5.00, Gardens only: Adult £6.00, Child Free, Student Free, Groups of 20+ £8.50.

Key facts: Beautiful venue for Weddings and Celebrations. Plant Hunters Fair Sunday 7 May 2017. Corporate hospitality available - please call or check website for more detail. WCs. Tea Room open on Hall open days. Offering a selection of hot and cold drinks and homemade cakes and scones. Groups of 20 or more by arrangement. Well behaved dogs allowed in the grounds on leads.

CAPESTHORNE HALL

SIDDINGTON, MACCLESFIELD, CHESHIRE SK11 9JY

www.capesthorne.com

Capesthorne Hall, built between 1719 and 1732 and set in 100 acres of picturesque Cheshire parkland, has been touched by nearly 1,000 years of history. The Hall has a fascinating collection of fine art, marble sculptures, furniture and tapestries. In the grounds enjoy the family Chapel, the 18th Century Italian Milanese Gates, the beautiful lakeside gardens and woodland walks.

The hall can be hired for civil weddings and corporate events.

Location: Map 6:N2. OS Ref SJ840 727. 5m W of Macclesfield. 30 mins S of Manchester on A34. Near M6, M60 and M62.

Owner: Sir William and Lady Bromley-Davenport **Contact:** Christine Mountney

Tel: 01625 861221 **E-mail:** info@capesthorne.com

Open: Apr-Oct Suns\Mons & BHs. Hall: 1.30-4pm. Last admission 3.30pm. Gardens & Chapel: 12-5pm. Groups welcome by appointment.

Admission: Suns & BHs - Hall, Gardens & Chapel: Adult £9.00, Child (5-16 yrs) £5.00, Senior £8.00, Family £25.00. Suns - Gardens & Chapel only: Adult £6.50, Child (5-16 yrs) £3.00 and Senior £5.50. Mons Only- Park, Gardens & Chapel: per car £10.00. Hall Entrance: per person £3.00. Group discounts available.

Key facts: Available for civil weddings, filming, corporate functions, festivals, activity days, garden parties. Caravan Park 4* AA Rated, open Mar-Oct inclusive.

Catering can be provided for groups (full menus on request). Partial. WC.

The Butler's Pantry offers light refreshments including afternoon teas.

Guided tours available for pre-booked parties (except Suns).

100 cars/20 coaches on hard-standing and unlimited in park.

Pre-booked educational visits available.

Licensed for civil weddings.

CHOLMONDELEY CASTLE GARDEN

MALPAS, CHESHIRE SY14 8AH

www.cholmondeleycastle.com

Cholmondeley Castle Garden is said by many to be among the most romantically beautiful gardens they have seen. Even the wild orchids, daisies and buttercups take on an aura of glamour in this beautifully landscaped setting with extensive ornamental gardens dominated by a romantic Castle built in 1801 of local sandstone. Visitors can enjoy the tranquil Temple Water Garden, Ruin Water Garden, memorial mosaic designed by Maggy Howarth, Rose garden and many mixed borders. Lakeside walk, picnic area, children's play areas and adventure den, farm animals including llamas and alpacas. Tea Room.

Location: Map 6:L3. OS Ref SJ540 515. Off A41 Chester/Whitchurch Rd. & A49 Whitchurch/ Tarporley Road. 7m N of Whitchurch. Sat Nav. SY14 8ET.

Owner: The Marquess of Cholmondeley.

Contact: The Secretary **Tel:** 01829 720383

E-mail: dilys@cholmondeleycastle.co.uk

Open: Sun 2 Apr-Thu 29 Sep 2017 Wed, Thu, Sun & Bank Holidays 11am-5pm (last entry 4.30pm). Open Suns only in Oct for Autumn Tints.

Admission: Adult £7.00, Child £4.00 under 5's free. (reduction for groups to gardens of 25+). For special events and variations to opening dates please refer to our website www.cholmondeleycastle.com.

Key facts: Partial access, disabled WCs and access to Tea Room. Our friendly Tea Room is uniquely situated in the very heart of the gardens serving a range of specialist teas, homemade cakes, light lunches & Snugbury's ice cream etc. All freshly prepared to order. On leads.

LYME

DISLEY, STOCKPORT, CHESHIRE SK12 2NX

www.nationaltrust.org.uk/lyme

Much-loved home of the Legh family for more than 600 years, Lyme sits in 570 hectares (1,400 acres) of deer-park, with glorious views across Manchester and the Cheshire Plain. Its lavish interiors reflect the life of a great estate. Discover the stories of Lyme's Regency heyday when Thomas Legh brought a tired and neglected estate back to life. You may recognise Lyme as 'Pemberley' from the BBC adaptation of Pride and Prejudice, starring Colin Firth, and the 'Big House' in series two of The Village. Lyme's ever-changing gardens with the Reflection Lake, Orangery and Rose Garden, are an ideal place to relax and stroll.

Location: Map 6:N2. OS Ref SJ965 825.
Off the A6 at Disley. 6½m SE of Stockport. M60 J1.

Owner: National Trust

Contact: The Visitor Experience Manager

Tel: 01663 762023 **Fax:** 01663 765035 **E-mail:** lyme@nationaltrust.org.uk

Open: House: 11 Feb-5 Nov, 11am-5pm (last entry 4pm), Mon, Tue, Fri-Sun. House also open Thu, 27 Jul-31 Aug. Garden: 11 Feb-5 Nov, 11am-5pm (last entry 4.30pm), Mon-Sun. Please call for Winter opening times.

Admission: Please visit the website for ticket prices. NT members free.

Key facts: Licensed. Licensed. Limited for coaches. Guide dogs only. East Lodge. A beautiful Edwardian cottage built in 1904, with two bedrooms, sleeps 4 (one double, one twin), dogs welcome. Enjoy spectacular views of Manchester and the Peak District. Closed Christmas Day.

PEOVER HALL & GARDENS

OVER PEOVER, KNUTSFORD WA16 9HW

www.peoverhall.com

A Grade 2* listed Elizabethan family house dating from 1585. Situated within some 500 acres of landscaped 18th Century parkland with formal gardens designed between 1890-1900 that include a series of "garden rooms" filled with clipped box, lily ponds, Romanesque loggia, warm brick walls, unusual doors, secret passageways, beautiful topiary work, herb and walled gardens. The grounds of the Hall house working stables, estate cottages and the parish church of St Laurence which, contains two Mainwaring Chapels. The architectural jewel Grade I listed Carolean stables built in 1654, with richly carved stalls and original Tuscan columns and strap work.

Location: Map 6:M2. OS Ref SJ772 734. 4m S of Knutsford off A50 at Whipping Stocks Inn. Further directions on website, satnav leads down an unsuitable road.

Owner: Mr R Brooks

Contact: Fisher German LLP

General Enquiries: via Fisher German LLP - 01565 757980

E-mail: bookings@peoverhall.com

Open: 2017 May-Aug, Tue & Thu afternoons. Stables & Gardens open between 2-5pm. Tours of Peover Hall at 2.30pm & 3.30pm.

The Church is open 2pm-4pm.

Admission: Please see website for updated admission prices.

Key facts: Obligatory.

© @yvonnemetcalf2011

© @yvonnemetcalf2011

TABLEY HOUSE

TABLEY LANE, KNUTSFORD, CHESHIRE WA16 0HB

www.tableyhouse.co.uk

The finest Palladian House in the North West, Tabley a Grade I listing, was designed by John Carr of York for the Leicester family. It contains one of the first collections of English paintings, including works of art by Turner, Reynolds, Lawrence, Lely and Dobson. Furniture by Chippendale, Bullock and Gillow and fascinating family memorabilia adorn the rooms. Fine plasterwork by Thomas Oliver and carving by Daniel Shillito and Mathew Bertram. Interesting Tea Room and 17th Century Chapel adjoin, including Burne-Jones window.

Location: Map 6:M2. OS Ref SJ725 777.

M6/J19, A556 S on to A5033. 2m W of Knutsford.

Owner: The University of Manchester

Contact: The Administrator

Tel: 01565 750151 **E-mail:** tableyhouse@btconnect.com

Open: House: Apr-end Oct: Thu-Sun & BHs, 1-5pm.

Last admission at 4.30pm.

Tea Room open from 12-5pm.

Admission: Adult £5.00. Child/Student £1.50. Groups by arrangement.

Key facts: No photography in galleries. No stiletto heels. Heel guards can be provided. Suitable for drinks receptions & presentations for up to 100 people. Call the office before arriving to arrange for lift entrance to be opened. Serving light lunches, afternoon teas, refreshments & homemade cakes. By arrangement, also available outside normal opening hours, guides provided at no extra charge. Free. Suitable for post 16 students. Guide dogs only. Civil Wedding & Partnerships Licence. Naming Ceremonies & Renewal of Vows.

Register for news and special offers at www.hudsonsheritage.com

ARLEY HALL & GARDENS

Northwich, Cheshire CW9 6NA

www.arleyhallandgardens.com

A cherished family home owned for over 550 years. Renowned features include the double herbaceous border, pleached Lime Avenues, Ilex Columns, Cruck Barn and Chapel. The Hall (Grade II*) built in the Victorian Jacobean style, with elaborate ceilings & oak panelling, impressive fireplaces, intricate stained glass and beautiful contents. **Location:** Map 6:M2. OS Ref SJ675 809.

Owner: Viscount & Viscountess Ashbrook **Contact:** Helen Begent

Tel: 01565 777353 **E-mail:** helen.begent@arleyhallandgardens.com

Open: Gardens: Mar-Oct, Mon-Sun 11am-5pm. The Hall: Mar-Oct, Sun, Tue & BHs 12noon-5pm. Parts of the Gardens are also open Nov-Feb, 11am-dusk.

Admission: Gardens Mar-Oct: Adult £8.50, Child (5-12yrs) £3.50, Senior £8.00, Family (2+2) £20.00. Hall & Gardens Mar-Oct: Adult £11.00, Child (5-12yrs) £4.50, Senior £10.00, Family (2+2) £25.00. Group rates are available please visit the website. **Key facts:** Family Adventure Playzone, Filming, Weddings & Corporate Events. Contact the plant nursery on 01565 777 479 Downstairs in The Hall, most of the gardens, café and WCs. Free. All dogs on a lead. See website for details.

Capesthorne Hall

COMBERMERE ABBEY

Whitchurch, Shropshire SY13 4AJ

www.combermereabbey.co.uk

Combermere Abbey, its large mere and 1000 acre parkland celebrates almost 900 years of history. The Cistercian monastery est. in 1133 was dissolved in 1536. The estate offers luxury accommodation and is licensed for weddings.

Location: Map 6:L4. OS Ref SJ599 434. 5m E of Whitchurch, off A530.

Owner: Mrs S Callander Beckett **Contact:** Administrator

Tel: 01948 662880 **E-mail:** estate@combermereabbey.co.uk

Open: Public Tours: 4 Apr-8 Jul advance booking essential.
Group visits (20-30) by arrangement (Apr-Oct).
Bluebell Walk: Sun 23 Apr 1-4pm.
Garden Open Afternoons: Wed -31 May, 21 Jun, 26 Jul, 30 Aug, 27 Sep, 1-4pm.

Admission: Open days: Adult £7.00, Child (U16) £4.00. Group tours: £12.00pp incl of refreshments. Bluebell Walk & Garden Open Afternoons: Adult £5.00

Key facts: No photography in the house.

DORFOLD HALL

Acton, Nr Nantwich, Cheshire CW5 8LD

www.dorfoldhall.com

Jacobean country house built in 1616 for Ralph Wilbraham. Family home of the Roundells. Beautiful plaster ceilings and oak panelling. Attractive woodland gardens and summer herbaceous borders.

Location: Map 6:L3. OS Ref SJ634 525. 1m W of Nantwich on the A534 Nantwich-Wrexham road.

Owner/Contact: Charles Roundell

Tel: 01270 625245

Fax: 01270 628723

E-mail: info@dorfold.com

Open: Apr-Oct: Tue only and BH Mons, 2-5pm.

Admission: Adult £7.00, Child £3.00.

Key facts: Obligatory.
Limited. Narrow gates with low arch prevent coaches. Access for coaches from a different entrance. Please contact the hall.

© National Trust Images/Robert Thrift

DUNHAM MASSEY

Altrincham, Cheshire WA14 4SJ

www.nationaltrust.org.uk/dunhammassey

In 1856 Victorian carriages rolled along the avenues of Dunham's deer-park laden with the family's most treasured possessions. Having suffered the rejection of Cheshire society, Catherine, a former circus performer, and her husband, the 7th Earl, left Dunham and never returned. We take you on Catherine and George Harry's journey to consider what it might be like to leave this home. The newly-opened historic stable buildings tell the story of horses and the motor car at Dunham. **Location:** Map 6:M1. OS Ref SJ735 874. 3m SW of Altrincham off A56. M6/J19. M56/J7. Station Altrincham (Train & Metro) 3m.
Owner: National Trust **Contact:** Visitor Experience
Tel: 0161 941 1025 **E-mail:** dunhammassey@nationaltrust.org.uk
Open: Please see website. **Admission:** House & Garden: £14.00, Child £7.00, Family £35.00. Groups (15+) £11.50, Child £5.70. Garden only: £8.80, Child £4.40, Family £22.00 Groups (15+) £7.00, Child £3.50. Parking: Cars £6.00, Motorbikes £1.50, Coaches £20. **Key facts:** Photography permitted, no flash or tripods. Large gift shop selling homewares & local produce. Plant sales area; seasonal bulbs & ornamental plants. Good access to most of property. Access to house is limited. Indoor & outdoor seating, range of light meals & snacks. Licensed. £6.00 Free to NT members. Dedicated walking area in North Park. Park, garden, shop & café.

GAWSWORTH HALL

Macclesfield, Cheshire SK11 9RN

www.gawsworthhall.com

Fully lived-in Tudor half-timbered manor house with Tilting Ground. Former home of Mary Fitton, Maid of Honour at the Court of Queen Elizabeth I, and the supposed 'Dark Lady' of Shakespeare's sonnets. Fine pictures, sculpture, furniture and beautiful grounds adjoining a medieval church. Garden Theatre performances take place in the Hall courtyard in July and August.
Location: Map 6:N2. OS Ref SJ892 697. 3m S of Macclesfield on the A536 Congleton to Macclesfield road.
Owner: Mr and Mrs T Richards **Contact:** Mr J Richards
Tel: 01260 223456
E-mail: gawsworthhall@btinternet.com
Open: See www.gawsworthhall.com.
Admission: Adult £7.50, Child £3.50. Groups (20+) £6.00.
Key facts: Partial. WCs. Licensed. Licensed. Guided tours by arrangement. In grounds.

RODE HALL

Church Lane, Scholar Green, Cheshire ST7 3QP

www.rodehall.co.uk

Rode Hall is a fine early 18th Century country house with a beautiful collection of English porcelain, set in a Repton landscape. Home to the Wilbraham family since 1669, the extensive gardens include a woodland garden, formal rose garden designed by Nesfield in 1860 and a stunning two acre walled kitchen garden which provides produce for the monthly farmers' market and delightful Tea Rooms. Rode Pool has its own heronry on Birthday Island and the icehouse in the park is well worth a visit. **Location:** Map 6:M3. OS Ref SJ819 573. 5m SW of Congleton between the A34 & A50. Kidsgrove railway station 2m NW of Kidsgrove.
Owner/Contact: Randle Baker Wilbraham
Tel: 01270 873237 **E-mail:** enquiries@rodehall.co.uk
Open: 5 Apr-27 Sep, Weds & BH Mons. Gardens 11am-5pm, House 12-4pm. Groups welcome by appointment on alternative days. The gardens are also open alongside the monthly farmers' market on the first Sat of every month, (exc Jan) 9am-1pm. Snowdrop Walks 4 Feb-5 Mar, Tue-Sun 11am-4pm (Closed Mons). Bluebell Walks 29 Apr-7 May. **Admission:** House & Garden: Adult £8.00, Conc £7.00, Child £2.00. Gardens: Adult £5.00, Child £2.00.
Key facts: Light lunches & cream teas. Homemade cakes & refreshments. On leads.

BEESTON CASTLE

Chapel Lane, Beeston, Tarporley, Cheshire CW6 9TX

Standing majestically on a sheer rocky crag, Beeston offers perhaps the most stunning views of any castle in England. **Location:** Map 6:L3. OS Ref SJ537 593.
Tel: 01829 260464 **Website:** www.english-heritage.org.uk/beeston
Open: 2 Jan-Mar & Nov-Dec, Sat & Sun, 10-4pm; daily at half term; Apr-Oct, daily, 10-5pm. **Admission:** Adult £7.40; Child £4.40.

LITTLE MORETON HALL

Congleton, Cheshire CW12 4SD

Begun in 1504 and completed 100 years later, Little Moreton Hall is regarded as the finest example of a timber-framed moated manor house in the country.
Location: Map 6:N3. OS Ref SJ832 589. **Tel:** 01260 272018 **E-mail:** littlemoretonhall@nationaltrust.org.uk **Website:** www.nationaltrust.org.uk
Open: Apr-Oct, Wed-Sun, 11-5pm; School Hols (except Xmas), daily, 11-5pm; 4 Nov-17 Dec, Sat & Sun, 11-4pm. **Admission:** Adult £9.05; Child £4.50.

TATTON PARK

Knutsford, Cheshire WA16 6QN

A complete historic estate with 1,000 acres of deer park, 200 year old 50 acre gardens and Tudor Old Hall. **Location:** Map 6:M2. OS Ref SJ745 815.
Tel: 01625 374400/01625 374435 **E-mail:** tatton@cheshireeast.gov.uk
Website: www.tattonpark.org.uk
Open: Gardens: Winter, daily, 10-4pm; Apr-Oct, daily, 10-6pm. House: Apr-Oct, Tue-Sun & BH Mons, 1-5pm. **Admission:** Adult £11; Child £5.50.

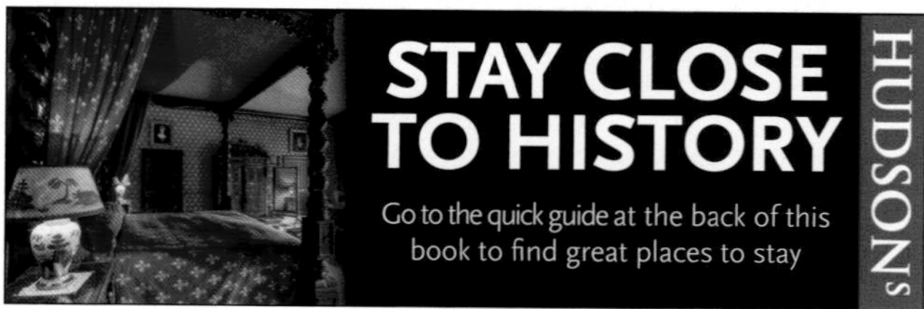

KIRKLINTON HALL AND GARDENS

KIRKLINTON, CARLISLE CA6 6BB

www.kirklintonhall.co.uk

Adjacent to the 12th Century de Boyville stronghold, Kirklinton Hall is said to have been built from its stone. Begun in the 1670's, extended in the 1870's and ruined in the 1970's, the Hall has been a Restoration Great House, an RAF base, a school, a gangsters' gambling den and worse. Walk in the footsteps of Norman Knights, Cavalier Commanders, Victorian Plutocrats and the Kray twins. Now, Kirklinton Hall and its Gardens are being restored by the Boyle family to its former glory, a painstaking and fascinating process. It is also the official home of SlowFood Cumbria and is available for weddings and events.

'Spectacularly sinister ruin' - Pevsners Buildings of England.

Location: Map 10:K3. OS Ref NY433 672. 6 miles north east of M6 junction 44, follow A7 towards Longtown. At Blackford turn right following sign to Kirklinton 5 miles. Stay on road and follow Brown Signs.

Owner: Mr & Mrs Christopher Boyle **Contact:** Annabel Candler, Venue Manager
Tel: 01697 748850 **Facebook:** Kirklinton Hall. **Twitter:** @kirklintonhall.
E-mail: info@kirklintonhall.co.uk
Open: 1 Apr-30 Sep, 12-5pm weekdays and Suns. Sats for Public or Private Events. Available for Wedding Receptions. **Admission:** Adult £4.00, Child £1.00 (under 16). Free to HHA and MyCumbria Card Holders.
Key facts: Gifts, Treats, Postcards, David Austen Roses Books & Hudson's Heritage. Specialising in David Austin Roses & Rare Rhododendrons. Disabled WC. Tea, coffee, cake, ice cream, biscuits & soft drinks. By arrangement for groups. Free Car parking. Contact property. On leads. Yurt hire & camping. Contact for information about holding special celebrations at the Hall. Exclusive use, flexible space & truly unique.

LEVENS HALL

KENDAL, CUMBRIA LA8 0PD

www.levenshall.co.uk

Levens Hall is an Elizabethan mansion built around a 13th Century pele tower. The much loved home of the Bagot family, with fine panelling, plasterwork, Cordova leather wall coverings, paintings by Rubens, Lely and Cuyp, the earliest English patchwork and Wellingtoniana combine with other beautiful objects to form a fascinating collection. The world famous Topiary Gardens were laid out by Monsieur Beaumont from 1694 and his design has remained largely unchanged to this day. Over 90 individual pieces of topiary, some over nine metres high, massive beech hedges and colourful seasonal bedding provide a magnificent visual impact.

Location: Map 10:L7. OS Ref SD495 851.
5m S of Kendal on the A6. Exit M6/J36.

Owner: C H Bagot
Contact: The Administrator
Tel: 015395 60321 **E-mail:** houseopening@levenshall.co.uk
Open: Apr-mid Oct, Sun-Thu (closed Fri & Sat). Garden, Tea Room, Gift Shop & Plant Centre: 10am-5pm. House: 12 noon-4pm. Groups (20+) please book. Please see www.levenshall.co.uk for full details.
Admission: House & Gardens or Gardens Only. Please see www.levenshall.co.uk for full details, special offers & current events. Group Rates on application.
Key facts: No indoor photography. Gift shop. Partial. WCs. Licensed. Licensed. By arrangement. Free on-site parking. Assistance dogs only.

© Tony West Photography

ABBOT HALL ART GALLERY

Abbot Hall, Kendal, Cumbria LA9 5AL

www.abbothall.org.uk

Abbot Hall Art Gallery is housed in one of Kendal's most important buildings, a Grade I listed villa, on the banks of the River Kent. The galleries offer two floors of light-filled spaces in which to see art. The Gallery holds an impressive collection of 18th, 19th and 20th Century British art. The Gallery also hosts an ambitious temporary exhibition programme.

Location: Map 10:L7. OS Ref SD517 921. 10 min drive from M6 J36. Follow signs to south Kendal & then for Abbot Hall. Nearest train stations: main line, Oxenholme, the Lake District, local line, Kendal.

Owner/Contact: Lakeland Arts

Tel: 01539 722464 **E-mail:** info@abbothall.org.uk

Open: Mon-Sat, 10.30am-5pm (4pm Nov-Feb). Jan-Dec 2017.

Admission: Adult £7.00 (without donation £6.35). Children & students free, 50% discount for National Art Pass.

Key facts: The Gallery Shop is packed with books on art & culture, artists' prints & materials. Serving a menu of freshly prepared sandwiches, soups & cakes. Pay & display parking on site. See our website for details. See our website for details.

© Lakeland Arts

BLACKWELL, THE ARTS & CRAFTS HOUSE

Bowness-on-Windermere, Cumbria LA23 3JT

www.blackwell.org.uk

Blackwell, completed in 1900, is the largest and most important surviving example of work by architect Mackay Hugh Baillie Scott. Designed as a holiday retreat for Sir Edward Holt, the house survives in a truly remarkable state of preservation retaining many original decorative features. Visitors are encouraged to sit and soak up the atmosphere in Blackwell's fireplace inglenooks and are free to enjoy the house as it was originally intended, without roped-off areas. The period rooms are furnished with Arts & Crafts furniture and decorative arts, which are complemented by exhibitions of historical applied arts and contemporary craft.

Location: Map 10:K7. OS Ref SD401 945. 1.5 m S of Bowness just off the A5074 on the B5360. **Owner:** Lakeland Arts **Contact:** Blackwell **Tel:** 015394 46139 **E-mail:** info@blackwell.org.uk **Open:** Daily 10.30am-5pm (4pm Nov-Feb). Jan-Dec 2017. **Admission:** Adult £8.50 (without donation £7.70), Children & Students free, 50% discount for National Art Pass. **Key facts:** Shop stocks contemporary craft by leading craft-makers selected for its quality & beauty. WCs. Café menu emphasises quality & the handmade, reflecting the philosophy of Arts & Crafts Movement. Free for cars, coaches by appointment. See website. Guide dogs only. See website.

ASKHAM HALL AND GARDENS

Askham, Penrith, Cumbria CA10 2PF

www.askhamhall.co.uk

Meander through the beautiful gardens, visit the animals and enjoy lunch in the Kitchen Garden Café. Askham Hall is grade I listed, dating back to the late 1200s. It has recently been transformed from a stately family home into a stylish retreat also with a restaurant, 15 bedrooms and a wedding barn.

Location: Map 10:L5. OS Ref NY514 237. Askham Hall in Cumbria is situated in a quiet and picturesque village within easy access (about ten minutes' drive) from Penrith and junction 40 of the M6. Follow the brown tourist signs.

Owner: Charles Lowther **Contact:** Marie-Louisa Raeburn

Tel: 01931 712350

E-mail: enquiries@askhamhall.co.uk

Open: Gardens and café: Every day except Sat. 10am-5pm in high season, reduced hours and times in low season. Restaurant and accommodation: Tue-Sat for dinner and overnight stays.

Admission: Entry to the gardens and animals: Adult £4.00, Child free.

Key facts: www.askhamhall.co.uk/gardens-and-cafe Free to enter. Groups by arrangement. Free. Permitted in café but not gardens.

Kirklinton Hall

DALEMAIN MANSION & GARDENS

Penrith, Cumbria CA11 0HB

www.dalemain.com

A fine mixture of Medieval, Tudor & early Georgian architecture. Lived in by the same family since 1679 and home to the World's Original Marmalade Awards & Festival. Award-winning gardens, richly planted with unusual combinations of flowers and shrubs. Highlights include the Rose Walk, Ancient Apple Trees, Tudor Knot Garden, Blue Himalayan Poppies, Earth Sculpture and Stumpery.

Location: Map 10:L5. OS Ref NY477 269. On A592 1m S of A66. 4m SW of Penrith. London, M1, M6/J40. Edinburgh, A73, M74, M6/J40.

Owner: Robert Hasell-McCosh Esq **Contact:** Florence Lindeman - Marketing

Tel: 017684 86450 **Fax:** 017684 86223 **E-mail:** marketing@dalemain.com

Open: 9 Apr-26 Oct, Sun-Thu. Gardens, Tea Room & Gift Shop: 10am-4.30pm (3pm in Oct). House 10.30am-3.30pm. Groups (12+) please book.

Admission: House & Gardens or Gardens Only. Please see website for details. Group Prices on application.

Key facts: No photography in house. Phone for event enquiries. Gift Shop. Plant Sales. Partial. WCs. Licensed Tea Room. 1hr tours. German and French translations. Garden tours available. Guided tour details on website. 50 yds. Free. Guide dogs only.

© Holker Hall & Gardens

HOLKER HALL & GARDENS

Cark-In-Cartmel, Grange-Over-Sands, Cumbria LA11 7PL

www.holker.co.uk

Holker is the family home of the Cavendish family, set amongst beautiful countryside surrounding the Lake District. Steeped in history, this magnificent Victorian Mansion of neo-Elizabethan Gothic style was largely re-built in the 1870's following a fire, but origins date back to the 1600's. The glorious gardens, café, brasserie, food hall & gift shop complete the visitor experience.

Location: Map 10:K8. OS Ref SD360 770.
From Motorway M6/J36, Signed Barrow A590.

Owner: Cavendish Family **Contact:** Jillian Rouse

Tel: 015395 58328 **Fax:** 015395 58378 **E-mail:** info@holker.co.uk

Open: 25 Mar-29 Oct, Wed-Sun & BH Mons (closed Mon & Tue)
Hall: 11-4pm. Gardens: 10.30-5pm, Café, Food Hall & Gift Shop: 10.30-5pm

Admission: Hall & Gardens: Adult £12.50, Child FOC. Gardens only: Adult £8.50, Child FOC. Hall only: Adults £8.00, Child FOC. Group Rates (10+)
Hall & Gardens: Adult £8.50, Gardens only: Adult £6.00.

Key facts: No photography in house. Food Hall & Gift Shop. For groups, by arrangement. Dogs on leads (in park).

MIREHOUSE

Keswick, Cumbria CA12 4QE

Melvyn Bragg described Mirehouse as 'Manor from Heaven'. Set in stunning landscape, Mirehouse is a literary house linked with Tennyson and Wordsworth. Live piano music and children's history trail in house. Natural playgrounds, serene bee garden and lakeside walk.

Location: Map 10:J5. OS Ref NY235 284. Beside A591, 3½m N of Keswick.

Owner: James Fryer-Spedding

Contact: Janaki Spedding

Tel: 017687 72287

E-mail: info@mirehouse.com

Website: www.mirehouse.com

Open: Please see website for open dates.

Admission: Please see website for admission rates.

Key facts: No photography in house. Good bus service to property. By arrangement. Pay and display. On leads in grounds.

CARLISLE CASTLE

Carlisle, Cumbria CA3 8UR

Standing proudly in the city it has dominated for nine centuries, Carlisle Castle was a constantly updated working fortress until well within living memory.

Location: Map 10:K3. OS Ref NY396 562. **Tel:** 01228 591922 **E-mail:** customers@english-heritage.org.uk **Website:** www.english-heritage.org.uk/carlisle **Open:** 2 Jan-Mar & Nov-Dec, Sat & Sun, 10-4pm; daily at half term; Apr-Oct, daily, 10-5pm. **Admission:** Adult £7.10; Child £4.30.

HUTTON-IN-THE-FOREST

Penrith, Cumbria CA11 9TH

The home of Lord Inglewood's family since 1605. Built around a medieval pele tower with later additions. Fine collections and outstanding grounds.

Location: Map 10:L5. OS Ref NY460 358. **Tel:** 017684 84449

E-mail: info@hutton-in-the-forest.co.uk **Website:** www.hutton-in-the-forest.co.uk **Open:** Gardens: Apr-Oct, daily, 10-5pm. House: Easter-Oct, Wed, Thu, Sun & BH Mons, 11.30-4pm. **Admission:** Adult £10; Child Free.

LANERCOST PRIORY

Lanercost, Brampton, Cumbria CA8 2HQ

This Augustian Priory was founded c1166. The east end of the noble 13th Century church survives to its full height. **Location:** Map 10:L3. OS Ref NY556 637.

Tel: 01697 73030 **E-mail:** customers@english-heritage.org.uk

Website: www.english-heritage.org.uk/lanercost

Open: 2 Jan-Mar & Nov-Dec, Sat & Sun, 10-4pm; daily at half term; Apr-Oct, daily, 10-5pm. **Admission:** Adult £7.10; Child £4.30.

MUNCASTER CASTLE GARDENS

Muncaster Castle, Ravenglass, Cumbria CA18 1RQ

Muncaster was described by Ruskin as Heaven's Gate. Grade II* woodland gardens are famous for rhododendrons and breathtaking views. The Castle is a treasure trove of paintings, silver, embroideries and more. **Location:** Map 10:J7. OS Ref SD103 965. **Tel:** 01229 717614 **E-mail:** info@muncaster.co.uk

Website: www.muncaster.co.uk **Open:** Gdns: Feb-Mar & Oct-22 Dec, 11-4pm. Castle: Apr-Oct, Sun-Fri, 12-4pm. **Admission:** Adult £13.50; Child £6.75.

SIZERGH CASTLE AND GARDEN

Sizergh, Kendal, Cumbria LA8 8AE

Beautiful medieval house, with rich gardens and estate.

Location: Map 10:L7. OS Ref SD499 872.

Tel: 015395 60951 **E-mail:** sizergh@nationaltrust.org.uk

Website: www.nationaltrust.org.uk

Open: Gardens: All year, daily, 10-4pm. House Apr-Oct, Sun-Thu, 12-4pm.

Admission: Adult £9.90; Child £4.95.

WRAY CASTLE

Low Wray, Ambleside, Cumbria LA22 0JA

Mock-Gothic castle sitting on the shores of Lake Windermere with turrets, towers and informal grounds. **Location:** Map 10:K6. OS Ref NY373 010.

Tel: 015394 33250 **E-mail:** wraycastle@nationaltrust.org.uk

Website: www.nationaltrust.org.uk

Open: Apr-Oct & Feb half term, daily, 10-5pm; Nov, Sat & Sun, 10.30-4pm.

Admission: Adult £8.50; Child £4.25.

BROWSHOLME HALL

Clitheroe, Lancashire BB7 3DE

www.browsholme.com

Browsholme Hall has been the ancestral home of the Parkers, Bowbearers of the Forest of Bowland since the time Tudor times. Today it is still the family's home and Robert and Amanda Parker invite visitors to enjoy its magnificent architecture, fabulous interiors, antique furnishings and lovely gardens set in the beautiful landscape of the Forest of Bowland. Superb oak chests, Gillow furniture, portraits, porcelain, Civil War arms and many unique relics, including mementos of Bonnie Prince Charlie, and even a fragment of a Zeppelin reflect the continuous occupation of the Hall by the Parkers for over 500 years.

A beautifully restored 18th Century barn has a Tea Room for refreshments; also used for concerts, theatre, events and weddings. Browsholme is open to visitors for a special fortnight before Christmas, decorated in style for the family.

Location: Map 10:M10. OS Ref SD683 452. 5m NW of Clitheroe off B6243. What3Words: rumble.crunchy.roost

Owner: Robert & Amanda Parker **Contact:** Catherine Turner

Tel: 01254 827160 **E-mail:** info@browsholme.com

Open: Gardens & Tea Room 11am–4.30pm. Hall Tours from 12pm. May-end Sep, every Wed. May & Jun-1st Sun. Spring & Aug-Bank Holiday Mon. Dec-1st & 2nd Sun Christmas special. Booked parties & groups welcome at other times, including Christmas (3-14 Dec) **Admission:** See website for full details.

Key facts: Guide dogs only.

© Hoghton Tower Preservation Trust

HOGHTON TOWER

Hoghton, nr Preston, Lancashire PR5 0SH

www.hoghtontower.co.uk

A Tudor fortified Manor House, the ancestral home of the de Hoghton family. Join a tour of the staterooms to learn about the history of the house. Stroll through the stunning walled gardens. Browse the gift shop and finish with an afternoon tea in our Vaio Tea Room. Self-catering accommodation is available in your very own tower. Private and school tours welcome by pre-booking. Wedding Venue.

Location: Map 10:L11. OS Ref SD622 264. M65/J3. Midway between Preston & Blackburn on A675.

Owner: Hoghton Tower Preservation Trust

Tel: 01254 852986 **E-mail:** mail@hoghtontower.co.uk

Open: May-Sep (Sun-Thu), BHs (except Christmas & New Year) and every 3rd Sun of the Month. Mon-Thu 11am-5pm, Sun 10am-5pm (First Tour 11:30am, last tour 3:30pm). Tea Room Mon-Thu 11am-5pm, Sun 10am-5pm. Group visits by appointment all year round. Please see our website for variations.

Admission: Please check website.

Key facts: Gift ideas. Conferences. Tea Room. House, Gardens & Dolls Houses available. Pre-book only. Assistance dogs only. Self-catering.

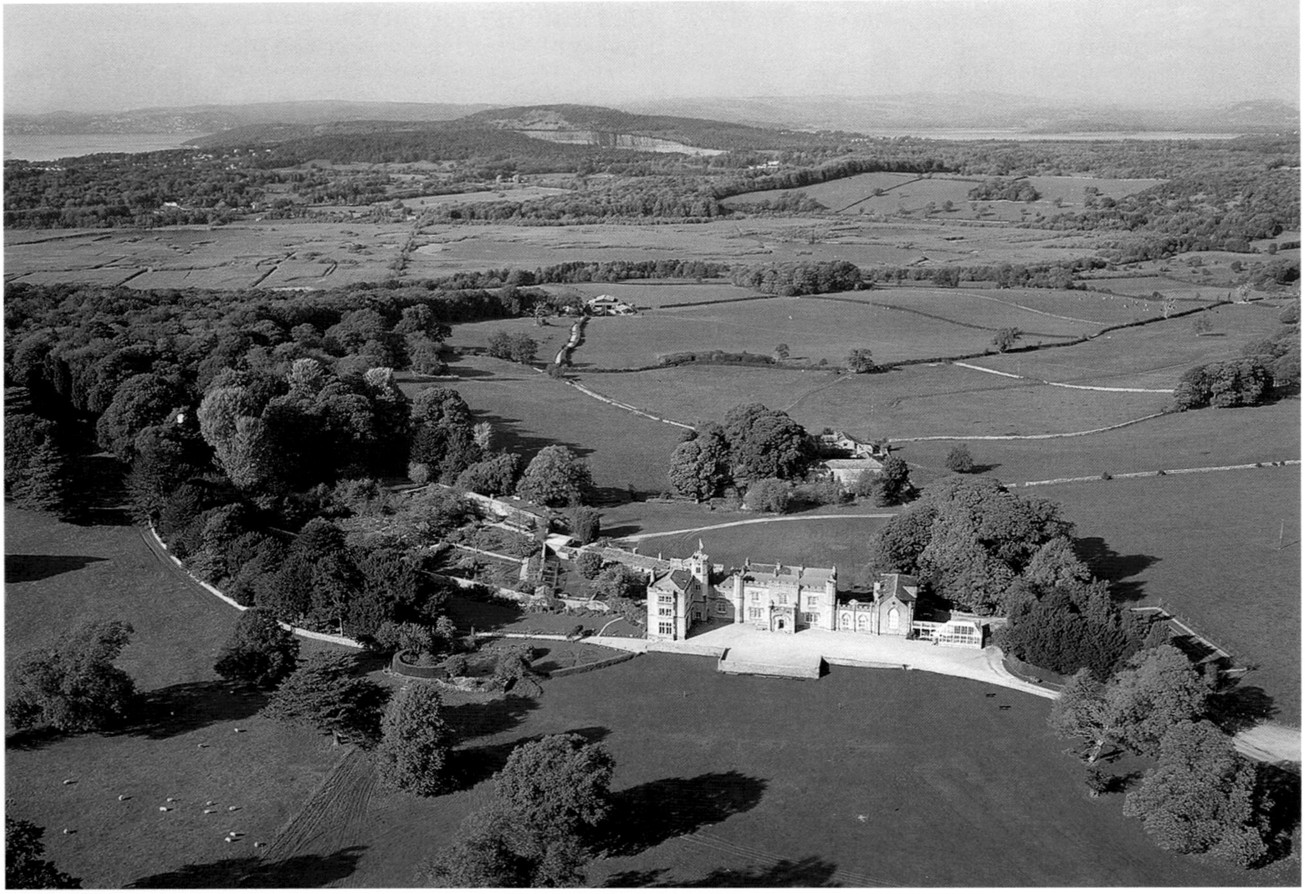

Leighton Hall

LEIGHTON HALL

Carnforth, Lancashire LA5 9ST

www.leightonhall.co.uk

Award winning Leighton Hall's setting can deservedly be described as spectacular. Nestled in 1,550 acres of lush grounds, this romantic, Gothic house is the lived-in home of the famous Gillow furniture making family. Visits include: informal and entertaining house tours, birds of prey displays, charming Tea Rooms, children's play area, plant conservatory, beautiful gardens and parkland.
Location: Map 10:L8. OS Ref SD494 744. 9m N of Lancaster, 10m S of Kendal, 3m N of Carnforth. 1½ m W of A6. 3m from M6/A6/J35, signed from J35
Owner: Richard Gillow Reynolds Esq **Contact:** Mrs C S Reynolds
Tel: 01524 734474 **Fax:** 01524 720357 **Additional Contact:** Mrs Lucy Arthurs
E-mail: info@leightonhall.co.uk **Open:** May-Sept, Tue-Fri (also BH Sun and Mon, Suns in Aug) 2-5pm. Pre-booked groups (25+) all year by arrangement. Group rates. **Admission:** Adult £8.50, OAP/Student £7.50, Child (5-12 years) £5.50, Family (2 adults and up to 3 children) £28.00, Grounds only £4.75.
Key facts: No photography in house. Partial. WCs. Regrettably the halls first floor is inaccessible for unaccompanied wheelchair users. Child friendly, enthusiastic guides bring Leighton's history to life. Informal, relaxed tours. Free and ample parking. 3 themed packages available covering the new cross curriculum. On leads, on the parkland only.

ASTLEY HALL, COACH HOUSE AND PARK

Astley Park, Off Hallgate, Chorley PR7 1NP

Astley Hall "the most exhilarating house in Lancashire" (Simon Jenkins).
Location: Map 10:L11. OS Ref SD574 183.
Tel: 01257 515151 **E-mail:** astley.hall@chorley.gov.uk
Website: www.chorley.gov.uk/astleyhall
Open: All year, Sat, Sun & BH Mons, 12-4.30pm; school hols. Sat-Wed, 12-4.30pm. **Admission:** Donations welcome.

GAWTHORPE HALL

Padiham, Nr Burnley, Lancashire BB12 8UA

Built in 1600-05 and restored by Sir Charles Barry in the 1850s, with Barry's designs recreated in the principal rooms. Gawthorpe was the home of the Shuttleworths and the Shuttleworth textile collection is on display.
Location: Map 10:N10. OS Ref SD806 340. **Tel:** 01282 771004
E-mail: gawthorpehall@nationaltrust.org.uk **Open:** Gardens: All year, daily, 8-7pm. House: May-Oct, Wed-Sun, 11-5pm. **Admission:** Adult £4.

LANCASTER CASTLE

Shire Hall, Castle Parade, Lancaster, Lancashire LA1 1YJ

Situated on a hill fortified by the Romans, Lancaster Castle is one of the most iconic buildings in the north-west of England.
Location: Map 10:L9. OS Ref SD473 618. **Tel:** 01524 64998
E-mail: lancastercastle@lancashire.gov.uk **Website:** www.lancastercastle.com
Open: All year, daily, 10-4pm; closed Christmas week. **Admission:** Adult £8.

ORDSALL HALL

322 Ordsall Lane, Ordsall, Salford M5 3AN

Grade I listed Tudor manor house first recorded in 1177. It has been home to medieval gentry, Tudor nobility, Catholics loyal to the crown, butchers, farmers, an Earl, an artist, priests, scout troops, mill workers, cows and several ghosts!
Location: Map 6:N1. OS Ref SJ816 970. **Tel:** 0161 872 0251 **E-mail:** ordsall.hall@scll.co.uk **Website:** www.salfordcommunityleisure.co.uk/culture/ordsall-hall **Open:** All year, Mon-Thu, 10-4pm; Sun, 1-4pm. **Admission:** Free.

RUFFORD OLD HALL

Rufford, Nr Ormskirk, Lancashire L40 1SG

One of the finest 16th Century buildings in Lancashire. The magnificent Great Hall contains an intricately carved movable screen and suits of armour.
Location: Map 10:L11. OS Ref SD463 160. **Tel:** 01704 821254
E-mail: ruffordoldhall@nationaltrust.org.uk **Website:** www.nationaltrust.org.uk
Open: Mar-Oct, Sun-Wed, 11-4pm; School hols (except Xmas), daily, 11-5pm; 11 Nov-17 Dec, Sat & Sun, 11-4pm **Admission:** Adult £8; Child £4.

MANCHESTER CATHEDRAL

Victoria Street, Manchester M3 1SX

Manchester Cathedral Grade I listed masterpiece. **Location:** Map 6:N1. OS Ref SJ838 988. **Tel:** 0161 833 2220 **Fax:** 0161 839 6218
E-mail: office@manchestercathedral.org
Website: www.manchestercathedral.org
Open: Every day. Times vary, please check website for up-to-date information.
Admission: Donations welcome.

MEOLS HALL

Churchtown, Southport, Merseyside PR9 7LZ

17th Century house with subsequent additions. Interesting collection of pictures and furniture. Tithe Barn available for wedding ceremonies and receptions all year.
Location: Map 10:K11. OS Ref SD365 184.
3m NE of Southport town centre in Churchtown. SE of A565.
Owner: The Hesketh Family
Contact: Pamela Whelan
Tel: 01704 228326 **Fax:** 01704 507185
E-mail: events@meolshall.com
Website: www.meolshall.com
Open: May BH Mon: 1 & 29 May. 20 Aug-14 Sep. 1.30-5.30pm.
Admission: Adult £4.00, Child £1.00. Groups welcome but Afternoon Tea is only available for bookings of 25+.
Key facts: Wedding ceremonies and receptions available in the Tithe Barn.

SPEKE HALL GARDEN & ESTATE

The Walk, Speke, Liverpool L24 1XD

Superb half-timbered Tudor house, with rich Victorian interiors, fine gardens and estate. Close to Liverpool - but with room to breathe. **Location:** Map 6:K2. OS Ref SJ418 825. **Tel:** 0151 427 7231 **Website:** www.nationaltrust.org.uk
Open: Feb half term, Wed-Sun, 11-4pm; Apr-Oct, Wed-Sun, BH Mons, 11-5pm; Tue in Aug; 4 Nov-10 Dec, Sat & Sun, 11-4pm.
Admission: Adult £9.81; Child £4.91.

Browsholme Hall

NESS BOTANIC GARDENS
Neston Road, Ness, Cheshire CH64 4AY
Tel: 0845 030 4063 **E-mail:** nessgdns@liv.ac.uk

ALLAN BANK
Grasmere, Cumbria LA22 9QZ
Tel: 015394 35143 **E-mail:** allanbank@nationaltrust.org.uk

BRANTWOOD
Coniston, Cumbria LA21 8AD
Tel: 01539 441396 **E-mail:** enquiries@brantwood.org.uk

BROUGHAM CASTLE
Penrith, Cumbria CA10 2AA
Tel: 01768 862488 **E-mail:** customers@english-heritage.org.uk

CARLISLE CATHEDRAL
Carlisle, Cumbria CA3 8TZ
Tel: 01228 548151

DOVE COTTAGE & WORDSWORTH MUSEUM
Grasmere, Cumbria LA22 9SH
Tel: 01539 435544 **E-mail:** enquiries@wordsworth.org.uk

HALECAT GARDEN NURSERY & GARDENS
Witherslack, Grange-over-Sands, Cumbria LA11 6RT
Tel: 015395 52096 **E-mail:** matthewbardgett@hotmail.com

HILL TOP
Near Sawrey, Hawkshead, Ambleside, Cumbria LA22 0LF
Tel: 015394 36269 **E-mail:** hilltop@nationaltrust.org.uk

Holker Hall

HOLEHIRD GARDENS
Patterdale Road, Windermere, Cumbria LA23 1NP
Tel: 015394 46008 **E-mail:** maggie.mees@btinternet.com

LOWTHER CASTLE & GARDENS TRUST
Penrith, Cumbria CA10 2HG
Tel: 01931 712192

NAWORTH CASTLE
Naworth Castle Estate, Brampton, Cumbria CA8 2HF
Tel: 016977 3229. **E-mail:** office@naworth.co.uk

RYDAL MOUNT & GARDENS
Rydal, Cumbria LA22 9LU
Tel: 01539 433002 **E-mail:** info@rydalmount.co.uk

STOTT PARK BOBBIN MILL
Colton, Ulverston, Cumbria LA12 8AX
Tel: 01539 531087 **E-mail:** stott.park@english-heritage.org.uk

SWARTHMOOR HALL
Swarthmoor Hall Lane, Ulverston, Cumbria LA12 0JQ
Tel: 01229 583204 **E-mail:** info@swarthmoorhall.co.uk

TOWNEND
Troutbeck, Windermere, Cumbria LA23 1LB
Tel: 015394 32628 **E-mail:** townend@nationaltrust.org.uk

TULLIE HOUSE MUSEUM & ART GALLERY
Castle Street, Carlisle, Cumbria CA3 8TP
Tel: 01228 618718 **E-mail:** enquiries@tulliehouse.org

WINDERWATH GARDENS
Winderwath, Temple Sowerby, Penrith, Cumbria CA10 2AG
Tel: 01768 88250

WORDSWORTH HOUSE AND GARDEN
Main Street, Cockermouth, Cumbria CA13 9RX
Tel: 01900 820884 **E-mail:** wordsworthhouse@nationaltrust.org.uk

THE BEATLES CHILDHOOD HOMES
Woolton and Allerton, Liverpool L18 9TN
Tel: 0151 427 7231 **E-mail:** thebeatleshomes@nationaltrust.org.uk

LYTHAM HALL
Ballam Road, Lytham FY8 4JX
Tel: 01253 736652 **E-mail:** lytham.hall@htnw.co.uk

SAMLESBURY HALL
Preston New Road, Samlesbury, Preston PR5 0UP
Tel: 01254 812010 **E-mail:** info@samlesburyhall.co.uk

SMITHILLS HALL
Smithills Dean Road, Bolton BL7 7NP
Tel: 01204 332377 **E-mail:** historichalls@bolton.gov.uk

TOWNELEY HALL ART GALLERY & MUSEUMS
Burnley BB11 3RQ
Tel: 01282 447130

HEATON HALL
Heaton Park, Prestwich, Manchester M25 9WL
Tel: 0161 235 8815

Register for news and special offers at **www.hudsonsheritage.com**

Muncaster Castle Garden, Ravenglass

Alnwick Castle, Northumberland

Co. Durham
Northumberland
Tyne & Wear

Durham Cathedral, Co. Durham

North East

The lands either side of Hadrian's Wall are full of castles and the legacy of industrial wealth. From the Romans to the present day, houses, castles and gardens will show its distinctive history and culture.

© Critical Tortoise

© Sean Elliott Photography

AUCKLAND CASTLE

MARKET PLACE, BISHOP AUCKLAND, COUNTY DURHAM DL14 7NR

www.aucklandcastle.org

Historic palace of the Bishop of Durham, Auckland Castle is set within the heart of County Durham in the town of Bishop Auckland. Recently opened to the public it offers a changing programme of exhibitions, majestic State Rooms, the Library Tea Room and deer park. The building will temporarily close its doors in 2016 for a multi-million pound renovation and redevelopment. To see our full programme of events and sign up to the mailing list, please visit aucklandcastle.org

Location: Map 10:P5. OS Ref NZ213 302. From the A1 motorway take the A688 (J61) to Bishop Auckland. Follow signs to North Bondgate car park.

Owner: Auckland Castle Trust

Contact: Visitor Services 01388 743 797 for opening, admissions & group bookings etc.

Tel: 01388 743 750

Facebook: /aucklandcastle

Twitter: @aucklandcastle

E-mail: enquiries@aucklandcastle.org

Open: Closed to daily visits in 2017 for major restoration. Check our website for new developments.

Key facts: We stock a range of locally sourced items in our gift shop. Available for private hire. The Library Tea Room serves light lunches, afternoon teas and a range of hot and cold beverages. Daily guided tours at 11.30am and 2.30pm (Except Tue). We have an active education programme and work with many schools across County Durham. Guide Dogs Only. Dog walkers welcome in Bishop's Park. We offer a limited number of Chapel weddings in St Peter's Chapel.

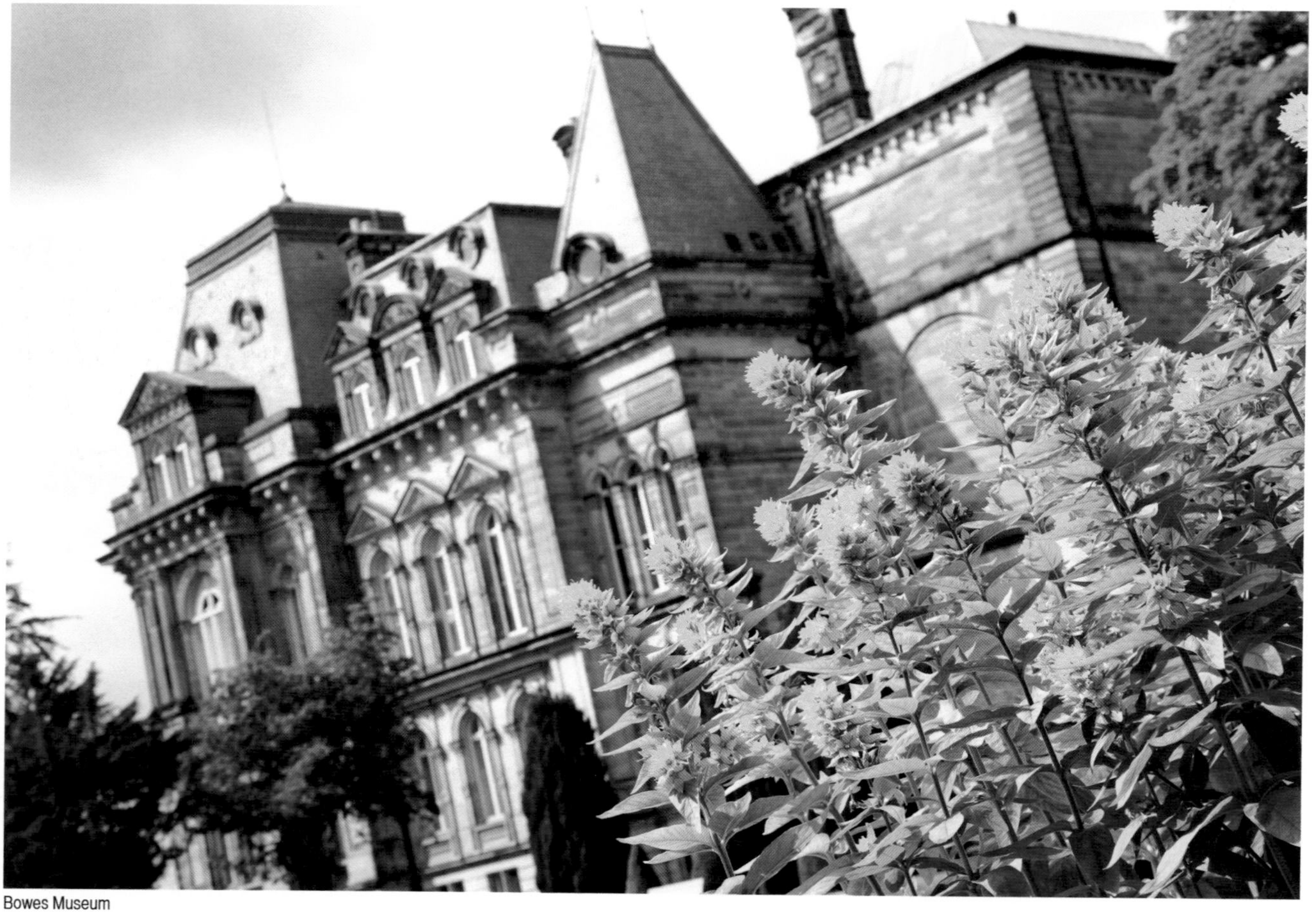

Bowes Museum

RABY CASTLE

STAINDROP, DARLINGTON, CO. DURHAM DL2 3AH

www.rabycastle.com

Raby Castle is surrounded by a large deer park, with two lakes and a beautiful walled garden with formal lawns, yew hedges and an ornamental pond. It was built by the mighty Nevill family in the 14th Century, and has been home to Lord Barnard's family since 1626. Highlights include the vast Barons' Hall, where it is reputed 700 knights gathered to plot the doomed 'Rising of the North' rebellion, and the stunning Octagon Drawing Room. With Meissen porcelain, fine furniture and paintings by Munnings, Reynolds, Van Dyck, Batoni, Teniers, Amigoni and Vernet. Also in the grounds is the 18th Century Stable block with impressive horse-drawn carriage collection, and a delightfully converted Gift Shop and Tea Rooms, and woodland play area.

Location: Map 10:O5. OS Ref NZ129 218. On A688, 1m N of Staindrop. 8m NE of Barnard Castle, 12m WNW of Darlington.

Owner: The Lord Barnard **Contact:** Castle Admin Office

Tel: 01833 660202 **E-mail:** admin@rabycastle.com

Open: 15 Apr-1 Oct 2017

Castle: Wed-Sun. (plus bank hols) Jul & Aug, Daily except Mon, 12.30-4.30pm.

Park & Gardens: As Castle, 11am-5pm.

Admission: Castle, Park & Gardens: Adult £12.00, Child (5-15yrs) £6.00, Conc. £11.00, Family discounts available. Groups (12+)*: Adult £10.00.

Park & Gardens: Adult £7.00, Child £3.00, Conc. £6.00. Season Tickets available.

*Groups please book in advance.

Key facts: No photography or video filming is permitted inside. Colour guidebook on sale. Gift Shop. Limited access to Castle interior. Accessible WCs, designated parking, free wheelchair loan. Tea Room. Castle Tours available on certain dates. Ample car parking on grass and coach parking on hard standing. Schools by arrangement. Dogs welcome on leads in deer park only. No dogs are allowed in the Walled Gardens or inside buildings.

THE BOWES MUSEUM

Barnard Castle, County Durham DL12 8NP

www.thebowesmuseum.org.uk

The recently transformed Museum houses fine art, fashion & textiles, silver & metals, ceramics, furniture and the iconic Silver Swan musical automation. A rolling exhibition programme is complemented by varied indoor and outdoor events. The acclaimed Café Bowes, a high quality gift shop, tranquil gardens and woodland walks add to the enjoyment. **Location:** Map 10:O6. OS Ref NZ055 163. Situated on Newgate in Barnard Castle. Just off the A66 in the heart of the North Pennines. **Tel:** 01833 690606 **Fax:** 01833 637163 **E-mail:** info@thebowesmuseum.org.uk **Open:** 10am-5pm. Closed only 25 & 26 Dec & 1 Jan. **Admission:** Adults £10.50, Conc. £9.50, 6 month pass £16.00. Admission to all exhibitions included. Accompanied children Free (U16). Accompanying carers Free. Free access to Café Bowes, Shop & Grounds.

Key facts: Souvenirs & gifts. 10am-4.45pm hire@thebowesmuseum.org.uk. Access to all areas. Locally produced seasonal menu, speciality teas, coffees & wines. Mon-Sat 9am-4.30pm Sun 10am-4.30pm. Available via group visits or selected days in Sum. Children's Audio available. Ample free parking & coach & accessible parking bays. education@thebowesmuseum.org.uk. Except guide dogs. hire@thebowesmuseum.org.uk.

DURHAM CATHEDRAL

Durham DH1 3EH

www.durhamcathedral.co.uk

One of the finest examples of Romanesque architecture in Europe, located at the heart of a UNESCO World Heritage Site. Burial place of St Cuthbert and the Venerable Bede. Explore Open Treasure, a new world-class visitor experience, and discover 2,000 years of history as the remarkable story of Durham Cathedral and its incredible collections is revealed.

Location: Map 10:P4. OS Ref NZ274 422. Durham City Centre.

Contact: The Cathedral Office **Tel:** 0191 3864266

E-mail: enquiries@durhamcathedral.co.uk

Open: Daily 7.30am-6pm (8pm Summer), with services three times daily.

Admission: Free, donations welcome. Admission applies to guided tours and Open Treasure. Groups contact visits@durhamcathedral.co.uk

Key facts: Souvenirs and gifts. Mon-Sat 9am-5.30pm, Sun 12noon-5pm. events@durhamcathedral.co.uk Partial. Locally-sourced food and drink served daily, 10am-4.30pm Restaurant available for hire. Adults £5.00, Conc. £4.50. Children free (U16). Limited disabled, public parking nearby. education@durhamcathedral.co.uk Guide dogs only.

VISITOR INFORMATION

Owner
His Grace The Duke of Northumberland

Address
Alnwick Castle
Alnwick
Northumberland
NE66 1NQ

Location
Map 14:M11
OS Ref. NU187 135
Well signposted less than a mile off A1; 35 miles north of Newcastle and 80 miles south of Edinburgh.
Bus: Regular bus services to Alnwick from around the region
Rail: 4 miles from Alnmouth Station (3.5 hours from London King's Cross)
Air: 34 miles from Newcastle Airport
Sea: 37 miles from North Sea ferry terminal

Contact
Tel: 01665 511100
Group bookings: 01665 511184
Media & filming: 01665 511794.
E-mail: info@alnwickcastle.com

Opening Times
24 Mar-29 Oct 2017
10am-5.30pm
(last admission 3.45pm).

State Rooms are open 11am-5pm
(last admission 4pm, Chapel closes at 2.30pm).
Check alnwickcastle.com for up-to-date opening dates and times.

Admission
Adult:	£14.95
Concession:	£12.50
Child (5-16yrs):	£7.75
Family (2+up to 4):	£40.00

(2016 prices shown, subject to change).

Tickets can be validated for unlimited free visits for 12 months, at no extra cost (see website for T&Cs)

Discounted rates available for groups of 14 or more.

Special Events
Daily events include guided tours of the State Rooms and grounds, Knight's Quest activities, and broomstick training. Seasonal events include knights tournaments, falconry displays, jester performances, and visits from skilled artisans. See website for details.

Conference/Function
Venue	Size	Max cap
Guest Hall	100' x 30'	300
Hulne Abbey	varies	500

ALNWICK CASTLE

www.alnwickcastle.com

Home to the Duke of Northumberland's family, the Percy's, for over 700 years; Alnwick Castle offers history on a grand scale.

Alnwick Castle's remarkable history is brimming with drama, intrigue, and extraordinary people; from a gunpowder plotter and visionary collectors, to decadent hosts and medieval England's most celebrated knight: Harry Hotspur.

Combining magnificent medieval architecture with sumptuous Italianate State Rooms, Alnwick Castle is one of the UK's most significant heritage destinations. In recent years it has also taken starring roles in a number of film and television productions, featuring as a location for ITV's Downton Abbey and as Hogwarts School of Witchcraft and Wizardry in the Harry Potter films.

With a history beginning in the Norman Age, Alnwick Castle was originally built as a border defence, before eventually being transformed from a fortification into a family home for the first Duke and Duchess of Northumberland in the 1760s.

The castle's State Rooms were later recreated by the 4th Duke in the lavish Italian Renaissance style that we see today, now boasting one of the country's finest private collections of art and furniture.

This remarkable collection includes works by Canaletto, Titian, Van Dyck, Turner, and Dobson; an extensive gallery of Meissen, Chelsea, and Paris porcelain; and the priceless Cucci cabinets, originally created for Louis XIV of France.

Alnwick Castle aims to create a vibrant and engaging heritage experience for families, with opportunities aplenty for children to get hands-on with history in the Knight's Quest arena, with dressing up, swordplay, medieval crafts and games.

KEY FACTS

- Storage available for suitcases. Photography is not permitted in the State Rooms.
- Gift Shop open daily.
- Team-building, banqueting, dinner dances. Call 01665 511086.
- Accessible WCs. Free wheelchair and mobility scooter hire available. Limited access in areas.
- Licensed.
- Free daily tours of the State Rooms and grounds.
- Coach parking also available.
- Workshops, activities and discounted admission available. Call 01665 511184.
- Assistance dogs only.
- Wedding ceremonies and receptions. Call 01665 511086.
- See website for details.

Register for news and special offers at **www.hudsonsheritage.com**

CHILLINGHAM CASTLE

www.chillingham-castle.com

20 Minutes from seaside or mountains. 4 stars in Simon Jenkins' 'Thousand Best Houses' and the very first of The Independent's '50 Best Castles in Britain & Ireland'.

This remarkable and very private castle has been continuously owned by just one family line since the 1200's. A visit from Edward I in 1298 was followed by many other Royal visits right down through this century. See Chillingham's alarming dungeons as well as active restoration in the Great Halls and State Rooms which are gradually brought back to life with tapestries, arms and armour. We even have a very real torture chamber.

The 1100s stronghold became a fortified castle in 1344, see the original Royal Licence to Crenellate on view. Wrapped in the nation's history Chillingham also occupied a strategic position during Northumberland's bloody border feuds being a resting place to many royal visitors. Tudor days saw additions but the underlying medievalism remains. 18th and 19th Centuries saw decorative extravagances including 'Capability' Brown lakes and grounds with gardens laid out by Sir Jeffrey Wyatville, fresh from his triumphs at Windsor Castle. Prehistoric Wild Cattle roam the park beyond more rare than mountain gorilla (a separate tour) and never miss the family tomb in the church.

Gardens

With romantic grounds, the castle commands breathtaking views of the surrounding countryside. As you walk to the lake you will see, according to season, drifts of snowdrops, daffodils or bluebells and an astonishing display of rhododendrons. This emphasises the restrained formality of the Elizabethan topiary garden, with its intricately clipped hedges of box and yew. Lawns, the formal gardens and woodland walks are all fully open to the public.

KEY FACTS

Corporate entertainment, lunches, drinks, dinners, wedding ceremonies and receptions.

By arrangement.

Avoid Lilburn route, coach parties welcome by prior arrangement. Limited for coaches.

Guide dogs only.

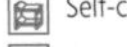

Self-catering apartments.

VISITOR INFORMATION

Owner

Sir Humphry Wakefield Bt

Address

Chillingham Castle
Northumberland
NE66 5NJ

Location

Map 14:L11
OS Ref. NU062 258
45m N of Newcastle between A697 & A1. 2m S of B6348 at Chatton.
6m SE of Wooler.
Rail: Alnmouth or Berwick.

Contact

The Administrator
Tel: 01668 215359
E-mail: enquiries@chillingham-castle.com

Opening Times

Summer
Castle, Garden & Tea Room

Easter-31 Oct.
Closed Sats, 12 noon-5pm.

Winter
Oct-Apr.
Groups & Coach Tours any time by appointment.
All function activities available.

Admission

Adult	£9.50
Children	£5.50
Conc.	£8.50
Family Ticket	£23.00

(2 adults and 3 children under 15).

BAMBURGH CASTLE

Bamburgh, Northumberland NE69 7DF

www.bamburghcastle.com

These formidable stone walls have witnessed dark tales of royal rebellion, bloody battles, spellbinding legends and millionaire benefactors. With 14 public rooms and over 3000 artefacts, including arms and armour, porcelain, furniture and artwork. The Armstrong and Aviation artefacts Museum houses artefacts spanning both World Wars as well as others relating to Lord Armstrongs ship building empire on the Tyne.

Location: Map 14:M10. OS Ref NU184 351. 42m N of Newcastle-upon-Tyne. 20m S of Berwick-upon-Tweed. 6m E of Belford by B1342 from A1 at Belford.
Owner: Francis Watson-Armstrong **Contact:** Chris Calvert, Director
Tel: 01668 214208 **E-mail:** administrator@bamburghcastle.com
Open: 11 Feb-29 Oct 2017, 10am-5pm. Last admission 4pm. 30 Oct 2017-10 Feb 2018, Weekends only, 11am-4.30pm. Last admission 3.30pm.
Admission: Adult £10.85, Child (5-16 yrs) £5.00, Family (2 adults and up to 3 dependents under 18) £25.00. For groups please contact.
Key facts: No flash photography in the State Rooms. WCs. Licensed. By arrangement at any time, min charge out of hours £150. 100 cars, coaches park on tarmac drive at entrance. Welcome. Guide provided if requested. Guide dogs only.

© Ford & Etal Estates

LADY WATERFORD HALL & GALLERY

Ford, Berwick-Upon-Tweed, Northumberland TD15 2QA

www.ford-and-etal.co.uk

At the heart of Ford & Etal Estates this 'must see venue' is the hidden gem of North Northumberland. Built as a school in 1860, the building houses an unique collection of magnificent watercolour murals (1861-1883) and smaller original paintings & sketches by Louisa Waterford, one of the most gifted female artists of the 19th Century. The fascinating story of Louisa's life & work is depicted through interpretation & film. Quizzes & games available for children to enjoy.

Location: Map 14:K10. OS Ref NT945 374. Midway between Edinburgh & Newcastle-upon-Tyne. Signed from A1 Berwick-upon-Tweed/A687 Cornhill-on-Tweed **Owner:** Ford & Etal Estates / Lady Waterford Hall Trust
Contact: Geoff Bavidge **Tel:** 07790 457580 / 07971 326177 / 01890 820338
E-mail: ladywaterfordhall@gmail.com
Open: 11am-5pm daily (times may vary slightly early & late season), late Mar-end Oct. Last entry 30 minutes before closing. **Admission:** Adult £3.00, Conc/Child £2.70, Family £8.00. U-5's Free. Joint tickets (Heatherslaw Cornmill & Lady Waterford Hall) 20% off normal admission. Discounts for pre-booked groups.
Key facts: Occasionally closed for private functions - please phone before travelling. Level access. Tea Rooms nearby Free Contact tourism@ford-and-etal.co.uk for information Guide dogs only.

Bamburgh Castle

THE ALNWICK GARDEN

Denwick Lane, Alnwick, Northumberland NE66 1YU

One of the world's most contemporary gardens, The Alnwick Garden combines provocative and traditional landscapes in the heart of Northumberland. Featuring Europe's largest wooden treehouse, a Poison Garden and Bamboo Labyrinth, The Garden also offers an expansive Rose Garden, climbing clematis and honeysuckle, as well as interactive water features and stunning Ornamental Garden.

Location: Map 14:M11. OS Ref NU192 132. Just off the A1 at Alnwick, Northumberland.
Owner: The Alnwick Garden Trust **Tel:** 01665 511350
E-mail: info@alnwickgarden.com **Website:** www.alnwickgarden.com
Open: Apr-Oct 10am-6pm. Nov-Mar 10-4pm.
Admission: Please check website for details.
Key facts: WCs. Licensed. By arrangement. Cars & coaches. Assistance dogs only.

BELSAY HALL, CASTLE & GARDENS

Belsay, Nr Morpeth, Northumberland NE20 0DX

Belsay has something for everyone. A fine medieval castle, which was later extended to include a magnificent Jacobean mansion.

Location: Map 10:O2. OS Ref NZ095 784.
Tel: 01661 881636 **Website:** www.english-heritage.org.uk/belsay
Open: 2 Jan-Mar & Nov-Dec, Sat & Sun, 10am-4pm; Apr-Oct & School Hols, 10am-5pm; 27-31 Dec, 10am-4pm. **Admission:** Adult £9.70; Child £5.80.

CHIPCHASE CASTLE

Wark, Hexham, Northumberland NE48 3NT

Jacobean castle set in formal and informal gardens **Location:** Map 10:N2. 10m NW of Hexham via A6079 to Chollerton. 2m SE of Wark.
Tel: 01434 230203 **E-mail:** info@chipchasecastle.com
Website: www.chipchasecastle.com
Open: Castle: 1-28 Jun, 2-5pm daily. Gardens & Nursery: Easter-31 Aug, Thu-Sun Incl. & BH Mon, 10am-5pm. **Admission:** Castle £6, Garden £4.

Register for news and special offers at www.hudsonsheritage.com

CRAGSIDE

Rothbury, Morpeth, Northumberland NE65 7PX

Revolutionary home of Lord Armstrong, Victorian inventor and landscape genius, Cragside sits on a rocky crag high above the Debdon Burn.
Location: Map 14:L12. OS Ref NU073 022. **Tel:** 01669 620333
E-mail: cragside@nationaltrust.org.uk **Website:** www.nationaltrust.org.uk/cragisde **Open:** Feb Half Term & Apr-Oct, daily, 11-5pm. Gardens: 10-6pm; 3 Nov-17 Dec, Fri-Sun, 11-4pm. **Admission:** Adult £10.20; Child £5.10.

DUNSTANBURGH CASTLE

Dunstanburgh Road, Craster, Northumberland NE66 3TT

Reached by a beautiful coastal walk, this 14th Century castle rivals any castle of its day. **Location:** Map 14:M11. OS Ref NU257 200.
Tel: 01665 576231 **Website:** www.english-heritage.org.uk/dunstanburghcastle
Open: Winter, Sat & Sun, 10-4pm; daily at half term; Apr-Sep, daily, 10-6pm; Oct, daily, 10-4pm. **Admission:** Adult £5.20; Child £3.10.

LINDISFARNE CASTLE

Holy Island, Berwick-Upon-Tweed, Northumberland TD15 2SH

Built in 1550 to protect Holy Island harbour from attack, the castle was restored and converted into a private house for Edward Hudson in 1903.
Location: Map 14:L10. OS Ref NU136 417. **Tel:** 01289 389244
E-mail: lindisfarne@nationaltrust.org.uk **Website:** www.nationaltrust.org.uk
Open: Apr-Oct, Tue-Sun & BH Mons, 10-3pm or 12-5pm; Aug, daily, 10-3pm or 12-5pm. Alternate times depend on tides. **Admission:** Adult £7.30; Child £3.60.

PRESTON TOWER

Chathill, Northumberland NE67 5DH

Built by Sir Robert Harbottle in 1392. **Location:** Map 14:M11. OS Ref NU185 253. Follow Historic Property signs on A1 7m N of Alnwick.
Tel: 01665 589227 / 07966 150216
Website: www.prestontower.co.uk
Open: All year daily, 10am-6pm, or dusk, whichever is earlier.
Admission: Adult £2.00, Child 50p, Concessions £1.50. Groups £1.50.

SEATON DELAVAL HALL

The Avenue, Seaton Sluice, Northumberland NE26 4QR

Seaton Delaval Hall was designed by Sir John Vanbrugh for Admiral George Delaval. Beautiful formal gardens. **Location:** Map 11:A2. OS Ref NZ322 765.
Tel: 0191 237 9100 **E-mail:** seatondelavalhall@nationaltrust.org.uk
Website: www.nationaltrust.org.uk **Open:** Jan-Feb & Nov-Dec, Sat & Sun, 11-3pm; Mar, Thu-Mon, 11-5pm; Apr-Oct, daily, 11-5pm.
Admission: Adult £6.30; Child £3.15.

WALLINGTON

Cambo, Morpeth, Northumberland NE61 4AR

Impressive, yet friendly, house with a magnificent interior and fine collections. Home to many generations of the unconventional Trevelyan family.
Location: Map 10:O2. OS Ref NZ030 843. **Tel:** 01670 773600
E-mail: wallington@nationaltrust.org.uk **Website:** www.nationaltrust.org.uk/wallington **Open:** All year, daily, 10-30-5.30pm (4.30pm in winter); 27 Dec-31 Dec, Tue-Sun, 10.30-4.30pm. **Admission:** Adult £11.80; Child £5.90.

WHALTON MANOR GARDENS

Whalton, Morpeth, Northumberland NE61 3UT

The three-acre garden is bursting with inspirational planting, influenced by Gertrude Jekyll, and magnificent architectural structures designed by Sir Edwin Lutyens. **Location:** Map 10:O2. OS Ref NZ132 814.
Tel: 01670 775205 **E-mail:** gardens@whaltonmanor.co.uk
Website: www.whaltonmanor.co.uk
Open: By appointment only. Available for Group Visits.

GIBSIDE

Nr Rowlands Gill, Burnopfield, Newcastle upon Tyne NE16 6BG

Gibside is an 18th Century 'forest' landscape garden, created by wealthy coal baron George Bowes. **Location:** Map 10:P3. OS Ref NZ172 584. **Tel:** 01207 541820
E-mail: gibside@nationaltrust.org.uk **Website:** www.nationaltrust.org.uk/gibside
Open: All year, daily, 10-6pm (4pm in winter).
Admission: Adult £8.70; Child £4.50.

The Alnwick Garden

BARNARD CASTLE ⌗
Nr Galgate, Barnard Castle, Durham DL12 8PR
Tel: 01833 638212 **E-mail:** barnard.castle@english-heritage.org.uk

BEAMISH, THE LIVING MUSEUM
Beamish Museum, Beamish, County Durham DH9 0RG
Tel: 0191 370 4000 **E-mail:** museum@beamish.org.uk

BOWES CASTLE ⌗
Bowes, Barnard Castle, County Durham DL12 9HP
Tel: 01912 691215 **E-mail:** grace.dunne@english-heritage.org.uk

CROOK HALL & GARDENS
Sidegate, Durham DH1 5SZ
Tel: 0191 3848028

DURHAM CASTLE
Palace Green, Durham DH1 3RW
Tel: 0191 3343800

ROKEBY PARK
Barnard Castle, County Durham DL12 9RZ
Tel: 01609 748612 **E-mail:** admin@rokebypark.com

AYDON CASTLE ⌗
Corbridge, Northumberland NE45 5PJ
Tel: 01434 632450 **E-mail:** customers@english-heritage.org.uk

BRINKBURN PRIORY ⌗
Long Framlington, Morpeth, Northumberland NE65 8AR
Tel: 01665 570628 **E-mail:** customers@english-heritage.org.uk

CHERRYBURN
Station Bank, Mickley, Stocksfield, Northumberland NE43 7DD
Tel: 01661 843276 **E-mail:** cherryburn@nationaltrust.org.uk

CHESTERS ROMAN FORT ⌗
Chollerford, Hexham, Northumberland NE46 4EU
Tel: 01434 681379 **E-mail:** customers@english-heritage.org.uk

CORBRIDGE ROMAN TOWN ⌗
Corchester Lane, Corbridge, Northumberland NE45 5NT
Tel: 01434 632349 **E-mail:** customers@english-heritage.org.uk

EDLINGHAM CASTLE ⌗
Edlingham, Alnwick NE66 2BW
Tel: 0191 269 1200

Lady Waterford Hall

ETAL CASTLE ⌗
Cornhill-On-Tweed, Northumberland TD12 4TN
Tel: 01890 820332 **E-mail:** customers@english-heritage.org.uk

GEORGE STEPHENSON'S BIRTHPLACE
Wylam, Northumberland NE41 8BP
Tel: 01661 853457 **E-mail:** georgestephensons@nationaltrust.org.uk

HERTERTON HOUSE GARDENS
Hartington, Cambo, Morpeth, Northumberland NE61 4BN
Tel: 01670 774278

HOUSESTEADS ROMAN FORT ⌗
Haydon Bridge, Hexham, Northumberland NE47 6NN
Tel: 01434 344363 **E-mail:** customers@english-heritage.org.uk

HOWICK HALL GARDENS & ARBORETUM
Alnwick, Northumberland NE66 3LB
Tel: 01665 577285 **E-mail:** estateoffice@howickuk.com

LINDISFARNE PRIORY ⌗
Holy Island, Berwick-Upon-Tweed, Northumberland TD15 2RX
Tel: 01289 389200 **E-mail:** lindisfarne.priory@english-heritage.org.uk

MELDON PARK KITCHEN GARDEN
Morpeth, Northumberland NE61 3SW
Tel: 01670 772341 **E-mail:** michelle@flyingfox.co.uk/james@flying-fox.co.uk

NORHAM CASTLE ⌗
Norham, Northumberland TD15 2JY
Tel: 01289 304493 **E-mail:** customers@english-heritage.org.uk

PRUDHOE CASTLE ⌗
Prudhoe, Northumberland NE42 6NA
Tel: 01661 833459 **E-mail:** customers@english-heritage.org.uk

WARKWORTH CASTLE ⌗
Warkworth, Alnwick, Northumberland NE65 0UJ
Tel: 01665 711423 **E-mail:** warkworth.castle@english-heritage.org.uk

BESSIE SURTEES HOUSE ⌗
41-44 Sandhill, Newcastle, Tyne & Wear NE1 3JF
Tel: 0191 269 1200 **E-mail:** customers@english-heritage.org.uk

HYLTON CASTLE ⌗
Craigavon Road, Sunderland, Tyne and Wear SR5 3PB
Tel: 01912 611585

NEWCASTLE CASTLE
Castle Garth, Newcastle, Tyne & Wear NE1 1RQ
Tel: 0191 230 6300 **E-mail:** info@newcastlecastle.co.uk

SOUTER LIGHTHOUSE
Coast Road, Whitburn, Sunderland, Tyne & Wear SR6 7NH
Tel: 0191 529 3161 **E-mail:** souter@nationaltrust.org.uk

TYNEMOUTH CASTLE AND PRIORY ⌗
Tynemouth, Tyne & Wear NE30 4BZ
Tel: 01912 691215 **E-mail:** customers@english-heritage.org.uk

WASHINGTON OLD HALL
The Avenue, Washington Village, Tyne & Wear NE38 7LE
Tel: 0191 416 6879 **E-mail:** washington.oldhall@nationaltrust.org.uk

Register for news and special offers at **www.hudsonsheritage.com**

Durham Cathedral, Durham

Scone Palace, Perth

Glamis Castle, Strathmore

Borders

South West Scotland, Dumfries & Galloway, Ayrshire & The Isle of Arran

Edinburgh City, Coast & Countryside

Greater Glasgow Glasgow & The Clyde Valley

Tayside Perthshire, Angus, Dundee, & The Kingdom of Fife

West Highlands & Islands, Loch Lomond, Stirling & Trossachs

Grampian Highlands, Aberdeen & North East Coast

Highlands & Skye

Scotland

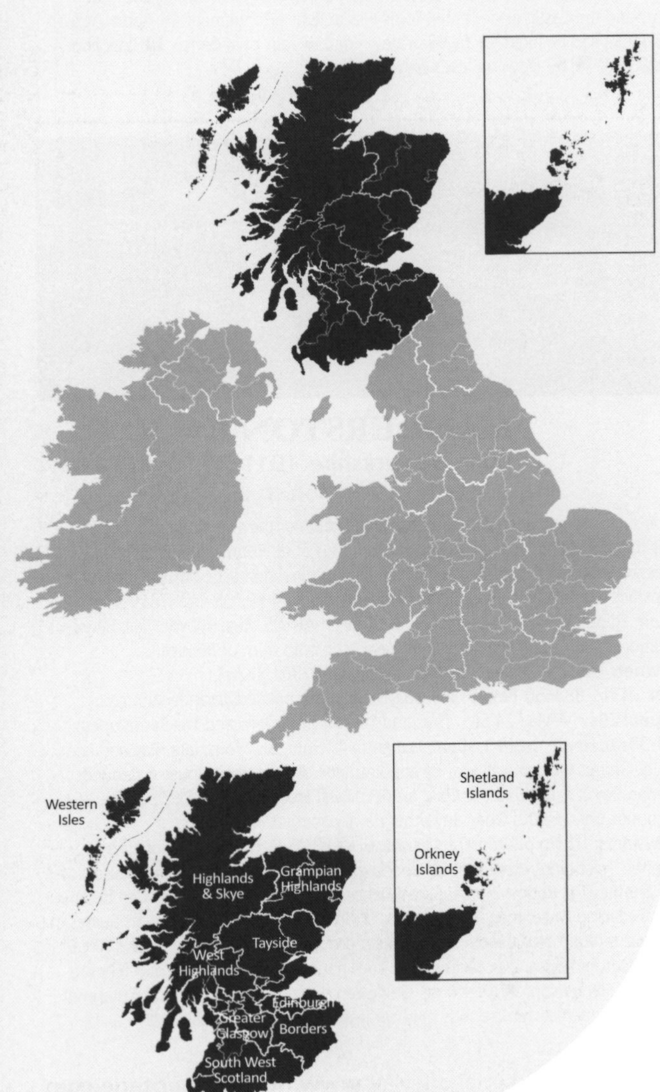

Come & visit Scotland in its Year of History, Heritage & Archaeology. Discover its rich history for yourself at the region's many castles, palaces and exceptional gardens.

FLOORS CASTLE

KELSO, THE SCOTTISH BORDERS TD5 7SF

www.floorscastle.com

Explore the spectacular State Rooms with outstanding collections of paintings, tapestries and furniture. Find hidden treasures like the collections of porcelain and oriental ceramics. Enjoy the picturesque grounds and gardens including the beautiful Victorian walled gardens. Stop at the Courtyard Café and enjoy a morning coffee or delicious lunch. For special events, please check our website.
Location: Map 14:J10. OS Ref NT711 347. From South A68, A698. From North A68, A697/9 In Kelso follow signs.
Owner: His Grace the Duke of Roxburghe **Contact:** Louise Rattray/Sarah Hepple
Tel: 01573 223333 **Fax:** 01573 226056
E-mail: estates@floorscastle.com **Open:** May-Oct

Admission: Floors Castle, Gardens & Grounds pass: Adult £12.50, Child (8–16yrs) £6.00, Family £32.00, Under 8yrs Free.
Key facts: Dogs must be kept on leads and under control at all times. Photography is not permitted within the Castle. We have 2 delightful gift shops to browse and shop. Exclusive lunches, dinner weddings and film shoots. Partial. WCs. 2 café, one open all year round serving the most delicious homemade Castle kitchen food. Team of Castle Guides dotted around the Castle or dedicated tours available by arrangement Audio App on a tablet can be hired for £2.99 or download to your own device. Cars and coaches. Dogs on leads only.

© The Abbotsford Trust

ABBOTSFORD, HOME OF SIR WALTER SCOTT

The Abbotsford Trust, Abbotsford, Melrose, Roxburghshire TD6 9BQ

www.scottsabbotsford.com

Abbotsford, the home world renowned author & poet Sir Walter Scott built on the banks of the River Tweed within the beautiful landscape of the Scottish Borders. Stunning state of the art visitor centre with restaurant, gift shop & free to access Exhibition on the Life & Legacy of Sir Walter Scott. Luxury accommodation in the Hope Scott Wing, beautiful gardens, woodland play trail, riverside & estate walks.
Location: Map 14:I10. OS Ref NT508 342. 2 miles from Melrose & Galashiels. Edinburgh 35 miles, Glasgow & Newcastle approx 70 miles. Major routes: A1, A68 and A7. **Owner:** The Abbotsford Trust **Tel:** 01896 752043 **Fax:** 01896 752916
E-mail: enquiries@scottsabbotsford.co.uk
Open: Visitors Centre: 1 Apr-30 Sep, 10am-5pm. 1 Oct-31 Mar, 10am-4pm. House & Gardens: 1-31 Mar 10am-4pm, 1 Apr-30 Sep 10am-5pm, 1 Oct-30 Nov, 10am-4pm.
Admission: House & Gardens: £8.95, £7.70 Conc, £4.50 U17 (free for 5 yrs and under). Gardens only: £3.60, £2.60 Conc & U17, Group rates available.
Key facts: Licensed. House only for groups. In house. Except in walled gardens. Hope Scott Wing, self-catering accommodation. Visitor Centre & wider Estate only.

MANDERSTON

Duns, Berwickshire TD11 3PP

www.manderston.co.uk

The supreme country house of Edwardian Scotland: the swansong of its era. Visitors are able to see not only the sumptuous State Rooms and bedrooms, decorated in the Adam manner, but also all original domestic offices, in a truly 'upstairs downstairs' atmosphere. **Location:** Map 14:K9. OS Ref NT810 544. From Edinburgh 47m, 1hr. 1½m E of Duns on A6105. Bus: 400yds. Rail: Berwick Station 12m. Airport: Edinburgh or Newcastle both 60m or 80mins.
Owner: The Lord Palmer **Contact:** Secretary: 01361 88263
Tel: 01361 883450 **Fax:** 01361 882010 **E-mail:** palmer@manderston.co.uk
Open: 2017: 4 May-24 Sep, Thus and Sun only. Gardens and Tea Room/open 11.30am. House opens 1.30pm, last entry 4.15pm. BH Mons, late May and late Aug. Groups welcome all year by appointment. **Admission:** House & Grounds (Open Days): Adult £10.00, Child (under 12yrs) Free, Groups (15+) £9.50, Grounds only: £6.00. Open any other day by appointment.
Key facts: No photography in house. Available. Buffets, lunches & dinners. Wedding receptions. Special parking available outside the house. Snaffles Tea Room - homemade lunches, teas, cakes & tray bakes. Can be booked in advance, menus on request. Included. Available in French. Guides in rooms. If requested, the owner may meet groups. Tour time 1¼ hrs. 400 cars 125yds from house, 30 coaches 5yds from house. Appreciated if group fees are paid by one person. Welcome. Guide can be provided. Biscuit Tin Museum of particular interest. Grounds only, on leads. 6 twin, 4 double.

Register for news and special offers at **www.hudsonsheritage.com**

© Mellerstain Trust

MELLERSTAIN HOUSE & GARDENS

Mellerstain, Gordon, Berwickshire TD3 6LG

www.mellerstain.com

One of Scotland's finest stately homes, this outstanding Georgian mansion house is a unique eg. of Adam design, begun in 1725 by Scottish architect William Adam & completed in 1778 by his more famous son, Robert. Some say this is one of Robert Adam's finest works, complemented by the fine art, period furniture, china & embroidery collections. Its idyllic location does not disappoint, with acres of parkland, gardens, lakeside walks, playground, coffee shop & holiday cottages.
Location: Map 14:J10. OS Ref NT648 392.
From Edinburgh A68 to Earlston, turn left 5m, signed.
Owner: The Mellerstain Trust
Contact: The Trust Administrator
Tel: 01573 410225 **Fax:** 01573 410636 **E-mail:** enquiries@mellerstain.com
Open: Easter weekend (4 days), May-Sep on Fri-Mon. House: 12.30-5pm.
Last ticket 4.15pm. Coffee shop & gardens: 11.30am-5pm.
Admission: Please see our website or call us.
Key facts: Partially suitable for visitors with limited mobility. By arrangement. Free onsite parking. Dogs on leads. Guide dogs only in the house.

© Copyright: Thirlestane Castle Trust

THIRLESTANE CASTLE

Lauder, Scottish Borders TD2 6RU

www.thirlestanecastle.co.uk

Set in the Scottish Borders at Lauder, Thirlestane Castle has its origins in the 13th Century. It was rebuilt as the Maitland's family home in 1590 and greatly enhanced by The Duke of Lauderdale in the 1670s. In 1840 it was extended and refurbished with the edition of two new wings. Thirlestane has exquisite 17th Century plasterwork ceilings, a fine portrait collection and historic toy collection. Facilities include free parking, Tea Room, playground, woodland walks and picnic area.
Location: Map 14:I9. OS Ref NT540 473. 35 minutes south of Edinburgh, signposted off A68 at Lauder. **Owner:** Thirlestane Castle Trust
Tel: 01578 722430 **E-mail:** enquiries@thirlestanecastle.co.uk
Open: Please check website for 2017 opening dates. **Admission:** Castle and Grounds: Adults £8.00; Children £3.50; Senior Citizens £6.50; Family (2+3) £20. Grounds Only: Adults £3.50; Children; £1.50. **Key facts:** Beautiful events venue for weddings, private dining, corporate and large outdoor events. Restricted access, no lift for first floor Enjoy delicious cakes or light lunch with tea and coffee in our cosy Tea Room. Groups welcome. Guided tours are available by arrangement. Free parking for cars and coaches. Stay at Thirlestane Castle in the Lauderdale Apartment.

TRAQUAIR HOUSE

Innerleithen, Peeblesshire EH44 6PW

www.traquair.co.uk

Dating back to 1107, Traquair was originally a hunting lodge for the kings and queens of Scotland. Later a refuge for Catholic priests in times of terror the Stuarts of Traquair supported Mary Queen of Scots and the Jacobite cause. Today, Traquair is a unique piece of living history.
Location: Map 13:H10. OS Ref NY330 354. On B709 near junction with A72. Edinburgh 1hr, Glasgow 1½ hrs, Carlisle 1½ hrs.
Owner/Contact: Catherine Maxwell Stuart, 21st Lady of Traquair
Tel: 01896 830323 **Fax:** 01896 830639 **E-mail:** enquiries@traquair.co.uk
Open: 1 Apr-29 Oct, 11am-5pm & 11am-4pm in Oct.
Weekends only in Nov, 11am-3pm.
Admission: House & Grounds: Adult £8.80; Child £4.50; Senior £7.80, Family £24.50 (2+3). Groups (20+): Adult £7.80; Child £3.80; Senior £6.80. Grounds only: Adults £4.50; Conc £3.50. Guide Book £4.50.
Key facts: Brewery & Gift Shops. Craft shops on site. Tours, Ale Tastings & Dinners available. Ground floor access with video about Traquair House. Disabled toilet behind restaurant. Licensed. Traquair App and tablet hire. Coaches; please book. In grounds only, on leads. Three double en suite bedrooms with antique furniture.

BOWHILL HOUSE & COUNTRY ESTATE

Bowhill, Selkirk TD7 5ET
Rich history and beautiful landscape combine at the Scottish Borders home of the Duke of Buccleuch & Queensberry KBE.
Location: Map 13:H10. OS Ref NT427 279.
Tel: 01750 22204
Open: Gardens: Apr-Oct, daily, House: Easter Weekend, 11-30-3.30pm; July, 1-5pm. **Admission:** Adult £10; Child £4.

HERMITAGE CASTLE

Scottish Borders TD9 0LU
Eerie fortress at the heart of the bloodiest events in the history of the Borders. Mary Queen of Scots make her famous ride here to visit her future husband.
Location: Map 10:L1. OS Ref NY495 960.
Tel: 01387 376222
Open: Apr-Sep, daily, 9.30-5.30pm.
Admission: Adult £4.50; Child £2.70.

MERTOUN GARDENS

St. Boswells, Melrose, Roxburghshire TD6 0EA
26 acres of beautiful grounds. Walled garden and well preserved circular dovecot.
Location: Map 14:J10. OS Ref NT617 318.
Tel: 01835 823236 **Fax:** 01835 822474 **E-mail:** estateoffice@mertoun.com
Website: www.mertoungardens.co.uk
Open: Apr-Sep, Fri-Mon 2-6pm. Last Admission 5.30pm.
Admission: Adult £5.00; Child Free.

PAXTON HOUSE, GALLERY & COUNTRY PARK

Berwick-Upon-Tweed TD15 1SZ
Palladian country house by John Adam built 1758. 12 period rooms, magnificent Picture Gallery - Partner of the National Galleries of Scotland, working Georgian kitchen. **Location:** Map 14:K9. OS Ref NT931 520.
Tel: 01289 386291 **E-mail:** info@paxtonhouse.com
Website: www.paxtonhouse.com **Open:** Apr-Oct, daily, 10-5pm.
Admission: Adult £8.50; Child U16 free.

VISITOR INFORMATION

■ Owner
The Great Steward of Scotland's Dumfries House Trust

■ Address
Dumfries House
Cumnock
East Ayrshire
Scotland
KA18 2NJ

■ Location
Map 13:C11
OS Ref. NS539 200
Dumfries House is in East Ayrshire, South West Scotland. Access is from the A70.
Rail: Auchinleck
Air: Prestwick or Glasgow

■ Contact
Visitor Services Tel:
01290 427975
Tel: Booking Line:
01290 421742
E-mail:
DHtours@dumfries-house.org.uk

■ Opening Times
Summer season:
Apr-Oct (inclusive)
7 days/week - tours from 10.45am-3.30pm (check website for Sat openings).
Guided tours at frequent intervals.
Winter season:
Nov-Mar (inclusive)
Sat and Sun only.
Sat -please check website
Sun-12.15pm and 1.45pm only.
Please note: The House is closed over the Christmas and New Year period.

Please be advised that you should go to www.dumfries-house.org.uk to confirm any House closures before your visit.

■ Admission
House Tour

Adults	£9.00
Art Fund	Free
Historic Scotland Members 25% discount	
Child (5-16 yrs)	£4.00
Grand Tour	
Adults	£13.00
Art Fund 50% discount	
Child (5-16 yrs)	£4.00
Art Tour	
Wed Only (Jul-Sep)	
Adults	£13.00
Art Fund 50% discount.	

■ Special Events
Special Events information available at www.dumfries-house.org.uk.
House available for private functions and corporate events.

DUMFRIES HOUSE

www.dumfries-house.org.uk

A Georgian Gem, nestling within 2,000 acres of scenic Ayrshire countryside in south-west Scotland.

Commissioned by William Crichton Dalrymple, the 5th Earl of Dumfries, the House was designed by renowned 18th Century architect brothers John, Robert and James Adam and built between 1754 and 1759.

Recognised as one of the Adam brothers' masterpieces it remained unseen by the public since it was built 250 years ago until it opened its doors as a visitor attraction in June 2008. The former home of the Marquesses of Bute, it was saved for the nation at the eleventh hour by a consortium of organisations and individuals brought together by HRH The Prince Charles, Duke of Rothesay.

The house holds the most important collection of works from Thomas Chippendale's 'Director' period. It is widely recognised that Scotland was a testing ground for Thomas Chippendale's early rococo furniture and the Dumfries House collection is regarded as his key project in this area.

Dumfries House also holds the most comprehensive range of pieces by Edinburgh furniture makers Alexander Peter, William Mathie and Francis Brodie. Indeed, the Scottish furniture together with the Chippendale collection is of outstanding worldwide historical significance.

KEY FACTS

- Prebooking of Tours is recommended.
- Visitor Centre and Gift Shop.
- Stairlift. WCs. 1 wheelchair per tour.
- Hot and cold food throughout the day.
- Thur-Sat evenings and Sunday Lunch.
- Obligatory.
- On leads in grounds only. Guide dogs only in the house.
- Exclusive 5 star country Guest House accommodation.
- Licensed for weddings.
- Grounds only.
- Check website for information - www.dumfries-house.org.uk.

AUCHINLECK

Ochiltree, Ayrshire KA18 2LR

www.landmarktrust.org.uk

Once diarist James Boswell's family seat, this grand 18th Century country house has its own grounds, river, ice-house and grotto. The large dining room and its elaborate plasterwork makes any meal special while the library lends itself to conversation and contemplation, just as it did for James Boswell and Dr Johnson.
Location: Map 13:C11. OS Ref NS510 226.
Owner: The Landmark Trust
Tel: 01628 825925
E-mail: bookings@landmarktrust.org.uk
Open: Self-catering accommodation. Parts of house open Easter-Oct, Wed afternoons. The Grounds are open dawn-dusk Spring and Summer.
Admission: Free on Open Days and visits by appointment.
Key facts: This building has grand, elegant rooms, a sweeping staircase, large dining and sitting rooms and plenty of open fires.

Gardens at Dumfries House

CASTLE KENNEDY GARDENS

Castle Kennedy, Stranraer
Dumfries and Galloway DG9 8SJ

www.castlekennedygardens.com

Famous 75-acre gardens situated between two large natural lochs. Ruined Castle Kennedy at one end overlooking beautiful herbaceous walled garden; Lochinch Castle at the other. Proximity to the gulf-stream provides an impressive collection of rare trees, including 20 Champion Trees, magnolias, and spectacular rhododendron displays. Guided walks, children's activities, regular ranger activities, open air theatre, bird hide, gift shop, plant centre and charming Tea Room - a 'must-visit'. **Location:** Map 9:D3. OS Ref NX109 610. 3m E of Stranraer on A75.
Owner: The Earl and Countess of Stair **Contact:** Stair Estates
Tel: 01776 702024 / 01581 400225 **E-mail:** info@castlekennedygardens.com
Open: Gardens and Tea Room: 1 Apr-31 Oct: daily 10am-5pm.
Feb & Mar: Weekends only.
Admission: Adult £5.50; Child £2.00; Conc. £4.50; Family (2+2) £12.00.
Groups of 20 or more 10% discount.
Key facts: WCs On leads only.

© National Trust for Scotland

CULZEAN CASTLE & COUNTRY PARK

Maybole, Ayrshire
KA19 8LE

www.nts.org.uk

Robert Adam's 18th Century masterpiece - a real 'castle in the air' - is perched on a cliff high above the crashing waves of the Firth of Clyde.
Location: Map 13:B11. OS Ref NS232 103. On A719, 4m west of Maybole and 12m south of Ayr. KA19 8LE
Owner: The National Trust for Scotland
Tel: 0844 493 2149
E-mail: culzean@nts.org.uk
Open: Garden: All year, daily, 9.30-5.30pm or dusk. House: Apr-Oct, daily, 10.30-5pm.
Admission: Adult £15.50.
Key facts:

GLENMALLOCH LODGE

Newton Stewart, Dumfries And Galloway DG8 6AG

www.landmarktrust.org.uk

A fairytale cottage in a wild and beautiful glen, this diminutive former schoolroom makes a perfect hideaway or writing retreat for two, or even one.

Location: Map 9:F3. OS Ref NX418 677.
Owner: The Landmark Trust
Tel: 01628 825925
E-mail: bookings@landmarktrust.org.uk
Open: Self-catering accommodation. Visits by appointment.
Admission: Free for visits by appointment.
Key facts: Although not far from Newton Stewart, the Lodge feels remote and looks out over the unspoilt and geologically interesting Galloway landscape.

CRAIGDARROCH HOUSE

Moniaive, Dumfriesshire DG3 4JB

Built by William Adam in 1729, over the old house dating from 14th Century (earliest records). The marriage home of Annie Laurie, the heroine of 'the world's greatest lovesong', who married Alexander Fergusson, 14th Laird of Craigdarroch, in 1710 and lived in the house for 33 years.

Location: Map 9:G1. OS Ref NX741 909.
S side of B729, 2m W of Moniaive, 19m WNW of Dumfries.
Owner/Contact: Mrs Carin Sykes
Tel: 01848 200202
Open: Jul: daily except Mons, 2-4pm.
Admission: £3.00.

DRUMLANRIG CASTLE

Thornhill, Dumfriesshire DG3 4AQ

Home to the Dukes of Buccleuch & Queensberry KBE. Built between 1679 and 1691 by William Douglas, 1st Duke of Queensberry.

Location: Map 10:I2. OS Ref NX851 992. **Tel:** 01848 331555
E-mail: info@drumlanrigcastle.co.uk **Website:** www.drumlanrigcastle.co.uk
Open: Apr-Sept, 10-5pm. House: Easter & May BHs, 11-4pm; Jul-Aug, daily, 11-4pm. **Admission:** Adult £6; Child £3.50.

RAMMERSCALES

Lockerbie, Dumfriesshire DG11 1LD

Fine Georgian house with views over Annan valley

Location: Map 10:I2. OS Ref NY080 780. Directions available on website.
Tel: 01387 810229 **E-mail:** malcolm@rammerscales.co.uk
Website: www.rammerscales.co.uk
Open: 1-26 May, 1pm-4pm. Bus parties by appointment.
Admission: Adult £5.00.

Auchinleck

HOPETOUN HOUSE

SOUTH QUEENSFERRY, EDINBURGH, WEST LOTHIAN EH30 9SL

www.hopetoun.co.uk

As you approach Hopetoun House the impressive panoramic view of the main façade is breathtakingly revealed. Designed by William Bruce and then altered and extended by William Adam, Hopetoun House is one of the finest examples of 18th Century architecture in Britain. Hopetoun House is filled with stunning collections and has been home to the Hope Family since the late 1600s, with the present Lord Hopetoun and his family still living in the House. As a five star Visitor Attraction, Hopetoun offers something for everyone with daily tours, 100 acres of majestic grounds with nature trails and scenic walks. The Stables Tea Room is also a must see, with traditional afternoon teas served in stunning surroundings.

Location: Map 13:F7. OS Ref NT089 790. Exit A90 at A904, Follow Brown Signs.
Owner: Hopetoun House Preservation Trust **Contact:** Reception
Tel: 0131 331 2451 **E-mail:** enquiries@hopetoun.co.uk

Open: Daily From Easter - last weekend Sep; 10.30am-5pm. Last admission 4pm. Groups (20+) welcome out of season by appointment.

Admission: House and Grounds: Adult £9.20; Child (5-16yrs)* £4.90; Conc/ Student £8.00; Family (2+2) £25.00. Grounds only: Adult £4.25; Child (5-16yrs)* £2.50; Conc/Student £3.70; Family (2+2) £11.50. *Under 5yrs Free. Winter group rates on request. Tea Room only admission is free.

Key facts: Visit www.hopetoun.co.uk/events to see our calendar of events. Private functions, wedding celebrations, banquets & gala evenings, meetings, conferences, exhibitions, incentive groups, outdoor activities, media & filming location. Lift to 1st floor, Virtual access to upper floors. WCs. Licensed. Daily tour at 2pm. Groups by arrangement. Cars & coaches welcome. Dogs permitted (on leads) in grounds. €

DALMENY HOUSE

South Queensferry, Edinburgh EH30 9TQ

www.dalmeny.co.uk

Dalmeny House, the family home of the Earls of Rosebery for over 300 years, boasts superb collections of porcelain and tapestries, fine paintings by Gainsborough, Raeburn, Reynolds and Lawrence, together with exquisite 18th Century French furniture and a superb Napoleonic collection.

Location: Map 13:G8. OS Ref NT167 779. From Edinburgh A90, B924, 7m N, A90 ½m. On south shore of Firth of Forth.
Owner: The Earl of Rosebery
Contact: The Administrator
Tel: 0131 331 1888 **Fax:** 0131 331 1788 **E-mail:** events@dalmeny.co.uk
Open: Jun & Jul Sun-Wed 2-5pm. Entry is by guided tour only and tours are 2.15pm and 3.30pm. Open at other times by appointment only for groups (20+).
Admission: Summer: Adult £10.00; Child (14-16yrs) £6.50; OAP £9.00; Student £9.00 & Groups (20+) £9.00.
Key facts: Lunches & Dinners. WCs. Obligatory. Special interest tours can be arranged outside normal opening hours. 60 cars, 3 coaches. Parking for functions in front of house. Dogs on leads in grounds only.

Edinburgh Castle

EDINBURGH CASTLE

Castle Hill, Edinburgh EH1 2NG

www.edinburghcastle.gov.uk

Edinburgh Castle, built on an extinct volcano, dominates the skyline of Scotland's capital city. Attractions include: The Honours of Scotland, The Stone of Destiny, The Great Hall, Laich Hall and St Margaret's Chapel, Prisons of War Experience, National War Memorial, the famous One O'clock Gun - fired daily Mon-Sat.

Location: Map 13:G8. OS Ref NT252 736. At the top of the Royal Mile in Edinburgh **Owner:** Historic Scotland **Tel:** 0131 225 9846

E-mail: hs.explorer@scotland.gsi.gov.uk **Open:** Apr-Sep, daily, 9.30-6pm; Oct-Mar, 9.30-5pm. Last tickets sold 1 hour before closing. Closed Christmas Day and Boxing Day. Visit the website for New Year opening times.

Admission: Adult £16.50, Conc £13.20, Child £9.90.

Key facts: Disabled parking only, blue disabled badge required. Private evening hire. WCs. Regular tours included in admission price. Check website for details. In 8 languages. Assistance dogs only. €

GOSFORD HOUSE

Longniddry, East Lothian EH32 0PX

www.gosfordhouse.co.uk

1791 the 7th Earl of Wemyss, aided by Robert Adam, built one of the grandest houses in Scotland, with a 'paradise' of lakes and pleasure grounds. New wings, including the celebrated Marble Hall were added in 1891 by William Young. The house has a fine collection of paintings and furniture.

Location: Map 14:17. OS Ref NT453 786. Off A198 2m NE of Longniddry.

Owner/Contact: The Earl of Wemyss

Tel: 01875 870201

Open: Please check our website for most up-to-date opening times/days.

Admission: Adult £8.00, O.A.P./Students £5.00, Child under 16 Free.

Key facts:

By arrangement.

Limited for coaches.

Hopetoun House

© VisitBritain/Britain on View

PALACE OF HOLYROODHOUSE

Edinburgh
EH8 8DX

www.royalcollection.org.uk

The Palace of Holyroodhouse, the official residence of Her Majesty The Queen, stands at the end of the Royal Mile against the spectacular backdrop of Arthur's Seat.
Location: Map 13:G8. OS Ref NT110 735. Central Edinburgh.
Owner: Official Residence of Her Majesty The Queen
Contact: Ticket Sales & Information Office
Tel: +44 (0)131 556 5100
E-mail: bookinginfo@royalcollection.org.uk
Open: Nov-Mar, daily, 9.30-4.30pm; Apr-Oct, daily, 9.30-6pm.
Admission: Adult £12; Child £7.20.
Key facts: Assistance dogs welcome.

AMISFIELD MAINS

Nr Haddington, East Lothian EH41 3SA
Georgian farmhouse with gothic barn and cottage.
Location: Map 14:I8. OS Ref NT526 755.
Between Haddington and East Linton on A199.
Tel: 01875 870201 **Fax:** 01875 870620
Open: Exterior only: By appointment, Wemyss and March Estates Office, Longniddry, East Lothian EH32 0PY. **Admission:** Please contact for details.

ARNISTON HOUSE

Gorebridge, Midlothian EH23 4RY
Magnificent William Adam mansion started in 1726. Beautiful country setting beloved by Sir Walter Scott. **Location:** Map 13:H9. OS Ref NT326 595. 1 mile from A7 at Gorebridge **Tel:** 01875 830515 **E-mail:** info@arniston-house.co.uk **Website:** www.arniston-house.co.uk **Open:** May & Jun: Tue & Wed; Jul-10 Sep: Tue, Wed & Sun, guided tours at 2pm & 3.30pm. Pre-arranged groups. **Admission:** Adult £6.00, Child £3.00.

BEANSTON

Nr Haddington, East Lothian EH41 3SB
Georgian farmhouse with Georgian orangery.
Location: Map 14:I8. OS Ref NT450 766.
Between Haddington and East Linton on A199.
Tel: 01875 870201
Open: Exterior only: By appointment, Wemyss and March Estates Office, Longniddry, East Lothian EH32 0PY. **Admission:** Please contact for details.

GLADSTONE'S LAND

477B Lawnmarket, Royal Mile EH1 2NT
The house of wealthy merchant and landlord Thomas Gledstanes showcases high-rise living, 17th Century style, at the heart of Edinburgh's historic Royal Mile.
Location: Map 13:G8. OS Ref NT255 735.
Tel: 0131 226 5856
Website: www.nts.org.uk/property/gladstones-land
Open: Apr-Oct, daily, 10-5pm. **Admission:** Adult £7.

HARELAW FARMHOUSE

Nr Longniddry, East Lothian EH32 0PH
Early 19th Century 2-storey farmhouse built as an integral part of the steading. Dovecote over entrance arch. **Location:** Map 14:I8. OS Ref NT450 766. Between Longniddry and Drem on B1377. **Tel:** 01875 870201
Open: Exteriors only: By appointment, Wemyss and March Estates Office, Longniddry, East Lothian EH32 0PY. **Admission:** Please contact for details.

LINLITHGOW PALACE

Linlithgow, West Lothian EH49 7AL
The royal pleasure palace was the birthplace of Mary Queen of Scots. Visit the great hall where Monarchs hosted banquets.
Location: Map 13:F8. OS Ref NS996 774.
Tel: 01506 842896 **E-mail:** hs.explorer@scotland.gsi.gov.uk
Website: www.historic-scotland.gov.uk
Open: Apr-Sep, daily, 9.30-5.30pm. **Admission:** Adult £5.50; Child £3.30.

NEWLISTON

Kirkliston, West Lothian EH29 9EB
Late Robert Adam house. 18th Century designed landscape, rhododendrons, azaleas and water features.
Location: Map 13:G8. OS Ref NT110 735. 9miles W of Edinburgh, 4miles S of Forth Road Bridge, off B800. **Tel:** 0131 333 3231
Open: 3 May–4 Jun: Wed–Sun, 2–6pm. Also by appointment.
Admission: Adult: £4.00; Child (under 12) Free of charge.

RED ROW

Aberlady, East Lothian EH32 0DE
Terraced Cottages.
Location: Map 14:I7. OS Ref NT464 798. Main Street, Aberlady, East Lothian.
Tel: 01875 870201 **Fax:** 01875 870620
Open: Exterior only. By appointment, Wemyss and March Estates Office, Longniddry, East Lothian EH32 0PY.
Admission: Please contact for details.

Arniston House

© New Lanark Trust

NEW LANARK WORLD HERITAGE SITE

New Lanark Mills, Lanark, South Lanarkshire ML11 9DB

www.newlanark.org

Close to the famous Falls of Clyde, this cotton mill village c1785 became famous as the site of Robert Owen's radical reforms. Beautifully restored as a living community and attraction, the fascinating history of the village has been interpreted in New Lanark Visitor Centre.

Location: Map 13:E9. Sat Nav code ML11 9BY. Nearest train station is Lanark. Glasgow > Lanark Bus from Buchanan Bus Station. **Owner:** New Lanark Trust

Contact: Trust Office **Tel:** 01555 661345 **E-mail:** trust@newlanark.org

Open: 10am-5pm Apr-Oct, 10am-4pm Nov-Mar. Shops/catering open until 5pm daily. Closed 25 Dec and 1 Jan.

Admission: Visitor Centre: Adult £9.50, Conc. (senior/student) £8.00, Child £7.00. Family (2+2) £30.00. Groups: 1 free/11 booked.

Key facts: Mill Shop. New Lanark Mill Hotel. Suitable. WC Mill Café. Mill One Restaurant. Book guided tours in advance. Cars & coaches. 5 min walk. Contact for information. Only service dogs inside buildings. Hotel, Self-catering & Hostel.

COREHOUSE

Lanark ML11 9TQ

Designed by Sir Edward Blore and built in the 1820s, Corehouse is a pioneering example of the Tudor Architectural Revival in Scotland.

Location: Map 13:E9. OS Ref NS882 416. Located on South bank of Clyde above Kirkfieldbank. At West Lodge, drive to bottom of hill. **Tel:** 01555 663126

Open: 1-29 May & 5-8 Aug: Sat–Wed. Tours: weekdays: 1 & 2pm, weekends: 2 & 3pm. Closed Thu & Fri. **Admission:** Adult £7.00, Child (under 16yrs)/OAP £4.00.

GLASGOW CATHEDRAL

Castle Street, Glasgow G4 0QZ

The only Scottish mainland medieval cathedral to have survived the Reformation complete. Built over the tomb of Kentigern.

Location: Map 13:D8. OS Ref NS602 655.

Tel: 0141 552 6891 **Website:** www.glasgowcathedral.org.uk

Open: Apr-Sep, Mon-Sat, 9.30-5.30pm; Sun, 1-5pm.

Admission: Free.

THE HILL HOUSE

Upper Colquhoun Street, Helensburgh G84 9AJ

Charles Rennie Mackintosh set this 20th Century masterpiece high on a hillside overlooking the Firth of Clyde. Mackintosh also designed furniture, fittings and decorative schemes to complement the house.

Location: Map 13:B7. OS Ref NS299 838.

Tel: 0844 493 2208 **E-mail:** thehillhouse@nts.org.uk

Open: Apr-Oct, daily, 11.30-5pm. **Admission:** Adult: £10.50.

POLLOK HOUSE

2060 Pollokshaws Road, Glasgow G43 1AT

The present house dates from around 1750 and contains a fine collection of Spanish art, together with furniture and furnishings appropriate to an Edwardian country house. **Location:** Map 13:C8. OS Ref NS557 612.

Tel: 0844 493 2202 **E-mail:** information@nts.org.uk **Website:** www.nts.org.uk

Open: Apr-Oct, daily, 10-5pm; Nov-24 Dec, Mon-Fri, 11-5pm; Sat & Sun, 10-5pm.

Admission: Adult £6.50.

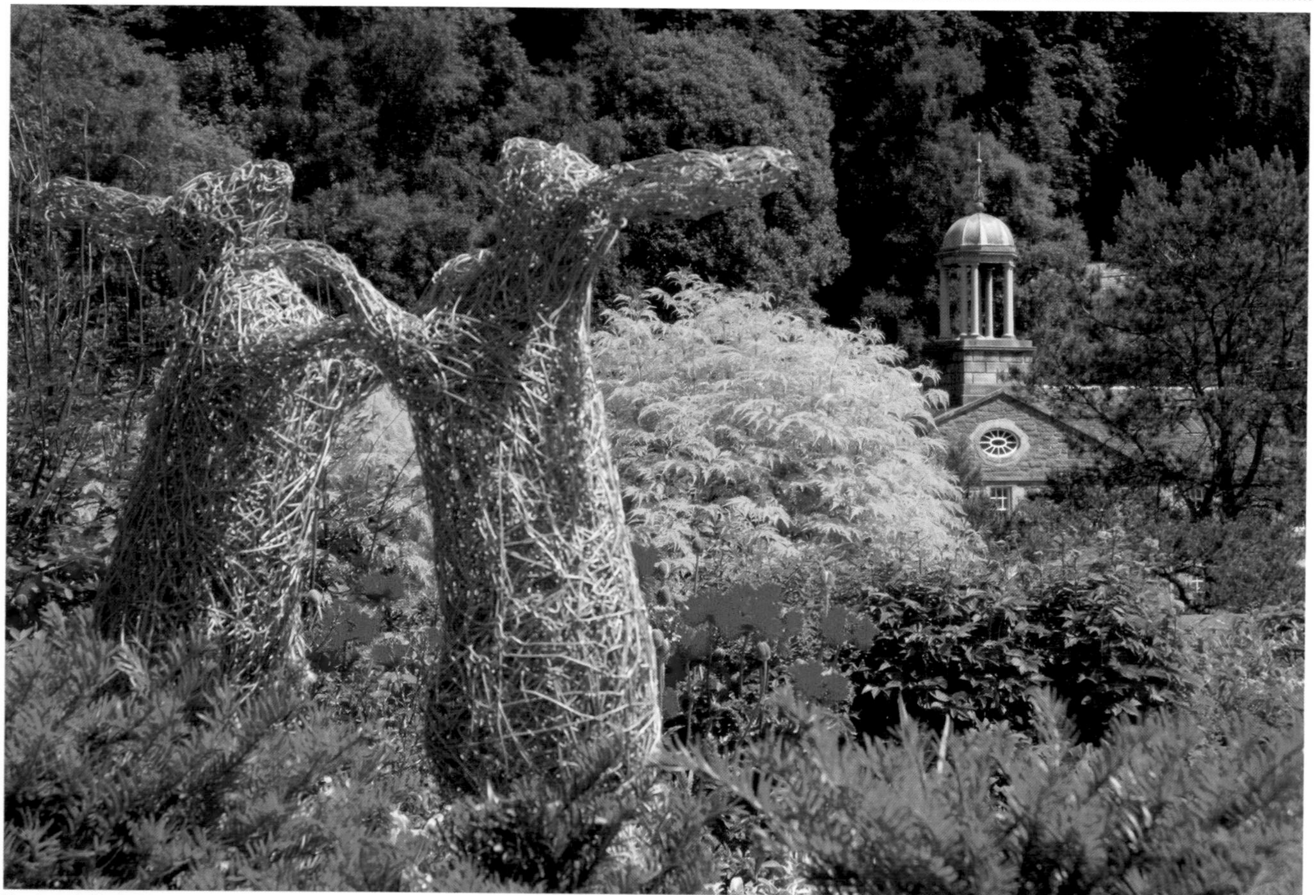

New Lanark Gardens

GLAMIS CASTLE & GARDENS

GLAMIS, FORFAR, ANGUS DD8 1RJ

www.glamis-castle.co.uk

Ancestral home of the Earls of Strathmore and Kinghorne. Childhood home of the Queen Mother. A fairytale castle of both history and mystery, also renowned as the most haunted castle in Scotland. Ghost stories abound on the 10 room guided tour which takes approximately one hour. Hear about the card playing earls, the Grey Lady and the ghostly servant boy in the Royal Apartments as well as seeing a snapshot of one family's contribution to Scottish history. Extend your visit to include a walk round our Italian and walled gardens or have lunch in our Victorian Kitchen Restaurant. We have special admission rates for groups and can offer group lunches to be booked in advance.

Location: Map 13:H4. OS Ref NO386 480.

15 min from Dundee. 35 min from Perth, one hour from Aberdeen and 1 hr 30min from Edinburgh and Glasgow. Turn off the A90 at Forfar and take the A94 to Glamis approx 5 miles.

Owner: The Earl of Strathmore & Kinghorne

Contact: Thomas Baxter, General Manager

Tel: 01307 840393

Fax: 01307 840733

E-mail: enquiries@glamis-castle.co.uk

Open: Daily 1 Apr-29 Oct from 11am-5.30pm (last admission 4.30pm)

Admission: Please see website for admission rates.

Key facts: No photography in castle. Gala corporate dinners and weddings a speciality. Limited disabled access in castle, free mobile scooter can be reserved. Schools are very welcome and Guided Tours of the castle are tailored for all ages and interests. On lead, in grounds only. By appointment out of season.

BLAIR CASTLE & GARDENS

Blair Atholl, Pitlochry, Perthshire PH18 5TL

www.blair-castle.co.uk

Blair Castle has a centuries old history as a strategic stonghold at the gateway to the Grampians and the route North to Inverness.

Location: Map 13:E3. OS Ref NN880 660.

Owner: Blair Charitable Trust **Contact:** Administration Office

Tel: 01796 481207 **E-mail:** bookings@blair-castle.co.uk

Open: Easter-Oct, daily, 9.30-5.30pm.

Admission: Adult £10.70; Child £6.40.

Key facts: Photography allowed in Ballroom only. Licensed Gift Shop. Private functions, civil and religious weddings. Partial. WCs. Licensed. Licensed. Guides available when booked in advance. 200 cars, 20 coaches. Coach drivers/couriers free, plus meal and shop voucher and information pack. Nature walks, ranger service, pony trekking and adventure playground. Dogs in grounds only Guide dogs only. Civil Wedding Licence. Regular winter opening.

DRUMMOND GARDENS

Muthill, Crieff, Perthshire PH7 4HN

www.drummondcastlegardens.co.uk

Scotland's most important formal gardens. The Italianate parterre is revealed from a viewpoint at the top of the terrace. First laid out in the 17th Century and renewed in the 1950s. The perfect setting to stroll amongst the manicured plantings and absorb the atmosphere of this special place.

Location: Map 13:E5. OS Ref NN844 181. 2m S of Crieff off the A822.

Owner: Grimsthorpe & Drummond Castle Trust, a registered charity SC03964

Contact: The Caretaker **Tel:** 01764 681433 **Fax:** 01764 681642

E-mail: info@drummondcastlegardens.co.uk

Open: Easter weekend, then daily. May, Sep, Oct at 1-6pm. Jun, Jul, Aug at 11-6pm. Last admission 5pm.

Admission: Adult £5.00; Child £2.00; Groups (20+) £4.50.

Special rates available for out of hours visits and guided garden tours.

Key facts: Partial. WCs. Viewing platform. Special vehicle access, ask on arrival. Gravel paths. By arrangement for groups Dogs on leads.

SCONE PALACE & GROUNDS

Perth
PH2 6BD
www.scone-palace.co.uk

1500 years ago it was the capital of the Picts. In the intervening centuries, it has been the seat of parliaments and the crowning place of the Kings of Scots.
Location: Map 13:G5. OS Ref NO114 266.
Owner: The Earl of Mansfield
Contact: The Administrator
Tel: 01738 552300 **E-mail:** visits@scone-palace.co.uk
Open: Gardens only: 3 Feb-Mar & 3 Nov-17 Dec, Fri-Sun, 10-4pm. House: Mar, Apr, Oct, daily, 10-4pm; May-Sep, daily, 10-5pm.
Admission: Adult £11; Child £8.
Key facts: No photography in state rooms. Gift shop and food shop. Grand dinners in state rooms (inc. buffets and cocktail parties). WCs. By Arrangement. Guides in each room. Private tours. 300 cars and 15 coaches (coaches - booking preferable). Couriers/drivers free meal and admittance. Welcome. Dogs in grounds only. By Appointment.

BALCARRES

Colinsburgh, Fife KY9 1HN
16th Century tower house with 19th Century additions by Burn and Bryce. Woodland and terraced gardens.
Location: Map 14:I6. OS Ref NO475 044.
½m North of Colinsburgh.
Owner: Balcarres Heritage Trust
Contact: Lord Balniel
Tel: 01333 340206
Open: Woodland & Gardens: 1 Mar-30 Sep, 2-5pm.
House not open except by written appointment and 1-30 Apr, excluding Sun.
Admission: House £8.00
Garden £8.00
House & Garden £15.00
Key facts: Partial.
By arrangement.
Dogs on leads only.

CORTACHY ESTATE

Cortachy, Kirriemuir, Angus DD8 4LX
Countryside walks including access through woodlands to Airlie Monument on Tulloch Hill with spectacular views of the Angus Glens and Vale of Strathmore. Footpaths are waymarked and colour coded. **Location:** Map 13:H3. OS Ref N0394 596. Off the B955 Glens Road from Kirriemuir. **Owner:** Trustees of Airlie Estates
Contact: Estate Office **Tel:** 01575 570108 **Fax:** 01575 540400
E-mail: office@airlieestates.com **Website:** www.airlieestates.com
Open: Walks all year. Gardens 19-22 Apr; 1 & 15 May-4 Jun inclusive; 14 Aug & 4 Sep. Last admission 3.30pm.
Admission: Please contact estate office for details.
Key facts: The estate network of walks are open all year round. The gardens and grounds can be hired for the location and setting of wedding ceremonies and photographs. Unsuitable. By arrangement. Limited. Dogs on leads only. Licensed to hold Civil Weddings and can offer wedding receptions, either a marquee in the grounds or a reception within the Castle.

CHARLETON HOUSE

Colinsburgh, Leven, Fife KY9 1HG
The house is protected as a category A listed building, and the grounds are included on the Inventory of Gardens and Designed Landscapes in Scotland, the national listing of significant gardens. **Location:** Map 14:I6. OS Ref NO464 036. Off A917. 1m NW of Colinsburgh. 3m NW of Elie.
Tel: 01333 340249 **Open:** 1 Sep-2 Oct: daily, 12 noon-3pm.
Guided tours obligatory, admission every ½hr. **Admission:** £12.00.

FALKLAND PALACE & GARDEN

Falkland, Fife KY15 7BU
The Royal Palace of Falkland, built between 1502 and 1541 and set in the heart of a unique medieval village. **Location:** Map 13:G6. OS Ref NO252 073.
On A912, 10 miles from M90, junction 8.
Tel: 0844 493 2186 **E-mail:** information@nts.org.uk **Website:** www.nts.org.uk
Open: Mar-Oct. See our website or call us for more up-to-date opening times.
Admission: Please see our website or call us for up-to-date prices.

GLENEAGLES

Auchterarder, Perthshire PH3 1PJ
Gleneagles has been the home of the Haldane family since the 12th Century. The 18th Century pavilion is open to the public by written appointment.
Location: Map 13:F6. OS Ref NS931 088.
0.75 miles S of A9 on A823. 2.5m S of Auchterarder.
Tel: 01764 682388 **Fax:** 01764 682535 **E-mail:** jmhaldane@gleneagles.org
Open: By written appointment only.

MONZIE CASTLE

Crieff, Perthshire PH7 4HD
Built in 1791. Destroyed by fire in 1908 and rebuilt and furnished by Sir Robert Lorimer.
Location: Map 13:E5. OS Ref NN873 244. 2miles NE of Crieff.
Tel: 01764 653110 **Open:** 13 May- 11 Jun: daily, 2-4.30pm.
By appointment at other times. **Admission:** Adult £5.00, Child £1.00.
Group rates available, contact property for details.

STRATHTYRUM HOUSE & GARDENS

St Andrews, Fife KY16 9SF
Location: Map 14:I5. OS Ref NO490 172. Entrance from the St Andrews/Guardbridge Road which is signposted when open.
Tel: 01334 473600 **E-mail:** info@strathtyrumhouse.com
Open: Mon-Thu weeks beginning 3, 10, 17, 24 April, 1, 8 & 15 May: Guided tours at 2pm and 3pm.
Admission: Adult £5.00, Child + Concessions £2.50.

TULLIBOLE CASTLE

Crook Of Devon, Kinross KY13 0QN
Scottish tower house c1608 with ornamental fishponds, a roofless lectarn doocot, 9th Century graveyard.
Location: Map 13:F6. OS Ref NO540 888. B9097 1m E of Crook of Devon.
Tel: 01577 840236 **E-mail:** info@tullibole.co.uk **Website:** www.tullibole.co.uk
Open: Last week in Aug-30 Sep: Tue-Sun, 1-4pm.
Admission: Adult £5.50, Child/Conc. £3.50. Free for Doors Open weekend.

Diana's Grove at Blair Castle

Register for news and special offers at **www.hudsonsheritage.com**

INVERARAY CASTLE & GARDENS

www.inveraray-castle.com

Inveraray Castle & Gardens - Home to the Duke & Duchess of Argyll and ancestral home of the Clan Campbell.

The ancient Royal Burgh of Inveraray lies about 60 miles north west of Glasgow by Loch Fyne in an area of spectacular natural beauty. The ruggedness of the highland scenery combines with the sheltered tidal loch, beside which nestles the present Castle built between 1745 and 1790. The Castle is home to the Duke and Duchess of Argyll. The Duke is head of the Clan Campbell and his family have lived in Inveraray since the early 15th Century. Designed by Roger Morris and decorated by Robert Mylne, the fairy-tale exterior belies the grandeur of its gracious interior. The Clerk of Works, William Adam, father of Robert and John, did much of the laying out of the present Royal Burgh, which is an unrivalled example of an early planned town. Visitors enter the famous Armoury Hall containing some 1,300 pieces including Brown Bess muskets, Lochaber axes, 18th Century Scottish broadswords, and can see preserved swords from the Battle of Culloden. The fine State Dining Room and Tapestry Drawing Room contain magnificent French tapestries made especially for the Castle, fabulous examples of Scottish, English and French furniture and a wealth of other works of art. The unique collection of china, silver and family artefacts spans the generations which are identified by a genealogical display in the Clan Room.

The castle's private garden which was opened to the public in 2010 for the first time is also not to be missed, especially in springtime with its stunning displays of rhododendrons and azaleas.

KEY FACTS

- No flash photography. Guide books in French, Italian and German translations.
- A wide range of Scottish gifts, books and Clan Campbell memorabilia.
- A varied selection of plants & shrubs available for purchase.
- Inveraray Castle provides the perfect location for corporate events of all sizes.
- Partial. Disabled Toilet inside the Castle.
- Licenced Tea Room serving lunches, tea/coffee, soft drinks and home baking.
- Available for up to 46 people per group. Tour time: approx 1 hr.
- 100 cars. Car/coach park close to Castle.
- £4.00 per child. Areas of interest include a woodland walk.
- Guide dogs only.

VISITOR INFORMATION

Owner
Duke of Argyll

Address
Inveraray Castle
Inveraray
Argyll
Scotland
PA32 8XE

Location
Map 13:A6
OS Ref. NN100 090
From Edinburgh 2½-3hrs via Glasgow. Just NE of Inveraray on A83. W shore of Loch Fyne.
Bus: Bus route stopping point within ½ mile.

Contact
Argyll Estates
Tel: 01499 302203
Fax: 01499 302421
For all corporate events and wedding enquiries please contact Jane Young
Email: manager@inveraray-castle.com.
E-mail: enquiries@inveraray-castle.com

Opening Times
1 Apr-31 Oct
Open 7 days 10am-5.45pm

(Last admission 5pm).

Admission
Castle & Gardens\ Group Rate*

Adults	£11.00 £8.80*
Senior Citizens	£10.00 £8.00*
Students (only valid with student card)	£10.00 £8.00*
Schools	£4.00*
Children (under 16)	£8.00 £6.40*
Family Ticket (2 adults & 2 or more children)	£32.00
Children Under 5	Free
Garden Only	£5.00

A 20% discount is allowed on groups of 20 or more persons (as shown with *).

Coach/Car Park Charge per vehicle (for non-Castle visitors) £3.00 redeemable in Tea Room or Gift shop when spending £10.00 or more.

Special Events
Check website www.inveraray-castle.com for details of forthcoming events.

MOUNT STUART

ISLE OF BUTE PA20 9LR

www.mountstuart.com

One of the world's finest houses - Mount Stuart, ancestral home of the Marquess of Bute, is a stupendous example of Victorian Gothic architecture set amidst 300 acres of gloriously landscaped gardens. Spectacular interiors include the stunning white Marble Chapel and magnificent Marble Hall complete with kaleidoscopic stained glass. A Fine Art Collection and astounding architectural detail presents both stately opulence and unrivalled imagination. With something for all the family, this award-winning visitor attraction offers facilities including way-marked walks, Tea Room, Gift Shop, picnic areas, Adventure Play Area and Contemporary Visual Arts Exhibition.

Location: Map 13:A9. OS Ref NS100 600.
SW coast of Scotland, 5 miles S of Rothesay.

Owner: Mount Stuart Trust
Contact: Mount Stuart Office
Tel: 01700 503877
Fax: 01700 505313
E-mail: contactus@mountstuart.com
Open: Seasonal opening. May be closed occasionally for private functions, please check website before travelling.
Admission: Please see our website for up-to-date information.
Key facts: Photography permitted. Gardens - Partial disabled access. Ample. Well behaved dogs on leads welcome. Assistance dogs only in House. Exclusive - House/Self-Catering - Grounds.

Castle Stalker

© Duart Castle, Isle of Mull

DUART CASTLE

Isle Of Mull, Argyll PA64 6AP

www.duartcastle.com

The 13th Century Castle of the Clan Maclean proudly guards the sea cliffs of the Isle of Mull. Explore the ancient island fortress with dungeons, keep, state rooms, great hall, museum & battlements. Discover our Summer Events, award-winning Tea Room, Gift Shop, Cottage Garden, Millennium Wood and coastal walks around Duart Point. The set for 1999 film "Entrapment" with Sean Connery.
Location: Map 12:O4. OS Ref NM750 350. Off A849, 3.5 miles from Craignure Ferry Terminal. The Duart Coach operates between the Ferry and the Castle.
Owner/Contact: Sir Lachlan Maclean Bt
Tel: 01680 812309
E-mail: guide@duartcastle.com
Open: 2 Apr-8 Oct 2017. The castle will be shut in Apr on Fris and Sats except over the Easter weekend.
Admission: For 2017 prices, please see our website for more details.
Key facts: Summer events calendar Gift Shop Award-winning Tea Room Dining Events 50m away Schools welcome Dogs welcome Duart cottage Weddings

STIRLING CASTLE

Stirling FK8 1EJ

www.stirlingcastle.gov.uk

Experience the refurbished 16th Century Royal Palace where you can explore the richly decorated King's and Queen's apartments. Other highlights include the Great Hall, Chapel Royal, Regimental Museum, Tapestry Studio and the Great Kitchens. Don't miss our guided tour where you can hear tales of the castle's history.
Location: Map 13:E7. OS Ref NS790 941. Leave the M9 at junction 10. and follow road signs for the castle.
Owner: Historic Scotland
Tel: 01786 450000
E-mail: hs.explorer@scotland.gsi.gov.uk
Open: Apr-Sep, daily, 9.30-6pm; Oct-Mar, daily, 9.30-5pm. Last ticket is sold 45 minutes before closing. Visit website for New Year opening times.
Admission: Adult £14.50; Concessions £11.00; Child £8.20.
Key facts: Private hire. Partial. WCs. Licensed. Licensed. Obligatory. Limited for coaches. Car parking is available £4.00. Assistance dogs only. €

ARDKINGLAS HOUSE & WOODLAND GARDEN

Estate Office, The Square, Cairndow, Argyll PA26 8BH

Situated on the shores of Loch Fyne in Argyll, against a spectacular background of mountain and forest, Ardkinglas Estate covers about 4800 hectares.
Location: Map 13:A6. OS Ref NN180 106. **Tel:** 01499 600261
E-mail: info@ardkinglas.com **Website:** www.ardkinglas.com
Open: Gardens: All year, daily, dawn-dusk. House: Apr-Oct, Fri, pre-book only.
Admission: £5 donation.

ARDTORNISH ESTATE & GARDENS

Morvern, Nr. Oban, Argyll & Bute PA80 5UZ

30 acres of garden including over 200 species of rhododendron, extensive planting for year round interest. **Location:** Map 12.O4. OS Ref NM702 472. In Ardtornish (Highland region, nr Loch Aline) - just off the A884 to Mull **Tel:** 01967 421288
E-mail: stay@ardtornish.co.uk **Website:** www.ardtornishgardens.co.uk
Open: Mar-Nov, Mon-Sun, 9am-6pm. **Admission:** £4.00 per person.

CASTLE STALKER

Portnacroish, Appin, Argyll PA38 4BL

Early 15th Century tower house and seat of the Stewarts of Appin. Set on an islet 400 yds off the shore of Loch Linnhe. **Location:** Map 12:P3. OS Ref NM930 480.
Tel: 01631 730354 **E-mail:** houseofkeil@hotmail.com
Website: www.castlestalker.com
Open: Please refer to website for tour dates.
Admission: Adult £20.00, Child £10.00.

DOUNE CASTLE

Doune FK16 6EA

A formidable 14th Century courtyard castle, built for the Regent Albany. The striking keep-gatehouse combines domestic quarters including the splendid Lord's Hall with its carved oak screen, musicians' gallery and double fireplace.
Location: Map 13:D6. OS Ref NN730 011. **Tel:** 01786 841742
Open: Apr-Sep, daily, 9.30am-5.30pm; Oct-Mar, daily, 10am-4pm.
Admission: Adult £5.50; Child £3.30.

Inveraray Castle and Gardens

CRAIGSTON CASTLE

Turriff, Aberdeenshire AB53 5PX

www.craigston-castle.co.uk

Built between 1604 and 1607 by John Urquhart Tutor of Cromarty. Two wings were added in the early 1700s. The beautiful sculpted balcony, unique in Scottish architecture, depicts a piper, two grinning knights and David and Goliath. Remarkable carved oak, panels of Scottish kings' biblical heroes, originally from the family seat at Cromarty castle were mounted in doors and shutters in the early 17th Century. The house is a private home and is still owned and lived in by the Urquhart family.

Location: Map 17:D8. OS Ref NJ762 550. On B9105, 4.5m NE of Turriff.
Owner: William Pratesi Urquhart **Contact:** Claus Perch
Tel: 01888551707 **E-mail:** info@craigston.co.uk
Open: 31 Mar-10 Apr & 13-30 Oct 2017, from 1-4pm.
Plus throughout the year by appointment. **Admission:** Adult £6.00, Child £2.00, Conc. £4.00. Groups: Adult £5.00, Child/School £1.00.
Key facts: Bespoke events can be organised with partner organisations. The house can be let on an exclusive self-catering basis. Very limited wheelchair access. Obligatory.

DELGATIE CASTLE

Turriff, Aberdeenshire AB53 5TD

www.delgatiecastle.com

'Best Visitor Experience' Award Winner. Dating from 1030 the Castle is steeped in Scottish history yet still has the atmosphere of a lived in home. It has some of the finest painted ceilings in Scotland, Mary Queen of Scots' bed-chamber. Clan Hay Centre. Scottish Home Baking Award Winner. Victorian Christmas Fayre held the last weekend in November and first weekend December. The castle is decorated throughout this period with decorations, Christmas trees and much more. Santa is here for the children with a pre-christmas present, crafters in many of the rooms throughout the Castle and staff in period costume.

Location: Map 17:D9. OS Ref NJ754 506. Off A947 Aberdeen to Banff Road.
Owner: Delgatie Castle Trust
Contact: Mrs Joan Johnson
Tel: 01888 563479 **E-mail:** joan@delgatiecastle.com
Open: Daily 15 Jan-20 Dec. 1 Apr-30 Sep, 10am-5pm. 1 Oct-31 Mar, 10am-4pm.
Admission: Adult £8.00, Child/Conc. £5.00, Family £21.00 (2 Adults & 2 Children), Groups (10+): £5.00. B&B in Symbister Suite £60.00 pppn.
Key facts: No photography. WCs. By arrangement. Guide dogs only. 2 self-catering apartments in Castle.

CRIMONMOGATE

Lonmay, Fraserburgh, Aberdeenshire AB43 8SE

Situated in Aberdeenshire, Crimonmogate is a Grade A listed mansion house and one of the most easterly stately homes in Scotland, it is now owned by William and Candida, Viscount and Viscountess Petersham. Pronounced 'Crimmon-moggat', this exclusive country house stands within beautiful and seasonally-changing parkland and offers one of Aberdeenshire's most outstanding and unusual venues for corporate events, parties, dinners and weddings.

Location: Map 17:F8. OS Ref NK043 588.
Owner/Contact: Viscount Petersham **Tel:** 01346 532401
E-mail: info@cmg-events.co.uk **Website:** www.cmg-events.co.uk
Open: 1-8 May, 18-30 Jun, Aug 27-1 Sep. Tours at 10.30am, 11.30am, and 12.30pm, or by appointment.
Admission: Adult £7.00, Conc. £6.00, Child £5.00.
Max of 12 at any one time, guided tours only.
Key facts: Weddings & special events: max 60 in hall & up to 200 in Marquee. Only the principal rooms are part of the tour. No dogs.

BALFLUIG CASTLE

Alford, Aberdeenshire AB33 8EJ

Small 16th Century tower house, restored in 1967. Its garden and wooded park are surrounded by farmland.

Location: Map 17:D11. OS Ref NJ586 151. Alford, Aberdeenshire.
Tel: 020 7624 3200
Open: Please write to M I Tennant Esq, 30 Abbey Gardens, London NW8 9AT.

CRATHES CASTLE, GARDEN & ESTATE

Banchory, Aberdeenshire AB31 3QJ

Fairytale-like turrets, gargoyles of fantastic design and the ancient Horn of Leys given in 1323 by Robert the Bruce are just a few features of this historic castle.

Location: Map 17:D12. OS Ref NO735 967. **Tel:** 0844 493 2166
E-mail: crathes@nts.org.uk **Website:** www.nts.org.uk
Open: All year, daily, 11-4pm. House: Jan-Mar, Sat & Sun, 11-3pm; Apr-Oct, daily, 10-30-5pm; 1 Nov-23 Dec, Sat & Sun, 11-3pm. **Admission:** Adult £12.50.

DRUMMUIR CASTLE

Drummuir, By Keith, Banffshire AB55 5JE

Castellated Victorian Gothic-style castle built in 1847 by Admiral Duff. 60ft high lantern tower with fine plasterwork, family portraits and interesting artefacts.

Location: Map 17:B9. OS Ref NJ372 442. Between Keith and Dufftown, off the B9014. **Tel:** 01542 810332 **Open:** Sat 3 Jun-Sun 2 Jul: daily, 2-5pm (last tour 4.15pm). **Admission:** Adult £4.00, Child £2.50. Groups by arrangement.

DUFF HOUSE

Banff AB45 3SX

One of the finest houses built in Scotland, Duff House is a magnificent Georgian mansion designed by William Adam. It houses a beautiful collection on loan from the National Galleries of Scotland. **Location:** Map 17:D8. OS Ref NJ 690 633.
Tel: 01261 818181 **E-mail:** hs.explorer@scotland.gsi.gov.uk
Website: www.duffhouse.org.uk **Open:** Apr-Oct, daily, 11-5pm; Nov-Mar, Thu-Sun, 11-4pm. **Admission:** Adult £7.10; Child £4.30.

LICKLEYHEAD CASTLE

Auchleven, Insch, Aberdeenshire AB52 6PN

Beautifully restored Laird's Castle, built by the Leslies c1450, renovated in 1629 by John Forbes of Leslie. Boasts many interesting architectural features.

Location: Map 17:C10. OS Ref NJ628 237. 2m S of Insch on B992.
Tel: 01464 820200
Open: 1-21 May. Sats throughout Jun. 10am-12 noon.
Admission: Free.

DAVID WELCH WINTER GARDENS

Duthie Park, Polmuir Road, Aberdeen AB11 7TH

One of Europe's large indoor garden, exotic plants

Location: Map 17:E11. OS Ref NJ939 046.
Just N of River Dee, 1m S of city centre.
Tel: 01224 585310 **E-mail:** wintergardens@aberdeencity.gov.uk
Website: www.aberdeencity.gov.uk
Open: All year: daily from 9.30pm. **Admission:** Free.

Register for news and special offers at **www.hudsonsheritage.com**

© @MacLeod Estate
Dunvegan Castle

DUNVEGAN CASTLE & GARDENS

www.dunvegancastle.com

Experience living history at Dunvegan Castle, the ancestral home of the Chiefs of Clan MacLeod for 800 years.

Any visit to the Isle of Skye is incomplete without savouring the wealth of history on offer at Dunvegan Castle & Gardens, the ancestral home of the Chiefs of Clan MacLeod for 800 years. Originally designed to keep people out, it was first opened to visitors in 1933 and is one of Skye's most famous landmarks. On display are many fine oil paintings and Clan treasures, the most famous of which is the Fairy Flag. Legend has it that this sacred Banner has miraculous powers and when unfurled in battle, the Clan MacLeod will defeat their enemies.

Another of the castle's great treasures is the Dunvegan Cup, a unique 'mazer' dating back to the Middle Ages. It was gifted by the O'Neils of Ulster as a token of thanks to one of the Clan's most celebrated Chiefs, Sir Rory Mor, for his support of their cause against the marauding forces of Queen Elizabeth I of England in 1596.

Today visitors can enjoy tours of an extraordinary castle and Highland estate steeped in history and clan legend, delight in the beauty of its formal gardens, take a boat trip onto Loch Dunvegan to see the seal colony, enjoy an appetising meal at the MacLeods Table Café or browse in one of its four shops offering a wide choice to suit everyone. Over time, we have given a warm Highland welcome to visitors including Sir Walter Scott, Dr Johnson and Queen Elizabeth II and we look forward to welcoming you.

KEY FACTS

- Boat trips to seal colony. Fishing trips & loch cruises. Boat trips dependent upon weather. No photography in castle.
- Our gift shops sell a wide range of quality items, Harris Tweed products, knitwear, jewellery & small gifts.
- Partial. WCs. Laptop tour of Castle available.
- MacLeod Table Café (seats 76).
- By appointment. Self-Guided.
- 120 cars & 10 coaches. Coaches please book if possible.
- Welcome by arrangement. Guide available on request.
- Dogs on leads in Gardens only.
- Self-catering holiday cottages.

© @MacLeod Estate
Dunvegan Castle Gardens

© @MacLeod Estate
Boat Trips to Seal Colony

VISITOR INFORMATION

Owner
Hugh Macleod of Macleod

Address
Dunvegan Castle
Dunvegan
Isle of Skye
Scotland
IV55 8WF

Location
Map 15:F9
OS Ref. NG250 480
1m N of village. NW corner of Skye. Kyle of Lochalsh to Dunvegan via Skye Bridge.
Rail: Inverness to Kyle of Lochalsh
Ferry: Maillaig to Armadale

Contact
Lynne Leslie,
Office Manager
Tel: 01470 521206
Fax: 01470 521205
E-mail: info@dunvegancastle.com

Opening Times
1 Apr-15 Oct
Daily 10am-5.30pm
Last admission 5pm

16 Oct-31 Mar
Open by appointment for groups only on weekdays.

Castle and Gardens closed Christmas and New Year.

Admission
Castle & Gardens

Adult	£13.00
Child (5-15yrs)	£9.00
Senior/Student/Group (Group min. 10 adults)	£10.00
Family Ticket (2 Adults, 4 Children)	£31.00

Gardens only

Adult	£11.00
Child (5-15yrs)	£7.00
Senior/Student/ Group	£8.00

Seal Boat Trips (Prices valid with a Castle or Gardens Ticket)

Adult	£7.50
Child (5-15yrs)	£5.50
Senior/Student/ Group	£6.50
Infant (under 3yrs)	Free

Wildlife Loch Cruises (1 hour)

Adult from	£18.00
Child (5-15yrs) from	£13.00

Fishing Trips (2 hours)

Adult	£45.00
Child	£35.00

Special Events
A unique location for film, TV or advertising. Check website for details.

© Cawdor Castle

© Derek Hosie

CAWDOR CASTLE AND GARDENS

CAWDOR CASTLE, NAIRN, SCOTLAND IV12 5RD

www.cawdorcastle.com

This splendid romantic castle, dating from the late 14th Century, was built as a private fortress by the Thanes of Cawdor, and remains the home of the Cawdor family to this day. The ancient medieval tower was built around the legendary holly tree. Although the house has evolved over 600 years, later additions, mainly of the 17th Century, were all built in the Scottish vernacular style. It has three gardens to enjoy: the earliest dating from the 16th Century with the symbolic gardens and maze: an 18th Century flower garden, and a 19th Century wild garden with rhododendrons and spring bulbs as well as splendid trees. Two further gardens, the Tibetan Garden and the Traditional Scottish Vegetable Garden, are at the Dower House at Auchindoune.

Location: Map 16:O9. OS Ref NH850 500. From Edinburgh A9, 3.5 hrs, Inverness 20 mins, Nairn 10 mins. Main road - A9, 14m.

Owner: The Dowager Countess Cawdor **Contact:** Ian Whitaker

Tel: 01667 404401 **Fax:** 01667 404674 **E-mail:** info@cawdorcastle.com

Open: 1 May-1 Oct 2017 Daily 10am-5.30pm. Last adm 4.45pm. Groups by appointment. Private tours can be arranged out of season by appointment.

Admission: Adult £11.50, Child (5-15 yrs) £7.00, Conc. £10.50, Family (2+up to 5) £32.00. Gardens, Grounds and Nature Trails £6.50. Adult Groups (12+) £10.00, Child Groups (12+ children, 1 adult free per 12) £6.00. Auchindoune Gardens (May-Jul only) £4.00.

Key facts: 9 hole golf course. No flash photography in the castle. Gift, Highland & Wool shops. WC. Parts of ground floor & gardens accessible. Courtyard Café & Coffee House By arrangement. 250 cars & 25 coaches. £6.00 per child. Guide dogs only.

ARMADALE CASTLE & GARDENS

Armadale, Sleat, Isle of Skye IV45 8RS

www.armadalecastle.com

The romantic ruin of Armadale Castle is a stunning backdrop to the most amazing views across the Sound of Sleat. With beautiful historic gardens and walks through 40 acres of ancient woodland, this iconic building sits at the heart of the 22,000 acres estate. Home to Museum of the Isles with 7 galleries & audio guides. Wildlife trips across the estate in all-terrain vehicle with picnic and Guide. Traditional shooting estate. Outdoor activities. Conservation in Action continues in 2017.

Location: Map 15:H11. OS Ref NG633 036. From Skye Bridge, 16 miles south of Broadford on the A851; or, take ferry from Mallaig to Amadale and follow signs.

Owner: Clan Donald Lands Trust **Contact:** Jan Wallwork Clarke

Tel: 01471 844305 **Fax:** 01471 844275 **E-mail:** jan@armadalecastle.com

Open: Good Fri-31 Oct, 9:30am-5:30pm. Nov-Mar, gardens open during daylight hours and weather permitting. Check website for updates.

Admission: Adults £8.50, Children & Conc. £6.50, Family (2 adults & 3 children) £25.00. Groups (10 or more) £6.50 per person. Children under 5 free.

Key facts: At the Ticket Office & in the Museum of the Isles Mobility scooters available. Pre-booking advisable. Various languages & visually impaired.

CASTLE & GARDENS OF MEY

Mey, Thurso, Caithness, Scotland KW14 8XH

www.castleofmey.org.uk

The home of The Queen Mother in Caithness. She bought the Castle in 1952, developed the gardens and it became her holiday home because of the beautiful surroundings and the privacy she was always afforded. There is a Visitor Centre with shop and Tea Room and an Animal Centre for children. There is also a wonderful walled garden.

Location: Map 17:B2. OS Ref ND290 739. On A836 between Thurso and John O'Groats, just outside the village of Mey.

Owner: The Queen Elizabeth Castle of Mey Trust **Contact:** Shirley Farquhar

Tel: 01847 851473 **Fax:** 01847 851475 **E-mail:** enquiries@castleofmey.org.uk

Open: 15 May-30 Sep 2017. Closed 25 Jul-8 Aug inclusive. Please check website as these dates may vary. Or alternatively, please telephone for details.

Admission: Adult £11.50, Child (5-16yrs) £6.50, Concession £9.75. Family £30.00. Booked groups (15+): £9.75. Gardens and Grounds only: Adult £6.50. Garden and Grounds family ticket £18.00.

Key facts: No photography in the Castle. Limited disabled access, please phone ahead for advice. Licensed. Guide dogs only.

BALLINDALLOCH CASTLE

Ballindalloch, Banffshire AB37 9AX

Ballindalloch Castle has been occupied by its original family, the Macpherson-Grants, since 1546. You'll enjoy this beautiful home, its decor, paintings, china, furniture and family photographs. Beautiful rock and rose gardens, children's play area, a grass labyrinth and river walks. The estate is home to the famous Aberdeen-Angus cattle breed. A superb family day out. **Location:** Map 17:A9. OS Ref NJ178 366. 14m NE of Grantown-on-Spey on A95. 22m S of Elgin on A95.
Owner: Mr & Mrs Guy Macpherson-Grant **Contact:** Fenella Corr
Tel: 01807 500205 **E-mail:** enquiries@ballindallochcastle.co.uk
Website: www.ballindallochcastle.co.uk
Open: Good Fri-30 Sep: 10am-5pm (last entry 4pm).
Closed on Sats (with the exception of Easter Sat).
Admission: Castle & Grounds: Adult £11.00, Senior Citizens £9.00, Child (6-16) £5.00, Family (2+3) £27.00, Individual Season Ticket £35.00.
Key facts: Please enquire. Partial. Short film. Cars & coaches. Designated areas only.

DUNROBIN CASTLE & GARDENS

Golspie, Sutherland KW10 6SF

Dating from the 13th Century with later additions. Wonderful furniture, paintings & Victorian museum set in woodlands overlooking the sea. Magnificent formal gardens, featuring French/Scottish formal parterres. And Falconry displays.
Location: Map 16:O6. OS Ref NC850 010. 50m N of Inverness on A9.
Owner: The Sutherland Dunrobin Trust
Contact: Scott Morrison, Managing Director **Tel:** 01408 633177
Fax: 01408 634081 **Additional Contact:** Scott Clark, Manager
E-mail: info@dunrobincastle.co.uk **Website:** www.dunrobincastle.co.uk
Open: 1 Apr–15 Oct: Apr, May, Sep & Oct, Mon-Sat, 10.30am-4.30pm, Sun, 12noon-4.30pm. Jun, Jul & Aug, daily, 10am-5pm. Please call ahead for Falconry timings. **Admission:** Adult £11.00, Child £6.50, OAP/Student. £9.00, Family (2 +3) £32.00. Groups (minimum 10): Rates on request. Rates include castle, falconry display, museum & gardens.
Key facts: Unsuitable for wheelchairs.

THE DOUNE OF ROTHIEMURCHUS

By Aviemore PH22 1QP

The family home of the Grants of Rothiemurchus since 1560.
Location: Map 16:P11. OS Ref NH900 100.
2m S of Aviemore. On B970 to Feshiebridge.
Tel: 01479 812345 **E-mail:** info@rothie.net
Website: www.rothiemurchus.net **Open:** Please see website for open dates.
Admission: Please see website for admission rates.

EILEAN DONAN CASTLE

Dornie, Kyle Of Lochalsh, Wester Ross IV40 8DX

A fortified site for eight hundred years, Eilean Donan now represents one of Scotland's most iconic images. **Location:** Map 16:J10. OS Ref NG880 260.
Tel: 01599 555202 **E-mail:** eileandonan@btconnect.com
Website: www.eileandonancastle.com
Open: Feb-Mar, daily, 10-5pm; Mar-Oct, daily, 10-6pm; Oct-Dec, daily, 10-4pm.
Admission: Adult £7.

INVEREWE GARDEN

Poolewe IV22 2LG

A lush, sub-tropical-style, oasis perched on a peninsula at the edge of Loch Ewe amid the rugged landscape of Wester Ross, this world-famous historic garden is one of Scotland's most popular botanical attractions. **Location:** Map 16:I7. OS Ref NG863 816. **Tel:** 01445 712952 **Fax:** 01445 712950 **E-mail:** inverewegarden@nts.org.uk **Open:** Gdns: Apr-Sep, daily 10-5pm; Oct, 10-4pm; Nov-Mar, daily, 10-3pm. Hse: Sep-Oct, daily, 11-4pm. **Admission:** Adult £10.50.

URQUHART CASTLE

Drumnadrochit, Loch Ness, Inverness-shire IV63 6XJ

Discover more than 1,000 years of history centred on the Great Glen. Urquhart Castle, on the shore of Loch Ness, has seen some of the most dramatic chapters in our nation's story. **Location:** Map 16:M10. OS Ref NH518 270.
Tel: 01456 450551 **Website:** www.historic-scotland.gov.uk
Open: Apr-Oct, daily, 9.30-6pm; Oct, 9.30-5pm; Nov-Mar, daily, 9.30-4.30pm.
Admission: Adult £8.50, Child £5.10.

Cawdor Castle and Gardens

BEMERSYDE GARDENS
Melrose, Roxburghshire, Scotland TD6 9DP
Tel: 01968 678465

BUGHTRIG GARDEN
Bughtrig, Coldstream TD12 4JP
Tel: 01890 840777 **E-mail:** ramsay@bughtrig.co.uk

DUNS CASTLE
Duns, Berwickshire TD11 3NW
Tel: 01361 883211

FERNIEHIRST CASTLE
Jedburgh, Roxburghshire, Scottish Borders TD8 6NX
Tel: 01450 870051 **E-mail:** curator@clankerr.co.uk

HIRSEL ESTATE
Coldstream TD12 4LP
Tel: 01555 851536 **E-mail:** joy.hitchcock@daestates.co.uk

SMAILHOLM TOWER
Smailholm, Kelso TD5 7PG
Tel: 01573 460365

ARDWELL GARDENS
Ardwell House, Ardwell, Stranraer, Wigtownshire DG9 9LY
Tel: 01776 860227 **E-mail:** info@ardwellestate.co.uk

BLAIRQUHAN CASTLE
Maybole, Ayrshire, Scotland KA19 7LZ
Tel: 01655 770239

BRODICK CASTLE
Isle Of Arran KA27 8HY
Tel: 0131 243 9300

CAERLAVEROCK CASTLE
Glencaple, Dumfries DG1 4RU
Tel: 01387 770244

KELBURN CASTLE & COUNTRY CENTRE
Fairlie, By Largs, Ayrshire KA29 0BE
Tel: 01475 568685/568595 **E-mail:** admin@kelburncountrycentre.com

SORN CASTLE
Sorn, Mauchline, Ayrshire KA5 6HR
Tel: 01290 551476 **E-mail:** info@sorncastle.com

BLACKNESS CASTLE
Blackness, Linlithgow EH49 7NH
Tel: 01506 834807

DIRLETON CASTLE
North Berwick EH39 5ER
Tel: 01620 850 330

HOUSE OF THE BINNS
Linlithgow, West Lothian EH49 7NA
Tel: 0844 493 2127 **E-mail:** information@nts.org.uk

INVERESK LODGE GARDEN
24 Inveresk Village, Musselburgh EH21 7TE
Tel: 0131 6651855 **E-mail:** inveresk@nts.org.uk

Craigston Castle

LENNOXLOVE HOUSE
Haddington, East Lothian EH41 4NZ
Tel: 01620 828614 **E-mail:** ken-buchanan@lennoxlove.com

ROSSLYN CHAPEL
Chapel Loan, Roslin, Midlothian EH25 9PU
Tel: 0131 440 2159 **E-mail:** mail@rosslynchapel.com

ABERDOUR CASTLE
Aberdour KY3 0SL
Tel: 01383 860519

ARBROATH ABBEY
Arbroath, Tayside DD11 1EG
Tel: 01241 878756

ARBUTHNOTT HOUSE & GARDEN
Arbuthnott, Laurencekirk AB30 1PA
Tel: 01561 361226

BRANKLYN GARDEN
116 Dundee Road, Perth PH2 7BB
Tel: 0844 493 2193 **E-mail:** information@nts.org.uk

BRECHIN CASTLE
Brechin, Angus DD9 6SG
Tel: 01356 624566 **E-mail:** enquiries@dalhousieestates.co.uk

CAMBO GARDENS
Cambo Estate, Kingsbarns, St. Andrews, Fife KY16 8QD
Tel: 01333 450054 **E-mail:** cambo@camboestate.com

Register for news and special offers at **www.hudsonsheritage.com**

CLUNY HOUSE
Aberfeldy PH15 2JT
E-mail: wmattingley@btinternet.com

DUNNINALD, CASTLE AND GARDENS
Montrose, Angus DD10 9TD
Tel: 01674 672031 **E-mail:** visitorinformation@dunninald.com

EDZELL CASTLE
Perthshire DD9 7UE
Tel: 01356 648 631

HILL OF TARVIT MANSION HOUSE
Cupar, Fife KY15 5PB
Tel: 0844 493 2185 **E-mail:** hilloftarvit@nts.org.uk

HOUSE OF DUN
Montrose, Angus DD10 9LQ
Tel: 0844 493 2144 **E-mail:** houseofdun@nts.org.uk

HOUSE OF PITMUIES GARDENS
Guthrie, By Forfar, Angus DD8 2SN
Tel: 01241 828245

HUNTINGTOWER CASTLE
Perth PH1 3JL
Tel: 01738 627 231

KELLIE CASTLE & GARDEN
Pittenweem, Fife KY10 2RF
Tel: 0844 493 2184 **E-mail:** information@nts.org.uk

ST ANDREW'S CASTLE
St Andrews, Fife KY16 9AR
Tel: 01334 477196

ARDCHATTAN PRIORY GARDENS
Connel, Argyll, Scotland PA37 1RQ
Tel: 01796 481355

ARDENCRAIG GARDENS
Ardencraig, Rothesay, Isle Of Bute, West Highlands PA20 9ZE
Tel: 01700 504644 **E-mail:** enquires@argyll-bute.gov.uk

ARDUAINE GARDEN
Arduaine, Oban PA34 4XQ
Tel: 0844 493 2216 **E-mail:** information@nts.org.uk

ATTADALE GARDENS
Attadale Gardens, Strathcarron, Wester Ross IV54 8YX
Tel: 01520 722217 **E-mail:** info@attadale.com

CRARAE GARDEN
Inveraray, Argyll, Bute & Loch Lomond PA32 8YA
Tel: 0844 493 2210 **E-mail:** CraraeGarden@nts.org.uk

KISIMUL CASTLE
Castlebay, Isle of Barra HS9 5UZ
Tel: 01871 810313

CASTLE FRASER & GARDEN
Sauchen, Inverurie AB51 7LD
Tel: 0131 243 9300

CRAIG CASTLE
Rhynie, Huntly, Aberdeenshire AB54 4LP
Tel: 01464 861705

DRUM CASTLE & GARDEN
Drumoak, By Banchory, Aberdeenshire AB31 3EY
Tel: 0844 493 2161 **E-mail:** information@nts.org.uk

DUNOTTAR CASTLE
Stonehaven, Aberdeenshire AB39 2TL
Tel: 01569 762173 **E-mail:** dunnottarcastle@btconnect.com

FORT GEORGE
Grampian Highlands IV2 7TD
Tel: 01667 460232

FYVIE CASTLE & GARDEN
Turriff, Aberdeenshire AB53 8JS
Tel: 0844 493 2182 **E-mail:** information@nts.org.uk

GORDON CASTLE
Estate Office, Fochabers, Morayshire IV32 7PQ
Tel: 01343 820244

HADDO HOUSE
Tarves, Ellon, Aberdeenshire AB41 0ER
Tel: 0844 493 2179 **E-mail:** information@nts.org.uk

HUNTLY CASTLE
Huntly, North and Grampian, Scotland AB54 4SH
Tel: 01466 793191

KILDRUMMY CASTLE
Alford, Aberdeenshire AB33 8RA
Tel: 01975 571331

PITMEDDEN GARDEN
Pitmedden Garden, Ellon, Aberdeenshire AB41 7PD
Tel: 01651 842352 **E-mail:** information@nts.org.uk

SPYNIE PALACE
Spynie Palace, Elgin IV30 5QG
Tel: 01343 546358

SKAILL HOUSE
Breckness Estate, Sandwick, Orkney, Scotland KW16 3LR
Tel: 01856 841501 **E-mail:** info@skaillhouse.co.uk

Mellerstain House

Treowen, Monmouth

Gregynog Hall, Powys

South Wales
Mid Wales
North Wales

Wales

Wales is a nation with a distinctive language and culture. Explore its historic buildings to find out more about its turbulent past, its pride in its history, its affluent Tudor merchants and its coal barons. Don't miss some of the most outstanding castles in Britain.

Find stylish hotels with a personal welcome and good cuisine in Wales. More information on page 348.

- Crug-Glas Country House
- Glen Yr Afon House Hotel
- The Hand at Llanarmon
- Sychnant Pass House
- Tre-Ysgawen Hall Hotel & Spa
- Warpool Court Hotel
- Wolfscastle Country Hotel

www.signpost.co.uk

© Fonmon Castle

© The Hall

FONMON CASTLE

FONMON, BARRY, VALE OF GLAMORGAN CF62 3ZN

www.fonmoncastle.com

Just 25 minutes from Cardiff and the M4, Fonmon is one of few medieval castles still lived in as a home, since being built c1200, it has only changed hands once. Visitors are welcomed by an experienced guide and the 45 minute tour walks through the fascinating history of the Castle, its families, architecture and interiors. The Fonmon gardens are an attraction in their own right for enthusiasts and amateurs alike and visitors are free to wander and explore. Available as an exclusive wedding and party venue, corporate and team building location, visitor attraction and host for product launches and filming.

Location: Map 2:L2. OS Ref ST047 681. 15miles W of Cardiff, 1miles W of Cardiff airport. **Owner:** Sir Brooke Boothby Bt

Contact: Casey Govier **Tel:** 01446 710206 **E-mail:** Fonmon_Castle@msn.com

Open: Public opening: 1 Apr- 30 Sep on Tue & Wed afternoons for individuals, families & small groups. Midday-5pm, no need to book. Tours at 2pm, 3pm & 4pm & last 45 mins, last entrance to gardens at 4pm. Groups 20+ welcome by appointment throughout the year. Varied hospitality options with very popular Afternoon Teas. **Admission:** Entry and tour of the Castle priced at £6.00, Children free. Access to garden and grounds is free.

Key facts: Conferences. By arrangement. Suitable. WCs. Guided Tour obligatory. Ample free parking for cars and coaches. Guide dogs only. Licensed for Civil Ceremonies for up to 110 people.

Tredegar House

ABERGLASNEY GARDENS

Llangathen, Carmarthenshire, Wales SA32 8QH

www.aberglasney.org

Made famous by the BBC television series 'A Garden Lost in Time', this followed its restoration. Today it is quite simply one of Wales' finest gardens. A renowned plantsman's paradise with a unique Elizabethan cloister garden at its heart, Aberglasney offers the opportunity to explore more than 10 acres of magnificent gardens which along with the fully restored ground floor of Aberglasney's Grade II* listed mansion offer a stunning venue for weddings, exhibitions and events.
Location: Map 5:F10. OS Ref SN579 221. Aberglasney is 12 miles east of Carmarthen and 4 miles west of Llandeilo on the A40 at Broad Oak
Owner: Aberglasney Restoration Trust (Private Charitable Trust).
Contact: Booking Dept **Tel/Fax:** 01558 668998 **E-mail:** info@aberglasney.org
Open: All year: daily (except Christmas day). Apr-Oct: 10am-6pm, last entry 5pm. Nov-Mar: 10.30am-4pm, last entry 3pm **Admission:** Adult/ Concessions £8.50, Children 16 years and under FREE, Booked groups (10+) Adult £7.25.
Key facts: Free entry. Free entry. Contact for info on corporate events & weddings. Mostly suitable. Licensed. Pre-booked for groups. Free parking, also large coach park. Guide dogs only. Two 5* self-catering holiday cottages on site. Mansion House and Garden weddings. Closed on Christmas Day.

LLANCAIACH FAWR MANOR

Gelligaer Road, Nelson, Treharris
Caerphilly County Borough CF46 6ER

www.llancaiachfawr.co.uk

This superbly restored gentry manor house is no ordinary heritage attraction. History here is tangible. The costumed servants of the house are living and working in 1645 and allow you to share and engage in their world. Fires crackle, candles flicker and the sounds and smells of domestic life make your visit a memorable experience of the past. Meet ordinary people living in extraordinary times.
Location: Map 2:M1. OS Ref ST114 967. S side of B4254, 1m N of A472 at Nelson. **Owner:** Caerphilly County Borough Council **Contact:** Reception
Tel: 01443 412248 **E-mail:** llancaiachfawr@caerphilly.gov.uk
Open: 10am-5pm Tue-Sun and BH Mons all year round. Last entry to the Manor 4pm Closed 24 Dec-1 Jan inclusive. **Admission:** Adults £8.50, Conc £6.95, Child £6.95, Family £25.00 (2 adults + 3 children) **Key facts:** No photography indoors. Boutique gift shop. Accessible WCs. Lift for access to upper floors. Licensed. 10am-4pm. Hot & cold drinks, sandwiches cakes & snacks, hot food between 12pm & 2pm. Licensed. Sun lunches & private functions. Costumed 17th Century servants lead tours. Approx 1.5 hours. 90 free spaces. Disabled spaces close to visitor centre entrance. Tours, activities, trails & workshops. Dogs in grounds only. Not in walled gardens.

ABERCAMLAIS HOUSE

Abercamlais, Brecon, Powys LD3 8EY

Splendid Grade I mansion dating from middle ages, altered extensively in early 18th Century with 19th Century additions, in extensive grounds beside the river Usk. Exceptional octagonal pigeon house, formerly a privy.
Location: Map 6:I10. OS Ref SN965 290. 5m W of Brecon on A40.
Owner: Mrs S Ballance
Contact: Francis Chester-Master
Tel: 01982 553248
Fax: 01982 553154
E-mail: admin@chester-master.co.uk
Website: www.abercamlais.com
Open: Apr-End Sep: by appointment.
Admission: Adult £5.00, Child Free.
Key facts: No photography in house. Obligatory. Dogs on leads only.

CRESSELLY

Kilgetty, Pembrokeshire SA68 0SP

Home of the Allen family for 250 years. The house is of 1770 with matching wings of 1869 and contains good plasterwork and fittings of both periods. The Allens are of particular interest for their close association with the Wedgwood family of Etruria and a long tradition of foxhunting.
Location: Map 5:C11. OS Ref SN065 065. W of the A4075.
Owner/Contact: H D R Harrison-Allen Esq MFH
E-mail: hha@cresselly.com
Website: www.cresselly.com
Open: May 2-16 inclusive and Aug 3-14 inclusive. Guided Tours only, on the hour 10am, 11am & 12 noon. 28 Aug. Guided Tours only on the hour 1pm, 2pm & 3pm. Coaches at other times by arrangement.
Admission: Adult £4.00, no children under 12.
Key facts: Ground floor only. Obligatory. Coaches by arrangement.

LLANDAFF CATHEDRAL

Llandaff Cathedral Green, Cardiff CF5 2LA

Discover Llandaff Cathedral, a holy place of peace and tranquillity, art, architecture and music with a very warm welcome. Over 1500 yrs of history, standing on one of the oldest Christian sites in Britain. Works include Epstein, Piper, Pace, Rossetti, William Morris, Goscombe John, Frank Roper and Burne Jones. Services daily, some sung by the Cathedral Choir. Details on the Cathedral website: www.llandaffcathedral.org.uk.
Location: Map 2:L2. OS Ref ST155 397. At Cardiff Castle, drive West and cross River Taff; turn right into Cathedral Road (A4119) and follow signs to Llandaff.
Owner: Representative body of the Church In Wales **Contact:** Cathedral Office
Tel: 02920 564554 **E-mail:** office@llandaffcathedral.org.uk
Website: www.llandaffcathedral.org.uk
Open: Every week day 9am-6pm; Sun 7.30am-4.30pm.
Admission: Free. Donations gratefully received.
Key facts: By arrangement. Nearby. Guide dogs only.

LLANVIHANGEL COURT

Nr Abergavenny, Monmouthshire NP7 8DH

Grade I Tudor Manor. The home in the 17th Century of the Arnolds who built the imposing terraces and stone steps leading to the house. The interior has a fine hall, unusual yew staircase and many 17th Century moulded plaster ceilings. Delightful grounds. 17th Century features, notably Grade I stables.
Location: Map 6:K11. OS Ref SO325 205. 4m N of Abergavenny on A465.
Owner/Contact: Julia Johnson
Tel: 01873 890217
E-mail: jclarejohnson@googlemail.com
Website: www.llanvihangelcourt.com
Open: 1-13 May & 14-25 Aug. Inclusive, daily 2.30-5.30pm. Tours 2.30pm, 3.30pm & 4.30pm.
Admission: Entry and guide, Adult £8.00, Child/Conc. £5.00.
Key facts: No inside photography. Private hire. Partial. Obligatory. Limited, no coaches. Dogs on leads only.

CARDIFF CASTLE

Castle Street, Cardiff CF10 3RB

2000 years of history has shaped Cardiff Castle into a spectacular and fascinating site at the heart of one of the UK's most vibrant cities. From Roman fort and Norman stronghold to a Victorian fairytale Castle, find a surprise around every corner. **Location:** Map 2:M1. OS Ref ST181 765. **Tel:** 029 2087 8100 **Website:** www.cardiffcastle.com **Open:** Mar-Oct, daily, 9-5pm; Nov-Feb, daily, 9-4pm. **Admission:** Adult £12 (+£3 for house tour); Child £9 (+£2).

CASTELL COCH ✠

Tongwynlais, Cardiff CF15 7JS

A fairytale castle in the woods, Castell Coch embodies a glorious Victorian dream of the Middle Ages. The castle is a by-product of a vivid Victorian imagination, assisted by untold wealth. **Location:** Map 2:L1. OS Ref ST131 826.
Tel: 029 2081 0101 **Website:** www.cadw.wales.gov.uk
Open: Mar-Jun, daily, 9.30-5pm; Jul-Aug, daily, 9.30-6pm; Sep-Oct, daily, 9.30-5pm; Nov-Jan, daily, 11-4pm. **Admission:** Adult £6; Child £4.20.

CORNWALL HOUSE

58 Monnow Street, Monmouth NP25 3EN

Town house, Georgian street façade, walled garden.
Location: Map 6:L11. OS Ref SO506 127. Half way down main shopping street, set back from street. Please use centre door.
Tel: 01600 712031 **E-mail:** jane2harvey@ tiscali.co.uk
Open: 2-5pm on Weds in Jul and Aug and on 8/9 Apr, 13-17 Apr, 29 Apr-1 May, 27-29 May, 26-28 Aug **Admission:** Adult £4.00, Concessions £2.00.

DINEFWR

Llandeilo, Carmarthenshire SA19 6RT

National Nature Reserve, historic house and 18th Century landscape park, enclosing a medieval deer park. **Location:** Map 5:C11. OS Ref SN614 225.
Tel: 01443 336000 **E-mail:** cadw@wales.gsi.gov.uk
Open: Gardens: All year, daily, 10-4pm; 6pm in Summer. House: 2 Jan-Mar & Nov-17 Dec, Fri-Sun, 11-4pm; Apr-Oct, daily, 11-6pm; Dec hols, daily, 11-4pm.
Admission: Adult £6.50; Child £3.50.

DYFFRYN GARDENS

St Nicholas, Vale of Glamorgan CF5 6SU

Grade I listed gardens featuring a collection of formal lawns, intimate garden rooms an extensive arboretum and reinstated glasshouse.
Location: Map 2:L2. OS Ref ST094 717. **Tel:** 02920 593328
E-mail: dyffryn@nationaltrust.org.uk **Website:** www.nationaltrust.org.uk
Open: All year, daily, 10-4pm; Mar-Sep, 1-6pm. House: Apr-Sep, daily, 12-4pm; Oct-Mar, Thu-Sun, 12-3. **Admission:** Adult £7.80; Child £3.90.

RAGLAN CASTLE ✠

Raglan, Monmouthshire NP15 2BT

Undoubtedly the finest late medieval fortress-palace in Britain, begun in the 1430s by Sir William ap Thomas who built the mighty 'Yellow Tower'.
Location: Map 6:K12. OS Ref SO415 084. **Tel:** 01291 690228
Website: www.cadw.wales.gov.uk **Open:** Mar-Oct, daily, 9.30-5pm; Nov-Feb, daily, 11-4pm. **Admission:** Adult £6; Child £4.20.

ST DAVIDS BISHOP'S PALACE ✠

St Davids, Pembrokeshire SA62 6PE

The city of St Davids boasts the most impressive medieval bishop's palace in Wales. The palace is lavishly decorated with finely carved stonework and still conveys the power and affluence of the medieval church. **Location:** Map 5:B11. OS Ref SM750 254. **Tel:** 01437 720517 **Website:** www.cadw.wales.gov.uk
Open: Mar-Oct, daily, 9.30-5pm; Nov-Feb, daily, 11-4pm.
Admission: Adult £3.50; Child £2.50.

TINTERN ABBEY ✠

Tintern NP16 6SE

Tintern was only the second Cistercian foundation in Britain, and the first in Wales. The present-day remains are a mixture of building works covering a 400-year period between 1131 and 1536. **Location:** Map 6:L12. OS Ref SO529 002.
Tel: 01291 689251 **E-mail:** TinternAbbey@wales.gsi.gov.uk
Open: Mar-Oct, daily, 9.30-5pm; Nov-Feb, daily, 11-4pm.
Admission: Adult £6; Child £4.

TREBINSHWN

Llangasty, Nr Brecon, Powys LD3 7PX

16th Century mid-sized manor house. Extensively rebuilt 1780. Fine courtyard and walled garden.
Location: Map 6:I10. OS Ref SO136 242. 1½m NW of Bwlch.
Tel: 01874 730653 **Fax:** 01874 730843
E-mail: liza.watson@trebinshunhouse.co.uk
Open: Easter-31 Aug: Mon-Tue, 10am-4.30pm. **Admission:** Free.

TREDEGAR HOUSE & PARK

Newport, South Wales NP10 8YW

Tredegar House is one of the most significant late 17th Century houses in Wales, if not the whole of the British Isles. **Location:** Map 2:M1. OS Ref ST290 852.
Tel: 01633 815880 **E-mail:** tredegar@nationaltrust.org.uk
Website: www.nationaltrust.org.uk/tredegarhouse
Open: Feb half term, daily, 11-4pm; Mar-Oct, daily, 11-5pm; 25 Nov-17 Dec, Sat & Sun, 11-5pm. **Admission:** Adult £7.70; Child £3.60.

TREOWEN

Wonastow, Monmouth NP25 4DL

The most important early 17th Century gentry house in the county. Particularly fine open well staircase. **Location:** Map 6:K11. OS Ref SO461 111. 3m WSW of Monmouth. **Tel:** 07530 357390 **E-mail:** john.wheelock@treowen.co.uk
Website: www.treowen.co.uk **Open:** May-Aug Fri 10am-4pm. Also Sat & Sun 25-26 Mar, 22-23 Apr, 6-7 May and 16-17 & 23-24 Sep 2-5pm.
Admission: £6.00. Free to HHA Friends on Fridays only.

USK CASTLE

Monmouth Road, Usk, Monmouthshire NP5 1SD

Best kept secret, romantic ruins overlooking Usk.
Location: Map 6:K12. OS Ref SZ539 924. Off Monmouth Road in Usk.
Tel: 01291 672563 **E-mail:** info@uskcastle.com
Website: www.uskcastle.com
Open: Castle: All year, see website. House: May (not Mons), 2-5pm and BHs. Guided tours only. **Admission:** £7.00; Gardens £4.00.

Castell Coch

Register for news and special offers at **www.hudsonsheritage.com**

GREGYNOG

Tregynon, Nr Newtown, Powys SY16 3PW

www.gregynog.org

Once a landed estate, now a vibrant conference centre, wedding venue and tourist destination. Set amidst 750 acres, Wales' newest National Nature Reserve and SSSI site offers 56 bedrooms and peace and tranquillity. We pride ourselves on the quality of our home-produced locally sourced food from an extensive menu choice put together by our Chef. Grade 1 listed gardens, historic oak panelled rooms, an extensive library and a fine collection of furniture add to the unique ambience.
Location: Map 6:I6. OS Ref SO 084974. From the A483 follow the brown sign (Gregynog) or Bettws Cedewain. From Bettws follow Tregynon & look for large sign at end of drive. **Owner/Contact:** Gregynog **Tel:** 01686 650224
E-mail: enquiries@gregynog.org **Open:** Estate: every day. Café: please see website. **Admission:** Gardens Adult £3.00, Child £1.00.
Key facts: Open daily from 9am. Plants for sale are on display in the Courtyard. Bespoke packages tailored to your requirements. Shop/Café/ some trails around the Hall. Open (except in winter) from 11am. Menu on website. Regular & various tours available - see website. Safe accessible parking. £2.50 charge. School visits welcomed - and to our Forest School. 4 of the historic rooms are licensed. Estate/grounds open all year.

THE JUDGE'S LODGING

Broad Street, Presteigne, Powys LD8 2AD

Explore the fascinating world of the Victorian judges, their servants and felonious guests at this award-winning, totally hands-on historic house. Through sumptuous judge's apartments and the gas-lit servants' quarters below, follow an 'eavesdropping' audio tour featuring actor Robert Hardy. Damp cells, vast courtroom and new interactive local history rooms included.
Location: Map 6:K8. OS Ref SO314 644. In town centre, off A44 and A4113. Within easy reach from Herefordshire, Shropshire and mid-Wales.
Owner: The Judge's Lodging Trust **Contact:** Gabrielle Rivers **Tel:** 01544 260650
E-mail: info@judgeslodging.org.uk **Website:** www.judgeslodging.org.uk
Open: 1 Mar-31 Oct: Tues-Sun, 10am-5pm. 1 Nov-31 Nov: Wed-Sun, 10am-4pm, 1 Dec-22 Dec: Sat-Sun 10am-4pm. Open BH Mons.
Admission: Adult £7.95, Child £3.95, Conc. £6.95, Family £21.50. Groups (10-80): Adult £7.50, Conc. £6.50, Schools £5.50.
Key facts: Partial. In town. Guide dogs only.

POWIS CASTLE & GARDEN

Welshpool, Powys SY21 8RF

Once a stark medieval fortress, Powis Castle has been transformed over 400 years into an extravagant family home with an exceptional collection of art, sculpture and furniture collected from Europe, India and the Orient. Outside you can enjoy the delights of a world famous garden with dramatic 17th Century terraces, lavish herbaceous borders and breath taking panoramic views. **Location:** Map 6:J6. 1 mile South of Welshpool. Signed from A483. **Tel:** 01938 551929

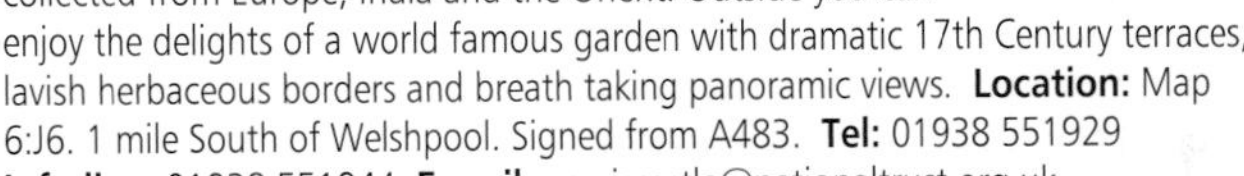

Info line: 01938 551944 **E-mail:** powiscastle@nationaltrust.org.uk
Website: www.nationaltrust.org.uk/powis-castle
Open: Castle: 1 Jan-31 Dec 11am-4pm (11am-5pm 27 Mar-1 Oct)*. Garden: 1 Jan-31 Dec 10am-4pm (10am-6pm 27 Mar-1 Oct). For shop & restaurant times, please see website. *Last entry 30 mins before closing. Reduced number of staterooms 1 Jan-17, Feb & 30 Oct-31 Dec. **Admission:** See website for prices.
Key facts: Licensed. Courtyard only. Closed 25 Dec.

CANOLFAN OWAIN GLYNDWR

Heol Maengwyn, Machylleth, Powys SY20 8EE

Historic building on site of Glyndwr Parliament of 1404. Interactive exhibition, historic artefacts and murals by Murray Urquhart.
Location: Map 5:G6. OS Ref SH748 008.
Tel: 01654 703336 **E-mail:** glyndwr.enquiries@canolfanglyndwr.org
Website: www.canolfanglyndwr.org
Open: Easter-Sep, daily, 10am-4pm. **Admission:** By donation.

GLANSEVERN HALL GARDENS

Glansevern, Berriew, Welshpool, Powys SY21 8AH

Romantically positioned on the banks of the River Severn in Mid Wales, Glansevern Hall Gardens offer over 25 stunning acres of diverse landscape and exotic planting.
Location: Map 6:J6. OS Ref SJ195 001.
Tel: 01686 640644 **E-mail:** glansevern@yahoo.co.uk
Open: Mar-Oct, Tue-Sat & BH Mons, 10.30-5pm; Nov-Feb, Tue-Sat, 10.30-4pm.
Admission: Adult £7; Child £3.50.

HAFOD ESTATE

Pontrhyd-y-groes, Ystrad Meurig, Ceredigion SY25 6DX

Ten miles of restored walks, the epitome of the Picturesque and Sublime. Set in 500 acres of wood and parkland featuring cascades, bridges and wonderful views.
Location: Map 5:G8. OS Ref SN768 736. 15 miles E of Aberystwyth, free car park.
Tel: 01974 282568 **E-mail:** trust@hafod.org **Website:** www.hafod.org
Open: All year - daylight hours. **Admission:** Free.

LLANERCHAERON

Ciliau Aeron, Nr Aberaeron, Ceredigion SA48 8DG

This rare example of a self-sufficient 18th Century Welsh minor gentry estate has survived virtually unaltered. Designed in the 1790s, is the most complete example of the early work of John Nash. **Location:** Map 5:F9. OS Ref SN479 601.
Tel: 01545 570200 **E-mail:** llanerchaeron@nationaltrust.org.uk
Open: Gardens: Feb-Dec, 11.30-3.30pm. House: Feb half term, 11.30-3.30pm; Apr-Oct, 10.30-5.30pm. **Admission:** Adult £6.90; Child £3.45.

The Judge's Lodging Bathroom

ISCOYD PARK

NR WHITCHURCH, SHROPSHIRE SY13 3AT

www.iscoydpark.com

A red brick Georgian house in an idyllic 18th Century parkland setting situated on the Welsh side of the Shropshire/Welsh border. After extensive refurbishment of the house and gardens we are now open for Weddings, parties, photography and film shoots, conferencing and corporate events of all kinds.

The house is only let on an exclusive basis meaning there is never more than one event occurring at any time. We offer a wide range of B&B and self-catering accommodation, The Secret Spa and beautiful gardens all within the context of a family home.

Location: Map 6:L4. OS Ref SJ504 421. 2m W of Whitchurch off A525.
Owner: Mr P C Godsal
Contact: Mr P L Godsal
Tel: 01948 780785
E-mail: info@iscoydpark.com
Open: House visits by written appointment.
Key facts: Private dinners and weddings a speciality. WCs. Licensed. Obligatory. Limited for coaches. Assistance dogs only permitted Licensed. Open All Year.

DOLBELYDR

Trefnant, Denbighshire LL16 5AG

www.landmarktrust.org.uk

Set in a timeless, quiet valley this 16th Century gentry house has many of its original features, including a first floor solar open to the roof beams. It also has good claim to be the birthplace of the modern Welsh language.
Location: Map 6:I2. OS Ref SJ027 698.
Owner: The Landmark Trust
Tel: 01628 825925
E-mail: bookings@landmarktrust.org.uk
Open: Self-catering accommodation. Open days on 8 days per year. Other visits by appointment.
Admission: Free on open days and visits by appointment.
Key facts: There is an open plan kitchen and dining area in front of a huge inglenook fireplace.

GWYDIR CASTLE

Llanrwst, Conwy LL26 0PN

www.gwydircastle.co.uk

Gwydir Castle is situated in the beautiful Conwy Valley and is set within a Grade I listed, 10 acre garden. Built by the illustrious Wynn family c1500, Gwydir is a fine example of a Tudor courtyard house, incorporating re-used medieval material from the dissolved Abbey of Maenan. Further additions date from c1600 and c1828. The important 1640s panelled Dining Room has now been reinstated, following its repatriation from the New York Metropolitan Museum.
Location: Map 5:H3. OS Ref SH795 610. ½m W of Llanrwst on B5106.
Owner/Contact: Mr & Mrs Welford
Tel: 01492 641687 **E-mail:** info@gwydircastle.co.uk
Open: 1 Apr-31 Oct: daily, 10am-4pm. Closed Mons & Sats (except BH weekends). Limited openings at other times. Please telephone for details.
Admission: Adult £6.00, Child £3.00, Concessions £5.50. Group discount 10%.
Key facts: Partial. By arrangement. By arrangement. 2 doubles.

Register for news and special offers at **www.hudsonsheritage.com**

COCHWILLAN OLD HALL

Halfway Bridge, Bangor, Gwynedd LL57 3AZ

A fine example of medieval architecture with the present house dating from 1450. It is thought to have been built by William Gryffydd who fought for Henry VII at Bosworth. Once owned in the 17th Century by John Williams who became Archbishop of York. The house was restored from a barn in 1971.

Location: Map 5:G2. OS Ref OS Ref. SH606 695. 3 ½ m SE of Bangor. 1m SE of Talybont off A55.
Owner: R C H Douglas Pennant
Contact: Mark & Christopher Chenery
Tel: 01248 355139
E-mail: risboro@hotmail.co.uk
Open: By appointment.
Admission: Please email or telephone for details.

HARTSHEATH

Pontblyddyn, Mold, Flintshire CH7 4HP

18th and 19th Century house set in parkland. Viewing is limited to 7 persons at any one time. Open by appointment. No toilets or refreshments.

Location: Map 6:J3. OS Ref SJ287 602. Access from A5104, 3.5m SE of Mold between Pontblyddyn and Penyffordd.
Owner: Dr M.C. Jones-Mortimer Will Trust
Contact: Dr Miranda Dechazal
Tel/Fax: 01352 770204
Open: 2pm-5pm
May 1, 6, 7, 27, 28, 29
Jun 11, 28
Jul 2
Aug 26, 27, 28
Sep 21, 22, 23, 24, 25, 26, 27, 28
Admission: £5.00.
Key facts:

PLAS BRONDANW GARDENS, CAFFI & SHOP

Plas Brondanw, Llanfrothen, Gwynedd LL48 6SW

Italianate gardens with topiary.

Location: Map 5:G4. OS Ref SH618 423. 3m N of Penrhyndeudraeth off A4085, on Croesor Road.
Owner: Trustees of the Clough Williams-Ellis Foundation.
Tel: 01766 772772 / 01743 239236
E-mail: enquiries@plasbrondanw.com
Website: www.plasbrondanw.com
Open: Mar-Sep daily,10am-5pm.
Coaches accepted, please book.
Admission: Adult £4.00, Children under 12 £1.00.
Key facts:

WERN ISAF

Penmaen Park, Llanfairfechan, Conwy LL33 0RN

This Arts and Crafts house was built in 1900 by the architect H L North as his family home and contains much of the original furniture and William Morris fabrics. Situated in a woodland garden with extensive views over the Menai Straits and Conwy Bay.

Location: Map 5:G2. OS Ref SH685 753. Off A55 midway between Bangor and Conwy.
Owner/Contact: Mrs P J Phillips
Tel: 01248 680437
Open: 2-31 Mar (excluding Weds) 11:30am-2:30pm
Admission: Free.

Iscoyd Park

Y FFERM

Pontblyddyn, Mold, Flintshire CH7 4HN

17th Century farmhouse. Viewing is limited to 7 persons at any one time. Open by appointment. No toilets or refreshments.

Location: Map 6:J3. OS Ref SJ279 603. Access from A541 in Pontblyddyn, 3½m SE of Mold.
Owner: Dr M.C. Jones-Mortimer Will Trust
Contact: Dr Miranda Dechazal
Tel: 01352 770161
Open: 2pm-5pm
May 1, 6, 7, 27, 28, 29
Jun 11, 28
Jul 2
Aug 26, 27, 28
Sep 21, 22, 23, 24, 25, 26, 27, 28
Admission: £5.00.
Key facts:

BODNANT GARDEN

Tal-Y-Cafn, Colwyn Bay LL28 5RE

One of the finest gardens in the country not only for its magnificent collections of rhododendrons, camellias and magnolias but also for its idyllic setting above the River Conwy. **Location:** Map 5:H2. OS Ref SH801 723. **Tel:** 01492 650460
E-mail: bodnantgarden@nationaltrust.org.uk **Website:** www.nationaltrust.org.uk
Open: Mar-Oct, daily, 10-5pm; Jan, Feb, Nov, Dec, daily, 10-4pm; 20 Dec-31 Dec, Tue-Sun, 10-4pm. **Admission:** Adult £11.25; Child £5.63.

CAERNARFON CASTLE

Castle Ditch, Caernarfon LL55 2AY

The most famous and perhaps the most impressive castle in Wales, built by Edward I. Distinguished by polygonal towers and colour-banded stone.
Location: Map 5:F3. OS Ref SH477 626. **Tel:** 01286 677617
Website: www.cadw.wales.gov.uk **Open:** Mar-Oct, daily, 9.30-5pm; Nov-Feb, daily, 11-4pm. **Admission:** Adult £9.95; Child £5.60.

ERDDIG

Wrexham LL13 0YT

Widely acclaimed as one of Britain's finest historic houses, Erddig is a fascinating yet unpretentious early 18th Century country house.
Location: Map 6:K3. OS Ref SJ326 482. **Tel:** 01978 355314
E-mail: erddig@nationaltrust.org.uk **Website:** www.nationaltrust.org.uk/erddig
Open: Mar-Oct, daily, 12.30-3.30pm; Feb, Mar, Nov, Dec, daily, 11.30-2.30pm.
Admission: Adult £11.25; Child £5.60.

PLAS MAWR

High Street, Conwy LL32 8DE

The best-preserved Elizabethan town house in Britain, Plas Mawr reflects the status of its builder Robert Wynn. **Location:** Map 5:H2. OS Ref SH781 776.
Tel: 01492 580167 **Website:** www.cadw.wales.gov.uk
Open: Apr-Sep, daily, 9.30-5pm; Oct, daily, 9.30-4pm.
Admission: Adult £6; Child £4.20.

ABERDEUNANT ✿
Taliaris, Llandeilo, Carmarthenshire SA19 6DL
Tel: 01588 650177 E-mail: aberdeunant@nationaltrust.org.uk

CAERPHILLY CASTLE ✠
Caerphilly CF83 1JD
Tel: 029 2088 3143

CARDIGAN CASTLE
Green Street, Cardigan, Ceredigion SA43 1JA
Tel: 01239 615131 E-mail: cadwganbpt@btconnect.com

CARREG CENNEN CASTLE ✠
Tir y Castell Farm, Llandeilo, Carmarthenshire SA19 6UA
Tel: 01558 822291

CHEPSTOW CASTLE ✠
Chepstow, Monmouthshire NP16 5EY
Tel: 01291 624065

CILGERRAN CASTLE ✿ ✠
Cardigan, Pembrokeshire SA43 2SF
Tel: 01239 621339 E-mail: cilgerrancastle@nationaltrust.org.uk

GROSMONT CASTLE ✠
Nr Abergavenny, Monmouthshire NP7 8EQ
Tel: 01443 336000 E-mail: cadw@wales.gsi.gov.uk

KIDWELLY CASTLE ✠
Kidwelly, Carmarthenshire SA17 5BQ
Tel: 01554 890104

THE KYMIN ✿
The Round House, The Kymin, Monmouth NP25 3SF
Tel: 01600 719241 E-mail: kymin@nationaltrust.org.uk

LAUGHARNE CASTLE ✠
King Street, Laugharne, Carmarthenshire SA33 4SA
Tel: 01994 427906

MARGAM COUNTRY PARK & CASTLE
Margam, Port Talbot, West Glamorgan SA13 2TJ
Tel: 01639 881635 E-mail: margampark@npt.gov.uk

MONMOUTH CASTLE ✠
Castle Hill, Monmouth NP25 3BS
Tel: 01443 336000 E-mail: cadw@wales.gsi.gov.uk

NATIONAL BOTANIC GARDEN OF WALES
Llanarthne, Carmarthenshire SA32 8HG
Tel: 01558 667149 E-mail: info@gardenofwales.org.uk

OGMORE CASTLE AND STEPPING STONES ✠
Ogmore, St Brides Major, Vale Of Glamorgan CF32 0QP
Tel: 01443 336000 E-mail: cadw@wales.gsi.gov.uk

OXWICH CASTLE ✠
Oxwich, Swansea SA3 1NG
Tel: 01792 390359

PEMBROKE CASTLE
Pembroke SA71 4LA
Tel: 01646 681510 E-mail: info@pembrokecastle.co.uk

Llancaiach Fawr

Register for news and special offers at **www.hudsonsheritage.com**

PICTON CASTLE & WOODLAND GARDENS
The Rhos, Nr Haverfordwest, Pembrokeshire SA62 4AS
Tel: 01437 751326 **E-mail:** info@pictoncastle.co.uk

ST FAGANS: NATIONAL HISTORY MUSEUM
Cardiff CF5 6XB
Tel: 029 2057 3500

SKENFRITH CASTLE
Skenfrith, Nr Abergavenny, Monmouthshire NP7 8UH
Tel: 01443 336000 **E-mail:** cadw@wales.gsi.gov.uk

STRADEY CASTLE
Llanelli, Carmarthenshire, Wales SA15 4PL
Tel: 01554 774626 **E-mail:** info@stradeycastle.com

TRETOWER COURT & CASTLE
Tretower, Crickhowell NP8 1RD
Tel: 01874 730279

TUDOR MERCHANT'S HOUSE
Quay Hill, Tenby, Pembrokeshire SA70 7BX
Tel: 01834 842279 **E-mail:** tudormerchantshouse@nationaltrust.org.uk

ABERYSTWYTH CASTLE
Aberystwyth, Ceredigion SY23 2AG
Tel: 01970 612125

THE HALL AT ABBEY-CWM-HIR
Nr Llandrindod Wells, Powys LD1 6PH
Tel: 01597 851727 **E-mail:** info@abbeycwmhir.com

TREWERN HALL
Trewern, Welshpool, Powys SY21 8DT
Tel: 01938 570243

ABERCONWY HOUSE
Castle Street, Conwy LL32 8AY
Tel: 01492 592246 **E-mail:** aberconwyhouse@nationaltrust.org.uk

BEAUMARIS CASTLE
Beaumaris, Anglesey LL58 8AP
Tel: 01248 810361

BODRHYDDAN HALL
Bodrhyddan, Rhuddlan, Rhyl, Denbighshire LL18 5SB
Tel: 01745 590414

CHIRK CASTLE
Chirk LL14 5AF
Tel: 01691 777701 **E-mail:** chirkcastle@nationaltrust.org.uk

CONWY CASTLE
Conwy LL32 8AY
Tel: 01492 592358

CRICCIETH CASTLE
Castle Street, Criccieth, Gwynedd LL52 0DP
Tel: 01766 522227 **E-mail:** cadw@wales.gsi.gov.uk

FLINT CASTLE
Castle St, Flint, Flintshire CH6 5HF
Tel: 01443 336000

Powis Castle Gardens

HARLECH CASTLE
Castle Square, Harlech LL46 2YH
Tel: 01766 780552

PENRHYN CASTLE
Bangor, Gwynedd LL57 4HN
Tel: 01248 353084 **E-mail:** penrhyncastle@nationaltrust.org.uk

PLAS NEWYDD
Hill Street, Llangollen, Denbighshire LL20 8AW
Tel: 01978 862834 **E-mail:** heritage@denbighshire.gov.uk

PLAS NEWYDD HOUSE & GARDENS
Llanfairpwll, Anglesey LL61 6DQ
Tel: 01248 714795 **E-mail:** plasnewydd@nationaltrust.org.uk

PLAS YN RHIW
Rhiw, Pwllheli, Gwynedd LL53 8AB
Tel: 01758 780219 **E-mail:** plasynrhiw@nationaltrust.org.uk

PORTMEIRION
Minffordd, Penrhyndeudraeth, Gwynedd LL48 6ER
Tel: 01766 772311 **E-mail:** enquiries@portmeirion-village.com

RHUDDLAN CASTLE
Castle Street, Rhuddlan, Rhyl LL18 5AD
Tel: 01745 590777

TOWER
Nercwys Road, Mold, Flintshire CH7 4EW
Tel: 01352 700220 **E-mail:** enquiries@towerwales.co.uk

Carrickfergus Castle, County Antrim

Hillsborough Castle, Co. Down

Antrim
Armagh
Down
Fermanagh
Londonderry
Tyrone

Northern Ireland

A beautiful and undervalued part of the country, Northern Ireland is easy to get to from the mainland, small enough to explore and packed with historic places that will help you understand its unique history.

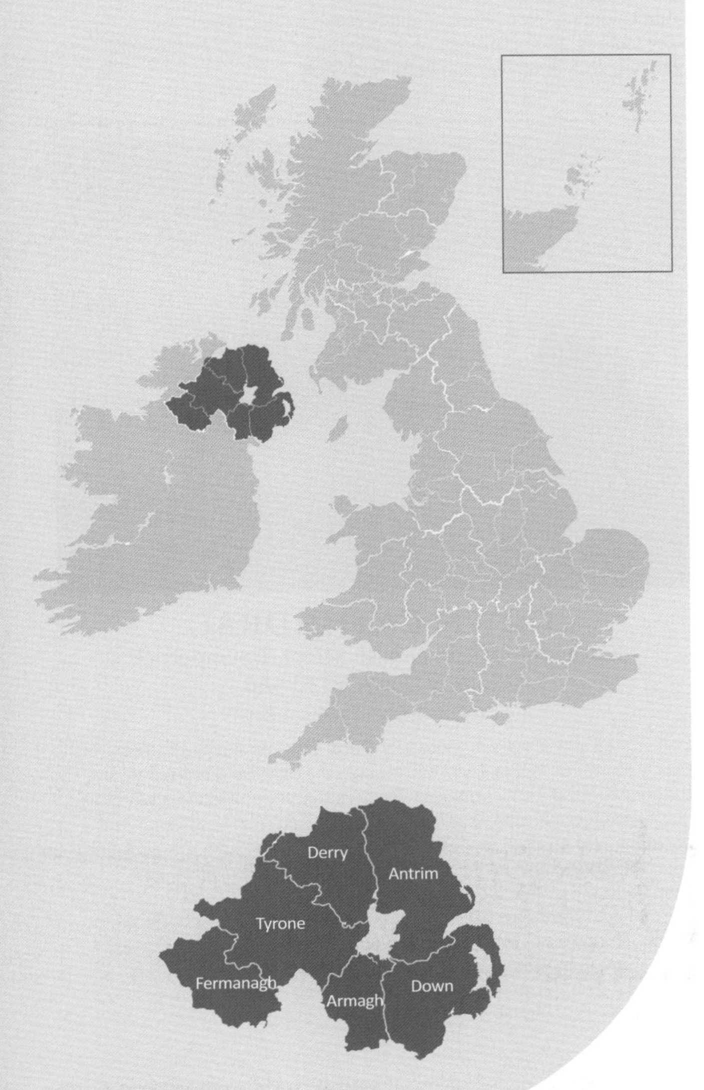

ANTRIM CASTLE GARDENS AND CLOTWORTHY HOUSE

RANDALSTOWN ROAD, ANTRIM BT41 4LH

www.antrimandnewtownabbey.gov.uk/antrimcastlegardens

Antrim Castle Gardens and Clotworthy House is a hidden gem waiting to be explored, these 400 year old Gardens have been transformed into a unique living museum.

Few historic gardens in Northern Ireland offer such evolutionary garden design characteristics with layer upon layer of design features and planting added over the centuries; including the magnificent 17th Century Anglo Dutch style canals, ponds, avenues, tunnels and pump house.

The award winning Antrim Castle Gardens offers a breathtaking walk into history but, also much more. While you are here why not stay for a coffee or lunch in the Garden Coffee Shop, browse the visitor shop and have a look round the Garden Heritage Exhibition and Art Gallery.

Location: Map 18:N4. OS Ref J186 850. Outside Antrim town centre off A26 on A6. Follow Brown Signs for Antrim Castle Gardens.
Owner: Antrim and Newtownabbey Borough Council
Contact: Samuel Hyndman - Garden Operations and Development Officer
Tel: 028 9448 1338
E-mail: culture@antrimandnewtwonabbey.gov.uk
Open: All year except Christmas Day, Boxing Day, New Year's Day and 12 July.
Mon, Wed and Fri 9.30am-5pm.
Tue and Thu 9.30am–9.30pm.
Sat and Sun 10am-5pm.
Admission: Free entry. Free guided group tours by arrangement only.
Key facts: Photographic shoots and filming by written permission only. WCs. Licensed.

BALLYWALTER PARK

Ballywalter, Newtownards, Co Down BT22 2PP

www.ballywalterpark.com

Ballywalter Park was built in the Italianate Palazzo style, by Sir Charles Lanyon for Andrew Mulholland. A Gentleman's wing was added in 1870 for Andrew's son, John Mulholland, later 1st Baron Dunleath. The house has a fine collection of original furniture and paintings, complemented by contemporary pieces.
Location: Map 18:P4. OS Ref J610 723. Off A2 on unclassified road, 1 km S of Ballywalter village. **Owner:** The Lord and Lady Dunleath
Contact: Mrs Sharon Graham, The Estate Office **Tel:** 028 4275 8264
Fax: 028 4275 8818 **E-mail:** enq@dunleath-estates.co.uk
Open: By prior appointment only; please contact The Estate Office.
Admission: House or Gardens: £9.50. House & Gardens: £17.00.
Groups (max 50): £9.50. Refreshments by arrangement.
Key facts: No photography indoors. The house is available for corporate & incentive events, lunches & dinners. Lunches & dinners can be booked by prior arrangement. Obligatory. Guide dogs only. Twelve en suite bedrooms available for group tours & corporate events. By appointment only. €

DOWN CATHEDRAL

Cathedral Office, English Street, Downpatrick County Down BT30 6AB

www.downcathedral.org

Built in 1183 as a Benedictine monastery, Down Cathedral is now a Cathedral of the Church of Ireland. Prominent and majestic, the cathedral is believed to have the grave of St Patrick in its grounds. There is also wonderful stained glass and a pulpit and organ of highest quality.
Location: Map 18:O6. OS Ref SB583 989.
Located in Downpatrick, in the heart of English Street. Follow brown signs.
Owner: Church of Ireland **Contact:** Joy Wilkinson
Tel: 028 4461 4922 **Fax:** 028 4461 4456 **E-mail:** info@downcathedral.org
Open: All year round. Mon-Sat: 9.30am-4pm. Sun: 2-4pm.
Admission: Donations. Guided tours by arrangement.
Key facts: By arrangement. Limited for cars and coaches. Guide dogs only.

Register for news and special offers at www.hudsonsheritage.com

HILLSBOROUGH CASTLE

Hillsborough BT26 6AG

www.hrp.org.uk/hillsborough

The late Georgian mansion was built in the 1770s and is a working royal residence, functioning as the official residence of the Royal Family when they are in Northern Ireland, and it has been the home of the Secretary of State since the 1970s. A tour of the house will guide you through the elegant State Rooms, still in use today, including the majestic Throne Room. Don't miss 98 acres of stunning gardens.
Location: Map 18:N5.
Owner: Historic Royal Palaces
Tel: 028 9268 1300
E-mail: hillsboroughcastle@hrp.org.uk
Open: Apr-Sep: House open specific days for guided tours. Year round: Gardens open 10am-5pm. Visit website or call for details before visiting.
Admission: See website. House by guided tour only, must book in advance.
Key facts: Weddings, receptions, conferences. No parking onsite.

BARONS COURT

Newtownstewart, Omagh, Co Tyrone BT78 4EZ

The home of the Duke and Duchess of Abercorn, Barons Court was built between 1779 and 1782, and subsequently extensively remodelled by John Soane (1791), William and Richard Morrison (1819-1841), Sir Albert Richardson (1947-49) and David Hicks (1975-76).
Location: Map 18:M3. OS Ref H236 382. 5km SW of Newtownstewart.
Contact: The Agent
Tel: 028 8166 1683 **E-mail:** info@barons-court.com
Website: www.barons-court.com
Open: By appointment only.
Admission: Tour of House and/or Gardens £13 per person. Tour inc. tea/coffee/scones £18 per person. Groups max. 50.
Key facts: No photography. The Carriage Room in the Stable Yard. Partial. By arrangement. Holiday cottages, 4 star rated by Northern Ireland Tourist Board. €

CASTLE WARD HOUSE & DEMESNE

Strangford, Downpatrick, Co Down BT30 7LS

Situated in a stunning location within an 820 acre walled demesne overlooking Strangford Lough.
Location: Map 18:P6. OS Ref J573 498. 7 miles north-east of Downpatrick, 1 mile from Strangford on A25
Owner: National Trust
Contact: Marketing & Communications Officer
Tel: 028 4488 1204
E-mail: castleward@nationaltrust.org.uk
Website: www.nationaltrust.org.uk/castle-ward
Open: Please see website for opening times and admission prices.
Key facts: Gift Shop WCs. Tea Room. By arrangement. On leads only. Caravan park. Holiday cottages. Basecamp. €

BENVARDEN GARDEN

Benvarden, Dervock, County Antrim BT53 6NN

This historic estate was built in the 1630s and owned by the Montgomery family since 1798. Most of the landscaping and planting of the mature trees was carried out by them in the years 1800-1820.
Location: Map 18:M1. OS Ref NW117 917. **Tel:** 028 2074 1331
Website: www.benvardin.com **Open:** Jun-Aug, Tue-Sun, BH Mons, 12-5pm.
Admission: Adult £5; Child U12 Free.

CARRICKFERGUS CASTLE

Marine Highway, Carrickfergus, County Antrim BT38 7BG

A Norman castle besieged in turn by the Scots, Irish, English and French, the castle played an important military role until 1928 and remains one of the best preserved medieval structures in Ireland. **Location:** Map 18:M1. OS Ref NW549 422.
Tel: 028 9335 1273 **E-mail:** scmenquiries@communities-ni.gov.uk
Open: All year, daily, 10-4pm. **Admission:** Adult: £5; Child £3.

CASTLE COOLE

Enniskillen, Co Fermanagh BT74 6JY

18th Century castle designed by James Wyatt and home of the Earls of Belmore is surrounded by its stunning landscape park. **Location:** Map 18:L4. OS Ref H245 436. On A4, 1½m from Enniskillen. **Tel:** 028 6632 2690 **E-mail:** castlecoole@nationaltrust.org.uk **Website:** www.nationaltrust.org.uk/castle-coole
Open: Easter, Jun-Aug, daily, 11-5pm; Mar & Apr, Sat & Sun, 11-5pm; May & Sep, Wed-Mon, 11-5pm. **Admission:** Adult £3.50; Child £2.

DUNLUCE CASTLE

87 Dunluce Road, Portrush, County Antrim BT57 8UY

The iconic ruin of Dunluce Castle bears witness to a long and tumultuous history. First built on the dramatic coastal cliffs of north County Antrim by the MacQuillan family around 1500, the earliest written record of the castle was in 1513.
Location: Map 18: M1. OS Ref NW087 999. **Tel:** 028 2073 1938
E-mail: scmenquiries@communities-ni.gov.uk
Open: All year, daily, 10-5pm. **Admission:** Adult: £5; Child £3.

KILLYLEAGH CASTLE

Killyleagh, Downpatrick, Co Down BT30 9QA

Oldest occupied castle in Ireland. Self-catering towers available, sleeps 4-9. Swimming pool and tennis court available by arrangement. Access to garden.
Location: Map 18:O5/6. OS Ref J523 529.
Tel: 028 4482 8261 **E-mail:** gawnrh@gmail.com
Website: www.killyleaghcastle.com **Open:** By arrangement.
Admission: Groups (30-50) by arrangement. Around £2.50 pp.

LISSAN HOUSE

Drumgrass Road, Cookstown, County Tyrone BT80 9SW

Lissan is an utterly enchanting country house set at the heart of a 267 acre demesne and nestling in a prime location in the valley of the Lissan Water.
Location: Map 18:L4. OS Ref NV937 413. **Tel:** 028 8676 3312
E-mail: lissan.house@btconnect.com **Website:** www.lissanhouse.com
Open: Easter-Sep, Sat & Sun, 12-5pm; Jul-Aug, Thu-Sun, 12-5pm.
Admission: Adult £4.50; Child £3.

MONTALTO ESTATE & CARRIAGE ROOMS

Ballynahinch, Co. Down BT24 8AY

Montalto is a privately owned estate nestled in the picturesque surroundings of the Co. Down countryside. **Location:** Map 18:O6. OS Ref NW117 917.
Tel: 028 9756 6100 **Fax:** 028 9756 6111
E-mail: info@montaltoestate.com **Website:** www.montaltoestate.com
Open: By appointment for weddings, events, luxury accommodation for up to 24.

MOUNT STEWART

Newtonards, Co Down BT22 2AD

Home of the Londonderry family since the early 18th Century, Mount Stewart was Lord Castlereagh's house and played host to many prominent political figures.
Location: Map 18:P5. OS Ref NW678 236. **Tel:** 028 4278 8387
E-mail: mountstewart@nationaltrust.org.uk **Website:** www.nationaltrust.org.uk/mount-stewart **Open:** 2 Jan-Mar & Nov-Dec, Sat & Sun, 11-3pm; Apr-Oct, daily, 11-5pm. **Admission:** Adult £7.72; Child £3.86.

SEAFORDE GARDENS

Seaforde, County Down BT30 8PG

Avenues of mature trees, a maze set in the middle of an old walled garden, rare plants and a Tropical Butterfly House.

Location: Map 18:O6. OS Ref SB497 984. On the A24 at Seaforde.
Tel: 028 4481 1225 **Fax:** 028 4481 1370 **E-mail:** info@seafordegardens.com
Website: www.seafordegardens.com **Open:** Easter-Sep, Mon-Sat, 10-5pm; Sun, 1-6pm. **Admission:** Adult £8.50; Child £4.85.

ARTHUR ANCESTRAL HOME

Cullybackey, County Antrim BT42 1AB

Tel: 028 2563 8494 **E-mail:** devel.leisure@ballymena.gov.uk

BELFAST CASTLE

Cave Hill, Antrim Road, Belfast BT15 5GR

Tel: 028 9077 6925

BOTANIC GARDENS

Stransmillis Road, Belfast BT7 1LP

Tel: 028 9031 4762

GLENARM CASTLE WALLED GARDEN

2 Castle Lane, Glenarm, Larne, County Antrim BT44 0BQ

Tel: 028 2884 1305

MONTALTO HOUSE

5 Craigaboney Road, Bushmills, County Antrim BT57 8XD

Tel: 028 2073 1257 **E-mail:** montaltohouse@btconnect.com

SENTRY HILL

Ballycraigy Road, Newtownabbey BT36 5SY

Tel: 028 9034 0000

ARDRESS HOUSE

64 Ardress Road, Portadown, Co Armagh BT62 1SQ

Tel: 028 8778 4753 **E-mail:** ardress@nationaltrust.org.uk

BENBURB CASTLE

Servite Priory, Main Street, Benburb, Co Tyrone BT71 7JZ

Tel: 028 3754 8241 **E-mail:** servitepriory@btinternet.com

DERRYMORE

Bessbrook, Newry, Co Armagh BT35 7EF

Tel: 028 8778 4753 **E-mail:** derrymore@nationaltrust.org.uk

GILFORD CASTLE ESTATE

Banbridge Road, Gilford BT63 6DT

Tel: 028 4062 3322 **E-mail:** gilford@irishfieldsports.com

AUDLEYS CASTLE

Strangford, County Down BT30 7LP

Tel: 028 9054 3034

BANGOR ABBEY

Bangor, County Down BT20 4JF

Tel: 028 9127 1200

BANGOR CASTLE

Bangor, County Down BT20 4BN

Tel: 028 9127 0371

CLOUGH CASTLE

Clough Village, Downpatrick, County Down

Tel: 028 9054 3034

SPRINGHILL HOUSE

20 Springhill Road, Moneymore, Co Londonderry BT45 7NQ

Described as 'one of the prettiest houses in Ulster'. A charming plantation house with a significant book collection, portraits and decorative arts.

Location: Map 18:M4. OS Ref NV998 422. **Tel:** 028 8674 8210
E-mail: springhill@nationaltrust.org.uk **Website:** www.ntni.org.uk
Open: Mar, Apr, Sep, Sat & Sun, 12-5pm; May, Fri-Sun, 12-5pm; Jun, Thu-Sun, 12-5pm; Jul-Aug, daily, 12-5pm. **Admission:** Adult £5; Child £2.27.

DUNDRUM CASTLE

Dundrum Village, Newcastle, County Down BT33 0QX

Tel: 028 9054 3034

GREENCASTLE ROYAL CASTLE

Cranfield Point, Kilkeel, County Down BT34 4LR

Tel: 028 9054 3037

GREY ABBEY

9-11 Church Street, Greyabbey, County Down BT22 2NQ

Tel: 028 9054 6552

GREY POINT FORT

Crawfordsburn Country Park, Helens Bay, Co. Down BT19 1LE

Tel: 028 9185 3621

HELENS TOWER

Clandeboye Estate, Bangor BT19 1RN

Tel: 028 9185 2817

INCH ABBEY

Downpatrick, County Down BT30 9AX

Tel: 028 9181 1491

KILCLIEF CASTLE

Strangford, County Down

Tel: 028 9054 3034

MAHEE CASTLE

Mahee Island, Comber, Newtownards BT23 6EP

Tel: 028 9182 6846

MOVILLA ABBEY

63 Movilla Road, Newtownards BT23 8EZ

Tel: 028 9181 0787

NEWRY CATHEDRAL

38 Hill Street, Newry, County Down BT34 1AT

Tel: 028 3026 2586

THE PRIORY

Newtownards, County Down

Tel: 028 9054 3037

PORTAFERRY CASTLE

Castle Street, Portaferry, County Down BT22 1NZ

Tel: 028 9054 3033

QUOILE CASTLE

Downpatrick, County Down BT30 7JB

Tel: 028 9054 3034

RINGHADDY CASTLE

Killyleagh, County Down

Tel: 028 9054 3037

ROWALLANE GARDEN ✿
Ballynahinch, Co Down BT24 7LH
Tel: 028 9751 0721 **E-mail:** rowallane@nationaltrust.org.uk

SKETRICK CASTLE
Whiterock, County Down BT23 6QA
Tel: 028 4278 8387

STRANGFORD CASTLE
Strangford, County Down
Tel: 028 9054 3034

CROM ESTATE ✿
Newtownbutler, County Fermanagh BT92 8AP
Tel: 028 6773 8118

ENNISKILLEN CASTLE ✿
Castle Barracks, Enniskillen, County Fermanagh BT74 7HL
Tel: 028 6632 5000 **E-mail:** castle@fermanagh.gov.uk

FLORENCE COURT ✿
Enniskillen, Co Fermanagh BT92 1DB
Tel: 028 6634 8249 **E-mail:** florencecourt@nationaltrust.org.uk

BELLAGHY BAWN
Castle Street, Bellaghy, County Londonderry BT45 8LA
Tel: 028 7938 6812

DUNGIVEN CASTLE
Main Street, Dungiven, Co Londonderry BT47 4LF
Tel: 028 7774 2428 **E-mail:** enquiries@dungivencastle.com

DUNGIVEN PRIORY AND O CAHANS TOMB
Dungiven, County Londonderry BT47 4PF
Tel: 028 7772 2074

THE GUILDHALL
Guildhall Square, Londonderry BT48 6DQ
Tel: 028 7137 7335

KINGS FORT
7 Connell Street, Limavady, Co Londonderry BT49 0HA
Tel: 028 7776 0304 **E-mail:** tourism@limavady.gov.uk

MOUNTSANDAL FORT
Mountsandal Road, Coleraine, Co Londonderry BT52 1PE
Tel: 027 7034 4723 **E-mail:** coleraine@nitic.net

PREHEN HOUSE
Prehen Road, Londonderry BT47 2PB
Tel: 028 7131 2829 **E-mail:** colinpeck@yahoo.com

ROUGH FORT
Limavady TIC, 7 Connell Street, Limavady BT49 0HA
Tel: 028 7084 8728

SAINT COLUMBS CATHEDRAL
London Street, Derry, County Londonderry BT48 6RQ
Tel: 028 7126 7313 **E-mail:** stcolumbs@ic24.net

SAMPSONS TOWER
Limavady TIC, 7 Connell Street, Limavady BT49 0HA
Tel: 028 7776 0307

THE ARGORY ✿
Moy, Dungannon, Co Tyrone BT71 6NA
Tel: 028 8778 4753 **E-mail:** argory@nationaltrust.org.uk

CASTLEDERG CASTLE
Castle Park, Castlederg, County Tyrone BT81 7AS
Tel: 028 7138 2204

HARRY AVERYS CASTLE
Old Castle Road, Newtownstewart BT82 8DY
Tel: 028 7138 2204

THE KEEP OR GOVERNORS RESIDENCE
Off Old Derry Road, Omagh, County Tyrone
Tel: 028 8224 7831 **E-mail:** omagh.tic@btconnect.com

KILLYMOON CASTLE
Killymoon Road, Cookstown, County Tyrone
Tel: 028 8676 3514

NEWTOWNSTEWART CASTLE
Townhall Street, Newtownstewart BT78 4AX
Tel: 028 6862 1588 **E-mail:** nieainfo@doeni.gov.uk

OMAGH GAOL
Old Derry Road, Omagh, County Tyrone
Tel: 028 8224 7831 **E-mail:** omagh.tic@btconnect.com

SAINT MACARTAN'S CATHEDRAL
Clogher, County Tyrone BT76 0AD
Tel: 028 0478 1220

SIR JOHN DAVIES CASTLE
Castlederg, County Tyrone BT81 7AS
Tel: 028 7138 2204

TULLYHOGUE FORT
B162, Cookstown, County Tyrone BT80 8UB
Tel: 028 8676 6727

Conservatory at Ballywalter Park

Opening Arrangements at places grant-aided by Historic England

Holkham Hall Vinery, Norfolk

Historic England is the public body that looks after England's historic environment. Each year they give grants to historic buildings in need in return for public access. Check here for details of opening times for many of the places recently in receipt of grants.

H Denotes opening for Heritage Open Days in September www.heritageopendays.org.uk.

Please note that parking and wheelchair access may be limited and toilets for people with disabilities are not always available. If you are travelling from afar or have special requirements, please check in advance. More details are available on www.historicengland.org.uk

LONDON

Benjamin Franklin's House, 36 Craven Street, London WC2N 5NF
A 1730s terraced house the site retains a majority of original features and is the world's only remaining home of Benjamin Franklin.
Location: Behind Charing Cross station. Rail: Charing Cross. Tube: Charing Cross. Bus: 6, 9, 11, 13, 15, 23, 77a , 91 and 176
Recipient: Friends of Benjamin Franklin House
Telephone: 020 7839 2006
Contact: Ms Sally James
Email: info@benjaminfranklinhouse.org
Website: www.benjaminfranklinhouse.org
Open: Mon, Wed-Sun, 10.30am-5.30pm. Tours and Historical Experience shows running at specific times.
Admission Adult: £7.00 **Child:** Free
H

Bromley Hall, Gillender Street, Tower Hamlets, London E14 6RN
A rare surviving 15th Century house and one of the oldest brick built houses in London.
Location: East side of A12. Rail: Devons Road. Tube: Bromley-by-Bow. Bus: 108.
Recipient: Leaside Regeneration
Telephone: 0845 262 0846
Contact: Mr David Black
Email: dblack@leasideplanning.co.uk
Open: By prior appointment.
P ♿ H

The Charles Dickens Museum, 48 & 49 Doughty Street, London WC1N 2LX
Dating from c1807-9 Charles Dickens wrote Oliver Twist and Nicholas Nickleby whilst living there. Includes manuscripts, rare editions, personal items and paintings.
Location: East Bloomsbury on accessible road with parking. Rail: Kings Cross/St Pancras 1m., Farringdon 1m., Euston 1m. Bus: 7, 17, 19, 38, 45, 46, 55, 243. Tube: Russell Square, Chancery Lane, Holborn, or Kings Cross St Pancras.
Recipient: The Charles Dickens Museum
Telephone: 020 7405 2127
Contact: Mr Robert Moye
Email: info@dickensmuseum.com
Website: www.dickensmuseum.com
Open: All year, Mon-Sun, 10am-5pm. Temporary closures are advertised on website. Closed 25, 26 Dec and 1 Jan.
Admission Adult: £8.00 **Child:** £4.00
♿

Headstone Manor, Pinner View, Harrow, London HA2 6PX
Grade I listed timber framed manor house, surrounded by a water filled moat and original residence of Archbishops of Canterbury until the Reformation.
Location: Access via Pinner View. Rail: Headstone Lane 1m. Bus: H9, H10 & H14.
Recipient: London Borough of Harrow
Telephone: 020 8863 6720
Contact: Ms Jo Saunders
Email: harrow.museum@harrow.gov.uk
Website: www.harrow.gov.uk/museum, www.harrowmuseum.org.uk
Open: Open most of year and for historic talks and school visits.
Admission Adult: £3.00 for tours
Child: Free
P ♿ H

Red House, Red House Lane, Bexleyheath DA6 8JF
Strongly influenced by gothic medieval architecture and constructed with an emphasis on natural materials. Unaltered interior with numerous original features including wall paintings and stained glass.
Location: Follow A221 Bexleyheath from A2. Rail: Bexleyheath 0.75m.
Recipient: The National Trust
Telephone: 020 8303 6359
Contact: Mr James Breslin
Email: redhouse@nationaltrust.org.uk
Website: www.nationaltrust.org.uk
Open: Feb-Nov, Wed-Sun, Nov-Dec, Fri-Sun and all BH Mons, 11am-5pm. Pre booked guided tours tel: 020 8304 9878.
Admission Adult: £8.00 **Child:** £4.00
P ♿

Strawberry Hill, Waldegrave Road, Twickenham, London TW1 4SX
Georgian house and a fine example of gothic revival architecture and interior decoration including extraordinary rooms, towers and battlements.
Location: 268 Waldegrave Road, Twickenham A309. Rail: Strawberry Hill ¼m. Bus: 33, R68
Recipient: Strawberry Hill Trust
Telephone: 020 8744 1241
Contact: Mr Nicholas Smith
Email: nicholas.smith@strawberryhillhouse.org.uk
Website: www.strawberryhillhouse.org.uk
Open: Mar-Nov, Mons, Tues, Weds, Sats and Suns, Weekdays 2pm-6pm, Weekends 12pm-6pm. Guided tours available.
Admission Adult: £12 **Child:** Under 16 free
P ♿

Opening Arrangements at places grant-aided by Historic England

SOUTH EAST

Basildon Park, Lower Basildon, Reading, Berkshire RG8 9NR
Designed in the 18th Century and set in 400 acres of parkland the site include rich interiors with fine plasterwork, small flower garden, pleasure ground and woodland walks.
Location: Between Pangbourne and Streatley. Rail: Pangbourne 2½m., Goring and Streatley 3m. Bus: 132
Recipient: The National Trust
Telephone: 01491 672382
Contact: Ms Amanda Beard
Email: basildonpark@nationaltrust.org.uk
Website: www.nationaltrust.org.uk
Open: Daily, 10am-5pm, closes at dusk if earlier. Closed 24 and 25 Dec
Admission Adult: £14.00 (House and Grounds) **Child:** £7.00 (House and Grounds)
P ♿ H

Bletchley Park Mansion, Wilton Avenue, Milton Keynes, Buckinghamshire MK3 6BN
Victorian and Edwardian mansion, the estate was taken over in WWII and used for substantially developing the UK's code breaking centre.
Location: In central Bletchley, access from Sherwood Drive. Rail: Bletchley
Recipient: Bletchley Park Trust
Telephone: 01908 640404
Contact: Mr Iain Standen
Email: istanden@bletchleypark.org.uk
Website: www.bletchleypark.org.uk
Open: Mar-Oct, 9.30am-5pm (last admission 4pm). Nov-Feb, 9.30am-4pm (last admissinon 3pm. Closed 24, 25, 26 Dec &1 Jan.
Admission Adult: £16.75 **Child:** £10.00 under 12s free
P ♿ H

Brambletye House Ruins, Brambletye Lane, Forest Row, East Sussex RH18 5EH
Ruins of a house built in 1631 and destroyed during the civil wars by Cromwellian troops.
Location: Off A22, private road where double white lines end. 2m. from East Grinstead.
Recipient: Mrs Anne Crawford
Telephone: 01342 826646
Contact: Mrs Anne Crawford
Email: annecrawford111@gmail.com
Open: Reasonable times by appointment.

Chantry House, St Mary the Virgin, Hart Street, Henley on Thames, Oxfordshire RG9 2AR
14th-15th Century three storey timber framed building with exposed interior timbering and early leaded glazing.
Location: Adjacent to churchyard on Hart Street. Rail: Henley on Thames 0.3m.
Recipient: PCC of St Mary the Virgin
Telephone: 01491 577340
Contact: Parish Secretary
Email: office.hwr@lineone.net
Website: www.stmaryshenley.org.uk
Open: May-Sept, Suns, 2.00-5.00pm. At other times by prior appointment.
♿

Cobham Hall and Dairy, Cobham, Kent DA12 3BL
Gothic-style dairy in grounds of Cobham Hall, built by James Wyatt c1790.
Location: Adj. to A2, 8m.from M25 jct.2. Rail: Sole Street, Meopham.
Recipient: Cobham Hall Heritage Trust
Telephone: 01474 823371
Contact: Mrs J Brace
Email: enquiries@cobhamhall.com or BraceJ@cobhamhall.com
Open: Specific dates only, as site is an independent boarding and day school for girls. Please check website for details.
Admission Adult: £5.50 **Child:** £4.50
P ♿

The Durdans Riding School, Chalk Lane, Epsom and Ewell, Surrey KT18 7AX
An indoor riding school built in 1881, Lord Rosebery bred three Derby winners; Lados, Cicero and St Visto here.
Location: Follow Chalk Lane from Epsom Racecourse, through double doors on left. Rail: Epsom 4m.
Telephone: 07930 915243
Contact: Mr Philip Buckman
Email: philip@psbconsultancy.co.uk
Website: www.thedurdansliverystables.co.uk
Open: By prior appointment.
P ♿ H

Firle Place, Lewes, East Sussex BN8 6LP
A grade I listed mansion the exterior dates mainly from 18th Century, but the western half was built in the early 16th Century, probably by Sir John Gage who was Constable of the Tower in Henry VIII's reign (d. 1557).
Location: 4m. E of Lewes, signposted on A27. Rail: Glynde Station 1m. Bus: Route 125
Recipient: Trustees of the Firle Estate Settlement
Telephone: 01273 858307
Contact: Mr Josh Feakins
Email: josh@firle.com
Website: www.firle.com
Open: Apr, Jun-Sept and May BH, Specific days, 1pm-4.30pm, check website for details
Admission Adult: £8.50 **Child:** £4.00
P ♿

Great Dixter House and Gardens, Northiam, nr. Rye, East Sussex TN31 6PH
Original medieval hall house built c1450 comprising three rooms, the Great Hall, Parlour and Solar.
Location: Off A268 in Northiam. Rail: Rye 7m.
Recipient: Ms O Eller
Telephone: 01797 252878 ext 3
Contact: Mr Perry Rodriguez
Email: office@greatdixter.co.uk
Website: www.greatdixter.co.uk
Open: Mar-Oct, Tues-Sun and BHs, 2pm-5pm. Gardens open from 11am.
Admission Adult: £10 (House and Garden) **Child:** £3.50 (House and Garden)
P ♿

Hall Barn Estate, Beaconsfield, Buckinghamshire HP9 2SG
Garden buildings situated in landscaped garden laid out in 1680s including gothic temple, classical temple and stone obelisk.
Location: 300yds S. of Beaconsfield Church. Rail: Beaconsfield 1½m. Bus: local services to Beaconsfield
Recipient: Hall Barn Trustees Ltd
Telephone: 01494 673 020
Contact: Estate Office
Email: giles.paddison@hallbarnestate.co.uk
Open: By prior appointment or written arrangement with Mr Farncombe, Hall Barn, Windsor End, Beaconsfield, Buckinghamshire HP9 2SG.
P ♿

Hardham Priory, London Road, Hardham, Chichester, West Sussex RH20 1LD
Ruins of an Augustinian monastery founded in the mid-13th Century and dissolved in 1534 with interesting Chapter House ruins.
Location: Rail: Pulborough 2m.
Telephone: 07881 788556
Contact: Mr John Rowell
Email: johnny.g.rowell@gmail.com
Open: Jun, specific dates, 10am to 4pm. Check website for details.
P ♿

The Hermitage, Carshalton House, Carshalton, Surrey SM5 3PS
One of three garden follies in an historic landscape, The Hermitage has a stone façade and is designed in a classical manner.
Location: A232 between Sutton and Croydon, off Pound Street.
Rail: Carshalton. Bus: 27, 157
Recipient: Carshalton Water Tower and Historic Garden Trust
Telephone: 020 8669 1546
Contact: c/o Jean Knight
Email: irvineknight@btinternet.com
Website: www.carshaltonwatertower.co.uk
Open: Apr-Sept, 1st and 3rd Sun of each month, 2.30pm-5pm. Tours available by arrangement. Please see website for details.
Admission Adult: £3.00 (also includes Water Tower entry) **Child:** Free
[♿] [H]

Highclere Castle and Park (Temple of Diana), Highclere, Newbury, Hampshire RG20 9RN
Early Victorian mansion rebuilt by Sir Charles Barry in 1842, surrounded by 'Capability' Brown parkland.
Location: 5m. S of Newbury off A34.
Rail: Newbury 5m.
Recipient: Executors of the 7th Earl of Carnarvon & Lord Carnarvon
Telephone: 01223 368771
Contact: Mr Alec Tompson
Email: alec.tompson@carterjonas.co.uk
Website: www.highclerecastle.co.uk
Open: View from car when exiting on Castle open days or on foot from permissive footpath. Please see website for details.
Admission Adult: £22 (Castle, Exhibition and Gardens) **Child:** £13.50 (Castle, Exhibition and Gardens)
[P] [♿]

Homeside, 7 Church Road, Oare, Kent ME13 0QA
Site including historic painted wallpaper dating from 1836 located in the current kitchen.
Telephone: 07977 531952
Contact: Mr Pierre Haincourt
Open: Jul, specific dates. Check website for details

Ightham Mote, Ivy Hatch, Sevenoaks, Kent TN15 0NT
Moated manor house covering nearly 700 years of history from medieval times to 1960s including a Tudor Chapel, Billiards Room and Drawing Room.
Location: 6m. E of Sevenoaks, off A25, 2½m. S of Ightham off A227. Rail: Borough Green and Wrotham 3½m. Bus: 222 ½m., 404 ¾m.
Recipient: The National Trust
Telephone: 01732 810378 exn 100
Contact: Property Manager
Email: ighthammote@nationaltrust.org.uk
Website: www.nationaltrust.org.uk
Open: All year except 24 and 25 Dec, daily, specific times. Estate open all year dawn-dusk.
Admission Adult: £12.00 **Child:** £6.00
[P] [♿] [H]

King George VI Memorial Park, Italianate Greenhouse, Ramsgate, Kent CT11 8BD
Early 19th Century glasshouse curved in design to maximise heat and light, attached to former East Cliff Lodge outbuilding and stable block courtyards.
Location: Accessed by Montefiore Avenue. Rail: Dumpton Park ½m.
Recipient: Thanet District Council
Telephone: 01843 853839
Contact: Mr Phil Dadds
Email: phil@phildadds.co.uk
Website: www.thanet.gov.uk/pdf/greenhouse_lowres.pdf
Apr-Sept, Mon-Fri, 9am-5pm.
At other times by prior appointment, tel: 01843 853839
[♿]

Knole, Sevenoaks, Kent TN15 0RP
The largest private house in England and a fine example of late medieval architecture the Cartoon Gallery contains six large copies of Raphael's cartoons.
Location: Off A22 at Sevenoaks High Street. Rail: Sevenoaks 1.5m.
Recipient: The National Trust
Telephone: 01732 462100
Contact: Steven Dedman
The Property Manager
Email: knole@nationaltrust.org.uk
Website: www.nationaltrust.org.uk/knole
Open: House: Mar-Nov; Tues-Sun, 12-4pm. Garden: Apr-Sept; Tues only 11am-4pm. Check website for details
Admission Adult: £11.50 **Child:** £5.75
[P] [♿] [H]

Painshill Park, Portsmouth Road, Cobham, Surrey KT11 1JE
158 acres of restored, 18th Century landscape garden with follies, a Serpentine lake, ruined Abbey, Turkish Tent and recently restored crystal grotto.
Location: 200m E. of A245/A307 roundabout. Rail: Cobham 2m. Walton on Thames or Weybridge. Bus: 408, 515 and 515A.
Recipient: Painshill Park Trust Ltd
Telephone: 01932 868113
Contact: Mr Michael Gove
Email: info@painshill.co.uk
Website: www.painshill.co.uk
Open: Mar-Oct: 10.30am-6pm, Nov-Feb: 10.30am-4pm . Closed 25 and 26 Dec. Guided tours by prior appointment at additional cost.
Admission Adult: £7.70 **Child:** £4.20
[P] [♿]

Provender, Provender Lane, Norton, Faversham, Kent ME13 0ST
A grade II* listed timber framed country house dating from 14th Century, restored using traditional methods of craftsmanship and historic materials.
Location: S off A2 between Faversham and Sittingbourne. Rail: Teynham 2m., Faversham and Sittingbourne.
Recipient: Princess Olga Romanoff
Telephone: 07583 859790-bookings
Contact: Princess Olga Romanoff
Email: olgaromanoff@aol.com
Website: www.provenderhouse.co.uk
May-Oct, tours on 1st and last Sun and first Tues of the month and BHs. Open all year for pre-booked group tours (minimum 15).
Admission Adult: £11.00 **Child:** £9.50
[P] [♿]

Stowe House, Buckingham, Buckinghamshire MK18 5EH
Mansion built in 1680 and surrounded by important 18th Century gardens and one of the most complete neo-classical estates in Europe.
Location: 3m. NW of Buckingham.
Rail: Milton Keynes 15m. Bus: X5
Recipient: The Stowe House Preservation Trust
Telephone: 01280 818002
Contact: Ms Ruth Peters
Email: rpeters@stowe.co.uk
Website: www.stowehouse.org
Open: Throughout the year.
Please see website for details or information line tel:01280 818166.
Admission Adult: £5.75 **Child:** free
[P] [♿] [H]

Opening Arrangements at places grant-aided by Historic England

Stowe Landscape Gardens, New Inn Farm, Buckingham, Buckinghamshire MK18 5EQ
Extensive and complex pleasure grounds and park around a country mansion, the park and gardens contain over 30 buildings, many of great architectural importance.
Location: 3m. NW of Buckingham off A422. Rail: Bicester North 9m., Milton Keynes Central 14m. or Aylesbury 20m. Bus: X5, 32, 66 3m.
Recipient: The National Trust
Telephone: 01280 822850
Contact: Property Manager
Email: stowe@nationaltrust.org.uk
Website: www.nationaltrust.org.uk
Open: Parkland: Open daily all year, dawn till dusk. Closed 25 December. See website for details and café and shop opening times
Admission Adult: £11.00 **Child:** £5.50
P ♿ H

Watts Gallery, Down Lane, Compton, Guildford, Surrey GU3 1DH
Gallery and house built 1903-4 to contain the paintings and sculptures of George Frederick Watts.
Location: B3000 from A3, onto Down Lane. Rail: Guildford 2½m. Bus: 46
Recipient: The Watts Gallery
Telephone: 01483 810235
Contact: Ms Perdita Hunt
Email: director@wattsgallery.org.uk
Website: www.wattsgallery.org.uk
Open: Tues-Sun and BHs, 11am-5pm.
Admission Adult: £7.50 **Child:** free
P ♿ H

Westenhanger Castle and Barns, Westenhanger, Kent CT21 4HX
Complex of 14th Century castle and 16th Century barns visited by Queen Elizabeth I. Now mostly ruinous, many features remain including Tudor fireplaces and dovecote tower.
Location: From M20 follow signs for Folkestone racecourse & take horsebox entrance. Rail: Westenhanger ¼m. Bus: Nearest bus stop Newing Green.
Recipient: G Forge Ltd
Telephone: 01227 738451
Contact: Mr Graham Forge
Email: grahamforge@btinternet.com
Website: www.westenhangercastle.co.uk
Open: Group tours and weddings by appointment.
P ♿

SOUTH WEST

Castle House, Taunton Castle, Castle Green, Taunton, Somerset TA1 4AA
15th Century lodging house, built by the Bishops of Winchester.
Location: Centre of Taunton in Castle Green. Rail: Taunton 1m.
Bus: Coach station adjacent
Recipient: Somerset Building Preservation Trust
Telephone: 01823 337363
Contact: Mr Chris Sidaway
Email: chrismsidaway@btconnect.com
Website: wwww.castlehousetaunton.org.uk
Open: Please see website for opening details.
♿ H

Cotehele, St Dominick, Saltash, Cornwall PL12 6TA
Built mainly between 1485-1627 the granite and slate-stone walls contain chambers adorned with tapestries, original furniture and armour.
Location: 1m. W of Calstock by steep footpath. Rail: Calstock 1¼m. Bus: 79
Recipient: The National Trust
Telephone: 01579 351346
Contact: General Manager, National Trust
Email: cotehele@nationaltrust.org.uk
Website: www.nationaltrust.org.uk
Open: House: Mar-Nov, daily, 11am-4.30pm. Garden: daily all year 10am-dusk.
Admission Adult: £10.50 (House, Garden & Mill), £6.50 **Child:** £5.50 (House, Garden & Mill)
P ♿ H

Manor Farm House, Meare, Glastonbury, Somerset BA6 9SP
14th Century summer residence of The Abbots of Glastonbury, now a farmhouse. The interior has a former open hall with large stone hooded fireplace.
Location: B3151 on E side of church. Rail: Castle Cary 12m. Bus: 668
Recipient: Mr Look
Telephone: 01458 860242
Contact: Mr Robyn Look
Email: robynlook@yahoo.co.uk
Open: Apr, May, Jul, Aug, specific dates, 9am-5pm. Wall paintings by prior appointment. Please see website for details.
P

Mapperton House, Beaminster, Dorset DT8 3NR
Grade I listed manor house, Elizabethan in origin, enlarged in late 1660s including the manor, church, stables and dovecote.
Location: Approach via B3163.
Rail: Crewkerne 7m. Dorchester 17m.
Recipient: The Earl & Countess of Sandwich
Telephone: 01308 862645
Contact: Lord Sandwich
Email: office@mapperton.com
Website: www.mapperton.com
Open: House: May, Jul-Aug, Mon-Fri, 2pm-4.30pm. Gardens: Mar-Oct. Contact property or check website for details. Other times by prior appointment.
Admission Adult: £6.00 (Garden), £6.00 (House) **Child:** £3 (Garden, under 18). Free (Garden, under 5).
P ♿ H

Old Duchy Palace, Quay Street, Lostwithiel, Cornwall PL22 0BS
Previously the administrative centre for the Duchy of Cornwall from 1878 it was a Freemasons' temple, becoming redundant in 2008.
Location: On A390 halfway between Liskeard and St Austell, turn left to Quay Street. Rail: Lostwithiel
Recipient: The Prince's Regeneration Trust
Telephone: 0203 262 0560
Contact: Dr Paul Gardner
Email: paul.gardner@princes-regeneration.org
Website: www.princes-regeneration.org/projects/old-d
Open: Ground floor, daily during trading hours, 10am-5pm. Most of the building is accessible apart from the upper second floor.

Porthmeor Studios, Back Road West, St Ives, Cornwall TR26 1NG
Grade II* listed lofts and cellars for the pilchard fishing industry, now used by fishermen and artists.
Location: Porthmeor beach 200metres from Tate St Ives. Rail: St Ives. Bus: Tate St Ives shuttle bus
Recipient: Borlase Smart John Wells Trust Ltd
Telephone: 01736 339339
Contact: Mr Chris Hibbert
Email: chris@bsjwtrust.co.uk
Website: www.bsjwtrust.co.uk
Open: Moffat Lindor Rm: Spring, daily, normal office hrs. Installation 'The Maritime Artist' and pilchard cellars open by request. Guided tours avail. Please contact for further details.
♿

Powderham Castle, Kenton, Devon EX6 8JQ
Pseudo medieval gothic tower built 1717-1774 in the deer park of Powderham Castle, modelled on the Shrub Hill Belvedere at Windsor.
Location: 6m. SW of Exeter, 4m. miles from M5 jct.30, A379 in Kenton Village. Rail: Starcross station 2m. Bus: 2. Ferry: Exeter to Starcross
Recipient: The Earl of Devon Estate
Telephone: 01626 890243
Contact: The Estate Office
Email: castle@powderham.co.uk
Website: www.powderham.co.uk
Open: March-Oct, Sunday-Friday, 11am-4.30pm. Access to Belvedere Tower (exterior only) by paid admission. Check website or telephone before visiting
Admission Adult: £11.00 (includes guided tour) **Child:** £8.00 (4-16, includes guided tour)
P

The Red House, Painswick Rococo Gardens, Painswick, Gloucestershire GL6 6TH
Principal folly building within landscaped garden, displaying many of the classic attributes of the Rococo period.
Location: On B4073 ½ mile outside Painswick. Rail: Stroud 4m. Bus: 61 ½m.
Recipient: Painswick Rococo Garden Trust
Telephone: 01452 813204
Contact: Mr Paul Moir
Email: info@rococogarden.co.uk
Website: www.rococogarden.org.uk
Open: Jan-Oct, daily, 11am-5pm.
Admission Adult: £7.00 **Child:** £3.30
P ♿

Saltram House, Plympton, Plymouth, Devon PL7 1UH
George II mansion, complete with its original contents and state rooms worked on by Robert Adam, set in a landscaped park.
Location: 3½m. E of Plymouth centre between A38 and A379. Rail: Plymouth 3½m. Bus: 19/A/B, 20-2 or 51 ¾m.
Telephone: 01752 333500
Contact: Carol Murrin
Email: saltram@nationaltrust.org.uk
Website: www.nationaltrust.org.uk
Open: House: Feb-Dec, daily, 11am-4:30pm until 1 Nov, 11am-3.30pm Nov-Feb. Please see website for details. Special events, tours throughout, timed house tickets.
Admission Adult: £11.40 **Child:** £5,80
P ♿ H

Tyntesfield, Wraxall, Bristol BS48 1NX
Large country house built in 1813 the house has survived with almost all its Victorian fittings and still retains much of its original hot-air heating and ventilation system.
Location: On B3128. Rail: Nailsea and Backwell 2m. Bus: frequent services from Bristol
Recipient: The National Trust
Telephone: 01275 461900
Contact: The Property Manager
Email: tyntesfield@nationaltrust.org.uk
Website: www.nationaltrust.org.uk
Open: Please see website
Admission Adult: £15.30 **Child:** £7.70
P ♿ H

The Walronds, 6 Fore Street, Cullompton, Devon EX15 1JL
Built between 1602 and 1605 the site has a panelled hall with a large fireplace with decorated plaster overmantel and a parlour with a decorated plaster ceiling.
Location: Leave M5 Jct. 28 following Cullompton. Rail: Tiverton Parkway 5m. Bus: 1, 1A
Recipient: Cullompton Walronds Preservation Trust
Telephone: 01884 33394
Contact: Colonel Michael Woodcock
Email: michaelwoodcock46@yahoo.com
Website: www.walronds.com
Sept, specific dates, 10am-4pm. Please check website for details.
♿ H

EAST OF ENGLAND

173 High Street, Berkhamsted, Hertfordshire HP4 3HB
13th Century timber framed building, thought to be one of the oldest shops in England.
Location: High Street in Berkhamsted opp. Old Town Hall. Rail: Berkhamsted.
Recipient: Mr B Norman
Email: barrie@landfind.co.uk
Open: By prior appointment, tel: 01442 879996
♿

Bawdsey Manor, Ferry Road, Suffolk IP12 3BH
Enjoying a magnificent position at the mouth of the River Deben, the Estate was bought by the MOD in 1936 to provide facilities for the development of Radar.
Location: B1083 to Melton, Sutton, Bawdsey village, then to Bawdsey Quay.
Recipient: Niels Toettcher
Telephone: 01394 412395
Contact: Mr Niels Toettcher
Email: ann@skola.co.uk
Website: www.bawdseymanor.co.uk
Open: By prior appointment only
Admission Adult: £5.00 **Child:** £5.00 (open days free)
P

Church of St Mary, Ickworth Park, Suffolk IP29 5QE
Grade II* church, located within the Grade II registered park at Ickworth.
Location: Off A143 between Bury St Edmunds and Haverhill. Bus: Routes between Bury St Edmunds and Haverhill
Recipient: Ickworth Conservation Trust
Telephone: 01284 763521
Contact: Mr Simon Pott
Website: www.ickworthchurch.org.uk
Open: Summer, daily, 10am - 5pm. Winter, daily, 11am - 3.30pm.
♿

Clare Castle, Clare, Suffolk CO10 8HG
Remains of a 13th Century shell-keep, the north bailey contained the earliest foundation of Augustinian friars in England (1090).
Location: S. of Clare, two minutes walk from centre.
Recipient: Suffolk County Council
Telephone: 01284 757088
Contact: Mr David Robertson
Email: clerk@clare-uk.com
Website: www.stedmundsbury.gov.uk
Open: All year during daylight hours.
♿

Hoveton Hall (Glasshouse), Hoveton, Norwich NR12 8RJ
Glasshouse dated to early 19th Century, constructed of predominately cast iron with brick wall and bothies behind and set amongst 15 acres of informal gardens.
Location: 150m NW of Hoveton Hall, 9m. N of Norwich on A1151. Rail: Hoveton, Wroxham 1m.
Recipient: A E Buxton
Telephone: 01603 782798
Contact: Mr A E Buxton
Email: andrew-buxton@tiscali.co.uk
Website: www.hovetonhallestates.co.uk
Open: May-June, Mon-Fri, 10.30am-4.30pm.
Admission: £7.50 for access to the gardens which include the glasshouse.
P

Opening Arrangements at places grant-aided by Historic England

Holkham Hall Vinery, Wells-next-the-Sea, Norfolk NR23 1AB
Range of six late 19th Century Glasshouses repaired to include early and late peach houses, a muscat house, fig house and early and late vineries.
Location: B1105 from A149 Fakenham to Wells. Rail: King's Lynn. Bus: Hunstanton to Cromer.
Recipient: Coke Estates Ltd
Telephone: 01328 710227
Contact: Ms Celia Deeley
Email: enquiries@holkham.co.uk
Website: www.holkham.co.uk
Open: Mar-Oct, 10am-5pm, other times by appointment.
Admission Adult: £2.50 **Child:** £1.00 (age 5-16)
♿

Knebworth House, Knebworth, nr. Stevenage, Hertfordshire SG1 2AX
Originally a Tudor manor house, rebuilt in gothic style in 1843 containing rooms in various styles including a Jacobean banqueting hall. Set in 250 acres of parkland with 28 acres of formal gardens.
Location: Jct7 A1(M) at Stevenage South. Rail: Stevenage.
Recipient: Knebworth House Education & Preservation Trust
Telephone: 01438 812661
Contact: Mrs Julie Loughlin
Email: info@knebworthhouse.com
Website: www.knebworthhouse.com
Open: Mar - Sept, check website for details
Admission Adult: £13.00 (£12.50 Snr/group) **Child:** £13.00 (£12.50 group)
P ♿

Moggerhanger House, Moggerhanger, Bedfordshire MK44 3RW
Country House including 18th Century core, refurbished by Sir John Soane -1790 -99 and set in 33 acres of parkland.
Location: Signposted from A603 in Moggerhanger. Rail: Sandy 3m. Bus: M3
Recipient: Harvest Vision Ltd
Telephone: 01767 641007
Contact: Mrs Tracy Purser
Email: enquiries@moggerhangerpark.com
Website: www.moggerhangerpark.com
Open: Jun-Sept, daily, guided tours Sun and Wed at 2.30pm. Grounds open throughout year. 10am-5pm. Check website for specific dates.
Admission Adult: £5.00 **Child:** Free
♿

Queen Anne's Summerhouse, Old Warden Bedfordshire SG18 9HQ
Standing on the Shuttleworth estate, the building is a foursquare folly of the early 18th Century featuring exceptionally fine brickwork of the period.
Location: 4m. W of Biggleswade. Access by foot from Old Warden village. Rail: Biggleswade 4m.
Recipient: The Landmark Trust
Telephone: 01628 825920
Contact: Ms Victoria O'Keefe
Email: vokeefe@landmarktrust.org.uk
Website: www.landmarktrust.org.uk
Open: Exterior: All reasonable times. Interior: specific dates and times by prior appointment.
H

The Shell House, Hatfield Forest, Takeley, Nr Bishops Stortford, Essex CM22 6NE
Rare garden house/folly, c1759, constructed of knapped and boulder flints, shells, glass fragments and brickwork with a low pitched pantile pediment gabled roof.
Location: Signposted from B1256. Rail: Stanstead Airport 3m. Bus: 307 ½m.
Recipient: The National Trust
Telephone: 01279 870678
Contact: Mrs Nicky Daniel
Email: hatfieldforest@nationaltrust.org.uk
Website: www.nationaltrust.org.uk
Open: Sats and Suns, 10am-4.30pm.
P ♿

South Elmham Hall, St. Cross, Harleston, Norfolk IP20 0PY
Ruined gatehouse, possibly 14th Century situated on a designated walk to adjacent ruined minster.
Location: A143 SW of Bungay, signed from B1062 at Homerfield Halesworth
Recipient: John Sanderson
Telephone: 07958793298
Contact: Mr John Sanderson
Email: info@southelmham.co.uk
Website: www.batemansbarn.co.uk
Open: Any reasonable time. Gatehouse is included on tours of South Elmham Hall, May-Sept: Thurs and Suns at 2pm and 3pm.
P ♿ H

The Tower, Dilham Hall, Dilham, Norfolk NR28 9PN
Remains of a tower, said to be part of gatehouse dating from 15th Century, the tower stands to almost the original height of two storeys with a parapet above.
Location: A1151 from North Walsham. Rail: North Walsham 5m.
Recipient: Bindwell Ltd
Telephone: 01692 536777
Contact: Mr Alistair Paterson
Open: By prior appointment.
H

EAST MIDLANDS

Belvoir Castle Riding Ring, Grantham, Leicestershire NG32 1PD
Grade II* listed circular exercise ring for horses constructed of colour washed brick, timber superstructure and slate roof over curved rafters.
Location: Between villages Knipton, Woolsthorpe-by-Belvoir and Redmile.
Recipient: Trustees of Frances, Duchess of Rutland's 2000 Settlement
Telephone: 01904 756301
Contact: Mr A R Harle
Email: andrew.harle@smithsgore.co.uk
Website: www.belvoircastle.com
Open: Apr-Jun, specific dates, exterior viewed when gardens are open. Access at other times by prior appointment only
Admission Adult: £15.00 (Castle and Gardens), £8.00 (Gardens) - charge to view ring included in fee. £2.50 at other times
Child: £8.00 (Castle & Gardens), £5.00 (Gardens) - charge to view ring included. £2.50 at other times.
P ♿

The Gatehouse Lodges and Gatepiers, Drakeholes, Nottinghamshire DN10 5DF
Once the entrance to Wiseton Hall they were used as living accommodation for the gate keeper and his wife who lived in the south lodge and slept in the north.
Location: Adj. to B6045 in Drakeholes, nr. to the Chesterfield canal basin opp. the White Swan pub. Rail: Retford (8m.).
Recipient: Mr Mike Deakin
Telephone: 01777 816285
Contact: Mr Mike Deakin
Email: mike@proviso-systems.co.uk
N, S and W elevations: viewed all yr. from the public highway. To view in more detail please contact tel: 07970 823574. Gatehouse interiors unrenovated and unavailable for public viewing.
P

KEY
P CAR PARKING AVAILABLE
♿ PARTIALORFULLWHEELCHAIRACCESS
H HERITAGE OPEN DAYS

www.historicengland.org.uk

Porthmeor Studios, Cornwall

Opening Arrangements at places grant-aided by Historic England

Elizabeth Gaskell's House, Manchester

Hardwick Hall, Doe Lea, Chesterfield, Derbyshire S44 5QJ
Late 16th Century 'prodigy house' designed for Bess of Hardwick containing an outstanding collection of 16th Century furniture, tapestries and needlework.
Location: Just off J29 of M1, 9½m. SE of Chesterfield. Rail: Chesterfield 8m. Bus: Chesterfield train and bus stations.
Recipient: The National Trust
Telephone: 01246 858400 or 858430
Contact: Denise Edwards
Email: hardwickhall@nationaltrust.org.uk
Website: www.nationaltrust.org.uk
Open: Feb-Nov, Wed-Sun and BH Mons, 12pm-4.30pm. Nov-Dec, Wed-Sun, 10.30am-3.30pm. Park, garden, shop and restaurant 9am-6pm all year, closed 25 Dec.
Admission Adult: £12.60 (Hall and Garden) **Child:** £6.30 (Hall and Gardens)
P ♿ H

King John's Palace Ruins, Kings Clipstone, Nottinghamshire NG21 9BJ
Three standing walls of 12th Century ruin of King John's Palace; outstanding views overlooking Sherwood Forest.
Location: B6030 from Mansfield on entrance to Old Kings Clipstone.
Recipient: Michelle Bradley
Telephone: 01623 823559
Contact: Ms Michelle Bradley
Email: mabradley@talltalk.net
Website: www.mercian-as.co.uk
Open: Aug, specific dates. At other times by prior appointment.
♿

Melbourne Hall, Melbourne, Derbyshire DE73 8EN
Small detached hexagonal garden building within Melbourne Hall Gardens. The building comprises buff stone walls, Westmoreland slate surrounding an ogee shaped roof, timber sash windows and internal plasterwork.
Location: Off Church Sq. via Church St/ Blackwell Lane. Rail: Derby 7m. Bus: 61
Recipient: Trustees of the Melbourne Trust Fund
Telephone: 01530 410859
Contact: Mr William Gagie
Email: william.gagie@fishergerman.co.uk
Website: www.melbournehall.com
Open: By appt. only. Please see website for details.
Admission Adult: £4.50 **Child:** £3.50
P ♿

Padley Hall and Chapell, Upper Padley, Grindleford, Derbyshire S32 2JA
Remains of medieval manor house dating back to 14th century
Location: Follow B6521 from Sheffield to park at Grindleford Railway station. 400 yds walk along unmade road to site.
Recipient: Mr Tom Garrud
Telephone: 0114 256 6420
Contact: Mr Tom Garrud
Email: property@hallam-diocese.com
Website: www.hallam-diocese.com/padley
Open: All yr.

HEART OF ENGLAND

119-123 Upper Spon Street, Coventry, West Midlands CV1 3BQ
Late medieval terrace of houses, the site is one of few timber framed structures in Coventry to survive in situ. No.122 restored as a medieval weavers cottage.
Location: Jct.7 from Coventry ring road. Rail: Coventry 1m. Bus: 6, 6a, 10 and 18.
Recipient: Spon End Building Preservation Trust
Telephone: 024 7625 7117
Contact: Ms Debbie Rowley
Email: info@sebpt.org.uk or deb.be@hotmail.co.uk
Website: www.theweavershouse.org
Open: Apr-Sept, every 2nd wkend, 11am-4pm and specific open days. School and group visits by prior appointment.
♿ H

Astley Castle, Astley, North Warwickshire CV10 7QD
In continuous occupation since the Saxon period, the site includes the moated castle, gateway and curtain walls, lake, church and pleasure gardens.
Location: Nuthurst Lane, then follow parking signs. Rail: Nuneaton.
Recipient: The Landmark Trust
Telephone: 01628 825920
Contact: Ms Victoria O'Keeffe
Email: vokeeffe@landmarktrust.org.uk
Website: www.landmarktrust.org.uk
Open: May, Jun, Sept, specific dates. At other times by appointment only. Access to moated site (exterior) from 10am-4pm on specific dates. Check website for details.
Admission: Free
♿

Baginton Castle Remains, Church Road, Baginton, Warwickshire CV8 3AR
13th Century castle ruin including buried remains of a Saxon settlement, the ruins of Bagot's Castle and 18th Century gazebo and remains of a WWII tank testing site.
Location: Nr. Jct. with A45, B4115. Follow signs to Baginton. Rail: Coventry 4m. Bus: 529
Recipient: David Hewer, The Custodian
Telephone: 07714 673450 / 07786 438711
Contact: Mr David Hewer
Email: david.hewer@yahoo.co.uk
Website: www.bagotscastle.org.uk
Open: Apr-Oct, weekends including BHs, 12pm-5pm. All year by appointment.
Admission Adult: £4.00 **Child:** £2.00 (Under 5s free)
P ♿ H

Bayley Lane Medieval Undercroft, 38 and 39 Bayley Lane, Jordan Well, Coventry, West Midlands CV1 5QP
Late medieval stone-vaulted undercroft, originally positioned to the rear of numbers 38 and 39 Bayley Lane. Now under Herbert Art Gallery.
Location: Opp. Coventry Cathedral. Rail: Coventry. Bus: Earl St or Little Park St.
Recipient: Coventry City Council
Telephone: 024 7623 7538
Contact: Mr David Bancroft
Email: david.bancroft@culturecoventry.com
Website: www.theherbert.org
Open: Daily, Mon-Sat, 10am-4pm. Sun 12pm-4pm.
Admission: Free
H

Castle House, Castle Square, Ludlow, Shropshire SY8 1AY
Grade II* listed house within Ludlow Castle, interior includes decorative plaster ceilings and pendants, fireplaces with fireback and imported panelling.
Location: A456 west of Birmingham, A49 from Hereford. Rail: Ludlow 0.4m. Bus: 435, 292, 492.
Recipient: Powys Castle Estate
Telephone: 01938 552554
Contact: Mr Tom Till
Email: info@ludlowcastle.com
Website: www.ludlowcastle.com
Open: Open as part of Ludlow Castle. Closed 25 Dec. Please check website for details.
[♿]

Chillington Hall, Codsall Wood, nr. Wolverhampton, Staffordshire WV8 1RE
House by Sir John Soane with earlier wing by Francis Smith (1724) with extensive grounds with gardens landscaped by 'Capability' Brown.
Location: A5 via Brewood or M54(J2) via Coven/Brewood. Rail: Codsall. Bus: Brewood or Codsall
Recipient: Mr J W Giffard
Telephone: 01902 850236
Contact: Mr J W Giffard
Email: info@chillingtonhall.co.uk
Website: www.chillingtonhall.co.uk
Open: Apr-Aug, 2pm-4pm, specific days only, check website for details
Admission Adult: £8.00 **Child:** £4.00
[P] [♿]

Hagley Hall, Hagley Lane, Hagley, Worcestershire DY9 9LG
Great Palladian House built in 1760 and situated in Grade I listed parkland including fine interior plasterwork.
Location: Off A456, just outside Stourbridge. Rail: Hagley 1m.
Recipient: The Executors of 11th Viscount Cobham
Telephone: 01562 882 5823
Contact: Lord Cobham
Email: cobham@hagleyhall.com
Website: www.hagleyhall.com
Open: Jan-Mar, Guided Tours 1.30pm-4.30pm (last tour 3.30pm).
Admission Adult: £10.00 **Child:** £3.50 (under 14)
[P] [♿]

Hanbury Hall, School Road, Hanbury, Droitwich, Worcestershire WR9 7EA
Built in 1701, containing painted ceilings, orangery, ice house and Moorish gazebos. The re-created 18th Century garden is surrounded by parkland and has a parterre, fruit garden and bowling green.
Location: Follow brown signs from A38 to B4090. Rail: Droitwich Spa 4m. Bus: 142/4 2½m.
Recipient: National Trust
Telephone: 01527 821214
Contact: General Manager
Email: hanburyhall@nationaltrust.org.uk
Website: www.nationaltrust.org.uk
Open: Jan-Feb and Nov-Dec (except 29 Jan, 24 and 25 Dec), house admission by guided tour. Admission by timed ticket on busy days. Check website for details
Admission Adult: £11.10 (House, Garden & Park), £7.50 (Garden, Park & Winter House), £5.20 (Winter Garden & Park)
[P] [♿] [H]

Hopton Castle Tower Keep, Hopton Castle, Craven Arms, Shropshire SY7 0QF
14th Century tower house, in 1644 it was the scene of a civil war siege held by 31 Roundheads, only 3 of whom survived.
Location: B4367 to Hopton Heath. Rail: Hopton Heath 1¼m., Craven Arms 7m.
Recipient: Hopton Castle Preservation Trust
Telephone: 01547 530 696
Contact: Mr P. Marquis
Email: p.m.marquis@bham.ac.uk
Website: www.hoptoncastle.org.uk
Open: Daily during daylight hours.
[P]

Old Grammar School, 81 Kings Norton Green, Birmingham, West Midlands B38 8RU
Early 15th Century house, probably the priests' house for St Nicholas Church, includes half-timbered first floor with faint remnants of Tudor decoration.
Location: A441 towards Birmingham city centre then turn left into The Green. Rail: Kings Norton. Bus: 18, 45, 49, 84, 145 and 146.
Recipient: Kings Norton PCC
Telephone: 0121 458 3289
Contact: Mrs Judy Ash
Email: info@saintnicolasplace.co.uk
Website: www.saintnicolasplace.co.uk
Open: Tues-Sat 10am to 3pm.
[♿] [H]

Stoneleigh Abbey, Kenilworth, Warwickshire CV8 2LF
16th Century house built on site and incorporating remains of Cistercian Abbey founded in 1155. Also has restored Regency riding stables, 19th Century conservatory and landscaped riverside gardens.
Location: B4115 to Ashow off A452. Rail: Leamington Spa or Warwick Parkway.
Recipient: Stoneleigh Abbey Preservation Trust (1996) Ltd
Telephone: 01926 858535
Contact: The Estate Office
Email: enquire@stoneleighabbey.org
Website: www.stoneleighabbey.org
Open: Weekdays and Suns, 11.30am-2.30pm, check website for details
Admission Adult: £8.50
Child: £3.50 (age 5-15)
[P] [♿]

The Summerhouse, Homme House, Much Marcle, Ledbury, Herefordshire HR8 2NJ
Late 17th century summerhouse. An important and little altered early example of a Gothic garden building.
Location: A449 between Ledbury and Ross on Wye. Rail: Ledbury 6m.
Recipient: Jocelyn D Finnigan
Telephone: 01531 660 419
Contact: Mrs Jocelyn D Finnigan
Email: jocelyn@hommehouse.co.uk
Website: www.hommehouse.co.uk
Open: By prior appt.
[P] [H]

Whittington Castle, Castle Street, Whittington, Oswestry, Shropshire SY11 4DF
One of a chain of fortresses along the English and Welsh border, the moated ruin consists of a bridge, gatehouse, towers and water frontage.
Location: 2m. E of Oswestry on A495 Rail: Gobowen 2m. Bus: D70
Recipient: Whittington Castle Preservation Trust
Telephone: 01691 662 500
Contact: Sue Ellis
Email: info@whittingtoncastle.co.uk
Website: www.whittingtoncastle.co.uk
Open: Castle: Mar-Oct, Wed-Sun, 10am-4pm, Nov-Feb, Thurs-Sun, 10am-4pm. Grounds: Free access all year.
[P] [♿] [H]

Opening Arrangements at places grant-aided by Historic England

Wilton Castle, Bridstow, nr. Ross on Wye, Herefordshire HR9 6AD
12th Century castle; a dry moat surrounds restored curtain walls which include three fortified accommodation towers.
Location: Between Wilton Bridge and Wilton roundabout on A40. Rail: Hereford 16m. and Gloucester 16m. Bus: routes 37, 38 and 32.
Recipient: Mr & Mrs A K Parslow
Telephone: 07836 386317 or 01989 565759
Contact: A K Parslow
Email: sue@wiltoncastle.co.uk
Website: www.wiltoncastle.co.uk
Open: Apr-May, specific dates, 12pm-5pm, every Weds and Sun afternoon in Jun, Jul and Aug. Check website for details.
Admission Adult: £5.00 **Child:** £2.00 (Under 11s Free)
P ♿

YORKSHIRE

Beningbrough Hall, Gallery and Garden, Beningbrough, North Yorkshire YO30 1DD
Country house containing an impressive Baroque interior exhibiting over one hundred 18th Century portraits, fine woodcarving and other ornate decoration, a Victorian laundry and walled garden.
Location: 8m. NW of York, signposted from A19. Rail: York 10m. Bus: 31/A/X.
Recipient: The National Trust
Telephone: 01904 472027
Contact: Property Manager
Email: jane.whitehead@nationaltrust.org.uk
Website: www.nationaltrust.org.uk
Open: House: Feb-Nov, Tues-Sun, 11am-5pm, Jul-Aug, daily, 11am-5pm. Also BHs. Please check website for details.
Admission Adult: £11.00 (House and Grounds) **Child:** £5.50 (House and Grounds)
P ♿ H

Bramham Park, Wetherby, West Yorkshire LS23 6LR
Early 19th Century Queen Anne house set in an early 18th Century landscape.
Location: 5m. S of Wetherby off A1(M). Rail: Garforth 8m. Bus: 770
Recipient: Mr G. C. N. Lane Fox
Telephone: 01937 846000
Contact: Estate office
Email: NLF@bramhampark.co.uk
Website: www.bramhampark.co.uk
Open: Weekdays by appointment
Admission Adult: £4.00 **Child:** £2.00 (age 6-16) 5 & under Free
P ♿

Castle Howard (pyramid on St Anne's Hill), York, North Yorkshire YO60 7DA
Large stately home dating from the beginning of the 18th century and designed by Sir John Vanbrugh situated in 10,000 acres of landscaped grounds.
Location: 15m. N of York on A64. Rail: Malton 6m. or York 15m. Bus: Yorkshire Coachline.
Recipient: The Hon. Nicholas Howard, Castle Howard Estate Ltd
Telephone: 01653 648621 Visitor Services
Email: house@castlehoward.co.uk
Website: www.castlehoward.co.uk
Open: For information about accessing the Temple of the Four Winds or Pyramid please contact Visitor Services tel: 01653 648621
Admission Adult: £17.50 **Child:** £9.00
P ♿

The Medieval Rectory, Church Farm, Adlingfleet, Goole, East Riding DN14 8JB
A rare example of a medieval secular building, it was built from stones taken from an older church before being converted into an agricultural barn in the 18th Century.
Location: Centre of Adlingfleet village, 50m S of church on main road. Rail: Goole 9m. Bus: 360, 361
Recipient: Mr & Mrs Harding
Telephone: 01724 798575
Contact: Mr & Mrs Harding
Email: hardingsadlingfleet@yahoo.co.uk
Open: By prior appointment.
H

Ripley Castle, Ripley, Harrogate, North Yorkshire HG3 3AY
Large house with three storey mid 16th Century tower built for Sir William Ingilby.
Location: 4m. N of Harrogate off A61 in Ripley village. Rail: Harrogate 4m. Bus: 36A
Recipient: Sir Thomas Ingilby Bt.
Telephone: 01423 770152
Email: enquiries@ripleycastle.co.uk
Website: www.ripleycastle.co.uk
Open: Castle: Mar, Oct and Nov, weekends, Apr-Sept, daily, by guided tour only. Jan, Feb and Dec, group booked tours only. Gardens and parkland: open throughout the year. Please see website for details.
Admission Adult: £9.00; Gardens: £6.00 **Child:** £5.50 (age 5 -16)
P ♿

Shandy Hall, Coxwold, North Yorkshire YO61 4AD
Country house, originally built in 1450, now an accredited museum to promote the life and writings of the author Laurence Sterne.
Location: A19 N of York, signposted Coxwold. Rail: Thirsk 7m. Bus: service by Stephensons and Hutchinson's
Recipient: Laurence Sterne Trust
Telephone: 01347 868465
Contact: Mr Patrick Wildgust
Email: shandyhall@dsl.pipex.com
Website: www.laurencesternetrust.org.uk
Open: May-Sept, Weds and Suns, 2.30pm-4.30pm. Wall painting tours available at specific times. Other times by appointment
Admission Adult: £4.50 **Child:** £1.00
P ♿ H

Wentworth Castle Gardens and Stainborough Park, Lowe Lane, Stainborough, Barnsley, South Yorkshire S75 3ET
500 acres of parkland and a 60 acre pleasure garden containing 26 listed buildings and monuments. The gardens are home to the National Plant collections of rhododendrons, camellias and magnolias.
Location: 2m. from M1 Jct. 37 in Stainborough, near Barnsley. Rail: Dodworth 1m., Barnsley Interchange 4m. Bus: 23, 24
Recipient: Wentworth Castle and Stainborough Park Heritage Trust
Telephone: 01226 776040
Contact: Ms Claire Herring
Email: heritagetrust@wentworthcastle.org
Website: www.wentworthcastle.org
Open: Parkland: all year, daily, Gardens: Apr-Sept, 10am-5pm, daily, Oct-Mar, check website for details. Closed 25 Dec.
Admission Adult: £6.50 **Child:** £3.25
P ♿

King George VI Memorial Park, Kent

Chillington Hall, Staffordshire

NORTH WEST

Adlington Hall, Mill Lane, Adlington, Macclesfield, Cheshire SK10 4LF
Manor house built around a medieval hunting lodge, the Great Hall houses a 17th Century organ, once played by Handel.
Location: 5m. N of Macclesfield off A523. Rail: Adlington ½m and Wilmslow or Macclesfield 5m.
Recipient: Mrs C J C Legh
Telephone: 01625 829206
Contact: Mrs Camilla J C Legh
Email: camilla@adlingtonhall.com
Website: www.adlingtonhall.com
Open: Private group tours available on request, contact 0191 2413 986.
Admission Adult: £9 (House and Garden), £6 (Garden only) and students £5 (House and Garden), free (Garden only)
[P] [♿]

Brackenhill Tower, Carlisle, Cumbria CA6 5TU
14th Century Pele Tower and 16th Century Jacobean cottage with Victorian extension.
Location: 3m. E of Longtown on minor road. Rail: Carlisle 12m.
Recipient: Lightning Protection Services
Telephone: 01461 800323
Contact: Mr Andrew Ritchie
Email: Andy@lightningconductor.co.uk
Website: www.brackenhilltower.co.uk
Open: By prior appointment
Admission Adult: £5.00 **Child:** £2.50
[P] [♿] [H]

Dacre Hall, Lanercost, Brampton, Cumbria CA8 2HQ
Part of the cloister of Lanercost Priory founded in 1168, contains unique remnants of 16th Century murals in the 'grotesque' style.
Location: 2m. NE of Brampton. Rail: Brampton 3m. Bus: 685 1½m.
Recipient: Lanercost Hall Committee
Telephone: 01697 741811
Contact: Mr G Sheridan
Email: gerry.sheridan16@btinternet.com
Open: Apr-Oct, Weekends and BHs, 10am-4pm. Check before travelling if Hall is closed for private hire.
[P]

Elizabeth Gaskell's House, 84 Plymouth Grove, Manchester M13 9LW
Detached regency style villa; the writer Elizabeth Gaskell wrote all but the first of her books whilst living here.
Location: A6 Stockport Road then A5184 Plymouth Grove. Rail: Manchester Piccadilly 1½m. Bus: 192, 197 and 157.
Recipient: Manchester Historic Buildings Trust
Telephone: 01663 744233
Contact: Janet Allan
Email: janetrallan@googlemail.com
Website: www.elizabethgaskellhouse.co.uk
Open: Wed, Thurs, Sun, 11am-5pm.
Admission Adult: £4.95 **Child:** Free
[P] [♿] [H]

Isel Hall, Cockermouth, Cumbria CA13 0QG
An Elizabethan range with a fortified Pele Tower; the interior of hall has Tudor panelling with traces of contemporary painting and contains furniture, paintings and textiles.
Location: Signposted from A595 3½m. from Cockermouth. Rail: Penrith 35m.
Recipient: Miss Mary Burkett
Telephone: 01900 826127
Contact: Mr Esme Lowe
Email: ecelowe@gmail.com
Website: www.visitcumbria.com
Open: Mar-Oct, Mons including BHs, 1:30pm-4:30pm. Groups at other times by prior appointment.
Admission Adult: £6 **Child:** £3
[P] [♿] [H]

Lowther Castle, Penrith, Cumbria CA10 2HG
Country house built as a sham castle, now a ruin without roof.
Location: A6 to Askham and Lowther.
Recipient: Lowther Castle
Telephone: 01931 712577
Contact: Mr Ken Gribben
Email: ken.gribben@lowther.co.uk
Open: Open throughout year, check website or contact for dates and times.
Admission Adult: £8 **Child:** Free
[P] [♿]

Lyme Park, Disley, Stockport, Cheshire SK12 2NX
Early 18th Century hunting tower within the 1400 acre medieval deer park of Lyme Park.
Location: Bus: 1,10,11,21,22,30,31,36,38, 71,72,80,81,87,88,100.
Recipient: Mr John Darlington
Telephone: 01663 762023
Contact: National Trust Regional Director
Email: lymepark@nationaltrust.org.uk
Website: www.nationaltrust.org.uk
Open: House and Garden: February-October, daily excpt Weds and Thurs, 11am-5pm, Park: open all year, 8am-6pm.
Admission Adult: £9.50 **Child:** £4.95
[P] [♿]

Rydal Hall Mawson Gardens, Rydal, Ambleside, Cumbria LA22 9LX
Formal Italianate gardens designed in 1911 and set in 34 acres including an informal woodland garden, 17th Century summerhouse, fine herbaceous planting, orchard and apiary.
Location: Just off A591, 2m. N of Ambleside. Rail: Windermere 5m. Bus: 555/599
Recipient: Church of England/Carlisle Diocesan Board of Finance
Telephone: 01539 432050
Contact: Mr Jonathon Green
Email: mail@rydalhall.org
Website: www.rydalhall.org
Open: Daily, dawn-dusk.
[P] [♿]

Opening Arrangements at places grant-aided by Historic England

Samlesbury Hall, Preston New Road, Samlesbury, Preston, Lancashire PR5 0UP
Built in 1325, the hall is a black and white timbered manor house set in extensive grounds.
Location: A677 towards Blackburn, 3m. on left. Rail: Preston 4m. Bus: 59.
Recipient: Samlesbury Hall Trust
Telephone: 01254 812010/01254 812229
Contact: Ms Sharon Jones
Email: enquiries@samlesburyhall.co.uk
Website: www.samlesburyhall.co.uk
Open: Daily except Sat, 11am-4.30pm. Open BHs. For Christmas closing times please contact the Hall.
Admission Adult: £3.00 **Child:** £1.00 (4 to 16 years)
P ♿ H

Scarisbrick Hall, Southport Road, Ormskirk, Lancashire LA40 9RQ
Country house with some of the finest examples of Victorian Gothic architecture and 100 foot tower.
Location: On Southport Road.
Recipient: Scarisbrick Hall Ltd
Telephone: 07764 885003
Contact: Mr Greg Aylmer
Email: greg@scarisbrick-hall.co.uk
Open: Specific dates and times. Check website for details. Tickets booked prior to event.
Admission Adult: £5.00 **Child:** £5.00
P ♿

Staircase House, 30/31 Market Place, Stockport, Cheshire SK1 1ES
Timber framed town house dating from 1460 with early panelled rooms and an important 17th Century caged newel staircase.
Location: Stockport town centre, 5 mins from M60. Rail: Stockport ½m. Bus: 10 mins from bus station
Recipient: Stockport Metropolitan Borough Council
Telephone: 0161 474 2390
Contact: Mr Phil Catling
Email: philip.catling@stockport.gov.uk
Website: www.stockport.gov.uk/staircasehouse
Open: Daily, Tues-Fri, 1pm-5pm, Sat, 10am-5pm, Sun, 11am-5pm, BHs, 11am-5pm. Closed 25, 26 Dec and 1 Jan
Admission Adult: £4.75 **Child:** Free up to 16
P ♿

NORTH EAST

Bowes Museum, Newgate, Barnard Castle, Durham DL12 8NP
French style chateau, built between 1869-c1885 housing a collection of European fine and decorative arts with a programme of exhibitions and special events.
Location: Close to A66. Rail: Darlington 18m. Bus: No.75 and No.76
Recipient: Bowes Museum
Telephone: 01833 690606
Contact: Mr Richard Welsby
Email: richard.welsby@thebowesmuseum.org.uk
Website: www.thebowesmuseum.org.uk
Open: All year apart from 25, 26 Dec and 1 Jan, 10am- 5pm
Admission Adult: £9.50 (includes donation) **Child:** Free to under 16s (as part of family visit)
P ♿

Cockle Park Farm Pele Tower, Morpeth, Northumberland NE61 3EB
Early 16th Century tower house, the tower is thought to have been built *c*.1520 and in the 19th Century became the centre of the Duke of Portland's experimental farm.
Location: 2m. N of Morpeth follow signs. Rail: Morpeth 3.5m.
Telephone: 01670790227
Contact: Mr David Watson
Email: david.watson1@ncl.ac.uk
Website: www.ncl.ac.uk/afrd/business/cockle/index.htm
Open: Mar, Apr, May, Aug, specific dates. All visitors to contact Cockle Park Farm tel: 07894 560071 or email prior to visiting.
P ♿

Cragside, Rothbury, Morpeth, Northumberland NE65 7PX
High Victorian mansion with original furniture and fittings including stained glass and earliest wallpapers. Built for Lord Armstrong who installed the world's first hydro-electric lighting.
Location: 13m. SW of Alnwick, follow B6341, entrance 1m. N of Rothbury. Rail: Morpeth 16m. Bus: Very limited service
Recipient: The National Trust
Telephone: 01669 622001
Contact: National Trust, Cragside
Email: john.obrien@nationaltrust.org.uk
Website: www.nationaltrust.org.uk
Open: Please see website
Admission Adult: £16.50 (House, Garden & Woodland) **Child:** £8.30 (House, Garden & Woodland) ages 5-17
P ♿ H

Gibside Chapel, Orangery and Stables, Gibside, nr. Rowlands Gill, Burnopfield, Tyne and Wear NE16 6BG
Palladian chapel completed 1812. Site includes stables and orangery situated south-west of Gibside Hall.
Location: On B6314 between Burnopfield and Rowlands Gill. Rail: Blaydon 4m., Newcastle-upon-Tyne 6m. Bus: 45, 46/A, 611-3 and 621
Recipient: The National Trust
Telephone: 01207 541 820
Contact: Visitor Services Manager
Email: gibside@nationaltrust.org.uk
Website: www.nationaltrust.org.uk
Open: Check website for dates and times.
Admission Adult: £7.95 **Child:** £4.10
P ♿ H

Sandy Hill

Lowther Castle, Cumbria

Middridge Grange Farm, Shildon Road, Newton Aycliffe, Darlington DL4 2QE
Dating back to 1578 the interior still has some fine bolection panelled walls with cornices and doors dating from the 17th Century.
Location: Off A6072 on roundabout leading to Redworth Road. Rail: Shildon 1-2m. Bus: 1B
Recipient: Messrs J & E Scott
Telephone: 07984407176
Contact: Mr Edward Scott
Email: fordtw15@btinternet.com
Open: All year, Mon-Fri, 9am-5pm by prior appointment. Visits outside these times to be discussed with owner.
P ♿

Netherwitton Hall, Morpeth, Northumberland NE61 4NW
Mansion house built c1685 access is available to main ground floor rooms and external elevations.
Location: 8m. W of Morpeth, just before entering village. Rail: Morpeth
Recipient: Mr J H T Trevelyan
Telephone: 01670 772 249
Contact: Mr J H T Trevelyan
Email: john@netherwitton.com
Open: Prior appointment at least 24hrs in advance. Tours available on specific dates. Groups at other times by prior arrangement.
Admission Adult: £5.00 **Child:** £1.00
P ♿

Raby Castle, Staindrop, Darlington, Durham DL2 3AH
Medieval castle, built in the 14th Century. Contains collections of art, fine furniture and highly decorated interiors. Also deer park, gardens and carriage collection.
Location: A67 to Barnard Castle. Rail: Darlington 14m. Bus: 75 or 6 1m.
Recipient: Lord Barnard TD
Telephone: 01833 660888/660202
Contact: Ms Clare Owen
Email: admin@rabycastle.com
Website: www.rabycastle.com
Open: Easter Weekend, Sat-Mon, May, Jun and Sept, Sun-Wed, Jul-Aug, Daily except Sat. Castle 1pm-4.30pm. Garden and Park 11am-5pm. Check website for details.
Admission Adult:£10.00 (Castle, Park & Gardens) **Child:** £4.50 age 5-15 (Castle, Park & Gardens)
P ♿

Rock Hall, Rock, Northumberland NE66 3SB
Manor house with parts dating back to 13th Century or early 14th Century set in five acres of grounds.
Location: 5m. N of Alnwick. Rail: Alnmouth 8m.
Recipient: Rock Hall School Charitable Trust
Telephone: 01665 579228
Contact: Rock Settled Estate
Email: carltuer@yahoo.co.uk
Open: Access to the exterior and grounds all year. Access to interior by appointment only.
P ♿

Sallyport Tower, Tower Street, Newcastle upon Tyne NE1 2HY
Tower forming the Lesser Gateway in Newcastle's medieval town wall with Company of Ships' Carpenters' meeting hall above.
Location: Tower Street, Newcastle upon Tyne. Rail and Metro: Newcastle Central Station 1m.
Recipient: Newcastle City Council
Telephone: 0191 2778992
Contact: Ms Donna Alderson
Email: donna.alderson@newcastle.gov.uk
Open: Visits by appointment. Tower open for exhibitions held in the Radcliffe Gallery. Please check website, www.radcliffegallery.co.uk
H

Stephens Hall, Lead Road, Ryton, Tyne & Wear NE40 4JE
Stone manor house built in early 15th Century, interior has arch centred doorways and fragments of contemporary wall paintings.
Location: 8m. W of Gateshead on B6315, south of Greenside Village. Rail: Blaydon
Recipient: Mr B Armstrong
Telephone: 0191 413 6030
Contact: Mr B Armstrong
Email: brian1965@hotmail.com
Open: By prior appointment.
P ♿ H

Cockle Park Farm Pele Tower, Northumberland

SIGNPOST

RECOMMENDING THE UK'S FINEST HOTELS SINCE 1935

Motoring conditions may have changed since the founder of Signpost first took to the road in 1935, but inspectors' standards are still the same. Inspected annually, Signpost features the UK's Premier hotels who possess that something special – style, comfort, warmth of welcome, cuisine, location – which really make them worth the visit. Here are Signpost's recommendations, by region, of fantastic places to stay while you are visiting Britain's historic sites. A wonderful combination.

www.signpost.co.uk

San Domenico House, London

LONDON

San Domenico House
29-31 Draycott Place
Chelsea
London SW3 2SH
Tel: 0207 581 5757

SOUTH EAST

Chase Lodge Hotel
10 Park Road
Hampton Wick
Kingston Upon Thames
Surrey KT1 4AS
Tel: 020 8943 1862

Deans Place Hotel
Seaford Road
Alfriston
East Sussex BN26 5TW
Tel: 01323 870248

Drakes Hotel
44 Marine Parade
Brighton
East Sussex BN2 1PE
Tel: 01273 696934

The Millstream Hotel
Bosham Lane
Bosham
Chichester
West Sussex PO18 8HL
Tel: 01243 573234

PowderMills Hotel
Powder Mill Lane
Battle
East Sussex TN33 0SP
Tel: 01424 775511

The White Horse Hotel
Market Place
Romsey
Hampshire SO51 8ZJ
Tel: 01794 512431

SOUTH WEST

Alexandra Hotel
Pound Street
Lyme Regis
Dorset DT7 3HZ
Tel: 01297 442010

Berry Head Hotel
Berry Head
Brixham
Devon TQ5 9AJ
Tel: 01803 853225

The Cottage Hotel
Hope Cove
Salcombe
Devon TQ7 3HJ
Tel: 01548 561555

Hannafore Point Hotel
Marine Drive
West Looe
Cornwall PL13 2DG
Tel: 01503 263273

Ilsington Country House Hotel
Ilsington Village
Nr Newton Abbot
Devon TQ13 9RR
Tel: 01364 661452

The Inn at Fossebridge
Fossebridge
Cheltenham
Gloucestershire GL54 3JS
Tel: 01285 720721

The Lordleaze Hotel
Henderson Drive
Forton Road
Chard
Somerset TA20 2HW
Tel: 01460 61066

The Manor Hotel
Beach Road
West Bexington
Bridport
Dorset DT2 9DF
Tel: 01308 897660

Mortons House Hotel
45 East Street
Corfe Castle
Wareham
Dorset BH20 5EE
Tel: 01929 480988

Northcote Manor
Umberleigh
North Devon EX37 9LZ
Tel: 01769 560501

The Pear Tree at Purton
Church End
Purton
Swindon
Wiltshire SN5 4ED
Tel: 01793 772100

Plumber Manor
Sturminster Newton
Dorset DT10 2AF
Tel: 01258 472507

Purbeck House Hotel
91 High Street
Swanage
Dorset BH19 2LZ
Tel: 01929 422872

EAST OF ENGLAND

Beechwood Hotel
20 Cromer Road
North Walsham
Norfolk NR28 0HD
Tel: 01692 403231

Broom Hall Country Hotel
Richmond Road
Saham Toney
Thetford
Norfolk IP25 7EX
Tel: 01953 882125

Hintlesham Hall Hotel
Hintlesham
Ipswich
Suffolk IP8 3NS
Tel: 01473 652334

The Hoste
The Green
Burnham Market
King's Lynn
Norfolk PE31 8HD
Tel: 01328 738777

Hotel Felix
Whitehouse Lane
Huntingdon Road
Cambridge
Cambridgeshire CB3 0LX
Tel: 01223 277977

Maison Talbooth
Stratford Road
Dedham
Colchester
Essex CO7 6HW
Tel: 01206 322367

milsoms Kesgrave Hall
Hall Road
Kesgrave
Ipswich
Suffolk IP5 2PU
Tel: 01473 333741

Hote Felix, East of England

The Norfolk Mead Hotel
Church Loke
Coltishall
Norwich
Norfolk NR12 7DN
Tel: 01603 737531

The Old Rectory Restaurant with Rooms
103 Yarmouth Road
Norwich
Norfolk NR7 0HF
Tel: 01603 700772

The Pier at Harwich
Hall Road
Kesgrave
Ipswich
Suffolk IP5 2PU
Tel: 01255 241212

Wentworth Hotel
Wentworth Road
Aldeburgh
Suffolk IP15 5BD
Tel: 01728 452312

EAST MIDLANDS

Barnsdale Lodge Hotel
The Avenue
Rutland Water
Exton LE15 8AH
Tel: 01572 724678

Biggin Hall Hotel
Biggin by Hartington
Buxton
Derbyshire SK17 0DH
Tel: 01298 84451

The Cavendish Hotel
Church Lane
Baslow
Derbyshire DE45 1SP
Tel: 01246 582311

Washingborough Hall Hotel
Church Hill
Washingborough
Lincoln LN4 1BE
Tel: 01522 790340

Whittlebury Hall Hotel & Spa
Whittlebury Hall
Whittlebury
NN12 8QH
Tel: 01327 857857

HEART OF ENGLAND

Castle House
Castle Street
Hereford
Herefordshire
HR1 2NW
Tel: 01432 356321

Cottage in the Wood
Holywell Road
Malvern Wells
Malvern WR14 4LG
Tel: 01684 577459

Soulton Hall
Soulton
Wem
Shrewsbury SY4 5RS
Tel: 01939 232786

YORKSHIRE & THE HUMBER

The Coniston Hotel & Country Estate
Coniston Cold
Skipton
North Yorkshire
BD23 4EA
Tel: 01756 748080

The Feversham Arms Hotel & Verbena Spa
8 High Street
Helmsley
York
North Yorkshire
YO62 5AG
Tel: 01439 770766

Lastingham Grange Country House Hotel
Lastingham, York
North Yorkshire
YO62 6TH
Tel: 01751 417345

Sportsmans Arms Hotel
Wath-in-Nidderdale
Near Pateley Bridge
North Yorkshire
HG3 5PP
Tel: 01423 711306

The Traddock
Austwick
Nr Settle
North Yorkshire LA2 8BY
Tel: 01524 251224

NORTH WEST

Aynsome Manor Hotel
Cartmel
Grange-over-Sands
Cumbria LA11 6HH
Tel: 015395 36653

Gilpin Hotel & Lake House
Crook Road
Windermere
Cumbria LA23 3NE
Tel: 01539 488818

Holbeck Ghyll Country House Hotel
Holbeck Lane
Windermere
Cumbria LA23 1LU
Tel: 015394 32375

Lovelady Shield Country House Hotel
Nenthead Road
Alston
Cumbria CA9 3LF
Tel: 01434 381203

The Inn at Fossebridge, South West

NORTH EAST

Waren House Hotel
Waren Mill
Northumberland
NE70 7EE
Tel: 01668 214581

SCOTLAND

Atholl Palace Hotel
Pitlochry
Perthshire
Scotland PH16 5LY
Tel: 01796 472400

Blackaddie Country House Hotel
Blackaddie Road
Sanquhar
Dumfries and Galloway
Scotland DG4 6JJ
Tel: 01659 50270

Coul House Hotel
Contin
Strathpeffer
Ross-shire
Scotland IV14 9ES
Tel: 01997 421487

Eddrachilles Hotel
Badcall Bay
Scourie
The Highlands
Scotland IV27 4TH
Tel: 01971 502080

The Four Seasons Hotel
St Fillans
Perthshire
Scotland PH6 2NF
Tel: 01764 685333

Roman Camp Country House & Restaurant
Main Street
Callander
Perthshire
Scotland FK17 8BG
Tel: 01877 330003

Viewfield House
Portree
Isle of Skye
Scotland IV51 9EU
Tel: 01478 612217

WALES

Crug-Glas Country House
Abereiddy Road
Solva
Haverfordwest
Pembrokeshire
SA62 6XX
Tel: 01348 831302

Glen Yr Afon House Hotel
Pontypool Road, Usk
Monmouthshire
NP15 1SY
Tel: 01291 672302

The Hand at Llanarmon
Ceiriog Valley
Llangollen
Denbighshire LL20 7LD
Tel: 01691 600666

Sychnant Pass House
Sychnant Pass Road
Conwy
Gwynedd LL32 8BJ
Tel: 01492 596868

Tre-Ysgawen Hall Hotel & Spa
Capel Coch
Llangefni
Isle of Anglesey
LL77 7UR
Tel: 01248 750750

Warpool Court Hotel
St Davids
Pembrokeshire
SA62 6BN
Tel: 01437 720300

Wolfscastle Country Hotel
Wolfscastle
Haverfordwest
Pembrokeshire SA62 5LZ
Tel: 01437 741225

Kiplin Hall, North Yorkshire

Quick Guides

Plant Sales

LONDON

SOUTH EAST

SOUTH WEST

EAST OF ENGLAND

EAST MIDLANDS

HEART OF ENGLAND

YORKSHIRE & THE HUMBER

NORTH WEST

NORTH EAST

SCOTLAND

WALES

Boconnoc, Cornwall

Places to Stay

LONDON

SOUTH EAST

SOUTH WEST

EAST OF ENGLAND

EAST MIDLANDS

HEART OF ENGLAND

YORKSHIRE & THE HUMBER

NORTH WEST

NORTH EAST

Iscoyd Park, North Wales

Ballywalter Park, Northern Ireland

SCOTLAND

WALES

NORTHERN IRELAND

Doddington Hall & Gardens, Lincolnshire

Open All Year

LONDON

SOUTH EAST

SOUTH WEST

EAST OF ENGLAND

EAST MIDLANDS

HEART OF ENGLAND

YORKSHIRE & THE HUMBER

NORTH WEST

NORTH EAST

SCOTLAND

WALES

NORTHERN IRELAND

Burghley House, Lincolnshire

Weddings

LONDON

SOUTH EAST

SOUTH WEST

EAST OF ENGLAND

EAST MIDLANDS

HEART OF ENGLAND

YORKSHIRE & THE HUMBER

NORTH WEST

Capesthorne Hall, Cheshire

Adlington Hall, Cheshire

NORTH EAST

SCOTLAND

WALES

NORTHERN IRELAND

Chiddingstone Castle, Kent

Private Hire

LONDON

SOUTH EAST

SOUTH WEST

EAST OF ENGLAND

EAST MIDLANDS

HEART OF ENGLAND

YORKSHIRE & THE HUMBER

NORTH WEST

Montalto Estate & Carriage Rooms, Northern Ireland

NORTH EAST

SCOTLAND

WALES

NORTHERN IRELAND

Chiswick House and Gardens, London

Beamish Museum, County Durham

Guided Tours

LONDON

SOUTH EAST

SOUTH WEST

EAST OF ENGLAND

Lyme, Cheshire

EAST MIDLANDS

HEART OF ENGLAND

YORKSHIRE & THE HUMBER

NORTH WEST

NORTH EAST

SCOTLAND

WALES

NORTHERN IRELAND

Arundel Castle & Gardens, Sussex

Hartland Abbey, Devon

Dogs Welcome

EAST OF ENGLAND

EAST MIDLANDS

HEART OF ENGLAND

YORKSHIRE & THE HUMBER

NORTH WEST

NORTH EAST

SCOTLAND

WALES

NORTHERN IRELAND

Renishaw Hall and Gardens, Derbyshire

In The Movies

Gemma Arterton and Eddie Redmayne filming at Chavenage House, Gloucestershire

Burghley House, Lincolnshire

Special Events

JANUARY

until 29 Jan - Glastonbury Abbey, Somerset
Ruins & Riches - Textiles by Heptad

until 15 Jan - Somerset House, London
Malick Sidibé Exhibition

until 22 Jan - Somerset House, London
Rodin and Dance Exhibition

until 13 Apr - Tower of London, London
Life in the Medieval Palace

Jan-Mar - Bowes Museum, Co. Durham
Dining with The Bowes Exhibition

1 - Hinton Ampner, Hampshire
New Years Day walk

1 - Knole, Kent
New Year's Day Walk

1 - Sheffield Park and Garden, Sussex
New Year's Day Holly Hike

1 - Standen, Sussex
New Year's Day Stroll

1 Jan-23 Apr - Standen, Sussex
Kaffe Fassett Exhibition

1 Jan-31 Dec - Tower of London, London
The Ceremony of the Keys

2 - Durham Cathedral, Co. Durham
Textiles: Painting with the Needle

2 Jan-12 Feb (Sats & Suns) - Osborne House, Isle of Wight
Victoria: Queen Beyond The Screen Guided Tour

5 - Hughenden, Buckinghamshire
Conservation in focus

7-8 - Knebworth House, Hertfordshire
Bride: The Wedding Show at Knebworth Barns

9 - Hinton Ampner, Hampshire
Hampshire Artists' Co-operative Exhibition

10 - Leighton House Museum ,London
Life - Drawing In Leighton's Grand Studio

11 - Great Dixter House & Gardens ,Sussex
The Art and Craft of Gardening Term 3 Courses

11 - Hughenden, Buckinghamshire
Behind the scenes garden tour

11 - Peckover House & Garden, Cambridgeshire
Willow Weaving Workshop – Plant Support

12 - Peckover House & Garden, Cambs.
Willow Weaving Workshop – Bird Sculpture

14 Jan-4 Feb - Birmingham Botanical Gardens, West Midlands
Compact Cameras

14 - Kensington Palace, London
Panto and Performance

14-15, 21-22, 28-29 - Peckover House & Garden, Cambridgeshire
The Garden in Winter

15 - Charleston, Sussex
Create a Visual Diary

18 - Goodwood House, Sussex
Hunting the Northern Lights

18 - Temple Newsam, West Yorkshire
Conservation in action

19 - Bowes Museum, The, Co. Durham
Gallery Talk

19 Jan-26 Feb - Chiswick House and Gardens, London
Magical Lantern Festival

19 - Dover Castle, Kent
Dover's Cold War Tunnels

21 - Osterley Park and House, London
Osterley Night Run

21 - Weston Park, Shropshire
Burns Night with Prue Leith

22 - Powderham Castle, Devon
Silverton Point to Point

22 - Stirling Castle, West Highlands
Revel with Rabbie

25 - Glastonbury Abbey, Somerset
Hurdle Making

25 - Goodwood House, Sussex
Burns Night

26 - Hoghton Tower, Lancashire
Wedding Open Evening

26 - Hughenden, Buckinghamshire
Behind the scenes manor tour

27 - Bowes Museum, The, Co. Durham
Gallery Talk

27 - Durham Cathedral, Co. Durham
Holocaust Memorial Day, Talks and Workshops

27 - Great Dixter House & Gardens, Sussex
Getting the Garden Ready Study Day

28 Jan-19 Mar - Bowes Museum, The, Co. Durham
The Allure of Napoleon Exhibition

28-29 - Claydon House and Gardens, Buckinghamshire
Sensational Snowdrops

28 - Durham Cathedral, Co. Durham
Defiant Requiem: Verdi at Terezin

29 - Capesthorne Hall, Cheshire
Wedding Fair

29 - Holkham Hall, Norfolk
Volunteering on the Nature Reserve

30 - Dover Castle, Kent
Hands-On Conservation Of Dover's Fire Command Post

FEBRUARY

1 - Temple Newsam, West Yorkshire
Beaus and Belles

3 - Audley End, Essex
Churchill's Secret Army: The Second World War Secrets of Audley End House

3-11 - Fairfax House, North Yorkshire
Silver Screen 2017

3-5, 10-12, 17-19, 24-27 - Scone Palace & Grounds, Tayside
Celebration of Snowdrops

4-5 - Claydon House and Gardens, Buckinghamshire
Sensational Snowdrops

4-5 - Newark Park, Gloucestershire
Spectacular Snowdrop Weekend

4-5 , 11-12, 18-19 - Peckover House & Garden, Cambridgeshire
The Garden in Winter

5-26 Feb (Suns) - Kingston Bagpuize House, Oxfordshire
Snowdrop Sunday

6 - Charleston, Sussex
Art and Perfumery

8 - Great Dixter House & Gardens, Sussex
The Art and Craft of Gardening
Term 3 Courses

10 - Bowes Museum, The, Co. Durham
Gallery Talk

11-12 - Claydon House and Gardens, Buckinghamshire
Sensational Snowdrops

11 - Leeds Castle, Kent
Valentine's Dinner in the Castle

11-13, 15-19 - Newark Park, Gloucestershire
February Family Trail

11 - Weston Park, Shropshire
Valentine's Dine & Stay

12 - Doddington Hall & Gardens, Lincolnshire
Spring Bulb Pageant 2017

12 - Holkham Hall, Norfolk
Volunteering on the Nature Reserve

13-17 - Dover Castle, Kent
Fairytale Castle

13-17 - Sheffield Park and Garden, Sussex
50 Things mini kites

13-17 - Audley End, Essex
Spy School

14 - Leighton House Museum, London
Flaming June: A Practical Colour Workshop

14 - Osborne House, Isle of Wight
Victorian Valentines

14 - Painshill Landscape Garden, Surrey
Wild Woodland Camp

16 - Standen, Sussex
Kaffe Fassett Lecture

18-16 - Standen, Sussex
February half term: Children's Bothy Trail

19 - Bowood House & Gardens, Wiltshire
Bowood Wedding Fayre

19 - Caerhays Castle & Garden, Cornwall
Wedding Open Day 2017

19 & 26 - Deene Park, Northamptonshire
Snowdrop Sundays

20 - Great Dixter House & Gardens, Sussex
Planting in the Mixed Border Study Days

20-24 - Osborne House, Isle of Wight
Victorian Fun And Games

20-24 - Weald & Downland Open Air Museum, Sussex
Winter Half-Term Family Activities

21 - Bowes Museum, The, Co. Durham
125 Years: Celebrating The Bowes Museum. A Family Fun Day

23 Feb-2 Mar - Great Dixter House & Gardens, Sussex
Symposium: The Art of Gardening

23-24 - Bowes Museum, The, Co. Durham
Jays Animal Encounters

24 - Bowes Museum, The, Co. Durham
Gallery Talk

24-26 - Stirling Castle, West Highlands & Islands
Building Scotland Exhibition

25 Feb-18 Mar - Birmingham Botanical Gardens, West Midlands
DSLR Photography for Beginners

25 Feb-7 May - Bowes Museum, Co. Durham
Only In England Exhibition

25 - Glastonbury Abbey, Somerset
Hurdle Making

25 Feb-2 Mar - Peckover House & Garden, Cambridgeshire
Film making at Peckover House – Dean Spanley

26 - Holkham Hall, Norfolk
Volunteering on the Nature Reserve

28 - Tintagel Castle, Cornwall
Tintagel Castle: The Drink of Kings

TBC - Dunvegan Castle & Gardens, Highlands & Skye
Snowdrop Open Day

MARCH

3 Mar-2 Apr - Chiswick House and Gardens, London
Camellia Show 2017

3-5, 10-12 - Scone Palace, Tayside
Celebration of Snowdrops

3-9, 11-16, 18-19 - Peckover House & Garden, Cambridgeshire
Film making at Peckover House

5 - Powderham Castle, Devon
Mid Devon Point to Point

6 - Great Dixter House & Gardens, Sussex
Succession Planting in the Mixed Border Study

8 - Dover Castle, Kent
Disaster Preparedness - Constables Tower

8 - Great Dixter House & Gardens, Sussex
The Art and Craft of Gardening Term 1 Courses

10-12 - Scone Palace & Grounds, Tayside
Galloway Antiques Fair

13 - Great Dixter House & Gardens, Sussex
Good Planting Study Day

14 - Leighton House Museum, London
Life-Drawing In Leighton's Grand Studio

17 - Caerhays Castle & Garden, Cornwall
RHS Recommended Lecture: Caerhays Bred Magnolias

17 - Fairfax House, North Yorkshire
Eating with Victoria: A Greedy Queen

18 Mar-19 Jun - Compton Verney Art Gallery & Park, Warwickshire
Creating the Countryside 1600–2017

18 Mar-30 Apr - Burghley House, Lincolnshire
Opening of the South Gardens

18-19 - Dalemain Mansion & Gardens, Cumbria
World Original Marmalade Festival 2017

18 - Knebworth House, Hertfordshire
Muddy Mayhem

19 - Chiddingstone Castle, Kent
Wedding Fair

23 - Standen, Sussex
Kaffe Fassett Lecture

24 - Manor, Hemingford Grey, The, Cambridgeshire
A Warning to the Curious and Lost Hearts

26 - Peckover House & Garden, Cambridgeshire
Mothering Sunday Afternoon Tea

26 - Weald & Downland Open Air Museum, Sussex
Mothering Sunday Events

29 - Glastonbury Abbey, Somerset
Building the Medieval Kitchen Garden

31 - Audley End, Essex
Resisting The Invader - Audley End 1940

TBC - Leighton House Museum, London
The Muse, by Palimpsest

APRIL

1-13 - Peckover House & Garden, Cambridgeshire
Adult Easter Trail

1-2 - Boconnoc, Cornwall
Garden Society Spring Flower Show

1-3, 5-10, 12-17, 19-23 - Newark Park, Gloucestershire
Wild about Wild Garlic

7 - Caerhays Castle & Garden, Cornwall
RHS Recommended Lecture – A Century of Rhododendrons

9 - Arundel Castle & Gardens, Sussex
MG Owner's Club Gathering

9 - Sherborne Castle & Gardens, Dorset
BMW Concours

12 - Great Dixter House & Gardens, Sussex
The Art and Craft of Gardening Term 1 Courses 8

14 - Bowes Museum, The, Co. Durham
Easter – Family Fun Day

14 - Fairfax House, North Yorkshire
Terry & The Chocolate Orange

14-17 - Holkham Hall, Norfolk
Easter at Holkham

14-17 - Peckover House & Garden, Cambridgeshire
Cadbury Easter Egg Hunt

16-17 - Newby Hall & Gardens, North Yorkshire
Easter Family Fun Days

Mid Apr / Mid May - Arundel Castle & Gardens, Sussex
Tulip Festival

17 - Chenies Manor House, Buckinghamshire
Egg & Spoon Race

21 - Capesthorne Hall, Cheshire
Starlight Walk

22 - St Mary's House and Gardens, Sussex
Phoenix Of Drury Lane Book Launch & Signing by Peter Thorogood

24 - Great Dixter House & Gardens, Sussex
Succession Planting in the Mixed Border Study Day

28 Apr-20 May - Birmingham Botanical Gardens, West Midlands
Compact Cameras

29 - Ingatestone Hall, Essex
Spring Concert

29 Apr-1 May - Penshurst Place & Gardens, Kent
Weald of Kent Craft & Design Show

29 Apr-1 May - Weald & Downland Open Air Museum, Sussex
Food & Folk Festival

30 - Chiddingstone Castle, Kent
Chiddingstone Castle Literary Festival

30 Apr-1 May - Weston Park, Shropshire
Spring Plant Fair

MAY

1 - Chenies Manor House, Buckinghamshire
Tulip Festival

3 - Glastonbury Abbey, Somerset
Planting the Medieval Kitchen Garden

5 - Caerhays Castle & Garden, Cornwall
RHS Recommended Lecture – Late Flowering Magnolias

6-7 - Althorp, Northamptonshire
Althorp Food and Drink Festival

6 - Kirklinton Hall and Gardens, Cumbria
Holistics Fair

6-7 - Leeds Castle, Kent
Motors by the Moat

7, 14 & 21 - Boconnoc, Cornwall
Garden Open Days

10 - Great Dixter House & Gardens, Sussex
The Art and Craft of Gardening Term 1 Courses

13 - Ingatestone Hall, Essex
Re-Enactment: Tudor Festival

15 - Great Dixter House & Gardens, Sussex
Meadow Gardening Study Day

15-21 - Highclere Castle, Gardens & Egyptian Exhibition, Hampshire
Literature & Landscapes

20-21 - Lydiard Park, Wiltshire
Race For Life

25-27 - Goodwood House, Sussex
Festival of Food & Racing

27-29 - Arundel Castle & Gardens, Sussex
Castle Siege 2017

27-29 - Holkham Hall, Norfolk
Pedal Norfolk

28 - Kingston Bagpuize House, Oxfordshire
Rare Plant Fair

29 - Ingatestone Hall, Essex
Dancing Troupe: Morris Dancing

29 - Sherborne Castle & Gardens, Dorset
Sherborne Castle Country Fair

May / Jun TBC - Arundel Castle & Gardens, Sussex
Allium Extravaganza

JUNE

2 - Kirklinton Hall and Gardens, Cumbria
Drove t' Drink - The Call of the Hall

4 - Stonor, Oxfordshire
VW Owners' Rally

7-11 - Chatsworth, Derbyshire
RHS Chatsworth Flower Show

7 - Fairfax House, North Yorkshire
The Fall & Rise of English Wine

9-11 - Kirklinton Hall and Gardens, Cumbria
Stepping Stones Festival 2017

10-11 - Newby Hall & Gardens, North Yorkshire
Tractor Fest 2017

10-11 - Peckover House & Garden, Cambs.
Bee Weekend

10 Jun-1 Jul - Birmingham Botanical Gardens, West Midlands
DSLR Photography for Beginners

11 - Goodwood House, Sussex
Family Race Day

11 - Woburn Abbey and Gardens, Bedfordshire
Teddy Bear Festival

14 - Great Dixter House & Gardens, Sussex
The Art and Craft of Gardening Term 1 Courses

17-18 - Boconnoc, Cornwall
Endurance GB Ride

17 - Ingatestone Hall, Essex
Art Exhibition: By The Guide of Essex Craftsman

17 - Kirklinton Hall and Gardens, Cumbria
Kirklinton Opera - 'Rigoletto'

17-18 - Weald & Downland Open Air Museum, Sussex
Wood Show

17-18 - Weston Park, Shropshire
International Model Air Show

17-24 - Peckover House & Garden, Cambridgeshire
Marmalade Cake

18 - Caerhays Castle & Garden, Cornwall
Caerhays Summer Fete 2017

18 - Sherborne Castle & Gardens, Dorset
Cancer Research UK – Race for Life

22-25 - Goodwood House, Sussex
Festival of Speed

24 - Leeds Castle, Kent
Junior Aquathlon

24-25 - Leeds Castle, Kent
Leeds Castle Triathlon

24-25 - Sherborne Castle Dorset
Jousting Tournament – The Knights of Royal England

24-25 - Woburn Abbey and Gardens, Bedfordshire
Woburn Abbey Garden Show 2017

25 - Chiddingstone Castle, Kent
Summer Vintage Fair

26 - Great Dixter House & Gardens, Sussex
Good Planting Study Day

27 - Boconnoc, Cornwall
St John Ambulance Run

JULY

1 - Ingatestone Hall, Essex
Jazz Concert: Ingatestone Rotary Club

8 - Burghley House, Lincolnshire
Battle Proms

8 - Leeds Castle, Kent
Classical Concert

8-9 - Weston Park, Shropshire
Camper Jam

12 - Great Dixter House & Gardens, Sussex
The Art and Craft of Gardening Term 2 Courses

15-16 - Sherborne Castle & Gardens, Dorset
Sherborne Castle Classic and Supercars

16 - Chenies Manor House, Buckinghamshire
Famous Plant & Garden Fair

16 - Weald & Downland Open Air Museum, Sussex
Rare & Traditional Breeds Show

18 - Inveraray Castle & Gardens, West Highlands & Islands
Inveraray Highland Games

22-23 - Holkham Hall, Norfolk
Holkham Country Fair

25-30 - Arundel Castle & Gardens Sussex
Jousting & Medieval Tournament 2017

28-30 - Boconnoc, Cornwall
Boconnoc Steam Fair

28-30 - Hatfield House, Hertfordshire
The Game Fair

AUGUST

1-5 - Goodwood House, Sussex
Qatar Goodwood Festival

5-6 - Lydiard Park, Wiltshire
Cheese and Chilli Festival

9 - Great Dixter House & Gardens, Sussex
The Art and Craft of Gardening
Term 2 Courses

19 - Ingatestone Hall, Essex
Re-Enactment: Civil War Historical

19-20 - Weald & Downland Open Air Museum, Sussex
Vintage & Steam

19-20 - Weston Park, Shropshire
V Festival

25-27 - Goodwood House, Sussex
Friday Fireworks, '50s Fun & Frivolity

25-28 - Stonor, Oxfordshire
Chilterns Craft & Design Show

26-28 - Arundel Castle & Gardens, Sussex
History in Action

26 - Ingatestone Hall, Essex
Summer Concert

31 Aug-3 Sep - Burghley House, Lincolnshire
Burghley Horse Trials

SEPTEMBER

4 - Great Dixter House & Gardens, Sussex
Exotic Gardening Study Day

5 & 27 - Goodwood House, Sussex
Midweek Racing

8-10 - Goodwood House, Sussex
Goodwood Revival

8-10 - Leeds Castle, Kent
Food Festival

8-10 - Penshurst Place & Gardens, Kent
Weald of Kent Craft & Design Show

9-16 - Great Dixter House & Gardens, Sussex
Symposium: The Art of Gardening

10 - Chiddingstone Castle, Kent
Chiddingstone Castle Country Fair

13 - Great Dixter House & Gardens, Sussex
The Art and Craft of Gardening
Term 2 Courses

23 Sep-14 Oct - Birmingham Botanical Gardens, West Midlands
Compact Cameras

23-28 - Leeds Castle, Kent
Festival of Flowers

30 Sep-8 Oct - Burghley House, Lincolnshire
Flower Festival

TBC - Holker Hall & Gardens, Cumbria
Chilli Fest 2017

OCTOBER

5-8 - Althorp, Northamptonshire
The Althorp Literary Festival

7-8 - Weald & Downland Open Air Museum, Sussex
Autumn Countryside Show

11 - Great Dixter House & Gardens, Sussex
The Art and Craft of Gardening
Term 2 Courses

15 - Goodwood House, Sussex
Season Finale

25-26 - Chenies Manor House, Buckinghamshire
Dahlia Festival

28 Oct-4 Nov - Great Dixter House & Gardens, Sussex
Symposium: The Art of Gardening

NOVEMBER

4-11 - Birmingham Botanical Gardens, West Midlands
DSLR Photography for Beginners

4 Nov-3 Jan - Chatsworth, Derbyshire
Christmas at Chatsworth

8 - Great Dixter House & Gardens, Sussex
The Art and Craft of Gardening
Term 3 Courses

20 - Great Dixter House & Gardens, Sussex
Integrating and Using Bulbs Study Day

24 Nov-1 Jan - Blenheim Palace, Oxfordshire
Christmas at Blenheim

24 Nov-7 Jan - Hampton Court Palace, Surrey
Hampton Court Palace Ice Rink

DECEMBER

1 Dec-5 Jan - Shakespeare's Family Homes, Warwickshire
Christmas at the Shakespeare Family Homes

2 Dec-1 Jan - Leeds Castle, Kent
Christmas at Leeds Castle

9 - Ingatestone Hall, Essex
Christmas Concert

10 - Ingatestone Hall, Essex
Bra-vissi-ma Ladies Choir Concert

13 - Great Dixter House & Gardens, Sussex
The Art and Craft of Gardening
Term 3 Courses

16 Dec-1 Jan - Beaulieu, Hampshire
Victorian Christmas

21 Dec- 1 Jan - Hampton Court Palace, Surrey
Christmas at Hampton Court

©VisitBritain/Rod Edwards

Maps

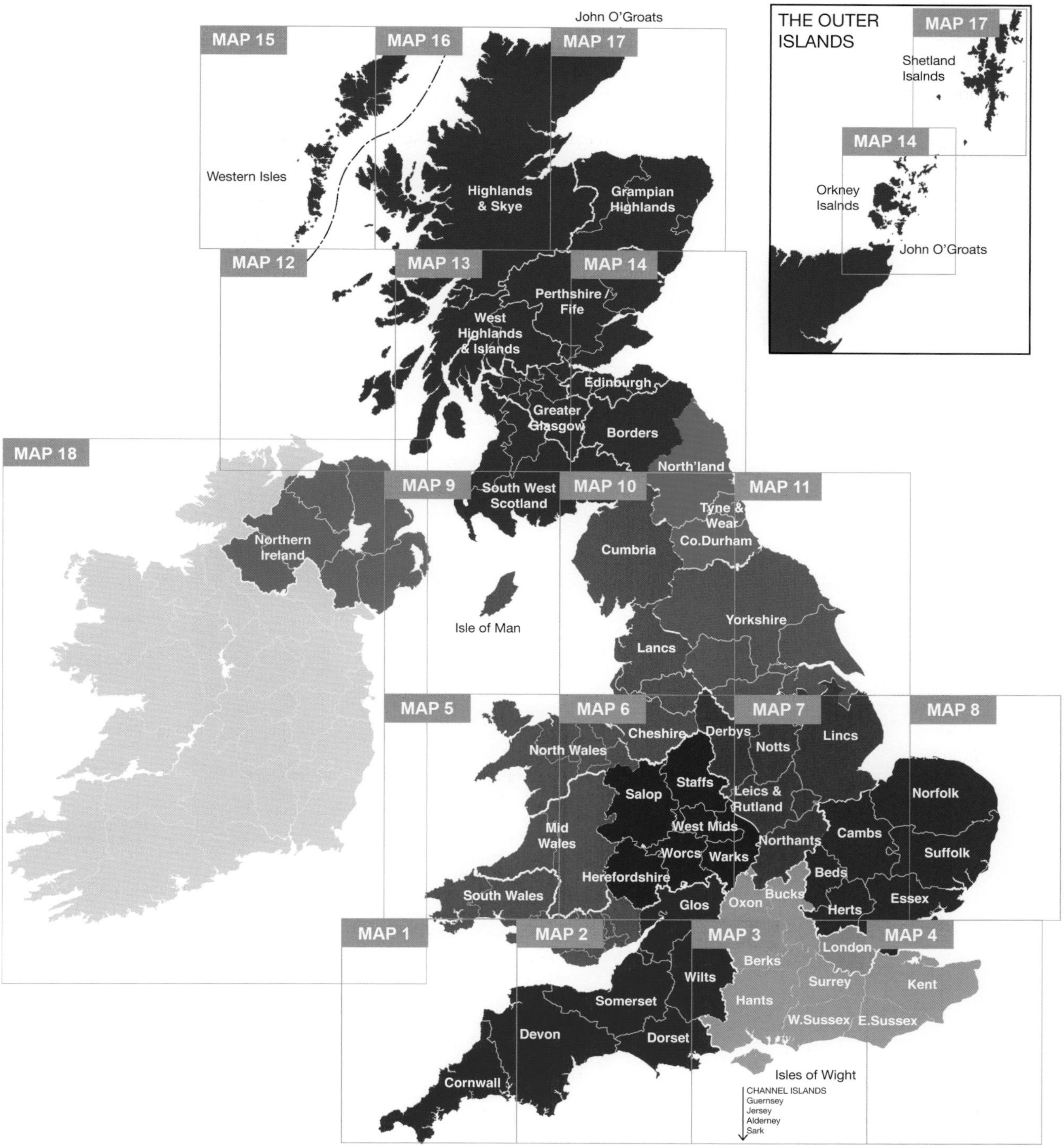

MAP 15
MAP 16
MAP 17
John O'Groats
Western Isles
Highlands & Skye
Grampian Highlands
MAP 12
MAP 13
MAP 14
Perthshire / Fife
West Highlands & Islands
Edinburgh
Greater Glasgow
Borders
MAP 18
North'land
MAP 9
South West Scotland
MAP 10
MAP 11
Tyne & Wear
Co.Durham
Northern Ireland
Cumbria
Isle of Man
Yorkshire
Lancs
MAP 5
MAP 6
MAP 7
MAP 8
Cheshire
Derbys
Lincs
North Wales
Notts
Staffs
Salop
Leics & Rutland
Norfolk
West Mids
Mid Wales
Northants
Cambs
Worcs
Warks
Suffolk
Herefordshire
Beds
South Wales
Glos
Oxon
Bucks
Herts
Essex
MAP 1
MAP 2
MAP 3
MAP 4
London
Berks
Wilts
Surrey
Kent
Somerset
Hants
W.Sussex
E.Sussex
Devon
Dorset
Isles of Wight
Cornwall
CHANNEL ISLANDS
Guernsey
Jersey
Alderney
Sark

THE OUTER ISLANDS
MAP 17
Shetland Isalnds
MAP 14
Orkney Isalnds
John O'Groats

MAP 1

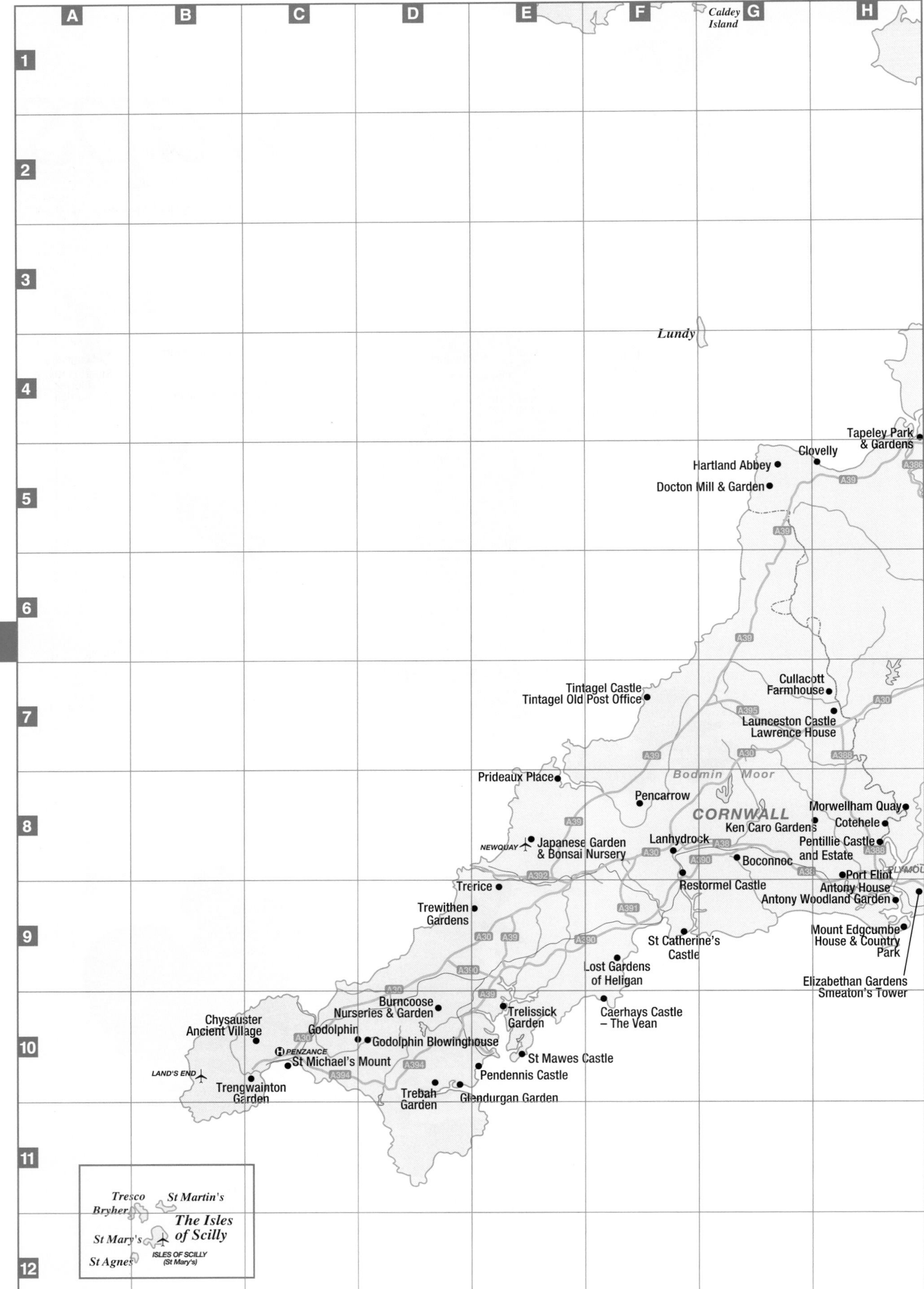
A
B
C
D
E
F
G
H
1
2
3
4
5
6
7
8
9
10
11
12
Caldey Island
Lundy
Tapeley Park & Gardens
Clovelly
Hartland Abbey
Docton Mill & Garden
Cullacott Farmhouse
Tintagel Castle
Tintagel Old Post Office
Launceston Castle
Lawrence House
Bodmin Moor
Prideaux Place
Pencarrow
CORNWALL
Morwellham Quay
Cotehele
Ken Caro Gardens
Pentillie Castle and Estate
Lanhydrock
NEWQUAY
Japanese Garden & Bonsai Nursery
Boconnoc
Port Eliot
Restormel Castle
Antony House
Antony Woodland Garden
Trerice
Trewithen Gardens
Mount Edgcumbe House & Country Park
St Catherine's Castle
Lost Gardens of Heligan
Elizabethan Gardens
Smeaton's Tower
Burncoose Nurseries & Garden
Trelissick Garden
Caerhays Castle – The Vean
Chysauster Ancient Village
Godolphin
Godolphin Blowinghouse
PENZANCE
St Michael's Mount
St Mawes Castle
LAND'S END
Pendennis Castle
Trengwainton Garden
Trebah Garden
Glendurgan Garden
Tresco
Bryher
St Martin's
The Isles of Scilly
St Mary's
St Agnes
ISLES OF SCILLY (St Mary's)

I
J
K
L
M
N
O
P
1
2
3
4
5
6
7
8
9
10
11
12
MAP 2
Weobley Castle
SWANSEA
Clyne Gardens
Oxwich Castle
Margam Country Park
St Fagans: National History Museum
BRIDGEND
Tythegston Court
RHONDDA CYNON TAFF
CAERPHILLY
Llancaiach Fawr Manor
Caerphilly Castle
Castell Coch
CARDIFF
Cardiff Castle
Dyffryn Gardens & Arboretum
VALE OF GLAMORGAN
Fonmon Castle
National Museum of Wales
Caerleon Roman Baths
NEWPORT
Tredegar House & Park
Chepstow Castle
Caldicot Castle
SOUTH GLOUCESTERSHIRE
Westbury Court Garden
Acton Court
Lady Margaret Hungerford Almshouses
BRISTOL
Blaise Hamlet
Dyrham Park
Bradford on-Avon Tithe Barn
Barton Grange Farm
Clevedon Court
Tyntesfield
Gatcombe Court
Beckford Tower
NORTH SOMERSET
American Museum & Gdns
Englishcombe Tithe Barn
29 Queen Square Railings
Arnos Vale Cemetery
British Empire & Commonwealth Museum
Georgian House
Lord Mayor's Chapel
Royal West of England Academy
St George's
No 1 Royal Crescent
Building of Bath Museum
Crowe Hall
Holburne Museum of Art
Museum of Costume & Assembly Rooms
Prior Park Landscape Garden
Roman Baths & Pump Room
William Herschel Museum
Peto Gardens at Iford Manor
Avoncliffe Aquaduct
Farleigh Hungerford Castle
Brean Down
King John's Hunting Lodge
Lynton Town Hall
Old Quay Head
Chambercombe Manor
Holnicote Estate
Exmoor
Exmoor Forest
Dunster Working Watermill
Dunster Castle
Arlington Court
Marwood Hill
Anderton House
Fairfield
St Andrews
Kentsford Orchard
Dodington Hall
Cleeve Abbey
Wyndham
Coleridge Cottage
Brendon Hills
Hall Farm High Barn
Quantock Hills
Combe Sydenham Country Park
Halswell House
Robin Hood's Hut
Maunsel House
Great House Farm
Milton Lodge Gardens
Nunney Castle
Wells Cathedral
SOMERSET
Longleat
Stourton House Flower Garden
Glastonbury Tribunal, Abbey & Tor
Stourhead
Higher Flax Mills
Stembridge Tower Mill
South Molton Town Hall Pannier Market
Hestercombe Gardens
Priest's House
Muchelney Abbey
Lytes Cary Manor
Sandford Orcas Manor House
Cothay Manor
Treasurer's House
Tintinhull Garden
Sherborne Old Castle
Sherborne Castle
Barrington Court
Ayshford Chapel
Rowlands Mill
Stoke sub-Hamdon Priory
Montacute House
RHS Garden Rosemoor
Knightshayes Court
Stock Gayland House
Tiverton Castle
Chard Guildhall
Lower Severalls
Merchant's House
Hemyock Castle
Lancin Farmhouse
Higher Melcombe
Killerton House
DEVON
Fursdon House
Loughwood Meeting House
Forde Abbey
Minterne Gardens
DORSET
Milton Abbey Church
Downes
Markers Cottage
Escot
Mapperton
Athelhampton House & Gardens
Clouds Hill
Okehampton Castle
Finch Foundry
Exeter Cathedral
Custom House Exeter
Shute Barton
Church of Our Lady & St Ignatius
Wolfeton House
Hardy's Cottage
EXETER
Cadhay
Sand
Castle Drogo
Culver House
21 The Mint
Max Gate
Kingston Maurward
Salem Chapel
Branscombe Mill
Abbotsbury Subtropical Gardens
Haldon Belvedere
Lawrence Castle
Bicton Park Botanical Gardens
Lulworth Castle & Park
Dartmoor
Powderham Castle
A La Ronde
Kilworthy Farm
Chesil Beach
Portland Castle
Portland Bill
The Garden House
Buckfast Abbey
Bradley Manor
TORBAY
Buckland Abbey
Compton Castle
Dartington Hall
Torre Abbey
PLYMOUTH
Totnes Castle
Greenway
Berry Pomeroy Castle
Oldway Mansion
Hemerdon House
Saltram House
Shilstone
Coleton Fishacre House & Garden
Dartmouth Castle
Overbeck's
GUERNSEY
Sausmarez Manor

MAP 3

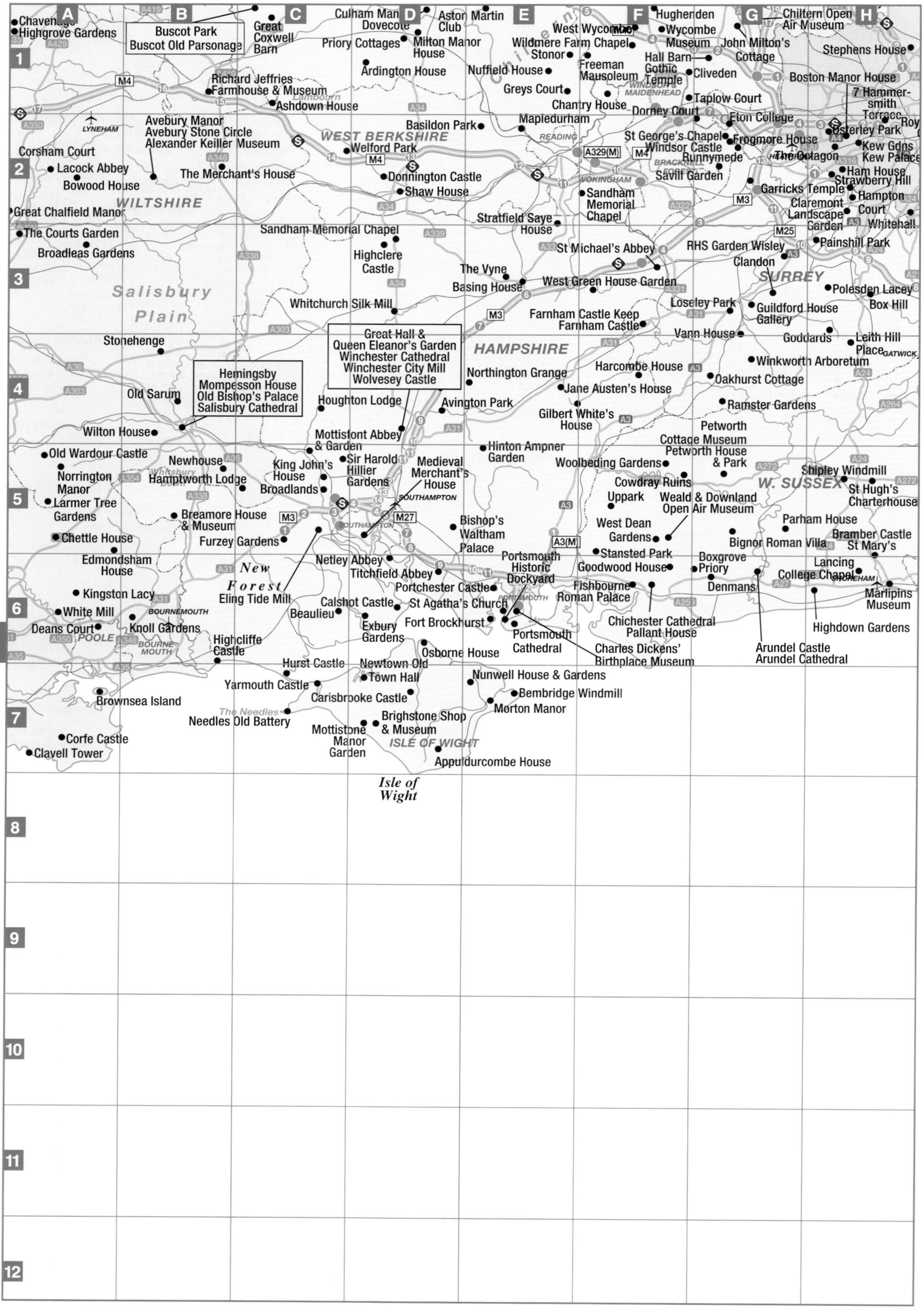

A B C D E F G H

1 2 3 4 5 6 7 8 9 10 11 12

Chavenage
Highgrove Gardens
Buscot Park
Buscot Old Parsonage
Great Coxwell Barn
Culham Manor Dovecote
Aston Martin Club
Milton Manor House
Priory Cottages
Ardington House
West Wycombe
Hughenden
Wycombe Museum
Wildmere Farm Chapel
Stonor
Freeman Mausoleum
Hall Barn
Gothic Temple
Cliveden
John Milton's Cottage
Chiltern Open Air Museum
Stephens House
Boston Manor House
7 Hammersmith Terrace
Nuffield House
Greys Court
Chantry House
Dorney Court
Taplow Court
Eton College
Richard Jeffries Farmhouse & Museum
Ashdown House
Lambourn
M4
LYNEHAM
Avebury Manor
Avebury Stone Circle
Alexander Keiller Museum
WEST BERKSHIRE
Basildon Park
Mapledurham
READING
WINDSOR & MAIDENHEAD
St George's Chapel
Windsor Castle
Frogmore House
Osterley Park
Kew Gdns
Kew Palace
Corsham Court
Welford Park
A329(M)
M4
Runnymede
The Octagon
Lacock Abbey
Bowood House
The Merchant's House
Donnington Castle
WOKINGHAM
BRACKNELL FOREST
Savill Garden
Ham House
Strawberry Hill
Shaw House
Sandham Memorial Chapel
M3
Garricks Temple
Hampton Court
WILTSHIRE
Great Chalfield Manor
Claremont Landscape Garden
Whitehall
The Courts Garden
Stratfield Saye House
Sandham Memorial Chapel
M25
RHS Garden Wisley
Painshill Park
Broadleas Gardens
Highclere Castle
St Michael's Abbey
Clandon
The Vyne
Basing House
West Green House Garden
SURREY
Polesden Lacey
Box Hill
Salisbury Plain
Whitchurch Silk Mill
Loseley Park
Guildford House Gallery
M3
Farnham Castle Keep
Farnham Castle
Vann House
Goddards
Leith Hill Place
GATWICK
Stonehenge
Great Hall & Queen Eleanor's Garden
Winchester Cathedral
Winchester City Mill
Wolvesey Castle
HAMPSHIRE
Winkworth Arboretum
Hemingsby
Mompesson House
Old Bishop's Palace
Salisbury Cathedral
Northington Grange
Harcombe House
Oakhurst Cottage
Jane Austen's House
Old Sarum
Houghton Lodge
Avington Park
Gilbert White's House
Ramster Gardens
Wilton House
Mottisfont Abbey & Garden
Petworth Cottage Museum
Petworth House & Park
Hinton Ampner Garden
Old Wardour Castle
Newhouse
King John's House
Sir Harold Hillier Gardens
Medieval Merchant's House
Woolbeding Gardens
Shipley Windmill
Norrington Manor
Hamptworth Lodge
Whitsbury Down
Cowdray Ruins
W. SUSSEX
St Hugh's Charterhouse
Broadlands
SOUTHAMPTON
Uppark
Weald & Downland Open Air Museum
Larmer Tree Gardens
Breamore House & Museum
M3
M27
Bishop's Waltham Palace
Parham House
Chettle House
Furzey Gardens
West Dean Gardens
Bignor Roman Villa
Bramber Castle
St Mary's
A3(M)
Edmondsham House
New Forest
Netley Abbey
Portsmouth Historic Dockyard
Stansted Park
Boxgrove Priory
Lancing College Chapel
Titchfield Abbey
Goodwood House
SHOREHAM
Kingston Lacy
Eling Tide Mill
Portchester Castle
Fishbourne Roman Palace
Denmans
Marlipins Museum
White Mill
Calshot Castle
St Agatha's Church
PORTSMOUTH
BOURNEMOUTH
Beaulieu
Fort Brockhurst
Chichester Cathedral
Pallant House
Highdown Gardens
Deans Court
Knoll Gardens
POOLE
BOURNEMOUTH
Exbury Gardens
Portsmouth Cathedral
Highcliffe Castle
Osborne House
Charles Dickens' Birthplace Museum
Arundel Castle
Arundel Cathedral
Hurst Castle
Newtown Old Town Hall
Nunwell House & Gardens
Yarmouth Castle
Bembridge Windmill
Brownsea Island
Carisbrooke Castle
Morton Manor
The Needles
Needles Old Battery
Brighstone Shop & Museum
Mottistone Manor Garden
ISLE OF WIGHT
Corfe Castle
Clavell Tower
Appuldurcombe House
Isle of Wight

Register for news and special offers at www.hudsonsheritage.com

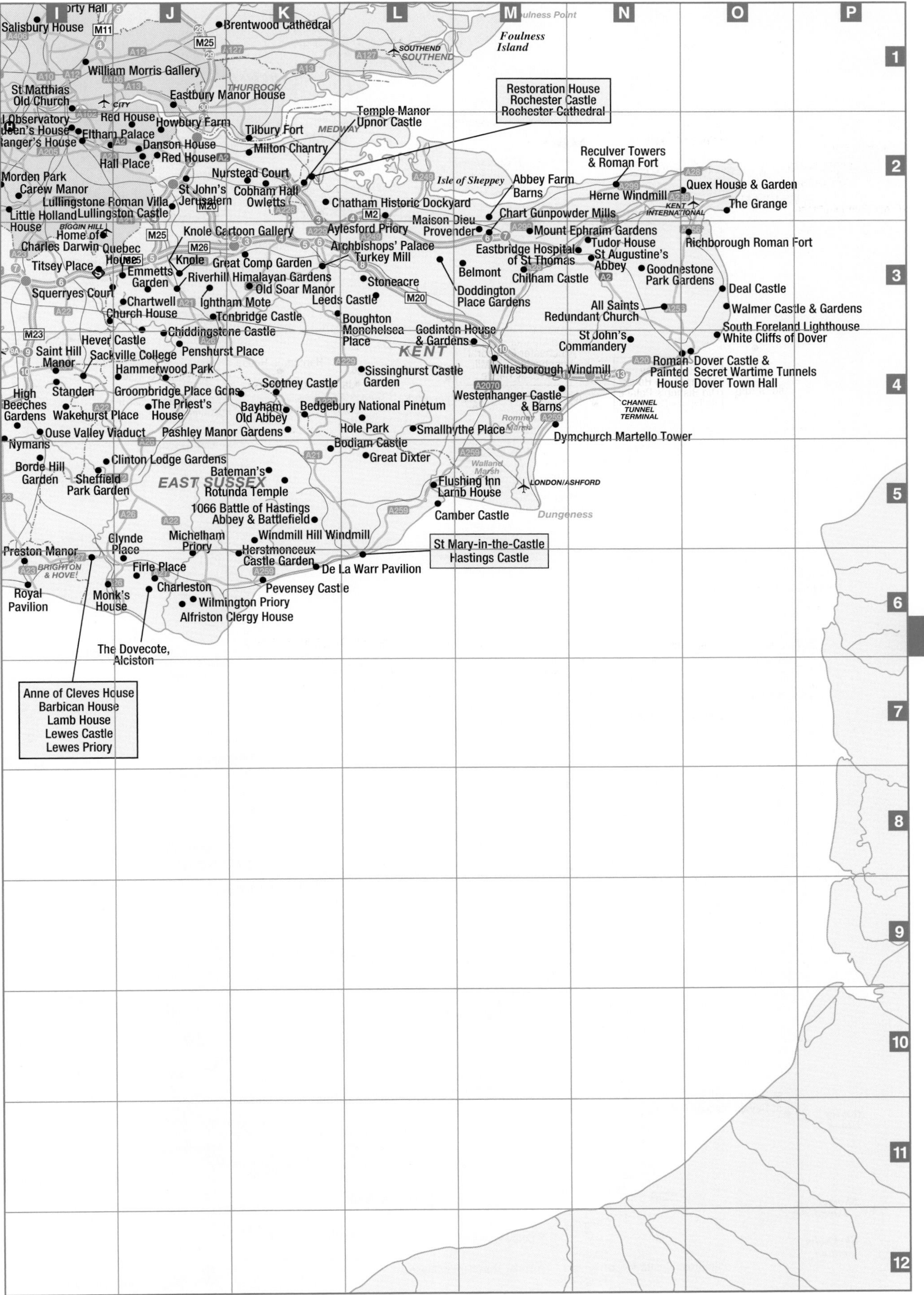
I
J
K
L
M
N
O
P
1
2
3
4
5
6
7
8
9
10
11
12
Salisbury House
Brentwood Cathedral
Foulness Point
Foulness Island
SOUTHEND
William Morris Gallery
THURROCK
St Matthias Old Church
CITY
Eastbury Manor House
Restoration House
Rochester Castle
Rochester Cathedral
Temple Manor
Upnor Castle
Observatory
Queen's House
Eltham Palace
Ranger's House
Red House
Howbury Farm
Danson House
Red House
Hall Place
Tilbury Fort
MEDWAY
Milton Chantry
Reculver Towers & Roman Fort
Morden Park
Carew Manor
Nurstead Court
St John's Jerusalem
Cobham Hall
Owletts
Isle of Sheppey
Abbey Farm Barns
Herne Windmill
Quex House & Garden
KENT INTERNATIONAL
The Grange
Lullingstone Roman Villa
Lullingstone Castle
Little Holland House
Chatham Historic Dockyard
Chart Gunpowder Mills
BIGGIN HILL
Home of Charles Darwin
Knole Cartoon Gallery
Aylesford Priory
Maison Dieu
Provender
Mount Ephraim Gardens
Richborough Roman Fort
Quebec House
Knole
Archbishops' Palace
Turkey Mill
Eastbridge Hospital of St Thomas
Tudor House
St Augustine's Abbey
Titsey Place
Emmetts Garden
Great Comp Garden
Belmont
Goodnestone Park Gardens
Riverhill Himalayan Gardens
Stoneacre
Chilham Castle
Deal Castle
Squerryes Court
Old Soar Manor
Chartwell
Ightham Mote
Leeds Castle
Doddington Place Gardens
All Saints Redundant Church
Walmer Castle & Gardens
Church House
Tonbridge Castle
Boughton Monchelsea Place
Godinton House & Gardens
South Foreland Lighthouse
White Cliffs of Dover
Hever Castle
Chiddingstone Castle
St John's Commandery
Saint Hill Manor
Sackville College
Penshurst Place
KENT
Roman Painted House
Dover Castle & Secret Wartime Tunnels
Dover Town Hall
Hammerwood Park
Sissinghurst Castle Garden
Willesborough Windmill
High Beeches Gardens
Standen
Groombridge Place Gdns
Scotney Castle
Westenhanger Castle & Barns
CHANNEL TUNNEL TERMINAL
Wakehurst Place
The Priest's House
Bayham Old Abbey
Bedgebury National Pinetum
Hole Park
Smallhythe Place
Romney Marsh
Ouse Valley Viaduct
Pashley Manor Gardens
Dymchurch Martello Tower
Nymans
Bodiam Castle
Great Dixter
Borde Hill Garden
Clinton Lodge Gardens
Sheffield Park Garden
Bateman's
EAST SUSSEX
Rotunda Temple
Walland Marsh
Flushing Inn
Lamb House
LONDON/ASHFORD
1066 Battle of Hastings Abbey & Battlefield
Camber Castle
Dungeness
Windmill Hill Windmill
Glynde Place
Michelham Priory
Preston Manor
Herstmonceux Castle Garden
St Mary-in-the-Castle
Hastings Castle
BRIGHTON & HOVE!
Firle Place
De La Warr Pavilion
Charleston
Pevensey Castle
Royal Pavilion
Monk's House
Wilmington Priory
Alfriston Clergy House
The Dovecote, Alciston
Anne of Cleves House
Barbican House
Lamb House
Lewes Castle
Lewes Priory

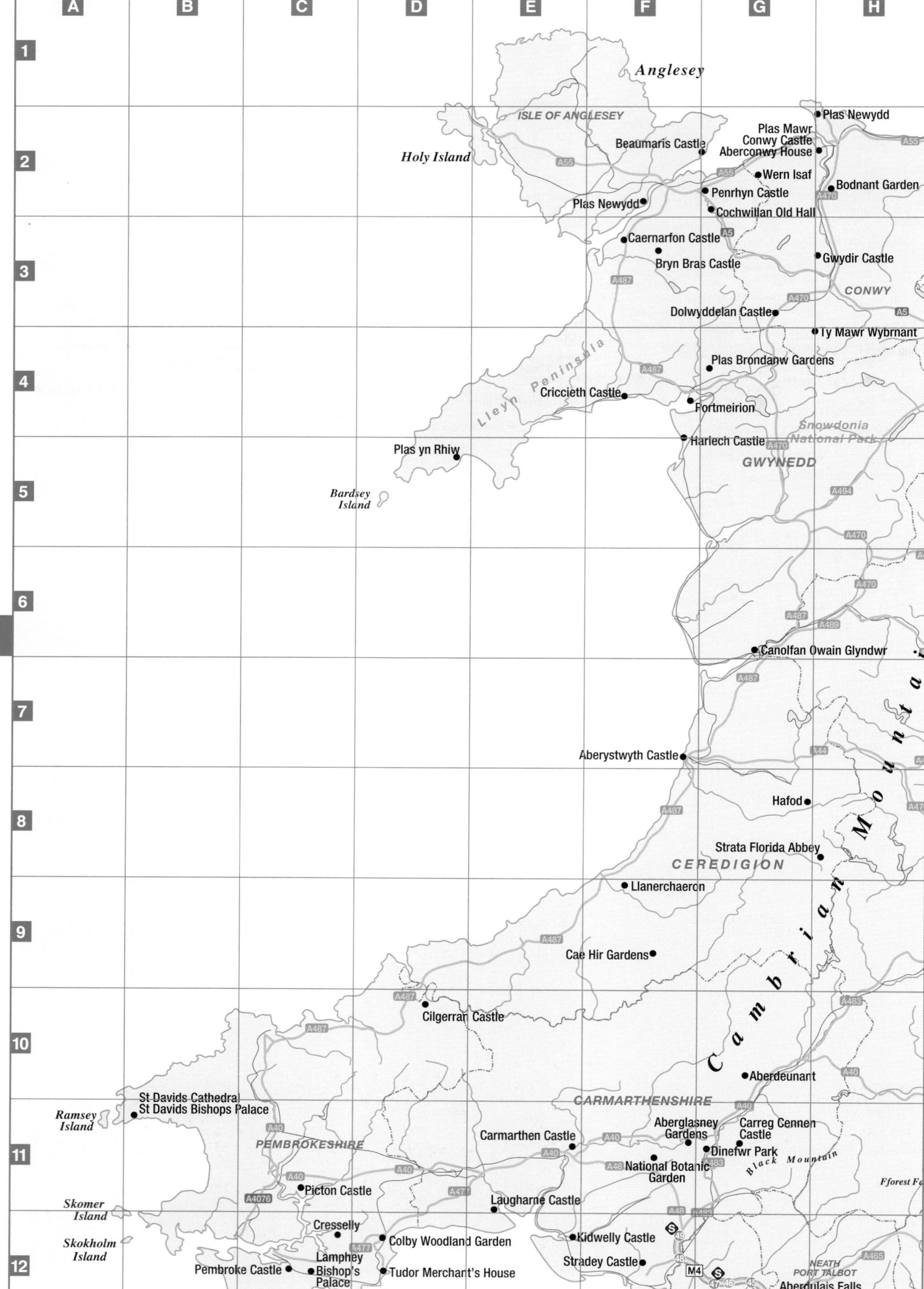

Register for news and special offers at www.hudsonsheritage.com

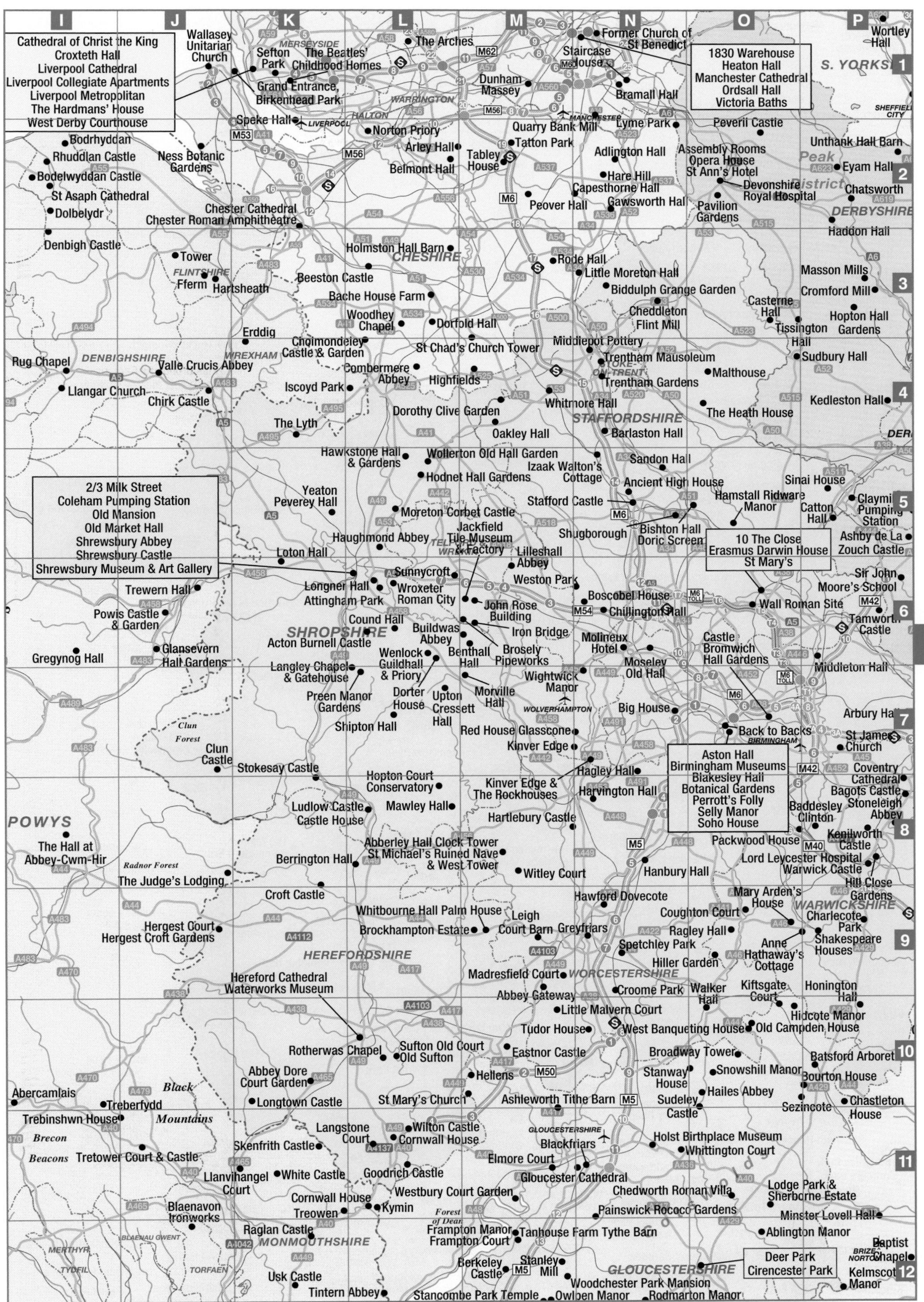

MAP 6
Cathedral of Christ the King
Croxteth Hall
Liverpool Cathedral
Liverpool Collegiate Apartments
Liverpool Metropolitan
The Hardmans' House
West Derby Courthouse
Wallasey Unitarian Church
Sefton Park
The Beatles' Childhood Homes
Grand Entrance, Birkenhead Park
The Arches
Former Church of St Benedict
Staircase House
1830 Warehouse
Heaton Hall
Manchester Cathedral
Ordsall Hall
Victoria Baths
Wortley Hall
Dunham Massey
Bramall Hall
Speke Hall
Norton Priory
Quarry Bank Mill
Lyme Park
Peveril Castle
Bodrhyddan
Rhuddlan Castle
Bodelwyddan Castle
St Asaph Cathedral
Dolbelydr
Denbigh Castle
Ness Botanic Gardens
Arley Hall
Belmont Hall
Tatton Park
Tabley House
Adlington Hall
Hare Hill
Capesthorne Hall
Gawsworth Hall
Peover Hall
Assembly Rooms
Opera House
St Ann's Hotel
Devonshire Royal Hospital
Pavilion Gardens
Unthank Hall Barn
Eyam Hall
Chatsworth
Haddon Hall
Chester Cathedral
Chester Roman Amphitheatre
Tower
Fferm
Hartsheath
Holmston Hall Barn
Beeston Castle
Bache House Farm
Woodhey Chapel
Dorfold Hall
Rode Hall
Little Moreton Hall
Biddulph Grange Garden
Cheddleton Flint Mill
Masson Mills
Cromford Mill
Casterne Hall
Tissington Hall
Hopton Hall Gardens
Erddig
Cholmondeley Castle & Garden
St Chad's Church Tower
Middleport Pottery
Trentham Mausoleum
Trentham Gardens
Sudbury Hall
Malthouse
Rug Chapel
Valle Crucis Abbey
Llangar Church
Chirk Castle
Combermere Abbey
Highfields
Iscoyd Park
Whitmore Hall
The Heath House
Kedleston Hall
The Lyth
Dorothy Clive Garden
Oakley Hall
Barlaston Hall
Hawkstone Hall & Gardens
Wollerton Old Hall Garden
Hodnet Hall Gardens
Izaak Walton's Cottage
Sandon Hall
Ancient High House
Sinai House
2/3 Milk Street
Coleham Pumping Station
Old Mansion
Old Market Hall
Shrewsbury Abbey
Shrewsbury Castle
Shrewsbury Museum & Art Gallery
Yeaton Peverey Hall
Moreton Corbet Castle
Stafford Castle
Hamstall Ridware Manor
Catton Hall
Claymills Pumping Station
Haughmond Abbey
Jackfield Tile Museum & Factory
Shugborough
Bishton Hall Doric Screen
10 The Close
Erasmus Darwin House
St Mary's
Ashby de La Zouch Castle
Loton Hall
Lilleshall Abbey
Sunnycroft
Weston Park
Sir John Moore's School
Trewern Hall
Longner Hall
Attingham Park
Wroxeter Roman City
John Rose Building
Boscobel House
Chillington Hall
Wall Roman Site
Powis Castle & Garden
Cound Hall
Buildwas Abbey
Iron Bridge
Tamworth Castle
Acton Burnell Castle
Benthall Hall
Broseley Pipeworks
Moliineux Hotel
Castle Bromwich Hall Gardens
Gregynog Hall
Glansevern Hall Gardens
Langley Chapel & Gatehouse
Wenlock Guildhall & Priory
Wightwick Manor
Moseley Old Hall
Middleton Hall
Preen Manor Gardens
Dorter House
Upton Cressett Hall
Morville Hall
Big House
Arbury Hall
Shipton Hall
Red House Glasscone
Back to Backs
St James Church
Clun Castle
Kinver Edge
Stokesay Castle
Aston Hall
Birmingham Museums
Blakesley Hall
Botanical Gardens
Perrott's Folly
Selly Manor
Soho House
Coventry Cathedral
Hopton Court Conservatory
Hagley Hall
Bagots Castle
Kinver Edge & The Rockhouses
Harvington Hall
Stoneleigh Abbey
Ludlow Castle
Castle House
Mawley Hall
Baddesley Clinton
Hartlebury Castle
Kenilworth Castle
POWYS
The Hall at Abbey-Cwm-Hir
Abberley Hall Clock Tower
St Michael's Ruined Nave & West Tower
Packwood House
Lord Leycester Hospital
Warwick Castle
Berrington Hall
Witley Court
Hanbury Hall
Hill Close Gardens
The Judge's Lodging
Croft Castle
Hawford Dovecote
Mary Arden's House
Coughton Court
Charlecote Park
Whitbourne Hall Palm House
Leigh Court Barn
Greyfriars
Ragley Hall
Hergest Court
Hergest Croft Gardens
Brockhampton Estate
Spetchley Park
Anne Hathaway's Cottage
Shakespeare Houses
Hiller Garden
Hereford Cathedral
Waterworks Museum
Madresfield Court
Croome Park
Walker Hall
Kiftsgate Court
Honington Hall
Abbey Gateway
Little Malvern Court
Hidcote Manor
Tudor House
West Banqueting House
Old Campden House
Rotherwas Chapel
Sufton Old Court
Old Sufton
Eastnor Castle
Broadway Tower
Batsford Arboretum
Abbey Dore Court Garden
Hellens
Stanway House
Snowshill Manor
Bourton House
Abercamlais
Treberfydd
Longtown Castle
St Mary's Church
Ashleworth Tithe Barn
Sudeley Castle
Hailes Abbey
Sezincote
Chastleton House
Trebinshwn House
Langstone Court
Wilton Castle
Cornwall House
Holst Birthplace Museum
Whittington Court
Skenfrith Castle
Tretower Court & Castle
Blackfriars
Elmore Court
Llanvihangel Court
White Castle
Goodrich Castle
Gloucester Cathedral
Chedworth Roman Villa
Lodge Park & Sherborne Estate
Blaenavon Ironworks
Cornwall House
Treowen
Kymin
Westbury Court Garden
Painswick Rococo Gardens
Minster Lovell Hall
Raglan Castle
Frampton Manor
Frampton Court
Tanhouse Farm Tythe Barn
Ablington Manor
Baptist Chapel
Berkeley Castle
Stanley Mill
Deer Park
Cirencester Park
Kelmscott Manor
Usk Castle
Woodchester Park Mansion
Tintern Abbey
Stancombe Park Temple
Owlpen Manor
Rodmarton Manor
MERSEYSIDE
CHESHIRE
FLINTSHIRE
DENBIGHSHIRE
WREXHAM
STAFFORDSHIRE
SHROPSHIRE
HEREFORDSHIRE
WORCESTERSHIRE
WARWICKSHIRE
GLOUCESTERSHIRE
MONMOUTHSHIRE
DERBYSHIRE
S. YORKS
Peak District
Clun Forest
Radnor Forest
Black Mountains
Brecon Beacons
Forest of Dean
I
J
K
L
M
N
O
P
1
2
3
4
5
6
7
8
9
10
11
12

MAP 7

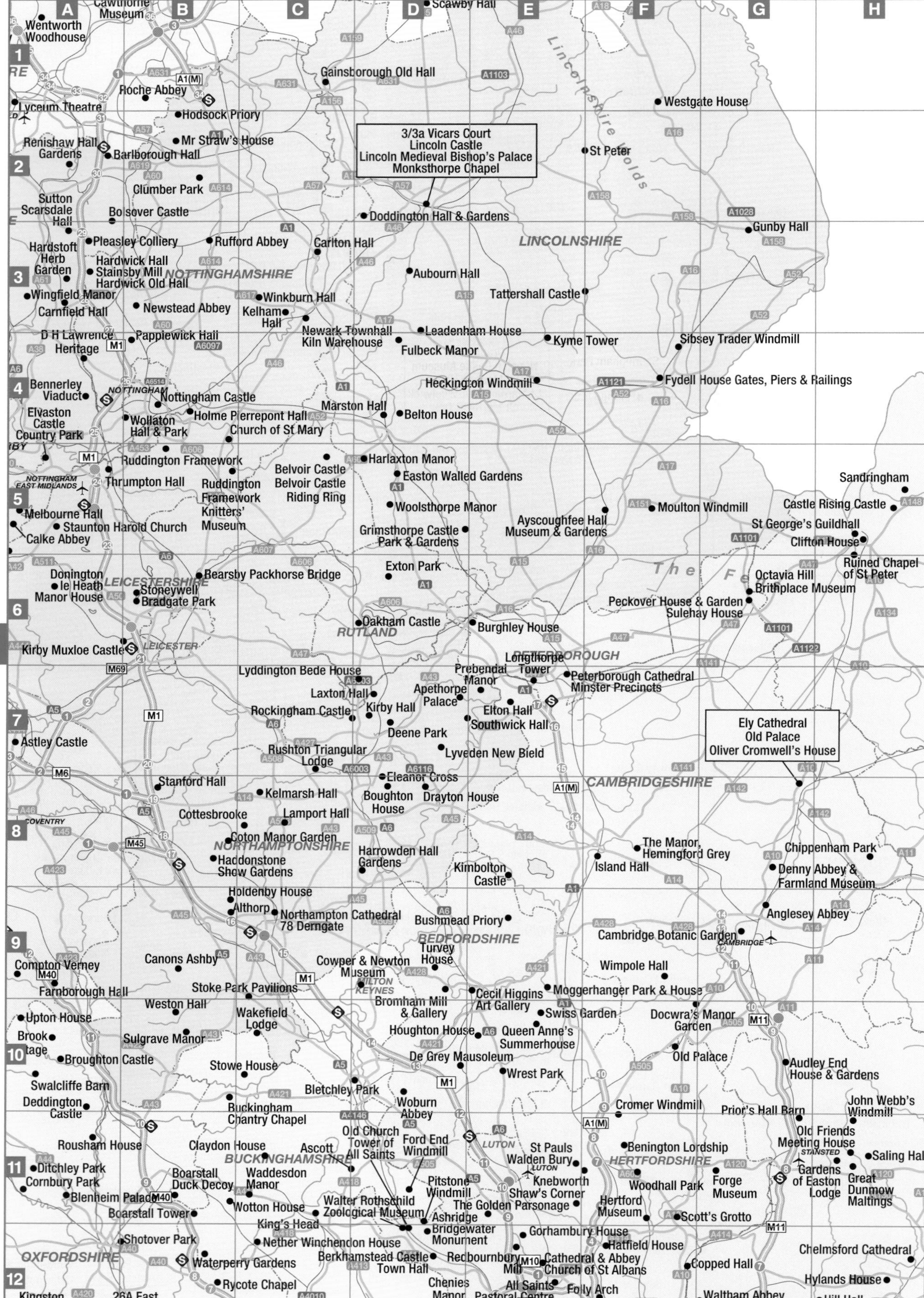

A
B
C
D
E
F
G
H
1
2
3
4
5
6
7
8
9
10
11
12
Cawthorne Museum
Scawby Hall
Wentworth Woodhouse
Lincolnshire Wolds
Gainsborough Old Hall
Roche Abbey
Lyceum Theatre
Hodsock Priory
Westgate House
Renishaw Hall Gardens
Mr Straw's House
Barlborough Hall
3/3a Vicars Court
Lincoln Castle
Lincoln Medieval Bishop's Palace
Monksthorpe Chapel
St Peter
Clumber Park
Sutton Scarsdale Hall
Bolsover Castle
Doddington Hall & Gardens
Gunby Hall
Hardstoft Herb Garden
Pleasley Colliery
Rufford Abbey
Carlton Hall
LINCOLNSHIRE
Hardwick Hall
Stainsby Mill
Hardwick Old Hall
NOTTINGHAMSHIRE
Aubourn Hall
Wingfield Manor
Winkburn Hall
Tattershall Castle
Carnfield Hall
Newstead Abbey
Kelham Hall
D H Lawrence Heritage
Papplewick Hall
Newark Townhall
Kiln Warehouse
Leadenham House
Fulbeck Manor
Kyme Tower
Sibsey Trader Windmill
Fydell House Gates, Piers & Railings
Heckington Windmill
Bennerley Viaduct
NOTTINGHAM
Nottingham Castle
Elvaston Castle Country Park
Wollaton Hall & Park
Holme Pierrepont Hall
Church of St Mary
Marston Hall
Belton House
Ruddington Framework
Belvoir Castle
Belvoir Castle Riding Ring
Harlaxton Manor
Easton Walled Gardens
NOTTINGHAM EAST MIDLANDS
Thrumpton Hall
Ruddington Framework Knitters' Museum
Sandringham
Melbourne Hall
Woolsthorpe Manor
Moulton Windmill
Castle Rising Castle
Staunton Harold Church
Calke Abbey
Grimsthorpe Castle Park & Gardens
Ayscoughfee Hall Museum & Gardens
St George's Guildhall
Clifton House
Ruined Chapel of St Peter
Donington le Heath Manor House
LEICESTERSHIRE
Bearsby Packhorse Bridge
Exton Park
The Fens
Octavia Hill Birthplace Museum
Stoneywell
Bradgate Park
Peckover House & Garden
Sulehay House
Oakham Castle
RUTLAND
Burghley House
Kirby Muxloe Castle
LEICESTER
PETERBOROUGH
Longthorpe Tower
Lyddington Bede House
Prebendal Manor
Peterborough Cathedral Minster Precincts
Apethorpe Palace
Laxton Hall
Kirby Hall
Elton Hall
Rockingham Castle
Southwick Hall
Deene Park
Ely Cathedral
Old Palace
Oliver Cromwell's House
Astley Castle
Rushton Triangular Lodge
Lyveden New Bield
Eleanor Cross
CAMBRIDGESHIRE
Stanford Hall
Kelmarsh Hall
Boughton House
Drayton House
COVENTRY
Cottesbrooke
Lamport Hall
Coton Manor Garden
NORTHAMPTONSHIRE
The Manor, Hemingford Grey
Chippenham Park
Haddonstone Show Gardens
Harrowden Hall Gardens
Island Hall
Denny Abbey & Farmland Museum
Kimbolton Castle
Holdenby House
Althorp
Northampton Cathedral
78 Derngate
Anglesey Abbey
Bushmead Priory
Cambridge Botanic Garden
CAMBRIDGE
BEDFORDSHIRE
Turvey House
Compton Verney
Canons Ashby
Cowper & Newton Museum
Wimpole Hall
MILTON KEYNES
Farnborough Hall
Stoke Park Pavilions
Cecil Higgins Art Gallery
Moggerhanger Park & House
Weston Hall
Bromham Mill & Gallery
Upton House
Wakefield Lodge
Swiss Garden
Docwra's Manor Garden
Brook Cottage
Sulgrave Manor
Houghton House
Queen Anne's Summerhouse
Broughton Castle
Old Palace
De Grey Mausoleum
Stowe House
Audley End House & Gardens
Swalcliffe Barn
Wrest Park
Bletchley Park
Deddington Castle
Woburn Abbey
Buckingham Chantry Chapel
Cromer Windmill
Prior's Hall Barn
John Webb's Windmill
Old Church Tower of All Saints
Ford End Windmill
Old Friends Meeting House
Rousham House
Claydon House
Ascott
LUTON
St Pauls Walden Bury
Benington Lordship
STANSTED
Saling Hall
BUCKINGHAMSHIRE
HERTFORDSHIRE
Ditchley Park
Boarstall Duck Decoy
Waddesdon Manor
Knebworth
Gardens of Easton Lodge
Great Dunmow Maltings
Cornbury Park
Pitstone Windmill
Woodhall Park
Forge Museum
Blenheim Palace
Wotton House
Walter Rothschild Zoological Museum
Shaw's Corner
Hertford Museum
The Golden Parsonage
Boarstall Tower
Ashridge
Scott's Grotto
King's Head
Bridgewater Monument
Gorhambury House
Shotover Park
Nether Winchendon House
Hatfield House
Chelmsford Cathedral
OXFORDSHIRE
Waterperry Gardens
Berkhamstead Castle
Redbournbury Mill
Cathedral & Abbey Church of St Albans
Copped Hall
Town Hall
Rycote Chapel
Hylands House
Chenies Manor House
All Saints Pastoral Centre
Folly Arch
Waltham Abbey Gatehouse & Bridge
Hill Hall
Kingston Bagpuize
26A East St Helen Street

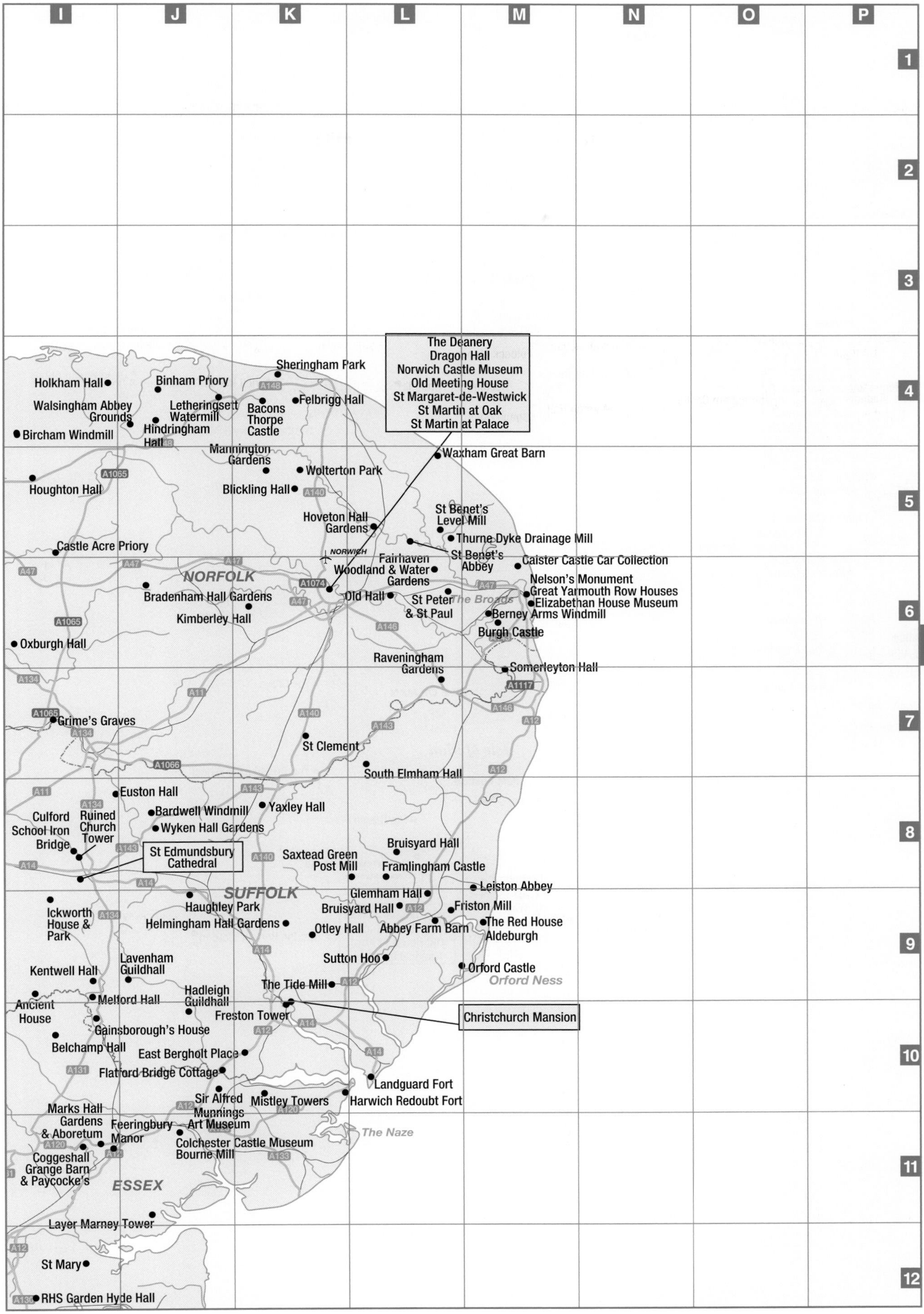

I J K L M N O P

1 2 3 4 5 6 7 8 9 10 11 12

The Deanery
Dragon Hall
Norwich Castle Museum
Old Meeting House
St Margaret-de-Westwick
St Martin at Oak
St Martin at Palace

Sheringham Park
Holkham Hall
Binham Priory
Walsingham Abbey Grounds
Letheringsett Watermill
Bacons Thorpe Castle
Felbrigg Hall
Bircham Windmill
Hindringham Hall
Mannington Gardens
Wolterton Park
Waxham Great Barn
Houghton Hall
Blickling Hall
St Benet's Level Mill
Hoveton Hall Gardens
Thurne Dyke Drainage Mill
Castle Acre Priory
St Benet's Abbey
Caister Castle Car Collection
NORWICH
Fairhaven Woodland & Water Gardens
NORFOLK
Nelson's Monument
Great Yarmouth Row Houses
Elizabethan House Museum
Bradenham Hall Gardens
Old Hall
St Peter & St Paul
The Broads
Kimberley Hall
Berney Arms Windmill
Burgh Castle
Oxburgh Hall
Raveningham Gardens
Somerleyton Hall
Grime's Graves
St Clement
South Elmham Hall
Euston Hall
Bardwell Windmill
Yaxley Hall
Culford School Iron Bridge
Ruined Church Tower
Wyken Hall Gardens
Bruisyard Hall
St Edmundsbury Cathedral
Saxtead Green Post Mill
Framlingham Castle
Leiston Abbey
SUFFOLK
Glemham Hall
Ickworth House & Park
Haughley Park
Bruisyard Hall
Friston Mill
Helmingham Hall Gardens
Otley Hall
Abbey Farm Barn
The Red House Aldeburgh
Lavenham Guildhall
Sutton Hoo
Kentwell Hall
Orford Castle
Orford Ness
The Tide Mill
Hadleigh Guildhall
Ancient House
Melford Hall
Freston Tower
Christchurch Mansion
Gainsborough's House
Belchamp Hall
East Bergholt Place
Flatford Bridge Cottage
Landguard Fort
Sir Alfred Munnings Art Museum
Mistley Towers
Harwich Redoubt Fort
Marks Hall Gardens & Aboretum
Feeringbury Manor
The Naze
Colchester Castle Museum
Bourne Mill
Coggeshall Grange Barn & Paycocke's
ESSEX
Layer Marney Tower
St Mary
RHS Garden Hyde Hall

A148 A1065 A140 A47 A1074 A146 A1065 A134 A11 A1117 A140 A143 A146 A12 A1065 A134 A1066 A12 A11 A134 A143 A140 A14 A14 A134 A12 A14 A14 A12 A14 A131 A12 A120 A120 A12 A133 A12 A130

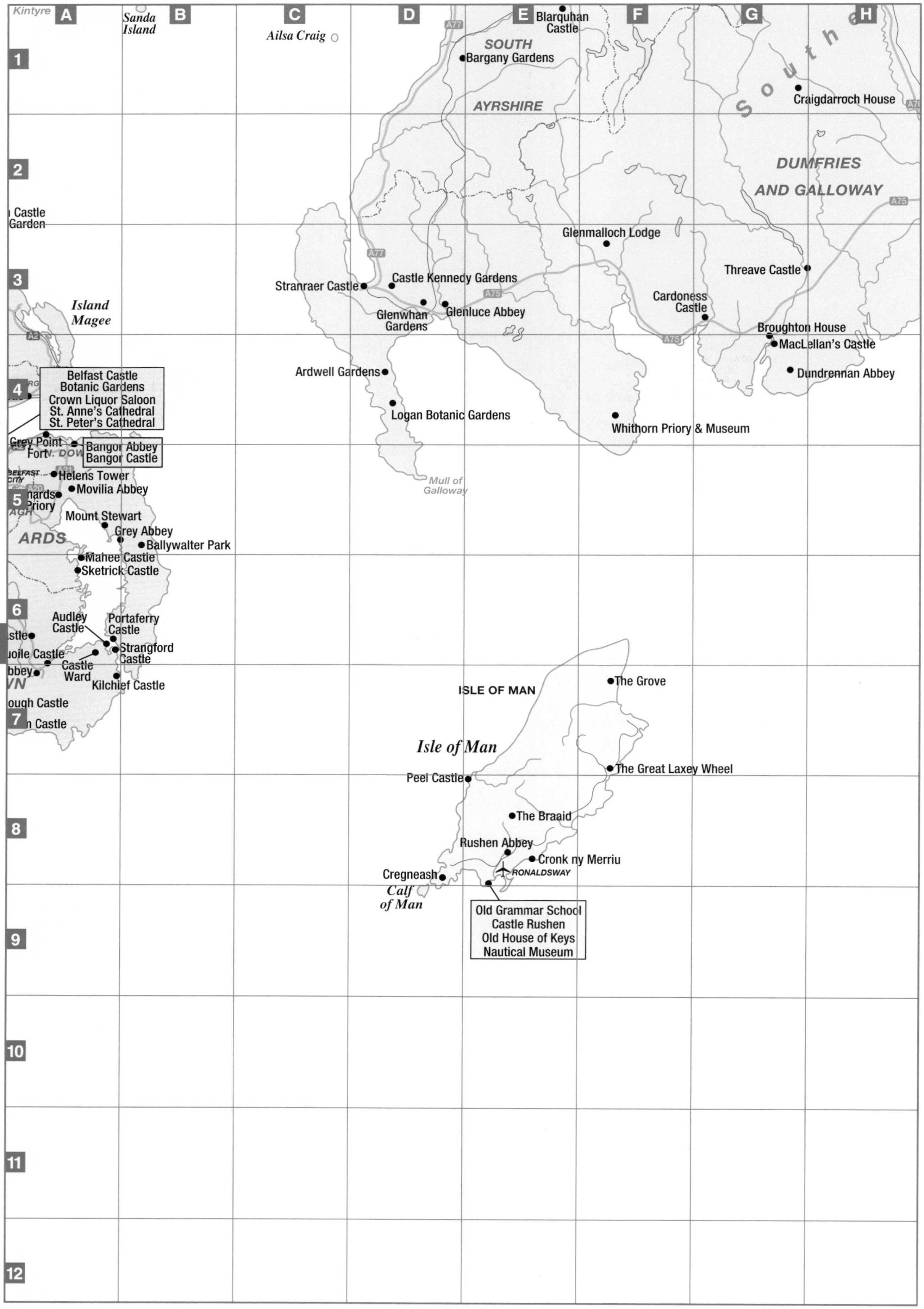

MAP 9

Kintyre
Sanda Island
Ailsa Craig

Blarquhan Castle
SOUTH AYRSHIRE
Bargany Gardens
South
Craigdarroch House
DUMFRIES AND GALLOWAY
Glenmalloch Lodge
Threave Castle
Stranraer Castle
Castle Kennedy Gardens
Glenwhan Gardens
Glenluce Abbey
Cardoness Castle
Broughton House
MacLellan's Castle
Dundrennan Abbey
Ardwell Gardens
Logan Botanic Gardens
Whithorn Priory & Museum
Mull of Galloway

Castle
Garden
Island Magee
Belfast Castle
Botanic Gardens
Crown Liquor Saloon
St. Anne's Cathedral
St. Peter's Cathedral
Grey Point Fort
Bangor Abbey
Bangor Castle
Helens Tower
Movilia Abbey
Priory
Mount Stewart
Grey Abbey
ARDS
Ballywalter Park
Mahee Castle
Sketrick Castle
Audley Castle
Portaferry Castle
Strangford Castle
Castle Ward
Kilclief Castle
Castle
Castle

ISLE OF MAN
Isle of Man
The Grove
The Great Laxey Wheel
Peel Castle
The Braaid
Rushen Abbey
Cronk ny Merriu
RONALDSWAY
Cregneash
Calf of Man
Old Grammar School
Castle Rushen
Old House of Keys
Nautical Museum

Register for news and special offers at www.hudsonsheritage.com

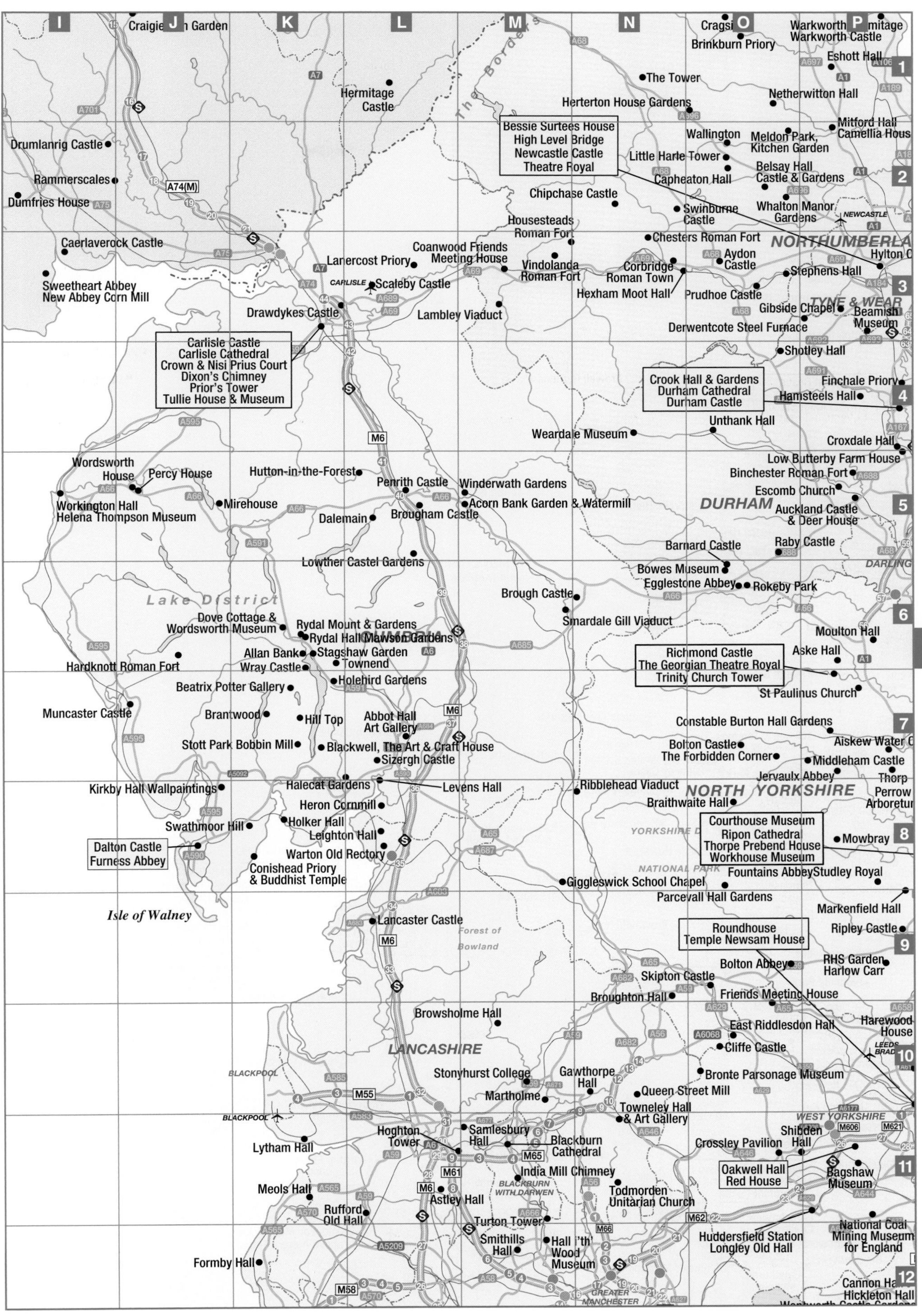

I
J
K
L
M
N
O
P
1
2
3
4
5
6
7
8
9
10
11
12
Craigieburn Garden
Cragside
Warkworth Hermitage
Warkworth Castle
Brinkburn Priory
Eshott Hall
The Borders
The Tower
Hermitage Castle
Herterton House Gardens
Netherwitton Hall
Bessie Surtees House
High Level Bridge
Newcastle Castle
Theatre Royal
Wallington
Meldon Park, Kitchen Garden
Mitford Hall
Camellia House
Drumlanrig Castle
Little Harle Tower
Belsay Hall Castle & Gardens
Rammerscales
Capheaton Hall
A74(M)
Dumfries House
Chipchase Castle
Swinburne Castle
Whalton Manor Gardens
NEWCASTLE
Housesteads Roman Fort
Caerlaverock Castle
Chesters Roman Fort
NORTHUMBERLAND
Coanwood Friends Meeting House
Aydon Castle
Hylton Castle
Lanercost Priory
Vindolanda Roman Fort
Corbridge Roman Town
Sweetheart Abbey
New Abbey Corn Mill
CARLISLE
Scaleby Castle
Hexham Moot Hall
Stephens Hall
Prudhoe Castle
TYNE & WEAR
Drawdykes Castle
Lambley Viaduct
Gibside Chapel
Beamish Museum
Derwentcote Steel Furnace
Carlisle Castle
Carlisle Cathedral
Crown & Nisi Prius Court
Dixon's Chimney
Prior's Tower
Tullie House & Museum
Shotley Hall
Crook Hall & Gardens
Durham Cathedral
Durham Castle
Finchale Priory
Hamsteels Hall
M6
Unthank Hall
Weardale Museum
Croxdale Hall
Wordsworth House
Percy House
Hutton-in-the-Forest
Low Butterby Farm House
Binchester Roman Fort
Penrith Castle
Winderwath Gardens
Escomb Church
Workington Hall
Helena Thompson Museum
Mirehouse
Acorn Bank Garden & Watermill
DURHAM
Auckland Castle & Deer House
Dalemain
Brougham Castle
Raby Castle
Barnard Castle
Lowther Castel Gardens
Bowes Museum
DARLINGTON
Egglestone Abbey
Rokeby Park
Lake District
Brough Castle
Dove Cottage & Wordsworth Museum
Rydal Mount & Gardens
Rydal Hall
Mawson Gardens
Smardale Gill Viaduct
CUMBRIA
Moulton Hall
MAP 10
Allan Bank
Stagshaw Garden
Townend
Aske Hall
Hardknott Roman Fort
Wray Castle
Richmond Castle
The Georgian Theatre Royal
Trinity Church Tower
Holehird Gardens
Beatrix Potter Gallery
St Paulinus Church
Muncaster Castle
Brantwood
Hill Top
Abbot Hall Art Gallery
Constable Burton Hall Gardens
Stott Park Bobbin Mill
Blackwell, The Art & Craft House
Bolton Castle
Aiskew Water
Sizergh Castle
The Forbidden Corner
Middleham Castle
Jervaulx Abbey
Thorp Perrow Arboretum
Kirkby Hall Wallpaintings
Halecat Gardens
Levens Hall
Ribblehead Viaduct
NORTH YORKSHIRE
Heron Cornmill
Braithwaite Hall
Swarthmoor Hill
Holker Hall
Courthouse Museum
Ripon Cathedral
Thorpe Prebend House
Workhouse Museum
Leighton Hall
YORKSHIRE DALES
Mowbray
Dalton Castle
Furness Abbey
Warton Old Rectory
Conishead Priory & Buddhist Temple
NATIONAL PARK
Fountains Abbey
Studley Royal
Giggleswick School Chapel
Parcevall Hall Gardens
Markenfield Hall
Isle of Walney
Lancaster Castle
Forest of Bowland
Ripley Castle
Roundhouse
Temple Newsam House
Bolton Abbey
RHS Garden Harlow Carr
Skipton Castle
Friends Meeting House
Broughton Hall
Browsholme Hall
Harewood House
East Riddlesdon Hall
Cliffe Castle
LANCASHIRE
LEEDS BRADFORD
BLACKPOOL
Stonyhurst College
Gawthorpe Hall
Bronte Parsonage Museum
M55
Queen Street Mill
Martholme
Towneley Hall & Art Gallery
WEST YORKSHIRE
Hoghton Tower
Samlesbury Hall
Blackburn Cathedral
Shibden Hall
Crossley Pavilion
Lytham Hall
M65
India Mill Chimney
Oakwell Hall
Red House
Bagshaw Museum
M61
BLACKBURN WITH DARWEN
Meols Hall
Astley Hall
Todmorden Unitarian Church
Rufford Old Hall
Turton Tower
M62
National Coal Mining Museum for England
Smithills Hall
Hall i'th' Wood Museum
Huddersfield Station
Longley Old Hall
M66
Formby Hall
Cannon Hall
Hickleton Hall
M58
GREATER MANCHESTER

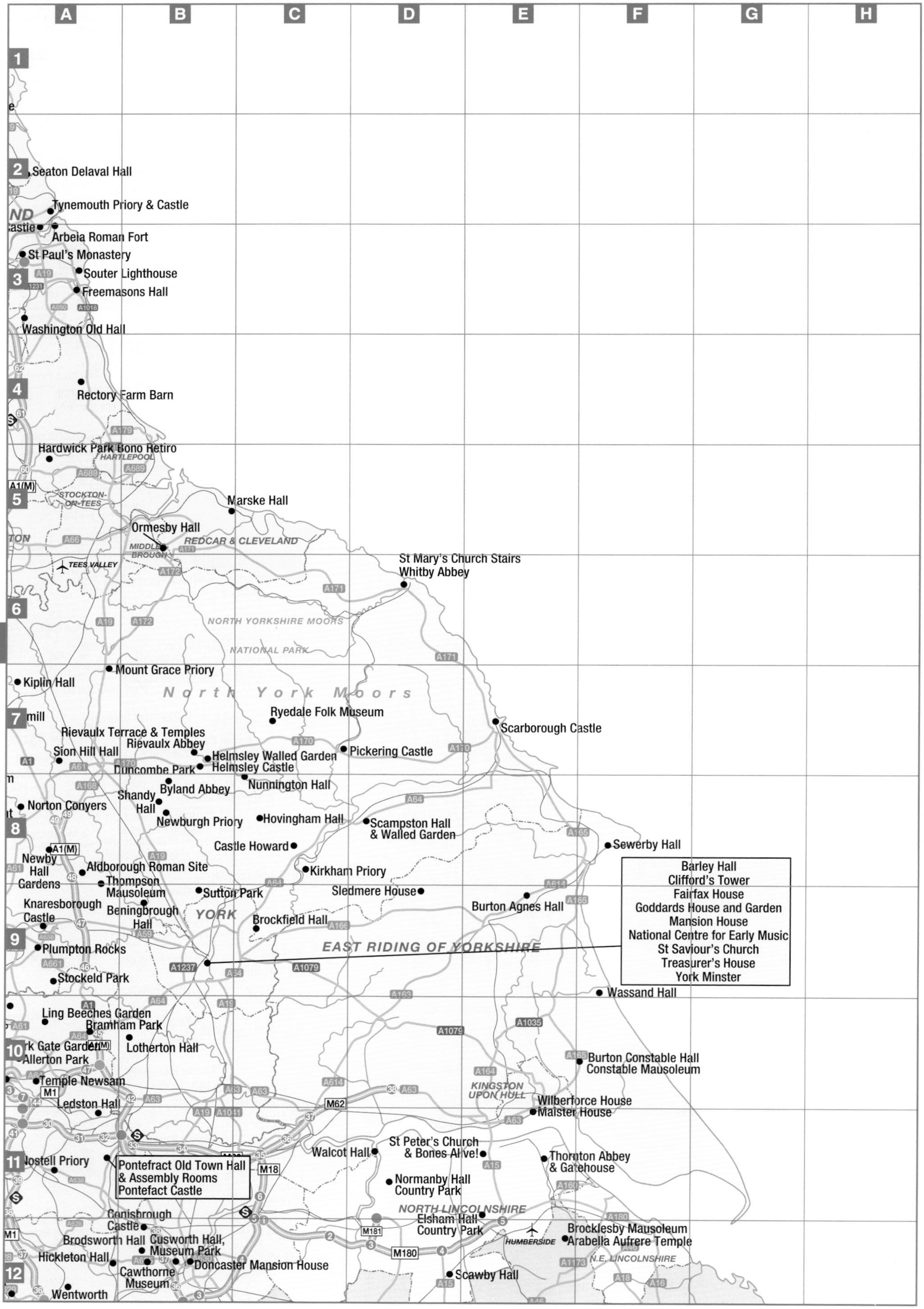

MAP 11

A B C D E F G H

1

2 Seaton Delaval Hall

Tynemouth Priory & Castle

Arbeia Roman Fort

St Paul's Monastery

3 Souter Lighthouse

Freemasons Hall

Washington Old Hall

4 Rectory Farm Barn

Hardwick Park Bono Retiro

HARTLEPOOL

5 STOCKTON-ON-TEES

Marske Hall

Ormesby Hall

MIDDLESBROUGH

REDCAR & CLEVELAND

TEES VALLEY

St Mary's Church Stairs
Whitby Abbey

6 NORTH YORKSHIRE MOORS NATIONAL PARK

Mount Grace Priory

Kiplin Hall

North York Moors

7 Ryedale Folk Museum

Scarborough Castle

Rievaulx Terrace & Temples

Rievaulx Abbey

Sion Hill Hall

Helmsley Walled Garden

Pickering Castle

Duncombe Park

Helmsley Castle

Nunnington Hall

Byland Abbey

Shandy Hall

Norton Conyers

8 Newburgh Priory

Hovingham Hall

Scampston Hall & Walled Garden

Castle Howard

Sewerby Hall

Newby Hall Gardens

Aldborough Roman Site

Kirkham Priory

Thompson Mausoleum

Sutton Park

Sledmere House

Knaresborough Castle

Beningbrough Hall

YORK

Burton Agnes Hall

Brockfield Hall

9 Plumpton Rocks

EAST RIDING OF YORKSHIRE

Barley Hall
Clifford's Tower
Fairfax House
Goddards House and Garden
Mansion House
National Centre for Early Music
St Saviour's Church
Treasurer's House
York Minster

Stockeld Park

Wassand Hall

Ling Beeches Garden

Bramham Park

10 Lotherton Hall

Burton Constable Hall
Constable Mausoleum

Allerton Park

Temple Newsam

KINGSTON UPON HULL

Ledston Hall

Wilberforce House

Maister House

St Peter's Church & Bones Alive!

11 Nostell Priory

Pontefract Old Town Hall & Assembly Rooms
Pontefact Castle

Walcot Hall

Thornton Abbey & Gatehouse

Normanby Hall Country Park

NORTH LINCOLNSHIRE

Conisbrough Castle

Elsham Hall Country Park

Brocklesby Mausoleum

Brodsworth Hall

Cusworth Hall, Museum Park

HUMBERSIDE

Arabella Aufrere Temple

Hickleton Hall

N.E. LINCOLNSHIRE

12 Doncaster Mansion House

Cawthorne Museum

Scawby Hall

Wentworth

Register for news and special offers at www.hudsonsheritage.com

I J K L M N O P

Kisimul Castle

Sanndraigh (Sandray)

Rum

Eigg

Muck

Inner Hebrides

1

2

Coll

Tiree

Ard Daraich Hill Gardens

Oransay

3

Castle Stalker

Ardtornish Gardens

Lip na Cloiche Garden

Ulva

Isle of Mull

Lismore

4

Ardchtton Priory Gardens

Dunstaffnage Castle

Ardchattan Priory Gardens

Duart Castle

Kerrera

Bonaw Iron Furnac

Iona

Iona Abbey

Angus's Garden

5

Ardmaddy Castle Gardens

Luing

Garvellachs

Arduaine Gardens

Lunga

Scarba

6

ARGYLL AND BUTE

MAP 12

Colonsay

Crarae Garden

Oronsay

7

Jura

8

Islay

ISLAY

Gigha

9

Kintyre

Brodick Castle

Arran

10

hull

11

Rathlin Island

Giant's Causeway

Giant's Causeway

Mull of Kintyre

WEN (Bun an Phobail)

Downhill Demesne Mussenden Temple

Hezlett House & Farmyard

Dunluce Castle

Sanda Island

Ailsa Crag

12

A830 A828 A816 A83

MAP 13

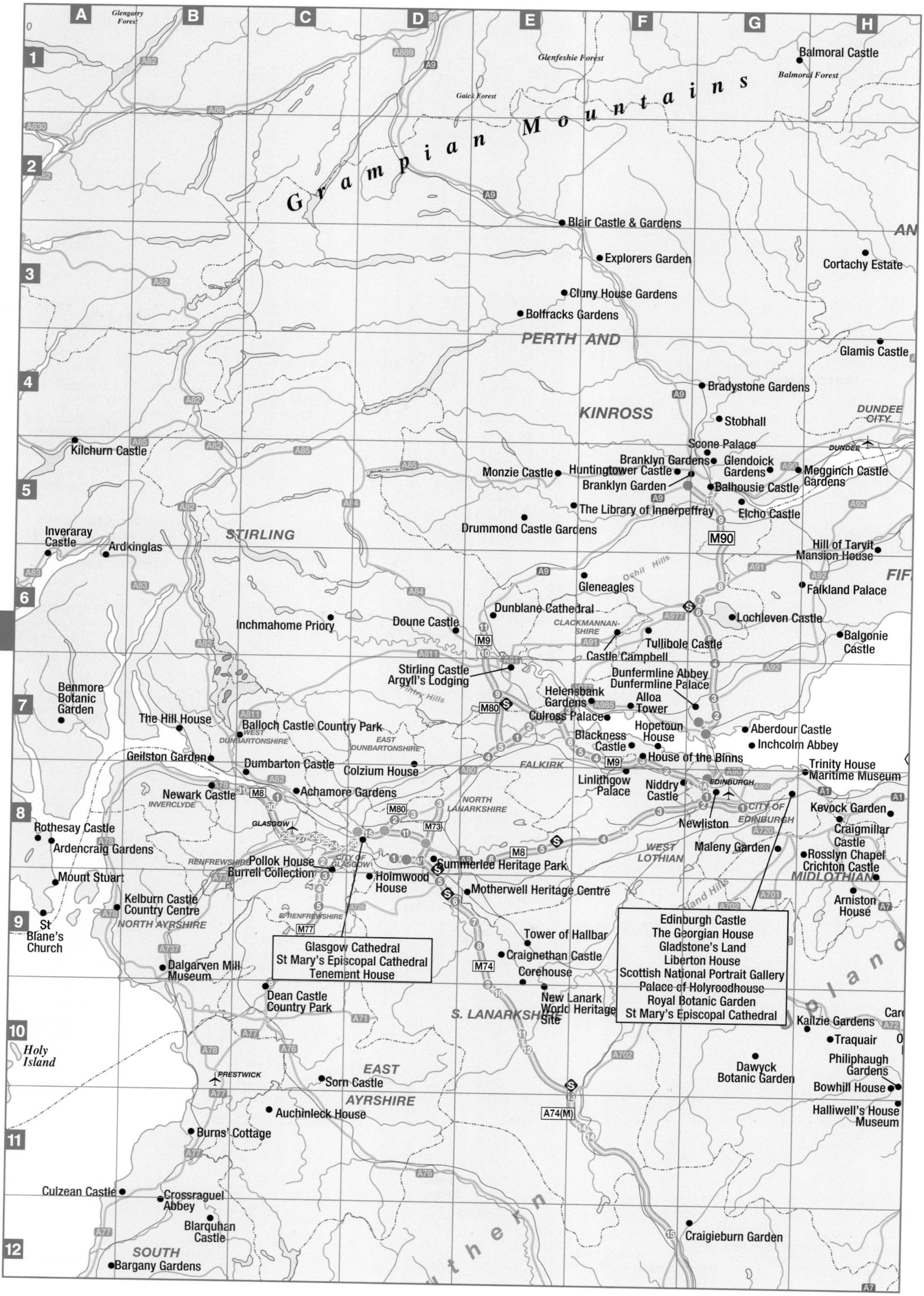

Grampian Mountains

Balmoral Castle
Balmoral Forest
Glenfeshie Forest
Gaick Forest
Glengarry Forest
Blair Castle & Gardens
Explorers Garden
Cortachy Estate
Cluny House Gardens
Bolfracks Gardens
PERTH AND KINROSS
Glamis Castle
Bradystone Gardens
Stobhall
DUNDEE CITY
Scone Palace
Kilchurn Castle
Branklyn Gardens
Glendoick Gardens
Megginch Castle Gardens
Monzie Castle
Huntingtower Castle
Branklyn Garden
Balhousie Castle
The Library of Innerpeffray
Elcho Castle
Drummond Castle Gardens
Inveraray Castle
Ardkinglas
STIRLING
Hill of Tarvit Mansion House
Ochil Hills
Gleneagles
Falkland Palace
FIFE
Dunblane Cathedral
Lochleven Castle
Inchmahome Priory
Doune Castle
CLACKMANNAN-SHIRE
Tullibole Castle
Balgonie Castle
Castle Campbell
Stirling Castle
Argyll's Lodging
Dunfermline Abbey
Dunfermline Palace
Fintry Hills
Benmore Botanic Garden
Helensbank Gardens
Alloa Tower
The Hill House
Culross Palace
Balloch Castle Country Park
Hopetoun House
Aberdour Castle
WEST DUNBARTONSHIRE
EAST DUNBARTONSHIRE
Blackness Castle
Inchcolm Abbey
Geilston Garden
House of the Binns
FALKIRK
Dumbarton Castle
Colzium House
Trinity House Maritime Museum
Linlithgow Palace
Niddry Castle
EDINBURGH
Newark Castle
Achamore Gardens
INVERCLYDE
NORTH LANARKSHIRE
Kevock Garden
CITY OF EDINBURGH
GLASGOW
Rothesay Castle
Newliston
Craigmillar Castle
Ardencraig Gardens
WEST LOTHIAN
Maleny Garden
Rosslyn Chapel
Pollok House
CITY OF GLASGOW
RENFREWSHIRE
Summerlee Heritage Park
Crichton Castle
Burrell Collection
MIDLOTHIAN
Mount Stuart
Holmwood House
Motherwell Heritage Centre
Arniston House
Kelburn Castle Country Centre
E RENFREWSHIRE
NORTH AYRSHIRE
St Blane's Church
Tower of Hallbar

Edinburgh Castle
The Georgian House
Gladstone's Land
Liberton House
Scottish National Portrait Gallery
Palace of Holyroodhouse
Royal Botanic Garden
St Mary's Episcopal Cathedral

Glasgow Cathedral
St Mary's Episcopal Cathedral
Tenement House

Craignethan Castle
Dalgarven Mill Museum
Corehouse
Dean Castle Country Park
New Lanark World Heritage Site
S. LANARKSHIRE
Kailzie Gardens
Traquair
Holy Island
EAST AYRSHIRE
PRESTWICK
Sorn Castle
Dawyck Botanic Garden
Philiphaugh Gardens
Bowhill House
Auchinleck House
Halliwell's House Museum
Burns' Cottage
Culzean Castle
Crossraguel Abbey
Blarquhan Castle
Craigieburn Garden
SOUTH
Bargany Gardens
Southern Uplands

Register for news and special offers at www.hudsonsheritage.com

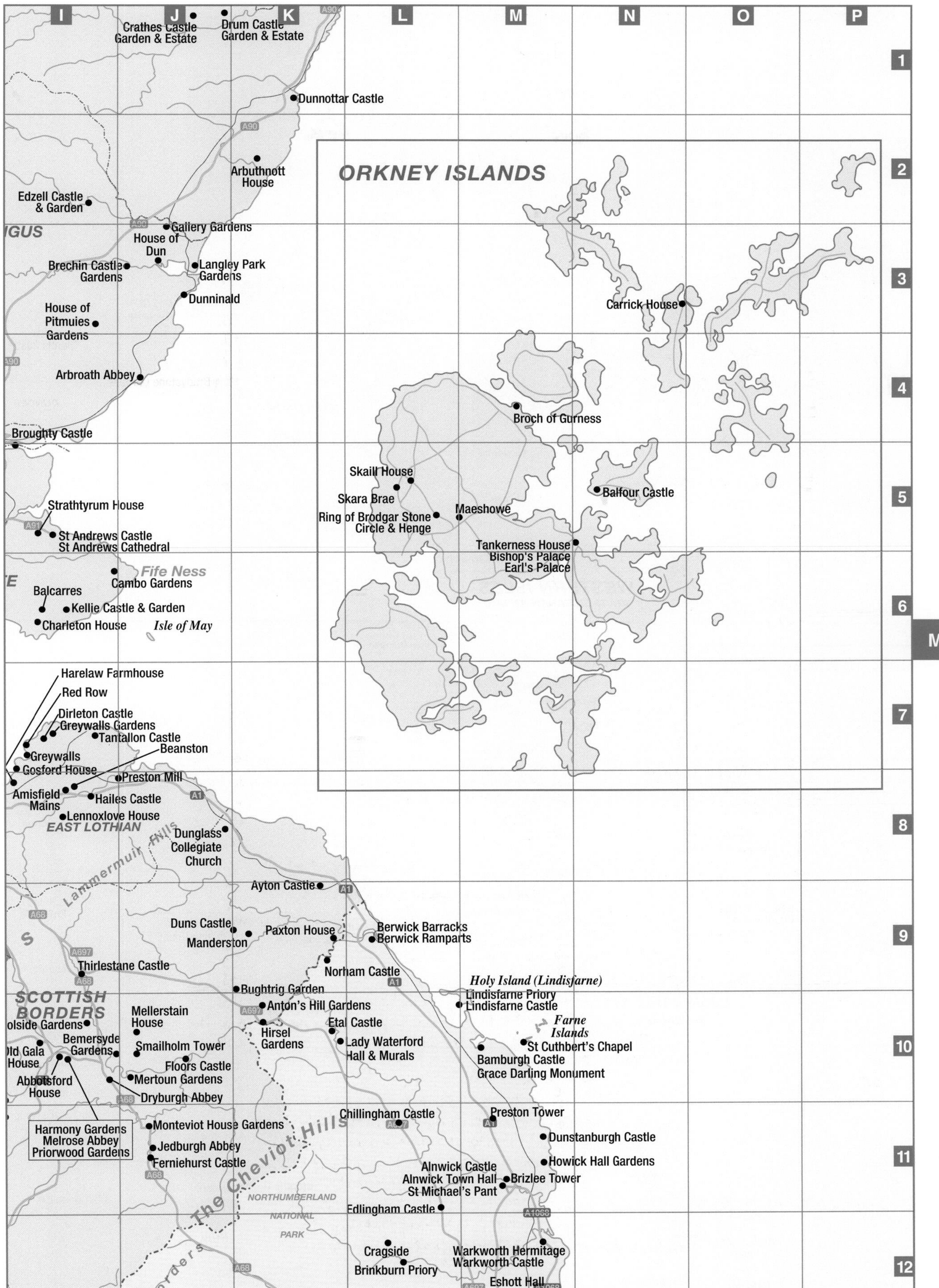

I
J
K
L
M
N
O
P
1
2
3
4
5
6
7
8
9
10
11
12
MAP 14
Crathes Castle Garden & Estate
Drum Castle Garden & Estate
Dunnottar Castle
Arbuthnott House
Edzell Castle & Garden
Gallery Gardens
House of Dun
Brechin Castle Gardens
Langley Park Gardens
Dunninald
House of Pitmuies Gardens
Arbroath Abbey
Broughty Castle
Strathtyrum House
St Andrews Castle
St Andrews Cathedral
Fife Ness
Cambo Gardens
Balcarres
Kellie Castle & Garden
Charleton House
Isle of May
ORKNEY ISLANDS
Carrick House
Broch of Gurness
Skaill House
Skara Brae
Ring of Brodgar Stone Circle & Henge
Maeshowe
Balfour Castle
Tankerness House
Bishop's Palace
Earl's Palace
Harelaw Farmhouse
Red Row
Dirleton Castle
Greywalls Gardens
Tantallon Castle
Beanston
Greywalls
Gosford House
Preston Mill
Amisfield Mains
Hailes Castle
Lennoxlove House
EAST LOTHIAN
Lammermuir Hills
Dunglass Collegiate Church
Ayton Castle
Duns Castle
Manderston
Paxton House
Berwick Barracks
Berwick Ramparts
Thirlestane Castle
Norham Castle
SCOTTISH BORDERS
Bughtrig Garden
Holy Island (Lindisfarne)
Lindisfarne Priory
Lindisfarne Castle
Mellerstain House
Anton's Hill Gardens
Hirsel Gardens
Etal Castle
Farne Islands
Bemersyde Gardens
Smailholm Tower
Lady Waterford Hall & Murals
St Cuthbert's Chapel
Abbotsford House
Floors Castle
Mertoun Gardens
Bamburgh Castle
Grace Darling Monument
Dryburgh Abbey
Harmony Gardens
Melrose Abbey
Priorwood Gardens
Monteviot House Gardens
Chillingham Castle
Preston Tower
Dunstanburgh Castle
Jedburgh Abbey
Ferniehurst Castle
The Cheviot Hills
Howick Hall Gardens
Alnwick Castle
Alnwick Town Hall
St Michael's Pant
Brizlee Tower
NORTHUMBERLAND NATIONAL PARK
Edlingham Castle
Cragside
Brinkburn Priory
Warkworth Hermitage
Warkworth Castle
Eshott Hall
Borders
A90
A91
A1
A68
A697
A1068

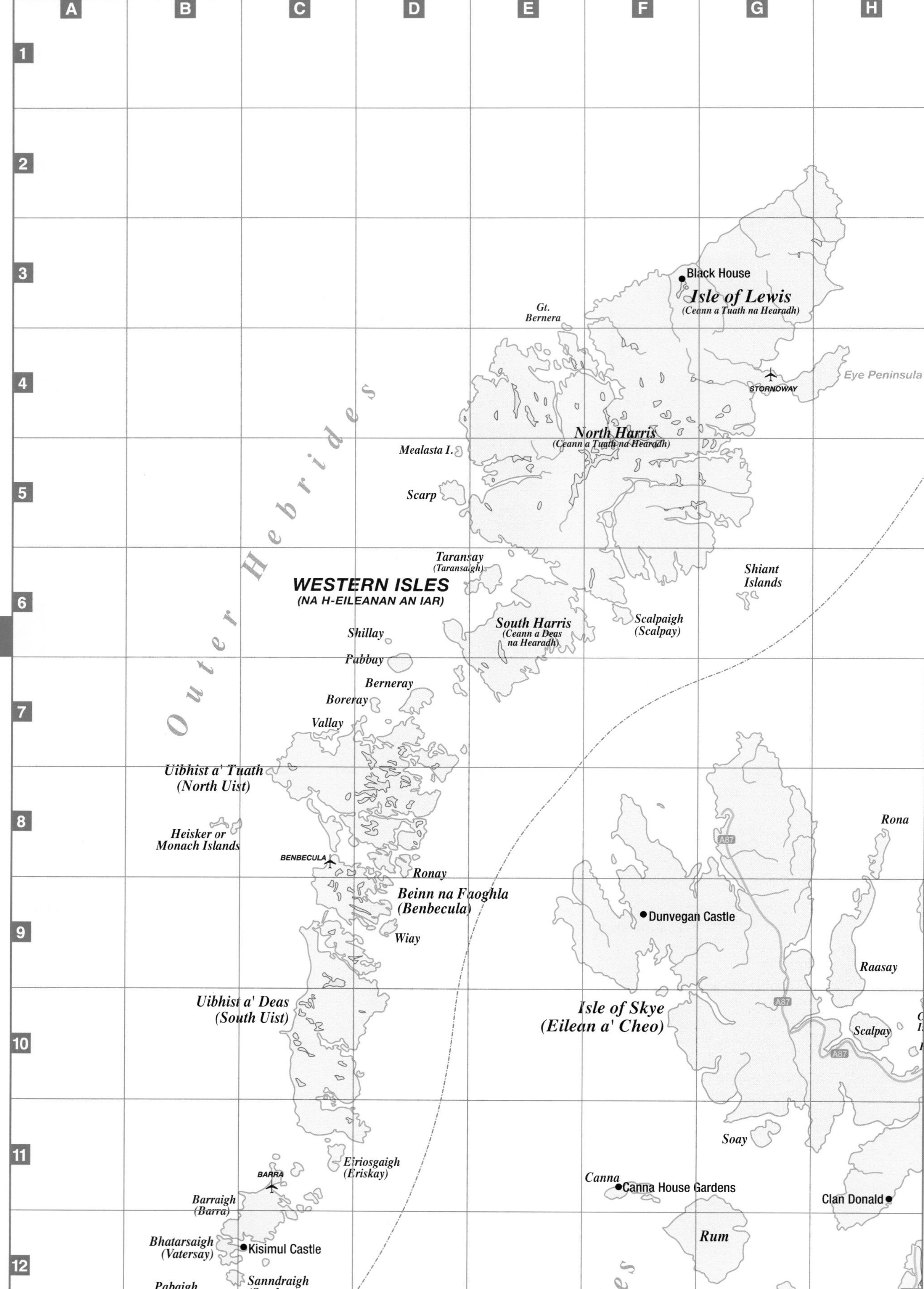

Register for news and special offers at **www.hudsonsheritage.com**

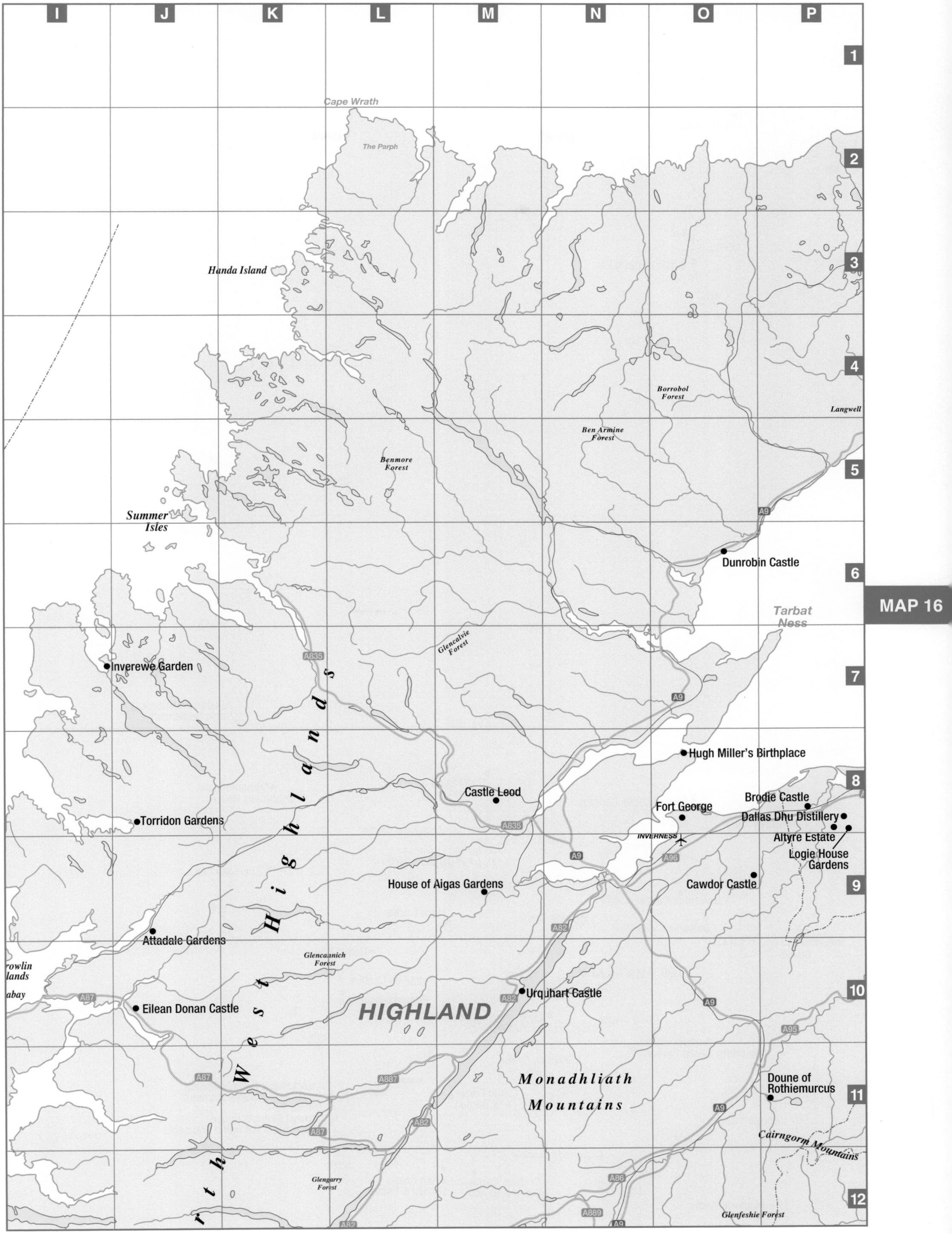

I J K L M N O P

1 2 3 4 5 6 7 8 9 10 11 12

MAP 16

Cape Wrath

The Parph

Handa Island

Summer Isles

Benmore Forest

Ben Armine Forest

Borrobol Forest

Langwell

Dunrobin Castle

Tarbat Ness

Glencalvie Forest

Inverewe Garden

Hugh Miller's Birthplace

Castle Leod

Fort George

Brodie Castle

Dallas Dhu Distillery

Altyre Estate

Logie House Gardens

INVERNESS

Torridon Gardens

House of Aigas Gardens

Cawdor Castle

Attadale Gardens

Glencaanich Forest

Urquhart Castle

Eilean Donan Castle

HIGHLAND

North West Highlands

Monadhliath Mountains

Doune of Rothiemurcus

Cairngorm Mountains

Glengarry Forest

Glenfeshie Forest

A9 A835 A96 A82 A87 A887 A95 A86 A889

MAP 17

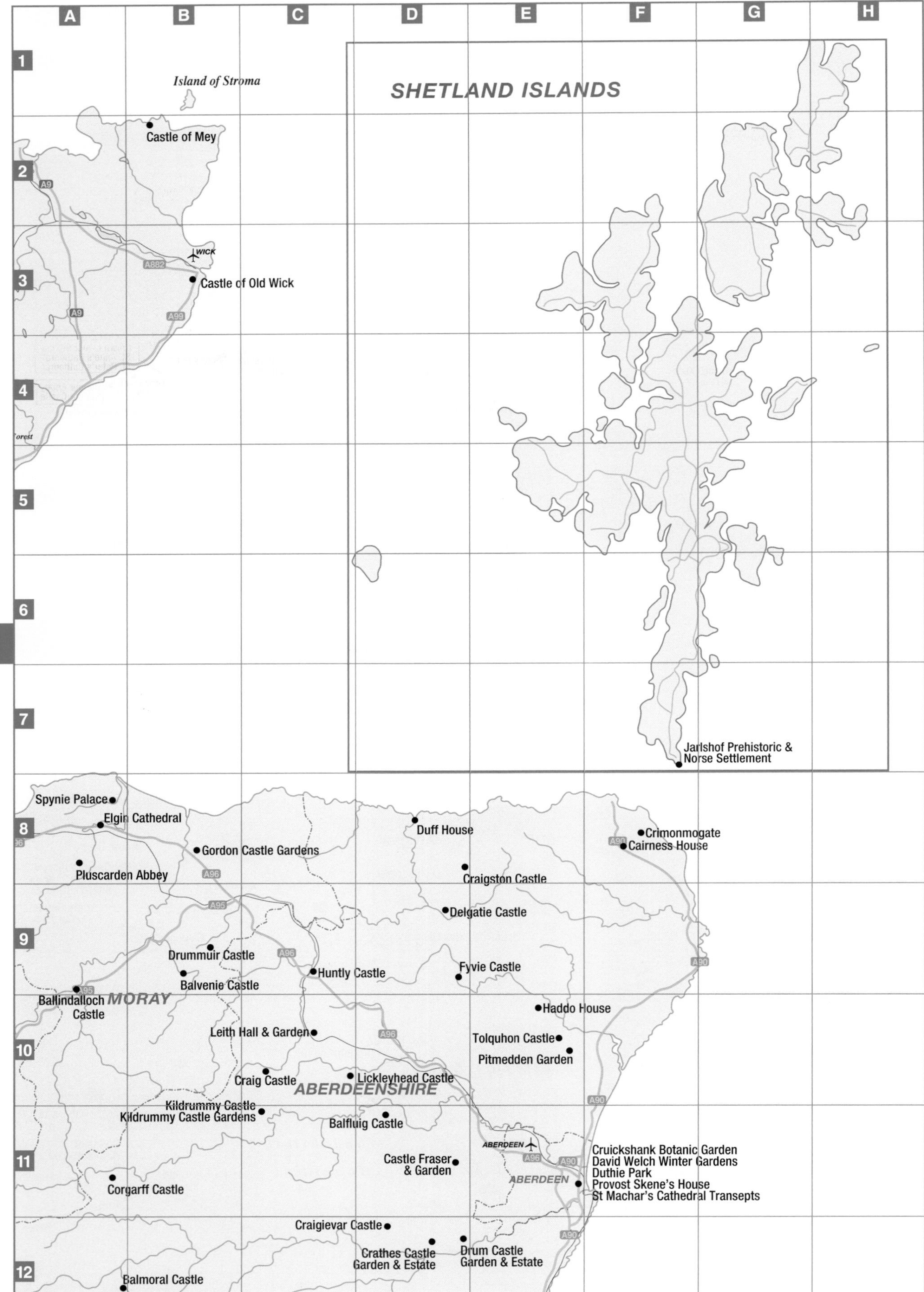

Register for news and special offers at **www.hudsonsheritage.com**

MAP 18
Downhill Demesne
Mussenden Temple
Hezlett House & Farmyard
Dunluce Castle
Giant's Causeway
Benvarden Gardens
Mountsandel Fort
The Guildhall
St. Columb's Cathedral
LONDONDERRY
(Derry)
Kings Fort
Limavady
Prehen House
Dungiven Priory & O'Cahan's Tomb
Glenarm Castle Walled Garden
Arthur Ancestral Home
Gray's Printing Press
Bellaghy Bawn
Antrim Castle Gardens
Stewart Castle
Harry Averys Castle
Barons Court
Belfast Castle
Botanic Gardens
Crown Liquor Saloon
St. Anne's Cathedral
St. Peter's Cathedral
Carrickfergus Castle
Sentry Hill
Patterson's Spade Mill
Lissan House
Omagh Keep & Geol
Wellbrook Beetling Mill
Springhill House & Costume Collection
Tullyhogue Fort
Grey Point Fort
Bangor Abbey
Bangor Castle
BELFAST
Helens Tower
Movilia Abbey
Newtownards Priory
Mount Stewart
Grey Abbey
Lisburn Cathedral
Mahee Castle
Sketrick Castle
The Argory
Templetown Mausoleum
Hillsborough Castle
Ardress House
Benburb Castle
Rowallane Garden
Enniskillen Castle
Castle Coole
Audley Castle
Portaferry Castle
Killyleagh Castle
Strangford Castle
Quoile Castle
Florence Court
Montalto
Inch Abbey
Castle Ward
Kilclief Castle
Clough Castle
Seaforde Gardens
Dundrum Castle
Crom
Derrymore House
Newry Cathedral
Greencastle Royal Castle
DUBLIN
(BAILE ÁTHA CLIATH)
INISHOWEN
MOYLE
COLERAINE
BALLYMONEY
LIMAVADY
DERRY
ANTRIM HILLS
BALLYMENA
LARNE
STRABANE
SPERRIN MTS
MAGHERAFELT
ANTRIM
OMAGH
LISBURN
CRAIGAVON
ARDS
DUNGANNON
FERMANAGH
ARMAGH
BANBRIDGE
DOWN
MONAGHAN
NEWRY & MOURNE
MOURNE MTS
CAVAN
LOUTH
LONGFORD
WESTMEATH
MEATH
DUBLIN
OFFALY
KILDARE
Island Magee
Lambay Island
Mull of Kintyre
Sanda Island
Inch I.
(Bun an Phobail)
(Bun Cranncha)
(Leitir Ceanainn)
(Leifear)
(Srath an Urláir)
(Bealach Feich)
(Muineachán)
(Cluain Eois)
(Baile na Lorgan)
(An Cabhán)
(Carrig Mhachaire)
(Dun Dealgan)
(An Longfort)
(Ceanannus Mór)
(Droichead Átha)
(Baile Brigin)
(Na Sceirí)
(An Ros)
(Sord)
(Mullach Íde)
(An Muileann gCearr)
(Baile Átha Troim)
(Maigh Naud)
(Tulach Mhór)
(An Nás)
(Mainistir Eimhin)
(Mointeach Milie)
(Bré)
(Na Clocha Liathe)
I J K L M N O P
1 2 3 4 5 6 7 8 9 10 11 12

GREATER LONDON

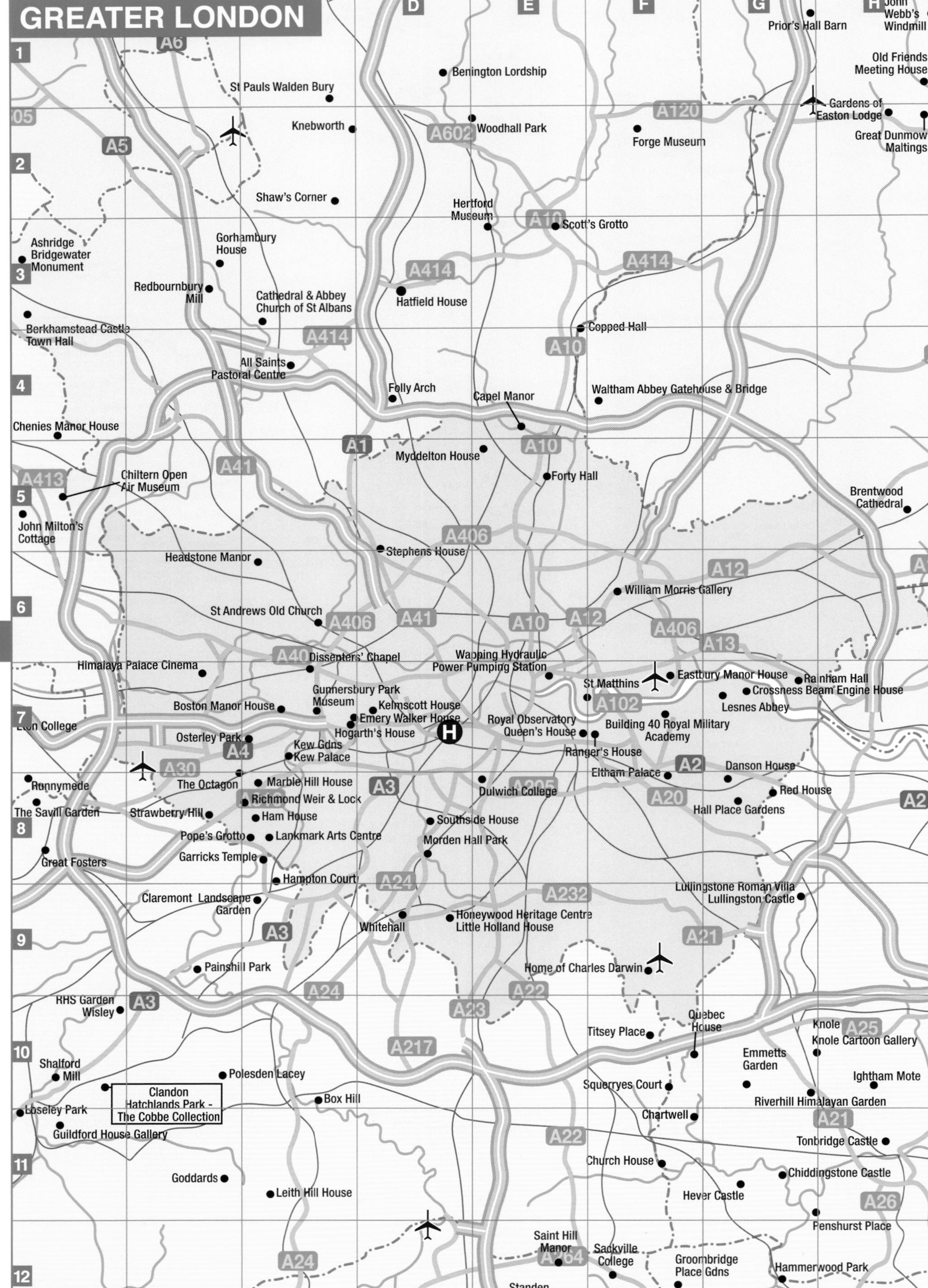

CENTRAL LONDON

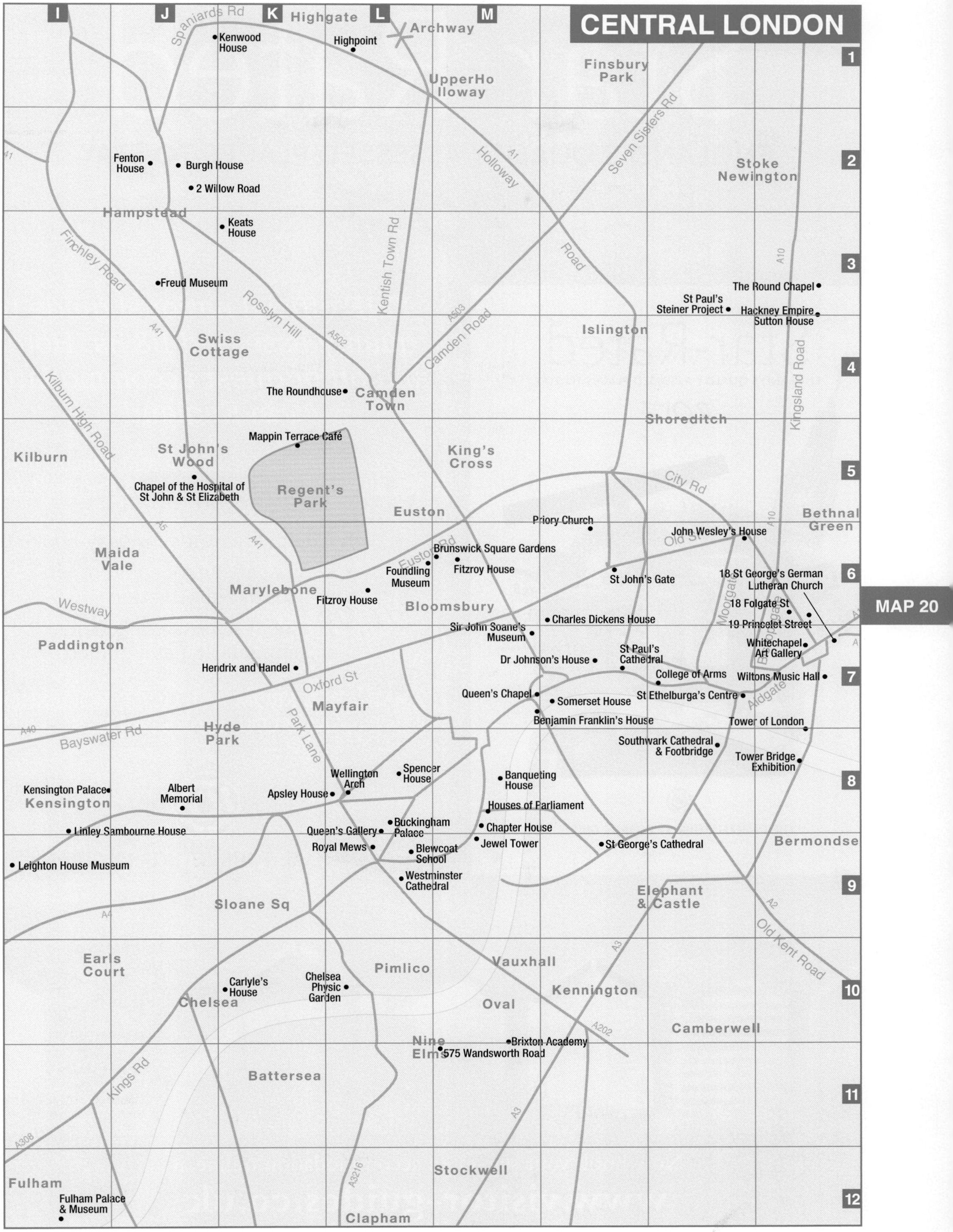
I
J
K
L
M
1
2
3
4
5
6
7
8
9
10
11
12
Spaniards Rd
Highgate
Archway
Kenwood House
Highpoint
Upper Holloway
Finsbury Park
Seven Sisters Rd
Holloway Road
A1
A41
Fenton House
Burgh House
2 Willow Road
Stoke Newington
Hampstead
Keats House
Kentish Town Rd
Finchley Road
Freud Museum
Rosslyn Hill
A10
The Round Chapel
St Paul's Steiner Project
Hackney Empire
Sutton House
A502
A503
Camden Road
Swiss Cottage
Islington
Kingsland Road
Kilburn High Road
The Roundhouse
Camden Town
Shoreditch
Mappin Terrace Café
Kilburn
St John's Wood
King's Cross
Chapel of the Hospital of St John & St Elizabeth
Regent's Park
City Rd
A5
Euston
Priory Church
Bethnal Green
John Wesley's House
Old St
Maida Vale
Euston Rd
Brunswick Square Gardens
Foundling Museum
Fitzroy House
St John's Gate
18 St George's German Lutheran Church
Marylebone
Fitzroy House
Moorgate
Westway
Bloomsbury
18 Folgate St
Charles Dickens House
19 Princelet Street
Sir John Soane's Museum
Paddington
Whitechapel Art Gallery
Dr Johnson's House
St Paul's Cathedral
Hendrix and Handel
Oxford St
College of Arms
Wiltons Music Hall
Queen's Chapel
Somerset House
St Ethelburga's Centre
Mayfair
Aldgate
A40
Benjamin Franklin's House
Tower of London
Bayswater Rd
Hyde Park
Park Lane
Southwark Cathedral & Footbridge
Tower Bridge Exhibition
Wellington Arch
Spencer House
Banqueting House
Kensington Palace
Albert Memorial
Kensington
Apsley House
Houses of Parliament
Buckingham Palace
Chapter House
Queen's Gallery
Linley Sambourne House
Royal Mews
Blewcoat School
Jewel Tower
St George's Cathedral
Bermondsey
Leighton House Museum
Westminster Cathedral
Elephant & Castle
Sloane Sq
A4
A2
Old Kent Road
A3
Earls Court
Vauxhall
Pimlico
Carlyle's House
Chelsea Physic Garden
Kennington
Chelsea
Oval
A202
Camberwell
Nine Elms
Brixton Academy
575 Wandsworth Road
Kings Rd
Battersea
A308
A3216
Stockwell
Fulham
Fulham Palace & Museum
Clapham
MAP 20

Star-Rated

ENGLAND'S QUALITY ASSESSED PLACES TO STAY

★★★★★ 2017 ★★★★★

THE official national guide to quality-assessed B&Bs, Hotels and other guest accommodation in England

Packed with information and easy to use, it's all you need for the perfect English break

- Web-friendly features for easy booking
- Events, attractions and other tourist information
- National Accessible Scheme accommodation at a glance

AVAILABLE FROM ALL GOOD BOOKSHOPS AND ONLINE RETAILERS

OFFICIAL TOURIST BOARD GUIDE

Now book your star-rated accommodation online at

www.visitor-guides.co.uk

Index

Places listed by name in alphabetical order

Stokesay Court, Shropshire

C

D

Chatsworth, Derbyshire

E

Stansted Park, Sussex

I

J

K

L

Q

R

S

T

U

V

W

Y

Display Advertisers